Communications
in Computer and Information Science 532

Hamido Fujita · Guido Guizzi (Eds.)

Intelligent Software Methodologies, Tools and Techniques

14th International Conference, SoMeT 2015
Naples, Italy, September 15–17, 2015
Proceedings

 Springer

Editors
Hamido Fujita
Iwate Prefectural University
Takizawa
Japan

Guido Guizzi
University of Naples "Federico II"
Napoli
Italy

ISSN 1865-0929 ISSN 1865-0937 (electronic)
Communications in Computer and Information Science
ISBN 978-3-319-22688-0 ISBN 978-3-319-22689-7 (eBook)
DOI 10.1007/978-3-319-22689-7

Library of Congress Control Number: 2015945329

Springer Cham Heidelberg New York Dordrecht London

Printed on acid-free paper

Springer International Publishing AG Switzerland is part of Springer Science+Business Media
(www.springer.com)

Preface

Software is the essential enabler for science and the new economy. It creates new markets and new directions for a more reliable, flexible, and robust society. It empowers the exploration of our world in ever more depth. However, software often falls short of our expectations. Current software methodologies, tools, and techniques remain expensive and are not yet sufficiently reliable for a constantly changing and evolving market, and many promising approaches have proved to be no more than case-by-case oriented methods.

This book explores new trends and theories that illuminate the direction of developments in this field, developments that we believe will lead to a transformation of the role of software and science integration in tomorrow's global information society.

By discussing issues ranging from research practices, techniques, and methodologies, to proposing and reporting solutions needed for global world business, it offers an opportunity for the software science community to think about where we are today and where we are going.

The book aims to capture the essence of a new state of the art in software science and its supporting technology, and to identify the challenges that such a technology will have to master. It contains extensively reviewed papers presented at the 14th International Conference on New Trends in Intelligent Software Methodology, Tools, and Techniques (SoMeT 2015) held in Naples, Italy, with the collaboration of the University of Naples Federico II, during September 15–17, 2015 (http://www.impianti. unina.it/somet2015/). This round of SoMeT 2015 celebrated its 14th anniversary. The SoMeT[1] conference series is ranked as B+ rank among other high-ranking computer science conferences worldwide.

This conference brought together researchers and practitioners to share their original research results and practical development experience in software science and related new technologies.

This volume forms part of the conference and the SoMeT series by providing an opportunity for the exchange of ideas and experiences in the field of software technology; by opening up new avenues for software development, methodologies, tools, and techniques, especially with regard to intelligent software by applying artificial intelligence techniques in software development; and by tackling human interaction in the development process for a better high-level interface. The focus is on human-centric software methodologies, end-user development techniques, and emotional reasoning, for an optimally harmonized performance between the design tool and the user.

---

[1] Previous related events that contributed to this publication are: SoMeT_02 (the Sorbonne, Paris, 2002); SoMeT 2003 (Stockholm, Sweden, 2003); SoMeT 2004 (Leipzig, Germany, 2004); SoMeT 2005 (Tokyo, Japan, 2005); SoMeT 2006 (Quebec, Canada, 2006); SoMeT 2007 (Rome, Italy, 2007); SoMeT 2008 (Sharjah, UAE, 2008); SoMeT 2009 (Prague, Czech Republic, 2009); SoMeT 2010 (Yokohama, Japan, 2010), and SoMeT 2011 (Saint Petersburg, Russia), SoMeT 2012 (Genoa, Italy), SoMeT 2013 (Budapest, Hungary), and SoMeT 2014 (Langkawi, Malaysia).

The word "intelligent" in the name SoMeT emphasizes the need to apply artificial intelligence issues to software design for systems application, for example, in disaster recovery and other systems supporting social services through sustainable recovery planning.

A major goal of this conference was to assemble the work of scholars from the international research community to discuss and share research experiences of new software methodologies and techniques. One of the important issues addressed is the handling of cognitive issues in software development to adapt it to the user's mental state. Tools and techniques related to this aspect form part of this book. Another subject raised at the conference was intelligent software design in software ontology and conceptual software design in the practice of human-centric information system applications.

The book also investigates other comparable theories and practices in software science, including emerging technologies, from their computational foundations in terms of models, methodologies, and tools. This is essential for a comprehensive overview of information systems and research projects, and to assess their practical impact on real-world software problems. This represents another milestone in mastering the new challenges of software and its promising technology, addressed by the SoMeT conferences, and provides the reader with new insights, inspiration, and concrete material to further the study of this new technology.

The book is a collection of carefully selected refereed papers by the reviewing committee and covering (but not limited to):

- Software engineering aspects of software security programs, diagnosis, and maintenance
- Static and dynamic analysis of software performance models
- Software security aspects and networking
- Agile software and lean methods
- Practical artifacts of software security, software validation and diagnosis
- Software optimization and formal methods
- Requirement engineering and requirement elicitation
- Software methodologies and related techniques
- Automatic software generation, re-coding and legacy systems
- Software quality and process assessment
- Intelligent software systems design and evolution
- Artificial intelligence techniques on software engineering, and requirement engineering
- End-user requirement engineering, programming environment for Web applications
- Ontology, cognitive models and philosophical aspects of software design
- Business-oriented software application models
- Emergency management informatics, software methods and application for supporting civil protection, first response and disaster recovery
- Model-driven development (DVD), code-centric to model-centric software engineering
- Cognitive software and human behavioral analysis in software design

All 48 papers selected and organized in this book have been carefully reviewed, on the basis of technical soundness, relevance, originality, significance, and clarity, by up to four reviewers. They were then revised before being selected by the SoMeT 2015 international reviewing committee. These papers are categorized into ten chapters and classified according to the paper's topic and its relevance to each chapter theme:

Chapter 1 "Embedded and Mobile Software Systems, Theory and Application"
Chapter 2 "Real-Time Systems"
Chapter 3 "Requirement Engineering, High-Assurance and Testing System"
Chapter 4 "Social Networks and Big Data"
Chapter 5 "Cloud Computing and the Semantic Web"
Chapter 6 "Artificial Intelligence Techniques and Intelligent System Design"
Chapter 7 "Software Development and Integration"
Chapter 8 "Security and Software Methodologies for Reliable Software Design"
Chapter 9 "New Software Techniques in Image Processing and Computer Graphics"
Chapter 10 "Software Applications Systems for Medical Health Care"

This book is the result of the collective effort of many industrial partners and colleagues throughout the world. In particular, we would like to acknowledge our gratitude to the University of Naples, Italy, Iwate Prefectural University, Japan, and all authors who contributed their invaluable time to this work. We would especially like to thank the reviewing committee and all those who participated in the rigorous reviewing process and the lively discussion and evaluation meetings that led to the selected papers in this book. Last and not least, we would also like to thank the Microsoft Conference Management Tool team for their expert guidance on the use of the Microsoft CMT System as a conference-support tool during all the phases of SoMeT 2015.

July 2015   Hamido Fujita
                                                             Guido Guizzi

Organization

SoMeT 2015 was held in Naples, Italy

General Chair

Hamido Fujita   Iwate Prefectural University, Japan

Program Chair

Guido Guizzi   University of Naples Federico II, Italy

Program Co-chair

Roberto Revetria   University of Genoa, Italy

Honorary Chairs

Dave Parnas	McMaster University, Hamilton, Canada
Imre J. Rudas	O'buda University, Budapest, Hungary
Colette Rolland	Paris 1 University, Paris, France
Danilo Iervolino	Telematic University Pegaso, Italy
Tina Santillo	University of Naples Federico II, Italy
Atsuto Suzuki	Iwate Prefectural University, Japan

Organizing Committee

Antonio Tufano	Telematic University Pegaso, Italy
Teresa Murino	University of Naples Federico II, Italy
Mosè Gallo	University of Naples Federico II, Italy
Francesco Fabbrocino	Telematic University Pegaso, Italy
Gajo Petrovic	Iwate Prefectural University, Japan

Reviewers and Program Committee

Abdul Syukor Mohamad Jaya	Universiti Teknikal Malaysia Melaka, Malaysia
Adzhar Kamaludin	Universiti Malaysia Pahang, Malaysia
Akram Zeki	International Islamic University Malaysia, Malaysia
Alexander Vazhenin	University of Aizu, Fukushima, Japan
Ali Selamat	Universiti Teknologi Malaysia, Malaysia
Andreas Speck	Kiel University, Germany

Anna-Maria Di Sciullo	University de Quebec de Montreal, Canada
Antoni Wibowo	Universiti Teknologi Malaysia, Malaysia
Antonio Tufano	Telematic University Pegaso, Italy
Azlan Mohd Zain	Universiti Teknologi Malaysia, Malaysia
Azrulhizam Shapii	Universiti Kebangsaan Malaysia, Malaysia
Azurah Abu Samah	Universiti Teknologi Malaysia, Malaysia
Balsam A. Mustafa	Universiti Malaysia Pahang, Malaysia
Beata Czarnacka-Chrobot	Warsaw School of Economics, Poland
Bipin Indurkhya	IIIT, Hyderabad, India
Burairah Hussin	Universiti Teknikal Malaysia Melaka, Malaysia
Chawalsak Phetchanchai	Suan Dusit Rajabhat University, Thailand
Cheah Wai Shiang	Universiti Malaysia Sarawak, Malaysia
Claudio De Lazzari	IFC-CNR, Rome, Italy
Clemens Schäfer	IT Factum GmbH, Germany
Colette Rolland	University of Paris 1-Pantheon Sorbonne, France
Dayang Norhayati Abang Jawawi	Universiti Teknologi Malaysia, Malaysia
Dewi Nasien	Universiti Teknologi Malaysia, Malaysia
Dmitry Mouromtsev	University of Information Technologies, St. Petersburg, Russia
Enrique Herrera Viedma	University of Granada, Spain
Fernando Barbosa	Universidade do Porto, Portugal
Francisco Chiclana	De Montfort University, England
Fritz Solms	Solms TCD, Johannesburg, South Africa
Gajo Petrovic	Iwate Prefectural University, Japan
Habibollah Haron	Universiti Teknologi Malaysia, Malaysia
Hamido Fujita	Iwate Prefectural University, Japan
Hamzah Asyrani Sulaiman	Universiti Teknikal Malaysia Melaka, Malaysia
Hassan Chizari	Universiti Teknologi Malaysia, Malaysia
Hector Perez-Meana	National Polytechnic Institute, Mexico
Hoshang Kolivand	Universiti Teknologi Malaysia, Malaysia
Huzara Zulzalil	Universiti Putra Malaysia, Malaysia
Igor Kotenko	St. Petersburg Institute for Informatics and Automation, Russia
Jamal Bentahar	Concordia University, Montreal, Canada
Jun Hakura	Iwate Prefectural University, Japan
Jun Sasaki	Iwate Prefectural University, Japan
Kamal Zuhairi Zamli	Universiti Malaysia Pahang, Malaysia
Kasem Saleh	Kuwait University, Kuwait
Liberatina Carmela Santillo	University of Naples Federico II, Italy
Love Ekenberg	Stockholm University, Sweden
Marite Kirikova	Riga Technical University, Latvia
Masaki Kurematsu	Iwate Prefectural University, Japan
Milan Vlach	Charles University Prague, Czech Republic
Mohamed Mejri	Laval University, Quebec, Canada

Mohd Fahmi Mohamad Amran	Universiti Industri Selangor, Malaysia
Ngoc-Thanh Nguyen	Wroclaw University of Technology, Poland
Mosè Gallo	University of Naples Federico II, Italy
Nikolay Mirenkov	Aizu University, Fukushima, Japan
Paul Johannesson	Royal Institute of Technology, Sweden
Peter Brida	University of Zilina, Slovakia
Peter Sosnin	Ulyanovsk State Technical University, Russia
Piero Giribone	University of Genoa, Italy
Radziah Mohamad	Universiti Teknologi Malaysia, Malaysia
Remigijus Gustas	Karlstad University, Sweden
Reza Masinchi	Universiti Teknologi Malaysia, Malaysia
Riccardo De Carlini	University of Naples Federico II, Italy
Rimantas Butleris	Kaunas University of Technology, Lithuania
Riza Sulaiman	Universiti Kebangsaan Malaysia, Malaysia
Roberto Mosca	University of Genoa, Italy
Roberto Revetria	University of Genoa, Italy
Roliana Ibrahim	Universiti Teknologi Malaysia, Malaysia
Roman Barták	Charles University Prague, Czech Republic
Rosalina Abdul Salam	Universiti Sains Islam Malaysia, Malaysia
Roselina Sallehuddin	Universiti Teknologi Malaysia, Malaysia
Rudolf Keller	PMOD, Zurich, Switzerland
Rusli Abdullah	Universiti Putra Malaysia, Malaysia
Samir Ouchani	University of Luxembourg, Luxembourg
Sarina Sulaiman	Universiti Teknologi Malaysia, Malaysia
Sergei Gorlatch	University of Münster, Germany
Sigeru Omatu	Osaka Institute of Technology, Japan
Siti Sophiayati Yuhaniz	Universiti Teknologi Malaysia, Malaysia
Soundar Kumara	Pennsylvania State University, Pennsylvania, USA
Stuart Charters	Lincoln University, New Zealand
Suhaila Mohamad Yusuf	Universiti Teknologi Malaysia, Malaysia
Sunday Olatunji	University of Dammam, Saudi Arabia
Suziyanti Marjudi	Universiti Industri Selangor, Malaysia
Takeru Yokoi	Tokyo Metropolitan University, Japan
Tatiana Gavrilova	Saint Petersburg University, Russia
Teresa Murino	University of Naples Federico II, Italy
Tokuro Matsuo	Tokyo Metropolitan University, Japan
Tutut Herwan	Universiti Malaya, Malaysia
Victor Malyshkin	Russian Academy of Sciences, Russia
Volker Gruhn	University of Duisburg-Essen, Germany
Yasuaki Nishitani	Iwate University, Japan
Yury Zagorulko	A.P. Ershov Institute of Informatics System, Russia

Contents

Social Networks and Big Data

Cloud Computing and the Semantic Web

Artificial Intelligence Techniques and Intelligent System Design

Software Development and Integration

Security and Software Methodologies for Reliable Software Design

New Software Techniques in Image Processing and Computer Graphics

Software Applications Systems for Medical Health Care

Embedded and Mobile Software Systems, Theory and Application

Towards Automated UI-Tests for Sensor-Based Mobile Applications

Tobias Griebe$^{(\boxtimes)}$, Marc Hesenius, and Volker Gruhn

Paluno - The Ruhr Institute for Software Technology,
University of Duisburg-Essen, Gerlingstr. 16, 45127 Essen, Germany
tobias.griebe@paluno.uni-due.de, remove@gmail.com
http://www.paluno.de

Abstract. Mobile devices changed human-computer interaction, caused the need for specialized software engineering methods and created new business opportunities. The mobile app market is highly competitive and software developers need to maintain high software quality standards for long-lasting economic success. While powerful software development kits support developers in creating mobile applications, testing them is still cumbersome, time-consuming and error-prone. Especially interaction methods depending on sensor input like device motion gestures prevent automated UI testing – developers and testers are forced to manually test all different aspects. We present an approach to integrate sensor information into user acceptance tests and use a sensor simulation engine to enable automatic test case execution for mobile applications.

Keywords: Software engineering · Testing · Test automation · Mobile applications · Sensor simulation

1 Introduction

Mobile devices caused an immense paradigm shift in computing, especially in Human Computer Interaction (HCI). In mobile applications, device sensors like accelerometers and gyroscopes can be used to identify device movements. While users typically benefit from a multitude of possible input methods and can choose their preferred interaction style satisfying the need for the individual User Experience (UX), software developers and testers face challenging problems. Processing device motion as a means of interaction requires developers to analyze a stream of data from sensors and is therefore more complex than classic Point'n'Click (PnC) interaction following the WIMP[1] paradigm. As a consequence, additional error sources are introduced and User Interface (UI) testing becomes a crucial activity. However, suitable test automation technology barely exists: test frameworks typically focus on classic PnC interfaces, but do not take recent HCI techniques into account. To our knowledge, tool support for

---

[1] windows, icons, menus, pointers.

H. Fujita and G. Guizzi (Eds.): SoMeT 2015, CCIS 532, pp. 3–17, 2015.
DOI: 10.1007/978-3-319-22689-7_1

testing motion gestures in applications is non-existent. Test automation frameworks do not support device motion gesture simulation. Hence, cumbersome and error-prone manual testing cannot be avoided. To alleviate this issue, we present an extension to the popular mobile testing framework Calabash[2], enabling application developers to simulate sensor information and mimic device motions in automatically processed user acceptance tests.

The remainder of this paper is structured as follows: Sect. 2 describes recent practices and the current situation regarding the development and test of mobile applications in general and sensor-based applications in particular. We will then present our approach to test automation for applications depending on sensor input in Sect. 3, followed by an evaluation and discussion of our approach to test automation in Sect. 4. Section 5 discusses related work. Section 6 concludes the paper and presents tasks for future work.

2   Developing and Testing Motion-Based Mobile Applications

App stores made the mobile application market highly competitive and user ratings have become an important metric for choosing one application over the other. Good quality and short release cycles are therefore vital for a project's economic success. Consequently, testing activities claim a major portion of a developer's daily routine and up to 90 % of the total development effort [11]. Manufacturers have released powerful Software Development Kits (SDKs) and development environments to support developers, but failed to add sufficient testing capabilities to their tools and – even more important – their devices.

2.1   Mobile Application Testing

Traditional testing tasks such as selecting an appropriate set of test cases, determining adequate test oracles and specifying test input data remain important activities in mobile testing. However, mobile-specific and interaction-specific factors need special attention as they significantly increase an application's vulnerability to potential defects. Interaction-specific factors include properties that are inherently bound to mobile HCI, e.g. rotating the device from landscape to portrait orientation. These factors multiply the testing effort, as the typical testing process is extended by the additional testing targets *interaction testing* (a special form of UI testing) and *testing in the wild* [4].

Mobile- and interaction-specific factors have to be paired, subsequently executed and the outcome examined. The large number of test cases required to assure adequate coverage easily exceeds a single developer's, tester's or even mid-sized company's capabilities in terms of effort invested in testing time as well as in budget. Besides being expensive due to the dependency on human resources, manual testing can hardly guarantee a reproducible test environment, especially when applications depend on sensor data.

---

[2] http://calaba.sh.

Sensors are prone to noise that may significantly influence data integrity and hence corrupt methods processing sensor data. For example, the magnetic field sensor will pick up any magnetic field surrounding the device, including external disturbances caused by ferromagnetic objects in the device's vicinity. The developer, on the other hand, in most cases expects to measure the magnetic field of the earth. Technically, sensor noise is a random variable that cannot effectively be controlled in manual testing using real sensors. Appropriate test automation technology can help to remedy these factors. Unfortunately, such technology barely exists and seldom meets the immediate requirements in terms of adequately handling interaction-specific factors.

The quality assurance process for applications using sensor input faces three key challenges: (1) sensor data needs to be exactly specified; (2) test cases must be reproducible in a reliable manner; (3) parameters for realistic sensor noise must be configurable. The lack of sensor simulation technology prevents the use of efficient test automation methods, even in cases where existing technology can automate the testing process in other aspects. However, test automation is a key technology to reliable test execution reproduction. In this work, we focus on aspects (1) and (2) and demonstrate how sensor input can be integrated into existing test automation technology.

2.2 Behavior-Driven Development

Several recent test automation tools use a Behavior-Driven Development (BDD) approach to automate mobile UI-testing. Test-Driven Development (TDD), the originator of BDD, turns the development process upside down: applications are developed after creating a series of tests to verify a program's correctness. Tests describe the program's expected output depending on a set of input variables. While this approach allows developers to verify correctness of a program during all stages of development (especially when maintaining existing code), it effectively excludes non-technical project team members from test creation: the basic software test component – the *Unit Test* – is typically a piece of software itself, enforcing the need of at least basic programming skills.

TDD focuses on an important part of software development and introduces a valid approach to ensure application quality. Unfortunately, it highly depends on programmers and testers correctly interpreting specification documents. Without clearly understanding the application under development, TDD may lead to testing the wrong functionality. Ideally, the developed application can be automatically validated against its specification. Suitable test automation technology capable to process *executable specifications* is desirable. Furthermore, the specification documents should be used as a common base for all stakeholders – technical as well as non-technical.

BDD evolved from TDD for this purpose [12]. The approach centers around a set of *user acceptance tests* describing the application's behavior from a user's point of view in a – preferably – near-natural language syntax. The user's actions result in system reactions – *given* the system is in a known, active state, *when* the user does something, *then* the system should respond in a certain way.

This natural style of describing interaction is reflected in the basic structure of user acceptance tests. Listing 1.1 demonstrates how an action in a hypothetical Android application can be specified using the BDD style. The example is written in *Gherkin*, a Domain Specific Language (DSL) specifically tailored to describe application behavior in near-natural language syntax. Notice how the *given-when-then*-approach is reflected, making the specification easy to read for all stakeholders.

```
1 Scenario: Activation of push services
2 Given my app is running
3 Then the ''GameMain'' activity should be open
4 And the view with id ''push-ind'' should not be visible
5 When I touch the ''Activate Push'' button
6 Then the view with id ''push-ind'' should be visible
```

Listing 1.1. Example of a BDD user acceptance test for an Android application expressed in Gherkin.

The BDD approach goes beyond specification. With suitable frameworks such as *Calabash*[3] for mobile applications or *SpecFlow*[4] for the .NET platform, user acceptance tests can be executed, allowing for application specification as well as test automation. Recent research has demonstrated how BDD can be used for mobile-specific aspects like multi-touch gestures [5] and multimodality [6].

2.3   Testing Sensor-Based Mobile Applications

Mobile application developers heavily rely on predefined components. Besides the capabilities manufacturers provide in their respective SDKs, third party components bring additional functionality to simplify the various aspects of application development. Typical examples are libraries for common or specialized operations or frameworks providing automated testing capabilities. For developing sensor-based applications, tool support strongly focuses on implementation aspects; testing capabilities are typically left out.

When creating sensor-based applications, developers have to analyze the stream of incoming data to determine the desired aspects of sensor input – an error-prone and mathematically sophisticated task. For example, motion gestures are detected using various sensors (e.g. accelerometer and gyroscope). Manually implementing individual motion detection code increases the danger of introducing bugs and complicates maintenance, especially when extending the application in a later stage of the lifecycle. Suitable test automation technology is therefore highly desirable.

For efficient test automation, a framework must provide three core capabilities: describing sensor input, deriving artificial sensor data, and injecting data into the tested application. We aim to integrate these abilities into Calabash and therefore have to extend Gherkin, the language used for specifying user acceptance tests, and add additional modules for sensor data generation.

---

[3] http://calaba.sh.
[4] http://www.specflow.org.

3 Test Automation for Motion Gesture Based Applications

3.1 Test Execution Automation Engine

Test automation for mobile applications is currently supported by a variety of tools operating on different levels of abstraction (e.g. JUnit[5], CUnit[6], Robotium[7], Calculon[8]). On the far side of close-to-code testing, unit testing frameworks are popular. While these are sufficient for tests that directly work on source code artifacts (e.g. individual classes or member functions), they are inadequate for test case specification on the far side of UI and user acceptance tests.

We decided to use Calabash's Android incarnation[9] to integrate test automation for sensor-based applications. In Calabash, test cases are expressed as Cucumber[10] features written in Gherkin. At the current stage of our research, we focus on the Android platform, since it is more accessible for the integration of sensor-data simulation as comparable mobile platforms. However, specialization to a specific platform is introduced only late in the process, so that our approach can be applied to other mobile platforms as well.

Our approach to sensor-based mobile application testing consist of three major building blocks: a modified version of the Calabash-Android test framework enhanced to deliver pseudo sensor data into the Application Under Test (AUT), a sensor-data specification interpreter accepting sensor expressions and a sensor simulator module generating a stream of pseudo sensor data.

Calabash builds on top of a technology stack consisting of two compartments: host platform and target platform. Test cases run on the host platform where the Calabash-Android framework interprets test cases expressed as Gherkin scripts. These are decomposed into separate instructions and subsequently transferred into the target platform compartment utilizing the HTTP-based communication link a in Fig. 1. At the target platform compartment, native instrumentation technology is used to remote-control the AUT by generating artificial user interaction events (e.g. click on a button, enter/read value into/from text fields).

To allow for motion gesture-based application testing, we modified the Calabash-Android framework by adding a sensor simulator module (see Fig. 1). At the host platform compartment, the sensor simulator module extends the original Calabash functionality with a sensor data simulation facility. It is used to transfer fake sensor data via communication link b in Fig. 1 into the AUT. At the target platform compartment, the sensor simulator receives test sensor data and submits it to the AUT. From the AUT's perspective, faked sensor data is handled using a shadow implementation of the original platform sensor Application Programming Interface (API).

---

[5] http://junit.org.
[6] http://cunit.sourceforge.net.
[7] https://code.google.com/p/robotium/.
[8] https://github.com/mttkay/calculon.
[9] https://github.com/calabash/calabash-android.
[10] http://cukes.info.

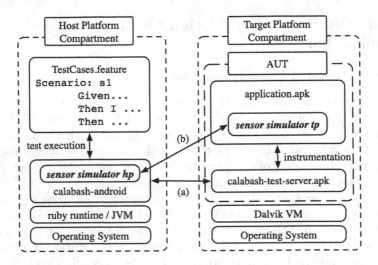

Fig. 1. The Calabash test automation technology stack extended with our *sensor simulator* module.

3.2 Sensor Simulator

No mobile platform currently allows to simulate sensor data when running on actual handsets. On the Android emulator, however, test sensor data can be enforced on the AUT by using a Telnet connection to the emulator environment. Commands may be issued to enforce specified sensor data on the sensors present in the emulated system using the emulator's console. However, we do not consider emulators as valid test case platforms, since they deliberately abstract from realistic execution environments to a degree that test results are non-representative.

Coherent with the Calabash framework architecture, the sensor data simulator module is split into two largely independent sub modules: one for each compartment. At the target platform compartment, we currently employ a heavily modified compilation of the SensorSimulator[11] library initially created by the open source project OpenIntents[12]. The library enables the spoofing of sensor data by replacing the systems's standard sensor framework APIs with a shadow implementation that, besides the package identifier, mimics the system's API down to class and method names. The library accepts incoming data streams from a HTTP socket and feeds that data into the shadow implementation of Android's sensor framework. The AUT subsequently uses that data just as if it were delivered by the original platform's hardware sensors.

At the host platform compartment, we completely replaced the original Open-Intents implementation with our own set of sensor models. These expose two interfaces: one accepting data from the Calabash-Android stack and one exposing that data to a worker thread. A transmit looper periodically reads data from

---

[11] https://code.google.com/p/openintents/wiki/SensorSimulator.
[12] http://www.openintents.org.

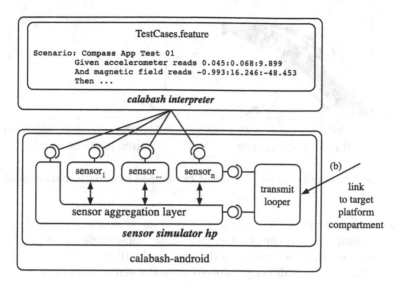

Fig. 2. Simplified excerpt from our custom Calabash implementation showing the sensor simulator module with a scheme of the sensor model.

the sensor model and transmits it through communication link b in Fig. 2 into the target platform compartment.

The sensor model implementation allows sensor data simulation at two modes of operation: the test case can directly specify the data to be read from the sensor model (explicit mode) or use the sensor aggregation layer (implicit mode) to simulate sensor data corresponding to device movement at a higher level of abstraction using either Gherkin short-cuts or compound sensor commands. At runtime of the simulation, the sensor aggregation model enforces specific data onto a set of sensors according to the device motion model: a shake gesture for example will alter primarily the values of the accelerometer. However, since the device is physically relocated by the shake gesture, the values of the gyroscope, the magnetic field sensor and others are affected as well.

The sensor models are designed to generate data according to a mathematical model describing the sensor's behavior on an idealized level and a per-axis base. The left side of Fig. 3, for example, depicts actual sensor data obtained in a series of experiments on multiple handsets from the x-axis value of the accelerometer when the device is held parallel to earth's surface in landscape orientation and then tilted around the longitudinal axis by 90° within approximately 1000 ms. The right side depicts the model derived from that data, in this specific case an approximation by a cosine function.

Possible use cases for the explicit operation mode are test cases either using a single sensor or non-complex combination of multiple sensors. Single sensor use cases measure properties of the execution environment (e.g. ambient temperature, ambient light) or properties of device movement derived from one sensor only. Non-complex combinations of multiple sensors combine sensor data, such

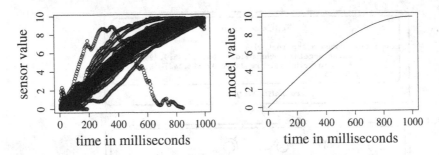

Fig. 3. Experimentally obtained sensor data mapped to a mathematical model.

as acceleration and magnetic field e.g. to calculate azimuth, pitch and roll of a device. An exemplary excerpt of a test case using non-complex sensor combination expressed as Gherkin scenario is depicted in Listing 1.2. The values stated in the Gherkin script are directly enforced onto the sensor simulator.

```
1 Feature: sensor based app test
2 Scenario: sensor based test scenario
3    ...
4    Given Magnetic field measures
5       8.318:0.392:-34.007
6    And Accelerometer measures
7       -0.0286:0.043:9.938
8    ...
```

Listing 1.2. Example of a Calabash user acceptance test for an Android application using a the accelerometer and the magnetic field sensor.

Possible use cases for the implicit operation mode are test cases specifying motion gestures as short-cut Gherkin expressions. Line 6 in Listing 1.3 depicts such a case. The expression *shake gesture* is recognized by the framework as a reserved term advising the system to generate a stream of sensor data characteristic for a shake gesture on the device's accelerometer and gyroscope. The data stream is calculated from a mathematical model derived from statistical data.

```
1 Feature: sensor based app test
2 Scenario: sensor based test scenario
3    ...
4    Given my app is running
5    Then the activity "MainActivity" should be open
6    And I shake the device
7    ...
```

Listing 1.3. Example of a Calabash user acceptance test for an Android application using a short-cut Gherkin expression, from which sensor data is derived.

4   Evaluation and Discussion

This work is based on OpenIntent's SensorSimulator library, leading to the side effect that spoofing sensor data is realized at application level within the AUT. This limitation currently prevents black-box-testing applications and is an important matter of future research as discussed in Sect. 4.2. We evaluated our test automation framework using white-box tests on a set of Android applications specifically built to demonstrate the test frameworks capabilities.

4.1 Evaluation

We evaluated our test automation framework by implementing two Android applications that rely on sensor data. To evaluate the explicit mode of our framework (explicit sensor data specification in test cases), we implemented a three-axis compass application that determines the device's orientation relative to the earth's surface and graphically indicates the device's heading towards the magnetic north pole. To evaluate the implicit mode, we implemented an application that uses standard motion gestures to control application behavior: rotating the device from portrait to landscape orientation and back.

Three-Axis Compass Application Evaluation. To implement a three-axis compass application, the Android platform allows for orientation determination based on the locally measured force of gravity and magnetic field strength. In our evaluation, we settled with this option allowing for the design of test cases that explicitly specify sensor data. The application uses the three-axis measurement of the magnitude and direction of gravitational force and the three-axis measurements of the magnetic field strength to obtain a rotation matrix describing the device's orientation. To generate a meaningful representation of this information, we present the user a graphical indication of the device's heading towards the magnetic north pole (see screenshot in Fig. 4). We achieve this by mapping the orientation information to a coordinate system defined by the device's longitudinal axis and a normal vector perpendicular to the device's display.

To obtain reference data, we conducted a series of manual test cases, where we compared the application's display output with the heading indication of a physical compass. This, of course, gave only rough estimates since the mechanical compass does not print out exact numbers. However, we used this to record the raw sensor data acquired by the magnetic field sensor and the accelerometer using different Android devices[13].

To perform the actual evaluation of our test automation framework, we created a set of Gherkin scenarios describing sensor data preconditions and the expected results of the orientation calculation. The nominal values for the sensor data were derived by averaging the recorded data from the manual test series. This evaluation demonstrates how test automation using reproducible sensor data can be used to reduce manual effort. One of the test cases we used to evaluate our approach is printed in Listing 1.4. We also executed further test cases taking sensor data representative for pitch and roll values into account.

We evaluated the test automation framework with the compass application on a set of different Android handsets and a number of different emulator configurations. We found that the test cases could be successfully completed in each

---

[13] Nexus 4 and 7, Nexus S, LG Optimus 3D, HTC Desire S510e.

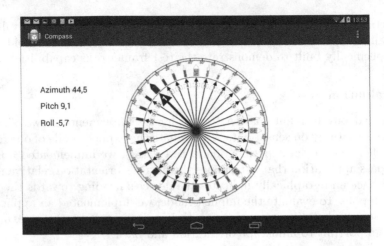

Fig. 4. Screenshot of the three-axis compass app used in our evaluation.

scenario. Especially could be verified that the sensor data as specified by the test case was correctly transferred into the AUT. This technique of transferring spoofed sensor data onto a AUT for test purposes is our main contribution to test automation for sensor-based applications: the reliable reproduction of sensor data in test environments.

```
1 Feature: sensor based digital compass
2
3 Scenario: Phone sits flat table and is rotated to 274, 356 degrees
4
5    Given Magnetic field measures
6       8.318:0.392:-34.007
7       with zero noise
8    And Accelerometer measures
9       -0.0286:0.043:9.938
10      with zero noise
11         Then I see "Azimuth 274"
12
13   Given Magnetic field measures
14      1.011:12.923:-36.538
15      with standard noise
16   And Accelerometer measures
17      0.000:0.004:9.950
18      with standard noise
19         Then I see "Azimuth 356"
```

Listing 1.4. Sample test case for a sensor-based app using spoofed data for the accelerometer and the magnetic field sensor with different noise models.

Sensor-Based Landscape/Portrait Switching. Today's mobile platforms provide API interfaces to detect changes in display orientation by using device sensors, so that developers may implement different application behavior depending on display orientation (e.g. orientation specific UI layout). To evaluate the implicit mode of our test automation framework, we implemented a simple application providing different UIs for landscape and portrait orientation.

When executing test cases for orientation-related UI events, the tester needs to physically rotate the device into the desired orientation. Using our approach, the desired device orientation can be stated within the test scenario by either using a compound sensor command to set the device orientation or a short-cut Gherkin expression defined by the test automation framework. In either case, the sensor simulator module selects the appropriate sensors (i.e. accelerometer, gyroscope, etc.) and supplies values corresponding to the specified orientation.

```
1 Scenario: UI reorientation according to device orientation
2   Given my app is running
3   And the device lays on the table
4   Then the view with id "portrait-only-button" should be visible
5   And the view with id "lst-landscape-detail" should not be visible
6   Given device orientation is 0:-90:90
7   Then the view with id "landscape-only-button" should be visible
8   And the view with id "lst-landscape-detail" should be visible
9   Given device orientation is portrait
10  Then the view with id "portrait-only-button" should be visible
11  And the view with id "lst-landscape-detail" should not be visible
```

Listing 1.5. Sample test case for a mobile application providing different UIs for portrait and landscape mode.

In Listing 1.5, we instruct the test automation framework to initially set all sensors to a default setting where the device lays flat on a table (line 3). This corresponds to a setting where rotation angles around the device's native coordinate system are zero. Line 6 instructs the test execution framework to simulate sensor events that correspond to tilting the device into a upward position representing the user holding the device in landscape mode. Line 9 instructs the test framework to rotate the device into portrait mode using a Gherkin short-cut. Lines 4, 5, 7, 8, 10 and 11 perform checks on the application's UI. Despite specifying concrete values in line 6, this statement is considered an implicit sensor data specification since internally multiple sensors are affected.

Upon test case execution, we carefully examined the raw sensor data supplied to the application and compared the per-axis graph of the sensor values to previously recorded data from a test series manually conducted on actual handsets (see Sect. 3.2). We found that the sensor values generated by our sensor simulator matched the averaged data obtained from the manual experiments scaled to fixed overall motion gesture duration within an error margin that allowed for the correct identification of the device's orientation, i.e. the data read from the sensor simulator was close to the values generated by underlying mathematical model. Minor deviations occurred due the lag of the network connection used to transmit the data, in which case some data arrived late at the target platform compartment causing the data to lag behind its actual timestamp. This is a minor issue we plan to eradicate in our future work.

4.2   Discussion

We used a modified version of the SensorSimulator library provided by the open source project OpenIntents that replaces the system's core sensor framework at application level to inject spoofed sensor data into the AUT. However, our current approach requires the AUT's source code to be accessible to include an additional library, causing two problems: the use of third-party test-only code not adding functionality to the application and a limitation on white-box testing.

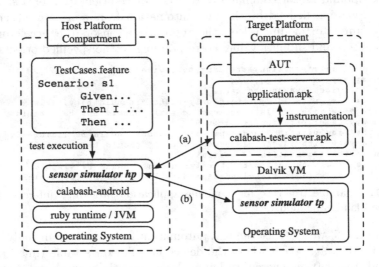

Fig. 5. The Calabash test automation technology stack extended with our *sensor simulator* module integrated into the Android OS at HAL level.

Using test-only code in the test case requires this code to permanently remain in the AUT, although it is never actually used by the application at runtime. Since the sensor simulator library requires an accessible network socket when running test cases, leaving the library in the AUT is a major security risk. However, removing the library after the testing is done voids the test results.

This problem is tightly connected to the limitations of white-box testing. In business environments, the development and testing of a software product may be delegated to different teams, often separated not only by distance but also by time or even by juristic interest. Especially the latter might be the case when a software product is subject to a third-party audit. In this case, the ability to black-box test an application is a major concern. As a consequence, we aim to improve our approach to support black-box testing.

To achieve black-box testing, we added the sensor simulator to the operating system's HAL (see Fig. 5) and compiled a custom Android-ROM implementing a series of mock sensor interfaces. This approach allows for real black-box testing by simulating sensor data without manipulating the AUT. However, this is ongoing research and needs further evaluation.

5   Related Work

Haller identifies two new test types – *device tests* and *tests in the wild* – when analyzing the special requirements of mobile application testing [4]. The author emphasizes the main challenge: the need for sufficient automation technology. The quickly evolving mobile platforms introduce new test triggers that must be handled efficiently. Our approach addresses these issues by automating the testing process for applications heavily depending on sensor input.

The challenges software developers face when testing mobile applications have been investigated in several research projects. Possible strategies are: describing test cases in a structured manner before test execution; analyzing log files; or *UI-Ripping*, a technique where test cases are automatically derived from algorithmically inspecting the AUT's UI, identifying possible input elements, and triggering all possible combinations of user input. To our best knowledge, all existing test automation solutions are more or less bound to classic PnC interfaces and do not take sensor input information into account, effectively excluding an important subset of recent application features.

UI-rippers like *SwiftHand* [3] and *AndroidRipper* [1] typically inspect an AUT's interface by analyzing the hierarchical structure created by UI elements and widgets. They try to determine a set of possible input sequences subsequently seen as test cases and automatically executed. UI elements with an event handler are triggered with corresponding events. As a consequence, only interaction means with UI representations can be tested, effectively limiting the test capabilities to classic PnC interaction. Sensor input is typically excluded, hence speech-, motion- or touch-based applications cannot be tested.

Structured tests depend on a dedicated test specification, either written or pre-recorded. *Hermes* [10] uses an XML-based dialect to configure virtual users, injecting necessary input information into the AUT. The authors do not specifically include sensor input information and instead focus on classic PnC interaction. TouchToolkit [9] is an automated testing tool for .NET-based applications focusing multi-touch gestures. Testers can record gestures and reuse them in unit tests. MobileTest [2] uses pre-recorded and replayed test scenarios to send commands to virtual agents running on mobile devices. Events such as *incoming call*, *inbox full* or *memory low* are the basic test cases and allow cross-device tests: tests can be executed on different devices interacting with each other. The authors do not specifically state whether or not sensor input information can be simulated and tested. Testdroid [8] allows to upload manually recorded AUT sessions to an online platform to be automatically executed on a set of physical devices. The system solves a common problem especially for Android developers – device heterogeneity – but the authors specifically exclude tests for applications depending on speech, movement or gestural input.

Another approach to application testing is collecting and analyzing log files created by the AUT. Hu and Neamtiu [7] conducted a bug study and present a framework for automatically generating and performing test cases resulting in a collection of log files for subsequent analysis. They were able to rediscover known bugs as well as reveal new ones in the examined applications. They do not use a structured approach to write test cases and rely on the pseudo-random user events create by Android's UI/Application Exerciser Monkey.

iSimulate[14] is a framework available for Apple's iOS platform consisting of a library and an iOS application. The library listens on a network socket for spoofed sensor data and is used to modify the sensor access layer within the iOS simulator with artificial input events. The application is installed on an iOS device to capture sensor data and send them via a network link to the library running inside the iOS simulator. iSimulate requires developers to add the respective SDK to their development project.

6　Conclusion and Future Work

We presented an extension to the testing framework Calabash allowing to integrate sensor information into user acceptance tests written in Gherkin. We created a sensor simulator that feeds artificial sensor data into the AUT, simulating information from the environment and mimicking a human user. The necessary data can be specified directly in within test scenarios. We demonstrated how our approach can be used with two applications depending on different sensor data and show how we remove the need for constant manual testing.

For our future research, different options remain. Incorporating different levels of inaccuracy leads to more realistic test results, but the extent of sensor data fuzziness needs empirical evidence. Statistical analysis of these research results will help to improve the mathematical sensor model.

Another interesting research topic is the description of sensor data in a human-readable manner. Motion gestures could be derived from formal gesture descriptions, but this aspect involves simulating several sensors in conjunction, e.g. accelerometer and gyroscope. As mobile device technology advances, new sensors become available allowing new kinds of interaction. To incorporate new sensors, a common ground must be developed to specify user acceptance tests in an easy manner, without the need for deep diving in to sensor data details. Formal languages offer interesting possibilities.

References

1. Amalfitano, D., Fasolino, A.R., Tramontana, P., De Carmine, S., Memon, A.M.: Using GUI ripping for automated testing of android applications. In: Proceedings of the 27th IEEE/ACM International Conference on Automated Software Engineering, ASE 2012, pp. 258–261. ACM, New York (2012)
2. Bo, J., Xiang, L., Xiaopeng, G.: MobileTest: a tool supporting automatic black box test for software on smart mobile devices. In: AST 2007 Proceedings of the Second International Workshop on Automation of Software Test, p. 8. IEEE Computer Society, Washington (2007)
3. Choi, W., Necula, G., Sen, K.: Guided GUI testing of android apps with minimal restart and approximate learning. In: Proceedings of the 2013 ACM SIGPLAN International Conference on Object Oriented Programming Systems Languages and Applications, OOPSLA 2013, pp. 623–640. ACM, New York (2013)

---

[14] http://www.vimov.com/isimulate/.

4. Haller, K.: Mobile testing. SIGSOFT Softw. Eng. Notes **38**(6), 1–8 (2013)
5. Hesenius, M., Griebe, T., Gries, S., Gruhn, V.: Automating UI tests for mobile applications with formal gesture descriptions. In: Proceedings of the 16th International Conference on Human-Computer Interaction with Mobile Devices and Services, MobileHCI 2014, pp. 213–222. ACM, New York (2014)
6. Hesenius, M., Griebe, T., Gruhn, V.: Towards a behavior-oriented specification and testing language for multimodal applications. In: Proceedings of the 2014 ACM SIGCHI Symposium on Engineering Interactive Computing Systems, EICS 2014, pp. 117–122. ACM, New York (2014)
7. Hu, C., Neamtiu, I.: Automating gui testing for android applications. In: Proceedings of the 6th International Workshop on Automation of Software Test, AST 2011, pp. 77–83. ACM, New York (2011)
8. Kaasila, J., Ferreira, D., Kostakos, V., Ojala, T.: Testdroid: Automated remote UI testing on android. In: Proceedings of the 11th International Conference on Mobile and Ubiquitous Multimedia, MUM 2012, pp. 28:1–28:4. ACM, New York (2012)
9. Khandkar, S.H., Sohan, S.M., Sillito, J., Maurer, F.: Tool support for testing complex multi-touch gestures. In: ACM International Conference on Interactive Tabletops and Surfaces, ITS 2010, pp. 59–68. ACM, New York (2010)
10. She, S., Sivapalan, S., Warren, I.: Hermes: a tool for testing mobile device applications. In: ASWEC 2009 Proceedings of the 2009 Australian Software Engineering Conference, pp. 121–130. IEEE Computer Society, Washington (2009)
11. Tassey, G.: The economic impacts of inadequate infrastructure for software testing. Technical report, National Institute of Standards and Technology (2002)
12. Wynne, M., Hellesoy, A.: The Cucumber Book: Behaviour-Driven Development for Testers and Developers. Pragmatic Bookshelf, Dallas (2012)

Indoor Position Detection Using BLE Signals Based on Voronoi Diagram

Kensuke Onishi[✉]

Tokai University, 4-1-1 Kitakaname, Hiratsuka, Kanagawa 259-1292, Japan
onishi@tokai-u.jp

Abstract. Bluetooth Low Energy (BLE) is a Bluetooth standard with low energy consumption. Beacons using BLE transmit BLE signals, which can be received by smart phones running iOS or Android OS. At present, demonstration experiments are conducted.

An indoor position detection using an ordered order-k Voronoi diagram was proposed. Beacons were installed in a building of Tokai University. Experiments are conducted to investigate position detection using the proposed approach. We have two results using the proposed system: (1) a floor decision success rate of 99.6 %; and (2) indoor position detection success rates of 85.5 % (first neighbor) and 48.9 % (second neighbor). Finally, we present some ideas for improving the proposed approach.

1 Introduction

Bluetooth Low Energy (BLE) [1] is a low-power Bluetooth standard. A machine called a *beacon* is developed for use in transmitting BLE signals. The beacon works for approximately one year on only a button battery.

BLE has been supported by iOS since 2013 and by Android OS (after version 4.3) since 2014. A BLE signal can be received by numerous types of smart phone. Thus, a number of demonstration experiments have been conducted in various locations. For example, beacons were placed on each aquarium at Hakkeijima Sea Paradise. When a person approaches one of the aquarium with a smart phone, the smart phone displays information on the sea animals in the aquarium ([2], until March 2015). A number of beacons have been placed in Tokyo Station to support position detection and navigation ([3], until February 2015). Finally, a system was constructed in which information related to bus stops was provided by beacons placed in busses in Kyoto City [4].

A number of studies have examined position detection based on a received signal: GPS (outdoors) and WiFi [5–7] (indoors). In a previous study, the Received Signal Strength Indicator (RSSI) of a WiFi access point was measured at many points, and a method of position detection using the measured data was proposed [5]. The covering method of directional sensor networks using Voronoi diagram was proposed [8]. While the directional sensor distributes signals for a pie-shaped region, the beacon distributes for all range. Moreover, an experiment using BLE signals had been conducted [9], in which 50 beacons were placed in a real field and the RSSIs of the BLE signals were measured. The position decision

© Springer International Publishing Switzerland 2015
H. Fujita and G. Guizzi (Eds.): SoMeT 2015, CCIS 532, pp. 18–29, 2015.
DOI: 10.1007/978-3-319-22689-7_2

by BLE signal was performed with an accuracy of 10 m to 20 m, and a hybrid method using the BLE signal and pedestrian dead reckoning was proposed.

We consider the problem for detecting own position from given field and installed beacons. It is necessary that the BLE signals from beacons cover the field. When many beacons are installed, the problem can be solved easily. BLE signals are collected by user's smart phone, then it is decided that the user is near the beacon with strongest RSSI. It has expensive cost that many beacons install on a real field. We consider indoor position detection under small number of beacons where the BLE signals cover the field.

In the present paper, we propose a method for position detection based on an ordered order-k Voronoi diagram. The Voronoi diagram is easily computed at a desk, and a number of configurations of beacons can be planned. We decided a configuration of beacons for a building of Tokai University, then installed 30 beacons on the building and measured the RSSIs of the BLE signal. We then evaluate the proposed method based on the measurement data. We explain the ordered order-k Voronoi diagram in Sect. 2, and the proposed method is described in Sect. 3. In Sect. 4, we describe the beacons used in the experiments, the building in which the experiments are conducted, and the experiments themselves. The experiments are further discussed floor decision and indoor position detection in Sect. 5.

2   Related Research

2.1   Ordered Order-k Voronoi Diagram

In this section, we explain the ordered order-k Voronoi diagram. Consider a set of points $P = \{p_1, p_2, \ldots, p_n\}$. Each point in the set is called a *site*. Let $(p_{i_1}, p_{i_2}, \cdots, p_{i_k})$ be ordered sites selected from P. An ordered order-k Voronoi diagram [10, pp. 144–151], called an *OO-k Voronoi diagram*, is a tessellation and consists of ordered order-k Voronoi polygons $R(P; i_1, i_2, \ldots, i_k)$. The ordered order-$k$ Voronoi polygon is defined as follows:

$$R(P; i_1, i_2, \ldots, i_k)$$
$$= \{x \in \mathbf{R}^2 \mid d(x, p_{i_1}) < d(x, p_{i_2}) < \cdots < d(x, p_{i_k}) < d(x, p_j),$$
$$j \neq i_1, i_2, \ldots, i_k\},$$

where $d(x, y)$ is the Euclidean distance between x and y. This polygon is a convex subset of the Euclidean plane. Every point in the polygon is near p_{i_1}, p_{i_2}, ..., p_{i_k} in the order. The set of Voronoi polygons for all ordered k sites is referred to as an OO-k Voronoi diagram.

Figure 1 is an OO-3 Voronoi diagram for P, which has six sites. The solid lines in Fig. 1 form the (OO-1) Voronoi diagram for the point set, which gives the nearest region of each site. The solid and dashed lines form the OO-2 Voronoi diagram. Each OO-k Voronoi polygon is divided into a number of OO-$(k + 1)$ Voronoi polygons. In Fig. 1, $R(P; 4, 3)$ is divided into $R(P; 4, 3, 2)$, $R(P; 4, 3, 5)$, and $R(P; 4, 3, 6)$.

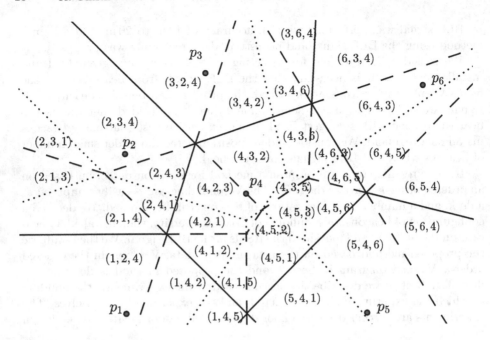

Fig. 1. Ordered order-3 Voronoi diagram.

The OO-k Voronoi diagram is constructed in $O(nk^2 \log n + nk \log^3 n)$ time and $O(k(n - k))$ storage [11]. Lee et al. proposed a computation method of generalized higher-order Voronoi diagram (HOVD) and applied HOVD to map segmentation [12].

2.2   Arrangement

The arrangement is formed by lines in a Euclidean plane. Consider n lines in the plane. The plane is divided into regions consisting of segments formed by given lines. The arrangement of n lines is computed in $O(n^2)$ time and $O(n^2)$ space [13]. The OO-n Voronoi diagram for n sites has the same structure with an arrangement of perpendicular bisectors of all pair of sites.

3   Proposed Method

In this section, we describe the proposed algorithm for position detection. The proposed algorithm uses position detection by an ordered order-k Voronoi diagram, or an arrangement of perpendicular bisections of all pair of sites.

Suppose that the configuration of beacons is known. We compute the OO-k Voronoi diagram, or the arrangement of beacon sites. Each OO-k polygon is regarded as position in indoor position detection. So we evaluate the difference among the OO-k polygon and the ordered sequence of beacons sorted by RSSI on a real field. Then, we clarify the problems of proposed method.

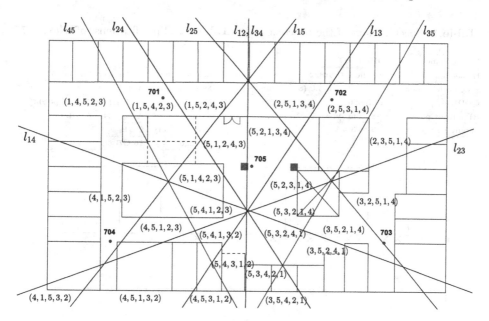

Fig. 2. Ordered order-5 Voronoi diagram on the seventh floor of Building 18 at Tokai University.

Figure 2 shows an OO-5 Voronoi diagram of the seventh floor of Building 18 at Tokai University. We installed five beacons (701–705) on the seventh floor, and five beacons were placed on the other floors. The configuration of beacons was planed to cover the field by small number of beacons. The seventh floor was divided into a number of OO-5 Voronoi polygons.

When position detection is performed using BLE signals, a smart phone collects signals from the beacons. The beacons are then sorted by RSSI and the beacon order is used to determine current position. For example, suppose that the sorted sequence of beacons is *704, 705, 701, 804, 702, 604, 703, 601, 801*, as shown in Fig. 2. Suppose that we already know that we are on the seventh floor. Since beacons *6*** and *8*** are on the sixth and eighth floors, respectively, we use only the *7*** beacons: *70$\underline{4}$, *70$\underline{5}$, 70$\underline{1}$, 70$\underline{2}$, 70$\underline{3}$. Then our position on the seventh floor is decided as $R(\overline{P}; 4, 5, 1, 2, 3)$.

The floor can be also decided based on the sorted sequence of beacons from the frequencies of first digits. If two first-digit values have the same number of occurrences, then we select the value corresponding to stronger BLE signals. In the above example, the first digits are $(7, 7, 7, 8, 7, 6, 7, 6, 8)$. Since 6, 7 and 8 appear once, five times and two times, respectively, in the sequence, the floor is decided as the seventh.

Table 1. Specifications of the beacons.

Model Name	HRM1017
Embedded BLE chip	Nordic nRF51822
Bluetooth version	Bluetooth LE 4.0 (Single mode)
QDID	B020660
RF output power	−8 dBm type
Supply voltage	1.8 to 3.6 V

Table 2. Specifications of Nexus 7 (2013, WiFi).

Model Name	Nexus 7 (2013, WiFi)
Manufacturer	ASUS
OS	Android 5.0.2 (Lollipop)
CPU	APQ8064(1.5 GHz)
Main Memory	2 GB
Storage	16 GB

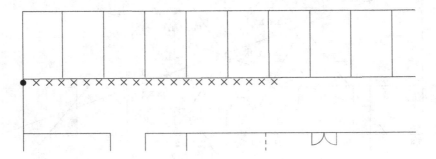

Fig. 3. Measurement points at the upper left corner of the seventh floor. •: beacon, ×: measurement point.

4   Measurement of the Beacon Field

4.1   Beacons and Smart Phone

First, we explain the beacon (Houwa System Design K.K.) and the smart phone used in the present study. The BLE module in the beacon is an HRM1017 (Hosiden Corp.). The supply voltage is approximately 3.0 V. The beacon can change the output power from −20 dBm to +4 dBm. Since the floor area is 32.8 m by 52.8 m and keeping the power as low as possible, we use −8 dBm in our experiment. The specifications of the beacons are shown in Table 1.

We use the Nexus 7 (2013, WiFi) as the BLE signal receiver. The Nexus 7 runs on Android 5.0.2 and supports a BLE device. The specifications of the receiver are shown in Table 2.

4.2   Preliminary Experiment

In this section, we describe the basic performance of beacons in a real location. We place one beacon in the upper left corner of the seventh floor. We measured the RSSI from 1 to 20 m at intervals of 1 m (Fig. 3). On average 46.5 measurements were taken at each measurement point, where a measurement consisted of sensing in four directions, each requiring 10 s. Measurements were then averaged over the four directions in order to account for local variation in a real location.

Figure 4 shows a box-and-whisker plot of the measurements. The x axis indicates the distance from the beacon and the y axis indicates the dBm level.

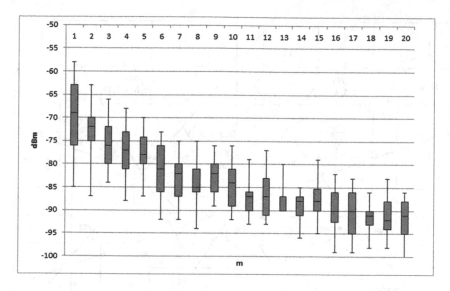

Fig. 4. Measurement results: RSSI (dBm) vs. distance (m)

In general, RSSI decreased with increasing distance, although there was some variation.

In this situation, we can find two thresholds: -65 dBm and -80 dBm. When the RSSI is larger than -65 dBm, the smart phone is closest to the beacon (corresponding to *Immediate* in the iOS SDK [14]). When the RSSI is larger than -80 dBm, the smart phone is near the beacon (corresponding to *Near* in the iOS SDK). Thus, we can divide the distance from the beacon into four parts: *Immediate* (RSSI > -65 dBm), *Near* (-80 dBm $<$ RSSI < -65 dBm), *Far*[1] (RSSI < -80 dBm) and *Unknown* (BLE is not detected).

4.3   Experiment on the Beacon Field

In this section, we describe the arrangement of beacons on the seventh floor of Building 18 at Tokai University. The arrangement of beacons is referred to as the *beacon field* and, in the following, we describe the measurement results on the beacon field.

Figure 5 shows the measurement points in the beacon field. The beacons are indicated by • symbols and measurement points are indicated by × symbols. We measured 136 points in the field. At each point, we measured in four directions, each requiring approximately 10 s. The average number of measurements is 41.7 per measurement point. The average number of measured beacons used in a measurement is 8.47.

---

[1] *Immediate, Near, Far* and *Unknown* are the return values for a method in the iOS SDK.

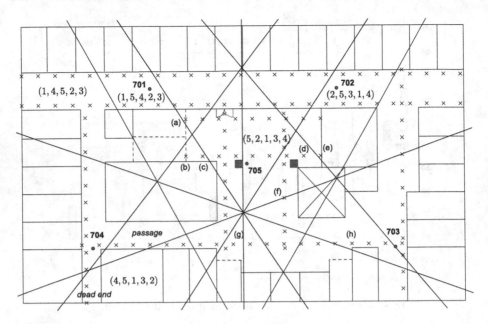

Fig. 5. Measurement points (×) and ordered order-5 Voronoi diagram for beacons (•) on the seventh floor.

Table 3. Floor decision rate statistics.

Measurement point	All	(a)	(b)	(c)	(d)	(e)	(f)	(g)	(h)
Correct rate	0.9961	0.8684	0.8837	0.8974	0.8205	1.0000	1.0000	1.0000	0.9767
Mistake rate	0.0039	0.1316	0.1163	0.1026	0.1795	0.0000	0.0000	0.0000	0.0233
Same rate	0.0580	0.4211	0.3023	0.5385	0.3333	0.3721	0.4524	0.4048	0.2093

Table 3 lists the correct and mistake rates for all and the measurement points (a), (b), ..., (h) shown in Fig. 5. The table also lists the *same rate*, which is the rate that two first-digit values have the same number of occurrences.

Table 4 lists the *correct rates* of OO-k Voronoi polygons in the experiments. The correct rate is computed as follows. Each measurement point is contained in an OO-5 Voronoi polygon. Thus, every point has a correctly sorted sequence of beacons $(c_1, c_2, c_3, c_4, c_5)$. In a measurement, we have a measured sequence of beacons $(b_1, b_2, \ldots b_k)$. The number k of measured beacons is not always five, but the maximum number of measured beacons is five. If b_j is equal to c_j $(j = 1, \ldots, i)$, we decide that these b_j are correctly ordered. When b_{i+1} is not equal to c_{i+1}, the beacons $b_{i+1}, \ldots, b_k$ are counted as an incorrect answer if $b_k = c_k$. As the index i increases, the correct rate decreases. The correct rate r_i of a OO-i Voronoi polygon is the number of correct beacons divided by the number of ith measurement beacons.

Table 4. Correct rates of ordered order-k Voronoi polygons.

Region	First	Second	Third	Fourth	Fifth	Number of measurement points
average	0.854648086	0.489470890	0.285739910	0.160785054	0.076366359	136
14523	0.840579710	0.378870674	0.113382900	0.075848303	0.000000000	14
15243	0.809224319	0.360379347	0.198505870	0.087640449	0.002074689	10
15423	0.848962656	0.309166667	0.156565657	0.068904594	0.001533742	6
23514	0.879654614	0.352685838	0.180011044	0.120669056	0.064893617	15
25134	0.841876629	0.353839442	0.211061947	0.132672332	0.074738416	11
25314	0.857825129	0.381180812	0.202616822	0.135124457	0.070960048	10
32514	0.870627063	0.386808088	0.223759703	0.135416667	0.066773504	7
35241	0.871857013	0.409671533	0.238995660	0.142051112	0.063383715	6
41523	0.882191781	0.448693260	0.262111453	0.138688327	0.064183124	9
45123	0.886483633	0.457195865	0.27015368	0.142237641	0.068365180	3
45132	0.89107413	0.470260693	0.284684685	0.152509653	0.074918567	4
51243	0.870967742	0.473364801	0.298333714	0.168042739	0.079146593	12
51423	0.865112225	0.468299082	0.290279627	0.163169064	0.076411960	3
52134	0.858987497	0.472245066	0.301878914	0.173893805	0.084502746	7
52314	0.857312959	0.482085987	0.303152789	0.174080411	0.083625731	4
53214	0.859652547	0.476311668	0.299284579	0.171848739	0.081621005	2
53241	0.857302326	0.488337376	0.293961764	0.168696347	0.080610605	6
53421	0.858171745	0.486015929	0.292692091	0.168350168	0.081102571	1
54123	0.857011916	0.484096341	0.290509043	0.167026921	0.080293886	1
54132	0.855686695	0.489418938	0.286000000	0.163030999	0.077743902	3
54312	0.854648086	0.489470890	0.285739910	0.160785054	0.076366359	2

For example, a measurement point is contained in $R(P; 1, 5, 2, 4, 3)$. We measured a sorted sequence of beacons (*701, 801, 704, 805, 702, 602, 505, 703, 804, 705, 502, 803*) on the seventh floor. We only use *7***: (*701, 704, 702, 703, 705*). We judge the first beacon *701* to be correct and the other beacons to be incorrect.

Figure 6 is a graph of the correct rates of average regions, good regions $R(P; 4, 5, 1, 3, 2)$, $R(P; 5, 2, 1, 3, 4)$ and worse regions $R(P; 1, 5, 4, 2, 3)$, $R(P; 1, 4, 5, 2, 3)$.

5 Discussion

Floor Decision

The floor decision is successful for 5,652 out of 5,674 measurements. The mistake rate is only 3.9 % in Table 3. The measurement points from (a) to (h) in Fig. 5 and in Table 3 includes ones with mistake decisions, or same rates higher rather than 40 %. We divide these points into three groups: {(a), (b), (c)}, {(d), (e), (f)} , and {(g), (h)}. The first group {(a), (b), (c)} is near staircases. The area indicated by the dashed lines containing (a) and (b) in Fig. 5 is the foot of the staircases. Since the staircases connect to the sixth and eighth floors, the smart phone collects BLE signals from other floors. This is why incorrect floor decisions

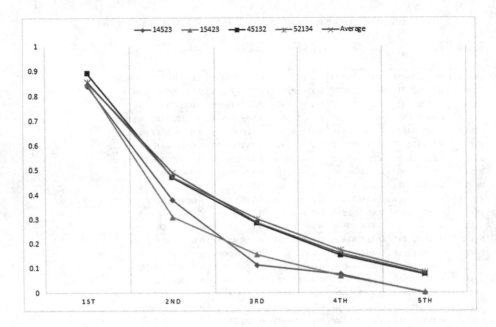

Fig. 6. Correct rates of some Voronoi polygons.

are made. Each of the third group {(g), (h)} is also near the foot of staircases, again indicated by dashed lines.

The second group {(d), (e), (f)} is not near staircases, but rather the measurement points are near a glass-enclosed open ceiling space, as expressed by ⊠ in Fig. 5. The BLE signal from the upper floor comes in through the glass.

Position Detection

[**Average Rate**]. First, we discuss the average correct rate of OO-k Voronoi polygons in Table 4. The first and second neighbors have correct rates of 85.5 % and 48.9 %, respectively. The remaining neighbors are 28.6 %, 16.0 %, and 7.6 %, in sequence. The first and second neighbors can be used for position detection, whereas the other neighbors cannot.

[**Good Correct Rates**]. In this section, we focus on polygons $R(P; 4, 5, 1, 3, 2)$ and $R(P; 5, 2, 1, 3, 4)$. Polygon $R(P; 4, 5, 1, 3, 2)$ is the lower left region in Fig. 5 and contains five measurement points. The measurement points are divided into two regions: the *dead end* and the *passage*. While the BLE signals from beacons *704 and 705* are received in the passage, the signal from beacon *704* is received in the dead end. Although the measurement point in the dead end is near beacon *705*, the RSSI of beacon *705* is smaller than that of beacon *701*, since there are walls between beacon *705* and the measurement points. Thus, the correct ratio of the points in the passage is better than that of the points in the dead end.

Polygon $R(P; 5, 2, 1, 3, 4)$ is the middle region in Fig. 5. There are seven measurement points in $R(P; 5, 2, 1, 3, 4)$, six of which are near beacon *705* and one of which is on the other side of a glass wall. At the point on the other side of glass, the RSSIs of beacons *701* and *702* are larger than that of beacon *705*. Thus, the correct rate is lower at the point and the average correct rate of $R(P; 5, 2, 1, 3, 4)$ is also lower. For better indoor position detection, it is necessary to omit such a point from the polygon, or to take the attenuation by the glass wall into consideration.

[**Poor Correct Rates**]. We discuss OO-5 Voronoi polygons $R(P; 1, 5, 4, 2, 3)$ and $R(P; 1, 4, 5, 2, 3)$. The polygon $R(P; 1, 5, 4, 2, 3)$ is located in the upper left corner of the beacon field (see Fig. 5). Among the measurement points of polygon $R(P; 1, 5, 4, 2, 3)$, the RSSIs of beacons *702* and *704* are larger than those of beacon *705*. The reason for this is that a glass wall and a staircase exist between the polygon and beacon *705*. The RSSI of *705* is weakened by the wall and by the large interference from beacons on other floors. The situation of polygon $R(P; 2, 5, 3, 1, 4)$ is similar to that of polygon $R(P; 1, 5, 4, 2, 3)$ from the symmetry of the configuration of beacons. The differences of situation between these polygons is near the staircases, or not. While beacon *705* is found 38 % measurement in polygon $R(P; 2, 5, 3, 1, 4)$, *705* is 30 % in polygon $R(P; 1, 5, 4, 2, 3)$. It is consider that the difference of correct rate is interference from other floors.

The polygon $R(P; 1, 4, 5, 2, 3)$ is also located in the upper left corner of the beacon field. The correct rates are 84 %, 38 %, 11 %, 8 % and 0 %, in sequence. Whereas the first rate is about the same as the average, the remaining rates are below the average. Thus, beacons *702* and *704* are detected and beacon *705* is not detected. The reason for this is also the above-mentioned interference.

6   Conclusion

In the present paper, we propose a method for indoor position detection using an ordered order-k Voronoi diagram. The proposed method involves two steps: floor decision and position detection. In the floor step, the floor number is decided based on the measured RSSIs. Position detection is based on a sequence of beacons arranged in strength order. The beacon field is divided into OO-k Voronoi polygons for sites that correspond to beacons.

We installed beacons in Building 18 of Tokai University and measured RSSIs at several points on seventh floor. We evaluated the measurements based on *floor decision* and *position detection*.

The floor decision success rate was approximately 99.6 %. At a few measurement points, the decision fails because of BLE signals from other floors. One idea is that used beacon is limited by their RSSIs (> -65 dBm) for detail decision. Since the beacons at other floor are far from a measurement point in a floor, the BLE signals from the beacons are weak. By the limitation, such beacons can be pruned from the sequence of beacons.

The position detection success rates are 85.5 % (first neighbor), 48.9 % (second neighbor) and 28.6 % (third neighbor). The first and second neighbors can be used for position detection. Two problem for position detection are found. One is interference of signals, another is variations of wall. First problem is a reason of worse correct ratio in higher order. The essential solution is difficult. We only take measure by the adjustment of neighbor region on real field. Another problem is solved by considering transmittance of wall. The glass wall above partially transmits BLE signals whereas the concrete wall does not transmit at all. So, we consider transmittance of wall and apply to proposed method.

For the effective use of these neighbors, it is better to use an *order-k Voronoi diagram*. A polygon $R(P; \{i_1, \ldots, i_k\})$ of an order-k Voronoi diagram is constructed by combining all OO-k Voronoi polygons $R(P; \sigma(i_1), \ldots, \sigma(i_k))$, where σ is a permutation of $i_1, i_2, \ldots, i_k$. For example, $R(P; \{2, 4\})$ in Fig. 1 is the combination of $R(P; 2, 4)$ and $R(P; 4, 2)$. Since the number of order-k Voronoi polygons is less than the number of OO-k polygons, we place more beacons on the field. HOVD [12] is also useful for indoor position detection when all wall does not transmit BLE signals.

The adjacency of an OO-k Voronoi polygon is useful for better detection. When a person is in an OO-k Voronoi polygon, in general, the person can only move to adjacent polygons.[2] For example, $R(P; 2, 4, 3)$ is adjacent to only $R(P; 2, 3, 4)$, $R(P; 4, 2, 3)$ and $R(P; 2, 4, 1)$.

Acknowledgments. The author would like to thank Professor Yoshimi ISHIHARA, Dean of the School of Science, Tokai University, for allowing the installation of beacons on Building 18 and for providing the opportunity to conduct the present study. Thanks are also due to Professor Masanori ITAI for suggesting the beacon installation and to the Open Beacon Field Trial (OBFT) (http://openbeacon.android-group.jp/) for providing beacons as well as the opportunity to conduct the present study. Special thanks are due to Daiki KANAI, a student in my laboratory, for measuring the RSSIs of the beacons.

References

1. Bluetooth specifications version 4.0, June 2010. https://www.bluetooth.org/
2. Yokohama Hakkeijima Sea paradise. http://www.seaparadise.co.jp/english/
3. Tokyo station navigation, East Japan Railway Company. http://www.jreast.co.jp/e/
4. Kyoto City Bus. http://www2.city.kyoto.lg.jp/koho/eng/access/transport.html
5. Hatami, A., Pahlavan, K.: A Comparative performance evaluation of RSS-based positioning algorithms used in WLAN networks. In: Proceedings of the IEEE Wireless Communications and Networking Conference (WCNC 2005), vol. 4, pp. 2331–2337, New Orleans, USA, March 2005
6. Evennou, F., Marx, F.: Advanced integration of WiFi and inertial navigation systems for indoor mobile positioning. EURASIP J. Appl. Signal Process 2006, Article ID 86706, 1–11 (2006). doi:10.1155/ASP/2006/86706

---

[2] Two Voronoi polygons are adjacent when the polygons share a segment.

7. Lloret, J., Tomas, J., Garcia, M., Canovas, A.: A hybrid stochastic approach for self-location of wireless sensors in indoor environments. Sensors **9**, 3695–3712 (2009). doi:10.3390/s90503695
8. Sung, T.-W., Yang, C.-S.: Voronoi-based coverage improvement approach for wireless directional sensor networks. J. Netw. Comput. Appl. **39**, 202–213 (2014)
9. Ishizuka, H., Kamisaka, D., Kurokawa, M., Watanabe, T., Muramatsu, S., Ono, C.: A fundamental study on a indoor localization method using BLE signals and PDR for a smart phone. IEICE Technical report, vol. 114, no. 31, MoNA2014-10, pp. 133–138 (in Japanese)
10. Okabe, A., Boots, B., Sugihara, K., Chiu, S.N.: Spatial Tessellations: Concepts and Applications of Voronoi Diagrams, 2nd edn. Wiley, New York (2000)
11. Aurenhammer, F., Schwarzkopf, O.: A simple on-line randomized incremental algorithm for computing higher order Voronoi diagrams. Int. J. Comput. Geom. Appl. **2**, 363–381 (1992)
12. Lee, I., Torpelund-Bruin, C., Lee, K.: Map segmentation for geospatial data mining through generalized higher-order Voronoi diagrams with sequential scan algorithms. Expert Syst. Appl. **39**(12), 11135–11148 (2012)
13. Halperin, D.: Arrangement. In: Goodman, J.E., O'Rourke, J. (eds.) Handbook of Discrete and Computational Geometry, 2nd edn, pp. 529–562. CRC Press, Boca Raton (2004)
14. Apple Inc., iOS: Understanding iBeacon. http://support.apple.com/kb/HT6048

Mobile Application Testing in Industrial Contexts: An Exploratory Multiple Case-Study

Samer Zein[1(✉)], Norsaremah Salleh[1], and John Grundy[2]

[1] Department of Computer Science, International Islamic University,
Kuala Lumpur, Malaysia
samer.m.zain@gmail.com, norsaremah@iium.edu
[2] Centre for Computing and Engineering Software Systems,
Swinburne University of Technology, Melbourne, Australia
jgrundy@swin.edu.au

Abstract. Recent empirical studies in the area of mobile application testing indicate the need for specific testing techniques and methods for mobile applications. This is due to mobile applications being significantly different than traditional web and desktop applications, particularly in terms of the physical constraints of mobile devices and the very different features of their operating systems. In this paper, we presented a multiple case-study involving four software development companies in the area of mobile and smartphones application. We aimed to identify testing techniques currently being applied by developers and challenges that they are facing. Our principle results are that many industrial teams seem to lack sufficient knowledge on how to test mobile applications, particularly in the areas of mobile application life-cycle conformance, context-awareness, and integration testing. We also found that there is no formal testing approach or methodology that can facilitate a development team to systematically test a critical mobile application.

Keywords: Software testing · Mobile applications · Case study

1 Introduction

Mobile applications are becoming very popular in that they are currently being integrated into almost all IT domains and their usage is widespread in everyday life [1]. Mobile applications nowadays are not only developed to serve the entertainment or social media sector, but also target safety and time critical domains, such as payment systems, m-government, military, and mobile health initiatives, to mention just a few [1, 2]. Therefore, users fully expect that such applications are easy, reliable and safe to use. Applications should thus be well-integrated, well-designed, accessible, robust and reliable. However, this makes mobile application solutions not only more complex and challenging to develop, but are also difficult to test and to validate [3].

It has been reported that the peculiarities of mobile application testing are due in part to the diversity of mobile platforms and features of mobile devices [1, 4]. Additionally, an important finding from the literature shows that there is a lack of studies on how to elicit specific testing requirements related to mobile application life cycle

© Springer International Publishing Switzerland 2015
H. Fujita and G. Guizzi (Eds.): SoMeT 2015, CCIS 532, pp. 30–41, 2015.
DOI: 10.1007/978-3-319-22689-7_3

properties from requirements specifications [5]. These issues motivate the need for better mobile testing approaches, techniques and tools [1, 5].

In a recent study we conducted a systematic mapping study that analyzed 45 empirical studies of mobile application testing techniques and challenges [5] and revealed significant gaps in the current body of research, suggesting several areas for further investigation. Among the issues we identified were most notably the needs for research in real-world industrial contexts, specific testing techniques, life cycle conformance and integration testing of mobile applications.

Since little information on mobile application testing techniques and issues is currently available in the context of industrial development companies, we undertook this research using an exploratory multiple-case study methodology. Understanding the developers' and test engineers' perception of the peculiarities, testing techniques and issues of mobile application testing are a challenge [1]. Such an understanding can reveal important insights and produce new perspectives on how mobile applications are developed in industrial contexts. It can also influence the research into new testing techniques and tools and importantly, how these techniques and tools might be most effectively transitioned into industrial practice. Each industrial case in our study represents a software development company in the field of mobile applications development located in Palestine, to which the lead author had good access to the company and staff. In this study, we analyzed the results from these multiple-case studies and compared them with mobile application testing techniques and challenges identified from our mapping study. The novelty of our study is that it represents the first attempt to explore and investigate mobile application testing techniques and challenges in four different companies and to help reveal key developer needs in such context. Based on our motivation above, the following study objectives were formulated:

- to investigate specific testing challenges and issues faced by industrial teams as well as how such teams currently tackle testing requirements of mobile applications.
- to compare the results of our case study with the state of the art from our mapping study to help increase the generalizability of others findings to date;
- to identify key future research areas in mobile application development testing that would be of benefit to industrial developers.

2   Related Work

Amalfitano et al. [3] present approaches to test context-aware applications and conduct case studies on real mobile applications to evaluate their approaches. In this present case study, we focused on any specific method or procedure that is used in testing mobile applications. The state-of-art of mobile application testing challenges and techniques can be summarized into four important aspects as below:

Life-cycle conformance: For mobile applications, the life-cycle is regarded as the different states that an application can go through during its run time and the transitioning between these states [4]. When developing mobile applications running on modern mobile operating systems such as Android, iOS and J2ME, the developer has to be fully aware of the states of the life-cycle in order to ensure correct behavior of application under all cases [4]. Such understanding will ensure that developers can build a reliable and robust mobile applications that operates correctly and is able to maintain data integrity [6–8]. Findings from our mapping study showed that there are only two studies that have proposed and evaluated such approaches to test conformance of mobile applications to life cycle models [4, 9]. However, the suggested approaches are very basic and that most of the critical steps proposed are manual and depend on the developer or tester's perception on the problem in hand.

Integration testing: Integration testing for mobile applications refers to the testing of mobile applications taking into account inter-application communication via intents or content providers in Android platform [1]. Similarly, mobile applications often require communication with other external applications such as social networking sites (e.g. Facebook, Twitter and MySpace) [6].

Automation testing: Most mobile application development is considered to be rapid development and teams should deliver applications to market in a short period of time to keep up with the market demand [10]. With the help of test automation, test engineers are more likely to be able to keep pace with developers to maintain agility [11, 12]. Automated UI testing and regression testing [12] are important requirements for agile teams. In our industrial case studies, we wanted to explore how teams apply test automation and which testing activities are involved.

Testing techniques: Our literature review also showed that there are several methods and procedures that can be used to test mobile applications under the categories of unit testing, functional UI testing, performance testing, and usability testing [13–15]. Additionally, several techniques have been introduced to test context-aware applications. For instance, Sama et al. [16] defines a new model based on finite-state machine for the detection of faults of incorrect adaptation logic and asynchronous updating of context information. In another study by Amalfitano et al. [3], an approach based on the definition of reusable design patterns is presented for automatic generation of test cases. In general, context-aware mobile applications are known to be very challenging applications to test [1, 3, 16]. In our industrial case studies, we investigated the type of testing techniques applied and compared them with those described in the research literature.

3 Research Methodology

In this section we discuss the case study methodology we used for our study. According to [17], case studies represent an empirical enquiry, investigating a contemporary phenomenon within its real life context, especially when the boundaries between phenomenon and context cannot be clearly specified. Case studies provide key value and deeper understanding of phenomena under study within real-world settings [18]. In case of exploratory case study research, it is important to include industrially-based cases because the context can play an important role in defining an emerging theme or theory [19].

3.1 Case Study Design

The design of this case study is based on multiple-case holistic design. Results and evidence from multiple-case designs is more convincing and compelling and thus, the overall study is considered to be more robust as compared to single-case design [17]. This case study investigates and draws conclusions from four different industrial cases. Figure 1 shows our approach to multiple-case study design, inspired by [17].

It is highly recommended to define a theoretical frame of reference that makes the context of the study clear to those who conduct the research and to those who review the results. Nevertheless, since theories in general are underdeveloped in software engineering, the frame of reference can be expressed in terms of related work that the study builds upon [18]. We have constructed the following three (3) key factors affecting mobile application testing that can be used as a basis for our data collection. These factors emerged from our literature review as well research direction reported by Muccini et al. [1]:

- Life cycle conformance – how and to what extent does mobile application testing take into account the life-cycle states of mobile applications?
- Integration testing – how and to what extent does testing examine the particularly critical issue of mobile application integration, including app-to-app data exchange, app-to-server data exchange, moving from one app to another, seamless and consistent user interfaces, context-awareness and so on?
- Testing techniques and test automation – what are the automated testing techniques employed by industrial mobile application testers and what further opportunities appear to automate additional laborious tasks?

3.2 Research Questions

We have formulated the following research questions:

- **RQ1:** How do teams in industrial mobile application development contexts approach testing?

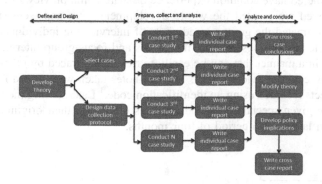

Fig. 1. Multiple case-study design [17]

- **RQ2:** What are the testing techniques applied and how effective are they compared to the state of the art?

3.3 Case Selection and Context

In software engineering, the cases and units of analysis can be anything that is contemporary software engineering phenomenon in its real-life context [18]. In our case study, the cases are the four software development companies in the field of mobile application development and unit of analysis are the development teams that consist of developers and testers working in the companies. The selection of the case study companies was based on availability of team members, willingness of company management, personal relationship with the main author and past working experience.

3.4 Data Collection and Analysis Procedures

Data was collected through interviews, observations and focus groups. The three principles of data collection which we used are: (1) use multiple sources of evidence; (2) use of a case study database; and (3) maintaining a chain of evidence [17, 20]. These were all applied in the case study design and its data collection and analysis.

Data collection through observations was done through taking field notes on the behavior and activities of developers and test engineers in mobile application development teams (i.e. observant without participation). For the interviews, the first author conducted a face-to-face as well as email and online interviews with test engineers and other software development team members. The interview protocol was designed prior to data collection. Each interview consisted of three parts and lasted for half an hour. In the first part the interviewees were given an introduction of study purpose and why they were selected. In second part, the interviewees were asked to give brief introduction about their work and experience. In the final part, the interviewees answered the interview questions defined in the protocol.

We also conducted a focus group discussion in order to get more insights, different data patterns and to apply data triangulation [21]. The groups are focused because the individuals gathered have common experience or share common views [22]. Since the group interviewed represented the whole development team and were small in size (4 persons), we treated the groups as adjuncts of interviewing individuals [23].

Data collected during observation, interviews and focus group interviews needs to be maintained in a manner that can be easily retrieved and traced by other researchers and to maintain chain of evidence [17, 18]. All notes taken were stored in documents and spread sheets recorded using an identification code.[1] Later, during thematic coding, sentences were given special codes and were also linked to their original documents. Data collection lasted for a period of four months.

---

[1] Case study protocol and summary data is available at https://sites.google.com/site/casestudymobileapp/.

We applied the thematic coding process reported in several qualitative studies [17, 18, 23, 24]. During this process, case study material such as interview answers, observation notes and researcher's reflections were studied. Then, a set of codes were formulated. Next, the whole material was divided in sentences and passages, given appropriate codes, and stored in spreadsheets. Then the spreadsheets, providing our case study database, were analyzed together to apply triangulation of data. Triangulation was used to combine the different data sources to corroborate our findings and conclusions and to minimize bias [17].

4 Results

In this section, we presented the results from our multiple case-studies. To preserve confidentiality, we refer to our case studies as C1, C2, C3 and C4. The first case study was C1, a startup company with a small development team consisting of two (2) developers applying agile and prototype-based processes. The team is working on a new daily task management system that deals with web and smartphone clients built for Android and iPhone platforms. The application complexity is high due to the fact that the application has many functional requirements and has to work on both online and offline modes with complex data synchronization logic and rules.

The second case, C2 is a well-established and large software development company developing software applications of various types such as cloud-based, web and mobile solutions. This company applies the SCRUM agile method and provides business and software solutions and a wide range of IT services. C2 has three mobile application development teams, each consisting of four (4) members, and offers custom mobile applications targeting personal assistant, navigation, and sales to mention a few.

The third case study, C3, is a software development company applying a strict SCRUM method and has an established and proven history of developing mobile applications as solutions to organizations with different sizes. They have specialized and skilled mobile specialists building mobile applications and applying best practices. This company, in contrast with C2, specializes in developing mobile applications for Android, iPhone and Blackberry platforms. Each platform has special development team of 4 members.

The forth case, C4, is a relatively old and established software development company building web and mobile applications for the enterprise level. What makes this company interesting is that their mobile application team is concerned with developing critical applications in the areas of e-billing and banking services. The development process applied in this company is waterfall and the mobile development team consists of three developers. The demographic profile of the companies is shown in Table 1. The companies are small and medium in size and the organization size varied from 3 to 125 people.

A summary of tools used by mobile application development teams, testing techniques applied and the average knowledge of the properties and conditions of life-cycle (LC) model for all cases are shown in Table 2. Except for fourth case C4 which used MS Team Foundation, the rest of cases used MS Excel to record bugs. During the

Table 1. Demographics of four cases

Case ID	Mobile apps domain	Dev. method	Org. size	Team size
C1	Task and project management	Prototype based, Waterfall	Small	2
C2	Navigation, search, personal assistant, traffic, sales	SCRUM	Large	3 teams (4 members each)
C3	Social apps, business apps	SCRUM	Medium	3 teams (4 members each)
C4	e-Banking, e-Billing, HR	Waterfall	Medium	3

Table 2. Tools and techniques applied

Case#	Tools used	Platform	Testing techniques	Average LC knowledge %
C1	Eclipse	Android, iPhone	Functional testing, performance testing	70 %
C2	Eclipse, Android Robotium, Traceview, Node JS, JUnit	Android, iPhone,	Functional testing, performance testing, automated GUI testing, unit testing	52 %
C3	Android studio, XCode, Eclipse, JUnit	Android, iPhone, Blackberry	Functional testing, performance testing, unit testing	80 %
C4	Eclipse, Team Foundation System	Android, iPhone	Functional testing, performance testing	65 %

Note: LC = Life cycle

four months of data collection, we have conducted observations and interviews with a total of nine (9) developers and a focus-group discussion involving four (4) developers.

In the following we provide a broad discussion of the development process and environment used, and then we move to more specific areas of life-cycle conformance, integration testing, and testing techniques.

Environment and development process: In general, it was observed that mobile application development is rapid in nature in most of companies studied (except for C4) and teams have to deliver increments of about one week sprints (iterations). On the other hand the development process applied by investigated cases ranged from waterfall, prototype-based to strict SCRUM. The dominant platforms between all companies for mobile applications are Android and iPhone. Regarding the development platform, one of the team leaders in C4 mentioned that: *"building for Android platform is very flexible compared to iPhone platform as we have to invoke many of the OS services. For instance, we are developing an application that keeps track and manages other running applications. This cannot be done on iPhone"* – Team leader, C4.

We noticed that a considerably a small amount of testing was done during the initial sprints and that comprehensive testing is done only in the final sprints before major releases. This implies that agile best practices such as test driven development are not strictly followed, as claimed by C2 and C3. This also implies that certain types of bugs are sometimes overlooked and missed [12].

We also noticed that since the mobile development community available online is considered relatively young and small, developers in the C1 company very often find it much more time consuming to search for a solution or certain examples of API usage. This is highlighted by one of the developers in C1: *"it is not easy to find solutions online when developing mobile apps, the community and available information is not that large"* – developer, C1.

Additionally, it was noticed that testing of mobile apps for their compatibility with different screen sizes consumes much effort and considerable time. Moreover, and since many mobile apps communicate with servers, it was observed for all cases that the testing process of such communication is also time consuming for the developers during the run-time.

Even though the dominant integrated development environment (IDE) used for Android development is Eclipse, all teams in all cases reported that they will move to Android Studio in the near future. This is because Google has announced that it will be the future supported platform for Android development [25]. *"We have one team that is using Android studio, soon the rest of the teams will join"* – Team leader, C3.

Additionally, in all cases the team size for all mobile application development was considered to be quite small, with team members ranging from two to four people including the team leader with no specialty between team members. *"we do not have specialty in our team, all team members perform all various tasks"*— developer, C1.

Life-cycle conformance testing: Testing of the life-cycle conformance of a mobile application is important to maintain a robust and reliable mobile application [4, 6, 7].

However, the findings from all cases revealed that none of the developers and test engineers showed deep and comprehensive understanding of the life-cycle properties and models of their mobile applications or applied specific testing techniques to test this important peculiarity.

An interesting result was noticed when the team members of the third case (C3) stated that they found some inconsistencies between the life-cycle model provided by Android Developers on their official website at [7], and the applications that they have developed. This result is also confirmed by the study at [4]. *"We noticed during the testing of one Android application using LogCat that the application followed a different path than that stated at Android Developer site"* – developer, C3.

Integration testing: Development teams in all cases in this study did not apply any specific method or procedure to test inter-application communication.

Testing techniques and test automation: Manual functional testing is the dominant testing techniques in all of the case studies. In fact, manual functional testing of mobile applications compromises about 80–90 % of total testing time and effort across each company. The researchers also noticed some use of record-and-replay tools such as Robotium. Furthermore, a test engineer stated that Robotium is not easy to use unless one has a thorough understanding of Android development: *"Android Robotium tool is not easy to be used by non-Android developers, for instance one has to know exactly how to access UI controls' Ids in order to build test scripts"* – developer, C2.

In another case (C3), one team reported that sometimes they use a special tool to monitor the application in the field after it is deployed to user. Specific testing techniques for context-awareness were totally absent with no application of specific testing techniques suggested by [26, 27].

Test automation on the other hand was applied on very limited basis and mostly at automating the execution of unit tests as well as the automation of GUI tests (regression testing) through special testing tool such as Android Robotium. Only one case (C2) reported that they used GUI record-and-replay tool in one of their projects.

On the other hand, several interviewees suggested other areas for automation such as the design of user interfaces in Android platforms: *"Considerable time is wasted when building user interfaces and the GUI designer for Android at Eclipse IDE is not very smart"* – team leader, C4.

5   Discussion and Threats to Validity

Prior work has documented the peculiarities of mobile applications and identified several testing approaches and techniques to address these peculiarities in the areas of life-cycle conformance, context-awareness and integration testing [1, 3, 4, 16]. However, there are no studies that investigate how much development teams in real industrial contexts are aware of such peculiarities, how testing is approached and what are the challenges faced by these teams.

Several issues can be concluded from the results. First and relating to research questions RQ1 and RQ2: It is apparent that testing of mobile applications is approached with a similar mind-set to traditional software testing techniques, with very little, if any, attention given to mobile application specific peculiarities and testing techniques. Furthermore, development teams are more concerned with developing highly responsive mobile applications with fancy user interfaces quickly and in short development cycles.

However, mobile applications are quite different than traditional web and desktop applications and therefore should be approached using different testing techniques [1, 10]. Manual functional testing is not sufficient to produce a robust and reliable mobile application, in particular if that application is considered to be critical [10]. A dedicated complementary testing technique should be applied to cover specific areas for mobile applications:

- For life-cycle conformance testing, the studies at [4, 9] provide a more robust life-cycle models than that defined by the Android Developer website.
- Regarding testing of context-aware apps, the study at [3] presents an approach based on the definition of reusable event patterns for the manual and automatic generation of test cases for mobile application testing. In another study by [28],

the authors target the problem of identifying and exposing faults of buggy context providers and propose a fault tolerant application design. Additionally, the study at [16] defines a new model for detecting faults of incorrect adaptation logic, asynchronous updating of context information and defines algorithms to automatically detect such faults.

- Test driven development (TDD) is one of the core practices in agile methods [12, 29]. This technique however, was not applied by teams using agile development. We strongly recommend careful consideration to applying TDD in mobile application testing, to improve early phase testing, to identify requirements problems [11].

Second, development teams should develop a specific testing strategy that is appropriate to the application under test. Such a strategy should contain appropriate testing techniques to address all aspects of mobile applications and not only the functional parts.

Third, it was noticed that the online documentation, forums, and community available on the Internet to assist mobile application developer are still relatively small and much less mature compared to other mature and large communities such as web application development.

Validity and reliability strategies were applied from the beginning in our study. The three criteria used to reach high level of rigor in our case studies are construct validity, external validity, and reliability [19]. As suggested by Yin [17], we applied the use of multiple evidence and chain of evidence strategies to address construct validity; use of theory strategy to address external validity case study protocol for reliability. The internal validity was not considered due to the type of this study that is exploratory in nature.

6 Conclusions and Future Research

This paper presents an exploratory multiple case-studies that aim to investigate how mobile application testing is approached in real world industrial contexts. Our industrial case studies can be characterized as the first attempt to explore and investigate how appropriate are such mobile application testing techniques to the challenges faced by industrial teams. We studied four mobile application development companies to see how they approach testing and the particular issues developers face when testing mobile applications.

We found that in virtually all cases we studied, developers and test engineers lack sufficient knowledge and skills with testing techniques and tools on how to develop or test a mobile application that conforms to life-cycle properties and models. Additionally, we found no awareness on how to test specifically mobile application inter-application communications issues, known as application integration testing. Instead, and in almost all cases, testing mostly relies on manual functional testing through the user interface. The findings from our study showed the absence of specialized testing techniques being used in four industry case studies to test specific and important issues of mobile applications such as life-cycle conformance and integration testing. In future work, we intend to design and implement a comprehensive testing framework for mobile applications.

Acknowledgment. This research was funded by the Ministry of Higher Education Malaysia under FRGS research grant (FRGS14-125-0366). We would like to thank the team leader and developers in the four companies who have participated in our case study.

References

1. Muccini, H., Di Francesco, A., Esposito, P.: Software testing of mobile applications: challenges and future research directions. In: 2012 7th International Workshop on Automation of Software Test (AST). IEEE (2012)
2. Payet, É., Spoto, F.: Static analysis of android programs. Inf. Softw. Technol. **54**(11), 1192–1201 (2012)
3. Amalfitano, D., Fasolino, A.R., Tramontana, P., Amatucci, N.: Considering context events in event-based testing of mobile applications. In: 2013 IEEE Sixth International Conference on Software Testing, Verification and Validation Workshops (ICSTW) (2013)
4. Franke, D., Kowalewski, S., Weise, C., Prakobkosol, N.: Testing conformance of life cycle dependent properties of mobile applications. In: 2012 IEEE Fifth International Conference on Software Testing, Verification and Validation (ICST) (2012)
5. Zein, S., Salleh, N., Grundy, J.: A systematic mapping study of mobile application testing techniques. J. Syst. Softw.: Under review (2015)
6. Lee, W.-M.: Beginning Android 4 Application Development. Wiley, Hoboken (2012)
7. Processes and Application Life Cycle, March 2014 (2014). http://developer.android.com/guide/topics/processes/process-lifecycle.html#
8. Haseman, C.: Creating Android Applications: Develop and Design. Peachpit Press, Berkeley (2011)
9. Franke, D., Elsemann, C., Kowalewski, S.: Reverse engineering and testing service life cycles of mobile platforms. In: 2012 23rd International Workshop on Database and Expert Systems Applications (DEXA) (2012)
10. Amalfitano, D., Fasolino, A.R., Tramontana, P.: A GUI crawling-based technique for android mobile application testing. In: 2011 IEEE Fourth International Conference on Software Testing, Verification and Validation Workshops (ICSTW) (2011)
11. Larman, C.: Agile and Iterative Development: A Manager's Guide. Addison-Wesley, Boston (2004)
12. Crispin, L., Gregory, J.: Agile Testing: A Practical Guide for Testers and Agile Teams. Pearson Education, Boston (2008)
13. Heejin, K., Byoungju, C., Wong, W.E.: Performance testing of mobile applications at the unit test level. In: Third IEEE International Conference on Secure Software Integration and Reliability Improvement, SSIRI 2009 (2009)
14. Amalfitano, D., Fasolino, A.R., Tramontana, P., De Carmine, S., Memon, A.M.: Using GUI ripping for automated testing of Android applications. In: 2012 Proceedings of the 27th IEEE/ACM International Conference on Automated Software Engineering (ASE) (2012)
15. Harrison, R., Flood, D., Duce, D.: Usability of mobile applications: literature review and rationale for a new usability model. J. Interact. Sci. **1**(1), 1–16 (2013)

16. Sama, M., Elbaum, S., Raimondi, F., Rosenblum, D.S., Zhimin, W.: Context-aware adaptive applications: fault patterns and their automated identification. IEEE Trans. Softw. Eng. **36**(5), 644–661 (2010)
17. Yin, R.K.: Case Study Research: Design and Methods. Sage Publications, Thousand Oaks (2009)
18. Runeson, P., Höst, M.: Guidelines for conducting and reporting case study research in software engineering. Empirical Softw. Eng. **14**(2), 131–164 (2009)
19. Woodside, A.G., Wilson, E.J.: Case study research methods for theory building. J. Bus. Ind. Mark. **18**(6/7), 493–508 (2003)
20. Lethbridge, T.C., Sim, S.E., Singer, J.: Studying software engineers: data collection techniques for software field studies. Empirical Softw. Eng. **10**(3), 311–341 (2005)
21. Creswell, J.: Research design: qualitative, quantitative, and mixed methods approaches. Sage Publications, Thousand Oaks (2009)
22. Tashakkori, A., Teddlie, C.: Sage Handbook of Mixed Methods In Social and Behavioral Research. Sage Publications, Thousand Oaks (2010)
23. Yin, R.K.: Qualitative Research From Start To Finish. Guilford Press, New York (2010)
24. Miles, M.B., Huberman, A.M.: Qualitative Data Analysis: A Sourcebook of New Methods. Sage publications, Thousand Oaks (1984)
25. Android Studio. http://developer.android.com/tools/studio/index.html
26. Ravindranath, L., Padhye, J., Agarwal, S., Mahajan, R., Obermiller, I., Shayandeh, S., AppInsight: mobile app performance monitoring in the wild. In: Proceedings of the 10th USENIX Conference on Operating Systems Design and Implementation, pp. 107–120. USENIX Association: Hollywood (2012)
27. Lettner, F. Holzmann, C.: Automated and unsupervised user interaction logging as basis for usability evaluation of mobile applications. In: Proceedings of the 10th International Conference on Advances in Mobile Computing and Multimedia, pp. 118–127. ACM, Bali (2012)
28. Bo, J., Xiang, L., Xiaopeng, G., Zhifang, L., Chan, W.K.: FLOMA: Statistical fault localization for mobile embedded system. In: 2011 3rd International Conference on Advanced Computer Control (ICACC) (2011)
29. Vu, J.H., Frojd, N., Shenkel-Therolf, C., Janzen, D.S.: Evaluating test-driven development in an industry-sponsored capstone project. In: Sixth International Conference on Information Technology: New Generations, ITNG 2009. IEEE (2009)

An Efficient Reconfiguration-Based Approach for Improving Smart Grid Performance

Syrine Ben Meskina[1,2][✉], Narjes Doggaz[3], and Mohamed Khalgui[1]

[1] LISI, INSAT, University of Carthage, Tunis, Tunisia
{bmeskinasyrine,khalgui.mohamed}@gmail.com
[2] FST, ISI, University of Tunis-El Manar, Tunis, Tunisia
[3] URPAH, FST, University of Tunis-El Manar, Tunis, Tunisia
narjes.doggaz@fst.rnu.tn

Abstract. In this research paper, we deal with power grid modeling and reconfiguration to improve electrical network performance for which we propose a new definition in terms of automatic recovery rate. We propose a novel and original methodology for, intelligently, optimizing the use of power energy in smart grids based on Mutli-Agent System composed of static and mobile agents. Our work presents an assistance-design approach as it proposes new and efficient reconfigurations to automatically resolve the maximum of failures in the aim of improving the power system reliability and performance. To optimize the cost of the automatic actions to be taken for reducing the costs of the human interventions, we identify a pertinent short list of failures based on a proposed relations of dominance and equivalence between failures. The efficiency of the proposed strategy is showed by the experimental study.

Keywords: Smart grid · Reconfiguration · Fault management · Performance evaluation · Software management and analysis

1 Introduction

The new generation of power networks called smart grids includes big amounts of multidimensional characteristics to make power networks intelligent such as multi-service communication, reliability, security and safety allowing a real-time monitoring and supervision. Moreover, it can be seen as the modernization of the current electric grid through the integration of renewable and green energies to decarbonize power systems and, even, the addition of new smart electric hardware devices and, also, distributed energy resources. The importance of the damages caused by power breaks and outages, as well as, the classical centralized production architecture have encouraged and inspired researchers to work on it in order to bring changes on power grids and, even, on their infrastructures. But the existing methods - dealing with power system recovery - do not handle the consequent failures and do not investigate the relations between them as each failure is handled separately. To overcome this disadvantage, we propose in [1]

© Springer International Publishing Switzerland 2015
H. Fujita and G. Guizzi (Eds.): SoMeT 2015, CCIS 532, pp. 42–55, 2015.
DOI: 10.1007/978-3-319-22689-7_4

to classify failures on dominant and equivalent ones. To experiment, test and validate the proposed approach, we have developed a software tool which is able to model, design, parameterize and simulate power networks [2]. It allows, also, the fault detection and an efficient recovery according to the structure and configuration of the simulated smart grid. However, the fault recovery is sometimes impossible because of a lack of electric power lines. To overcome this problem and to improve the reliability of power grid functioning, we propose new feasible reconfigurations, especially, in case of frequent power outages or for strategic zones such as hospitals or ministerial buildings. In this paper, we look for improving the reliability of power grid functioning and increasing its performance. In this aim, we present an extension and an adaptation of our multi-agent architecture for fault categorisation and recovery [1,2] to handle fault reconfiguration. It consists of searching the pertinent set of electrical lines to be deployed reducing the number of non resolvable failures to improve smart grid performance and, therefore, its service quality. For that, we propose a novel performance definition based on identifying the resolvable and non-resolvable faults aiming for increasing the recovery rate. In order to ensure efficient and automatic reconfigurations, we propose to search a short list of non-resolvable faults - using the fault classification proposed in [1] - for which the resolution implies the consequent resolution of other ones. The main gain of our approach consists of decreasing the human and manual recoveries while improving the importance of efficient automatic and distant recoveries with smaller costs and even to help and assist for smart grid re-design. We discuss, in Sect. 2, the recent related works and we, briefly, present, in Sect. 3 our previous research works. We propose a new definition for measuring smart grid performance in Sect. 4 illustrated by a simple case study. In Sect. 5, we detail the functioning of the proposed approach for power system reconfiguration as well as the proposed MAS. In Sect. 6, we expose the implemented algorithms and, then, an experimental study performed over different power grids.

2   State of the Art

Over the last years, many researchers worked on different topics and concepts relative to power networks and smart grids. There is an important number of works relative to the problematic of fault detection in power system, self-healing and system recovery, optimization and reconfiguration. These related studies investigate these problems and propose several approaches based on different concepts such as; Multi-Agent Systems (MAS), Petri-Nets, smart micro-grids using Distributed Energy Resources (DER), electric devices like Phasor Measurement Unit and smart storage devices... [3] develops an approach to efficiently identify the most probable failure modes in static load distribution for a given power network. [4] proposes a method using Petri Nets in order to model smart grids, detect and identify failures in transmission power grids. [5] present a new reconfiguration for power grids by evolving their infrastructure for improving their efficiency, reliability, and safety. The goal is to decentralize the control without waiting the response of the central protection system in case of power network failures. The decision of centralizing or decentralizing the control in power grids presents a fundamental concept to be studied and determined according to the encountered circumstances. [6] discusses the difference between central and distributed hierarchical control structures. The widespread failure is a, particularly, quite likely consequence to power grids having centralized infrastructure and, then, threatened with a cascading failures from which the benefit of dividing the network on subnetworks, called micro-grids or "islands", is highlighted. Distributed infrastructures decentralizing the control imply, generally, the deployment of DER and distributed generators and even energy storage systems and load controllers in order to reduce the transmission failures [7]. This concept is still under study in the last few years in several countries, as the extensive investment to install electric lines across large distances to supply few people is very expensive whenever projects relative to islanded micro grids provides great opportunities on the grid. [8] finds a very encouraging results, even, when introducing a small number of local generators into the grid, can reduce the likelihood of dramatically cascading failures. In fact, thanks to this strategy based on distributed energy resources and decentralized power system control, it will be possible to, efficiently, balance the demand and the generation at small-scale (micro-source) as shown in [9] during normal and outage operations. They proposes a concept of micro-grids working as islands independent of the main grid. [10] proposes a learning automata based data transmission path selection algorithm with multiple constraints such as cost, delay, and energy consumption to optimize the performance of smart grid in terms of fault tolerance and energy management. [11] proposes a new perspective to ameliorate the reliability by mixing three resources in smart grids (renewable, storage and demand resources) in a developed hierarchical framework based on intelligent agents. After these short observations on the literature, we count a multitude of research works working on power system recovery, reconfiguration, reliability and optimization of performance. In fact, all of them do not investigate the relation between failures. In the other hand, there is often some failures - resolvable or non-resolvable - depending on other ones. It is important to handle them efficiently by reducing the number of those to be automatically resolved. Moreover, we remark a lack of research works dealing with service quality of power networks an the majority of them propose manual recoveries without evaluating their costs as well as the required time for human interventions. We note, also, that it is important to analyze and investigate the load flowing the network and the benefit of the non-used available energy. We observe, also, that the power system reconfiguration in the literature is generally performed by radically changing its operating way, its infrastructure, integrating new electrical devices... While it is possible to investigate the current structure and propose new reconfigurations with smaller costs to assist the design of power gird with higher performance.

3 Background

We assume that a smart grid architecture involves, typically, three voltage levels: high, medium and low ones. It is generally, composed of power generators and transformers, consumers and electrical lines. In addition to it, we note, also, that it contains emergency lines which can be activated to resolve automatically some failures. In [1], we detail our multi-agent system for fault detection, localization and recovery in smart grids. We propose a set of operating conditions to be verified over smart grids based on useful characteristics of electrical components and lines in order to identify the, eventually, occurred faults. A fault corresponds to a failed component on which the operating conditions are not checked. In order to optimize the required time for power system recovery, we look for optimizing the cost of the resolution procedure while trying to solve, automatically and not manually, the maximum of the occurred faults. For that, we proposed new definitions for dominant and equivalent faults. Dominant faults correspond to faults engendering other ones in the connected components (belonging to the voltage level below or the same one with smaller rank). The rank presents the order of a component apparition in a power line. Equivalent faults correspond to faults occurring on components belonging to the same voltage level and having the same rank. These new relations facilitate the automatic failure recovery and allow the control and the reduction of the fault recovery time. In order to reduce the complexity of the faults to be resolved and, then, to accelerate the recovery procedure of power system recovery, we propose an efficient strategy for identifying the minimum set of pertinent faults. The developed simulator FDIRSY (Fault Detection, Isolation and Recovery SYstem), in [2], deploys a Multi-Agent System (MAS) ensuring an efficient strategy for power system recovery at realtime. We propose a local resolution thanks to the deployed static agents and a non-local resolution thanks to the integration of mobile agents. We show, also, that our system is able to find the best solution among the existent ones according to the proposed heuristics in a short time compared to related works. We prove mathematically the completeness and the efficiency of the optimized version of the recovery protocol. These observations were confirmed empirically by the experimental study and tests performed over several simulated smart grids having different structures over which we injected multiple problems at the same time. We showed, if there exists a solution for a detected problem, then our system is able to find it. But, there exist some faults for which FDIRSY can not find solution due to the lack of electrical lines in the configuration of the studied smart grids (insufficiency of capacities, of emergency lines, etc.). The service quality of smart grid as well as its operating performance depends, highly, on its ability to automatically recover the occurred failures.

4   Evaluation of Smart Grids: New Challenges for Design Assistance

4.1   Performance of Smart Grid

We propose a new definition and calculus of smart grid performance to asses them in terms of detectable faults which can be resolved compared with the whole set of possible faults. We look for analyzing this percentage in the aim of improving SG performance and automatize as much as possible the recovery procedure. We denote, by $Perf(SG)$, the performance of a smart grid SG for which we propose the calculus as in (1):

$$Perf(SG) = \frac{|RF(SG)|}{|TF(SG)|} \tag{1}$$

where $TF(SG)$ is the set of all detectable and possible faults which can occur over SG and $RF(SG)$ is the set of all the faults occurring over SG and which can be resolved by FDIRSY. In fact, we remind that a fault corresponds to a failed electrical component [2]. Thus, $TF(SG)$ can be formed by all the electrical components belonging to SG. So, if SG contains n electrical components including generators, transformers and consumers, then, $|TF(SG)| = n$. In this paper, we restrict our study, only, on the consumers of the studied smart grid SG. Hence, the set $TF(G)$ contains all the faults occurring on the medium and low voltage consumers of the smart grid SG and is defined by 2:

$$TF(SG) = RF(SG) \cup NRF(SG) \tag{2}$$

where $RF(SG)$ is the set of faults that FDIRSY can recover and $NRF(SG)$ is the set of non resolvable faults by FDIRSY. As both of $RF(SG)$ and $NRF(SG)$ are two subsets forming the whole set $TF(SG)$, we propose the following relation:

$$|TF(SG)| = |RF(SG)| + |NRF(SG)| \tag{3}$$

As $|TF(SG)|$ is constant since the number of consumers is constant, so when we increase the number of resolvable faults ($|RF(SG)|$ ↗), then, the number of non-resolvable faults over SG will automatically decrease ($|NRF(SG)|$ ↘), and, then, the performance of the smart grid SG will, consequently, increase ($Perf(SG)$ ↗). We aim to decrease the number of non-resolvable faults in order to improve the performance of smart grid. For that, we look for searching and proposing new reconfigurations for smart grid based on adding new electrical emergency lines to allow the resolution of some non-resolvable faults. We look, then, for searching the minimum set of pertinent lines to be added in order to resolve the maximum of non-resolvable faults.

4.2   Case Study

To illustrate the proposed definition and calculus, we propose to measure the performance of the smart grid SG in Fig. 1. As we are focussed on investigating faults occurring, only, on consumers, we obtain $TF(SG) = \{MC_i,\ LC_j\}$, where $i,\ j \in \mathbb{N}$ such that $i = 1, ..., 5$ and $j = 1, ..., 15$. Thus, we have $|TF(SG)| = 20$. According to the new fault categorization - by dominance or equivalence - proposed in [1], we cite, for example, the fault occurring on LC_7 as a dominant one which dominates the ones occurring on LC_9, LC_{11}, LC_{12} and LC_{10}. On the other hand, the faults occurring on the consumers LC_3 and LC_4 are equivalent. According to the existing emergency lines - $eMVL_1$, $eLVL_1$, $eLVL_2$, $eLVL_3$,

$eLVL_4$ and $eLVL_5$ - and to the required and remaining loads, as indicated in Fig. 1, we can identify the set of resolvable faults. The possible solutions which can be ensured consists, respectively, on resolving MC_2 or (MC_1 and MC_3), LC_5 or LC_{12}, LC_{15} or LC_{12}, LC_{11} or LC_4, LC_3 or LC_4, (LC_6 and LC_8) or (LC_7 and LC_9 and LC_{10} and LC_{11} and LC_{12}). Using the proposed fault classification by dominance or equivalence, it is possible to resolve 11 faults in the best case while, only, 7 ones can be resolved in the worst case. The subset of resolvable faults contains, thus, $RF(SG) = \{MC_1, MC_2, MC_3, LC_3, LC_4, LC_5, LC_6,$ $LC_7, LC_8, LC_9, LC_{10}, LC_{11}, LC_{12}, LC_{15}\}$ such that $|RF(SG)| = 14$. The set of non-resolvable faults, contains the faults belonging to $TF(SG)$ and for which there is no solution. Thus, we obtain $NRF(SG) = \{MC_4, MC_5, LC_1, LC_2,$ $LC_{13}, LC_{14}\}$ such that $|NRF(SG)| = 6$ with compliance to the two equalities 2 and 3 proposed in Sect. 4.1. We calculate the performance of the considered smart grid - using the formula 1. We find that it is comprised between $\frac{7}{20} = 35\%$ in the worst case and $\frac{11}{20} = 55\%$ in the best case. We notice that, even in the best case, the calculated performance covers barely 50%. Our analysis is original and motivating as no one in related works proposes some ideas.

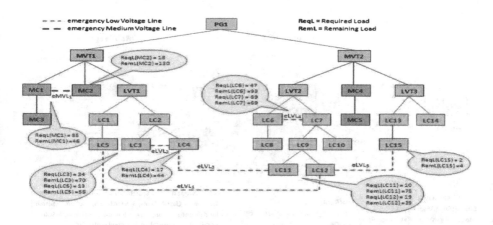

Fig. 1. Running example for measuring smart grid performance

5 New Approach for Improving Smart Grid Performance

5.1 Motivations

We propose, in [1,2], a recovery approach for flexible smart grid which consists of searching new local or non-local solutions for the detected failures by means of exploiting the existing emergency lines coming from components having remaining loads. Taking account of the unexploited remaining load, we propose in this paper the creation of new emergency lines in order to resolve even more faults ($\nearrow |RF(SG)|$) and that, in order to improve smart grid performance. We look for obtaining a software tool for design and reconfiguration assistance in the aim of obtaining a better or even best performance. To overcome these aims, we adapt the MAS architecture proposed in [1] which is composed of, only, one DataBase Agent, one Reconfiguration Agent per smart sub-grid and Mobile Agents instantiated by the second one(s). In this research paper, we propose an extension for this MAS taking into account the new reconfiguration functionality. In fact, we adapt our MAS to ensure, in addition to the efficient detection and recovery, the reconfiguration of flexible smart grid to improve its performance. In order to alleviate the tasks of the Reconfiguration Agent previously used, we introduce new agents; each one of them is specialized in handling a task (classification, managing local data base, local resolution, local reconfiguration, taking decision). These new agents are working as slave agents monitored and supervised by their Master Agent called SupAg. For that, we add two new agents for reconfiguration. The main role of the static agents consists of ensuring local recovery and reconfiguration while the mobile ones are dedicated to the global recovery and reconfiguration tasks. The proposed system has a distributed and hierarchical architecture at the same time as we associate one SupAg to each sub-grid. It is composed, as illustrated by Fig. 2, of the following cooperative agents.

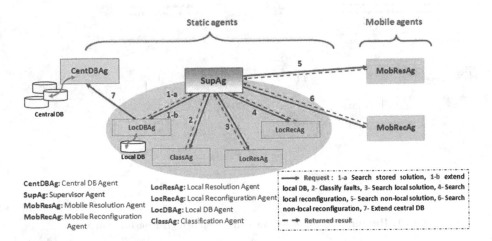

Fig. 2. New MAS architecture for smart grid recovery and reconfiguration

5.2 Multi-agent Architecture for Improving Smart Grid Performance

In this section, we describe briefly the role of the agents introduced in Sect. 5.1 as follows. The position of each one of them is illustrated by Fig. 3.

1- SupAg: is responsible of supervising the proper functioning of the sub-grid under its scope. In fact, we assign to each sub-grid belonging to the studied smart grid, one SupAg to which we associate the following Slave agents:

- **LocDBAg:** is responsible of managing the information relative to the concerned sub-grid as well as the history of the encountered problems and the corresponding solutions (encountered problem, fault category, failed components, solution type, number of occurrences...).
- **ClassAg:** is responsible of classifying, by dominance or equivalence, a given fault set in order to identify the short fault list corresponding to the components to be resolved or reconfigured.
- **LocResAg:** is responsible of searching all the existing local solution(s) to the encountered problem. A local solution consists of a local deactivated emergency line procuring sufficient loads to supply the failed component(s) of the identified short list.
- **LocRecAg:** is responsible of searching new feasible local reconfiguration(s) to the non-resolvable encountered problem. A new local reconfiguration consists of proposing to add new local emergency line(s).

In case of receiving multiple feasible local or non-local solutions/reconfigurations, the SupAg chooses the best one of them to be executed using a proposed heuristic: the one having the smaller remaining load from the components having the lower priority.

2- CentDBAg: is responsible of the management and the storage of all the information relative to the whole power grid structure as well as the history of the encountered problems and the corresponding solutions found by our MAS as well as the proposed new reconfigurations.

3- MobResBAg: is instantiated by the SupAg when there is no local solution to the encountered problem. It is responsible of searching new non-local solutions from the other sub-grids connected through emergency lines. A non-local solution consists of a non-local deactivated emergency line procuring sufficient loads to supply the failed component(s).

4- MobRecAg: is instantiated by the SupAg when there is no possible local reconfiguration to the encountered problem. It is responsible of searching new feasible non-local reconfiguration(s) to the non-resolvable encountered problem. A new non-local reconfiguration consists of proposing to add new non-local emergency line(s).

5.3   Reconfiguration Strategy for Performance of Smart Grid

The two agents LocRecAg and MobRecAg are, respectively, responsible of searching the feasible local and non-local reconfigurations. In fact, their search, respectively, the sets of local and non-local components to be linked to the one(s) of the short fault list through new emergency lines to be deployed. Let us denote by SSG_i the ith smart sub-grid belonging to the whole smart grid SG ($SSG_i \subset SG$). Let us denote by $FC(SSG_i)$ and $SL(FC(SSG_i))$, respectively, the failed components in SSG_i and the short list of the failed components over them such that $SL(FC(SSG_i)) \subset FC(SSG_i)$. We denote the remaining and required loads relative to component s, respectively, by $RemainL(s)$ and $ReqL(s)$.

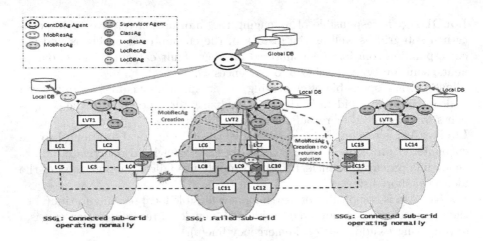

Fig. 3. Example for agent position (Color figure online)

The LocRecAg looks for finding the $LocRec(SL(FC(SSG_i)))$. It is the set of all the electrical components c such that: *(i)* c is local $(c \in SSG_i)$, *(ii)* c belongs to the same voltage level than the failed ones of the short list (Voltage Level(c) = Voltage Level$(SL(FC(SSG_i)))$), *(iii)* c is non-connected to the failed ones of the short list ($\nexists$ principal line between c and $SL(FC(SSG_i))$), *(iv)* c is not failed $(c \notin FC(SSG_i))$, *(v)* c procures sufficient loads to supply the failed one(s) of the short list (RemainL$(c) \geq \sum$ReqL(s) $\forall s \in SL(FC(SSG_i))$).

The MobRecAg looks for finding the $NonLocRec(SL(FC(SSG_i)))$. It is the set of all the electrical components c such that: *(i)* c is non-local $(c \notin SSG_i)$, *(ii)* c belongs to the same voltage level than the failed ones of the short list, *(iii)* c is non-connected to the failed ones of the short list ($\nexists$ emergency line between c and $SL(FC(SSG_i))$), *(iv)* c is not failed $(c \notin FC(SSG_j)$ $/i \neq j)$, *(v)* c procures sufficient loads to supply the failed one(s) of the short list. Applying this proposed strategy to the smart grid in Fig. 3 allows the deployment of two new emergency lines which are drawn in green.

6   Implementation and Experimentation

6.1   Algorithms

The first step of our methodology is to define the $RF(SG)$ and the $NRF(SG)$ sets (Algorithm 1). *SearchLocSolution* presents the task ensured by the LocResAg to search locally an existing solution for the encountered problem while *SearchNonLocSolution* is the principal task ensured by the MobResAg to perform a global search for solution.

Then the SupAg requests its ClassAgent to categorize the faults type by dominance and equivalence $(FT(NRF(SG)))$ as in Algorithm 2 in order to identify the relevant short list of faults to be recovered. It is denoted by $SL(NRF(SG))$

Algorithm 1. Identification of the $RF(SG)$ and $NRF(SG)$ subsets

---

Require: $TF(SG)$.
Ensure: $RF(SG)$, $NRF(SG)$
  $RF(SG) \leftarrow \emptyset$
  $NRF(SG) \leftarrow \emptyset$
  For each $f \in TF(SG)$ **do**
    If $(SearchLocSolution(f) = \emptyset)$ **and** $(SearchNonLocSolution(f) = \emptyset)$ **Then**
      $NRF(SG) \leftarrow NRF(SG) \cup \{f\}$
    Else
      $RF(SG) \leftarrow RF(SG) \cup \{f\}$
    End if
  End for

---

such that $SL(NRF(SG)) \subseteq NRF(SG)$. Thus, the number of consumers to be reconfigured is reduced ($|SL(NRF(SG))| \leq |NRF(SG)|$). In case of dominance, this short list contains, only, the dominant fault $DF(NRF(SG))$. We have, then, $|SL(NRF(SG))| = 1$ and we look for searching a new feasible reconfigurations only for this faults as the dominated ones will be, consequently, resolved. If there is no feasible reconfiguration for the component corresponding to the dominant fault, the SupAg requests its ClassAg to classify the dominated faults $Df(NRF(SG))$ in order to obtain a new short list and so on... In case of equivalence, the short list of faults $SL(NRF(SG))$ contains, only, the equivalent fault corresponding to the consumer having the higher priority. Thus, the system searches new reconfigurations only for this faults as the other equivalent ones will be consequently resolved. If we do not find feasible reconfiguration for the first one, we look for handling the fault corresponding the component having the second higher priority, and so on...

Algorithm 2. Fault Classification and Short List Identification

---

Require: $NRF(SG)$.
Ensure: $FT(NRF(SG)),SL(NRF(SG)),EF(NRF(SG)),DF(NRF(SG)),Df(NRF(SG))$.
  $min \leftarrow$ minimum Voltage Level over $NRF(SG)$
  $C_{min} \leftarrow \{c \in NRF(SG)/VoltageLevel(c) = min\}$
  If $(|C_{min}| = 1)$ **Then**
    $FT(NRF(SG)) =$ Dominance
    $DF(NRF(SG)) = C_{Min}$
    $Df(NRF(SG)) = NRF(SG) \setminus C_{Min}$
    $SL(NRF(SG)) = DF(NRF(SG))$
  Else
    $FT(NRF(SG)) =$ Equivalence
    $EqF(NRF(SG)) = C_{Min}$
    $SL(NRF(SG)) = f \in EqF(NRF(SG))/f$ has the higher priority
  End if

The proposed MAS contains two reconfiguration agents: the LocRecAg is working locally over the same sub-grid while the MobRecAg is working globally on the other sub-grids. In fact, the first one investigates the local consumers (belonging to the same sub-grid) which are not failed and not connected to $SL(NRF(SG))$ through emergency or principal lines. The second one investigates the non-local consumers (belonging to the other sub-grids) which are not failed and not connected to $SL(NRF(SG))$ through emergency lines. Algorithm 3 details how these two agents browse the network to find feasible reconfigurations $NewRec(SL(NRF(SG)))$.

Algorithm 3. Search for New Reconfigurations
***
Require: $SL(NRF(SG))$: Short List of Faults.
Ensure: $NewRec(SL(NRF(SG)))$
  $NewRec(SL(NRF(SG))) \leftarrow \emptyset$
  For each $c \in SL(NRF(SG))$
  For each *consumer cons* $\in SG$
    If (operating conditions are checked over *cons*) **and** (*Voltage Level*(*cons*) = *Votlage Level*(*c*)) **and** (Remaining Load(*cons*)$\geq$ Required Load(*c*)) and ($\nexists$ any line between *c* and *cons*) **Then**
      $NewRec(SL(NRF(SG))) \leftarrow NewRec(SL(NRF(SG))) \cup \{cons\}$
    End if
  End for{where *cons* belongs to the same sub-grid in case of local reconfigurations and to the other sub-grids in case of non-local reconfigurations}
  End for

When our agents find more than one feasible reconfiguration ($|NewRec| > 1$), the SupAg will choose the best one among them which has the smaller remaining load. The complexity of the proposed algorithms is similar to the complexity of the algorithms browsing tree data structures as we model the power networks using tree structures.

6.2   Evaluation

To evaluate our system, we study 5 smart grids having different structures and sizes (Table 1). The size of a smart grid is the number of all the contained electrical components.

As shown in Sect. 4.2, the performance of the smart grid $SG1$ (Fig. 1), is comprised between 35 % and 55 %, respectively, for the worst and best cases. Indeed, FDIRSY can not recover the faults occurring on the consumers MC_4 and MC_5. Thus, the obtained short list contains, only, the fault occurring on MC_4 to be reconfigured. The reconfiguration resolving this fault resolves all the problem since it corresponds to the dominant fault. The MobRecAg returns MC_3 as a new feasible reconfiguration as it has sufficient available remaining load, furthermore, it operates normally and it is not connected to MC_4. The reconfiguration to be performed consists on adding new emergency line linking MC_3 to MC_4. It allows

Table 1. The structure of the studied smart grids

SG		Electrical components				Electrical lines
Number	Size	PG	MVT	LVT	MC	LC	
SG1	26	1	2	3	5	15	31 lines including 6 emergency lines
SG2	50	2	6	9	9	24	64 lines including 15 emergency lines
SG3	100	4	14	22	21	39	119 lines including 20 emergency lines
SG4	200	6	21	31	58	84	231 lines including 32 emergency lines
SG5	300	8	29	42	62	159	348 lines including 68 emergency lines

where PG = Power Generator, MVT = Medium voltage Transformer, LVT = Low Voltage Transformer, MC = Medium Consumer and LC = Low Consumer.

to resolve at least one fault on MC_3 and at most two faults on MC_4 and MC_5. The performance increases, consequently, up to $\frac{8}{20} = 40\%$ in the worst case and to $\frac{13}{20} = 65\%$ in the best case. Our MAS proposes, also, a second new feasible reconfiguration, according to the available remaining load to the consumers LC_8 and LC_{14} by linking them through a new emergency line to be deployed. This reconfiguration resolves, exactly, one fault in both of worst and best cases to increase the performance up to $\frac{9}{20} = 45\%$ in the worst case and to $\frac{14}{20} = 70\%$ in the best case. Figure 4 illustrates the performance improvement of each of the studied smart grids. The horizontal axes present the number of consumers which can be resolved for each configuration of the power grids. The vertical axes present the performance of the investigated smart grid in percentage. The points A and C, in each graphic, present the initial performance measured for each investigated smart, respectively, in the worst and best cases. The initial performance is obtained for the initial configuration of the smart grid without adding any new emergency line. The points C and D, in each graphic, present the improved performance measured, respectively in the worst and best cases, for each studied smart grid taking into account the new found reconfigurations. The smart grid performance increases remarkably for each one of the power grids SG1, SG2, SG3, SG4 and SG5 by adding, respectively, only 2, 3, 4, 5 and 6 emergency lines. We remind that, as we discussed in the previous sections, that the deployment of only one new emergency line may resolve multiple faults.

As the studied smart grids have increasing sizes going from SG1 up to SG5, we are also interested on studying the improvement of the number of faults which can be resolved thanks to the new proposed reconfigurations in terms of the number electrical components contained in the grids. Figure 5 illustrates this relation between these two terms in both of worst and best cases. It shows that this improvement increases for larger power grids. This approach improves the number of non-resolvable faults which will be resolved without human intervention of technicians. It is also helpful for smart grid design to improve their quality of service.

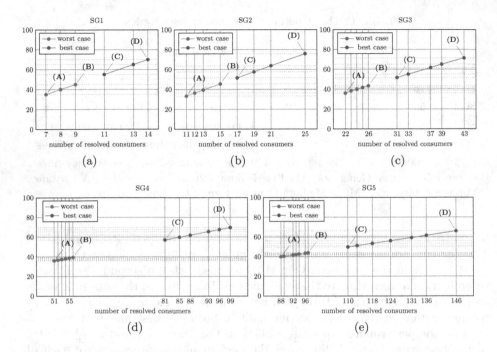

Fig. 4. Performance improvement for the smart grids SG1, SG2, SG3, SG4 and SG5

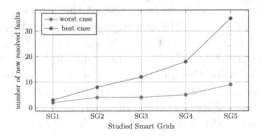

Fig. 5. Reconfiguration gain in terms new resolvable faults for each one of the studied smart grids

7   Conclusion

We propose, in this paper, a new approach for power smart grid reconfiguration to improve their performance. This approach is based on a distributed and hierarchical MAS deploying static and mobile agents to search feasible local and global recoveries and reconfigurations. It is helpful approach for the domain experts to design efficient and reliable smart grid. The experimental study demonstrates that the SG performance can be efficiently improved thanks to the used strategy of identifying the short list of components to be reconfigured by dominance and equivalence. Another advantage can be seen on decreasing the cost of electrical lines to be deployed since we try to handle a set of non-resolvable faults and not each one of them separately. We remark that the complexity and cost of the calculus increase for large power networks. For that, we are interested in future work to integrate the learning concept in order to automatize as much as possible the smart recovery and the efficient reconfiguration procedures for real large-scale networks.

References

1. Ben Meskina, S., Doggaz, N., Khalgui, M.: New solutions for fault detections and dynamic recoveries of flexible power smart grid. In: International Conference in Informatics in Control, Automation and Robotics (2014)
2. Ben Meskina, S., Doggaz, N., Khalgui, M.: An efficient simulator for fault detection and recovery in smart grid: FDIRSY. In: 5th International Conference on Pervasive and Embedded Computing and Communication Systems (2015)
3. Chertkov, M., Pan, F., Stepanov, M.G.: Predicting failures in power grids: the case of static overloads. J. IEEE Trans. SG **2**(1), 162–172 (2011)
4. Calderaro, V., Hadjicostis, C.N., Piccolo, A., Siano, P.: Failure identification in smart grids based on petri net modeling. J. IEEE Trans. Ind. Elec. **58**(10), 4613–4623 (2011)
5. Amin, M.: Scanning the technology: energy infrastructure defense systems. J. IEEE Proc. **93**, 861–875 (2005)
6. Rohbogner, G., Fey, S., Hahnel, U.J.J., Benoit, P., Wille-Haussmann, B.: What the term agent stands for in the smart grid definition of agents and multi-agent systems from an engineers perspective. In: Federated Conference on Computer Science and Information Systems (2012)
7. Oudalova, A., Fidigattib, A.: Adaptive network protection in microgrids. Int. J. Dist. En. Res. (2009)
8. Chen, J., Li, W., Lau, A., Cao, J., Wang, K.: Automated load curve data cleansing in power systems. J. IEEE Trans. SG **1**, 213–221 (2010)
9. Rahman, S., Pipattanasomporn, M., Teklu, Y.: Intelligent distributed autonomous power systems. In: IEEE Power Engineering Society General Meeting (2007)
10. Misraa, S., Krishnab, P.V., Sarithab, V., Agarwalb, H., Ahujac, A.: Learning automata-based multi-constrained fault-tolerance approach for effective energy management in smart grid communication network. J. Net. Comput. **44**, 212–219 (2014)
11. Moslehi, K., Kumar, R.: A reliability perspective of the smart grid. J. IEEE Trans. SG **1**(1), 57–64 (2010)

Real Time Systems

PEDASA: Priority, Energy and Deadline Aware Scheduling Algorithm

Maroua Gasmi[1,2]([✉]), Olfa Mosbahi[2], Mohamed Khalgui[2], and Luis Gomes[3]

[1] Faculty of Sciences of Tunis, University Tunis El Manar, Tunis, Tunisia
mra.gsm@gmail.com
[2] LISI Lab, INSAT Institute, University of Carthage, Tunis, Tunisia
{olfamosbahi,khalgui.mohamed}@gmail.com
[3] Universidade Nova de Lisboa, Lisbon, Portugal
lugo@fct.unl.pt

Abstract. We present a new approach for scheduling workloads containing periodic tasks in soft real-time systems. The proposed algorithm consists on finding a new set of priorities depending of the three main criteria identified in a real-time system: fixed priority initially assumed by user, deadline and energy efficiency. Our proposition involves a computational procedure that is responsible of extracting the new values of priorities out of the importance of the three factors previously mentioned. An eventual re-adjustment of the deadlines is also faced all along with the reloading of the system's power on specified instants. The resulting system is, therefore, feasible and effectively schedulable compared to the mono-criteria algorithms. This contribution allows also the definition of precise instants of reloading which enforces the new concept of extending the lifetime of the system.

Keywords: Real-time · Multi-criteria · Scheduling and optimization · Energy efficiency

1 Introduction

In a world where technology does not stop evolving, basic daily activities are substituted by extremely intelligent systems that keep getting optimized by time. Real-time systems offer a big range of services adapted. Moreover, these systems consist of one or more subsystems that should respond in a precise and finite time specified by the external world. Thus, a result obtained after a stated deadline remains false even if it is logically right. Consequently, the total correctness of an operation depends not only upon its logical correctness, but also upon the time in which it is performed which depends on several criteria. Although many scheduling algorithms concentrate only on timing constraints, others exist and need to be acknowledged as well. For this purpose, some works got oriented to the scheduling using a multi-criteria method. Nevertheless, it is more realistic to find compromises between the different parameters than to choose a single parameter at once. This way, it is possible to partially satisfy the varied objectives.

© Springer International Publishing Switzerland 2015
H. Fujita and G. Guizzi (Eds.): SoMeT 2015, CCIS 532, pp. 59–72, 2015.
DOI: 10.1007/978-3-319-22689-7_5

The basic problem in this paper is how to deal with scheduling the existing tasks while keeping an eye on all of the criteria at once. In the case of a soft real-time system, it seems crucial to watch the feasibility of most of the tasks while calculating the new priorities. As an example of works who got concerned about this matter, the author in [11] introduced a multi-criteria algorithm to schedule soft real-time tasks on uniform multiprocessor systems. This approach uses three criteria, namely deadline, laxity and interval. Similarly, In the work [2], the approach is carried considering the priority, the processing time as well as the waiting time of a task. The previously mentioned work, as well as the approach introduced in [10] treat several parameters while scheduling real-time tasks by considering a fuzzy reasoning. Although this reasoning is capable of dealing with uncertainties in a many-valued logic, there are more than the simple "true" or "false" responses. In fact, this logic only disposes of approximations rather than fixed and exact analysis especially when extreme precision is required. Another limiting factor of fuzzy reasoning is the extensive testing it needs to find an adequate decision. In the contrary, the algorithm RT-DBP [1] takes into account many scheduling parameters. All the criteria are associated with weight parameters in order to give more weight to one criterion in particular depending on the application requirements. Although this approach uses computational procedures instead of estimations, the calculations are made during run-time which can have an impact on the global time processing. Like all the mentioned works, our approach treats the setting of new priorities depending on the existing criteria. It computes the latter mentioned priorities and finds the exact moments where the reloading of the system energy should take place. As a matter of fact, the particularity of the work is that it does not totally ignore the predefined parameters. Alternatively, it relates to them when it comes to calculating the new ones. Among these parameters we specifically find the first set up priority which indicates the degree of importance that a prospective user accords to the task. The other parameters are eventually, the deadline which is a crucial real-time efficiency indicator and the level of energy consumption which has a great impact on the functioning of the system in general. Another advantage presented in our proposition is the calculation that is performed in an off-line mode. This way, no computational overheads are imposed on the system during its execution. In order to explicit our proposition, we expose in the following section the miscellaneous parameters defining a real-time system model as well as the most substantial static scheduling algorithms dealing, separately, with the priority, deadline and energy consumption parameters. The impact of applying each of these algorithms on a predefined set of tasks is pinpointed through Sect. 3. After mathematically formalizing the needed elements in Sect. 4, we detail the proposed solution PEDASA in the section that follows. We first start by analyzing the potential priorities carried out of the predefined parameters. The exact values of these priorities are, then, set by checking the possibility of a maximum regard to deadline in parallel with the consideration of the initial priorities respect all along with an adjustment of periods when necessary. Counting on the resulting set of priorities, we proceed to the search of the exact moments at which the energy level in a system can be reloaded. This enlarges the time span of the tasks and gives them the possibility to execute without any power constraints imposed on them.

2   Background

In this section we aim to introduce the basic axes on which stands the context of this work. Therefore, we conduct a definition of the elemental real-time model as well as an overview on the existing mono-criteria scheduling algorithms that allow a more effective arrangement of the latter.

2.1   Real-Time System Model

Concretely, a real-time system should necessarily guarantee a response within strict time constraints, referred to as deadlines. For this matter, three classes are introduced: (i) *Hard* where missing a deadline is totally fatal, (ii) *Firm* where few deadline misses are allowable, but may affect the quality of service within the system and (iii) *Soft*, like our chosen system, where the practicality of a result debases after its deadline, thereby altering the efficiency of the system [12]. In a multi-tasking method, several tasks can be part-way through execution at the same time, and more than one task is advancing over a specific period of time. The parameters of a real-time task, denoted as τ_i, are mainly: (i) P_i Static priority representing the degree of functional importance related to the task, (ii) $Order_i$ Order of execution of a task, (iii) A_i Arrival time, (iv) S_i Actual starting time, (v) C_i Computation time also known as Worst Case Execution Time (WCET), (vi) T_i Period, (vii) D_i Deadline, (viii) R_i Response time, (ix) F_i Actual time at which the task finishes its execution, (x) BF_i Best finishing time and (xi) E_i Percentage of power needed for each task. The execution of the periodic tasks within a system is repeated every hyper-period, denoted by T_{hyp}. The latter is introduced as the smallest interval of time after which the periodic patterns of all the tasks are repeated. It is typically defined as the LCM (least common multiple) of all the periods. In this paper, we are interested in computing a new set of priorities in order to maximize the number of feasible tasks.

2.2   Mono-criteria Scheduling Algorithms

A scheduling algorithm enables the orchestration of priorities to the set of tasks. The performance of such an algorithm is judged for how quickly or how predictably a scheduled real-time system can respond [8]. Therefore, the assigned priorities are based on deadline or some other timing constraint. In a time shared scheduling, such in a multi-tasking system, a scheduler has the power to preempt a task and to resume its execution after a while [9]. This change is known as a context switch and several scheduling algorithms use preemption in order to finish the execution of a higher priority task. In literature, two classes of real-time

scheduling algorithms are introduced: static or dynamic [5]. In static scheduling, decisions are made during compilation. The parameters of all the tasks are
assumed to be known in advance and a schedule is built based on this assumption. Consequently, no modification can be applied online once the scheduler is
set. On the other hand, the decisions related to the dynamic scheduling are done
at run-time. Although, dynamic schedulers are flexible and adaptive, they can
cause a significant overheads because of consuming run-time processing. Reason
why, several industrial propositions insist on making use of the static scheduling
algorithms instead. Usually, these algorithms use a single criteria for determining the priorities of the different tasks. This priority can be fixed ahead, as in
Fixed Priority Preemptive (FPP) algorithm, or concluded out of another parameter. By parameter we can refer to the period of the task, as in Rate Monotonic
Scheduling (RM), or energy consumption as in Low Energy First (LEF). In the
Fixed Priority Preemptive Algorithm (FPP), the scheduler makes sure that at
any instant, the processor executes the highest priority task among the rest of
the tasks that are currently waiting for execution [13]. As for the Rate Monotonic
scheduling algorithm (RM), the static priorities are assigned based on task
periods [6]. The task with the shortest period gets the highest priority, and
the one whose the period is the longest gets the lowest static priority. Since in
most cases, the period of the task is analogous with its deadline, the Deadline
Monotonic algorithm is an extension of RM. Considering the energy consumption parameter, several works treated the case where the lower the power consumption of a task the most prioritized it is [7]. Compared to the mentioned
algorithms, PEDASA introduces the possibility of assigning new priorities that
take into consideration the three criteria all at once. It also offers the ability of
defining a set of moments at which the energy reloads enhancing therefore the
efficiency of the complete system.

3   Case Study

Through this section, we show by a concrete example how choosing a single
scheduling criteria does not allow the satisfaction of others. For this matter,
let us take an example of a set of six tasks. As mentioned in Sect. 2, each one
is characterized by a static priority P, a period T that also corresponds to its
deadline, a percentage of energy consumption E and an execution time C. The
different values of these criteria are given by Table 1. It is to mention that the

Table 1. Parameters of the tasks.

	τ_1	τ_2	τ_3	τ_4	τ_5	τ_6
P	6	5	4	3	2	1
T	120	170	50	80	110	100
E	60	30	50	10	40	20
C	30	10	10	20	10	10

release time of all the tasks is 0 (e.g. all tasks are assumed to be synchronous). Each time, we use a scheduling algorithm based on one of the assumed criteria. At a first time, Fixed Priority Protocol (FPP) is applied to the set of tasks then Rate Monotonic (RM) and finally the Low Energy First Protocol (LEF).

3.1 Fixed Priority Protocol (FPP)

When using the FPP algorithm, the relation between the priorities of the different tasks is defined by the Eq. 1:

$$P_1 > P_2 > P_3 > P_4 > P_5 > P_6 \tag{1}$$

The values of the response times using this protocol are $\{R_1 = 30; R_2 = 40; R_3 = 50; R_4 = 80; R_5 = 120; R_6 = 220\}$. Although the tasks conserve their fixed priorities, it is obvious that some of them miss their deadlines. In fact, only the execution of the tasks τ_1, τ_2, τ_3 and τ_4 goes normally. As for the tasks τ_5 and τ_6, their response times exceed their deadlines. Considering the energy consumption when using this scheduling algorithm, τ_1 and τ_2 are the only ones executing since they consume 80 % of the battery.

3.2 Rate Monotonic (RM)

Since the scheduling of the tasks depends on their periods, the relation between the priorities of these tasks is given by the Eq. 2. This way none of the following tasks respects the initially given priorities.

$$P_3 > P_4 > P_6 > P_5 > P_1 > P_2 \tag{2}$$

Therefore, using this scheduling algorithm only τ_3, τ_4, τ_5 and τ_6 (the tasks with the highest priorities) respect their deadlines. Therefore, the values of the response time are $\{R_1 = 140; R_2 = 240; R_3 = 10; R_4 = 30; R_5 = 50; R_6 = 40\}$. Changing the order of execution allows τ_3, τ_4 and τ_6 to operate with the existing power.

3.3 Low Energy First Protocol

When using the Energy aware algorithm, the relation between the priorities of execution of the different tasks is defined by the Eq. 3 which is totally different from the initial one.

$$P_4 > P_6 > P_2 > P_5 > P_3 > P_1 \tag{3}$$

The execution of the tasks proves that the tasks τ_3 and τ_1 do not respect their deadlines. The corresponding response times are $\{R_1 = 160; R_2 = 40; R_3 = 60; R_4 = 20; R_5 = 50; R_6 = 30\}$. For a single criteria scheduler, it is difficult to concentrate on all the different parameters of a real-time system. In the works related to these scheduling algorithms, the focus on one criteria at a time leads to ignoring the other ones. This been said, the originality of the proposed approach lies in respecting all of the mentioned parameters in order to get a scheduled system that is aware of the deadline constraints and the energy effectiveness.

4   Formalization

Through this section, we tend to mathematically represent the underlying assumptions. Moreover, we expose the problem treated in this paper analytically. We also formalize all the aspects related to energy, deadline and initially fixed priorities in order to have a precise overview on the given problem.

4.1   Energy

The studied system Sys is composed of n tasks $\{\tau_1...\tau_n\}$ and takes into account the energy consumption aspect. We suppose that obtaining the information about the energy does not require any power consumption and that the battery level gets restored every specific amount of time. As a consequence, let E(t) be the level of available energy at the moment t. For a non preemptive scheduling algorithm, it is possible to know the amount of energy consumed at a specific moment. The function allowing such awareness is denoted by $E_i'(t)$ and given by Eq. 4. Therefore, a precise task τ_i (i = 1..n) does not consume any power before its starting time S_i and right after its best finishing time BF_i (at this level, we consider a non preemptive task). However inside of the interval limited by these two values, the energy consumption increases continuously following a general function $Consump$.

$$E_i'(t) = \begin{cases} 0 \; if \; t \leq S_i \vee t > BF_i \\ E_i \; if \; t = BF_i \\ Consump(t, BF_i, S_i) \; otherwise \end{cases} \tag{4}$$

where $Consump$ represents the exact equation related to the consumption. We assume that we do not really have a precise idea on the latter mentioned function. That's why in this paper we are supposing that the energy is consumed exponentially. The amount consumed at the starting moment is 0 and at the best finishing time the whole amount related to the task is drained. Therefore, we propose a function that allows having the previously mentioned characteristics and is given by Formula 5. The scope of this function denoted by β allows having a proportional increase of consumption and is calculated through the couple of values of $Consump$ obtained at S_i and BF_i.

$$Consump(t, BF_i, S_i) = 1 - \exp^{-\beta(t-S_i)}$$

$$\beta = \frac{-log(1-\frac{E_i}{100})}{BF_i - S_i} \tag{5}$$

The power consumption in the system is also dependent on the priority of the tasks. In fact, the energy is consumed starting from the more prioritized task and going on. In the best cases, all of the n tasks are executed before the total exhaustion of the battery. This means that if the energy is consumed in a specific order, it is preferable that the sum of the amount of energy consumed does not exceed 100 % of the available power. This case is represented by Eq. 6.

$$\sum_{i=1}^{n} EP(i)/100 < 1 \tag{6}$$

where EP(i), given by Eq. 7, represents the percentage of energy consumed by the task that the value of its priority is $n+1-i$ and, as a consequence, its range of execution is i.

$$EP(i) = \{E_j/\exists j, 0 < j \leq n \wedge P_j = n+1-i\} \qquad (7)$$

In the general case, let $T_{ES}(SA)$ be the set of tasks that are executed before the total exhaustion of the battery. The number of elements in this set, given by Eq. 8, totally depends on the chosen scheduling algorithm SA.

$$T_{ES}(SA) = \{\exists \tau_i/0 < i \leq n, \sum_{i=1}^{n} EP(i)/100 < 1\} \qquad (8)$$

In the best case the number of the elements of $T_{ES}(SA)$ corresponds to the total number of tasks in the system. This can be translated by the fact that all the tasks are applied without the total tiredness of the energy. This is described by Eq. 9.

$$Card(T_{ES}(SA)) = Card(T_s) = n \qquad (9)$$

4.2   Deadline

The respect of deadline within a real-time system is also a crucial need that demands attention. Therefore, the best real-time scheduling algorithm is the one that allows all the tasks to finish their execution before reaching their deadlines. Let $T_{DS}(SA)$ be the set of tasks that respect their deadlines under a given scheduling algorithm SA. This set is represented by Eq. 10 where the elements are only the tasks whose their execution (the sum of the arriving and the response times) does not exceed the predefined deadline.

$$T_{DS}(SA) = \{\forall i, \exists \tau_i/0 < i \leq n \wedge A_i + R_i \leq D_i\} \qquad (10)$$

The whole system is considered feasible when the number of elements in the set $T_{DS}(SA)$ is equal to n (the number of tasks in the set T_s). This is represented by Eq. 11.

$$Card(T_{DS}(SA)) = Card(T_s) = n \qquad (11)$$

4.3   Priority

The priorities initially fixed in the system are sometimes of extreme functional importance. Thus, ignoring them for the profit of other parameters can affect the whole system in an undesirable way. In the perspective of this criterion, let $T_{PS}(SA)$ be the set of tasks that conserve their initial priorities under a given scheduling algorithm SA. This set is represented by Eq. 12. We suppose that IR_i is the initial range corresponding to a task τ_i and resulting from the initial given priority. $FR_i(SA)$, on the other hand, corresponds to the final range obtained after applying a feasible scheduling algorithm SA. These values correspond to the order in which the task should be executed. The following set contains only the tasks that conserved their order (the ones where $IR_i = FR_i$).

$$T_{PS}(SA) = \{\forall i, \exists \tau_i / 0 < i \leq n \land IR_i = FR_i(SA)\} \tag{12}$$

Similarly, the system is completely feasible if the number of elements in the set $T_{PS}(SA)$ is equal to n (the number of tasks in the set T_s). This is represented by Eq. 13.

$$Card(T_{PS}(SA)) = Card(T_s) = n \tag{13}$$

4.4   Generalization

Generally speaking, applying a scheduling algorithm can affect the system in 3 different ways. In the first possibility (or the best case), the Eqs. 9, 11 and 13 are all perfectly verified. In the second case, only one of the two conditions is met and in the worst case none of them is verified. Let ES, DS and PS be respectively the Boolean verification functions of the Eqs. 9, 11 and 13. Therefore the formalization of the states that a system can have is given by formula 14.

$$\forall \tau_i \in T_s, State(Sys) : \begin{cases} ES \land DS \land PS(\textbf{State 1}) \\ \lor \\ \neg ES \land DS \land PS(\textbf{State 2}) \\ \lor \\ \neg ES \land \neg DS \land PS(\textbf{State 2}) \\ \lor \\ ES \land \neg DS \land \neg PS(\textbf{State 2}) \\ \lor \\ ES \land DS \land \neg PS(\textbf{State 2}) \\ \lor \\ \neg ES \land \neg DS \land \neg PS(\textbf{State 3}) \end{cases} \tag{14}$$

The pinpointed problem is basically how to get the priority, fixed by a user depending on its preferences, to be respected all along with the deadline, which is a crucial real-time parameter, and the energy efficiency. The following section details the proposed solution that solves this confusion in a simple and effective way.

5   Proposed Approach: PEDASA

The solution to the problem mentioned in Sect. 4 is given by the proposed scheduling algorithm entitled PEDASA. It is a static algorithm that consists on manipulating certain parameters in order to allow all of tasks to meet their deadlines and to execute before the exhaustion of the battery. The new suggested priorities take into consideration the importance of the 3 principle criteria: (i) fixed priority, (ii) deadline and (iii) energy efficiency in the perspective of each task.

5.1   Real-Time Reasoning

New Priorities Analysis. The procedure of computing the new priorities is based on the three importance factors previously mentioned. In fact, α_P, α_D and α_E are rates related to the importance of respectively the existing priority, the fixed deadline and the energy efficiency. The relation between these rates is given by Eq. 15.

$$0 \leq \alpha_P, \alpha_D, \alpha_E \leq 1, \alpha_P + \alpha_D + \alpha_E = 1 \tag{15}$$

The next step consists on sorting the tasks, each time depending on the parameter, while according a positive number that corresponds to their order. Let m_{ij} be the order factor; i $(1..n)$ corresponds to the index of the task and j to the parameter (1: Fixed Priority, 2: Deadline and 3: Energy consumption). This number does not exceed the number of elements in the task set T_s. When sorting the tasks, we consider an ascending order for the fixed priority and a descendant one for the deadline and the energy consumption. Let M be the matrix relating the order factors of the tasks to the defined parameters. This matrix, having as dimensions n (the number of tasks) rows and 3 (corresponds to the system parameters) columns, is composed of the elements m_{ij}. Let $K(\tau_i)$ be the value of the new priority of the task τ_i that depends on the importance factors α_P, α_D and α_E, and the order factors of this latter. We suppose that K is a vector that contains the new priorities of all the tasks. Therefore, Eq. 16 defines the value of these new priorities.

$$K = \begin{pmatrix} \alpha_P \\ \alpha_D \\ \alpha_E \end{pmatrix} * M \tag{16}$$

The idea behind this calculation, is to have resultant priorities issued from the existing ones. Instead of running through all the possibilities, we stay focused on the preferences given by the system at first place. This guarantees the respect of the first desired parameters.

Final Values of PEDASA Priorities. Finding the exact values of α_P, α_D and α_E should be based on a well-founded decision making. Accordingly, the main intent of this approach is to maximize the number of tasks respecting their deadlines without totally ignoring the delimited priorities. In fact, the predefined priority set does not allow the tasks to fully respect their deadlines. Hence, we aim for less than n tasks respecting the desired arrangement. Thus, while searching for the exact values of α_P, α_D and α_E, we start with a heuristic algorithm that runs through all the possibilities. Let $Vect_D$ and $Vect_P$ be the vectors containing, respectively, the number of tasks complying with their deadlines and initially fixed priorities under different values of the importance factors. Simply, these vectors refer to the number of elements of the Eqs. 10 and 12. Two constraints are considered while searching for the exact values of α_P, α_D and α_E: **(i)** when fixing these values we should have a number of tasks respecting their deadlines that is greater or equal to the number of tasks whose the old priorities correspond to the new ones, and **(ii)** the multiplication of these two numbers should be the maximum amongst all the possible values. The fact of considering the multiplication is based on the approximation to the logical operation *AND* exposed in [14]. This is mathematically described by Eq. 17. The choice behind this equation is founded on the desire of guaranteeing, so far, a higher number of tasks respecting their deadlines while partially obeying the predefined priorities. However, the complication occurs once the number of deadline-conducted tasks after calculation is lower than the one initially obtained by the FPP. This way, we focus on the set of priorities offered by this scheduling algorithm. Nevertheless, As long as there are tasks exceeding their deadlines, we proceed to changing the periods of the latter ones in order to have a fully functional system. The fundamental intention here consists on enhancing the values of a minimum number of periods related to the least prioritized tasks which outstrip their deadlines and replacing them by their multiples. Yet, the incrementation should obey to the constraint that we should not outpace the existing hyper-period.

$$\begin{aligned} \{Value(\alpha_P), Value(\alpha_D), Value(\alpha_E)\} = \{\alpha_P, \alpha_D, \alpha_E / \\ Vect_D(\alpha_P, \alpha_D, \alpha_E) \geq Vect_P(\alpha_P, \alpha_D, \alpha_E) \\ \wedge Vect_P(\alpha_P, \alpha_D, \alpha_E) * Vect_D(\alpha_P, \alpha_D, \alpha_E) = \\ max(Vect_D * Vect_P)\} \end{aligned} \tag{17}$$

5.2   Energy Consumption Adaptability

After finding the correct order in which the tasks should be executed based on the PEDASA computation, we introduce the concept of the system reloading. In fact, instead of manipulating the parameters of the set of tasks, it seems more efficient to reload the energy within the system, at a specific moment, in a way that its energy level gets restored. That is why in this part we search for the instants of energy reloading that enhance the lifespan of the whole system. Therefore, let t_{load} be the vector of instants, within a hyper-period T_{hyp}, at which the energy level attains 100 % again. This is analytically represented by Eq. 18.

$$\forall l, 0 < l \leq Size(t_{load}) : E(t_{load}(l)) = 100\% \tag{18}$$

Obviously, between the moments t and t_{load} the energy level can either decrease or remain the same. This depends on the energy required by each task. The chance of rewinding the system, allows the latter to execute all of its tasks without worrying about the exhaustion of the battery. We proceed in a determinist way, since the proposed scheduling algorithm is static. The first step consists on determining the instants at which each task got preempted by another one of a higher priority and the ones at which it resumed its execution. It is to mention that, in the real case, a task can be preempted one or several times during T_{hyp}. But it is also possible that the task never gets preempted. Generally speaking, let Pre_{ij} and Res_{ij} respectively be the instants of preemption and resumption number j for the task τ_i (i = 1..n). The second step takes in charge the definition of the new consumption functions that result from the several preemption cases that a task might have. For this matter, let $E_i''(t)$ be the real consumption function that, based on $E_i'(t)$, takes into consideration the preemption as well as the shift in the execution. This function is given by Eq. 19.

$$\forall i, j \in k_i : E_i''(t) = \begin{cases} E_i'(t + (S_i - A_i)) \; if \; t \geq S_i \vee t \leq Pre_{i1} \\ 0 \; if \; t \in \,]Pre_{ij}, Res_{ij}[\\ E_i'(t + (S_i - A_i) - \sum_{j=1}^{k_i}(Res_{ij} - Pre_{ij})) \; otherwise \end{cases} \tag{19}$$

The resulting function $E_{Ts}(t)$ (given by Eq. 20) represents the general survey on the energy consumption at any moment during T_{hyp}. This function is discontinuous and composed of the consumption functions related to each task. Let $\pi_{sys}(t)$ be the function that allows having an idea on the specific task executing at the instant t. This function is given by Eq. 21.

$$E_{Ts}(t) = \begin{cases} E_i''(t) \; if \; \pi_{sys}(t) = \tau_i \\ 0 \; if \; \pi_{sys}(t) = 0 \end{cases} \tag{20}$$

$$\pi_{sys}(t) = \begin{cases} \tau_i \; if \; \exists \tau_i / \pi_i(t) = 1 \\ 0 \; otherwise \end{cases} \tag{21}$$

Ultimately, the decrease in the available energy levels in the system during the same period, can be described by $E_{Sys}(t)$. Where this function (described by Eq. 22) is the difference between the available energy level at a precedent moment and the required energy at the moment that follows.

$$E_{Sys}(t) = E_{Sys}(t-1) - E_{Ts}(t) \tag{22}$$

Supposing that the procedure of reloading the battery is immediate and that the time it takes is insignificant, the reloading moment should more likely occur when $E_{Sys}(t)$ is zero. As a consequence, the system can dispose of a set of parameters ready for application without worrying about any future behavior since the periodicity is always predictable.

Running example: We consider the interval of time from 0 to 240 (the biggest period among all the tasks). During which, The task τ_1 got preempted only once. As a consequence, the following Figure exposes the function E_{Ts}, composed by the real consumption functions related to the tasks executing at that same time being.

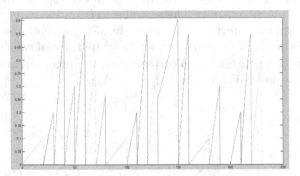

The graphical representation of the available energy level, during the chosen time, conducted from the general energy consumption is given by the following Figure.

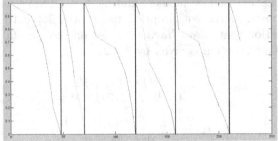

In fact, the graph demonstrates that the battery in this system needs to be reloaded around five times. Therefore the vector t_{load} is as follows (for the initially specified time in this running example).

$$t_{load} = \{48, 70, 119, 158, 210\}$$

6 Discussion

PEDASA is an optimal scheduling algorithm responsible of defining a new set of priorities without conducting an exhaustive calculation. In order to reduce this computation, we proceed to the strategy of limiting the possible priorities to the relation between the importance and the order factors. The aim of this strategy is to relate the new set of priorities to the first given parameters of the three criteria as well. The output of this algorithm is not only the new priorities, but also a new definition to the periods of the least prioritized tasks in a way that guarantees the feasibility of the scheduled task set. Moreover, the instants of reloading relevant to the battery are also resulted from the PEDASA algorithm. Compared to the mono-criteria scheduling algorithms (FPP, RM and LEF), the number of tasks respecting their deadlines and executing before battery exhaustion (Eqs. 9 and 11) is way important. However, even if the range of the tasks under the new set priorities is different from the initial ones it is still substantial compared to the RM and LEF algorithms. Through Fig. 1, where we consider the case study displayed in Sect. 3, it is noticeable that the surface of the PEDASA consideration is larger than that of RM, FPP or LEF schedulers which pinpoints its remarkable contribution. Additionally, compared to the existing multi-criteria real-time scheduling algorithms that are based on fuzzy logic, PEDASA offers a more determinist method to find the new adequate set of priorities and adjusts several parameters to enhance the performance of the system. Our approach is also reversible. This means that it can simply refer to a RM, FPP or LEF scheduling if the result that one of them offers is effectively performed. Consequently, it economizes in terms of energy and time computation.

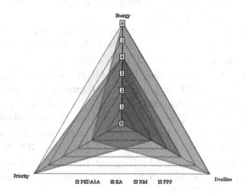

Fig. 1. Respect ratio of the parameters energy, deadline and initial priorities.

7 Conclusion

In this paper we introduced PEDASA as a static soft real-time scheduling algorithm that solves the multi-criteria decision making in a computational way. The performance of this algorithm is then compared with that of FPP, RM and LEF. It is put in display that our proposed approach not only confirms an important performance compared to these algorithms but also changes the system into a more versatile structure. Surely, the establishment of power reloading possibility in predetermined instants guarantees the continuous functioning of the system. Similarly, the feasibility of the task set is very accurate with the purpose of the real-time constraints. Therefore, this algorithm could be more appropriate for use on the real-time systems that are monitored by users and that require a consistent power level. As a perspective, we wish to apply this new algorithm to a system where the three criteria priority, deadline and energy efficiency are very important features and can be affected by different reconfiguration scenarios. The wireless sensor network is a potential application of this work [3, 4].

References

1. Baccouche, L., Eleuch, H.: Rt-Dbp: a multi-criteria priority assignment scheme for real-time tasks scheduling. Appl. Math. **6**(2), 383–388 (2012)
2. Fahmy, M.: A fuzzy algorithm for scheduling non-periodic jobs on soft real-time single processor system. Ain Shams Eng. J. **1**(1), 31–38 (2010)
3. Gasmi, M., Mosbahi, O., Khalgui, M., Gomes, L.: New pipelined-based solutions for optimal reconfigurations of real-time systems. In: Proceedings of the European Simulation and Modelling Conferences (2014)
4. Gasmi, M., Mosbahi, O., Khalgui, M., Gomes, L.: Reconfigurable priority ceiling protocol under rate monotonic based real-time scheduling. In: 2014 11th International Conference on Informatics in Control, Automation and Robotics (ICINCO), vol. 1, pp. 42–52. IEEE (2014)
5. Kopetz, H.: Real-Time Systems: Design Principles for Distributed Embedded Applications. Springer, New York (2011)
6. Lehoczky, J., Sha, L., Ding, Y.: The rate monotonic scheduling algorithm: exact characterization and average case behavior. In: 1989 Proceedings of Real Time Systems Symposium, pp. 166–171. IEEE (1989)
7. Lindberg, P., Leingang, J., Lysaker, D., Bilal, K., Khan, S.U., Bouvry, P., Ghani, N., Min-Allah, N., Li, J.: Comparison and analysis of greedy energy-efficient scheduling algorithms for computational grids. In: Zomaya, A., Lee, Y.C. (eds.) Energy Aware Distributed Computing Systems. Wiley, Hoboken (2012)
8. Park, S., Kim, J.H., Fox, G.: Effective real-time scheduling algorithm for cyber physical systems society. Future Gener. Comput. Syst. **32**, 253–259 (2014)
9. Peng, B., Fisher, N., Bertogna, M.: Explicit preemption placement for real-time conditional code via graph grammars and dynamic programming. Ph.D. thesis, Wayne State University (2014)
10. Rattanatamrong, P., Fortes, J.A.: Fuzzy scheduling of real-time ensemble systems. In: 2014 International Conference on High Performance Computing & Simulation (HPCS), pp. 146–153. IEEE (2014)
11. Salmani, V., Ensafi, R., Khatib-Astaneh, N., Naghibzadeh, M.: A fuzzy-based multi-criteria scheduler for uniform multiprocessor real-time systems. In: 10th International Conference on Information Technology, (ICIT 2007), pp. 179–184. IEEE (2007)
12. Shin, K.G., Ramanathan, P.: Real-time computing: a new discipline of computer science and engineering. Proc. IEEE **82**(1), 6–24 (1994)
13. Wang, Y., Saksena, M.: Scheduling fixed-priority tasks with preemption threshold. In: 1999 Sixth International Conference on Real-Time Computing Systems and Applications, RTCSA 1999, pp. 328–335. IEEE (1999)
14. Zadeh, L.A.: The Concept of a Linguistic Variable and Its Application to Approximate Reasoning. Springer, New York (1974)

New Pack Oriented Solutions for Energy-Aware Feasible Adaptive Real-Time Systems

Aymen Gammoudi[1,2]([⊠]), Adel Benzina[1,2], Mohamed Khalgui[1],
and Daniel Chillet[3]

[1] LISI Laboratory, INSAT, University of Carthage, Tunis, Tunisia
{aymen.gammoudi1,benzina.adel,khalgui.mohamed}@gmail.com
[2] Tunisia Polytechnic School, University of Carthage, Tunis, Tunisia
[3] IRISA Laboratory, ENSSAT, University of Rennes 1, Rennes, France
daniel.chillet@irisa.fr

Abstract. This paper addresses the management of tasks execution for
real-time reconfigurable systems powered by battery. In this context, one
of major problem concerns the management of battery life between two
different recharges. For this type of systems, a reconfiguration scenario
means the addition, removal or update of tasks in order to manage the
whole system at the occurrence of hardware/software faults, or also to
improve its performance at run-time. When such a scenario is applied,
the system risks a fatal increase in energy consumption, a violation of
real time constraints or a memory saturation. To prevent this type of
problems during the execution, a new scheduling strategy is necessary.
Our proposal is based on the definition of packs of tasks and the management of different parameters of these packs. For each reconfiguration
scenario, modifications will be performed on packs/tasks parameters in
order to respect the memory, real-time and energy constraints.

Keywords: Embedded system · Reconfiguration · Real-time and low-
power scheduling · OS software optimization · Software analysis

1 Introduction

Nowadays, reconfigurable real-time embedded systems are found in diverse application areas including; avionics, automotive electronics, telecommunications,
sensor networks, and consumer electronics. In all of these areas, there is rapid
technological progress, yet, energy concerns are still the bottleneck. The minimization of energy consumption is an important criterion for development of
real-time embedded systems due to limitations in the capacity of their batteries;
in addition battery life can be extended by reducing power consumption [11].
The new generation of real-time embedded systems is addressing new criteria
such as flexibility and agility [5]. For these reasons, there is a need to define
strategy/methodology in embedded software engineering and dynamic reconfigurable embedded technologies as an independent discipline. Concerning the
reconfiguration, two policies are defined in the literature: static and dynamic

© Springer International Publishing Switzerland 2015
H. Fujita and G. Guizzi (Eds.): SoMeT 2015, CCIS 532, pp. 73–86, 2015.
DOI: 10.1007/978-3-319-22689-7_6

reconfigurations. Static reconfigurations are applied off-line to apply changes before the system cold start for a required functional safety [4], whereas dynamic reconfigurations are applied during the execution (on-line) of the application, i.e. at run-time. Dynamic reconfiguration can be manually applied by users [9] or automatically applied by Intelligent Agents [6].

We consider here dynamic reconfiguration and we assume that the system executes n real-time tasks initially feasible towards real-time scheduling. We also assume that the system battery is recharged periodically with a recharge period RP. The general goal of this paper is to ensure that any reconfiguration scenario changing the implementation of the embedded system does not violate real-time constraints and does not result in fatal energy over consumption or in memory saturation. Several research studies [11,12] have focused on the modification of periods or WCETs of tasks in order to decrease the processor utilization. These studies are interesting, but the authors are not interested in the computation cost of the new parameters since they perform heavy calculations after any reconfiguration scenario. Moreover, non-logical values of parameters that do not meet user requirements can be generated. Finally, they do not consider the memory overflow problem after any reconfiguration scenario. Unlike [11,12], we are interested in this paper in deterministic solutions to control the computation cost of parameters that should be realistic while controlling energy and memory constraints.

As a major contribution of this paper, to respect the memory, real-time and energy constraints, a new strategy is defined where after each reconfiguration scenario, suitable and acceptable modifications are performed on parameters of tasks by using well-defined formulas. After each reconfiguration scenario, [12] proposes some solutions to be applied in an arbitrary manner in order to minimize the energy consumption, but it is hard to implement the approach proposed in an embedded platform because it is too complex to be executed on-line. In this paper, we propose a methodological strategy that solves this drawback. According to system and battery state, this strategy proposes quantitative techniques to modify periods, reduce execution times of tasks or remove some of them to ensure real-time feasability, avoiding memory overflow and ensuring a rational use of remaining energy until next recharge.

This paper is organized as follows: Sect. 2 presents the state of the art of reconfigurable embedded systems, low power consumption and real-time scheduling. The third section explains the formalization and a case study. In Sect. 4 we present the different proposed solutions. We evaluate this solution in Sect. 5. Finally, we conclude and present our future works in Sect. 6.

2   State of the Art

Several papers in recent years considered real-time and low-power scheduling policies [8,12,13].

2.1 Reconfiguration of Embedded Systems

Nowadays, a fair amount of research has been done to develop reconfigurable embedded systems. In [11] Wang et al. propose a study for feasible low power dynamic reconfigurations of real-time systems where additions and removals of real-time tasks are applied at run-time. They aim to minimize the energy consumption after any reconfiguration scenario. The research in [3] proposes an agent-based reconfiguration approach to save the whole system when faults occur at run-time. [1] develops an ontology-based agent to perform system reconfigurations that adapt changes in requirements and also in environment. They are interested in studying reconfigurations of control systems when hardware faults occur at run-time. Although these rich and useful contributions provide interesting results, no one is reported to address the problem of dynamic reconfigurations under memory, real-time feasability and energy constraints simultaneously.

2.2 Real-Time Scheduling

Real-time scheduling has been extensively studied in the last three decades [2]. These studies propose several Feasibility Conditions for the dimensioning of real-time systems. These conditions are defined to enable a designer to grant that timeliness constraints associated with an application are always met for all possible configurations. In this paper, Two main classical scheduling are generally used in real-time embedded systems: RM and EDF. Firstly, EDF is a dynamic scheduling algorithm used in real-time operating systems. EDF is an optimal scheduling algorithm on preemptive uniprocessors, in the following sense: if a collection of independent jobs (each one characterized by an arrival time, an execution requirement, and a deadline) can be scheduled (by any algorithm) such that all the jobs complete by their deadlines, then the EDF will schedule this collection of jobs such that all of them complete by their deadlines. On the other hand, if a set of tasks is not schedulable under EDF, then no other scheduling algorithm can feasibly schedule this task set. So, compared to fixed priority scheduling techniques like Rate-Monotonic scheduling, EDF can guarantee all the deadlines in the system at higher loading. When scheduling periodic processes that have deadlines equal to their periods, and when the context switching time is negligible, EDF has a utilization bound of 100 %. The necessary and sufficient condition for the schedulability of the tasks follows that for a given set of n tasks, τ_1, τ_2,..., τ_n with time periods T_1, T_2, ..., T_n, and computation times (worst case execution time, WCET) of C_1, C_2, ..., C_n assuming that $T_i = D_i$ (period equals to deadline) for each task, the deadline driven schedule algorithm is feasible if and only if $U = \sum_{i=1}^{n} \frac{C_i}{T_i} \leq 1$, [7]. Secondly, RM is an on-line preemptive static priority scheduling strategy for periodic and independent tasks assuming that $T_i = D_i$ (period equals to deadline) for each task τ_i. The idea is to determine fixed priorities by task frequencies: tasks with higher rates (shorter periods) are assigned with a higher priority. The necessary and sufficient condition for the schedulability of the tasks follows that for a given set of n tasks, τ_1, τ_2,..., τ_n with time periods T_1, T_2, ..., T_n, and computation times of C_1, C_2, ..., C_n, the deadline driven scheduling algorithm is feasible if $U = \sum_{i=1}^{n} \frac{C_i}{T_i} \leq n(2^{\frac{1}{n}} - 1)$. In our current work, to ensure the availability of energy after each reconfiguration scenario, we focus on adapting task parameters T_i or C_i. We propose to apply dynamic policy EDF when the performance of the system is well, otherwise the static policy RM with limited characteristics. We use as a notation for this real-time feasibility condition: $U = \sum_{i=1}^{n} \frac{C_i}{T_i} \leq \alpha_{policy}$, where $\alpha_{policy} = 1$ for EDF scheduling and $\alpha_{policy} = n(2^{\frac{1}{n}} - 1)$ for RM scheduling.

2.3 Low-Power Scheduling

Power reduction techniques can be classified into two categories: static [10] and dynamic. In [11], the power consumption P is proportional to the processor utilization U. If the processor utilization is minimized, then the power consumption is automatically minimized: $P = k.U^2$. Based on the previous formula, Wang et al. in [11,12], present a simple run-time strategy that reduces the energy consumption. They propose to modify the tasks period T_i, assigning a single value to all tasks which is not reasonable in practice [11]. Another solution proposed is to reduce WCETs (C_i) assigning a single value to all tasks which is not reasonable in practice [11]. The formulas proposed in [11,12] are simple with soft calculation, but the main disadvantage is that it is not acceptable for a real-time system to change the period of tasks more than a certain limit according to user requirement. Moreover if tasks have very diverse periods T_i, tasks that have small periods will be too much affected if they will be aligned with tasks that have large periods. The system overall will look like a synchronous system driven by the slowest task. [11,12] propose the same principle to modify WCETs.

To address this problem, we propose to group the tasks that have "similar" periods in packs by assigning a unique period to all tasks of a pack. This idea is formalized in Sect. 3. To reduce energy consumption, [11,12] propose to remove some tasks when the system lacks energy without any reasonable strategy. This is a suitable approach, but if we have to remove a task, we shall preserve critical real-time tasks and remove less important ones first. The complete formulation of this strategy is given in the next sections of this paper. To verify the system's behavior, we use the real-time simulator Cheddar.

3 Problem Formalization for Reconfigurable Real-Time Systems

This section defines a formalization of the problems exposed above illustrated by different case studies.

3.1 Task Model

We assume in this paper that a real-time embedded system Sys is composed of a set of tasks that should meet real-time constraints defined in user requirements:

$Sys = \{\tau_1, \tau_2, ..., \tau_n\}$. Like in [7], Each task τ_i of Sys is defined by (i) a release time R_i, (ii) its worst case execution time (WCETs) C_i, (iii) a period T_i, (iv) a maximum period $T_i max$, (v) a deadline D_i, (vi) an importance factor I_i and vii) a memory footprint MF_i. Let us explain some parameters: (a) $T_i max$: is the maximum period I_i can not exceed according to system specification, (b) I_i: is an Integer variable (between 0 and 15), called "importance factor" according to user functional requirements. If a task has a very high value I_i, then the task is less important, else the task is paramount. In case the embedded system has a low energy, so it should to remove some tasks according to their importance factor. Tasks that have $I_i = 0$ are considered critical real-time tasks that can not admit change in their parameters. Finally (c) MF_i: the memory space used by the task τ_i. In this paper, we assume that $T_i = D_i$, then each task τ_i will be described by: $\tau_i = \{R_i, C_i, T_i, T_i max, I_i, MF_i\}$. After each reconfiguration scenario, it is necessary to check the feasibility of real-time scheduling by verifying the equation: $\sum_{i=1}^{n} \frac{C_i}{T_i} \leq \alpha_{policy}$.

3.2 Energy Model

We consider that a real-time embedded system is periodically fully recharged, the energy model is characterized by (i) a quantity of energy available at full recharge E_{max}, (ii) an energy available at time $t : \Delta E(t)$, (iii) a recharge period RP and (iv) a time remaining until the next recharge Δt. As define in Sect. 2.3, the power consumption P is proportional to the processor utilization U. So, $P\alpha U$, it means $P = k.U^2$. Then the power consumption is calculated by:

$$P = k.U^2 = k.(\sum_{i=1}^{n} \frac{C_i}{T_i})^2 \tag{1}$$

We assume in this paper that $k = 1$. To ensure that the system will run correctly until the next recharge, it is necessary that at time t:

$$P(t).\Delta t \leq \Delta E(t) \tag{2}$$

$P(t)$ is the power consumption at t, that means the power consumption $P(t) \leq \frac{\Delta E(t)}{\Delta t}$. We define $P_{limit}(t) = \frac{\Delta E(t)}{\Delta t}$. After each reconfiguration scenario, we have to ensure that: $P(t) \leq P_{limit}(t)$: This is the Energy Constraint.

3.3 Memory Model

We suppose that the memory model in a real-time embedded system is characterized by (i) a memory size MS and (ii) an Available memory at time t, $AM(t)$. Each task occupies at run-time MF_i amount of memory. After each reconfiguration scenario, we must ensure that: $\sum_{i=1}^{n} MF_i < AM(t)$. This is the Memory Constraint.

3.4   Reconfiguration Problem

We suppose that Sys is initially composed of n tasks at t_1, $Sys(t_1) = \{\tau_1, \tau_2, ..., \tau_n\}$, we also suppose that $Sys(t_1)$ is feasible. We assume in the following that the system Sys is dynamically reconfigured at run-time such that its new implementation is $Sys(t_2) = \{\tau_1, \tau_2, ..., \tau_n, \tau_{n+1}, ..., \tau_m\}$. The subset $\{\tau_{n+1}, ..., \tau_m\}$ is added to the initial implementation $\{\tau_1, \tau_2, ..., \tau_n\}$. To ensure that the system will run correctly after this reconfiguration scenario, at time t, it is necessary to check whether the new configuration respects these three constraints:

1. Real-time scheduling feasability constraint, denoted FeasibleC, must verify

$$\sum\nolimits_{i=1}^{m} \frac{C_i}{T_i} \leq \alpha_{policy} \tag{3}$$

2. Energy constraint, denoted EnergyC, must verify

$$P(t) \leq P_{limit}(t) \tag{4}$$

3. Memory constraint, denoted MemoryC, must verify

$$\sum\nolimits_{i=1}^{m} MF_i < AM(t) \tag{5}$$

After each reconfiguration scenario, one or more of these constraints can be violated, we have to find the suitable solution to each problem.

3.5   Case Study Problems Illustrations

We present in this section a case study that can show the different problems. We use this notation to represent certain tasks $\tau_i = \{C_i, T_i, T_i max, I_i\}$. Let us assume that the system supports the following tasks: $\tau_1 = \{4, 40, 90, 1\}$, $\tau_2 = \{6, 15, 50, 1\}$, $\tau_3 = \{3, 29, 80, 2\}$ and $\tau_4 = \{4, 40, 70, 4\}$. It is assumed that we use the EDF scheduling ($\alpha_{policy} = 1$). We verify the system feasibility condition:

$$U = \sum_{i=1}^{4} \frac{C_i}{T_i} = 0.7034 \leq 1 \tag{6}$$

then the system is feasible. We suppose that at this time t, $P_{limit}(t) = 1.2\,\mathrm{W}$. It is assumed also that $k = 1$, then we calculate the power consumption at t:

$$P(t) = k * U^2 = 1 * (\sum_{i=1}^{4} \frac{C_i}{T_i})^2 = 0.4947\,\mathrm{W} \tag{7}$$

$P(t)$ is less than $P_{limit}(t)$, then the Energy constraint is respected.

We suppose now that after a certain execution time, a first reconfiguration is performed. For this reconfiguration, two tasks $\tau_5 = \{5, 20, 50, 1\}$ and

$\tau_6 = \{6, 25, 50, 5\}$ are added. Due to this reconfiguration, we must verify if the system respects the feasibility condition. We then compute U as,

$$U = \sum_{i=1}^{6} \frac{C_i}{T_i} = 1.193 > 1 \tag{8}$$

Because the value of U is greater than 1, the system is no more feasible after the reconfiguration. Furthermore, we must also verify the Energy constraint at this time t:

$$P(t) = k * U^2 = 1 * (\sum_{i=1}^{6} \frac{C_i}{T_i})^2 = 1.423 \, \text{W} \tag{9}$$

As $P(t)$ is higher than $P_{limit}(t)$, then the Energy constraint is not respected.

So, for this reconfiguration scenario, two constraints are then violated:

- *Problem1: Real-Time Constraint is violated.*
- *Problem2: Energy Constraint is violated.*

4   Solutions for Feasible Reconfigurable Real-Time Systems

In this section, we present the different solutions that we propose to extend [11, 12]. These solutions are mainly based on the modification of the periods (T_i) or the WCETs (C_i) of tasks in order to ensure that the system will run correctly until the next battery recharge after each reconfiguration scenario and to satisfy the real-time feasibility and memory constraints. In fact if we take Eqs. 1 and 3, we can see that T_i and C_i are parameters that can be adapted to apply a new configuration that respects the energy and feasibility constraints. To ensure that the system is feasible, Wang et al. in [11,12] propose an approche to modify the tasks period T_i assigning the same value to all tasks [11]. Another solution proposed is to reduce WCET while assigning also the same value to all tasks [11]. As stated in Sect. 2.3, this approach presents two main drawbacks and cannot be applied in practice. In this paper, we propose to group the tasks that have "similar" periods in several Packs, denoted Pk, by assigning a unique new period T^{New} to all tasks of the first pack Pk_1. Moreover all new periods affected to pack Pk_j are multiples of T^{New}, the period affected to tasks belonging to pack Pk_1. We have only to compute the suitable T^{New}. This solution controls the complexity of the problem.

4.1   Pack Model

Let us note that each time a new period T^{New} is affected to a task that has originally a period T_i, the cost is a delay penalty for this task of T^{New} - T_i. This is applicable for tasks of Pack Pk_1. For other packs Pk_j the period is $j* T^{New}$. So the cost for each task of Pk_j is: $(T^{New}-(T_i \bmod T^{New})) \bmod T^{New}$. The total cost for the approach is the sum of all these costs. We need to seek the value T^{New} that minimizes the cost of the new solution for the whole system:

$$\sum_{i=1}^{m} ((T^{New} - (T_i \bmod T^{New})) \bmod T^{New}) \text{ is minimal, with } T^{New} \geq Min(T_i)$$

$$(10)$$

***Running Example 1*: (Case study).** We have 6 tasks. According to Eq. 10 we seek a value of T^{New} that leads to a minimum cost. Possible values of T^{New} range from 15 s to 40 s. We found that $T^{New} = 26$ s is the optimal solution.

The same approach is applied when WCET is modified. It is necessary to seek C^{New} such that:

$$\sum_{i=1}^{m} ((C^{New} - (C_i \bmod C^{New})) \bmod C^{New}) \text{ is minimal, with } C^{New} \geq Min(C_i)$$

$$(11)$$

***Running Example 2*: (Case study).** We have 6 tasks. According to Eq. 11 we seek C^{New}, then we start the calculation of costs, with $C^{New} = 3$ until $C^{New} = 6$. So $C^{New} = 3$ is minimal with a cost equals to 5.

This approach leads to 2 solutions to make the system feasible denoted (T_{RT}^{New} and C_{RT}^{New}) and 2 solutions to be sure that the system respects the energy constraint denoted (T_{Eg}^{New} and C_{Eg}^{New}). We present the proposed solutions for each problem apart.

4.2   Solution A: Modification of Periods Under Real-Time Scheduling Constraint:

Proposition 1. The extended T_i of the task τ_i is multiple of T_{RT}^{New}:

$$T_{RT}^{New} = \left\lceil \frac{\sum_{Pk_1} C_i + \sum_{Pk_2} \frac{C_i}{2} + \dots + \sum_{Pk_j} \frac{C_i}{j}}{\alpha_{policy}} \right\rceil \qquad (12)$$

Proof. In order to respect the real-time scheduling constraint according to a scheduling policy "α_{policy}": $\sum_{i=1}^{m} \frac{C_i}{T_i} \leq \alpha_{policy}$. We assign each task to its Pack Pk_j according to its period T_i, Then:

$$\sum_{Pk_1} \frac{C_i}{T} + \sum_{Pk_2} \frac{C_i}{2.T} + \dots + \sum_{Pk_j} \frac{C_i}{j.T} \leq \alpha_{policy}$$

So,

$$\frac{1}{T}.(\sum_{Pk_1} C_i + \sum_{Pk_2} \frac{C_i}{2} + \dots + \sum_{Pk_j} \frac{C_i}{j}) \leq \alpha_{policy}$$

Then,

$$T_{RT}^{New} = \frac{\sum_{Pk_1} C_i + \sum_{Pk_2} \frac{C_i}{2} + \dots + \sum_{Pk_j} \frac{C_i}{j}}{\alpha_{policy}}$$

Since the periods are integer:

$$T_{RT}^{New} = \left\lceil \frac{\sum_{Pk_1} C_i + \sum_{Pk_2} \frac{C_i}{2} + ... + \sum_{Pk_j} \frac{C_i}{j}}{\alpha_{policy}} \right\rceil$$

Now, we assign T_{RT}^{New} to tasks of Pk_1, $2*T_{RT}^{New}$ to tasks of Pk_2, ..., $j*T_{RT}^{New}$ to tasks of Pk_j. After the modification of the periods, the processor utilization of tasks is reduced, and can satisfy the real-time scheduling.

Running Example 3: **Problem 1 (Case study).** According to Eq. 10, the optimal value of T^{New} is 15 s. Then we have three Packs: Pk_1 groups tasks that have periods between 1 and 15, Pk_2 groups tasks that have periods between 16 and 30 and Pk_3 groups tasks that have periods between 31 and 45. The new period T_{RT}^{New} that satisfies the real-time constraint is equal to 16 according to Eq. 12. Then, U is equal to $0.9791 \leq 1$. It is obvious that the real-time constraint is respected after applying a reconfiguration scenario.

4.3 Solution B: Modification of WCETs Under Real-Time Scheduling Constraint:

Proposition 2. The extended WCET C_i of task τ_i is multiple of C_{RT}^{New}:

$$C_{RT}^{New} = \left\lfloor \frac{\alpha_{policy}}{\sum_{Pk_1} \frac{1}{T_i} + \sum_{Pk_2} \frac{2}{T_i} + ... + \sum_{Pk_j} \frac{j}{T_i}} \right\rfloor \tag{13}$$

Proof. We followed the same used technique to calculate the new WCETs. After we reconfigure the WCETs, we should get $\sum_{i=1}^{m} \frac{C_i}{T_i} \leq \alpha_{policy}$. We assign each task to its Pack Pk_j according to its WCETs C_i, Then:

$$\sum_{Pk_1} \frac{C}{T_i} + \sum_{Pk_2} \frac{2.C}{T_i} + ... + \sum_{Pk_j} \frac{j.C}{T_i} \leq \alpha_{policy}$$

So,

$$C. \left(\sum_{Pk_1} \frac{1}{T_i} + \sum_{Pk_2} \frac{2}{T_i} + ... + \sum_{Pk_j} \frac{j}{T_i} \right) \leq \alpha_{policy}$$

Then,

$$C_{RT}^{New} = \left\lfloor \frac{\alpha_{policy}}{\sum_{Pk_1} \frac{1}{T_i} + \sum_{Pk_2} \frac{2}{T_i} + ... + \sum_{Pk_j} \frac{j}{T_i}} \right\rfloor$$

We assign C_{RT}^{New} to tasks of Pk_1, $2 * C_{RT}^{New}$ to tasks of Pk_2, ..., $j * C_{RT}^{New}$ to tasks of Pk_j. After the modification of the WCETs, the processor utilization of tasks is reduced, and can satisfy the real-time scheduling.

Running Example 4: **Problem 1 (Case study).** According to Eq. 11, the optimal value of C^{New} is 3 s. Then we have two Packs: Pk_1 groups tasks that have WCETs between 1 and 3 and Pk_2 groups tasks that have WCETs between 4 and 6. The new WCET C_{RT}^{New} satisfies the real-time constraint is equal to 2 according to Eq. 13. Then, U is equal to $0.895 \le 1$. It is obvious that the real-time constraint is respected after applying a reconfiguration scenario.

4.4   Solution C: Modification of Periods Under Energy Constraint:

Proposition 3. The extended T_i of task τ_i is multiple of T_{Eg}^{New}

$$T_{Eg}^{New} = \left\lceil \frac{\sum_{Pk_1} C_i + \sum_{Pk_2} \frac{C_i}{2} + \ldots + \sum_{Pk_j} \frac{C_i}{j}}{\sqrt{\frac{P_{limit}(t)}{k}}} \right\rceil \tag{14}$$

Proof. It is necessary that the current power $P(t) = k.U^2$ should be less than the critical power P_{limit}, with $P_{limit(t)} = \frac{\Delta E(t)}{\Delta t}$, then we should get $k.U^2 \le P_{limit}(t)$ $U \le \sqrt{\frac{P_{limit}(t)}{k}}$. So, $\sum_{i=1}^{m} \frac{C_i}{T_i} \le \sqrt{\frac{P_{limit}(t)}{k}}$. We assign each task to its Pack Pk_j according to its period, Then:

$$\sum_{Pk_1} \frac{C_i}{T} + \sum_{Pk_2} \frac{C_i}{2.T} + \ldots + \sum_{Pk_j} \frac{C_i}{j.T} \le \sqrt{\frac{P_{limit}(t)}{k}}$$

$$\frac{1}{T}.\left(\sum_{Pk_1} C_i + \sum_{Pk_2} \frac{C_i}{2} + \ldots + \sum_{Pk_j} \frac{C_i}{j}\right) \le \sqrt{\frac{P_{limit}(t)}{k}}$$

So,

$$T_{Eg}^{New} = \left\lceil \frac{\left(\sum_{Pk_1} C_i + \sum_{Pk_2} \frac{C_i}{2} + \ldots + \sum_{Pk_j} \frac{C_i}{j}\right)}{\sqrt{\frac{P_{limit}(t)}{k}}} \right\rceil$$

We assign T_{Eg}^{New} to tasks of Pk_1, $2 * T_{Eg}^{New}$ to tasks of Pk_2, ..., $j * T_{Eg}^{New}$ to tasks of Pk_j. After the modification of the periods, the processor utilization of tasks is reduced which can respect the energy constraint.

Running Example 5: **Problem 2 (Case study).** According to Eq. 10, the optimal value of T^{New} is 15 s. Then we have three Packs: Pk_1 groups tasks that have periods between 1 and 15, Pk_2 groups tasks that have periods between 16 and 30 and Pk_3 groups tasks that have periods between 31 and 45. The new period T_{Eg}^{New} that satisfies the energy constraint remains equal to 15 according to Eq. 14. Then, U is equal to 1.0392. So, $P = k.U^2 = 1 * U^2 = 1.08 \,\text{W} \le 1.2 \,\text{W}$. It is obvious that the energy constraint is respected after applying a reconfiguration scenario.

Note: In this running example the real-time constraint is violated because $U = 1.0392 > 1$, we should seek another period by using the solution A and choose the maximum to satisfy the two constraints.

4.5   Solution D: Modification of Periods Under Energy Constraint:

Proposition 4. The extended WCET C_i of task τ_i is multiple of C_{Eg}^{New}:

$$C_{Eg}^{New} = \left\lfloor \frac{\sqrt{\frac{P_{limit}(t)}{k}}}{(\sum_{Pk_1} \frac{1}{T_i} + \sum_{Pk_2} \frac{2}{T_i} + ... + \sum_{Pk_j} \frac{j}{T_i})} \right\rfloor \tag{15}$$

Proof. It is necessary that the current power $P(t) = k.U^2$ should be less than the critical power P_{limit}, with $P_{limit(t)} = \frac{\Delta E(t)}{\Delta t}$, then we should get $k.U^2 \leq P_{limit}(t)$ $U \leq \sqrt{\frac{P_{limit}(t)}{k}}$. So, $\sum_{i=1}^{m} \frac{C_i}{T_i} \leq \sqrt{\frac{P_{limit}(t)}{k}}$.

We assign each task to its Pack Pk_j according to its WCETs C_i, Then:

$$\sum_{Pk_1} \frac{C}{T_i} + \sum_{Pk_2} \frac{2.C}{T_i} + ... + \sum_{Pk_j} \frac{j.C}{T_i} \leq \sqrt{\frac{P_{limit}}{k}}$$

$$C. \left(\sum_{Pk_1} \frac{1}{T_i} + \sum_{Pk_2} \frac{2}{T_i} + ... + \sum_{Pk_j} \frac{j}{T_i} \right) \leq \sqrt{\frac{P_{limit}}{k}}$$

So,

$$C_{Eg}^{New} = \left\lfloor \frac{\sqrt{\frac{P_{limit}}{k}}}{\sum_{Pk_1} \frac{1}{T_i} + \sum_{Pk_2} \frac{2}{T_i} + ... + \sum_{Pk_j} \frac{j}{T_i}} \right\rfloor$$

We assign C_{Eg}^{New} to tasks of Pk_1, $2*C_{Eg}^{New}$ to tasks of Pk_2, ..., $j*C_{Eg}^{New}$ to tasks of Pk_j. After the modification of the WCETs, the processor utilization of tasks is reduced, and can respect the energy constraint.

Running Example 6: **Problem 2 (Case study).** According to Eq. 11, the optimal value of C^{New} is 3 s. Then we have two Packs: Pk_1 groups tasks that have WCETs between 1 and 3 and Pk_2 groups tasks that have WCETs between 4 and 6. The new WCET C_{Eg}^{New} that satisfies the energy constraint is equal to 2 according to Eq. 15. Then, U is equal to 0.894, then $Pk = k.U^2 = 1 * U^2 = 0.799 \leq 1.2$ W. It is obvious that the energy constraint is respected after applying a reconfiguration scenario.

Note: If the real-time constraint is violated ($U > 1$), we should seek another WCET by using the solution B and choose the minimum to satisfy the two constraints.

4.6   Solution E: Removal of Tasks

This solution proposes the removal of less important tasks according to the importance factor I_i in order to minimize the energy consumption after any reconfiguration scenario of an embedded system that affects the energy constraint.

4.7   New Deterministic Solution for Real-Time and Low-Power Scheduling of Reconfigurable Embedded Systems Under Memory Constraints

We can implement our approach by this algorithm with complexity $O(n)$. We use the following functions: $ProcessorUtilization(k)$: It is a function that returns the processor utilization value when it runs with a given tasks parameters denoted k. $Execution(k)$: System execution by applying k, $Execution()$: Regular execution, $Max(a, b)$: It is a function that returns the maximum between a and b, $Min(a, b)$: It is a function that returns the minimum between a and b.

Algorithm 1. Decision Strategy

---

  while Reconfiguration **do**
    if (!MemoryC) **then**
      $Execution(SolutionE)$
    else if (FeasibleC) AND (EnergyC) **then**
      $Execution()$
    else if (!FeasibleC) AND (EnergyC) **then**
      if $(ProcessorUtilization(SolutionA) < ProcessorUtilization(SolutionB))$ **then**
        $Execution(SolutionA)$
      else
        $Execution(SolutionB)$
      end if
    else if (FeasibleC) AND (!EnergyC) **then**
      if $(ProcessorUtilization(SolutionC) < ProcessorUtilization(SolutionD))$ **then**
        $Execution(SolutionC)$
      else
        $Execution(SolutionD)$
      end if
    else
      if $(ProcessorUtilization(Max\{SolutionA, SolutionC\})$ $<$
      $ProcessorUtilization(Min\{SolutionB, SolutionD\})$ **then**
        $Execution(Max\{SolutionA, SolutionC\})$
      else
        $Execution(Min\{SolutionB, SolutionD\})$
      end if
    end if
  end while

---

5   Evaluation of Performance

To evaluate the current paper's contribution to the related works (RW) in [11,12]. We assume a case of a system composed of 100 tasks that can be reconfigured at run-time under memory and energy constraints. For this purpose we adopted the same set of tasks used in [11] to evaluate this algorithm. We calculate the

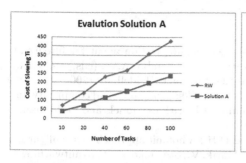
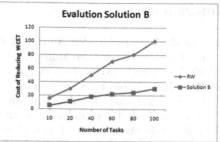

Fig. 1. Cost of modication of periods T_i (Solution A) and WCETs C_i (Solution B).

cost of our solutions compared to the proposed solution in [11,12]. The cost of a solution is the total delay introduced to periods T_i or to WCETs C_i as explained in Sect. 4.1. In Fig. 1, we show a comparison with RW when we apply Solution A (Fig. 1 left side) and Solution B (Fig. 1 right side). For each reconfiguration scenario, modifications will be performed on packs/tasks parameters in order to respect the memory, real-time and energy constraints. Thanks to this concept of packs, we can notice that our solution is less costly in both cases A and B than RW. Moreover, our solutions are implemented by an algorithm with complexity $O(n)$, but the complexity of the algorithm of these related works [12] is $O(n^2)$ (two nested for-loops).

More evaluation work has to be developed through simulation:

- The processor utilization while considering several random distributions of a set of tasks and comparison with [11,12].
- The total delay (Solution cost) also with randomly distributed set of tasks.

6 Conclusion

This paper is interested in reconfigurable real-time embedded systems when the battery recharges are done periodically. Our study concerns specifically the influence of the reconfiguration on memory, energy and real-time feasibility constraints. We propose a new strategy that ensures a low-cost feasible real-time and low-power reconfiguration of embedded systems while meeting memory limits. Thanks to the estimation of available energy after any reconfiguration, the system is temporally configured to run the embedded tasks with low-cost computation. In addition to the control of memory, our solution is more realistic since it generates logical values of real-time parameters to be assigned to different packs. This original contribution is more useful than related works in [11,12] since it is applicable in practice. In our future works, we will be interested in the implementation of the paper's contribution that will be evaluated by assuming real case studies.

References

1. Al-Safi, Y., Vyatkin, V.: An ontology-based reconfiguration agent for intelligent mechatronic systems. In: Mařík, V., Vyatkin, V., Colombo, A.W. (eds.) HoloMAS 2007. LNCS (LNAI), vol. 4659, pp. 114–126. Springer, Heidelberg (2007)
2. Baruah, S., Goossens, J.: Scheduling real-time tasks: algorithms and complexity. In: Leung, J.Y.T. (ed.) Handbook of Scheduling: Algorithms Models and Performance Analysis. CRC Press, Boca Raton (2003)
3. William Brennan, R., Fletcher, M., Norrie, D.H.: A holonic approach to reconfiguring real-time distributed control systems. In: Mařík, V., Štěpánková, O., Krautwurmová, H., Luck, M. (eds.) ACAI 2001, EASSS 2001, AEMAS 2001, and HoloMAS 2001. LNCS (LNAI), vol. 2322, pp. 323–335. Springer, Heidelberg (2002)
4. Angelov, C., Sierszecki, K., Marian, N.: Design models for reusable and reconfigurable state machines. In: Yang, L.T., Amamiya, M., Liu, Z., Guo, M., Rammig, F.J. (eds.) EUC 2005. LNCS, vol. 3824, pp. 152–163. Springer, Heidelberg (2005)
5. Gharsellaoui, H., Ben Ahmed, S.: Real-time reconfigurable scheduling of sporadic tasks. In: Cordeiro, J., Van Sinderen, M. (eds.) ICSOFT 2013. CCIS, vol. 457, pp. 24–39. Springer, Heidelberg (2014)
6. Khalgui, M., Mosbahi, O., Li, Z., Hanisch, H.: Reconfigurable multi-agent embedded control systems: from modelling to implementation. IEEE Trans. Comput. 60(4), 538–551 (2010)
7. Liu, C., Layland, J.: Scheduling algorithms for multiprogramming in a hard-real-time environment. J. ACM 20(1), 46–61 (1973)
8. Quan, G., Hu, X.: Minimum energy fixed-priority scheduling for variable voltage processors. IEEE Trans. Comput. Aided Des. Integr. Circ. Syst. 23(9), 1062–1071 (2003)
9. Rooker, M.N., Sünder, C., Strasser, T., Zoitl, A., Hummer, O., Ebenhofer, G.: Zero downtime reconfiguration of distributed automation systems: the εCEDAC approach. In: Mařík, V., Vyatkin, V., Colombo, A.W. (eds.) HoloMAS 2007. LNCS (LNAI), vol. 4659, pp. 326–337. Springer, Heidelberg (2007)
10. Shin, Y., Choi, K.: Power conscious fixed priority scheduling for hard real-time systems. In: 1999 36th Proceedings of Design Automation Conference, pp. 134–139 (1999)
11. Wang, X., Khalgui, M., Li, Z.: Dynamic low power reconfigurations of real-time embedded systems. In: Proceedings of the 1st International Conference on Pervasive and Embedded Computing and Communication Systems, Portugal (2011)
12. Wang, X., Khemaissia, I., Khalgui, M., Li, Z.: Dynamic low-power reconfiguration of real-time systems with periodic and probabilistic tasks. IEEE Trans. Autom. Sci. Eng. 12(1), 258–271 (2014)
13. Yao, F., Demers, A., Shenker, S.: A scheduling model for reduced CPU energy. In: 1995 Proceedings of the 36th Annual Symposium on Foundations of Computer Science, pp. 374–382 (1995)

New Solutions for Useful Execution Models of Communicating Adaptive RA2DL

Farid Adaili[1,2,3](✉), Olfa Mosbahi[1], Mohamed Khalgui[1], and Samia Bouzefrane[3]

[1] LISI Laboratory, INSAT, University of Carthage, Tunis, Tunisia
{olfamosbahi,khalgui.mohamed}@gmail.com
[2] Tunisia Polytechnic School, University of Carthage, Tunis, Tunisia
[3] CEDRIC Laboratory, National Conservatory of Arts and Crafts, Paris, France
{farid.adaili,samia.bouzefrane}@cnam.fr

Abstract. The paper deals with adaptive component-based control systems following the Reconfiguration Architecture Analysis and Design Language (denoted by RA2DL). A system is assumed to be composed a network of RA2DL in coordination. When a fault occurs in the plant, RA2DL component will have a lot of problems to solve such as: the management of the reconfiguration flow, the correction of execution, the synchronization of reconfiguration with the other RA2DL components and the coordination between them. A correction is proposed therefore to improve RA2DL by three layers: the first one is the Middleware reconfiguration (MR) to manage the reconfiguration of RA2DL, the second one is the Execution Controller (EC) which describes the executable and reconfiguration part of RA2DL and the third one is the Middleware Synchronization (SM) for synchronous reconfigurations. When the system is distributed on a network of RA2DL components, we propose a coordination method between them using well-defined matrices to allow feasible and coherent reconfigurations. A tool is developed to simulate our approach. All the contributions of this work are applied to a case study dealing with IEEE 802.11 Wireless LAN.

Keywords: Control system · RA2DL · Reconfiguration · Execution model · Coordination · Synchronization · Distribution

1 Introduction

Nowadays in the academy and manufacturing industry, many research works have been made to deal with real-time reconfiguration of embedded control systems. The new generation of these systems are addressing today a new criteria such as flexibility and agility. To reduce their cost, these systems have to be changed and adapted to their environment without any disturbance.

In the literature, two reconfiguration policies exist, (i) static reconfigurations [2] to be generally applied offline: (ii) and dynamic reconfigurations that can be applied at run-time. We generally define two solutions for the second case:

© Springer International Publishing Switzerland 2015
H. Fujita and G. Guizzi (Eds.): SoMeT 2015, CCIS 532, pp. 87–101, 2015.
DOI: 10.1007/978-3-319-22689-7_7

manual reconfigurations to be applied by users at run-time, and automatic reconfigurations which are generally handled by software autonomous agents [5]. We are interested in this paper in automatic reconfigurations of embedded control systems. In order to reduce their development and consequently their time to market, these systems are based on the component-based approach. A component is classically defined as a software unit to be composed with others in order to form the general control functions of the whole system [7]. Two families of components are proposed: the components to be composed at run-time such as .Net [3] and the components that should be composed off-line to check their respect of functional and temporal constraints such as IEC61499 [6] and AADL [11]. We are interested in this work in the AADL technology. AADL component is a software unit to be encoded with a set of algorithms that implement its control functions. Each algorithm is activated by corresponding external event-data inputs, and generally produces the results of its execution on corresponding data-event outputs. It is well-used in many industrial applications such as Avionics Software [12]. We note that a rich library is available today to develop applications in AADL. Nevertheless, these applications are not flexible and cannot be adapted to their environment since Society of Automotive Engineers (SAE) [9] does not provide technical solutions for the possible adaptation of the system based on AADL components at run-time. Moreover, no one in all related works deal with the flexibility of AADL components.

Adaptive systems such as IEEE 802.11 Wireless LAN are composed of networked components. Their logical structure is expressed by an architectural graph in which nodes represent components, and the arcs represent connections between components. In such systems, a dynamic reconfiguration means not only replacing individual components at run-time, but potentially also changing system architecture or structure by adding/removing components and/or changing the patterns of their interconnection between components.

In this work, we are interested in the extention and the logical correction of RA2DL by proposing a new execution model which is composed of three layers: (i) Middleware Reconfiguration level that handles the input reconfiguration flows, (ii) Execution Controller level to control the execution and reconfiguration of RA2DL and (iii) Middleware Synchronization level that controls and manages the synchronization of the reconfiguration. On the other hand, we propose a new approach about the coordination between several RA2DL components in a distributed architecture. The paper's contribution is applied to a case study of an IEEE 802.11 LAN Wireless system that will be followed as a running example. A tool called *ECReconf* is developed in a collaboration between LISI Lab at University of Carthage in Tunisia and CEDRIC Lab at CNAM in France to implement and simulate the case study.

We present in the next section the background of RA2DL, and define in Sect. 3 the case study of the IEEE 802.11 LAN Wireless. Section 4 proposes the execution model of RA2DL, Sect. 5 presents the coherent execution models of the communication between RA2DL components, and Sect. 6 defines the modelling and verification where an UPPAAL-based model checking is applied. We propose in Sect. 7 an implementation and simulation of our solution and conclude the paper in Sect. 8.

2 Background

We define in a previous paper [1] the concept of RA2DL dealing with the reconfigurable AADL components. RA2DL is composed of controller and controlled modules where the first one is a set of reconfiguration functions applied in AADL, and the second is a set of input/output events, algorithms, and data. We concentrate on three hierarchical reconfiguration levels in RA2DL: **(i) Form 1:**. Architectural level: modifies the component architecture when particular conditions are met. This is done by adding new algorithms, events and data or removing existing operations in the internal behaviors of the component. **(ii) Form 2:** Compositional level: modifies the composition of the internal components (algorithms) for a given architecture. **(iii) Form 3:** Data level: changes the values of variables without changing the component algorithms.

In [8] the authors describe the ADL features which permit the description of dynamic software architectures in which the organisation of components and connectors may change during the system execution, taken from Darwin language, a language used to describe the distributed system structure. In [4] the authors expose the *RUNES* approach (reconfigurable, ubiquitous, and networked embedded systems) which has the general goal of developing an architecture for networked embedded systems that encompasses dedicated radio layers and networks.

Several related works do not provide solutions to develop flexible RA2DL components of adaptive embedded systems. We mean by flexibility the facility to change correctly the behavior of a component according to user requirements and evolution of the environment. The current paper proposes new extended solutions to a correct execution and reconfiguration of a RA2DL component. However, in this work we want to extend this study by considering a distributed system controlled by several interacting RA2DL components.

3 Case Study

IEEE 802.11 Wireless LAN [10] is used as a running example in this paper in order to highlight the contributions of our work. It represents a collection of sensor nodes represented by two RA2DL components: *RA2DL − sender* and *RA2DL − receiver*, connected by a multihop backbone to a channel described by a *RA2DL − channel* component, which is in turn connected to a wired network. The description of the components of this case study is as follows:

RA2DL-Sender: is for sending packets in the network. It begins with a data packet ready to send, and senses the *RA2DL − channel*. If the channel remains free, then the *RA2DL − sender* enters its vulnerable period and starts sending a packet (event send), otherwise the *RA2DL − sender* enters a backoff via an urgent transition. The time taken to send a packet is non-deterministic (within T_{min} and T_{max}).

RA2DL-Channel: plays an intermediary role in the network, as a transmission canal of packets between components in the network. The success of the transmission depends on whether a collision has occurred, and is recorded by setting the variable status to the value of the $RA2DL - channel$ variable $c1$. The $RA2DL - sender$ then immediately tests the $RA2DL - channel$ (represented by the urgent location TEST C). If the channel is busy, the $RA2DL - sender$ enters the backoff procedure, otherwise it waits for an acknowledgement. If the packet was sent correctly ($status = 1$), then the destination $RA2DL - recever$ waits and sends the acknowledgement; the $RA2DL - sender$ then receives this acknowledgement. On the other hand, if the packet was not sent correctly ($status = 2$), then the destination $RA2DL - recever$ does nothing. In this case, the $RA2DL - sende$r time out and enters the backoff procedure.

RA2DL-Recever: represents the component for receiving the packets delivered by $RA2DL - sender$. Messages from $RA2DL - sender$ component need to be transmitted across the wired network. If the wired network is busy, these messages should be stored in the $RA2DL - channel$ delaying their processing and increasing the buffer space requirements in the $RA2DL - channel$.

The implementation of this case study with the classic RA2DL presents a set of problems: (i) problem of management of the reconfiguration flow if a component receives several reconfigurations at the same time. (ii) Execution problem to resolve the deadlock and the ambiguity when a reconfiguration execution of each RA2DL component occurs. (iii) Synchronization problem when synchronous reconfigurations occur between RA2DL components and (iv) Coordination problem, when RA2DL components are interconnected and communicated between them by reconfiguration flows, data and events.

The component $RA2DL - channel$, receives a set of reconfiguration flows as input at run-time from $RA2DL - sender$ and $RA2DL - recever$ components. For example, changing the frequency of sending (S_f) by giving a maximization or a minimization. $RA2DL - channel$ has two variables $c1$ and $c2$ which record respectively the status of the packet being sent by $RA2DL - sender$ and $RA2DL - recever$, and which are updated both when a station starts sending a packet ($event\ send$) or finishes sending a packet ($event\ finish$). These variables have the following interpretation: $ci = 0$ - nothing being sent by a station i; $ci = 1$ - packet being sent correctly from station i; $ci = 2$ - packet being sent garbled from station i. Let show some reconfiguration scenarios that can adapt and coordinate RA2DL components of this application to its environment at run-time. We suppose that the $RA2DL - sender$ sends M packets received by $RA2DL - recever$ at a particular time. Let us denote also by (i) Pi the i-th packet ($i \in [1:M]$) to be sent from the $RA2DL - recever$ with a frequency Fi and a transmission speed TS between $Tmin$ and $Tmax$. Each Pi has a size Se at the transfer moment from $RA2DL - sender$ and Sr in reception from $RA2DL - recever$ (ii) Pi the i-th packet ($i \in [1:P]$) which passes through the $RA2DL - channel$ and has a boolean variable C (0 if busy, 1 if free), and

(iii) we assume in the current paper that we have two threads allowing the emission of packets with two periods according to the channel conditions: the first sends the packet each 6 ms when the channel is busy (C = 0) whereas the second sends each 2 ms when the channel is free (C = 1). We assume the following 6 reconfiguration scenarios:

1. **Reconfiguration 1:** if $RA2DL - sender$ sends the packet by $RA2DL - channel$ to $RA2DL - recever$, then the content of the packet must not modify or change the $RA2DL - channel$ component.
2. **Reconfiguration 2:** if $RA2DL - channel$ receives conflicting reconfigurations to minimize or maximize frequency sending (S_f), then the $RA2DL - channel$ component reconfigures the parameter (S_f).
3. **Reconfiguration 3:** if $RA2DL - channel$ is busy $(C = 0)$ then the packet is periodically sent from the $RA2DL - recever$ by a thread $EV - T1$ each $6ms$.
4. **Reconfiguration 4:** if $RA2DL - channel$ is free $(C = 1)$ then the packet is periodically sent from the $RA2DL - recever$ by a thread $EV - T2$ each $2ms$.
5. **Reconfiguration 5:** if the packet size Se is large when the emission is done, then Se should be compressed in Sr by the $RA2DL - recever$.

4   Extension to RA2DL: New Execution Model of RA2DL

We define in [1] a new reconfiguration component RA2DL to control and adapt AADL-based systems to their environment. This RA2DL reacts when an error occurs in the plant and the decision taken may vary from changing the set of RA2DL components that constitute the system, adding-modifying-deleting the internal algorithms/ports, substituting the behavior of some RA2DL components by other behaviors or even modifying data. According to these functionalities, a RA2DL component presents some gaps which remain unresolved like the management of different reconfigurations, the synchronization, the coordination and the distribution. In this paper, we enrich RA2DL by an execution model that undergoes such a failure and to ensure better distribution between RA2DL components. The execution model is composed of three layers (Middleware reconfiguration, Execution Controller and Middleware synchronization) as presented in Fig. 1.

4.1   Middleware Reconfiguration Layer

The Middleware Reconfiguration layer (MR) is dedicated to receive all the reconfiguration Flows (RF) from the input port (IRF). Each RF has a token RT containing the necessary information such as the address of RA2DL destination DA, a binary variable V ($V = 1$ if the reconfiguration is synchronous, otherwise $V = 0$) and a priority factor PF given by the user. Secondly this layer represents the RA2DL manager; it decides whether the RF is associated to it or not, if not associated, it sends to its successor by ORF output. In the case it receives

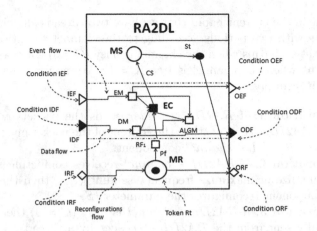

Fig. 1. Execution model of RA2DL

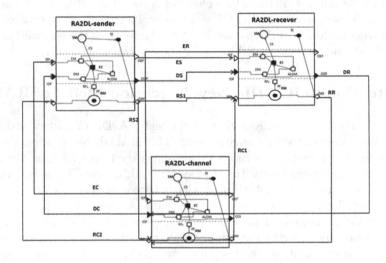

Fig. 2. RA2DL components

concurrent or contradictory RF, the layer decides which reconfiguration will be accepted using the PF.

Running Example: We suppose in Fig. 2 two reconfiguration scenarios $RS1$ and $RS2$. $RS1$ is assumed to amplify frequency Fs for $RA2DL - channel$ and $RS2$ is assumed to minimize the size of the packet for the $RA2DL - recever$, RR is the reconfiguration from $RA2DL - recever$ to change the value c of $RA2DL - channel$ and $RC1$ is to change size in $RA2DL - recever$. The token RT is represented in Table 1.

According to Table 1, we have two problems: (i) two contradictory reconfigurations appear at the same time in $RA2DL - channel$: $RS2$ from $RA2DL -$

Table 1. Token information

	DA (Destination address)	Synchronous	Asynchronous	PF
RS1	RA2DL-recever	0	1	1
RS2	RA2DL-channel	1	0	3
RR	RA2DL-channel	0	1	2
RC	RA2DL-sender	0	1	4

sender to amplify frequency Fs and RR from $RA2DL - recever$ to minimize Fs. In this case, RM compares the two priority factors $PF(RS1 = 3) > PF(RR = 2)$. $RS1$ will be accepted and RR will be rejected. (ii) We have synchronous and asynchronous reconfigurations. When the packet is well transmitted, the reconfiguration is asynchronous when $RA2DL - channel$ changes the variable $c1$ to $c2$. And when the reconfiguration $RC2$ adds a new byte in $RA2DL - sender$, this reconfiguration should be synchronized by also adding a byte with $RS1$ in $RA2DL - receiver$ and automatically passes to the middleware synchronization that will be explained later.

4.2   Execution Controller Layer

The *Execution Controller* (EC) layer is responsible of the reconfiguration execution part of RA2DL having two input/output ports (the first for data flow and the second for events flow) and algorithms (Alg) of RA2DL. The EC is assumed to be encoded in three hierarchical levels (a) Architecture Level (to be denoted by AL), (b) Composition Level (to be denoted by CL), and (c) Data Level (to be denoted by DL). We define in AL, all the possible architectures that can implement the RA2DL component at run-time. An architecture in AL is a set of algorithms (Alg) that perform control activities. A reconfiguration scenario can change the architecture of the $RA2DL$ component by adding or also removing algorithms. For each architecture in AL, we need to define an execution model of the corresponding algorithms. A composition is then defined in CL to affect a priority to each algorithm. For each architecture and for each composition of the corresponding algorithm, we define also in Data level, all the possible corresponding values of data to be handled at run-time.

Running Example: We have two architectures in the IEEE 802.11 Wireless LAN. The first one is when the $RA2DL - channel$ is busy $(C = 0)$, and is implemented with the first architecture $(ASM1)$. The second one is when the $RA2DL - channel$ is free $(C = 1)$ and is implemented with the second architecture $(ASM2)$.

4.3   Middleware Synchronization Layer

The reconfiguration of each RA2DL component in each round is independent of the other RA2DL components and the output generated by a RA2DL component in a round is the input of the next round. In RA2DL technology, such RA2DL components should be executed asynchronously. However, since the RA2DL components are independent in each round, the final states in each round are the same in both asynchronous and synchronous reconfigurations. This layer has a Synchronization Token (ST). If the reconfiguration is synchronized with the other RA2DL components, ST sends with the address, the RA2DL components involved in the reconfiguration pass to semaphore state (S). If the reconfiguration is asynchronous, this layer is not considered.

Running Example: The reconfiguration of the $RA2DL - channel$ component is synchronous or dependent with $RA2DL - sender$ and $RA2DL - recever$, when the $RA2DL - channel$ has collision problems. In this case, a synchronous flow of reconfiguration is sent to $RA2DL - sender$ and $RA2DL - recever$ to inform for a new reconfiguration to apply. Automatically, $RA2DL - sender$ and $RA2DL - recever$ pass to semaphore state (S).

```
Semaphore (RA2DL-sender, RA2DL-receiver)
RA2DL-sender(s:)
RA2DL-receiver(s):
n(s) := n(s) - 1;
if n(s)<0 then; {
State(RA2DL-sender) := blocked;
State(RA2DL-recever) := blocked;}
enter (RA2DL-sender, f(s))
enter (RA2DL-recever, f(s))
```

5   Coherent Reconfigurable Execution Models in Distributed Architectures

In this section, we define a new component named $RA2DL - coordinator$ for the coordination between all RA2DL components. Each RA2DL is specified by nested state machines that support all reconfiguration forms. Nevertheless, the coordination between execution models in this distributed architecture is extremely mandatory because any uncontrolled automatic reconfiguration applied in a RA2DL can lead to critical problems. To guarantee safe distributed reconfigurations, we define the concept of $Coordination\ Matrix\ (CM)$ that defines correct reconfiguration scenarios.

5.1   Distributed RA2DL Architecture

Let Sys be a distributed reconfigurable system composed of n RA2DL components, and let $RA2DL_1, ..., RA2DL_n$ be n RA2DL components to handle automatic distributed reconfiguration scenarios of these components. We denote in the following by $Reconfiguration^a_{ia,ja,ka}$ a reconfiguration scenario applied by $RA2DL_n$ ($a \in [1,n]$) as follows: (i) the corresponding ASM state machine is in the state ASM_{ia}. Let $cond^a_{ia}$ be the set of conditions to reach this state, (ii) the CSM state machine is in the state CSM_{ja}. Let $cond^a_{ja}$ be the set of conditions to reach this state, (iii) the DSM state machine is in the state DSM_{ka}. Let $cond^a_{ka}$ be the set of conditions to reach this state. To handle coherent distributed reconfigurations that guarantee safe behaviors of the whole system Sys, we define the concept of $Coordination\ Matrix$ of size (n, 3) that defines coherent scenarios to be simultaneously applied by different $RA2DL$ components as presented in Fig. 3. Let CM be such a matrix that we characterize as follows: each line $a(a \in [1;n])$ corresponds to a reconfiguration scenario $Reconfiguration^a_{ia,ja,ka}$ to be applied by $RA2DL_a$ as follows:

$$CM[a,1] = ia; CM[a,2] = ja; CM[a,3] = ka$$

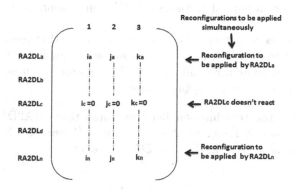

Fig. 3. Coordination matrix

5.2 Coordination Between Distributed RA2DL Components

We propose a new architecture for control systems following the Standard RA2DL to handle automatic distributed reconfigurations of components. To guarantee a coherent behavior of the whole distributed system, we define $RA2DL - coordinator$ (denoted by $CR(\Omega(Sys))$) which handles the Coordination Matrices of $\Omega(Sys)$ to control the rest of RA2DL components (i.e. $RA2DL_a \in [1:n]$) as follows: when a particular $RA2DL_a$ ($a \in [1:n]$) should apply a reconfiguration scenario $Reconfiguration^a_{ia,ja,ka}$ (i.e. under well-defined conditions), it sends the following request to $CR(\Omega(Sys))$ to obtain the authorization.

$$request(RA2DL_a, CR(\Omega(Sys)), Reconfiguration^a_{ia,ja,ka})$$

When $CR\Omega(Sys)$ receives this request that corresponds to a particular coordination matrix $CM \in \Omega(Sys)$ and if CM has the highest priority between all matrices of $\Omega(Sys)$, then $CR\Omega(Sys)$ informs the Control RA2DL that it should react simultaneously with RA2DL as defined in the CM. The following information is sent from $CR\Omega(Sys)$:

For each $RA2DL_b$, $b \in [1,n] \setminus \{a\}$ and $CM[b,i] \neq 0 \; \forall \; i, \in [1,3]$:

$reconfiguration\,((CR\Omega(Sys)), RA2DL_b, Reconfiguration^b_{(CM[b,1],CM[b,2],CM[b,3])})$

Running Example: In the communication IEEE 802.11 Wireless LAN, we distinguish three kinds of participating components:

- The $RA2DL-sender$ (station 1): Starts the communication and when an error occurs in a specific plant, the associate $RA2DL - recever$ tries to correct it and if it decides the necessity of reconfiguration in the whole network (i.e. the other RA2DL components must be aware of this modification) the informs the $RA2DL - coordinator$.
- The $RA2DL-coordinator(CR)$: it is the main component which aims to coordinate between the different RA2DL components. When it receives a reconfiguration request, it searches the list of RA2DL components which should be informed. It sends a request to these RA2DL components and waits for their response.
- The $RA2DL-recever$ (station 2): it is the component that receives a reconfiguration request from the $RA2DL - coordinator$ component. Firstly, it checks the possibility to apply a reconfiguration. If it is possible, it sends a positive answer, otherwise it sends a negative answer.

Figure 4 shows the coordination between these three RA2DL components when the packet size is large. In this case, the CR uses the Matrix CM to compress the size of packets in the $RA2DL - recever$.

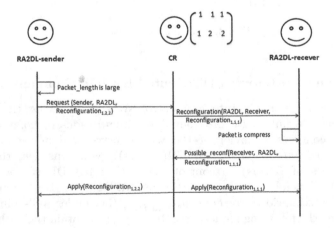

Fig. 4. Coordination between the RA2DL-sender and RA2DL-recever

6   Modeling and Verification of Distributed Architecture RA2DL

We propose in this section the modelling and verification of RA2DL by using UPPAAL. Firstly, we model the execution model of RA2DL with the three layers (RM, EC, SM) by Nested State Machines. Secondly, we model the coordination part with CR and the coordination matrix CM. Thirdly, we check a set of properties to ensure the security and flexibility of our case study.

6.1   Modelling of the Execution Model

The modelling of the execution model with the three layers is described by the state machine presented in Fig. 5.

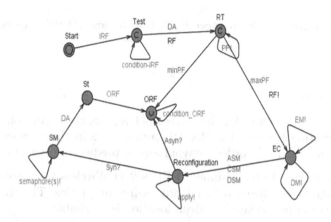

Fig. 5. Modeling of execution model

The states of execution model are described as follows: *start* to start the reconfiguration, *test* to test the condition $condition - IRF$ entering at the port IRF, RT state to test the reconfiguration acceptance with the reconfiguration token in MR if it corresponds to the greatest priority factor PF. EC state corresponds to the execution controller layer with EM for events and DM data of RA2DL, $Reconfiguration$ state to apply the reconfiguration request. It tests whether if the reconfiguration is synchronous or asynchronous. SM state describes the middleware synchronization. If the reconfiguration of the current component is synchronous with another RA2DL component, the semaphore (S) is used in *waiting* state. St is a state to send the reconfiguration to the target component. ORF corresponds to the final state of the execution model.

6.2   Modeling Coordination

We present in Fig. 6 the modeling of the RA2DL coordinator between the RA2DL components, and the communication process between them. $RA2DL - server$

state describes the packet transmission and $RA2DL - recever$ state describes the packet receiving when an error occurs in $RA2DL - server$. This component sends a reconfiguration request to $RA2DL - coordinator$. The latter with the coordination matrix CM ensures the passage of the requests between the two components while a reconfiguration is executing.

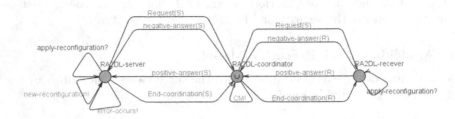

Fig. 6. Coordination between RA2DL-server and RA2DL-recever

6.3   Verification

We check a set of properties for the correct behavior of the execution model and better coordination between the RA2DL components in the systems after any reconfiguration scenario in order to avoid any unpredictable execution.

Running Example: In the assumed IEEE 802.11 Wireless LAN, we check simple reachability, safety, liveness and deadlock-free properties. The simple reachability properties are checked if a given location is reachable:

Property 1: $RT[].PF!.maxPF(RF)$: the execution model has to manage competition reconfigurations according to the PF and has to decide which reconfiguration should be executed the first.

Property 2: $SM[].semaphore(s) \Rightarrow St[]$: if the reconfiguration is asynchronous, the SM must necessarily send a token to block the target with a $semaphore(S)$.

Property 3: $RA2DL - server[].error - occurs \Rightarrow RA2DL - coordinator$: this property means that when an error occurs in RA2DL, the $RA2DL - coordinator$ is informed.

Property 4: $NOT(RA2DL - sender[]$ AND $RA2DL - recever[])$ This property means that we could not receive two different notifications from the $RA2DL - coordinator$ at the same time;

Property 5: $(RA2DL - sender[]$ AND $RA2DL - coordinator[]$ AND $RA2DL - recever[])$ not deadlock: the system is deadlock-free.

The verification of these properties is summarized in Table 2.

Table 2. Verification result

Property	Result	Time (s)	Memory (Mo)
Property 1	True	12.03	5.34
Property 2	True	5.9	3.56
Property 3	True	10.23	5.78
Property 4	True	11.34	4.23
Property 5	True	7.24	3.96

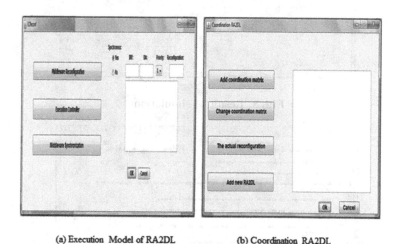

(a) Execution Model of RA2DL   (b) Coordination RA2DL

Fig. 7. ECReconf Tool

7   Implementation and Simulation

To simulate the behavior of a distributed Architecture RA2DL, we develop a prototype tool called ECReconf. First, we present the different graphical interfaces of the ECReconf with the execution model and its three layers as presented in Fig. 7(a). We start by showing the simulations of the coordination and the communication between the different RA2DL components, the $RA2DL - coordinator$ and the $coordination - matrix$ in Fig. 7(b). Second, we present a graph showing gains compared to the old RA2DL in response time and how the RA2DL component becomes correct. The result of the simulation after using the execution model is represented in Fig. 8.

Running Example: In IEEE 802.11 Wireless LAN, the $RA2DL - coordinator$ applies the reconfiguration for minimizing the packet size from Se in $RA2DL - sender$ to Sr in $RA2DL - recever$, the result is shown in Fig. 9.

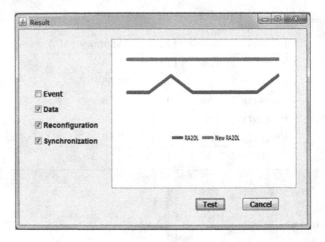

Fig. 8. Result of simulation

Fig. 9. Example of communication and reconfiguration

8   Conclusion

The paper deals with new solutions for a required flexibility of adaptive control systems. Firstly, we define an execution model which represents a correct model of RA2DL in three-layer: (i) Middleware Reconfiguration (MR), Execution controller (EC) and Middleware Synchronization (MS). Secondly, we propose a coordination and communication between execution models for each RA2DL for the distributed reconfigurations. These components use the coordination matrix to define for each RA2DL the applied reconfiguration according to predefined conditions. The model checking is used to prove the correctness of the execution model. The coordination model is represented by Nested state machine. Finally, the "ECReconf" tool is used to simulate the execution model with the three layers and the coordination between RA2DL components, it is applied to an IEEE 802.11 Wireless LAN.

The future works will deal with the security of RA2DL-based systems where the reconfigurable security will be an issue to be discussed on RA2DL.

References

1. Adaili, F., Mosbahi, O., Khalgui, M., Bouzefrane, S.: Ra2dl: new flexible solution for adaptive aadl-based control components. In: 5th International Conference on Pervasive and Embedded Computing and Communication Systems (2015)
2. Angelov, C., Sierszecki, K., Marian, N.: Design models for reusable and reconfigurable state machines. In: Yang, L.T., Amamiya, M., Liu, Z., Guo, M., Rammig, F.J. (eds.) EUC 2005. LNCS, vol. 3824, pp. 152–163. Springer, Heidelberg (2005)
3. Baudry, B., Fleurey, F., Jezequel, J.-M., Le Traon, Y.: Automatic test case optimization using a bacteriological adaptation model: application to .net components. In: Proceedings of the 17th IEEE International Conference on Automated Software Engineering, ASE 2002, pp. 253–256 (2002)
4. Costa, P., Coulson, G., Mascolo, C., Picco, G.P., Zachariadis, S.: The runes middleware: a reconfigurable component-based approach to networked embedded systems. In: IEEE 16th International Symposium on Personal, Indoor and Mobile Radio Communications, PIMRC 2005, vol. 2, pp. 806–810, September 2005
5. Khalgui, M.: Nces-based modelling and ctl-based verification of reconfigurable embedded control systems. Comput. Ind. **61**(3), 198–212 (2010)
6. Khalgui, M.: Distributed reconfigurations of autonomous iec61499 systems. ACM Trans. Embed. Comput. Syst. **12**(1), 18:1–18:23 (2013)
7. Lee, J., Kim, J.-S.: A methodology for developing component-based software with generation and assembly processes. In: The 6th International Conference on Advanced Communication Technology, vol. 2, pp. 696–699, February 2004
8. Magee, J., Kramer, J.: Dynamic structure in software architectures. In: Proceedings of the 4th ACM SIGSOFT Symposium on Foundations of Software Engineering, SIGSOFT 1996, pp. 3–14. ACM, New York (1996)
9. SAE: Architecture analysis & design language (standard SAE as5506), September 2004
10. Sokolsky, O., Chernoguzov, A.: Performance analysis of AADL models using real-time calculus. In: Choppy, C., Sokolsky, O. (eds.) Monterey Workshop 2008. LNCS, vol. 6028, pp. 227–249. Springer, Heidelberg (2010)
11. Vergnaud, T., Pautet, L., Kordon, F.: Using the AADL to describe distributed applications from middleware to software components. In: Vardanega, T., Wellings, A.J. (eds.) Ada-Europe 2005. LNCS, vol. 3555, pp. 67–78. Springer, Heidelberg (2005)
12. Wang, Y., Ma, D., Zhao, Y., Zou, L., Zhao, X.: An aadl-based modeling method for arinc653-based avionics software. In: 2011 IEEE 35th Annual Computer Software and Applications Conference (COMPSAC), pp. 224–229, July 2011

Requirement Engineering, High-Assurance and Testing System

Architectural Specification and Analysis of the Aegis Combat System

Mert Ozkaya[✉]

Department of Computer Engineering,
Istanbul Kemerburgaz University, Istanbul, Turkey
mert.ozkaya@kemerburgaz.edu.tr

Abstract. Software architecture is nowadays considered as a highly important design activity due to enabling the analysis of system behaviours and detecting the design errors before they propagate into implementation. There have been many architecture description languages developed so far that focus on analysing software architectures. However, these languages require the use of process algebras for specifying system behaviours, which are found unfamiliar by practitioners in general. XCD (Connector-centric Design) is one of the most recent languages that is instead based on the well-known Design-by-Contract approach. In this paper, XCD is illustrated in architectural modelling and analysis via the Aegis Combat System case-study. With the Aegis system, it is aimed to show how one of the most common design errors, i.e., the deadlocking components, can be caught in XCD and prevented in a modular way. In the paper, XCD is also compared with Wright, one of the most influencing architecture description languages, with which Aegis has been specified and analysed for deadlock too.

1 Introduction

Software architectures have always been one of the most crucial topics in software engineering since the early nineties. Although there have been various definitions provided, software architectures are commonly considered as the high-level design activity through which software systems can be specified in terms of components interacting with each other via connectors [4]. There have been so many architecture description languages (ADLs) developed to date [7]. These languages may differ in their scope of interest, some focussing on early code generation from software architectures while some focussing on architectural analysis. With the architectural analysis, it becomes possible to verify the behaviours of system components and connectors. To enable this, ADLs base their notations to some process algebras [9]. Indeed, process algebras are supported by model checkers, which can exhaustively verify algebraic architecture specifications for, e.g., deadlock. However, algebraic ADLs are found unfamiliar by practitioners in general, which has also been stated in Malavolta et al.'s survey [6].

XCD (Connector-centric Design) [11] is one of the most recent ADLs, which, unlike the algebraic ADLs, supports architectural modelling and analysis without

© Springer International Publishing Switzerland 2015
H. Fujita and G. Guizzi (Eds.): SoMeT 2015, CCIS 532, pp. 105–119, 2015.
DOI: 10.1007/978-3-319-22689-7_8

imposing process algebra. XCD is based on the well-known Design-by-Contract approach [8] and intended for the modular, reusable, and realisable specification of software architectures. To enable analysis, XCD has its semantical basis defined using SPIN's ProMeLa language [5]. This is also supported with a translator tool [12], which, given an XCD architecture, can produce a ProMeLa model in accordance with the semantics. Designers can then perform formal verification using SPIN's model checker and detect issues such as deadlock.

This paper aims at showing how XCD's contractual notation and modular nature facilitate the modelling and analysis of complex software architectures. This is achieved by specifying the Aegis Combat System and analysing its behaviour with XCD. The Aegis Combat System has already been addressed by Allen et al. [1] in their illustration of the Wright language [2]. Aegis is a command-and-control system developed by the US navy using a client-server approach, containing a number of sensors to establish the environment a ship is in and components that analyse this context in order to react to potential threats. Our initial attempt at specifying Aegis is given in [10], where our main purpose was essentially to introduce the basics of XCD's notation. So, the Aegis specification therein was quite simple as the main focus is not on the architectural analysis but on introducing XCD. Here, I extend the previous architecture specification of Aegis to a more complex one, specifying essentially the original Aegis behaviour described by Allen et al. using Wright [1]. By doing so, I show not only the architectural analysis capability of XCD but also compare XCD with Wright over the Aegis system.

In the rest of the paper, I summarise XCD's contractual notation first. Following that, I give the XCD specification of the Aegis system. Next, I give the analysis of the Aegis specification using the SPIN model checker and show how easily a deadlocking behaviour is detected and prevented thanks to XCD's modular nature. Lastly, I discuss XCD in a comparative manner with the Wright language.

2   Xcd's Contractual Notation

XCD extends Design-by-Contract (DbC) [8] in its notation. XCD's extension of DbC allows for the specification of contracts not only for the component provided services but for its required services too. This is because, unlike object classes for which DbC was initially designed, components also have required services in their public interfaces. At the same time, XCD proposes a different contract structure so as to better distinguish between the functional and interaction component constraints, which are usually mixed together in most DbC approaches. Finally, XCD uses DbC to specify connectors/protocols as well as components.

Component Contracts. Components are specified with (i) *ports* representing the points of interaction with their environment, and (ii) *data* representing the component state. Component ports can be either *provided* or *required* for two-way synchronous methods. Method ports consist of methods, and, the behaviours

```
 1 component client(int id){            15 component server(){
 2   byte data:=-1;                     16   bool isInitialised:=true;
 3   required port service{             17   provided port service{
 4     @interaction{waits:data == -1;}  18     @interaction{accepts:isInitialised;}
 5     @functional{                     19     @functional{
 6       promises: arg := id;           20       requires: arg >= 0;
 7       requires: \result >= 0;        21       ensures: \result := 5;
 8       ensures: data:=\result;        22       otherwise:
 9       otherwise:                     23         requires: arg < 0;
10         requires: \result < 0;       24         ensures: \result := 3;}
11         ensures: data:=-1;}          25     int request(int arg);
12     int request(int arg);            26   }
13   }                                  27 }
14 }
```

Fig. 1. Contractual specifications of client and server

of methods are specified with functional and interaction contracts. Figure 1 gives a simple specification of client and server components for illustrating the ports with contractual methods. So, for provided ports (e.g., lines 17–26 in Fig. 1), their method functional contracts are just like the classic contracts introduced by the familiar DbC-based approaches, represented with pre-conditions (*requires*) and post-conditions (*ensures*). It should, however, be noted that while pre-conditions are expressions, post-conditions in XCD are in fact assignments. So, whenever their pre-condition is met, their post-conditions are applied to update component state and to set method result. For required ports (e.g., lines 3–12 in Fig. 1), their functional contracts further include *promises* clause for assigning parameter arguments of methods to be requested.

To specify at which states the functional contracts of methods can be processed, XCD introduces *interaction* contracts. An interaction contract can be specified in two (*mutually exclusive*) ways. In the first (safe) way, a *delaying* pre-condition (*waits*) is employed to declare the component states where an method action can be processed (e.g., line 4 in Fig. 1). In all other states the actions are blocked from being processed, until the pre-condition is satisfied. In the second (unsafe) way, a designer can specify a pre-condition (*accepts*) to declare the states where a method call is acceptable and will be processed and those where it is not acceptable and potentially catastrophic (e.g., line 18 in Fig. 1). Rejected (i.e., not acceptable) calls lead to chaotic behaviours, indicating the wrong use of services.

Complex Methods of Provided Ports. Provided and required ports mentioned above operate their methods atomically. This means for provided ports that upon receiving a method-call, provided methods contracts are processed, and then, the response is sent back indivisibly as a single action. However, the atomic execution of provided methods may not necessarily be the case. Figure 2 shows a simple example where one component requests the result of $x^2 + x$ from another, which in its turn asks a third component for the value of x^2 so as to be able to compute the final value. In order to be able to model cases like these of Fig. 2, it is necessary to break a method request-response protocol further

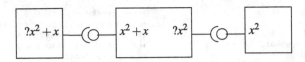

Fig. 2. Component method chaining

```
 1 provided port Name{
 2    // Method request: Event Consumption
 3    @interaction_req {
 4      accepts: pre-condition;
 5    //OR
 6      waits: pre-condition;
 7    }
 8    @functional_req {
 9      requires:pre-condition;
10      ensures:data-assignments;
11    }
12    // Method response: Event Emission
13    @interaction_res {
14      waits: pre-condition;
15    }
16    @functional_res {
17      promises:result-assignment;
18      ensures: data-assignments;   //(OR throws : exception;)
19    }
20    type method_id(type param,..) throws exception;
21 }
```

Fig. 3. Generic structure of a provided port with a complex method

into its two constituent events and no longer consider a provided methods as an atomic action. In XCD, such provided methods are called *complex methods*. A complex method is specified in two separate atomic blocks, where the first block serves for receiving the request event for the method and the second for emitting the response event.

As shown in Fig. 3, for a complex method, two pairs of interaction-functional contracts are specified, one corresponding to the request and the other to the response event for the complex method. A complex-method request event consumption has a contract like normal provided port methods. The complex-method response event emission also has another contract like a normal required port method, but now its promises cannot assign parameters. Instead, promises can be used herein to assign the result to be responded. Note that there is no requires for the response events as responses to be sent do not need to constrained with some conditions. Moreover, an exception may also be thrown via throws, which can be used as alternative to the ensures.

Connector Contracts. Connectors are specified with roles to be assumed by the components and instances of other connectors that they are using. Each role represents the interaction protocol of a component that assumes the role. A role is specified with *data* and *port-variables*, mirroring a component assuming the role. Note that when connectors are instantiated in configurations, components are passed via connector parameters to be associated with the roles. The role port-variables are bound to ports of the components assuming the role and constrain the port actions via their interaction contracts. So, a port can perform its method/event actions when both its own interaction constraint and the constraints of the role port-variables are satisfied. Figure 4 gives the specification of a connector for controlling the interaction of a client with a server. Therein, two roles are specified: *client_r* (lines 3–11) and *server_r* (lines 12–19). The role *client_r* constrains the client, guaranteeing that the client cannot request services before initialising the server (here, it is assumed that it is already initialised, i.e., *isInitialised* = *true*). The server is not constrained by the role *server_r*. Moreover, a basic link connector is provided by XCD to specify a simple asynchronous method call between role port-variables (so the component ports). In Fig. 4, for instance, one method-call link is instantiated in lines 17–18 for connecting the required port of the client with the provided port of the server.

```
1 connector client_server_conn(
2          client_r(service, initialisation),  server_r(service, initialisation)){
3 role client_r{
4   bool isInitialised := true;           12 role server_r{
5   required port_variable service{       13   provided port_variable service{
6     @interaction{                       14     int request(int arg);
7       waits:isInitialised;              15   }
8       ensures: \nothing; }              16 }
9     int request(int arg);               17 connector link1(client_r(service),
10  }                                      18                  server_r(service));
11 }                                       19 }
```

Fig. 4. Contractual specification of a connector for client and server

3 Aegis Case Study

As depicted in Fig. 5, the Aegis combat system consists of a set of components interacting with each other. The *ExperimentControl* at the top of the diagram provides information, obtained via sensors, to its connected components. The *TrackServer* requires the track information from the *ExperimentControl*, for determining the location of the enemies that operate around the ship. The *TrackServer* then provides the location information to its own connected components. The *DoctrineAuthoring* requires doctrine rules from the *ExperimentControl* and provides them to its connected components, which require rules to take actions. Using the doctrine rules and track information from its environment, the *GeoServer* calculates region information for enemies and provides them to the *DoctrineReasoning*. Lastly, the *DoctrineReasoning* makes the decision of which task(s) to take against the enemies.

My motivation for specifying the Aegis system is essentially that its component behaviours let me illustrate XCD's support for non-atomic provided methods, whose responses do not have to be sent back to the callers immediately upon receiving the method requests. Indeed, the Aegis components, such as

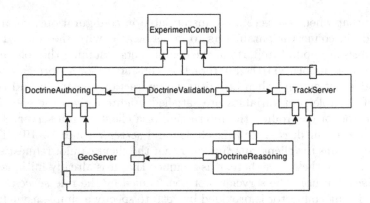

Fig. 5. Conceptual diagram of Aegis

TrackServer and *DoctrineAuthoring*, may need their required ports to obtain some data before they send back the responses of the provided methods whose requests have already been processed. Moreover, I also aim at showing how the first-class specification of connectors facilitates the detection of wrong interaction protocols that cause deadlocking component behaviours.

3.1 Xcd Specification of Aegis

I specify three types of components: *client*, *server*, and *mixedComponent*. To model the interactions between the components, I also specify the connector type *client2server*. Finally, I specify a composite component type to describe the configuration of client, server, and mixedComponent components as depicted in Fig. 5.

```
1 component client(int numOfPorts){
2  int data = 0,
3  int openedConns = 0;              13    @interaction{
4                                    14      waits:openedConns==numOfPorts;}
5  required port service[numOfPorts]{ 15   @functional{
6    @functional{                    16      ensures:data:=\result;}
7      ensures:openedConns:=pre(openedConns)+1;} 17 int request();
8    void open();                    18  }
9    @functional{                    19 }
10     ensures:
11       openedConns:=pre(openedConns)-1;}
12   void close();
```

Fig. 6. Client component type specification of aegis

Client Component. Figure 6 gives the specification of the client component type. The client data variables are specified in lines 2–3, representing the state of the client. The client consists of an array of the *service* required ports (lines 5–18), whose size is equal to the *numOfPorts* component parameter.

Each *service* port is used as a connection to a distinct server port, whose methods are requested. Three methods are specified in the *service* port: *open*, *close*, and *request*. The *open* (lines 6–8) and *close* (lines 9–12) methods can be requested at any time. Upon their request and the receipt of the response, the component state is updated using the methods' **ensures** functional constraint (line 7 for *open* and lines 10–11 for *close*). The method *request* (lines 13–17) can be requested only when all the server connections have been opened. Upon calling the *request* and receiving the response, the **ensures** functional constraint updates the state using the received *result* (line 16).

```
1 component server(int numOfPorts){
2 int data = 1;
3
4 provided port service[numOfPorts] {
5   void open();
6
7   void close();
8
9   @functional{ensures:\result:=data;}
10  int request();
11  }
12 }
```

Fig. 7. Server component type specification

Server Component. Figure 7 gives the specification of the *server* component type. In line 2, a data variable is specified, representing the server state. The server consists of an array of the *service* provided ports (lines 4–11). Each of these ports in the array is used as a connection to a specific required port of the client, receiving its requests and sending back the responses. Each *service* port has three methods, *open*, *close*, and *request*. Requests for these three methods can be received at any time, which does not change the state. Note that the *request* method assigns the result of a received request via its **ensures** functional constraint (line 9).

```
1 component mixedComponent(int CSize,int SSize){
2 int openedConns := 0,
3 int data := 3;                              17 provided port server[SSize]{
4 required port client[CSize]{                18 @interaction_req{waits:openedConns==CSize;}
5   @functional{ensures:openedConns++;}       19 void open();
6   void open();                              20
7                                             21 @interaction_req{waits:openedConns==CSize;}
8   @functional{ensures:openedConns--;}       22 void close();
9   void close();                             23
10                                            24 @interaction_req{waits:openedConns==CSize;}
11  @interaction{waits:openedConns=CSize;}    25 @functional_res{ensures:\result:=data;}
12  @functional{ ensures: data:=result;       26 int request();
13                 dataUpdated:=false;        27 }
14  }                                         28 }
15  int request();
16 }
```

Fig. 8. MixedComponent component type specification of aegis

MixedComponent Component. Figure 8 gives the specification of the *mixedComponent* component type. In lines 2–3, two data variables are specified, representing the component state. The mixedComponent has an array of the *client* required ports (lines 4–16), whose size is equal to the component parameter *CSize*. Herein, each *client* port behaves in the same way as those of the client component type, specified in Fig. 6. There is also an array of the *server* provided ports specified in lines 17–27, whose size is equal to the *SSize* parameter this time. Each *server* port has *open*, *close*, and *request* methods. These methods are *complex* – whose request and response are processed non-atomically. So, in their complex method specifications, the interaction and functional contracts are split into two atomic parts: the request part (*_req*), evaluated upon the receipt of the method request, and the response (*_res*) part, evaluated when the port is ready to send the method response. The requests for the complex methods can be received once the client ports have opened their connections, according to the method requests' interaction constraints (line 18 for *open*, line 21 for *close*, and line 24 for *request*). Unlike for *open* and *close*, the *request* method response has functional constraint (@functional_res), given in line 25. Its **ensures** assigns the value of *data* to the *result* that is sent back as a response. Note that I have not specified interaction constraints for the complex method responses. This is due to the fact that the mixedComponent can send back the *server*'s complex method responses immediately (non-atomically though) after processing the respective requests, while it still has the option of making some service requests via its client ports before sending the responses.

Client2Server Connector. Figure 9 gives the specification of the *client2server* connector type. The client2server has the roles *client* and *server*, played by client and server components. The *client* role is specified in lines 4–25. It has two data variables (lines 5–6) and the *service* port-variable (lines 7–25), corresponding to the *service* port of a client component. The *service* port-variable includes the *open*, *close*, and *request* methods. While the *open* method is delayed by its interaction constraint (line 9) until the client port's server connection is closed, the *close* method is delayed until the server connection is opened (line 14). Upon making a request and receiving the response for *open* or *close*, the role's state is updated using the method's **ensures** interaction constraint (line 10 for *open* and line 15 for *close*). The *request* method may be requested when the client's currently executing port[1] is the selected port of the client (i.e., initially the first port, determined via the *clientConnection* data specified in line 6) and that port's server connection is already opened. Upon its request and the receipt of the response, the role state is updated (lines 21–22), selecting another client port nondeterministically for the next method request.

The *server* role is specified in lines 27–49, which has again two data variables in lines 28–29 and the *service* provided port-variable, corresponding to the *service* port of the server component. The *service* port-variable has three methods: *open*,

---

[1] The currently executing port of a component, playing a connector role, is accessible via the @ symbol, which returns the current port index.

```
 1 connector client2server_deadlock(client{service}, server{service},
 2                                   byte numOfClients, byte numOfServers){
 3
 4   role client{                          27   role server{
 5     bool opened := false;               28     bool opened:=false;
 6     byte clientConnection := 0;         29     byte serverConnection := 0;
 7     required port_variable service{     30     provided port_variable service{
 8       @interaction{                     31
 9         waits: !opened ;                32       @interaction{
10         ensures: opened := true;        33         waits:!opened;
11       }                                 34         ensures:opened:=true;
12       void open();                      35       }
13       @interaction{                     36       void open();
14         waits: opened;                  37       @interaction{
15         ensures: opened := false;       38         waits: opened;
16       }                                 39         ensures:opened:=false;
17       void close();                     40       }
18       @interaction{                     41       void close();
19         waits: opened &&                42       @interaction{
20              clientConnection == @ ;    43         waits:opened && serverConnection==@;
21         ensures:clientConnection \in    44         ensures:serverConnection \in
22              [0, numOfClients-1];        45                 [0, numOfServers-1];
23       }                                 46       }
24       byte request();                   47       byte request();
25     }                                   48     }
26   }                                     49   }
                                           50
                                           51     connector link(client{service},
                                           52                    server{service});
                                           53 }
```

Fig. 9. Client2Server connector type specification of aegis

close, and *request*. While the requests for the *open* method are delayed until the server's port connection is closed (line 33), the *close* method requests are delayed until the connection is opened (line 38). Upon receiving and processing a method request, the role state is updated using the methods' **ensures** interaction constraint (line 34 for *open* and line 39 for *close*). Finally, the *request* method can be received when the connection is opened and the currently executing port of the server is the selected one (i.e., initially the first port, determined via the *serverConnection* data specified in line 29). Upon the successful receipt of the *request*, the role state is updated (lines 44–45) and a new server port is selected nondeterministically, from which the next request can be received.

The link connector instantiated in lines 51–52 specifies the connected role port-variables (and through them, the respective component ports).

Aegis Composite Component. Figure 10 gives the specification of the *aegis* composite component type. The Aegis component describes the configuration depicted in Fig. 5, instantiating the *client*, *server*, and *mixedComponent* component types, and controlling their interaction via the connector instances created from the *client2server* connector type.

```
1 component aegis(){
2
3   component server experimentControl(3);
4   component mixedComponent
5                doctrineAuthoring(1,3);
6   component client doctrineValidation(3);
7   component mixedComponent trackServer(1,3);
8   component mixedComponent geoServer(2,1);
9   component client doctrineReasoning(3);
10
11  connector client2server_deadlock c1(
12      1, 3,doctrineAuthoring{client[0]},
13          experimentControl{service[0]});
14  connector client2server_deadlock c2(
15      3, 3,doctrineValidation{service[0]},
16          experimentControl{service[1]});
17  connector client2server_deadlock c3(
18      1, 3,trackServer{client[0]},
19          experimentControl{service[2]});
20  connector client2server_deadlock c4(
21      3, 3,doctrineValidation{service[1]},
22          doctrineAuthoring{server[0]});
23  connector client2server_deadlock c5(
24      3, 3,doctrineValidation{service[2]},
25          trackServer{server[0]});
26  connector client2server_deadlock c6(
27      3, 3,doctrineReasoning{service[0]},
28          doctrineAuthoring{server[1]});
29  connector client2server_deadlock c7(
30      2, 3,geoServer{client[0]},
31          doctrineAuthoring{server[2]});
32  connector client2server_deadlock c8(
33      3, 3,doctrineReasoning{service[1]},
34          trackServer{server[1]});
35  connector client2server_deadlock c9(
36      2, 3, geoServer{client[1]},
37          trackServer{server[2]});
38  connector client2server_deadlock c10(
39      3, 1,doctrineReasoning{service[2]},
40          geoServer{server[0]});
41 }
```

Fig. 10. Aegis composite component type specification of aegis

3.2   Analysis of Aegis

As aforementioned, XCD is semantically based on SPIN's ProMeLa formal verification language. The informal definition of XCD's semantics can be found in [11], where it is shown how each main element of XCD can be translated into ProMeLa constructs. XCD's semantics also include the encoding of a number of property verifications. These properties are (i) component interaction constraint violations, (ii) incomplete functional behaviours of components, (iii) race conditions, (iv) deadlocks, and (v) the violation of system properties specified by designers. So, using XCD's tool [12] that implements the semantics and performs the translations into ProMeLa models automatically, designers can verify their architectures for any of these properties without any effort.

Having specified the Aegis system, I used XCD's tool to translate the Aegis architecture into a ProMeLa model for formal verification. While I have not received any verification errors for chaotic behaviours, wrong functional contracts, race conditions, and (global) deadlock, SPIN reported unreachable ProMeLa code for the executing components. SPIN's unreachable ProMeLa code indicates that some part of the component behaviours cannot be executed. More precisely, it indicates herein that (i) the clients may insist on a specific port connection for making requests; thereby, their other connections are ignored, and, (ii) the servers may accept calls from particular client connections and ignore the rest of their connections. Indeed, (i) the *experimentControl* server chooses to receive requests only from its connection with *doctrineAuthoring*, delaying the rest indefinitely; (ii) the *doctrineAuthoring* mixedComponent makes requests to *experimentControl* only; (iii) the *doctrineValidation* client chooses to make requests to *experimentControl* only, which is however delayed indefinitely by *experimentControl*; (iv) the *trackServer* mixedComponent chooses to make request to *experimentControl* only, which is delayed indefinitely again;

(v) the *geoServer* mixedComponent chooses to make request to *doctrineAuthoring* only, which is delayed indefinitely; and finally, *(vi)* the *doctrineReasoning* client chooses to make request to *doctrineAuthoring* only, which is delayed indefinitely by *doctrineAuthoring*. So, there are essentially *local* deadlocks here. While the *experimentControl* server can interact with the *doctrineAuthoring* client, the *trackServer* and *geoServer* servers cannot receive requests from their selected ports. This is because the *doctrineValidation* and *doctrineReasoning* clients, which are supposed to make requests to them, get stuck waiting indefinitely for their selected servers *experimentControl* and *doctrineAuthoring* respectively.

```
1  connector client2server(client{service},
2                          server{service}){
3  role client{                               19  role server{
4     bool opened := false;                    20     bool opened:=false;
5     required port_variable service{          21     provided port_variable service{
6        @interaction{                          22        @interaction{
7           waits: opened==false;               23           waits: !opened;
8           ensures: opened:=true;}             24           ensures: opened:=true;
9        void open();                           25        }
10       @interaction{                          26        void open();
11          waits: opened==true;                27        @interaction{
12             ensures: opened:=false;}         28           waits: opened;
13       void close();                          29           ensures: opened:= false;
14       @interaction{                          30        }
15          waits: opened==false;}              31        void close();
16       int request();                         32        @interaction{
17    }                                         33           waits: opened;
18 }                                            34           ensures: \nothing;
                                                35        }
                                                36        byte request();
                                                37     }
                                                38  }
                                                39  connector link(client{service},
                                                40                 server{service});
                                                41 }
```

Fig. 11. Deadlock-free Client2Server connector type specification of aegis

This situation is due to the protocols of the *client2server* connector specified in Sect. 3.1 (page 8). The connector protocols force the clients and servers to initially select their first ports to write and listen requests respectively. Then, each time the client and server complete their interaction, they both re-set their selections for the port. However, as already shown, this can lead to local deadlocks. To avoid this issue, I enhanced the freedom of the clients and servers so that they do not need to make selections among their ports – any port can be chosen at a time. I did this by introducing a new connector for client-server interaction as shown in Fig. 11. Unlike the previous connector given in Fig. 9, the new *client2server* connector does not impose any selection of ports. It simply guarantees via its protocols that the clients may make a request to a server via their port when they open the server connection. Likewise, the servers accept requests when their port connections are already opened by the clients.

When I replaced the connector instances in the configuration with the instances of the new connector, the new verification results shown in Table 1 did not report any unreachable code. This proves that now clients and servers can use either of their ports freely without the imposition of any selections.

Table 1. Verification results for Aegis – with the corrected connector given in Fig. 11

Model	State-vector	States		Memory	Time
	(in Bytes)	Stored	Matched	(in MB)	(in seconds)
Aegis	556	15527961	72314072	7024†	62
BITSTATE Aegis	556	68133665	3.1582694e+08	36	365

Spin (version 6.2.4) and gcc (version 4.7.2) used, with up to 7024MB of RAM and a search depth of 50,000:

spin –a configuration .pml

gcc –DMEMLIM=7024 –O2 –DXUSAFE –DSAFETY –DNOCLAIM –w –o pan pan.c

./pan –m50000 –c1

For bit-state verification, the **-DBITSTATE** option needs to be passed to gcc. Using a 64bit Intel Xeon CPU (W3503 @ 2.40 GHz × 2), 11.7 GB of RAM, and Linux version 3.5.0-39-generic.

Column "States Stored" shows the number of unique global system states stored in the state-space, while

column "States Matched" the number of states that were revisited during the search - see:

http://spinroot.com/spin/Man/Pan.html#L10

† Cases marked with † in the Memory column run out of memory.

4   Discussion

So far, we have seen that XCD can be used to specify the architectures of complex software systems, such as Aegis, and analyse their behaviours. The Aegis system helped in illustrating the use of XCD's DbC-based specifications and automated formal verifications with SPIN. Furthermore, with the Aegis system, I also showed the expressive power of XCD, which supports two types of provided methods, i.e., atomic and non-atomic complex ones. In Aegis, I used complex (i.e., non-atomic) provided methods for the *server* port of the *mixedComponent*, specified in Sect. 3.1 (page 7). When the server receives a request for one of its complex methods, the *server* port processes the request first, and then, the *client* required port can make some data calculations, requesting some data from their environments. Finally, the *server* port resumes, processing the method response and sending back the data as a method result to the requester. Figure 12 gives the Wright specification of the Aegis's mixed-component. Wright does not distinguish among port types, nor does it distinguish methods types too (e.g., provided methods and complex provided methods). So, the semantical differences among required methods, provided methods, and complex provided methods are left to designers, who are supposed to specify their behaviours using the CSP process algebra.

Unlike Wright using the CSP process algebra, XCD uses a contractual notation. Intuitively, considering the algebraic Wright specification of the mixed-component depicted in Fig. 12, the XCD specification of the *mixedComponent* depicted in Fig. 8 is closer to what practitioners use already, consisting of contracts that are specified as a pair of (pre-)conditions and assignments.

Component MixedComp(numServers : 1..; numClients : 1..) =
   Port Service$_{1..\text{numServers}}$ = ClientPullT
   Port Client$_{1..\text{numClients}}$ = ServerPushT
   Computation = OpenServices ; WaitForClient$_{\{\},\{\}}$
     where WaitForClient$_{O,C}$ = $\forall x :$ ((1..numClients) \ $(O \cup C))$ [] Client$_x$.open→ DecideNextAction$_{O \cup \{x\},C}$
       DecideNextAction$_{O,C}$ = WaitForClient$_{O,C}$ ⊓ $\forall x : O$ ⊓ ReadFromClient$_{x,O,C}$
                ⊓ (UseService ; DecideNextAction$_{O,C}$)
        $O \neq \{\} \wedge O \cup C \neq$ (1..numClients)
       DecideNextAction$_{O,C}$ = $\forall x : O$ ⊓ ReadFromClient$_{x,O,C}$ ⊓ (UseService ; DecideNextAction$_{O,C}$)
        $O \neq \{\} \wedge O \cup C =$ (1..numClients)
       DecideNextAction$_{\{\},C}$ = WaitForClient$_{\{\},C}$ ⊓ (UseService ; DecideNextAction$_{\{\},C}$)
        $C \neq$ (1..numClients)
       DecideNextAction$_{\{\},(1..\text{NumClients})}$ = (UseService ; DecideNextAction$_{\{\},(1..\text{numClients})}$) ⊓ Exit
       ReadFromClient$_{x,O,C}$ = Client$_x$.request→(OptionalUseService ; $\overline{\text{Client}}_x$.resultly→DecideNextAction$_{O,C}$)
             [] Client$_x$.close→DecideNextAction$_{O \setminus \{x\},C \cup \{x\}}$
       UseService = $\forall x :$ (1..numServers) ⊓ $\overline{\text{Service}}_x$.request→Service$_x$.result?y→§
       OptionalUseService = (UseService ; OptionalUseService) ⊓ §
       OpenServices = $\forall x :$ (1..numServers) ; $\overline{\text{Service}}_x$.open→§
       Exit = $\forall x :$ (1..numServers) ; $\overline{\text{Service}}_x$.close→§

Fig. 12. Wright specification of the mixed-component [1], whose XCD specification is depicted in Fig. 8

XCD is also highly modular that aids in detecting and preventing design errors, e.g., deadlock, easily. This is possible with the clean separation of the interaction protocols as a connector. Indeed, upon analysing the aegis specification above and tracing the resulting deadlock error, I understood easily that the deadlocking component behaviours derive from the wrong connector protocols. So, this saved me from revising the component specifications, which have been specified as protocol-independent. To avoid deadlock, I specified a new connector as an alternative to the deadlocking connector. The new connector is the simplified form of the deadlocking one, obtained essentially by re-using the current one. I basically removed from the deadlocking connector specification the parts (i.e., contractual expressions) that force a pre-selection of the server ports to listen requests from (and client ports to make requests for). Servers now accept any requests whose connection is open (and clients make requests to any server freely too). When I verified the Aegis configuration with the new connector, no deadlocks has been reported.

In Wright [1], the deadlocking behaviour of the Aegis system has been dealt with in a number of ways. One way is to change the protocols of the components and connectors so that servers no longer attempt at opening all of its client connections first. Instead, now, servers wait for receiving client requests upon that client opening the connection. Likewise, whenever a client opens a connection with the server, the client subsequently makes a request to the server. By doing so, deadlock is avoided as the clients can no longer make request to a server which

Component DynamicServerized (numServers : 0..;
                                numClients : 0..) =
Port Service$_{1..\text{numServers}}$ = DServerPullT
Port Client$_{1..\text{numClients}}$ = DServerPushT
Computation = WaitForService [] WaitForClient [] §
where WaitForService =
        ∀ i :1..numServers
            [] Service$_i$.open→Service$_i$.request?x
            →$\overline{\text{Service}_i.\text{result}}$→Service$_i$.close
            →**Computation**
    WaitForClient =
        ∀ i : 1..numClients [] Client$_i$.open
                                →Client$_i$.request
                                →Client$_i$.result!x
                                →Client$_i$.close
                                →**Computation**

Fig. 13. The deadlock-free specification of the mixed component in Wright [1]

expects some other client. While this approach avoids the deadlock, it requires the component specifications to be modified with the new protocols. Indeed, the *mixedComponent* depicted in Fig. 12 is modified as Fig. 13 so as to comply with the new protocols. Figure 13 has modified port protocols (i.e., *DServerPullT* and *DServerPushT*). Also, the computation has been modified to be consistent with the new protocols, where each *request* is preceded by an *open* event.

Asynchronous communication is another method applied in [1] for avoiding deadlock, in which clients/servers do not get stuck waiting for a request/response. So, when making a wrong guess, clients no longer need to wait indefinitely for a response. Likewise, servers will not wait for a request indefinitely. This solution requires a new connector to be specified from scratch, which comprises an unbounded buffer for storing message data that are communicated asynchronously. However, when unbounded buffers are employed in a model, the resulting state space during the formal verification is likely to be infinite. Worse, model checking infinite models is undecidable [3].

5   Conclusion

One of the major problems in architecture description languages is their complex algebraic notations for specifying software architectures. XCD has been developed recently as another architecture description language that allows for the modular specification of software architectures in a way that is far from being complex but instead contractual. XCD's formal semantics were defined using SPIN's ProMeLa language, which is supported by a tool that can translate any XCD architecture into a ProMeLa model. In this paper, to illustrate XCD and its tool, the Aegis combat system was specified and analysed for a number of properties. Aegis has initially been addressed by the pioneering language Wright. So, I followed a comparative approach in discussing how deadlocks can be caught and prevented thanks to XCD's contractual notation and modular nature.

References

1. Allen, R., Garlan, D.: A case study in architectural modelling: the aegis system. In: Proceedings of the Eighth International Workshop on Software Specification and Design (IWSSD-8), pp. 6–15, Paderborn, Germany, March 1996
2. Allen, R., Garlan, D.: A formal basis for architectural connection. ACM Trans. Softw. Eng. Methodol. **6**(3), 213–249 (1997)
3. Brand, D., Zafiropulo, P.: On communicating finite-state machines. J. ACM **30**(2), 323–342 (1983)
4. Garlan, D., Shaw, M.: An introduction to software architecture. Technical report, Pittsburgh, PA, USA (1994)
5. Holzmann, G.J.: The SPIN Model Checker - Primer and Reference Manual. Addison-Wesley, Reading (2004)
6. Malavolta, I., Lago, P., Muccini, H., Pelliccione, P., Tang, A.: What industry needs from architectural languages: a survey. IEEE Trans. Softw. Eng. **99** (2012)
7. Medvidovic, N., Taylor, R.N.: A classification and comparison framework for software architecture description languages. IEEE Trans. Softw. Eng. **26**(1), 70–93 (2000)
8. Meyer, B.: Applying design by contract. IEEE Comput. **25**(10), 40–51 (1992)
9. Ozkaya, M., Kloukinas, C.: Are we there yet? Analyzing architecture description languages for formal analysis, usability, and realizability. In: Demirörs, O., Türetken, O. (eds.) EUROMICRO-SEAA, pp. 177–184. IEEE (2013)
10. Ozkaya, M., Kloukinas, C.: Architectural specification and analysis with XCD - the aegis combat system case study. In: Pires, L.F., Hammoudi, S., Filipe, J., das Neves, R.C. (eds.) MODELSWARD 2014 - Proceedings of the 2nd International Conference on Model-Driven Engineering and Software Development, 7–9 January 2014, Lisbon, Portugal, pp. 368–375. SciTePress (2014)
11. Ozkaya,M., Kloukinas. C.: Design-by-contract for reusable components and realizable architectures. In: Seinturier, L., de Almeida, E.S., Carlson, J. (eds.) CBSE 2014, Proceedings of the 17th International ACM SIGSOFT Symposium on Component-Based Software Engineering (part of CompArch 2014), June 30 - July 4 2014, Marcq-en-Baroeul, Lille, France, pp. 129–138. ACM (2014)
12. Xcd. Website. Maintained by Mert Ozkaya (2013). http://www.staff.city.ac.uk/c.kloukinas/Xcd/

Visualization of Checking Results
for Graphical Validation Rules

Sören Witt[1,2]([⊠]), Sven Feja[1], Christian Hadler[1], Andreas Speck[1],
and Elke Pulvermüller[2]

[1] Kiel University, Kiel, Germany
{swi,svfe,cha,aspe}@informatik.uni-kiel.de
[2] Osnabrück University, Osnabrück, Germany
{soeren.witt,elke.pulvermueller}@informatik.uni-osnabrueck.de

Abstract. Graphically represented Business Process Models (BPMs)
are common artifacts in documentation as well as in early phases of (software) development processes. The Graphical Computation Tree Logic
(G-CTL) is a notation to define formal graphical validation rules on the
same level of abstraction as the BPMs, allowing to specify high-level
requirements regarding the content level of the BPMs. The research tool
Business Application Modeler (BAM) enables the automatic validation
of BPMs with G-CTL rules. While details of the validation procedure
are hidden from the user, the checking results need to be presented adequately. In this contribution, we present and discuss methods for visualization and analysis of the checking results in the context of G-CTL
based validations. We elaborate how artifacts, which are generated during a validation procedure, may be used to derive different visualizations,
and we show how these methods can be combined into more expressive
visualizations.

Keywords: Business Process Models · Validation · Verification · Visualization of checking results · Error visualization

1 Introduction

Business Process Models (BPMs) have become basic artifacts in documentation
as well as in early phases of (software) development processes for commercial
systems. Since BPMs are early artifacts in the development process, the costs
for repairing errors are very high. Moreover, in terms of requirements engineering
BPMs express requirements merely implicitly. For example a BPM depicts an
order of execution of certain activities, but it may not explain if this order is
actually mandatory or why it is mandatory. Hence, there is a high demand to
express requirements explicitly and validate the correctness.n this paper, we do
not address basic correctness criteria like e.g. absence of deadlocks which may be
checked for example by [5]. Instead we target correctness at the content level of
BPMs, addressing high-level requirements like e.g. compliance, economic aspects
or enterprise specific demands. Due to the increasing complexity of BPMs, the

© Springer International Publishing Switzerland 2015
H. Fujita and G. Guizzi (Eds.): SoMeT 2015, CCIS 532, pp. 120–136, 2015.
DOI: 10.1007/978-3-319-22689-7_9

application of automatic, formal techniques for checking the correctness of BPMs is worthwhile.

Automated verification requires formalization. The used BPM notations must comply to a formal syntax and semantic to a sufficient degree. Likewise, requirements need to be expressed formally and explicitly. Therefore, an additional notation is needed to express requirements, which, however, should be as close as possible to the BPM notation. In [8] we introduced the Business Application Modeler (BAM). It facilitates the specification of graphical validation rules, which are formal and reusable requirements close to the BPMs. The notation for these graphical validation rules is the Graphical Computation Tree Logic (G-CTL) [7,18]. Moreover, BAM enables the automatic checking of BPMs with G-CTL rules.

The challenge following the one of specifying requirements and finding violations in BPMs, is the one of supporting the user to understand the validation result and to deal with it. Providing visual notations for requirement specification virtually implies presenting visual feedback for checking results. We consider supporting modelers in this area as crucial.

In this paper, we elaborate methods for analyzing and visualizing checking results in the context of G-CTL-based validations as realized in BAM. In the following we will refer to these methods as *Checking Result Analysis and Visualization* (CAV) methods. In the context of a tool demonstration [17] we already mentioned some exemplary methods, but without any conceptual or detailed description.

The proposed CAV methods primarily rely on artifacts, which are needed for and generated during the validation process. The artifacts can be visualized directly, showing different aspects of the validation. Combining these basic methods allows even more expressive visualizations and analysis to support the user.

In the following section, we describe background concepts regarding BPMs and graphical validation rules. In Sect. 3, we present our CAV methods. There we introduce the artifacts, created during the validation and afterwards we elaborate on direct visualizations of these. Next we deal with combinations of these methods. Section 4 presents related work and Sect. 5 concludes this paper.

2   Background

2.1   Business Process Models

The basic concept of business process models (BPMs) is to describe processes with means of functionality and transitions linking these functions. Further process elements enhance the expressiveness of the BPMs. From the various notations that exist for modeling BPMs, in this contribution we make use of the extended Event-driven Process Chain (eEPC) [10]. An example for an eEPC model is depicted in Fig. 1. The example models a small, abstract process intended to introduce the eEPC notation briefly, and to demonstrate the CAV methods in confined space.

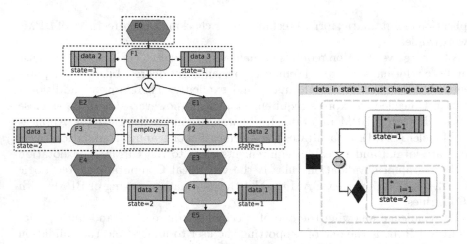

Fig. 1. A simple process in eEPC notation. Dashed borders expose examples for substates.

Fig. 2. A G-CTL example rule.

The rounded rectangles are *function* elements, representing activities. The hexagon symbols are called events, representing facts or conditions that hold before or after a function. So in classic eEPC models events and functions always alter along each path of the control flow. The control flow is given by the solid arrows and the control flow operators, which can split and join the control flow. Such operators are the circle elements, containing a symbol for their logic behavior.

The remaining kinds of elements in the eEPC belong to a class of elements, we call attached objects. In eEPC such objects can be connected by non-control-flow edges to functions or events or other attached objects. The attached objects are used to specify the object they are attached to more detailed. An example is the cluster symbol (rectangle with two bars on the outer left and on the outer right), which represents data. In general it is connected to functions with a directed data flow edge (dashed arrows). Other attached objects like the position are connected with a non-directed association edge. All elements can be annotated with arbitrary attributes, displayed as text beside the element.

From a semantic point of view, time proceeds along the control flow, which basically lines up the events and functions. We consider, therefore, each event and function as a core of a temporally atomic unit, which we call substate. In Fig. 1 some substates are exemplarily highlighted in dashed boxes. If attached objects are related to a function or event, they are part of the event's or function's substate. This is because they are considered to be active at the same time as the function or event they are associated to.

Hence, from a slightly more abstract perspective, the control flow defines the temporal order of substates and the set of active substates defines the overall state of the process at some point in time. A more general and detailed description is given in [18].

2.2   Graphical Computation Tree Logic

Beyond the modeling of processes, BAM enables the modeling of graphical validation rules. The notation for these rules is the Graphical Computational Tree Logic (G-CTL), first published in [7]. G-CTL allows explicit, formal and visual expression of requirements regarding the content level of BPMs[1] and the BPMs can be checked automatically with these rules.

The core principle of G-CTL is to embed *patterns of process elements* into a graphical logical expression. Such logical expressions are a straight forward representation of the textual Computation Tree Logic (CTL). Figure 2 shows a simple example for a G-CTL rule, which will be explained below. This is not a domain-specific example, since the presented approach is not domain-specific. However, multiple G-CTL examples from the privacy domain may be found in [19].

In G-CTL rules the logic expression of the rule can be read independently of the content of the patterns, which are boxed in solid rounded rectangles. The example rule with two patterns requires: In all states of the process *(Always Globally*, ■, **AG**) holds, if a substate matches the upper pattern, then *(implication)* from this state on always *(Always Future*, ♦, **AF**) a substate matching the second pattern must be reached. Hence, this rule is a response property in terms of [6].

The patterns of process elements allow to define facts or circumstances in the same way as in a BPM. These patterns can be built from all elements of the BPM notation except for the control flow, since these patterns will be matched to the temporally atomic substates. Furthermore, G-CTL rules allow specifications in a generic manner, enabling the reusability for multiple BPMs. Instead of concrete element names wildcards ("*") can be used and identity constraints (e.g. "$i = 1$", c.f. Fig. 2) facilitate to specify if elements inside of one and across different patterns refer to the same or different elements in the BPM (example follows).

The example rule in Fig. 2 has two simple patterns. The upper pattern matches on any substate with a data cluster that has the attribute *state=1*. The lower pattern is similar, but matches substates with a data cluster that has the attribute *state=2*. Moreover, there is an identity constraint, requiring the data clusters in the patterns to refer to identical (i.e. node type and name are equal) data clusters in the BPM.

Hence, the example rule requires: If in some substate of the process a data cluster with an arbitrary name x occurs that is tagged with an attribute "state 1", a substate must be reached in which the same data, i.e. a data cluster with name x, occurs that is tagged with the attribute "state 2".

[18] provides a detailed description, how G-CTL rules are applied to BPMs. Important for understanding this paper is the fact that multiple ways may exist in which a particular G-CTL rule can be applied to a particular BPM. We illustrate this in Fig. 3 for the case of applying the rule in Fig. 2 on the BPM in

---

[1] G-CTL is not intended to check for syntactical or semantic issues (e.g. deadlocks).

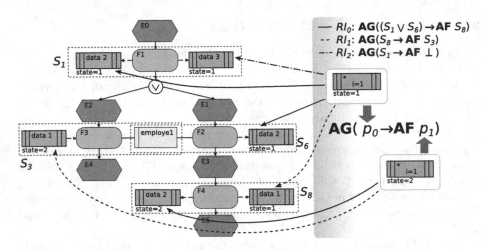

Fig. 3. Rule Instances for the examples in Figs. 2 and 1.

Fig. 1. On the left of Fig. 3 the example process is depicted. We marked (dashed boxes) and labeled the substates $(S_1, S3, S6, S8)$ that are relevant with respect to the example rule. On the right the patterns of the rule are shown. Between them the basic textual CTL statement is depicted, which is the skeleton for the final textual rules. It is a straight forward translation of the graphical logic expression with placeholders for the patterns (here p_0 and p_1).

On the upper right of the figure the final textual rules (RI_0, RI_1, RI_2) are listed, which are passed to the model checker. We call each of these final textual rules a *rule instance*. Each rule instance represents a specific way in which the G-CTL rule applies to the process model.

From the patterns on the right of Fig. 3 arrows point to places in the process model. Each arrow represents a *pattern match*, which is basically a mapping of the elements in the rule pattern to matching elements in a substate of the BPM. A pattern match contains precise information how the pattern matches a substate. A substate might be matched in different ways by one pattern, and each way is considered. For example, two arrows point from the upper pattern to substate S_1. One addresses the match of data 2, the other addresses the match of data 3.

Each rule instance is a way to assign the pattern matches to the placeholders in the textual rule skeleton, such that every match is considered in at least one rule instance, no identity constraint is violated in a rule instance, and as few rule instances as possible are created.

In Fig. 3, consistent combinations of matches are indicated by the line style of the arrows. Pattern matches with identical line style form a rule instance. The rule instances RI_0, RI_1, RI_2 in the upper right are also marked with the corresponding line style. The textual rules are finally created by replacing the placeholders in the skeleton with a conjunction of tests for the activity of the matched substates (e.g. $S_1 \lor S_6$) or false ($\bot$) if no match exists. Hence, in this case actually one rule instance is created for each data cluster *data 1, data 2* and *data 3*. For example data 2 in state 1 occurs in the substates S_1 and S_6. The adequate response data 2 in state 2 exists in substate S_8, which results in $RI_1 : \mathbf{AG}((S_1 \vee S_6) \rightarrow \mathbf{AF}S_8)$. In case of data 3: these data occur with the attribute state=1 in substate S_1. However, there is no occurrence of data 3 with attribute state=2 and, therefore, $RI_2 : \mathbf{AG}(S_1 \rightarrow \mathbf{AF}\perp)$ is created.

The rule instances are passed to the model checker with a state machine that represents all possible execution orders of the substates and each expression S_x can simply be interpreted as a test for the activity of substate x in the state machine.

3   Checking Result Analysis and Visualization

The primary goal of CAV is to improve the understanding of the BPM and the rule models as well as detected rule violations. CAV should help to understand and decide if and how to modify a BPM in case of detected errors, but it should also help to understand the reasons why a rule is actually correct. To achieve these goals basically any kind of analysis on the BPM or rule can be helpful, depending on the particular problem. In this contribution, we want to narrow the area down to CAV (closely) related to our validation method for the dynamic behavior of BPMs. This means that the presented methods will rely on analysis of artifacts created during the validation procedure. Such artifacts are the information carrier. Here, we will not involve heuristics or intend to detect further errors with these methods. Moreover, the visualization methods we are going to show are not optimized with respect to usability. They are intended to demonstrate that sufficient information is given to realize such a visualization.

In the following we are going to introduce the artifacts that appear by validating a BPM in BAM. Next we discuss basic and composed CAV methods as they are realized in BAM and how they contribute to the goals.

3.1   Artifacts

The basic artifacts we deal with are the BPMs and the graphical validation rules in the G-CTL notation. At a glance the procedure of validating BPMS with G-CTL rules can be outlined as follows: First the user chooses a BPM to be checked and a set of G-CTL rules. Then BAM starts with matching the patterns of process elements of the G-CTL with the substates in the BPM. Thereby the actual instances in which the rules can be applied to the BPM are determined and translated to textual CTL, as described in [18]. The next step is the computation of the execution semantics, allowing to transform the BPM into a state machine, readable by the model checker[2]. The model checker delivers a counterexample for violated rule instances. For valid rule instances, it simply returns *true*. The final step is to present the results to the user and give access to CAV.

---

[2] The model checker we currently use is the Cadence Symbolic Model Verifier [11].

We now give a detailed description of the artifacts that are generated during the validation process:

Pattern Matches and Rule Instances: Both were introduced in Sect. 2.2. The *pattern matches* represent the information in which ways the elements in the patterns of the G-CTL rules are matched to the elements in the substates of the BPM. The rule instances describe the possible arrangements of pattern matches and the corresponding textual rules, testing for the activity of the matched substates.

Reachability Graph: As a result from computing the execution semantic of the BPM, the reachability graph represents the state space of the BPM, allowing to determine possible execution orders of substates. It is used to transform the model to a state machine representation for the model checker. The reachability graph provides a mapping of the substates to the state space and vice versa. The concrete semantic we use is based on the one proposed in [12]. It might be exchanged by another semantic, as long as such a reachability graph can be computed.

Error Path: The model checker returns true for valid rule instances and a counterexample for each violated rule instance (similar for other model checkers). Such a counterexample is a path through the state space of the model, which exposes the behavior, violating the particular rule instance. Note that multiple other counterexamples may exist for this rule instance. However (in general) model checkers stop evaluating a CTL rule after discovering the first counterexample. We can map the states back into a path through the substates in the BPM, which we call the *error path*.

Parse Tree: This artifact encompasses the logic of the G-CTL rule, i.e. only the CTL expression, not the patterns. Hence, it is the same for all rule instances of a rule. The parse tree is used to create the textual CTL expressions.
Moreover, it allows trivial evaluations of rule instances, just by determining if patterns are matched or not. For example, assuming that no match exists for one of the patterns p_0, p_1 in a rule $\mathbf{AF}(p_0 \wedge p_1)$. Then this rule boils down to $\mathbf{AF}(\bot \wedge \text{some match}) = \bot$, no matter what matches p_1. Such trivial cases need not to be evaluated by the model checker, but an error path will of course not be available then.

3.2 Basic CAV

As mentioned above the artifacts are the information carrier for CAV. Basically, for some of them direct visualizations can be displayed in the BPM or the rule model.

Error Path Visualization. A counterexample created by the model checker and the resulting error path for a rule instance is the only output that is created by the checking tool itself. Therefore, it is probably the most obvious visualization approach to use the error path for exposing the affected elements in some way. In BAM this is currently realized by displaying the elements that do not occur on the error path transparently. Other tools or concepts use basically similar methods as pointed out in related work.

Another method to display the error path in the BPM is to follow the process elements on the error path step by step. The modeler can step forward or backward through the time steps. Substates that are active at the currently chosen time step are emphasized with a frame.

Both ways to display the error path use the same information, but show different aspects. The transparency method focuses more on the big picture, highlighting all parts of the process that are involved. The actual execution order must be concluded by reading the control-flow, which may be inconvenient with respect to issues related to looping, concurrency or if (mostly) all substates are involved. The step by step method exposes the execution order and concurrency explicitly. On the other hand, it does not help to keep the big picture in large models.

Combining these methods allows to overcome the mutual disadvantages. However, this visualization is not visually related to the violated rule instance, and it does not depict which elements on the error path are actually relevant with respect to the cause of the faulty behavior.

Rule Instance Visualization. As explained in Sect. 2.2, a rule instance is one of possibly multiple ways a G-CTL rule can be applied to the process model. Independent of a particular BPM, the modeler basically can understand the G-CTL rule as such and the requirement, it expresses. Nevertheless, it might not be obvious for a modeler how many and which rule instances of a rule exist for a specific BPM. Hence, it is desirable to visualize the relation of rule instances to the BPM.

The pattern matches allow to identify the elements in the BPM a particular rule instance deals with. It is possible to visualize the matches as well in the BPM as in the rule model. This method basically presents similar information as depicted by the arrows from the patterns to the substate elements in Fig. 3, focused on one violated rule instance. In BAM this is realized by highlighting affected elements in the BPM and in the rule model by showing these candidate elements via a mouseover. Instead of drawing arrows between the rule patterns and the BPM like in Fig. 3, the highlighted elements in the BPM and in the mouse over box are annotated with identifiers.

The screenshot in Fig. 4 exemplarily depicts the visualization of RI_0, introduced in Sect. 2.2. The pattern matches relevant in terms of RI_0 are highlighted in the BPM with rounded rectangles. The G-CTL rule is displayed beside the model. The mouse pointer is placed over the cluster element in the upper pattern, causing the display of the elements matched in the BPM for this pattern element. The arrow (not part of the screenshot) exemplarily links two identifiers, that clearly relate the element in the mouseover window and in the BPM.

If multiple instances of a G-CTL rule exist, rule instance visualization supports the understanding, in which respect the rule is valid and in which it is not. Moreover, this CAV is basically independent from a validation result and,

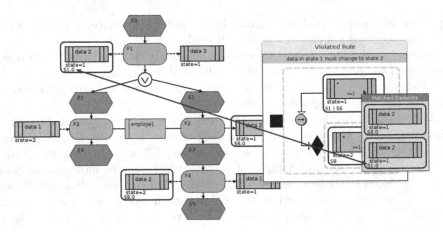

Fig. 4. Visualization of a pattern match. The blue arrow points to the annotation, identifying the matched element.

therefore, independent from the existence of an error path. Therefore, it can be a useful visualization for the trivial cases like $\mathbf{AF}(p_0 \wedge p_1)$ (c.f. Sect. 3.1), trivially evaluating to false if in a rule instance of this rule at least one pattern could not be assigned. Even if an error path existed in this trivial case, it would neither provide any benefit in understanding the cause of the error nor would it provide any information how to solve the problem. Nevertheless, considering the error path might be useful as we are going to show in Sect. 3.3.

Property Recognition. The parse tree catches the structure of the logic expression in a G-CTL rule. Next to the generation of textual CTL and evaluation of trivial cases, it allows to identify the type of the property defined by the rule. [6] defines various categories and types of CTL properties. There is actually a significantly small number of properties that covers a huge share of properties typically requested. As denoted above, the rule in Fig. 2 is an example for the so-called *response property*.

We use a simple XML-based description to specify *parse tree skeletons* for arbitrary types of properties. (Hence, this method is not limited to property types defined by [6].) The property recognition tries to find a parse tree skeleton that matches the actual parse tree of the rule to be recognized. Although no direct visualization is generated from this information, for example, an explaining text could be displayed for identified types of properties. In the next section, we will improve this property recognition by taking pattern matches and the error path into account in order to generate more specific hints for the modeler. Again, this method is basically independent from the validation result and can be applied to valid rule instances as well.

3.3 Combined CAV

In the previous section, we describe CAV methods informational based on particular artifacts. In the following, we will combine basic CAV methods and the underlying artifacts to visualize relations, to support the modeler in reasoning about the cause of errors.

Error Path Aware Rule Instance Visualization. The plain error path visualization does not show its relation to the violated rule instance. In fact, the rule instance visualization method can display how the particular BPM is related to the rule instance. Hence, it is rather obvious to combine these methods, which is illustrated in Fig. 5. The elements outside of the error path are displayed transparently in the BPM. Matched elements are highlighted with boxes of different colors[3] in the BPM and the G-CTL rule that is displayed beside the BPM.

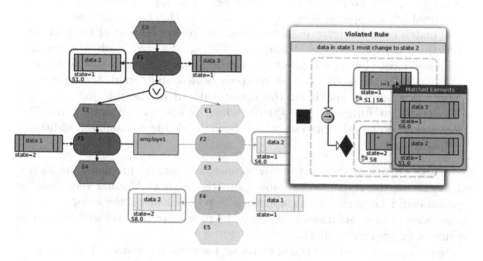

Fig. 5. Error path aware rule instance visualization for rule instance RI_0.

Matched elements, occurring on the error path are highlighted in blue in the BPM as well as in the mouseover box. Matched elements outside the error path are marked in red. Additionally, the pattern boxes of the rule model are colored, and an icon is displayed in the lower left corner, according to the cases listed in Table 1. These cases refer to the match situation of a particular pattern p in a particular rule instance r. We basically distinguish the case: 1) no match exists for p in r and 2) at least one match exists. For the latter we differentiate if all matches for p occur on the error path or just some or none. These distinctions can support the user to understand or even conclude why the rule instance is invalid (or valid).

---

[3] For grayscale prints: In the BPM and mouseover box: The elements with label S1.0 are highlighted in a blue box. S6.0 and S8.0 in a red box. In the rule, the border of the upper pattern is colored magenta, the box of the lower pattern is red.

Table 1. Frame color and icon indicate how the matches **for one particular pattern** in a rule instance relate to the error path.

box color	icon (abbr.)	meaning
Blue	(aEP)	All matches occur on error path.
Red	(nEP)	No matches occur on error path.
Magenta	(sEP)	Some matches occur on error path.
Gray	($\perp$)	Pattern not matched.

An example is provided in Fig. 5, which again reflects the case of RI_0, introduced in Sect. 2.2. Provided that the user understands that the logic of the rule is a response property (e.g. supported by basic rule recognition) the modeler can conclude:

1. Such a response property can only be false, if the upper pattern that triggers the need for a response is on the error path. In this particular case, exactly one match is on the error path and must, therefore, be part of the problem.
2. For this "data 2" element at function "F1" on the error path, the required response exists but is not always reachable. This is directly visible because the match for the second pattern has only been found outside the error path.
3. There is a second match for the upper pattern in the rule for the "data 2" element at function "F2" (S6.0), which is not on the error path. This is another potential violation, which became visible without an additional validation run.

To fix the violation, the control-flow could be changed to make the identified match for the response reachable from the trigger. Alternatively, another response could be placed at an appropriate position along the error path. Of course, none of these solutions guaranties the process to be valid with respect to the rule after another validation run.

Figure 6 presents an additional example for error path-aware Rule Instance Visualization, visualizing the violation of RI_1 (c.f. Sect. 2.2). Here both patterns were matched and both matches occur on the error path, which indicates an inadequate execution order. As recommended in Sect. 3.2 we visualize the error path stepwise then. In Fig. 6 are frames around the events "E4" and "E3". These frames indicate the activity of these elements in some step t in the error path. One step before at $t - 1$ the frames were on "F3" and "F2". In the next step at $t + 1$ the frame on "E3" moves to "F4". This means a path through the process exists, in which the substate matching the lower pattern occurs before the substate matching the upper pattern. Hence, this visualization makes it easier for the modeler to conclude and confirm that the execution order causes the violation.

Without Property Recognition, the modeler is not supported in understanding the logic of the rule, which is required to draw correct conclusions in the examples above. In the next section, we will elaborate how to improve plain Property Recognition by considering Rule Instances and the error path, and, therefore, also improve the error path aware Rule Instance Visualization.

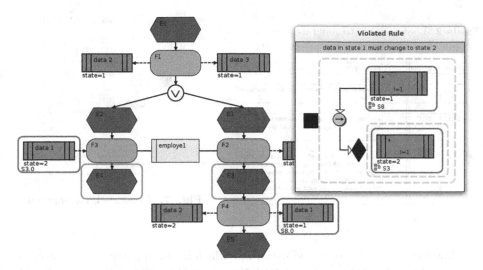

Fig. 6. Error path aware rule instance visualization for rule instance RI_1.

Rule Explanation. Plain property recognition enables the basic recognition of types of properties, e.g. according to [6]. In the previous section we listed conclusions the modeler could draw supported by the error path-aware Rule Instance Visualization for a specific rule instance. The CAV presented in this section delivers some of these conclusions automatically as textual hints or simple recommendations. This method is based on extending the XML definition for the property recognition with a lookup table. The table maps pattern matches, their relation to the error path and the validation result to recommendations.

An exemplary extract of a lookup table for the response property is shown in Table 2 (the letters on the left are only used to address rows from this text). For each pattern in the rule, one column is reserved, and each pattern is labeled. For a response property like in Fig. 2 we labeled the upper pattern in the G-CTL rule *"(trigger)"*, the lower pattern *"(response)"*. For the values in the pattern columns, we distinguish between the cases listed in Table 1. To indicate that a match exists for a pattern independent of its relation to the error path, we write ⊤. The pattern columns are followed by a column for the validation result, which are Boolean values. The last column contains messages to be displayed if the conditions in the aforegoing columns apply. The messages are presented at the bottom of the rule window as shown in Fig. 7.

As mentioned before Table 2 contains some exemplarily chosen lines of the table for the response property. Of course, the table also allows to capture cases in which the rule instance is not violated and no error path exists. One of these cases is shown in row a. It deals with the case that a match for the response pattern exists but not for the trigger pattern. The modeler might question if this is intended or if a trigger should exist in the model, since a response exists.

Table 2. Lookup table to generate hints or recommendations for the response property.

	(trigger)	(response)	result	messages
	...	...	...	...
a	$\perp$	$\top$	$\top$	• Response exists, but is not required with respect to this rule.
	...	...	...	...
b	aEP	aEP	$\perp$	• (trigger) and (response) exist on error path but (response) is not always reached. Check the execution order. ...
	...	...	...	...
c	sEP	nEP	$\perp$	• Candidate for (response) found, but is not reachable on **every** path from (trigger). • Alternatively, you might want to add an appropriate response on the error path. • Furter matches for (trigger) exist outside the error path. Potential additional violation.
	...	...	...	...

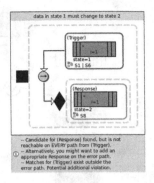

Fig. 7. Generated recommendations.

Row b reflects the case of a violation, at which for both patterns the matches occur on the error path. The hint that the execution order may be flawed will be presented in accord with the example of RI_1 in Fig. 6. Row c catches the case applying to RI_0 (Fig. 5). The trigger pattern was found inside and outside the error path. The response pattern was found outside the error path. Again, automatically the conclusions are shown, which the modeler could have drawn manually by analyzing the visualization.

These recommendations do not generally allow to isolate the specific cause of a violation, which might, in particular, be the case if more than one match for at least one of multiple patterns exist. Nevertheless, this method increases the visibility of such issues. In future work it might be refined by considering more information (e.g. number of matches on the error path) to present more specific recommendations.

4   Related Work

Naturally, verification tools deliver their results in the language used by the particular tool. A model checker, for example, delivers a counterexample (a sequence of states–the error path) in the language and terms of the model checker input. While this may be appropriate in specific contexts (e.g. in the NASA domain [14]) this is not accepted in the domain of BPM. Hence, a backward transformation of the results of checking tools into the (modeling) language used by the user of the particular domain is required. This is not only desired for the domain of BPM but also development tools for technical domains like the development of autonomous systems have "associated visualization tools that distill and present data from log files of actual runs of the system" [16].

Most error visualization techniques for business processes focus on structural and semantic checking. This kind of checking is based on the syntax and the semantics of the underlying modeling notation. Primarily, the approaches check for the correct connection of model elements as well as the overall control flow of the model. Besides control flow analysis [2] is focused in particular on the checking of dataflow aspects in workflow models. In order to identify control and data flow violations the authors introduce pre- and postconditions on activities and apply Integer Programming and Constraint Programming techniques to the models. In case of an error the trigger–a subgraph leading to the point "where the workflow gets stuck"–is shown (like an error path) in the (graphical) workflow model. [15] presents a first step towards a compiler for business processes which is why the approach strictly focuses on structural correctness. Errors found in a verification run are marked in the graphical model in the used modeling tool Activity (based on Eclipse). The authors provide so-called markers (in a typical Eclipse manner), which can highlight the errors in the model and deliver further information about the error (e.g. lack of Synchronization). The aforementioned highlighting mechanisms are similar or identical to the highlighting of an error path but most lack further analysis of the error and support for error correction (e.g. recommendations).

The generic model query language (GMQL) proposed by [3] allows the specification of textual compliance rules. Theses rules are used to identify matching parts of the process model, which basically can be understood as a pattern matching mechanism. Identified patterns are highlighted in the modeling tool. Further information about a possible violation is not provided. Although this approach allows the checking of processes on the content level it does not consider the execution semantics of the model.

In [9] presents a "generic visualization framework" for the visualization of errors found in UML models by verification tools (e.g. a model checker). On the one hand the framework provides an animation mechanism for behavioral models like state diagrams, which highlights different types of visited states as well as the firing of transitions. On the other hand the framework allows the generation of a sequence diagram. Both mechanisms are basically a visualization of the counterexample and error path respectively delivered by the checking tool applied. However, as stated in [4] often the sole existence of a counterexample is not sufficient to understand and correct the cause of the error. First of all, a counterexample must be comprehensible in terms of the, for example, underlying process model, which some approaches can not provide for technical reasons [16]. Furthermore, a particular error path may only be one way the model violates the particular rule. After the (possible) correction of the model a rerun of the checking tool is required, which, "in turn, is ineffective" [1]. Additionally, the proper correction of the model only based on the counterexample is not a straight forward task and frequently includes guessing by the modeler.

To ease the task of locating the cause of violations, [16] presents a verification approach for autonomous systems. It produces textual explanations of the problem based on the counterexample by employing a Truth Maintenance System (TMS) [13]. It delivers a hierarchical explanation of inconsistent propositions. These explanations are intended to help the modeler to focus on the "true source(s)" of the cause of the violation. This approach is similar to our recommendation mechanism in providing further artifacts for the analysis of found errors.

Instead of counterexamples as means to provide hints on the cause of an error the approach in [1] derives so-called anti-patterns from the violated compliance patterns. Each anti-pattern describes a possible violation, which provides the modeler hints on causes for the error enabling to further investigate the violation. In contrast, our approach combines further analysis of the error path as well as the analysis of the rules in order to provide hints and recommendations respectively for the correction of an error.

5   Conclusions

The application of validation and verification techniques in the business process management domain is not common, yet. Nevertheless, quite a long list of approaches exists that at least try to advance this situation. To enable the modelers of Business Process Models (BPMs) to use these (to some extend very formal) techniques the usability expectations, resulting from this specific context have to be considered. On the one hand the modeler should be supported with visualization and explanation mechanisms in order to ease the understanding and reasoning of checking results. On the other hand (as well as in other domains) it is desired to improve both the performance and expressiveness of the overall verification process.

In this paper, we introduced *Checking Result Analysis and Visualization* (CAV) methods that are based on the artifacts (c.f. Sects. 3.1 and 3.2) that emerge during the validation of BPMs with G-CTL rules. Moreover, we elaborated on combining these basic CAVs and their underlying artifacts to present additional information and relations to the modelers. Besides supporting to analyzing rule violations and their causes, CAV also contributes to understand which rule instances (c.f. Sect. 2.2) exist and how these are related to the BPM.

Basically, the presented CAVs are not limited to analyzing *in*valid rules. In future work we plan to elaborate more on CAV for valid rules, e.g. valuable during specifying and testing a G-CTL rule when a positive outcome was not expected. Current work in progress is to reduce verification time by reducing the state space of BPMs specifically for rule instances. We expect this to introduce additional information regarding the (ir)relevance of areas in the BPM with respect to the rule instance, which might especially advance visualizations in large models. Although the CAVs and findings are focused on the Business Application Modeler tool, the concepts might be applicable in other approaches as well.

References

1. Awad, A., Weidlich, M., Weske, M.: Visually specifying compliance rules and explaining their violations for business processes. J. Vis. Lang. Comput. **22**(1), 30–55 (2011)
2. Borrego, D., Eshuis, R., Gómez-López, M.T., Gasca, R.M.: Diagnosing correctness of semantic workflow models. Data Knowl. Eng. **87**, 167–184 (2013)

3. Bräuer, S., Delfmann, P., Dietrich, H.A., Steinhorst, M.: Using a generic model query approach to allow for process model compliance checking – an algorithmic perspective. In: 2013 Proceedings of the Wirtschaftsinformatik (2013)
4. Copty, Fady, Irron, Amitai, Weissberg, Osnat, Kropp, Nathan, Kamhi, Gila: Efficient debugging in a formal verification environment. In: Margaria, Tiziana, Melham, Thomas F. (eds.) CHARME 2001. LNCS, vol. 2144, pp. 275–292. Springer, Heidelberg (2001)
5. van Dongen, Boudewijn F., de Medeiros, Ana Karla Alves, Verbeek, HMW(Eric), Weijters, AJMMTon, van der Aalst, Wil M.P.: The ProM framework: a new era in process mining tool support. In: Ciardo, Gianfranco, Darondeau, Philippe (eds.) ICATPN 2005. LNCS, vol. 3536, pp. 444–454. Springer, Heidelberg (2005)
6. Dwyer, M.B., Avrunin, G.S., Corbett, J.C.: Patterns in property specifications for finite-state verification. In: Proceedings of the 21st International Conference on Software Engineering, pp. 411–420. ACM (1999)
7. Feja, S., Fötsch, D.: Model Checking with Graphical Validation Rules. In: International Conference on the Engineering of Computer-Based Systems. pp. 117–125. IEEE Computer Society (2008)
8. Feja, S., Witt, S., Speck, A.: BAM: a requirements validation and verification framework for business process models. In: 11th International Conference on Quality Software, pp. 186–191. IEEE Computer Society (2011)
9. Goldsby, Heather J., Cheng, Betty H.C., Konrad, Sascha, Kamdoum, Stephane: A visualization framework for the modeling and formal analysis of high assurance systems. In: Wang, Jilin, Whittle, Jon, Harel, David, Reggio, Gianna (eds.) MoDELS 2006. LNCS, vol. 4199, pp. 707–721. Springer, Heidelberg (2006)
10. Keller, G., Nüttgens, M., Scheer, A.W.: Semantische Prozessmodellierung auf der Grundlage Ereignisgesteuerter Prozessketten (EPK). Technical report Institut für Wirtschaftsinformatik Universität Saarbrücken, Saarbrücken (1992)
11. McMillan, K.: Cadence SMV and other downloads from Cadence Berkeley Labs. Technical reports, Cadence Berkeley Labs (2012)
12. Mendling, J.: Metric for Process Models-Empirical Foundations of Verification, Error Prediction, and Guidelines for Correctness. Springer, Berlin (2008)
13. Nayak, P.P., Williams, B.C.: Fast Context Switching in Real-Time Propositional Reasoning, pp. 50–56. AAAI Press (1997)
14. Pecheur, Charles, Simmons, Reid G.: From livingstone to SMV. In: Rash, James L., Rouff, Christopher A., Truszkowski, Walt, Gordon, Diana F., Hinchey, Michael G. (eds.) FAABS 2000. LNCS (LNAI), vol. 1871, pp. 103–113. Springer, Heidelberg (2001)
15. Prinz, Thomas M., Spieß, Norbert, Amme, Wolfram: A first step towards a compiler for business processes. In: Cohen, Albert (ed.) CC 2014 (ETAPS). LNCS, vol. 8409, pp. 238–243. Springer, Heidelberg (2014)
16. Simmons, R., Pecheur, C., Srinivasan, G.: Towards automatic verification of autonomous systems. In: International Conference on Intelligent Robots and Systems, pp. 1410–1415 (2000)
17. Witt, S., Feja, S., Speck, A., Hadler, C.: Business application modeler: a process model validation and verification tool. In: Requirements Engineering Conference, pp. 333–334 (2014)

18. Witt, S., Feja, S., Speck, A.: Applying pattern-based graphical validation rules to business process models. In: IEEE International Conference on Software Testing, Verification, and Validation Workshops, pp. 274–283. IEEE Computer Society (2014)
19. Witt, S., Feja, S., Speck, A., Prietz, C.: Integrated privacy modeling and validation for business process models. In: Proceedings of the 2012 Joint EDBT/ICDT Workshops, pp. 196–205. ACM (2012)

Processor Rescue

Safe Coding for Hardware Aliasing

Peter T. Breuer[1]([⊠]), Jonathan P. Bowen[1], and Simon Pickin[2]

[1] School of Computing, Telecommunications and Networks,
Birmingham City University, Birmingham, UK
`Peter.T.Breuer@gmail.com`, `Jonathan.Bowen@bcu.ac.uk`
[2] Facultad de Informática, Complutense University of Madrid, Madrid, Spain
`Simon.Pickin@fdi.ucm.es`

Abstract. What happens if a Mars lander takes a cosmic ray through the processor and thereafter $1 + 1 = 3$? Coping with the fault is feasible but requires the numbers 2 and 3 to be treated as indistinguishable for the purposes of arithmetic, while as memory addresses they continue to access different memory cells. If a program is to run correctly in this altered environment it must be prepared to see address 2 sporadically access data in memory cell 3, which is known as 'hardware aliasing'. This paper describes a programming discipline that allows software to run correctly in a hardware aliasing context, provided the aliasing is underpinned by hidden determinism.

Keywords: Hardware aliasing · Machine code · Compilation

1 Introduction

Imagine that a Mars lander has suffered a cosmic ray hit that damages a piece of internal circuitry in its arithmetic logic unit (ALU) so that $1 + 1 = 3$ is the new outcome from an addition. It continues to be the case that $2 + 0 = 2$ and $3 - 1 = 2$ as usual, but $1 + 1$ and possibly more come out wrong. What should the mission team do about that? We hope they have a backup processor ready to take over in the lander in the short term[1], but it turns out that we can rehabilitate the faulty processor via some reprogramming from back home on Earth, first adjusting fault handlers to tidy up the processor's arithmetic so that it works with less precision than before, then rewriting application machine codes in the lander to suit. Successful rehabilitation restores processing redundancy.

---

[1] The Curiosity rover now on Mars has a second processor that was signalled to take over on February 28, 2013, due to an issue with the active processor's flash memory that resulted in it continuously rebooting, draining power. The rover was not heard from again until March 4, the spacecraft nearly having been lost. The issue reoccurred late in March, 2013, and full normal operation was only finally resumed on March 25, 2013, after reloading programs to a different portion of flash memory.

© Springer International Publishing Switzerland 2015
H. Fujita and G. Guizzi (Eds.): SoMeT 2015, CCIS 532, pp. 137–148, 2015.
DOI: 10.1007/978-3-319-22689-7_10

A solution in the $1+1=3$ case is to ignore bits 0 and 1 everywhere, so that the bit-patterns 0, 1, 2, 3 are all taken to mean the same integer value 0, and the bit-patterns 4, 5, 6, 7 are all taken to mean the integer value 1, and so on. Viewed like that, arithmetic in the processor is not 32-bit, but 30-bit, with a four-way redundancy in how each integer is coded as a bit-pattern. Only the top 30 bits of each bit-pattern in memory or on disk remain meaningful. When the processor calculates $1+1=3$, it should be looked at as a concrete instance 'on the metal' of the sum $0+0=0$, with different bit patterns representing the integer 0. There is potentially a crack in the illusion when the processor checks for zero, because it needs on the metal to check for any of the four possible bit-patterns 0, 1, 2 or 3 representing 0, but programs can be altered to cope or it can be arranged that they fault on each branch-if-zero machine instruction and the four-fold check is run in the fault handler, avoiding any application code changes. The result is *fully homomorphically encrypted computation* [7,18]. The processor continues to work correctly, but using a multi-valued numerical encoding in registers and memory that is different from the standard encoding. The reader need not be concerned that it works correctly because a formal proof of correctness in the case of a Von Neumann processor architecture and 1-to-many encodings is given in [7], and for a rewrite-rule machine architecture in [18]. In the case of the Von Neumann machine, programs have to keep data addresses and program addresses separated according to the type discipline articulated in [5], because the former are encrypted and the latter are not, but that is the only restriction.

Memory access in a mended lander's processor is problematic, however, and is not so straightforward to handle. A memory offset that is intended by the programmer to be 0 may be expressed by the processor as any of the bit-patterns 0, 1, 2 or 3, and the memory circuits will access memory at any one of four corresponding locations, with apparently haphazard results from the point of view of the program. That is classically known as *hardware aliasing*, and this paper shows how to ensure that machine code modified for a damaged Mars lander continues to work correctly in the face of the hardware aliasing issues that arise in connection with memory addressing.

Aliasing in the more familiar sense – let us dub it 'software aliasing' in this context in order to distinguish it – is relatively well-studied. It occurs when two different addresses access the same location in memory. This kind of aliasing is broadly treated in most texts on computer architecture (see, e.g., Chap. 6 of [2]) and is common lore in operating systems kernel programming. In contrast, 'hardware' aliasing only nowadays commonly arises in embedded systems under certain circumstances[2] and awareness of it is restricted to a few embedded systems programmers. But programmers *do* have prior experience with hardware aliasing, although the era has been largely forgotten now. It used to be common in the early days of DOS and the IBM PC, when memory managers such

---

[2] Barr in [2] describes it thus: "Hardware Aliasing: ... [is] used to describe the situation where, due to either a hardware design choice or a hardware failure, one or more of the available address bits is not used in the memory selection process." That is, the available memory address bits do not serve to distinguish two different locations.

as Quarterdeck's expanded memory manager (QEMM) [11] allowed the same address to access both BIOS and RAM opportunistically just below 1024K.

The situation envisaged here is somewhat special with respect to that venerable era in that aliasing in a mended Mars lander is fully deterministic 'under the hood'. It may be observed that $1 + 1 = 3$ consistently, every time, because the damage is a physical open or short circuit, and running exactly the same sequence of machine code always produces exactly the same arithmetic results.

Axioms: the discussion in this paper is restricted to *hidden deterministic* hardware aliasing contexts, which means that:

I a saved address copy always accesses the same memory location on reuse;
II recalculating the address exactly the same way accesses the same location.

We are motivated particularly by one special case: the Krypto-Processor (KPU) is a processor design in which encrypted data circulates through memory and registers without ever being decrypted [8,9]. It is in principle secure from backdoors, privileged observers and malfeasants. Nevertheless, a KPU is in every way but one an ordinary CPU; the difference is that its ALU has been transformed mathematically so that it works natively on encrypted data.

Because practical encryptions encode each integer value as many alternative bit-patterns in the KPU, it looks from the outside rather like a Mars lander with a damaged ALU. To make sense of the numbers that come out of the KPU, or a damaged Mars lander's processor, one has to look at the numbers through the right kind of 'refracting lenses'. The right lens to look at the numbers coming out of a KPU with is the decrypting function for the cipher in use. In the case of the damaged Mars lander, it is the lens that sees no difference between the bit patterns 0, 1, 2, 3, equating them all to the intended number 0.

The canonical KPU design encrypts 32-bit integers in 64 bits, so up to 2^{32} different 64-bit patterns exist for each intended 32-bit address. While all are meant by the programmer to address the same location, they all in fact address different locations via the KPU's quite standard memory hardware, which is not privy to the encryption used in order that 'cold boot' attacks [12,13,17] that examine memory contents may not succeed – such attacks will discover no more than encrypted memory contents located at encrypted memory addresses, and many alternative encrypted addresses at that. The memory address decoder hardware in the KPU does not come equipped with the magic lenses that decrypt what the circulating bit-patterns mean, and the result is hardware aliasing.

The other case of note that produces hardware aliasing by design is a bespoke embedded processor with, say, 40 bits of arithmetic but provision for 64-bit addressing. The extra memory address lines might be grounded, or high, and it varies from design to design. The lines may be connected to 64-bit address registers in the processor, so their values change with the register contents and it is up to software to set the extra bits to zero, or one, or some consistent value, in order that calculating an address may yield a consistent result. The good news is that a single executable may be compiled that works for all design variants in the same generic class, just because the aliasing is deterministic underneath.

Indeed, given conditions (I), (II), it turns out to be not hard to write code that avoids aliasing. There is a programming discipline to be followed, and conventional assembly and machine code may be altered to follow it. The rationale behind the discipline is that (I), (II) say that the bit-pattern representing a memory address is just a number deterministically produced by the processor from its inputs. Provide exactly the same inputs again (identical bit-patterns) and the processor will repeat the same transformations to produce the same outputs. If every time an address is needed, the same instructions are used to calculate it in exactly the same way from the same bit-patterns as starting point, the same pattern of bits must result. So the discipline consists of using exactly the same calculation for the same address from the same starting point every time.

'Copying' (I) is just the trivial case, nevertheless it is one point where existing assembly and machine code almost always needs modification to work in a hardware aliasing context. Reduced instruction set (RISC) [16] architecture processors in particular have code that is written to move data between registers by adding zero through the ALU, not by shuffling data out of one register into another. That enables the instruction set to be comprised of one less instruction. But passing data through the ALU, even adding zero, may transform the bit-representation non-trivially in the setting considered here; programmers assume that adding zero to the bit-pattern 0x1 gives just the same bit-pattern 0x1 again, but in the context of a KPU or a broken Mars lander, the number 0 may be represented by the bit-pattern 0x2, and adding zero (in the form of the alternative bit-pattern 0x1) may produce the different bit-pattern 0x3 although it is just another encoding of the number 0.

We are not aware of any existing techniques to fix or accommodate a broken processor in the field. There is work on strategies to cope with ionising radiation (e.g., [19], which advocates for redundant caching hardware) but we have found none that contemplates repairing a chip's ability to calculate after damage to it.

The layout of this paper is as follows: Sect. 2 discusses mending processor arithmetic to the point where programs can run again. Section 3 introduces the consequent hardware aliasing problem, and Sect. 4 shows how to compile around hardware aliasing when the aliasing effect is underpinned by *hidden determinism*. Section 5 illustrates the procedure with a short example and references where to find larger examples and software tools related to this solution.

2   Processor Repair up to a Point

When a processor develops the idiosyncrasy that $1 + 1 = 3$, that gives rise to logical contradictions through the standard laws of algebra. Surely $1 + 2 = 1 + 1 + 1 = 3 + 1 = 4$ in consequence, yet $1 + 2 = 3$ may continue to be the output from the processor. So does $3 = 4$? In this section a full repair for $1 + 1 = 3$ will be examined for a hypothetical 3-bit CPU with the following arithmetic tables, incorporating the $1 + 1 = 3$ fault:

+	0	1	2	3	4	5	6	7
0	0	1	2	3	4	5	6	7
1	1	3	3	4	5	6	7	0
2	2	3	4	5	6	7	0	1
3	3	4	5	6	7	0	1	2
4	4	5	6	7	0	1	2	3
5	5	6	7	0	1	2	3	4
6	6	7	0	1	2	3	4	5
7	7	0	1	2	3	4	5	6

×	0	1	2	3	4	5	6	7
0	0	0	0	0	0	0	0	0
1	0	1	2	3	4	5	6	7
2	0	2	4	6	0	2	4	6
3	0	3	6	1	4	7	2	5
4	0	4	0	4	0	4	0	4
5	0	5	2	7	4	1	6	3
6	0	6	4	2	0	6	4	2
7	0	7	6	5	4	3	2	1

In this particular case a solution is to regard the bit-patterns 0, 1, 2, 3 as equivalent, meaning 0. In general the solution is always to develop a notion of equivalence among bit-patterns. An equivalence class proposed here is $\{0, 1, 2, 3\}$ meaning 0, and the equivalence it is part of is $x \equiv y$ iff $x - y \in \{0, 1, 2, 3\}$. The aim is to develop an equivalence such that all the variant answers that one may get for a particular result by varying the calculation through the stricken ALU lie within the same equivalence class. That requires adjustments in the arithmetic tables beyond the original fault. In this case $x +' y = (x_2 \wedge y_2).(x + y)_{1,0}$ and $x \times' y = (x_2 \& y_2).(x \times y)_{1,0}$ will do (giving the formulae bitwise here):

+'	0	1	2	3	4	5	6	7
0	0	1	2	3	4	5	6	7
1	1	3	3	0	5	6	7	4
2	2	3	0	1	6	7	4	5
3	3	0	1	2	7	4	5	6
4	4	5	6	7	0	1	2	3
5	5	6	7	4	1	2	3	0
6	6	7	4	5	2	3	0	1
7	7	4	5	6	3	0	1	2

×'	0	1	2	3	4	5	6	7
0	0	0	0	0	0	0	0	0
1	0	1	2	3	0	1	2	3
2	0	2	0	2	0	2	0	2
3	0	3	2	1	0	3	2	1
4	0	0	0	0	4	4	4	4
5	0	1	2	3	4	5	6	7
6	0	2	0	2	4	6	4	6
7	0	3	2	1	4	7	6	5

It can be seen that the modifications leave the four quarters of the tables each occupied by elements from only one of the two equivalence classes $\{0, 1, 2, 3\}$ and $\{4, 5, 6, 7\}$. That is, if $x' \equiv x$ and $y' \equiv y$ then $x' +' y' \equiv x +' y$, which means that the modified arithmetic 'makes sense' with respect to this equivalence.

While it is not hard to make these modifications in practice – the processor must be reconfigured to fault on arithmetic instructions and the fault handler must be programmed to produce the modified result using the functionality available –, in this particular case the fault handler might as well just correct the original result $1 + 1 = 3$ back to the intended $1 + 1 = 2$. However, in general that is not always convenient. It may be, for example, that one pin of the ALU output is stuck to the internal carry, so it is hard to force the correct value to appear in that bit position without also losing the carry. It is always the case, however, that whatever repair is effected, the repair either merely permutes all the bit-patterns available or else it makes equivalent some bit-patterns, which now represent the same integer just as 0, 1, 2, 3, 4 represent the integer 0 above.

The latter situation is of most interest. The equivalence classes can be viewed as the inverse images of decodings to integers under some function $\mathcal{D}$. In the example above the equivalence class $\{0,1,2,3\} = \mathcal{D}^{-1}\{0\}$ and $\{4,5,6,7\} = \mathcal{D}^{-1}\{1\}$, so $\mathcal{D}$ is $\mathcal{D}(x) = \lfloor x/4 \rfloor$, the integer part of $x/4$. The design of the repaired addition and multiplication operations is such that $\mathcal{D}(x +' y) = \mathcal{D}(x) + \mathcal{D}(y)$ mod 2 and $\mathcal{D}(x \times' y) = \mathcal{D}(x)\mathcal{D}(y)$ mod 2. That means that $\mathcal{D}$ is a mathematical *homomorphism* on the set of bit-patterns that turns the computer operations into the arithmetic operations mod 2 (more generally, 2^n, for some n). In repairing a faulty processor one is looking to create a homomorphism, and the arithmetic will then be a homomorphic image of arithmetic mod 2^{32} (for a 32-bit processor), and thus be an arithmetic mod 2^n for $n \le 32$. That means that the effective precision, or number of bits, of a repaired processor is reduced from 32 to n, and if any two bit-patterns represent some one integer, then $n < 32$ and there are exactly 2^{32-n} bit-patterns representing each integer value.

The reasoning in the paragraphs above explains why the KPU is relevant here. The arithmetic in a KPU is an altered form of computer arithmetic, such that the result of an addition $\mathcal{E}(a) + \mathcal{E}(b)$ in the processor of two encrypted values $\mathcal{E}(a)$ and $\mathcal{E}(b)$ is an encryption $\mathcal{E}(a+b \mod 2^{32})$ of the expected arithmetic result $a + b \mod 2^{32}$. In the canonical KPU design there are 2^{32} encryptions of every 32-bit integer, each fitting into a 64-bit word, and $\mathcal{E}$ is a 1-to-2^{32} 'many-valued function', or relation. Its inverse, the decrypting function $\mathcal{D}$, has $\mathcal{D}(\mathcal{E}(a) + \mathcal{E}(b)) = \mathcal{D}(\mathcal{E}(a + b \mod 2^{32})) = a + b \mod 2^{32}$. Writing $a' = \mathcal{E}(a)$ and $b' = \mathcal{E}(b)$, this says that $\mathcal{D}(a' + b') = a + b \mod 2^{32} = \mathcal{D}(a') + \mathcal{D}(b') \mod 2^{32}$, and $\mathcal{D}$ is a homomorphic function. The decryption $\mathcal{D}$ establishes equivalence classes for an equivalence $x \equiv_\mathcal{D} y$ iff $\mathcal{D}(x) = \mathcal{D}(y)$ that settles which bit-patterns x and y are alternate codings for the same integer value $\mathcal{D}(x) = \mathcal{D}(y)$.

Any strategy that allows programs to continue working in the context of the deliberately changed arithmetic in a KPU also enables continued working in the context of a repair to an impaired arithmetic in a conventional processor.

3   The Hardware Aliasing Problem

How code may go wrong when arithmetic in the processor is a reduced-precision image of the original, either through repair in a Mars lander or deliberately in a KPU, is illustrated by the way that a compiler renders machine code for the stack pointer movement around a function call.

Say the code of subroutine *foo* first decrements the stack pointer by 32 to make space for a *frame* of 8 local variables of one word (4 bytes) each on the stack. Before return from the routine, the code increments the pointer back to its original value sp_0. The following is the assembler/machine code emitted by a RISC compiler (*gcc 4.9* for MIPS):

```
foo:
addiu sp sp -32 # decrement stack pointer register by 32 (8 word frame)
...more code...
addiu sp sp 32  # restore initial stack pointer value by adding 32 again
jr ra           # jump back to return address stored in ra register
```

The 'restore ... by adding 32' calculates $sp_0 - 32 + 32$. That is a bit-pattern equivalent via the equivalence of the previous section to the intended result sp_0 but not necessarily identical to it. If sp_0 were, say, 0xb0000000, then $sp_0 - 32 + 32$ might be not 0xb0000000 but 0x12345678. Though both 0xb0000000 and 0x12345678 represent the same integer value, they are different encodings of it.

The outcome is that a different 'alias' bit-pattern of the initial stack pointer sp_0 ends up in the **sp** register. The caller gets back a pointer 0x12345678 that does not point to its own data, which was left at 0xb0000000. It restores from 0x12345678 so it will not recover the data it wrote at 0xb0000000 earlier. The following code sequence works instead:

```
foo:
move fp sp       # copy stack pointer register to fp register
addiu sp sp -32 # decrement stack pointer register by 32 (an 8 word frame)
...more code...
move sp fp       # copy stack pointer value back from fp register
jr ra            # jump back to return address stored in ra register
```

This code is not victim to the aliasing effect. It takes an extra register (**fp**) and needs an extra instruction (the initial **move**), but the old register content may first have been saved on the stack to be restored before return so it is not lost. The **fp** register may also be saved on the stack during execution of the interior code in the routine, and restored before return, so there is no loss of a slot.

How may one formally show the second code is aliasing-safe? One technique is described in [6]. There, semi-automatic decompilation [3,4] of RISC machine code to assembler code for a stack machine and its automatic validation via a Hoare logic [15] is used, and that can show that the code above (in full) is safe. The technique annotates the decompiled code in the style of verification frameworks such as VCC [10]. Where human assistance is required is in choosing between alternative decompilations of the machine code, which amounts to choosing between alternative logical rules of inference that may be applied at each point in the machine code (the different logical rules correspond to different decompilations). However, [6] shows that there are at most 32 different decompilations possible for each RISC machine code, corresponding to the different registers in which the stack pointer may reside at program start. If one assumes that the stack pointer is in the **sp** register, as is standard, then there is no ambiguity. An interesting point is that different decompilations of machine code correspond to different proofs that the machine code is safe, so while there may be several different decompilations available from point to point in the code, very few combinations of those will fit together coherently.

4   Constructing Hardware Alias-Safe Code

Another technique than validation of existing machine code after the fact is to construct the machine code to be safe in the first place, which means compiling appropriately. The validation technique of [6] establishes, inter alia, that:

(a) reads and writes of local variables within the current routine's stack frame are only by means of machine code memory load and store instructions that each address a fixed constant offset from the bottom of the frame;
(b) no read or write beyond the current routine's stack frame boundary, say to a parent frame's local variable, is attempted;
(c) no stack location is read before it is written.

Reading these criteria as a recipe for compiling machine code results in machine code that is safe against hardware aliasing by construction. Criterion (a) and (b) taken together mean there is only one way of accessing a local variable at offset 12 from the bottom of the frame. It is via a

$$\text{lw } r, 0\text{xabcd}(\textbf{fp}) \qquad \text{or} \qquad \textbf{sw } 0\text{xabcd}(\textbf{fp}), r$$

machine code instruction, respectively a load to and a store from register r, where 0xabcd is a fixed constant bit-pattern encoding the integer 12. Only one of the possible bit-patterns (aliases) representing the integer offset 12 is allowed and 0xabcd has been chosen here.

Following that recipe guarantees that every time the address of the variable is calculated during the subroutine call, it is by means of exactly the same calculation on exactly the same atomic components, namely fp + 0xabcd.[3] The integer offset encoded must be less than the frame size, so there is no possibility of accessing local variables in the parent frame from a subroutine – such accesses are often generated by compilers as optimisations [1,14]. That would amount to using two different calculations for the same intended address, which cannot be relied on to deliver the same bit-pattern.

Because the same calculation is used for the address of the local variable each time, down to the bit-patterns representing constant elements of the calculation, Axiom II of Sect. 1 applies, and the same memory location really is accessed each time, thereby avoiding hardware aliasing.

Exactly the same technique is used to access arrays:

(d) an array element may only be accessed via an explicit offset from the bottom of the array embedded in a load or store instruction, and the same bit-pattern must be used for the displacement each time, even if other bit-patterns exist that also represent the same integer offset;
(e) no access below zero or beyond the array extent may be attempted;
(f) no array element may be read before it is written.

---

[3] A more sophisticated version of this recipe relaxes the rule to allow different aliases than 0xabcd to be used provided that the same alias is always used for one write and the succeeding reads; the next write may use a different alias again.

In consequence, exactly the same calculation for the address of an array element is used each time it is needed, and Axiom II guarantees that the same memory location is accessed, avoiding aliasing.

Strings, however, are accessed via a different pattern. The idea is to use calculations for the address that have the form

$$\text{base} + 0, \ \text{base} + 1 + 0, \ \text{base} + 1 + 1 + 0, \ \ldots$$

for the consecutive elements of the string. That is done by incrementing the string pointer from the base address in constant amounts via immediate addition operations and then doing a final access via a load or store at a displacement of zero. Given that the base address of the string is in register r_1, the instruction sequence to read the second element of the string into register r_2 is

addi $r_1\ r_1$ 0xf000baaa; **addi** $r_1\ r_1$ 0xf000baaa; **lw** r_2 0xdeedd04e(r_1)

where 0xf000baaa is a bit-pattern representing the integer 1 and 0xdeedd04e is a bit-pattern representing the integer 0. That is:

(g) a string element may only be accessed by a sequence of constant increments from the base of the string, using the same bit-pattern for the increment each time, followed by a load or store instruction with displacement zero, expressed as the same constant bit-pattern each time;
(h) no access below the start of the string or beyond a null element in the string may be attempted;
(i) no string element may be read before it is written.

Because strings are set up in read-only memory during program load before the program runs, some calculation by the compiler at the time the executable file is constructed ensures that the string elements are specified at exactly that address bit-pattern where the program will look for them at runtime.

5 Example Code

A simple machine code program, safe from aliasing, that just calls 'printstr' with a string address as argument, then calls 'halt', is shown in Table 1. The reader may recognise it as a "hello world" program. It contains subroutine calls, conditionals, jumps, etc., as well as string accesses. The code was emitted by a modified standard compiler (*gcc* 4.9 for MIPS), so some compiler quirks are still visible. An address for the "hello world" string on the heap is introduced on line 7 of 'main' by the **li a0** (load immediate) instruction, which sets the **a0** ('0th argument') register for the call to 'printstr' on line 8. Execution stops in the 'halt' subroutine.

The 'main' code contains the safe-from-aliasing stack push and pop sequence described in Sect. 3. Line 1 saves the stack pointer in the frame pointer, line 2 changes the stack pointer, making a local frame in which those registers that will be clobbered by the subroutine calls can be saved (lines 3 and 4). The frame pointer itself is one of those saved registers (line 4). It is to be supposed that the called subroutines each execute a similar sequence as the 'main' program does in order to recover the value of the stack pointer that they had on entry. Therefore line 15 restores the frame pointer after the subroutine calls have returned, and line 16 moves it back into the stack pointer, reestablishing the value of the stack pointer that it had at entry to the subroutine.

Note that program addresses are here embedded 'as is' in program machine code. The processor and instruction set architecture is or should be designed so there is no calculation involved in going from the bit-pattern for an address that is embedded in a machine code jump or branch instruction to that which the fetch cycle in the processor uses to retrieve the target instruction from memory.

Table 1. Example code. For clarity the intended offsets and increments are shown, not the bit-patterns that code for them.

```
    main:
 1. move fp sp              ; copy stack pointer to frame pointer
 2. addiu sp sp -32         ; push stack for local frame
 3. sw ra 28(sp)            ; save ra in local frame
 4. sw fp 24(sp)            ; save old stack pointer in local frame
 7. li a0 <helloworld>      ; load string address
 8. jal <printstr>          ; call printstr subroutine
10. jal <halt>              ; call halt subroutine
11. nop
14. lw ra 28(sp)            ; restore ra
15. lw fp 24(sp)            ; prepare to restore old stack pointer
16. move sp fp              ; pop stack, deleting local frame
17. jr ra                   ; return
    helloworld:
    ⟨string data⟩
```

A KPU simulator based on the OpenRISC v1.1 processor (see homepage at http://opencores.org/or1k) is available at http://sf.net/p/or1ksim64kpu, and it exhibits 2^{32}-way hardware aliasing via its 32-bits-encrypted-in-64-bits architecture. A tool-chain is available at http://sf.net/p/or1k64kpu-binutils/. The OpenRISC 'or1ksim' test suite has been compiled for this KPU, and a typical arithmetic test in the suite (the 'is-add-test', for addition) comprises 205,582 executed instructions, 176,117 loaded. The test suite executes without error, which lends some empirical weight to the claim that the compilation strategy described in this paper is sound, and results in hardware aliasing-safe code.

Conclusion

In this paper, we have described a style of compilation to machine code that avoids hardware aliasing in an environment where the aliasing has *hidden determinism*. In that kind of environment, a program may choose to replay the same calculation for the same address, resulting in a unique bit-pattern being used to access that address at runtime, avoiding hardware aliasing.

A repeatable fault in a processor can be masked by regarding 'wrong' calculations as producing a bit-pattern that is an alternative to the conventional encoding of the result. Modulo an induced equivalence, conventional computer arithmetic is restored, albeit with fewer bits of precision. But the repair causes programs to exhibit hardware aliasing, because different bit-patterns intended to encode the same target address really access different memory locations. Recompiling programs in the style described here then completes the repair.

Acknowledgements. Simon Pickin's contribution to the research described in this paper has been partially supported by the Spanish MEC project ESTuDIo (TIN2012-36812-C02-01). Peter T. Breuer wishes to acknowledge the support of HecuSys Inc. (http://www.hecusys.com) in connection with KPU technology, described herein.

References

1. Allen, R., Kennedy, K.: Optimizing Compilers for Modern Architectures: A Dependence-Based Approach, vol. 289. Morgan Kaufmann, San Francisco (2002)
2. Barr, M.: Programming Embedded Systems in C and C++, 1st edn. O'Reilly & Associates Inc., Sebastopol (1998)
3. Bowen, J.P., Breuer, P.T.: Decompilation. In: van Zuylen, H. (ed.) The REDO Compendium: Reverse Engineering for Software Maintenance, chap. 10, pp. 131–138. John Wiley & Sons, Hoboken (1993)
4. Breuer, P.T., Bowen, J.P.: Decompilation: the enumeration of types and grammars. ACM Trans. Program. Lang. Syst. (TOPLAS) **16**(5), 1613–1647 (1994)
5. Breuer, P.T., Bowen, J.P.: Typed assembler for a RISC crypto-processor. In: Barthe, G., Livshits, B., Scandariato, R. (eds.) ESSoS 2012. LNCS, vol. 7159, pp. 22–29. Springer, Heidelberg (2012)
6. Breuer, P.T., Bowen, J.P.: Certifying machine code safe from hardware aliasing: RISC is not necessarily risky. In: Counsell, S., Núñez, M. (eds.) SEFM 2013. LNCS, vol. 8368, pp. 371–388. Springer, Heidelberg (2014)
7. Breuer, P.T., Bowen, J.P.: A fully homomorphic crypto-processor design. In: Jürjens, J., Livshits, B., Scandariato, R. (eds.) ESSoS 2013. LNCS, vol. 7781, pp. 123–138. Springer, Heidelberg (2013)
8. Breuer, P.T., Bowen, J.P.: Avoiding hardware aliasing: verifying RISC machine and assembly code for encrypted computing. In: Proceedings of the 25th IEEE Intlernational Symposium on Software Reliability Engineering Workshops (ISSRE 2014), 2nd IEEE International Workshop on Reliability and Security Data Analysis (RSDA 2014), pp. 365–370. IEEE, November 2014
9. Breuer, P.T., Bowen, J.P.: Towards a working fully homomorphic crypto-processor. In: Jürjens, J., Piessens, F., Bielova, N. (eds.) ESSoS. LNCS, vol. 8364, pp. 131–140. Springer, Heidelberg (2014)
10. Cohen, E., Dahlweid, M., Hillebrand, M., Leinenbach, D., Moskal, M., Santen, T., Schulte, W., Tobies, S.: VCC: a practical system for verifying concurrent C. In: Berghofer, S., Nipkow, T., Urban, C., Wenzel, M. (eds.) TPHOLs 2009. LNCS, vol. 5674, pp. 23–42. Springer, Heidelberg (2009)

11. Glosserman, P.: Quarterdeck Expanded Memory Manager: QEMM, Instant Power for 386, 486 or Pentium PCs. Quarterdeck Office Systems, Santa Monica (1985)
12. Gruhn, M., Müller, T.: On the practicability of cold boot attacks. In: 8th International Conference on Availability, Reliability and Security (ARES 2013), pp. 390–397, September 2013
13. Halderman, J.A., Schoen, S.D., Heninger, N., Clarkson, W., Paul, W., Calandrino, J.A., Feldman, A.J., Appelbaum, J., Felten, E.W.: Lest we remember: cold-boot attacks on encryption keys. Commun. ACM **52**(5), 91–98 (2009)
14. He, J., Bowen, J.P.: Specification, verification and prototyping of an optimized compiler. Formal Aspects Comput. **6**(6), 643–658 (1994)
15. Hoare, C.A.R.: An axiomatic basis for computer programming. Commun. ACM **12**(10), 576–580 (1969)
16. Patterson, D.A.: Reduced instruction set computers. Commun. ACM **28**(1), 8–21 (1985)
17. Simmons, P.: Security through amnesia: a software-based solution to the cold boot attack on disk encryption. In: Proceedings of the 27th Annual Computer Security Applications Conference (ACSAC 2011), pp. 73–82. ACM, New York (2011)
18. Tsoutsos, N.G., Maniatakos, M.: The HEROIC framework: encrypted computation without shared keys. IEEE Trans. Comput. Aided Des. Integr. Circuits Syst. **34**(6), 875–888 (2015)
19. Wang, S., Hu, J., Ziavras, S.G.: On the characterization of data cache vulnerability in high-performance embedded microprocessors. In: Proceedings of the IC-SAMOS 2006: International Conference on Embedded Computer Systems: Architectures, Modeling and Simulation, pp. 14–20, July 2006

Automatic Test Data Generation Targeting Hybrid Coverage Criteria

Ahmed El-Serafy[✉], Cherif Salama, and Ayman Wahba

Computers and Systems Engineering Department,
Ain-Shams University, Cairo, Egypt
a.elserafy@ieee.org,
{cherif.salama,ayman.wahba}@eng.asu.edu.eg

Abstract. Software used in safety critical domains such as aviation and automotive has to be rigorously tested. Since exhaustive testing is not feasible, Modified Condition/Decision Coverage (MC/DC) has been introduced as an effective structural coverage alternative. However, studies have shown that complementing the test cases satisfying MC/DC to also satisfy Boundary Value Analysis (BVA) increases the bug finding rate. Hence, the industry adopted its testing processes to accommodate both. Satisfying these coverage requirements manually is very expensive and as a result many efforts were put to automate this task. Genetic algorithms (GA) have shown their effectiveness so far in this area. We propose an approach employing GA techniques and targeting hybrid coverage criteria to increase BVA in addition to MC/DC.

Keywords: Testing · Search · Genetic · MC/DC · BVA

1 Introduction

Software testing is one of the major activities conducted during any software development life cycle [1]. Testing typically consumes at least 50 % of the total costs involved [2] without adding any functionality to the product. Nevertheless, it remains the primary method through which confidence in software is achieved. Typically, testers need to formulate as many test cases as possible to locate faults in the program and to verify that fixing bugs does not introduce new ones.

In an ideal world, we would want to test every possible permutation of a program's inputs (exhaustive testing); however, even a seemingly simple program can have hundreds or thousands of possible input combinations. Complete testing of a complex application would take too long and require too many human resources to be economically feasible. Instead, coverage is used to ensure the quality of a set of tests and to measure how much testing was done. There are two types of coverage: Structural coverage and Functional coverage. Structural coverage (Sect. 2.1) focuses on how the implemented code behaves; however, it misses out what should have been implemented. On the other hand, functional coverage (Sect. 2.2) focuses on the specifications without enough visibility to touch on every piece of written code. Hence, in the industry, both types are used to complement each other. Combining them was shown to be worth the extra cost due to the increased effectiveness in bug finding [3, 4].

© Springer International Publishing Switzerland 2015
H. Fujita and G. Guizzi (Eds.): SoMeT 2015, CCIS 532, pp. 149–160, 2015.
DOI: 10.1007/978-3-319-22689-7_11

However, manually generating test cases to achieve the highest levels of coverage is very expensive in terms of time and labor. This is particularly true for safety critical domains such as in aviation [5] and automotive [6, 7]. Automated test data generation has been proposed to reduce the development costs, to improve the quality, and to increase confidence in the software under test. For instance, search based approaches; in particular the Genetic Algorithm (GA) (Sect. 2.3), have shown very high potential in this area [8, 9].

In this paper, we propose an efficient technique (Sects. 3, 4, and 5) based on GA to automatically generate test data targeting Modified Condition/Decision Coverage (MC/DC) as a structural coverage criterion and Boundary Value Analysis (BVA) as a functional coverage criterion.

2 Background

In this section, we briefly present the background concepts necessary to understand the proposed methodology.

2.1 Structural Coverage

Structural testing is a white box testing technique and as such it is based on the program's source code [10]. There are several structural coverage criteria that can be used. They vary in their complexity and effectiveness, as follows:

- Statement coverage: Measures the percentage of statements that have been tested.
- Condition[1] coverage: Measures the percentage of condition outcomes that have been tested. 100 % condition coverage means that each single condition in every decision has taken both values true and false.
- Decision[2] coverage: Measures the percentage of decision outcomes that have been tested. 100 % decision coverage implies 100 % statement coverage.
- Condition/Decision coverage: Measures the percentage of all condition outcomes and decision outcomes that have been tested. 100 % condition/decision coverage implies both 100 % condition coverage and 100 % decision coverage.
- Modified Condition/Decision coverage (MC/DC): Measures the percentage of all single condition outcomes, which *independently* affect a decision outcome that have been tested. 100 % MC/DC implies 100 % condition/decision coverage [5].
- Multiple condition coverage: Measures the percentage of combinations of all single condition outcomes within each statement that have been tested. 100 % multiple condition coverage implies 100 % MC/DC. It is also referred to as exhaustive testing.

The relation between the various coverage criteria is illustrated in Fig. 1. In this paper, we target MC/DC as a structural coverage measurement criterion; it ensures a high

---

[1] A logical expression that can be evaluated as true or false, e.g. A > B.

[2] A program point where the control flow has two or more alternative paths.

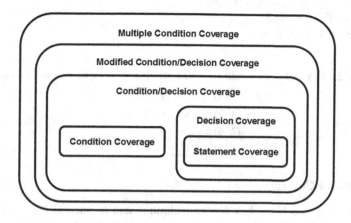

Fig. 1. The containment relation between structural coverage criteria

coverage level of control statements while maintaining relatively low testing costs. In fact, MC/DC was originally introduced by NASA [11] for airborne systems and has been widely used since then.

To further illustrate the MC/DC criterion, we provide the following decision expression as an example: (x > 0 && (y < 10 || z == 0)). The truth table of the expression is shown in Table 1.

Table 1. Truth table for the expression: (x > 0 && (y < 10 || z == 0))

Row ID	x > 0	y < 10	z == 0	Output
0	False	False	False	False
1	False	False	True	False
2	False	True	False	False
3	False	True	True	False
4	True	False	False	False
5	True	False	True	True
6	True	True	False	True
7	True	True	True	True

To systematically deduce the test cases necessary to satisfy MC/DC we need to follow these steps:

1. For each condition, extract the row pairs where only this condition's value changes and the output also changes, as illustrated in Table 2.
2. Form test sets by combining rows from each condition's pairs. Each test set must contain at least N + 1 test cases (truth table rows), where N is the number of conditions in the decision. Satisfying any of them is enough to satisfy MC/DC. As a result, we obtain the following sets:
   (a) Test set I: 3, 7, 4, 6, 5

(b) Test set II: 2, 6, 4, 5
(c) Test set III: 1, 5, 4, 6

Table 2. Row pairs per condition, where its change in value affects the output

x > 0	y < 10	z == 0
(3, 7)	(4, 6)	(4, 5)
(2, 6)		
(1, 5)		

2.2 Functional Coverage

Functional testing is a black box testing technique and as such is based on the program's specifications [10]. We focus on a couple of functional testing techniques:

- Equivalence partitioning: It is the process of dividing input domain into equivalent partitions for which the behavior of the program is assumed to be the same based on the specifications. Test cases are designed to execute representatives from each equivalence partition at least once.
- Boundary value analysis (BVA): It is the process of designing test cases based on input values lying on equivalence partitions' edges or at the smallest incremental distance on each side of each edge [12].

To further illustrate these two functional coverage criteria, we use a program that checks whether the input integer is a valid month as an example. In this example there are two equivalence partitions for inputs. The first partition consists of integers between 1 and 12 representing valid month numbers and the second partition consisting of all other integers representing invalid month numbers. For equivalence partitioning, inputs −5, 5, and 15 would be enough to test this program; however, for BVA, inputs 0, 1, 12 and 13 are additionally required as depicted in Fig. 2.

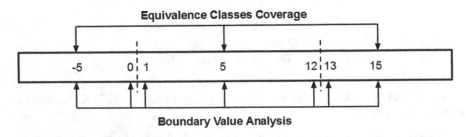

Fig. 2. Illustration of the difference between BVA and equivalence partitioning for an input representing the month to the program under test

In this paper, we target BVA as means to satisfy functional coverage. The key idea is that, statistically, developers are more likely to make mistakes at the boundaries of variables' ranges in contrast to the values lying within these ranges [13].

2.3   Genetic Algorithm

The Genetic Algorithm (GA) [14] has been extensively and successfully used to solve many software engineering optimization problems under the umbrella of Search Based Software Engineering (SBSE) [15, 16]. GA is a global search algorithm simulating the evolution cycle of individuals (known as chromosomes) in a population. The GA starts by randomly generating a set of possible solutions to a problem known as the initial population. Next, it iteratively generates more populations by probabilistically applying different evolutionary operators (such as selection, cross-over, and mutation) to the individuals of the current population. Each iteration is known as an epoch. This process is repeated until an individual corresponding to a satisfactory solution is found or until the iterations limit is reached. The GA uses a fitness function to assess how close each individual is to the optimal solution. This function may also be used by the selection operator. Figure 3 illustrates the algorithm.

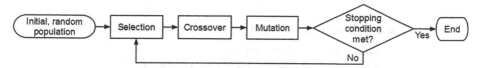

Fig. 3. Basic genetic algorithm flow chart

3   Our Approach

As stated earlier, in this paper we propose an algorithm to automatically generate test data achieving the maximum possible MC/DC and BVA coverage. Towards this goal, we extended the promising work of Awedikian et al. [8]. Awedikian et al. succeeded to automate test data generation for MC/DC using GA. In their work, they generate a set of test targets[3] for each decision and they run the GA once for each test target to find a program's input combination (test data) that satisfies the test target. Note that not all input combinations will lead to the decision under consideration to evaluate. Whether it will evaluate or not relies on data [8] and control dependencies [9]. In order to incorporate BVA, we need to extract equivalence partitions along with their boundaries and derive test targets accordingly. There are two possible ways to extract equivalence partitions in an automated framework:

1. Parse formally written specifications, if available.
2. Extract conditions from the program's source code.

Boundary Value Coverage (BVC) refers to using the latter approach to derive test cases. Since complete formal specifications are not always available, we opted to use BVC. Despite being a white box technique, BVC eventually leads to satisfying BVA provided that there is a one-to-one correspondence between all the conditions in the

---

[3] A test target corresponds to a row in the decision's truth table.

code and all the turning points in the specifications as explained below. This strict correspondence must be manually verified by the tester.

Equivalence partitions are actually abstractions of expected behavior. For example, if the predicate "temperature > 10" appears in code, it is expected that the application will behave in a certain manner if the temperature is more than 10 and differently if not. If we trace this condition back to the specifications' documents, the temperature being more than 10 must be a turning point in the application's expected behavior, or else it would be an inconsistency. It is then up to the tester to decide whether this inconsistency is a bug or just a missing piece in specifications.

Inherently, MC/DC satisfaction in its unique cause form implies weak satisfaction of equivalence partitions coverage [17]. Since this coverage is a subset of BVA, we seek to benefit from what the original algorithm [8] generates to satisfy MC/DC and complement it with the necessary test data to increase BVC. In order to do that, we map the problem of satisfying BVC to the context of GA optimization. We have to make two major adjustments to enable this:

Table 3. Test targets generated per condition adopted from [13]

Condition	Altered targets
x == y, x! = y	x == y, x == y + k^a, x == y − k
x < y, x > = y	x == y, x > y, x == y − k, x < y − k
x > y, x <= y	x == y, x < y, x == y + k, x > y + k

[a]k is the smallest incremental constant of the data type involved in the relational test

1. We alter the relational operator of each condition and its right hand side according to Table 3 [4]. This modification is done to include the boundary values of each equivalence partition. Each altered instance of the condition is added as a test target for the GA to satisfy.
2. C-like programming languages which are typically used in safety critical applications (and which we use in our work) feature short-circuiting of logical operators preventing some conditions from being evaluated. When generating the test targets associated with a certain condition as explained above, we have to ensure that the condition at hand is not masked. As a result, we derive the necessary values that all the other conditions forming the same decision should take and we add the resulting combination as a test target too.

The next section explains how all the pieces fit together forming the whole algorithm.

4   Implementation

The algorithm developed by Awedikian et al. [8] is illustrated in Fig. 4. It consists of the following steps:

1. Parsing module: Builds the abstract syntax tree (AST) of the code, extracts the decisions structure and divides it into conditions.

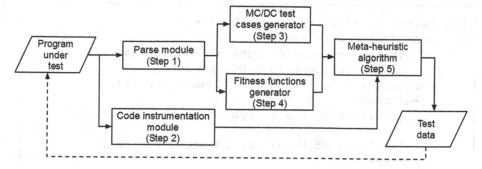

Fig. 4. Algorithm block diagram by Awedikian et al. [8]

2. Code instrumentation module: Instruments the code by probing the values used in each decision just before its execution, in order to trace the execution path of a given test datum.
3. MC/DC test cases generator: Generates the necessary test cases that would satisfy MC/DC for each decision.
4. Fitness functions generator: Generates the fitness function equation per decision in order to know how far each solution (test data) is from satisfying a certain test target, taking into account both data and control dependencies.
5. Meta-heuristic algorithm: Searches the input space using GA for a solution that satisfies each target generated from the MC/DC test cases generator, using the guidance provided by the instrumentation module and the fitness functions generated per decision.

We chose to mock the backend of the algorithm (steps 1 and 2) because our extension is only related to targeting an added coverage criterion and we used standard benchmarks (which were also used by Awedikian et al. [8]). The other steps were implemented and tuned where necessary to include BVC test targets. We used C# for implementation, along with the AForge.Net GA library [18] for the meta-heuristic search. The GA algorithm was configured as follows:

- The chromosome is an array of integers that represent the inputs.
- Input range: The whole range of 32-bit integers.
- Population size = 100.
- Iterations limit = 10000.
- Selection: Elite ranking selection where the best chromosome is moved between generations.
- Cross-over: whole arithmetic cross-over [8]. With a 70 % probability.
- Mutation: uniform mutation [8]. With a starting probability of 5 % that gradually increases to 100 %.

Figure 5 lists our algorithm's pseudo-code.

```
Population = InitializePopulation(size);
for each decision in ApplicationDecisions
  MCDCTestCases = decision.GenerateMCDCTestCases();
  for each MCDCTestCase in MCDCTestCases
    for (int i = 0; i < GAIterationsLimit; i++)
      RunEpoch();
      if(decision.Evaluate(Population.BestChromosome) ==
                                            MCDCTestCase)
        TestData.add(Population.BestChromosome);
        break;
      end if
    end for
  end for
  for each condition in decision.Conditions
    TargetDecisionPattern = decision.
                GetConditionsValuesToEvaluate(condition);
    BVCTestCases = condition.GenerateBVCTestCases();
    Population = InitializePopulation(size);
    for each BVCTestCase in BVCTestCases
      BVCTargetSatisfied = false;
      for each TestDatum in TestData
        if(decision.Evaluate(TestDatum) ==
                                    TargetDecisionPattern)
          BVCTargetSatisfied = true;
          break;
        end if
      end for
      if(BVCTargetSatisfied)
        continue;
      end if
      for (int i = 0; i < GAIterationsLimit; i++)
        RunEpoch();
        if(decision.Evaluate(Population.
            BestChromosome) == TargetDecisionPattern)
          TestData.add(Population.BestChromosome);
          break;
        end if
      end for
    end for
  end for
end for
```

Fig. 5. Pseudo-code of the algorithm

5 Experimental Results

We used the following well known benchmark applications frequently referenced in the software testing literature:

1. Triangle classification problem: Accepts three integers (a, b, and c) as its input, each of which is taken to be a triangle's side length. The values of these inputs are used to determine the type of the triangle (Equilateral, Isosceles, Scalene, or not a triangle).
2. Next date problem: A function that takes an input of three integers representing a day, a month, and a year. It returns the date of the next day.

As shown in Table 4, Figs. 6 and 7, by targeting BVC while taking the test data generated to satisfy MC/DC into account, we were able to increase BVC percentage while keeping the size of the test suite to a minimum.

The presented results are for 300 runs of the algorithm in order to avoid non-realistic biased data.

Table 4. Experimental results statistics

Problem	Next date	Triangle classification
Number of decisions	14	11
Number of MC/DC targets	34	29
Average MC/DC coverage	92.8 %	86.4 %
Maximum MC/DC coverage	97.1 %	93.1 %
Number of conditions	20	18
Number of BVC targets	67	64
Average BVC from MC/DC	55.7 %	42.6 %
Maximum BVC from MC/DC	62.7 %	50 %
Average enhanced BVC	74.9 %	66.8 %
Maximum enhanced BVC	77.6 %	71.88 %
Average increase in BVC	25.6 %	36.2 %
Average number of cumulative iterations consumed to satisfy MC/DC	62586	13593
Average cumulative iterations consumption increase required	42113	11584

6 Related Work

Testing is an activity that has been gaining more attention by researchers with different prospectives to emphasize the importance of producing quality software products [19, 20]. The area of Search Based Software Testing (SBST) as a subarea of SBSE has been studied from many perspectives in the literature. Mainly, there have been two major approaches: Meta-heuristic search and dynamic symbolic execution (DSE).

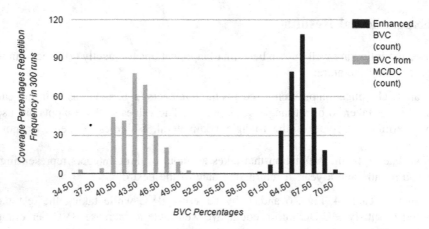

Fig. 6. Triangle classification problem BVC percentages

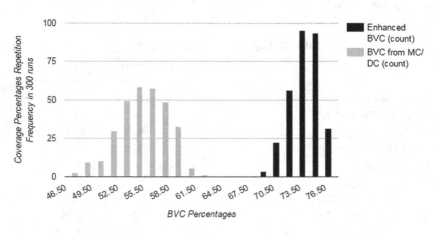

Fig. 7. Next date problem BVC percentages

DSE [21–23], although being efficient, requires deep understanding of the semantics of the written program. This level of understanding is not an easy task for C/C++ languages that use multi-level memory references. Additionally, DSE suffers from an exponential growth in paths that need to be explored rendering it impractical in many situations [24]. So we chose to go with the meta-heuristic search path due to its relative efficiency in the safety critical applications domain.

The meta-heuristic search technique itself has been subjected to many evaluations [8, 9, 16] using various search techniques. The fitness function used to evaluate the solution has evolved over the years from only containing control dependencies to including branch distance [25], control dependencies and data dependencies [8, 9].

Satisfying BVA along with a structural coverage criterion has been tackled by Pandita et al. using DSE [4]. To the best of our knowledge, this paper is the first attempt to combine structural coverage with BVA using meta-heuristics.

7   Conclusion and Future Work

We can conclude that BVA can be targeted using GA and benefit from its strengths in search for suitable test data. We also show that benefiting from the generated test data to cover MC/DC when targeting BVA massively decreases the search effort that would have been needed if we targeted BVA on its own.

We plan to explore how we can benefit from the extracted information describing each predicate's relational operator into enhancing the performance of the search algorithm. We are also planning to implement the mocked components in order to apply this enhanced algorithm in actual industrial projects to be able to measure the actual savings against real data compared to manual execution of this task.

References

1. Myers, G.J.: The Art of Software Testing, 3rd edn. Wiley, New York (2011)
2. Beizer, B.: Software Testing Techniques, 2nd edn. Thomson Computer Press, London (1990)
3. Suman, P.V., Muske, T., Bokil, P., Shrotri, U., Venkatesh, R.: Masking boundary value coverage: effectiveness and efficiency. In: 5th International Academic and Industrial Conference on Testing - Practice and Research Techniques, Windsor, UK (2010)
4. Pandita, R., Xie, T., Tillmann, N., DeHalleux, J.: Guided test generation for coverage criteria. In: ICSM (2010)
5. DO-178C: Software Considerations in Airborne Systems and Equipment Certification. RTCA, Washington, USA (2012)
6. ISO 26262: Road vehicles - Functional safety (2011)
7. IEC 61508: Functional Safety of Electrical/Electronic/Programmable Electronic Safety-related Systems (1997)
8. Awedikian, Z., Ayari, K., Antoniol, G.: MC/DC automatic test input data generation. In: GECCO, pp. 1657–1664 (2009)
9. McMinn, P.: Search-based software test data generation: a survey. Softw. Test. Verification Reliab. 14(2), 105–156 (2004)
10. ISTQB Standard Glossary of Terms used in Software testing, v.2.4. International Software Testing Qualifications Board (2014)
11. Hayhurst, K.J., Veerhusen, D.S., Chilenski, J.J., Rierson, L.K.: A Practical Tutorial on Modified Condition/Decision Coverage Report. NASA (2001)
12. Neate, B.: Boundary value analysis. Swansea University (2006). http://www.cs.swan.ac.uk/~csmarkus/CS339/dissertations/NeateB.pdf. Accessed 18 April 2015
13. Kosmatov, N., Legeard, B., Peureux, F., Utting, M.: Boundary coverage criteria for test generation from formal models. In: ISSRE, pp. 139–150 (2004)
14. Man, K.F., Tang, K.S., Kwong, S.: Genetic algorithms: concepts and applications. IEEE Trans. Industr. Electron. 43(5), 519–534 (1996)
15. Harman, M., McMinn, P., de Souza, J.T., Yoo, S.: Search based software engineering: techniques, taxonomy, tutorial. In: Meyer, B., Nordio, M. (eds.) Empirical Software Engineering and Verification. LNCS, vol. 7007, pp. 1–59. Springer, Heidelberg (2012)
16. Harman, M.: Software engineering meets evolutionary computation. IEEE Comput. 44(10), 31–39 (2011)

17. An Investigation of Three Forms of the Modified Condition Decision Coverage (MCDC) Criterion. Office of Aviation Research, Washington, USA (2001)
18. AForge.Net Library, v.2.2.5 (2013). http://www.aforgenet.com/framework/. Accessed 18 April 2015
19. Abaei, G., Selamat, A., Fujita, H.: An empirical study based on semi-supervised hybrid self-organizing map for software fault prediction. Knowl. Based Syst. **74**, 28–39 (2015)
20. Baumeister, J.: Advanced empirical testing. Knowl. Based Syst. **24**(1), 83–94 (2011)
21. Godefroid, P., Klarlund, N., Sen, K.: DART: directed automated random testing. In: PLDI, pp. 213–223 (2005)
22. Sen, K., Marinov, D., Agha, G.: CUTE: a concolic unit testing engine for C. In: ESEC/FSE, pp. 263–272 (2005)
23. Tillmann, N., de Halleux, J.: Pex–white box test generation for .NET. In: Beckert, B., Hähnle, R. (eds.) TAP 2008. LNCS, vol. 4966, pp. 134–153. Springer, Heidelberg (2008)
24. Sharma, A.: A critical review of dynamic taint analysis and forward symbolic execution. Technical report, NUS (2012)
25. Baresel, A., Sthamer, H., Schmidt, M.: Fitness function design to improve evolutionary structural testing. In: Genetic and Evolutionary Computation Conference, pp. 1329–1336 (2002)

Optimization of Generated Test Data for MC/DC

Ghada El-Sayed[(✉)], Cherif Salama, and Ayman Wahba

Computers and Systems Engineering Department, Ain-Shams University,
Cairo, Egypt
Ghada.ElSayed@ieee.org,
{Cherif.Salama,Ayman.Wahba}@eng.asu.edu.eg

Abstract. Structural coverage criteria are employed in testing according to the criticality of the application domain. Modified Condition/Decision Coverage (MC/DC) comes highly recommended by multiple standards, including, ISO 26262 and DO-178C in the automotive and avionics industries respectively. Yet, it is time and effort consuming to construct and maintain test suites that achieve high coverage percentages of MC/DC. Search based approaches were used to automate this task due to the problem complexity. Our results show that the generated test data could be minimized while maintaining the same coverage by considering that a certain test datum can satisfy multiple MC/DC test targets. This improves the maintainability of the generated test suite and saves the resources required to define their expected outputs and any part of the testing process that is repeated per test case.

Keywords: DO-178C · Search based testing · Maintainability · MC/DC · Optimization · Structural coverage

1 Introduction

Testing is a normal activity in every software development life cycle [1]. It exists in many forms: Unit testing, Integration testing, Validation... etc. Each level has its own scope, artifacts and expected results, but they are all unified in target, which is finding bugs. The earlier the bug is discovered, the less impact it has on the software under development. We are targeting the earliest phase of testing; Unit testing, in order to maximize the gain from our work.

1.1 Domain Requirements

The domain is a major factor in deciding the testing techniques to use and coverage levels to require. In safety critical applications, standards were instructed to the industry. The most commonly referenced ones are ISO 26262 [2] and DO-178C [3], meant for the automotive industry and aviation industry respectively. DO-178C defines the Modified Condition/Decision Coverage (MC/DC) specification. And both of them highly recommend or require MC/DC as a structural coverage criterion. We will explain MC/DC in details in Sect. 2.2.

© Springer International Publishing Switzerland 2015
H. Fujita and G. Guizzi (Eds.): SoMeT 2015, CCIS 532, pp. 161–172, 2015.
DOI: 10.1007/978-3-319-22689-7_12

1.2 Coverage

Coverage based testing quantifies the percentage of the software that is executed in the testing process [4], representing the degree of thoroughness of the test suite. It can be applied to any level of testing. Our concern is structural coverage which is a form of white-box testing. Structural coverage is measured against the internal structure of the program under test. Such form of testing can measure coverage at various levels, including statements, lines, blocks, conditions and functions. We target enhancing structural coverage automation. Structural coverage criteria are explained in Sect. 2.1.

This paper discusses minimizing the generated test data by exploring the subsumption relation between the generated test data to satisfy certain test cases and the other test cases in the program under test. This consequently improves the maintainability of the generated test suite. Furthermore, for each saved test case, any subsequent manual work required in documentation, expecting results and maintenance will be saved.

2 Background

In this section we summarize the basic notions used in this paper. In particular, we provide essential information on structural coverage, MC/DC, search-based software testing (SBST) and the basis on which we build our work.

2.1 Structural Coverage Criteria

There is a wide variety of structural coverage criteria that vary in their effectiveness and difficulty. Briefly, they are as follows [5]:

- Statement coverage: Every statement in the program is executed at least once.
- Decision[1] coverage: Also known as branch coverage. Every statement in the program is executed at least once, and every decision in the program has taken all possible outcomes at least once.
- Condition[2] coverage: Every condition in each decision has taken all possible outcomes at least once.
- Condition/decision coverage: Every statement in the program is executed at least once, every decision in the program has taken all possible outcomes at least once, and every condition in each decision has taken all possible outcomes at least once.
- Modified condition/decision coverage (MC/DC): Every point of entry and exit in the program has been invoked at least once, every condition and decision in the program has taken all possible outcomes at least once, and each condition has been shown to independently affect its decision's outcome.

---

[1] A decision is composed of one or multiple conditions connected by logical operators (And, Or, Not).

[2] A condition is an expression containing a relational operator.

- Multiple condition coverage: Every statement in the program is executed at least once, and all possible combinations of condition outcomes in each decision have been invoked at least once (exhaustive testing).

Table 1 summarizes the differences and commonalities between the different structural coverage criteria.

Table 1. Structural coverage criteria summary

Coverage criteria	Decision	Condition	Decision/Condition	MC/DC	Multiple condition
Entry/exit nodes	X	X	X	X	X
Decisions	X		X	X	X
Conditions		X	X	X	X
Conditions independently affect decisions				X	X
All combinations					X

Also we can compare coverage criteria according to the subsumption relation between them [6]. The relationship is defined as follows: "Criterion A is said to subsume criterion B if and only if; every test set that satisfies A also satisfies B". Decision coverage subsumes statement coverage; condition/decision coverage includes branch coverage. Figure 1 shows the subsumption hierarchy summary.

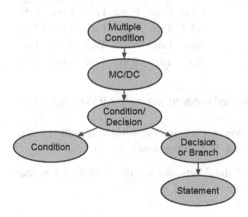

Fig. 1. Subsumption relation for structural coverage criteria

2.2 Modified Condition/Decision Coverage

The implemented programs are mostly built from combined predicates; the complexity of the expression becomes a concern in safety critical domains. MC/DC effectively tests the combined boolean expressions in comparison to simpler levels of structural coverage criteria without increasing the test cases number exponentially as it is the case in multiple conditions coverage [7]. In other words, MC/DC is a way of finding important combinations among all other combinations [8]. MC/DC could be satisfied by N + 1 test case for N basic conditions [8]. MC/DC has three criteria that must be met [7]:

(a) Every decision in the program has taken all possible outcomes at least once;
(b) Every condition in a decision has taken all possible outcomes at least once;
(c) Each condition in a decision has been shown to independently affect that decision's outcome.

How to generate MC/DC test cases systematically?

1. For each condition, we do the following steps:
    (a) Create a set.
    (b) Search for the pair of rows where only the value of this condition changes, and the rest of the conditions' values are the same.
    (c) Compare output of these 2 rows.
    (d) If the outputs do not match, add this rows pair to this condition's set.
2. MC/DC test sets are formed from the unions of pairs in each condition's set of pairs.

Example 1: A && B

This expression generates the first half of the truth table in Table 2.

Table 2. A && B and A || B truth tables

Row ID	A && B			A || B		
	A	B	O/P	A	B	O/P
0	False	False	False	False	False	False
1	False	True	False	False	True	True
2	True	False	False	True	False	True
3	True	True	True	True	True	True

Following the explained steps to generate MC/DC test cases

- The set for condition A contains the following pair: (1, 3).
- The set for condition B contains rows: (2, 3).

Taking the union of the 2 sets, we get the following test cases necessary to satisfy MC/DC: truth table rows 1, 2, and 3.

Example 2: A || B

This expression generates the second half of the truth table in Table 2.
Applying the same steps;

- The set for condition A contains the following pair: (0, 2).
- The set for condition B contains rows: (0, 1).

Taking the union of the 2 sets, we get the following test cases necessary to satisfy MC/DC: truth table rows 0, 1 and 2.

More complex expressions in more complex programs are time and labor intensive to cover using MC/DC. Hence, there have been recent efforts to automate the generation of such test data [9].

2.3 Search-Based Software Testing

Search-based software engineering (SBSE) is a reformulation of software engineering as a search problem, in which the solution to a problem is found by sampling a large search space of possible solutions [5].

SBSE has been utilized for a number of software engineering activities including test data generation [10]. Search-Based Software Testing (SBST) is the application of search optimization techniques such as Genetic Algorithms (GA) to solve problems in software testing. SBST is widely used to generate test data that satisfy a certain targeted coverage [10]. There is another technique used to automatically generate test inputs; that is Dynamic Symbolic Execution (DSE) [11–13]. DSE executes the program under test for some given test inputs and at the same time performs symbolic execution [14] in parallel to collect symbolic constraints obtained from predicates. However, DSE sometimes cannot represent the exact semantics of the program and that may cause divergence from that targeted solution [15]. Since our domain is safety critical applications, where languages with difficult semantics are used; C, C++, we target enhancing the SBST technique due to its efficiency.

2.4 Search Based Algorithms

Search based algorithms are iterative by design; they evolve to find a better solution over time. They are mostly inspired by nature, for example:

- Ant colony [16]: inspired by ants finding the shortest path between their nest and food source.
- Simulated annealing [17]: inspired by iron finding an equilibrium point in the annealing process.
- Particle swarm [18]: inspired by bird swarms and how they are guided to serve the seasonal migration cause.
- Genetic algorithms (GA) [19]: inspired by the generational evolution process and how the offspring has better survival chances.

Each of the above mentioned examples of search based algorithms has its suitable applications. The one that has proven its effectiveness in our problem is GA [20].

3 Problem Definition

Despite the automation efforts put in automation, manual work yet remains for the tester to complement, maintain, document and expect the outputs for each of the test data generated. This encouraged us to address the optimization of the generated test data. In this paper, we seek to explore the effect of the subsumption relation between test cases targeting different MC/DC objectives for different decisions in the program under test with the intention to optimize them in terms of size. The following section shows how we addressed this problem.

4 Our Approach

Looking at the literature on SBST revealed that the work done by Awedikian et al. [20] showed promising coverage percentages of MC/DC. So we decided to build our enhancement upon their approach to automatically generate test data satisfying MC/DC. The following steps summarize the original algorithm, also shown in Fig. 2:

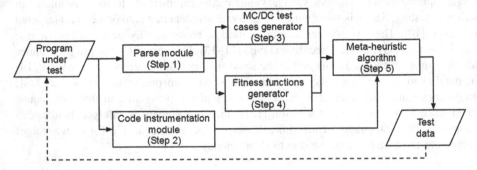

Fig. 2. Original approach components by Awedikian et al. [20]

1. Parse module: parses the program under test source code and converts it to the relevant data structures used in the developed solution.
2. Code instrumentation module: manipulates a version of the code under test to allow extracting values of variables used in each decision just before its execution.
3. MC/DC test cases generator: generates the required test sets to satisfy MC/DC per decision as we explained in Sect. 2.4.
4. Fitness function generator: runs the code under test with a given test data to evaluate their closeness to satisfy a test case target.[3] The used fitness function includes the following:
   (a) Control and data dependencies [20, 21].
   (b) Branching fitness function [22, 23].
5. Meta-heuristic algorithm: evolves/generates test data over iterations. Genetic algorithm, hill climbing and random search were all used separately, but genetic algorithms showed the best results of all.

---

[3] Each test case in the MC/DC set is targeted individually by GA, hence called "test case target".

4.1 Optimizing Generated Test Data

An extension component was added as shown in Fig. 3. It removes the redundant generated test data considering that a single generated test data may satisfy multiple test cases in different decisions. We made this enhancement in a separate component to allow its reusability later with other optimization algorithms.

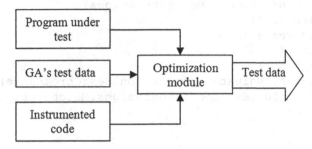

Fig. 3. Interactions of the optimization module

5 Implementation

From the components in Fig. 2, we only implemented the 3rd (MC/DC test cases generator), 4th (Fitness functions generator) and 5th (GA) components and statically simulated the other 2 components since we were targeting comparing our results relative to the results produced by the original implementation in the same environment. Here are the implementation details of our proposed enhancement:

5.1 GA Implementation

We implemented the basic GA with its standard operations [19]: crossover, mutation and selection as shown in Fig. 4. Each test target generated as described in Sect. 2.2 is set as an objective for GA to generate input test data that gets the target test case in the target decision to match.

We used GA configurations similar to the used in the original implementation [20]:

- Population size: 100.
- Uniform mutation with a starting rate of 0.05 and increased till it reaches 1 by the last generation.
- Whole-arithmetic crossover with a rate of 0.7.
- Elite ranking selection: A ranking selection where the best individual is moved between generations without changes.
- GA generations limit: 10000.

5.2 Optimizing Generated Test Data

Here, we implemented the extra component "Optimization module" as is illustrated in Fig. 5.

```
for each Decision in code_under_test.Decisions
  Decision.GenerateMCDCTests( )
  for each test_case in Decision.MCDC_tests
    generation = 0
    Initialize_Population ( )
    while (generation < max_generations)
      generation++
      Crossover ( )
      Mutate ( )
      Selection ( )
      Decision.Evaluate (population.BestChromosome)
      if(Decision.EvalConditionsValues.Match(test_case))
        Break
      end if
    end while
  end for
end for
```

Fig. 4. Pseudo code of the GA

In theory, the algorithm in Fig. 5 produces the minimal set of test cases while maintaining the exact same coverage percentage provided by the test data generated from the GA or any other meta-heuristic search implementation. This is basically done by sorting the test data according to their contribution in the overall MC/DC coverage percentage of the test suite which is represented by the counter named "NumberOf-SatisfyingTestCases" in Fig. 5. Furthermore, this algorithm can be used by other coverage criteria as well by substituting the way test targets are generated.

5.3   Technologies and Libraries Used

We are using C# to implement these algorithms. We used AForge.Net [24] library with some modifications to match our needs.

6   Experimental Results

We used the two commonly referenced benchmarks in this research domain:

- Triangle Classification program: A function that takes 3 numbers as input to determine the type of the triangle that takes these numbers as sides.
- Next Date program: A function that takes 3 numbers as input representing Day, Month and Year to calculate the date of the next day.

In order to provide realistic non-biased results, all the results we present are for 300 runs of the algorithm using the configurations listed in Sect. 5.1.

```
TestData[ ] TestDataArray = GenerateTestDataUsingGA( )
Decision[ ] Decisions = ProgUnderTest.ExtractDecisions( )
for each Decision in Decisions
  Decision.GenerateMCDCTestCases( )
end for
for each TestData in TestDataArray
  Program_under_test.Execute( TestData )
  for each Decision in Decisions
    for each TestCase in TestCases
      if(Decision.ExecutedTruthTableRow.Match(TestCase))
        TestData.NumberOfSatisfyingTestCases++
        break
      end if
    end for
  end for
end for
TestDataArray.Sort( )
for each TestData in TestDataArray
  TestData.NumberOfSatisfyingTestCases = 0
  Program_under_test.Execute( TestData )
  for each Decision in Decisions
    for each TestCase in TestCases
      if(TestCase.PreviouslySatisfied)
        continue
      end if
      if(Decision.ExecutedTruthTableRow.Match(TestCase))
        TestData.NumberOfSatisfyingTestCases++
        TestCase.PreviouslySatisfied = true
      end if
    end for
  end for
end for
TestDataArray = RemoveRedundantTestCases(TestDataArray)
```

Fig. 5. Pseudo code of the optimization algorithm used

The results obtained from our optimization are shown in Table 3 and Fig. 6. This table shows the decrease in test data count required to satisfy the same coverage percentages as the non-optimized version of test data.

The 1st and 2nd rows represent the number of decisions and MC/DC test targets in each test program. The 3rd and 4th rows represent the average and maximum reduction in generated test data from running the optimization module as explained in Fig. 5 over the original algorithm [20]. This illustrates the impact of our enhancement concerning test data count.

Table 3. The summary of obtained results from optimization

Problem	Triangle classification	Next date
Number of decisions	11	14
Number of MC/DC test targets	29	34
Average reduction in test data size after optimization	55.8 %	43.3 %
Maximum reduction in test data size after optimization	59.1 %	46.7 %

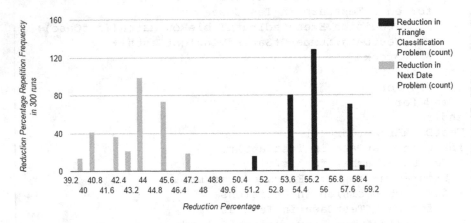

Fig. 6. Optimization percentages over the original algorithm

7 Related Work

In most evolutionary approaches for structural testing, the traditional fitness function is composed of two components: f(x) = approach level [25] + branch distance [9].

Tracey et al. [9] started by introducing the branch distance calculations for relational predicates.[4] Tracey has designed a fitness function that evaluates to zero if the relational predicate evaluates to the desired condition and will be positive otherwise. The larger the positive value, the further the test data is from achieving the desired outcome.

Then Bottaci [22, 23] extended this fitness function in 2001 and 2003. However, his approach lacked the guidance in case of dependencies. This was proposed by McMinn and Holcombe [21] in 2006 to resolve control and data dependencies by hybridizing evolutionary testing with an extended chaining approach. The chaining approach is a method which identifies statements on which the target structure is data dependent, and incrementally develops chains of dependencies in an event sequence. By incorporating this facility into evolutionary testing, the search can be directed into potentially promising, unexplored areas of the test subject's input domain.

---

[4] Predicates that consist of relational expressions connected with logical operators.

Then Awedikian et al. [20] integrated data dependencies via control dependencies in a new fitness function tailored for MC/DC, and incorporated this new fitness function into GA. Also in 2013, a workshop [26] was held about SBST that discussed the readability of test cases which directed us towards the importance of the generated test data optimization.

8 Conclusion

We can conclude from the obtained results that the proposed optimization on test data will always have a positive effect on the raw version of the generated test data. This is while maintaining the same coverage level obtained from the original algorithm, just with a smaller test suite in size. This benefits the users in many aspects, such as:

- Keeping the test suite maintainable, as the size of the test suite plays a major role in keeping it updated.
- Reducing the time required for defining the expected outputs per each generated test datum.

9 Future Work

In the future, we aim at implementing the mocked components of the algorithm in order to be able to explore its efficiency in real world projects with different data types of variables and varying inputs' sizes and search spaces.

We also aim at exploring the possibility of optimizing tests suite against an updated version of the code that it was previously designed to cover. This involves three essential steps:

- Mapping the old input/output fields to the new respective fields.
- Extract relevant test data from the old test suite.
- Complement the extracted test data with the necessary test data satisfying a specified coverage criterion.

References

1. Myers, G.J., Badgett, T., Sandler, C.: The Art of Software Testing, 3rd edn. Wiley, Hoboken (2012)
2. ISO 26262: Functional safety for road vehicles (2011)
3. DO-178C: Software Considerations in Airborne Systems and Equipment Certification. RTCA (2012)
4. Yang, Q., Li J.J., Weiss, D.: A survey of coverage based testing tools. In: International Workshop on Automation of Software Test, Shanghai, China (2006)
5. Maragathavalli, P., Anusha, M., Geethamalini, P., Priyadharsini, S.: Automatic test-data generation for modified condition/decision coverage using genetic algorithm. Int. J. Eng. Sci. Technol. 3(2), 1311–1318 (2011)

6. Sarabi, M.: Evaluation of Structural Testing Effectiveness in Industrial Model-Driven Software Development. Malardalen University, Sweden (2012)
7. Chilenski, J.J., Miller, S.P.: Applicability of modified condition/decision coverage to software testing. Softw. Eng. J. **9**(5), 193–200 (1994)
8. Pezze, M., Young, M.: Software Testing and Analysis: Process, Principles and Techniques. Wiley, Hoboken (2007)
9. Tracey, N., Clark, J., Mander, K., McDermid, J.: An automated framework for structural test-data generation. In: International Conference on Automated Software Engineering, pp. 285–288. IEEE Computer Society Press, Hawaii (1998)
10. Maragathavalli, P.: Search-based software test data generation using evolutionary computation. Int. J. Comput. Sci. Inf. Technol. **3**(1), 213–233 (2011)
11. Godefroid, P., Klarlund, N., Sen, K.: DART: directed automated random testing. In: PLDI, pp. 213–223 (2005)
12. Sen, K., Marinov, D., Agha, G.: CUTE: a concolic unit testing engine for C. In: ESEC/FSE, pp. 263–272 (2005)
13. Tillmann, N., de Halleux, J.: Pex–white box test generation for .NET. In: Beckert, B., Hähnle, R. (eds.) TAP 2008. LNCS, vol. 4966, pp. 134–153. Springer, Heidelberg (2008)
14. King, J.: Symbolic execution and program testing. Commun. ACM **19**(7), 385–394 (1976)
15. Seo, H.: A survey on dynamic symbolic execution for automatic test generation (2014). http://www.slideshare.net/hunkim/pqe-ver2-1. Accessed 18 April 2015
16. Dorigo, M., Blum, C.: Ant colony optimization theory: a survey. Theoret. Comput. Sci. **344**, 243–278 (2005)
17. Eglese, R.W.: Simulated annealing: a tool for operational research. Eur. J. Oper. Res. **46**, 271–281 (1990)
18. Bai, Q.: Analysis of particle swarm optimization algorithm. Comput. Inf. Sci. **3**(1), 180–184 (2010)
19. Melanie, M.: An Introduction to Genetic Algorithms. MIT Press, Cambridge (1999)
20. Awedikian, Z., Ayari, K., Antoniol, G.: MCDC automatic test input generation. In: 11th Annual Genetic and Evolutionary Computation Conference, GECCO 2009, pp. 1657–1664 (2009)
21. McMinn, P., Holcombe, M.: Evolutionary testing using an extended chaining approach. Evol. Comput. **14**(1), 41–64 (2006)
22. Bottaci, L.: A Genetic Algorithm Fitness Function for Mutation Testing (2001)
23. Bottaci, L.: Predicate expression cost functions to guide evolutionary search for test data. In: Cantú-Paz, E., Foster, J.A., Deb, K., Davis, L., Roy, R., O'Reilly, U.-M., Beyer, H.-G., Kendall, G., et al. (eds.) GECCO 2003. LNCS, vol. 2724. Springer, Heidelberg (2003)
24. AForge.Net Library, v.2.2.5 (2013). http://www.aforgenet.com/framework/. Accessed 18 April 2015
25. Wegener, J., Baresel, A., Sthamer, H.: Evolutionary test environment for automatic structural testing. Inf. Softw. Technol. **43**(14), 841–854 (2001)
26. Poulding S., Vos Tanja E.J.: Sixth international workshop in search-based software testing: workshop summary. In: IEEE 6th International Conference on Software Testing, Verification and Validation Workshops (2013)

Social Networks and Big Data

Hybridized Feature Set for Accurate Arabic Dark Web Pages Classification

Thabit Sabbah and Ali Selamat[✉]

Faculty of Computing, Universiti Teknologi Malaysia (UTM),
Skudai, Johor, Malaysia
Thabit.s.sabbah@gmail.com, aselamat@utm.my

Abstract. Security informatics and computational intelligence are gaining more importance in detecting terrorist activities as the extremist groups are misusing many of the available Internet services to incite violence and hatred. However, inadequate performance of statistical based computational intelligence methods reduces intelligent techniques efficiency in supporting counterterrorism efforts, and limits the early detection opportunities of potential terrorist activities. In this paper, we propose a feature set hybridization method, based on feature selection and extraction methods, for accurate content classification in Arabic dark web pages. The proposed method hybridizes the feature sets so that the generated feature set contains less number of features that capable of achieving higher classification performance. A selected dataset from Dark Web Forum Portal (DWFP) is used to test the performance of the proposed method that based on Term Frequency - Inverse Document Frequency (TFIDF) as feature selection method on one hand, while Random Projection (RP) and Principal Component Analysis (PCA) feature selection methods on the other hand. Classification results using the Support Vector Machine (SVM) classifier show that a high classification performance has been achieved base on the hybridization of TFIDF and PCA, where 99 % of F1 and accuracy performance has been achieved.

Keywords: Feature set · Terrorism detection · Dimensionality reduction · Random projection · PCA · SVM

1 Introduction

The Internet provides users with many facilities such as anonymity, inexpensive development and maintenance environment, and the huge possible audience. However these facilities are being misused by extremist groups to incite terrorism, propaganda, and fund-rising [1]. Moreover, these groups utilize various Internet data containers such as web sites, blogs, and social medias, this part of the web used by terrorists or extremist groups is referred as the Dark Web (DW) [2]. However, for more than a decade, researchers studied many different types of DW contents such as images, videos, and texts, to improve the understanding of the affinity of such groups and reveal potential terrorism. However, text content is the largest in DW collection [3] as well as in web data [4]. Therefore, many text classification based approaches were proposed to

© Springer International Publishing Switzerland 2015
H. Fujita and G. Guizzi (Eds.): SoMeT 2015, CCIS 532, pp. 175–189, 2015.
DOI: 10.1007/978-3-319-22689-7_13

detect terrorist activities from the web textual data, where data dimensionality is one of the well-known problems [5]. Even though Feature Selection (FS) and Feature Extraction (FE) methods are used to resolve the high dimensionality caused by the huge number of unique terms (words) in the corpus [6, 7] by identifying and selecting the most significant features of the feature space, still these approaches do not achieve satisfactory accuracy [4, 8, 9]. In this work, we propose a hybridized feature set that contains less number of features and capable of achieving higher detection performance.

The rest of this paper is structured as follows: Sect. 2 reviews some of the related works in terrorism detection domain. Section 3 presents the proposed hybridization method. While Sect. 4 describes the dataset and experimental setup, Sect. 5 shows and discusses the experimental results, and finally, this study is concluded in Sect. 5.

2 Related Works

Over the recent years, statistical text-classification methods have been used intensively in detecting potential terrorist activities on the web. Vector Space Model proposed by [10] is still an effective textual representation method, in which documents are presented as vectors of weighted features. The most common weighting method is the TFIDF, which is commonly used to determine the significant words (features) in the text [4]. However, statistical text representations based on features such as syntactic, lexical, stylistic [11–13], Bag of Words (BoW), n-grams [14–18], and Parts of Speech (PoS) [9] are frequently utilized in text classification approaches to detect terrorism activities. However, few studies such as [13] use combination of such features.

For example, in [18], n-gram based features were used on the level of roots, words, and characters. A set of 7,556 features was extracted from documents that have been collected from two radical international Jihadist Arabic forums. The Information Gain (IG) weighting scheme in conjunction with a Recursive Feature Elimination (RFE) technique were applied recursively for dimensionality reduction, and identifying the most appropriate and relevant features. The study aimed to measure the sentiment polarities, however, 22 % of the features were included in the final model and all sentiment classifiers demonstrated good results, with higher than 88 % accuracy in sentiment polarities, as reported by the study.

On the other hand, bi-gram, BoW, and PoS were utilized to detect racism in text, individually [9]. Greevy and Smeaton [9] applied the SVM classifier to conduct their experiments on four different datasets. It has been noted that the highest classification accuracy was achieved based on the BoW using the polynomial function as the classifier kernel.

In the manner of combined feature set based classification, [13] uses a feature set consisting of 270 features of four categories: lexical (character and word based), structural, syntactic, and content specific features, to identify the authorship of an online message in English and Chinese languages. Various statistical features were considered for different categories, such as the total number of characters and words, average word length, the total number of lines and sentences, and punctuations.

However, [13] reported the highest accuracy values (97.69 % and 83.33 %) have been achieved using SVM classifier for the English and Chinese datasets, respectively.

Similarly, a feature set of 418 features of the same categories as in [13] was extracted from bilingual (English and Arabic) documents in [11]. However, a special parser has been used to address the specific issues of Arabic language such as diacritics, word elongation, and infection. Moreover, many structural features such as hyperlinks, embedded images, and font size were also included in the feature set. Feature sets were added incrementally to two classifiers (C4.5 and SVM), however, the SVM classifier based on combined feature set performs the best in terms of accuracy (97 % and 94.83 %) on both English and Arabic datasets, respectively, as reported in the study.

As mentioned earlier, the performance of statistical methods in the domain of terrorist activities detection is reported to be insufficient [4, 8, 9] as the underlying statistical methods are unable to understand the semantics of a text. Therefore, some other techniques were proposed to overcome the deficiency of statistical methods. Knowledge-based tools that provide the conceptual hierarchy interconnections such as Wikipedia and WordNet has been utilized by [4, 19, 20], to measure the semantic relations between concepts and determine the important features. However, the improvements in classification performance have not been found to be significant relative to the existing statistical methods.

3 Proposed Method

As mentioned in Sect. 2, to resolve the dimensionality reduction of text classification, FS and FE methods are used widely to produce a reduced feature set that contains much fewer features than the original feature space. The challenging part of this procedure is finding the most relevant features without losing the accurate description of the data. Mainly, the difference between FS and FE methods lays in the procedure in which the reduced feature set is produced. FS methods are concerned with picking the most significant features to represent the feature space and produce a feature set which is a subset of the original feature space. However, FE methods are concerned with eliminating as much possible of less significant (redundant and irrelevant) features from the feature space, and usually generate a feature set that is of different dimension and not a direct subset of the original feature space.

3.1 Methodology

In this research, firstly we apply TFIDF as an FS method to generate a reduced feature set, while PCA and RP FE methods are applied to generate another reduced feature sets separately. Finally, the feature sets are hybridized by appending the reduced feature set produced by applying PCA and RP to the TFIDF feature set, separately. It is expected the hybridized feature set will overcome the problem of losing the significant data. Figure 1 shows our work process starting from the dataset preprocessing until the evaluation including the generating of proposed hybridized feature set.

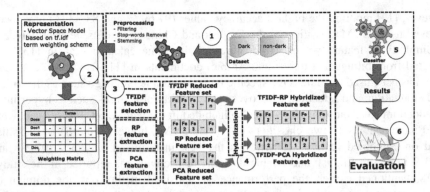

Fig. 1. Study processes.

As seen in Fig. 1, the first process in this work is the dataset preprocessing. Preprocessing includes tokenizing, filtering, stop-words removal, and stemming. In this research, tokenizing means converting document's text into an array of strings in which each string consists of one word. Filtering stands for removing non-Arabic characters, numbers, symbols, and special characters such as punctuations and Arabic diacritics. However, stop-words removal means removing the meaningless words from the text, where 450 common Arabic stop-words[1] were removed from the text. Stemming is the process of removing suffixes, prefixes and infixes from the words where the Larkey's Light Stemmer algorithm [21] is applied. Secondly, the textual data is represented using the Vector Space Model (VSM) based on the TFIDF term weighting scheme. The third process is the application of the FS and FE methods, where the TFIDF is considered in this study as an FS method, while RP and PCA are applied as an FE methods. The top features based on these methods have been selected to generate the reduced feature sets. Then in the fourth process, the reduced feature set generated based on TFIDF is hybridized with RP and PCA based feature sets individually. The hybridized feature sets will be referred as TFIDF-RP and TFIDF-PCA. Next process (process 5 in Fig. 1) is the classification process where the SVM classifier is applied, and finally the results are evaluated in process 6.

3.2 TFIDF Feature Selection Method

TFIDF is one of the most popular term weighting schemes for ranking the terms, in which the less frequent term in the collection is considered to be more significant in the document and vice versa. However, it consists of the dot product of the Term Frequency (TF) and the Inverse Document Frequency (IDF) of the term. The following formulations are used to calculate the weight of term t in document d (denoted as $TFIDF_{td}$).

$$TFIDF_{td} = \frac{fr_{td}}{\sqrt{\sum_{t \in d} fr_{td}^2}} \cdot \log\left(\frac{N}{DF_t} + 1\right) \tag{1}$$

Where fr_{td} is the raw frequency of term t in document d, N is the number of documents in the collection, and DF_t is the number of documents that the term t occurs.

TFIDF is used widely in IR domain [22], for example, it has been utilized by [23] for health professionals web information retrieval, and by [24] for effective ranking of terms, moreover, it has been used for text clustering by [25], and by [26–29] for DW analysis.

3.3 Random Projection (RP) Feature Extraction Method

RP is one of the popular efficient and simple linear dimensionality reduction techniques [30, 31]. The method of random projection uses random projection matrices to project the data into lower dimensional spaces [32]. The original data $X \in RP$ is transformed to the lower dimensional $S \in RK$ with $K < <P$ via $S = RX$, where the columns of R matrix are realizations of independent and identically distributed (i.i.d) zero-mean normal variables, normalized to have unit length. The dimensionality reduction using the random mapping method was proposed in the context of clustering text documents by Kaski [33], to diminish about 98 % of the original dimension (reduce the data dimensions from about 6000 into 100 features for the initial and the final dimensions respectively). Moreover, it has been shown empirically that results with the random projection method are comparable with results obtained with PCA [6], and take a fraction of the time that PCA requires [32, 33]. Using random projections is computationally significantly less costly than using some other dimensionality reduction methods such as PCA [6]. With a slight loss in accuracy, the random projection method computational burden can be reduced by setting the random projection matrix R values to −1 and +1, or by fixed number of ones (at random locations) while the rest of values in the matrix are zeros [32]. Details and proofs of RP and its formulation can be found in [33].

3.4 Principal Component Analysis (PCA) Feature Extraction Method

PCA is a linear dimensional reduction technique that is widely used in many fields. It was used by [34] in text classification, and image processing and neuro-science by [35, 36] respectively. As a multivariate technique, PCA reduces the dimensionality by transforming a set of possibly related data into a set of linearly uncorrelated variables known as Principal Components (PCs) [37]. In text classification, the number of features in principal components set is much less than the number of features in the original feature space. PCA transformation function is defined in such a way that the variance of each principal component is the highest possible variance considering the condition that it (i.e. the principal component) is not correlated with other components. The first principal component is the variable that has the highest possible variance.

Mathematically, PCA is an orthogonal linear transformation function that transforms data into a new coordinate system. The main purpose of PCA is to compute the most meaningful information to re-express a noisy data set. It involves the calculation of eigenvalue decompositions of a data co-variance matrix or the singular value decomposition of a data matrix, usually after mean centering the data for each attribute. Mathematical detail of PCA can be found in [30].

4   Experiments Setup

4.1   Dataset

As many of the existing studies in DW text classification such as [28, 38–43], we consider the Dark Web Forum Portal (DWFP) as the source of the experimental dataset. DWFP is the largest collection of crawled terrorist related documents, collected from 17 Arabic forums and many other forums [3] in different languages such as Russian, Dutch, French, and English. This research uses a balanced dataset consist of 1000 documents. However, this research focuses on the classification of Arabic web pages. Therefore, thousands of Arabic documents were downloaded from DWFP, and then, native Arabic domain experts examined the documents and labeled 500 documents as Dark. The experts labelled a document as dark if it contained a material related to terrorist activities such as explosives or weapons manufacturing, attack planes, bombing, and other such activities. Finally, the non-Dark documents were imported from the Open Source Arabic Corpora (OSAC) text classification dataset [44]. OSAC dataset includes documents in numerous categories such as Economy, Education, Foods, Health, History, and Religion. Figure 2 shows documents' categorized distribution of the considered dataset.

However, as in many of existing works, terrorism activities detection is considered as binary classification, in which the result is to label the document as Dark or non-Dark, Therefore, the categories of non-dark documents are not important, yet it is mentioned here to show the diversity of categories from which the dark content can be distinguished.

Though the dataset is balanced and number of documents in the dataset is seems to be relatively low, the size of feature space of this collection is high, as the total number of unique terms in the collection is 107523 terms.

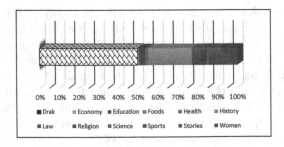

Fig. 2. Dataset categorical distribution.

4.2 Evaluation

In the domain of DW content classification, Precision, Recall, *F1*, and Accuracy are widely used in evaluating solutions and approaches [3, 4, 9, 45]. In the context of dark content classification evaluation, Precision is defined as the number dark documents correctly labeled, divided by the total number of all documents labeled as dark. While Recall is the ratio of correctly labeled dark documents to the dark document. However, *F1* measure combines precision and recall into a single measurement that attributes equal importance to both of them [46], and Accuracy evaluates the "correctness" of the technique. In DW classification, the following terms are used to indicate the corresponding definitions:

- True Positive (TP): Number of *dark* documents labeled correctly by the classifier.
- False Positive (FP): Number of *non-dark* documents labeled incorrectly as *dark* by the classifier.
- True Negative (TN): Number of *non-dark* documents labeled correctly by the classifier.
- False Negative (FN): Number of *dark* documents labeled incorrectly as *non-dark* by the classifier.

The evaluation measures are calculated as in Eqs. 2-5:

$$\text{Precision} = |TP| \, / \, (|TP| + |FP|) \tag{2}$$

$$\text{Recall} = |TP| \, / \, (|TP| + |FN|) \tag{3}$$

$$F1 = 2 \times (\text{Precision} \times \text{Recall}) \, / \, (\text{Precision} + \text{Recall}) \tag{4}$$

$$\text{Accuracy} = (|TP| + |TN|) \, / \, (|TP| + |FP| + |FN| + |TN|) \tag{5}$$

5 Experiments and Results Discussions

As mentioned before, this study proposes a feature set hybridization method that is capable to produce a reduced feature set for achieving higher content classification performance, based on TFIDF as FS method and RP and PCA as FE methods. Therefore, we conducted many experiments to find out the smallest (in term of the number of features) feature set that can achieve the highest performance. In the experiments, the *10*-fold cross validation method is applied, where the data is divided into 10 mutual exclusive (equal or approximately equal) subsets (known as folds) [47], and then the classification process was run for 10 rounds. In each round, the classifier uses 9 folds as training data and the remaining fold as testing data, however, a specific fold could not be used for testing more than once. The results of each round are saved, and then merged together to get the final classification results. The main results of these experiments are discussed in the following consecutive subsections.

5.1   TFIDF Based Results

In this experiment, classification performance has been measured using the top 15000 features based on TFIDF feature selection method as shown in Fig. 3. The highest performance (in terms of F1 and Accuracy measures) has been achieved based on 13000 features in the feature set. Yet, the number of features has been increased up to 30000 features, but the performance shows no increase. However, the number of features in this feature set is huge, and the performance is still needed to be enhanced.

From Fig. 3, it is seen that the performance based on number of features less than 1000 features, is very poor. However, because we are focusing on reducing the number of features, the results based on the top TFIDF 500 features are shown in Table 1.

Results in Table 1 show generally low classification performance in terms of F1 and accuracy. However, on the one hand, high Recall values and low Precision values are recorded while using 200 features and more, yet, on the other, low Recall values and high Precision values are achieved while using less than 200 features.

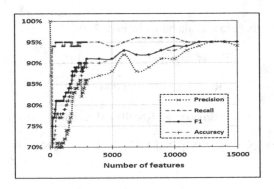

Fig. 3. TFIDF based classification performance results for to 15000 features.

Table 1. TFIDF based classification performance results top 500 features

Number of features	Precision %	Recall %	F1 %	Accuracy %
100	87.0	7.0	13.0	53.0
150	66.0	35.0	45.0	58.0
200	63.0	93.0	75.0	70.0
250	65.0	94.0	77.0	71.0
300	65.0	94.0	77.0	72.0
350	65.0	94.0	77.0	72.0
400	66.0	94.0	78.0	73.0
450	68.0	94.0	79.0	75.0
500	70.0	95.0	81.0	77.0

5.2   RP Based Results

In RP based experiment, the feature space was reduced to a series of feature sets of sizes 50 to 500 features (in 50 features interval). The classification performance based on these feature sets is illustrated in Fig. 4.

As seen in Fig. 4, a low-performance classification is achieved based on 50 features; however, the performance increases gradually as the number of features increases. The highest classification performance in terms of F1 and Accuracy (87 %) is achieved on the level of 400 features, and no more classification performance increment is seen as the increase in the number of features. Yet, even the number of features is relatively low, classification performance measures are needed to be enhanced.

In comparison to the TFIDF results based on 500 features (results from Table 1 and Fig. 4), it is noticeable that the classification performance of RP much higher than TFIDF based classification.

5.3   PCA Based Results

As discussed in Sect. 3, PCA technique reduces the feature space by transforming it into a set PCs. In this experiment, our feature space, which consists of 107523 features, is reduced to 939 features which the number of PCs; Fig. 5 shows the accumulated loading factor and the classification performance of the reduced feature set.

Figure 5 (a) shows that the first 50 features (PCs) of the reduced feature set generated by PCA FE method represent about 35 % of the original feature space. However, the first PC represents around 0.04 of the data while the first five PCs represent approximately one percent of the data, which means that the data is reduced by 99 %. Whereas, the classification performance based on the first 50 PCs, which is shown in Fig. 5 (b) shows that the classification performance (in terms of F1 and Accuracy) based on the first 50 PCs is between 88 % and 93 %, which is higher than the RP classification results (based on 500 features) shown if Fig. 4. However, in comparison to TFIDF based classification, the PCA results based on 50 PCs is approximately equal to TFIDF results using around 10000 features.

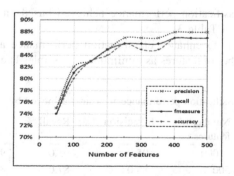

Fig. 4. RP based classification performance (500 feature).

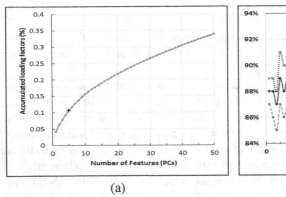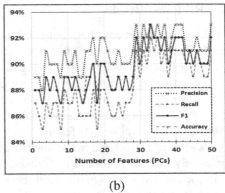

(a)   (b)

Fig. 5. Accumulative loading factor (a) and classification performance (b) of first 50 PCs.

Table 2. Classification performance results based on first 450 Pcs

Number of features	Accumulative Loading Factor	Precision %	Recall %	F1 %	Accuracy %
50	0.3387	94.0	92.0	93.0	93.0
150	0.5633	92.0	91.0	92.0	92.0
250	0.6943	91.0	90.0	91.0	91.0
350	0.7851	92.0	91.0	91.0	91.0
450	0.8535	94.0	93.0	93.0	93.0

However, there is no more enhancement in classification performance if more PCs are included in the classification, Table 2 shows the classification results based on 50 to 450 PCs, where the first 450 PCs represents more than 85 % of the original feature space.

5.4   Hybridized Feature Sets Based Results

So far, the highest classification performance achieved based on individual methods can be summarized as in Table 3.

However, the aim is to enhance classification performance as much as possible while keeping the number of features as minimum as possible, Therefore, on one hand,

Table 3. Highest classification performance measures achieved by individual methods

Feature set generating method	Number of features	Precision %	Recall %	F1 %	Accuracy %
TFIDF	13000	95.0	95.0	95.0	95.0
RP	500	88.0	87.0	87.0	87.0
PCA	50	94.0	92.0	93.0	93.0

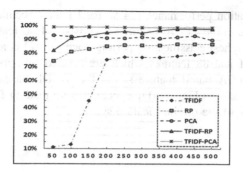

Fig. 6. Classification F1 performance for individual and hybridized feature sets.

the RP based feature set was hybridized to TFIDF based feature set by direct appending. On the other hand, the PCA feature set was hybridized to TFIDF based feature set. Figure 6 shows the classification results in term of F1 based on feature sets consisting of 50 to 500 features. However, the hybridized feature sets TFIDF-PCA and TFIDF-RP contain all the features of both feature sets. For example, the hybridized feature set TFIDF-PCA based on 50 features for each of the two feature sets (i.e. TFIDF and PCA) consists of 100 features, which are the summation of the number of features of TFIDF and PCA feature sets.

It is noticeable in Fig. 6 that F1 classification performance of the hybridized feature sets is higher than any of individual feature set based classification. Moreover, the hybridized feature set TFIDF-PCA outperforms the TFIDF-RP feature set where the F1 based on TFIDF-PCA feature set is 99 % for all feature sets consisting of 50 to 500 features.

Based on the results in Fig. 6, further experiment has been conducted to find out the minimum number of features in TFIDF-PCA feature set that can maintain the achieved classification performance. Therefore, one feature from PCA feature set is appended to TFIDF feature set, gradually. Figure 7 shows the results of this experiment, where it is

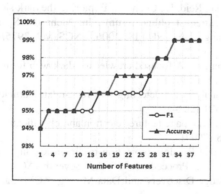

Fig. 7. TFIDF-PCA feature set performance with different number of PCs

seen that the classification performance (94 % for F1 and Accuracy) is achieved by appending the first PC to the TFIDF feature set consists of 50 features.

From Fig. 7, the highest classification performance (99 %) is achieved based on a feature set consists of just 88 features which are formed by appending the first 33 features (PCs) from PCA based feature set to the TFIDF based feature set of 50 features. However, as seen in Fig. 5 (a) the accumulative loading factor of the first 33 features is about 28 % of the original feature space.

6   Conclusions

This paper proposes feature set hybridization method, based on existing FS and FE methods. The TFIDF FS method is utilized to generate a reduced feature set, which is in turn individually hybridized with feature sets generated based on RP and PCA FE methods. From the results, it can be concluded that the achieved classification performance depending on the small hybridized feature set (in terms of number of features) based on TFIDF and PCA is outperforming individual feature sets and the hybridized feature set TFIDF-RP. Our future work will focus on testing the proposed method on the general text classification problem and evaluating its performance by benchmarking using different classifiers and common datasets.

Acknowledgment. The Universiti Teknologi Malaysia (UTM) and Ministry of Education Malaysia under Research University grants 00M19, 02G71 and 4F550 are hereby acknowledged for some of the facilities that were utilized during the course of this research work. Moreover, The Al-Quds Open University – Palestine is acknowledged for supporting and funding the first author during his PhD study.

References

1. Abbasi, A., Chen, H.: Affect intensity analysis of dark web forums. In: Proceedings of the 2007 IEEE International Conference on Intelligence and Security Informatics (ISI 2007). IEEE, New Brunswick (2007)
2. Zhou, Y., Qin, J., Lai, G., Reid, E., Chen, H.: Exploring the dark side of the web: collection and analysis of U.S. extremist online forums. In: Mehrotra, S., Zeng, D.D., Chen, H., Thuraisingham, B., Wang, F.-Y. (eds.) ISI 2006. LNCS, vol. 3975, pp. 621–626. Springer, Heidelberg (2006)
3. Fu, T., Abbasi, A., Chen, H.: A focused crawler for dark web forums. J. Am. Soc. Inf. Sci. Technol. **61**(6), 1213–1231 (2010)
4. Choi, D., et al.: Text analysis for detecting terrorism-related articles on the web. J. Netw. Comput. Appl. **38**, 16–21 (2014)
5. Selamat, A., Omatu, S.: Web page feature selection and classification using neural networks. Inf. Sci. **158**(1), 69–88 (2004)
6. Bingham, E., Mannila, H.: Random projection in dimensionality reduction: applications to image and text data. In: Proceedings of the Seventh ACM SIGKDD International Conference on Knowledge Discovery and Data Mining. ACM, San Francisco (2001)

7. Lee, Z.-S., et al.: Enhance term weighting algorithm as feature selection technique for illicit web content classification. In: Proceedings of the Eighth International Conference on Intelligent Systems Design and Applications (ISDA 2008). IEEE, Kaohsiung (2008)
8. Ran, L., Xianjiu, G.: An improved algorithm to term weighting in text classification. In: Proceedings of the International Conference on Multimedia Technology (ICMT), Ningbo, China (2010)
9. Greevy, E., Smeaton, A.F.: Classifying racist texts using a support vector machine. In: Proceedings of the 27th Annual International ACM SIGIR Conference on Research and Development in Information Retrieval. ACM, Sheffield (2004)
10. Salton, G., Wong, A., Yang, C.: A vector space model for automatic indexing. Commun. ACM **18**(11), 613–620 (1975)
11. Abbasi, A., Chen, H.: Applying Authorship Analysis to Extremist-Group Web Forum Messages. IEEE Intell. Syst. **20**(5), 67–75 (2005)
12. Abbasi, A., Chen, H.: Writeprints: a stylometric approach to identity-level identification and similarity detection in cyberspace. ACM Trans. Inform. Syst. **26**(2), 7 (2008)
13. Zheng, R., et al.: A framework for authorship identification of online messages: Writing-style features and classification techniques. J. Am. Soc. Inf. Sci. Technol. **57**(3), 378–393 (2006)
14. Chen, H.: IEDs in the dark web: genre classification of improvised explosive device web pages. In: Proceedings of the 2008 IEEE International Conference on Intelligence and Security Informatics (ISI 2008). IEEE, Taipei (2008)
15. Tianjun, F., Chun-Neng, H., Hsinchun, C.: Identification of extremist videos in online video sharing sites. In: Proceedings of the 2009 IEEE International Conference on Intelligence and Security Informatics (ISI 2009). IEEE, Dallas (2009)
16. Huang, C., Fu, T., Chen, H.: Text-based video content classification for online video-sharing sites. J. Am. Soc. Inform. Sci. Technol. **61**(5), 891–906 (2010)
17. Choi, D., et al.: Building knowledge domain N-Gram model for mobile devices. Inf. Int. Interdisc. J. **14**(11), 3583–3590 (2011)
18. Chen, H.: Sentiment and affect analysis of Dark Web forums: measuring radicalization on the internet. In: Proceedings of the 2008 IEEE International Conference on Intelligence and Security Informatics (ISI 2008). IEEE, Taipei (2008)
19. Hwang, M., Choi, C., Kim, P.: Automatic Enrichment of Semantic Relation Network and Its Application to Word Sense Disambiguation. IEEE Trans. Knowl. Data Eng. **23**(6), 845–858 (2011)
20. Choi, D., Kim, P.: Automatic image annotation using semantic text analysis. In: Quirchmayr, G., Basl, J., You, I., Xu, L., Weippl, E. (eds.) CD-ARES 2012. LNCS, vol. 7465, pp. 479–487. Springer, Heidelberg (2012)
21. Larkey, L.S., Ballesteros, L., Connell, M.E.: Light Stemming for Arabic Information Retrieval. In Soudi, A., van den Bosch, A., Neumann, G. (eds.) Arabic Computational Morphology, pp. 221–243. Springer, Netherlands (2007)
22. Chianga, D.-A., et al.: The Chinese text categorization system with association rule and category priority. Expert Syst. Appl. **35**(1–2), 102–110 (2008)
23. Ting, S.L., See-To, E.K., Tse, Y.K.: Web information retrieval for health professionals. J. Med. Syst. **37**(3), 1–14 (2013)
24. Paik, J.H.: A novel TF-IDF weighting scheme for effective ranking. In: Proceedings of the 36th International ACM SIGIR Conference on Research and Development in Information Retrieval. ACM, Dublin (2013)
25. Iezzi, D.F.: Centrality Measures for Text Clustering. Commun. Stat. Theory Methods **41**(16–17), 3179–3197 (2012)

26. Alghamdi, H.M., Selamat, A.: Topic detections in Arabic Dark websites using improved Vector Space Model. In: Proceedings of the 4th Conference on Data Mining and Optimization (DMO 2012). IEEE, Langkawi (2012)
27. Elovici, Y., Shapira, B., Last, M., Zaafrany, O., Friedman, M., Schneider, M., Kandel, A.: Content-based detection of terrorists browsing the web using an Advanced Terror Detection System (ATDS). In: Kantor, P., Muresan, G., Roberts, F., Zeng, D.D., Wang, F.-Y., Chen, H., Merkle, R.C. (eds.) ISI 2005. LNCS, vol. 3495, pp. 244–255. Springer, Heidelberg (2005)
28. L'Huillier, G., et al.: Topic-based social network analysis for virtual communities of interests in the dark web. In: Proceedings of the ACM SIGKDD Workshop on Intelligence and Security Informatics (ISI-KDD 2010). Association for Computing Machinery, Washington, DC (2010)
29. Yang, L., et al.: Discovering Topics from Dark Websites. In: Proceedings of the 2009 IEEE Symposium on Computational Intelligence in Cyber Security (CICS). IEEE, Nashville (2009)
30. Fodor, I.: A Survey of Dimension Reduction Techniques (2002)
31. Kabán, A., Durrant, R.J.: Dimension-Adaptive bounds on compressive FLD classification. In: Jain, S., Munos, R., Stephan, F., Zeugmann, T. (eds.) ALT 2013. LNCS, vol. 8139, pp. 294–308. Springer, Heidelberg (2013)
32. Kohonen, T., et al.: Self organization of a massive document collection. IEEE Trans. Neural Networks 11(3), 574–585 (2000)
33. Kaski, S.: Dimensionality reduction by random mapping: Fast similarity computation for clustering. In: Proceedings of the 1998 IEEE International Joint Conference on Neural Networks, IEEE World Congress on Computational Intelligence. IEEE, Anchorage (1998)
34. Gabrilovich, E., Markovitch, S.: Computing semantic relatedness using Wikipedia-based explicit semantic analysis. In: Proceedings of the 20th International Joint Conference on Artifical Intelligence. Morgan Kaufmann Publishers Inc., Hyderabad (2007)
35. Kwang In, K., Franz, M.O., Scholkopf, B.: Iterative kernel principal component analysis for image modeling. IEEE Trans. Pattern Anal. Mach. Intell. 27(9), 1351–1366 (2005)
36. Baldi, P., Hornik, K.: Neural networks and principal component analysis: Learning from examples without local minima. Neural Networks 2(1), 53–58 (1989)
37. Jolliffe, I.T.: Principal Component Analysis. Springer Series in Statistics. Springer, New York (2002)
38. Anwar, T., Abulaish, M.: Identifying cliques in dark web forums - An agglomerative clustering approach. In: Proceedings of the 2012 IEEE International Conference on Intelligence and Security Informatics (ISI 2012). IEEE, Washington, DC (2012)
39. Rios, S.A., Munoz, R.: Dark web portal overlapping community detection based on topic models. In: Proceedings of the ACM SIGKDD Workshop on Intelligence and Security Informatics (ISI-KDD 2012). Association for Computing Machinery, Beijing (2012)
40. Yang, C.C., Tang, X., Gong, X.: Identifying dark web clusters with temporal coherence analysis. In: Proceedings of the 2011 IEEE International Conference on Intelligence and Security Informatics (ISI 2011). IEEE, Beijing (2011)
41. Yang, C.C., Tang, X., Thuraisingham, B.M.: An analysis of user influence ranking algorithms on Dark Web Forums. In: Proceedings of the ACM SIGKDD Workshop on Intelligence and Security Informatics (ISI-KDD 2010). Association for Computing Machinery, Washington, DC (2010)
42. Kramer, S.: Anomaly detection in extremist web forums using a dynamical systems approach. In: Proceedings of the ACM SIGKDD Workshop on Intelligence and Security Informatics (ISI-KDD 2010). Association for Computing Machinery, Washington, DC (2010)

43. Sabbah, T., Selamat, A., Selamat, M.H.: Revealing Terrorism Contents form Web Page Using Frequency Weighting Techniques. In: International Conference on Artificial Life and Robotics (ICAROB), Japan (2014)
44. Saad, M.K., Ashour, W.: OSAC: Open Source Arabic Corpora. In: Proceedings of the 6th International Conference on Electrical and Computer Systems, Lefke, Cyprus (2010)
45. Zimbra, D., Chen, H.: Scalable sentiment classification across multiple dark web forums. In: Proceedings of the 2012 IEEE International Conference on Intelligence and Security Informatics (ISI 2012). IEEE, Washington, DC (2012)
46. Man, L., et al.: Supervised and traditional term weighting methods for automatic text categorization. IEEE Trans. Pattern Anal. Mach. Intell. **31**(4), 721–735 (2009)
47. Selamat, A., Ng, C.C.: Arabic script web page language identifications using decision tree neural networks. Pattern Recogn. **44**(1), 133–144 (2011)

Accelerating Keyword Search for Big RDF Web Data on Many-Core Systems

Chidchanok Choksuchat[1], Chantana Chantrapornchai[2]($^{\boxtimes}$),
Michael Haidl[3], and Sergei Gorlatch[3]

[1] Department of Computing, Silpakorn University, Bangkok, Thailand
cchoksuchat@hotmail.com
[2] Department of Computer Engineering, Kasetsart University,
Bangkok, Thailand
fengcnc@ku.ac.th
[3] University of Muenster, Münster, Germany
{m.haidl,gorlatch}@uni-muenster.de

Abstract. Resource Description Framework (RDF) is the commonly used format for Semantic Web data. Nowadays, huge amounts of data on the Internet in the RDF format are used by search engines for providing answers to the queries of users. Querying through big data needs suitable searching methods supported by a very high processing power, because the traditional, sequential keyword matching on a semantic web server may take a prohibitively long time. In this paper, we aim at accelerating the search in big RDF data by exploiting modern many-core architectures based on Graphics Processing Units (GPUs). We develop several implementations of the RDF search for many-core architectures using two programming approaches: OpenMP for systems with CPUs and CUDA for systems comprising CPUs and GPUs. Experiments show that our approach is 20.5 times faster than the sequential search.

Keywords: Resource Description Framework (RDF) · Parallel search · Graphics Processing Unit (GPU) · CUDA · Semantic web

1 Introduction

Resource Description Framework (RDF) format has recently become a standard model for data interchange in the Semantic Web area [1]. A large number of various websites are connected using the RDF standard; they are usually called Linked Data [2] and constitute large data sources for Semantic Web. When querying big RDF data, traditional keyword matching on a one-processor web server may take a prohibitively long time.

In this paper, we aim at accelerating the search in big RDF data by exploiting modern many-core architectures based on Graphics Processing Units (GPUs). While GPUs have become inexpensive processors that can be used for general-purpose computing, the restrictions of the GPU memory hierarchy prevent a direct use of GPUs for processing big data: (1) data transfers between the GPU

© Springer International Publishing Switzerland 2015
H. Fujita and G. Guizzi (Eds.): SoMeT 2015, CCIS 532, pp. 190–202, 2015.
DOI: 10.1007/978-3-319-22689-7_14

memory and CPU may incur a high run time overhead, (2) the size of GPU memory is not large enough to hold big amounts of data. Hence, in this paper, we aim to propose a software engineering solution for the search and management of the related data transfers, taking into account the constrained memory of GPU architectures. Our method is general enough and can be applied to search any large text data, but we specifically focus on the parallel search for the RDF data [3], because it is currently the most common format for semantic web applications.

Our contributions in this paper are as follows.

1. We develop several novel parallel search algorithms using the advantages of the CUDA architecture [4] for GPU programming.
2. We analytically and experimentally study the effect of the total data size on the average searching time per keyword, the transfers' time, and the throughput, i.e. the number of keywords searched per time unit.
3. We show that searching multiple keywords simultaneously leads to reducing the average search time per keyword by utilizing many cores in GPUs and re-using the data residing in memory.

The paper is structured as follows. We proceed with the background in Sect. 2. Then in Sect. 3, the parallelization of search algorithms is presented. Section 4 presents and discusses the experimental results on a system with many cores. We summarize our findings and suggest future work in Sect. 5.

2 Background and Related Work

Resource Description Framework (RDF) is a standard data model for exchanging data on the Web that facilitates combining data of different schemas. RDF is the extension of the Web representation which uses URIs to name the relationship between things and to name the two ends of the relationship link. The linked structure is represented as a directed, labeled graph, where the edges represent named links between resources, represented by the graph nodes. The basic structure is a triple denoted by $x \xrightarrow{y} z$, where x is the *subject*, y is the relationship *predicate*, and z is the *object*. RDF enables combining the structured and semi-structured data, as well as publishing and sharing the data across different applications.

Figure 1 shows an example of a simplified RDF graph for the Thailand tourism domain area from the data set http://health-tourism.cpe.ku.ac.th/huahinonto/index.html. In the figure, the circle nodes are concept classes, the dashed circles represent classes, and the dashed arrows represent relationships which are defined outside our data set. The rounded rectangles represent the keywords related to each concept. For example, point (I) defines the relationship Hua Hin District has a type of spa, called Wellness Spa., expressed by the triple $HuaHin\_district \xrightarrow{hasTypeOfSpa} WellnessSpa$. From this RDF, one may query "List all Wellness spas." This will involve keywords Spa and Wellness, to be searched for.

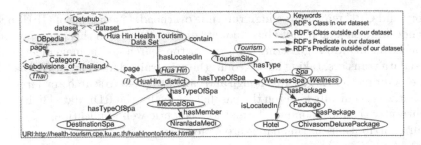

Fig. 1. Keyword samples from the health tourism domain linked to DBpedia.

Processing of large semantic web data using parallel architecture is a new and active area of research. Williams et al. [5] extract 784,783 triples from 1.6 billion triples on the IBM Blue Gene/L supercomputer and then use the BitMat system to compress the dataset in a triple store where it can be directly and efficiently queried by specific keywords on a laptop. They do not consider implementation using GPU. Falt et al. [6] presented a parallel framework Bobox providing a SPARQL query engine that utilizes the task, pipeline, and data parallelism.

Zhang et al. [7] use GPUs to accelerate the clustering algorithm for processing up to 500,000 documents on the cluster of 16 GTX280 GPUs (each with 240 cores) and observe the speedup of 30–50 times as compared to the cluster of 16 CPUs. The approach most close to ours is by Lee and Liu [8] who use 21 servers for several types of queries using hash partitioning over large RDF graphs, such as DBLP, Freebase, LUBM and SP^2Bench with maximum $1,068 \times 10^6$ triples; however, they did not use GPU. Scott et al. [9] employ GPUs for pattern matching of large data divided into blocks. Zenz et al. [10] create a system combining the keyword search with the expressivity of semantic queries and then to construct the query in a tree fashion. The authors searched the RDF data in the "Billion Triples Challenge 2009" data set of 249 GB.

In this paper, we consider data sets with up to $2,863 \times 10^6$ triples, which size is up to 400 GB, and accelerate the search using a Tesla K20c GPU with CUDA version 6.0 by utilizing both shared and global memory of the GPU.

3   Parallelising the RDF Search

We develop three versions of the RDF search algorithm as shown in Fig. 2.We start in Fig. 2(a) with the baseline sequential version. In Fig. 2(b) is the multi-threaded search using OpenMP [14]: several threads are performing the concurrent search. Both versions split the RDF data and read them in chunks, such that the keyword is searched within each chunk. Then, the results are collected and returned. The main memory of the CPU is used here. Figure 2(c) shows the implementation scheme of the search on a GPU using CUDA framework. In this version, the CPU manages the transfer of RDF data chunks, keywords and results between the CPU and GPU. The threads are created inside the GPU as *kernel threads* and are executed using both shared and global memory of GPU.

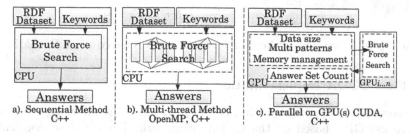

Fig. 2. The search algorithms: (a) using CPU sequentially; (b) multithreading search using OpenMP; (c) multithreading search using GPU(s).

For all algorithms presented below, the input parameters are the RDF file and the list of keywords. The output is the list of the positions found. In the following, we assume for simplicity that we have one keyword to be searched for.

In the pseudocodes of our algorithms, we use the following notation. Let n be the string length of the total text/RDF document, m be the keyword length, *dataArray* be the array storing RDF in chunks, *keywordArray* be the array in case of several keywords, *keyword* be a particular keyword to search, and *positionArray* be the array of resulting positions.

3.1 Sequential Search Algorithm

The sequential version runs the search for a keyword sequentially as shown in Algorithm 1. It reads the data chunks and then it loops through the data to match the given *keyword*.

Algorithm 1. Sequential algorithm (BFSEQ)

Input: *dataArray* and *keywordArray*
Output: Resulting positions in *positionArray*
1 **while** *not EOF* **do**
2   Read the RDF data file chunk in *dataArray*.
3   /* compare the data to *keyword* */
4   **for** $i = 0; i < n; i + +$ **do**
5   j=0
6   **while** $i < n$ *and* $j < m$ **do**
7   **if** *dataArray[i+j]* $! =$ *keyword[j]* **then**
8   **break**
9   **if** $j == m$ **then**
10   *positionArray[i]* $= true$

3.2 OpenMP Parallelization

The brute-force search version (Algorithm 1) is modified to use multi-threading by means of OpenMP. The pseudocode of Algorithm 1 is modified in Line 4 to use the OpenMP "parallel pragma" as follows:

$$\#pragma\ omp\ parallel\ for\ private(j).$$

The OpenMP version of the search algorithm is referred to as BFOMP.

3.3   First CUDA Implementation

In the sequential code of Algorithm BFSEQ, we make the following changes in order to use GPU based on the CUDA framework. The GPU version, called BFG, is shown as Algorithm 2.

Algorithm 2. Parallel search on GPU (BFG)

Input: *dataArray, keywordArray*
Output: *positionArray*
1 Allocate device memory for *dataArray, keywordArray, positionArray*.
2 **while** *not EOF* **do**
3   Read the RDF data file chunk in *dataArray*.
4   Copy *dataArray* to GPU
5   **for** *each keyword in keywordArray* **do**
6   *positionArray* (initialized to false) and copy *keyword* to GPU
7   Launch the following kernel code for threads for each *keyword*
8   **Kernel Code Begin(***Search***)**
9         $j = 0$
10   **for** $i = threadIdx$; $i < n$; $i+ = blockDim * gridDim$ **do**
11   **if** $dataArray[i] == keyword[0]$ **then**
12               $j = 1$
13   **while** $i + j < n\ and\ j < m$ **do**
14   **if** $dataArray[i+j] \neq keyword[j]$ **then**
15   **break**
16   **if** $j == m$ **then**
17               $positionArray[i] = true$
18   **Kernel Code End(***End Search***)**
19   Copy *positionArray* back to CPU and sum total positions found.
20 Free the memory.

The parallelisation is done in the manner analogous to BFOMP. In order to reduce the overhead of copying data to and from the GPU memory, the GPU kernel code works in a loop to generate more work per kernel thread and runs in a stride manner to take advantage of the memory coalescing [15]. In Line 11, each thread compares the string starting at position i. To search with multiple keywords, we iterate for each keyword in Line 5, copy the keyword to the GPU memory in Line 6, and launch GPU threads in Line 7.

3.4   Optimization: Using GPU Shared Memory

We further improve the Algorithm 2 by using the GPU shared memory; this version is called BFGSH and shown as Algorithm 3. Since the shared memory size is limited, we cannot put the whole data chunk in it. Therefore, we put a keyword in the shared memory. For simplicity, we assume that the keyword size equals to 16 elements of integer. The first 16 threads are responsible for copying the keyword to the shared memory, *s_keyword* as in Lines 10–11 in Algorithm 3. Therefore, the number of bytes transferred is in Eq. (1).

3.5   Optimization: Search with Multiple Keywords

Our further optimization is applied in case of the multiple keywords search. We copy all keywords to the shared memory of the GPU memory for a given *dataArray* inside a GPU thread in Line 4. This version is called BFGSHM (Algorithm 4).

In our example code, the number of keywords is assumed to be 8 and each keyword has the size of 16 integers. All keywords are copied at once to the GPU memory in Lines 10–12. We use the flag *match* to count the number of found keywords for *positionArray* in Line 13.

Algorithm 3. Brute-force search on a GPU with shared memory (BFGSH)

Input: *dataArray, keywordArray*
Output: *positionArray*
1 Allocate device memory for *dataArray, keywordArray, positionArray*.
2 **while** *not EOF* **do**
3 | Read the RDF data file chunk in *dataArray*.
4 | Copy *dataArray* to GPU
5 | **for** *each keyword in keywordArray* **do**
6 | | *positionArray* (initialized to false) and copy *keyword* to GPU
7 | | Launch the following kernel code for threads for each *keyword*
8 | | **Kernel Code Begin**(*Search*)
9 | | j = 0
10 | | Allocate shared memory of size int[16], called *s_keyword*.
11 | | **if** *thread_index* < 16 **then**
12 | | | *s_keyword*[*thread_index*] = *keyword*[*thread_index*]
13 | | *syncthreads*
14 | | /* The same as Lines 8-17 of Algorithm 2 **except that we use** *s_keyword* **for comparison** */
15 | | **Kernel Code End**(*End Search*)
16 | Copy *positionArray* back to CPU and sum total positions found.
17 Free the memory.

3.6   Data Transfer Analysis

In this section, we analyse the number of data transfers as the main source of overhead in the GPU-based algorithms. Our GPU algorithms attempt to bring data into the GPU memory and search keywords there. The larger the GPU memory, the larger chunk of data we can store and the fewer number of transfers are needed. Thus, we try to allocate the global memory as large as possible to store the *dataArray*, such that the number of transfers is reduced.

We denote the total number of transfers between the CPU memory and the GPU memory by N_{base}; it consists of: the transfer of all RDF data in *dataArray*, the transfer of all keywords *keywordArrays*, and the transfer of *positionArray* back. Let n be the total RDF data length, c be the chunk size in CPU, k be the number of keywords. The lower bound for the transferred number of bytes is

$$N_{base} = \lceil \frac{n}{c} \rceil \times |c| + \sum_{i=1}^{p}(|k_i| + \lceil \frac{n}{c} \rceil \times |c|) \tag{1}$$

The first term in Eq. (1) depends on the number of times to copy the text from CPU memory to GPU device $\lceil \frac{n}{c} \rceil$ and the size of each chunk $|c|$. In the second term, the sum of keywords in *keywordArray* is $|k_i|$, and $\lceil \frac{n}{c} \rceil \times |c|$ is the number of bytes for copying results which return with each keyword. Note that for receiving the result positions back, the array of the same size is required. We also reserve some part of the global memory for other data. E.g., on our test system, we can allocate 1.8 GB global memory for *dataArray* and *positionArray*, i.e., we read the chunk of 0.9 GB from the RDF file. In Algorithms 2 and 3, for searching each chunk, each keyword needs to be copied to the GPU memory in the kernel code. Because in Algorithms 2 and 3 we copy every keyword in each iteration.

For Algorithm 4, we copy the *keywordArray* to the GPU once in Line 2 and the position results are accumulated at Line 17 and are transferred back once for each chunk at Line 19. Thus, the total number of transfers are reduced as in Eq. 2. Thus, the total number N_{opt} of transfers between the CPU and GPU memory, for p keywords:

$$N_{opt} = \lceil \frac{n}{c} \rceil \times |c| + \sum_{i=1}^{p} |k_i| + \lceil \frac{n}{c} \rceil \times c \times p \tag{2}$$

As we will see in the next section, the data transfer time of Algorithm 4 grows slower as compared to that of Algorithms 2 and 3.

4   Experiments

This section presents the experimental methods and results: (1) we describe the hardware platform and our benchmark data set; (2) we present the performance of the proposed algorithms regarding speedup; (3) we show the throughput of our search algorithms and we analyse the data transfer time.

4.1   Hardware Specification and Data Sets

Our test machine is based on the Intel(R) Xeon(R) CPU E5-1620 v2 @ 3.70 GHz, 64-bit, 4 CPU cores. The two GPU devices are Tesla K20c, global memory

---

Algorithm 4. Brute-force search on a GPU with shared memory for multiple keywords (BFGSHM)

Input: *dataArray, keywordArray*
Output: *positionArray*

1 Allocate device memory for *dataArray, keywordArray, positionArray.*
2 Copy *keywordArray* to GPU.
3 **while** *not EOF* **do**
4   Read the RDF data file chunk in *dataArray.*
5   Copy *dataArray* , and *positionArray* (initialized to false) to GPU
6   Launch the following kernel code for threads
7   **Kernel Code Begin**(*Search*)
8   j = 0
9   Allocate shared memory of int [16*8] called *s_keyword*
10   **if** *(thread_index < 16 ∗ 8)* **then**
11   *s_keyword[thread_index] = keywordArray[thread_index]*
12   *syncthreads*
13   match = -*total_keyword;*
14   **for** *p = 0 to total_keyword* **do**
15   //replace the global memory pointer with the shared memory pointer.
16   *keyword = s_keyword + 16 ∗ p*
17   /* Here is the same as Lines 9-17, from Algorithm 2 **except that when** *j == m,* **we update** *match + +* **and set** *positionArray[i] = match* */
18   **Kernel Code End**(*End Search*)
19   Copy *positionArray* back to CPU and sum total positions found.
20 Free the memory.

Table 1. Tested data sets.

Data Source	Size	Triples $\times 10^6$
Freebase 4/10	5.1 G	41
DBpedia 2012	44.9 G	13
Geonames	10.0 G	4.4
Freebase Weekly	80 G	633
Freebase Weekly5	400G	2,863

of 4 GB. The number of multiprocessors (SM) is 13, each with 192 CUDA cores (706 MHz) per processor, totally 2,496 cores per GPU.

All implemented programs are compiled with the NVIDIA (R) CUDA compiler, release 6.0. We use OpenMP version 3.1 on the same gcc (Ubuntu 4.8.2-19ubuntu1) 4.8.2 for the BFOMP algorithm. As our final goal is to accelerate the semantic web search, we are interested in the real-world RDF data sets. Particularly, we are experimenting with an ontology for health tourism using the RDF data from [11]. The characteristics of the RDF data are shown in Table 1.

In our experiments, we search for keywords from the ontology of Health Tourism domain. These keywords are of the total length up to 48 characters, as follows: 1 word: "thai", 2 words: "thai spa", 4 words: "thai spa huahin tourism", and 8 words: "thai spa huahin tourism health wellness massage budget". Our source code is available at https://github.com/chidcha/Parallel_Search.

4.2 Speedup

The speedup is calculated for all parallel algorithms as compared to the sequential version. We first compare the performance of BFOMP to that of BFSEQ. The measured speedups are shown in Fig. 3.

Due to the limited space, the figure reports the performance of 4 data sets with sizes as 5.1 GB, 10.0 GB, 44.9 GB and 400 GB. They have similar trends of speedup between all keywords and datasets. It is obvious that BFOMP outperforms BFSEQ. Next,the speedup of all datasets are dramatically increased for BFG over BFSEQ, i.e. accelerating the search using the GPU is better than using only CPU for both single and multiple keywords. When using shared memory (BFGSH with 128 threads), we obtain the same speedup. However, BFGSHM yields a better speedup than BFG when multiple keywords are used, due to reuse of the shared memory. When copying all keywords to the shared memory once in BFSHM, we gain the maximum speedup over BFSEQ of up to 20.48.

4.3 Search Throughput and Average Search Time

Since we are interested in productive processing of semantic queries, we evaluate throughput, i.e. the number of queries processed per time unit. In our algorithm, we deal with the query for searching many keywords simultaneously. In the following, we calculate the throughput from the total execution time.

Let $T_{overall}$ be the total execution time, composed as

$$T_{overall} = T_{transfer} + T_{searchGPU} \tag{3}$$

In our following experiments, we calculate the throughput as the number of keywords that can be searched per hour:

$$Throughput\_per\_hr = \lfloor \frac{3,600 \times \sum_{i=1}^{p} |k_i|}{T_{overall}} \rfloor \tag{4}$$

The throughputs of keyword search per hour for our algorithms are shown in Fig. 4, as obtained by using Eq. (4) for the data size 400 GB.

We can see that BFGSHM provides the maximum throughput of 414 keywords searched per hour while BFSEQ yields throughput of only 20 keyword searches per hour. On the other hand, we also compute the average time spent per keyword search. The average search time per keyword is computed as $\frac{T_{overall}}{p}$, where p is the number of keywords.

Figure 5 shows the average search time per keyword for the cases of 1, 2, 4, and 8 keywords for varying data sizes. We found that the performance of BFGSHM with 8 keywords yields the smallest average search time for all data sizes.

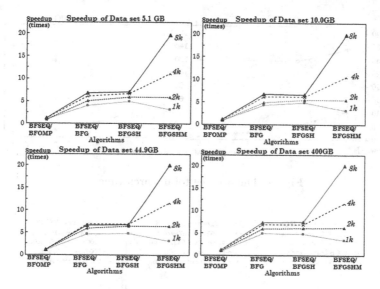

Fig. 3. Comparison of the speedup between 1, 2, 4, and 8 keywords with data size 5.1 GB, 10.0 GB, 44.9 GB and 400 GB for the chunk size = 1 MB.

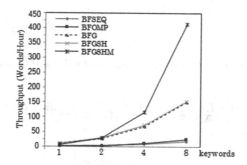

Fig. 4. The throughput of keyword search.

4.4 Transfer Time

• Figure 6 shows the search time and transfer time of two specific datasets, 80 GB and 400 GB; the solid lines show the transfer time. The figure shows the sharp growth in transfer time and search time of 1, 2, 4, 8 keywords for BFG and BFGSH due to the algorithm's behaviour as predicted by Eq. (1). However, the transfer time of BFGSHM remains constant for 1–8 keywords while the search time gradually grows up. This behaviour corresponds to Eq. (2).

We can break down the data transfer time further; $T_{transfer} = T_{data} + T_{keywords} + T_{position}$, which corresponds to the time to transfer data chunk, keywords and position results respectively. Figure 7 shows the transfer time

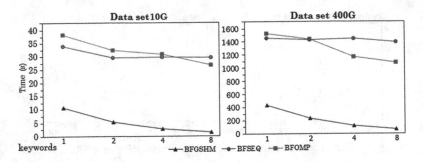

Fig. 5. The average total search time.

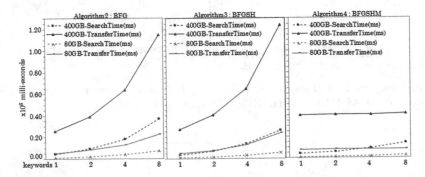

Fig. 6. The search and transfer time for data size 80 GB and 400 GB.

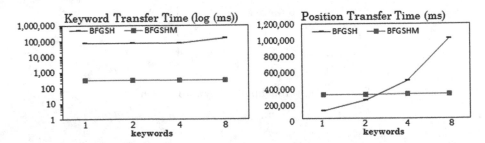

Fig. 7. The data transfer time of BFGSH and BFGSHM: data, keywords and position results varying the number of keywords for 80 GB and 400 GB data set.

of data, keywords, and positions of algorithms BFGSH and BFGSHM when searching for 1, 2, 4, and 8 keywords, in a log scale. In BFGSHM, we observe that the transfer time of the keywords is almost constant, due to the fact that we transfer all the keywords only once and put them in the shared memory. Also in BFGSHM, we accumulate the found positions for all keywords and we return the *positionArray*, specifying the number of found occurrences in each position for each data chunk only once, i.e. the time to transfer the results back is increasing linearly with the number of data chunks. In detail, this time is constant for every number of keywords, while for BFGSH it is increasing linearly with the number of keywords as implied by Eq. (2).

5 Conclusion

In this paper, we exploit the modern systems with GPU to accelerate the search in big data sets. We present parallel algorithms and we describe how to manage the data transfer for search algorithms in a large RDF file and to reuse the GPU global and shared memory for the multiple keyword search.

Our experiments compare the execution time, speedup, and throughput of our algorithms with the sequential and the multi-core version using OpenMP, when using varying number of keywords for various sizes of data files. Our fastest algorithm that uses GPU global and shared memory, BFGSHM, can optimise the transfer time and yields the speedup of 20.5 times over the sequential version. The average time per keyword search can be as low as 0.215 ms and it results in the maximum throughput of 414 keywords searched per hour. We observe that the more simultaneous keywords are searched, the more speedup and throughput are achieved.

As shown in Fig. 6, memory transfer adds a significant overhead to the search time, because of the slow connection between the GPU and the main memory. Newer technologies, e.g., NVLink [13] aim to provide a higher memory bandwidth and merge the CPU and GPU memory spaces. This will improve the performance of our approach to the big data RDF search.

In the future, we will consider other methods of GPU preprocessing, such as using the texture memory, multiple GPUs, etc. Finally, we plan to integrate our search algorithms into the reasoning process of a semantic web engine.

Acknowledgments. This work was supported by the following institutes and research programs: The Thailand Research Fund (TRF) through the Royal Golden Jubilee Ph.D. Program under Grant PHD/0005/2554, DAAD (German Academic Exchange Service) Scholarship project id: 57084841, the Faculty of Engineering at Kasetsart University Research funding contract no. 57/12/MATE, the DFG Cells-in-Motion Cluster of Excellence (EXC 1003 – CiM), University of Muenster, Germany, as well by the FP7 EU project MONICA (PIRSES-GA-2011-295222) and a hardware grant from NVIDIA Corporation.

References

1. RDF Working Group: RDF - Semantic Web Standards. http://www.w3.org/RDF/
2. Bizer, C., Heath, T., Berners-Lee, T.: Linked data: principles and state of the art. In: World Wide Web Conference (2008)
3. RDF 1.1 Test Cases. http://www.w3.org/TR/rdf11-testcases/
4. CUDA Toolkit Documentation: Programming Guide. http://docs.nvidia.com/cuda/cuda-c-programming-guide/index.html#asynchronous-concurrent-execution

5. Williams, G.T., Weaver, J., Atre, M., Hendler, J.A.: Scalable reduction of large datasets to interesting subsets. Web Semant. Sci. Serv. Agents World Wide Web **8**, 365–373 (2010)

6. Falt, Z., Cermak, M., Dokulil, J., Zavoral, F.: Parallel SPARQL query processing using bobox. Int. J. Adv. Intell. Syst. **5**, 302–314 (2012)

7. Zhang, Y., Mueller, F., Cui, X., Potok, T.: Data-intensive document clustering on Graphics Processing Unit (GPU) clusters. Data Intensive Comput. **71**, 211–224 (2011)

8. Lee, K., Liu, L.: Scaling queries over big RDF graphs with semantic hash partitioning. Proc. VLDB Endow. **6**, 1894–1905 (2013)

9. Scott, G., England, M., Melkowski, K., Fields, Z., Anderson, D.T.: GPU-based PostgreSQL extensions for scalable high-throughput pattern matching. In: 2014 22nd International Conference on Pattern Recognit (ICPR), pp. 1880–1885 (2014)

10. Zenz, G., Zhou, X., Minack, E., Siberski, W., Nejdl, W.: From keywords to semantic queries–incremental query construction on the semantic web. Web Data **7**, 166–176 (2009)

11. Choksuchat, C., Ngamphak, S., Maneesaeng, B., Chiwpreechar, Y., Chantrapornchai, C.: Parallel health tourism information extraction and ontology storage. In: 2014 11th International Joint Conference on Computer Science and Software Engineering (JCSSE), pp. 236–241 (2014)

12. RDF 1.1 N-Quads. http://www.w3.org/TR/n-quads/

13. NVIDIA NVLink TM High-Speed. http://info.nvidianews.com/rs/nvidia/images/NVIDIANVLinkHigh-SpeedInterconnectApplicationPerformanceBrief.pdf

14. OpenMP. http://openmp.org/wp/openmp-compilers/

15. Memory Coalescing. https://www.cac.cornell.edu/vw/gpu/coalesced.aspx

16. CUDA Toolkit Release Notes. http://developer.download.nvidia.com/compute/cuda/6_0/rc/docs/CUDA_Toolkit_Release_Notes.pdf

17. Kepler Tuning Guide. http://docs.nvidia.com/cuda/kepler-tuning-guide/index.html#ixzz3Uy7CMFqm

18. CUDA C Programming Guide. http://docs.nvidia.com/cuda/cuda-c-programming-guide/index.html\#axzz3Uy4AYkcS

19. NVIDIA Tesla K20 Compute Processor. http://www8.hp.com/h20195/v2/getpdf.aspx/c04111061.pdf?ver=1

Finding Target Users Interested in Regional Areas Using Online Advertising and Social Network Services

Jun Sasaki[1(✉)], Shizune Takahashi[1], Li Shuang[1], Issei Komatsu[2], Keizo Yamada[1], and Masanori Takagi[1]

[1] Faculty of Software and Information Science,
Iwate Prefectural University, Takizawa, Japan
jsasaki@iwate-pu.ac.jp
[2] Cheekit Incorporation, Takizawa, Japan
issei@cheekit.com

Abstract. There is a shift in the Japanese population from rural areas to urban areas. As a result, the economic power of rural areas is decreasing. Various combinations of information technology and tourism have been applied to preserve the historic and cultural heritage of rural areas with limited successes. One reason for this lack of success is that the relevant government or regional community does not concentrate on the target users who are interested in the area. This study proposes methods to discover the target users that are interested in regional areas. We find the target users via online advertising and social network services. The results show that our proposed methods are effective.

Keywords: Information system · Information strategy · Online advertising · Social network services · User profile

1 Introduction

Japan is experiencing a shift in its population from rural areas to urban areas [1]. This has resulted in a declining rural population and in rural areas experiencing a reduced economic strength. Such changes make it difficult for rural areas to preserve their historic and cultural heritage. It is necessary to undertake regional revitalization to resolve these issues and to re-establish rural economic strength. The Japanese government announced a regional creation plan [2] aimed toward increasing the rural population and to stimulating rural economic growth by establishing regional industries and creating rural employment.

This study focuses on the tourism industry that is expected to impart direct and early economic benefits. Tourism in this study encompasses eating out, participating in events, shopping and sightseeing. Tourism is an important economic driver and is a force for retaining historic and cultural values. The previous attempts to combine information technology with tourism to preserve the historic and cultural heritage in rural areas have had limited successes. This may be because the government or the regional community did not consider the target users who are interested in the area.

H. Fujita and G. Guizzi (Eds.): SoMeT 2015, CCIS 532, pp. 203–215, 2015.
DOI: 10.1007/978-3-319-22689-7_15

There are several destination recommendation system studies for tourists [3–7]; however, they do not clarify the target users (the tourists).

We propose methods to find the target users that are interested in regional areas. Information technology can be effectively applied in many instances. We find the target users via online advertising and social network services (SNSs). The online advertising distribution method used follows previous studies [8–11]. We undertake further online advertising distribution experiments and report the results. We use SNSs to find the target users who are interested in regional areas. We use two SNS types: a check-in service (such as Facebook and CheekiTrip[1], where users check in to the website to add material) and a photograph hosting and sharing service (in this case we use Flickr). We show that our proposed method effectively identifies the target users who are interested in regional areas.

2 Online Advertising Distribution

2.1 Online Advertising Distribution Method

The study analyzed the online advertising distribution effects and how to find the target users. Figure 1 shows the online advertising distribution method used. We created online advertisement pages containing links and submitted these to online advertising networks such as Yahoo! and Facebook. The online advertisements are distributed to users according to the rules implemented by the advertising network company. If a user clicks on a link in the online advertisement, then they visit a destination page. At the same time, the user's profile is stored in the advertising network's database. The visiting data requirements can be reported to the distributer and the data can be analyzed. The distributer can identify the destination page's target user group. This cycle is repeated until the target user group becomes clear.

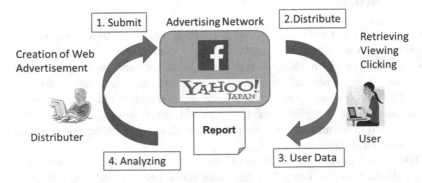

Fig. 1. Online advertising distribution method

---

[1] CheekiTrip is an SNS developed by the Cheekit Incorporation. It provides a sharing service of check-in data among friends.

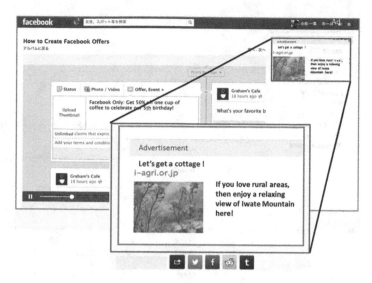

Fig. 2. Online advertisement example

Figure 2 shows an example of an online advertisement created for this study. This advertisement includes a picture, a catch phrase (*Let's get a cottage*), a short message (*If you love rural areas, then enjoy a relaxing view of Iwate Mountain here*), and a link to www.i-agri.or.jp, the Iwate Prefectural Agricultural Corporation's (the sponsor) webpage. This advertisement was distributed to Facebook users. Figure 3(a) shows the report settings that can be selected for such advertisements including the number of impressions (appearing in the user's display), the number of clicks and other items such as the user's profile data (such as access date and time, access device, location, gender and age). Figure 3(b) provides a report example. It is possible to identify the number of clicks (per session) for each user in different locations.

We carried out two experiments; the results of the first are reported in [8, 9, 11]. In the first experiment we produced online advertisements containing links to the following three Japanese websites: (1) the Iwate Prefectural Agricultural Corporation's webpage; (2) the Minamihata Area Council's webpage; and (3) a blog about living in rural Minamihata.

Regarding the advertisement's destinations, we selected the following three mediums (online advertising networks):

(i) Facebook Adverts.
(ii) Yahoo! JAPAN Promotional Ads.
  (ii-1) Sponsored Search (listing advertisement) that is related to keywords;
  (ii-2) Display Ad. (interest-matched advertisement) that is not related to keywords.

The online advertisements are evaluated according to the following criteria:

– Number of impressions (NI): the number of times that the advertisement appears on users' web browsers.

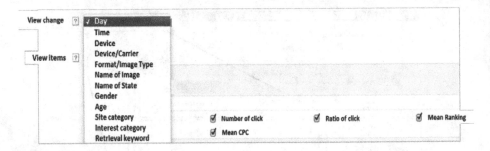

(a) Setting page of report

▲	A	B	C	D	E	F	G	H
1	Country/Area	Region	Sessions	New session	New users	Direct return	Page/Session	Mean Session
2	Japan	Tokyo	372	81.45%	303	86.83%	1.23	23.07
3	Japan	Iwate	137	29.93%	41	56.20%	1.96	193.45
4	Japan	Osaka Prefecture	92	94.57%	87	88.04%	1.27	17.95
5	Japan	Kanagawa	69	95.65%	66	86.96%	1.16	21.48
6	Japan	Aichi	60	88.33%	53	85.00%	1.28	26.73

(b) Example of report

Fig. 3. Online advertising distribution report settings and report example

- Number of clicks (NC): the number of clicks on an advertisement.
- Click-through rate (CTR): the percentage of clicks per impression:

$$CTR = NC/NI \times 100\,\%$$
(1)

The CTR is generally used to measure the effectiveness of online advertising. When the CTR is high then online advertisement is effective.

In the first experiment (Experiment 1), we delivered a total of 10 advertisements via three mediums. There was no charge for displaying the advertisements; however, they contained a charging mechanism when the links were followed (pay-per-click). The fee per click (unit price) differs depending on the medium and on the display conditions.

In Experiment 2, we wanted to evaluate cost limitations. Table 1 compares the two experiments. In Experiment 1 and Experiment 2, the cost limitations were 300 yen/day and 3,000 yen/day, respectively. However, because the research budget was limited for Experiment 2, it had fewer advertising networks and links than Experiment 1.

2.2   Online Advertising Distribution Results

The Experiment 1 results are reported in [8–11]; hence, we focus on the Experiment 2 results here and draw some comparisons with those of Experiment 1.

Figure 4 shows the change in the number of visitors (viewers) to the Minamihata Area Council's website as a result of the advertisements placed in Experiment 2.

Table 1. Experiment 1 and Experiment 2 conditions

Item	Experiment 1	Experiment 2
Period	Feb.1–28, 2014	Sep. 7–Oct. 6, 2014
Cost limitation	300 Yen/day	3,000 Yen/day
Advertising network	• Facebook Ad • Yahoo! Listing Ad • Yahoo! Display Ad	• Facebook Ad • Yahoo! Listing Ad
Link in advertise	(1) Webpage of Minamihata Area Council (2) Webpage of Iwate Prefectural Agricultural Corporation (3) Blog about living in rural areas of Minamihata (4) Facebook page of team Shizukuishi	(1) Webpage of Minamihata Area Council

The number of visitors significantly increased. The average daily visitor numbers were 10.97 in Experiment 1 and were 48.05 in Experiment 2. The cost limitations imposed in Experiment 2 were 10 times those of Experiment 1, showing a clear cost effect. It seems that there would be an optimum cost.

Figure 5 shows the relationship between the total number of visitors to the Minamihata Area Council's website and their area of domicile. These results were obtained using the free Google Analytics tool that tracks website traffic. In Experiment 1, most of the viewers were from Iwate Prefecture, followed by Tokyo and Kanagawa. In Experiment 2, most of the viewers were from Tokyo, followed by Iwate and Osaka. The cost limitations imposed in Experiment 1 may have had an impact because the visitors from Iwate Prefecture may have accessed the website early in the day (the morning) and the low daily cost limit placed on the advertisement meant that it would not appear on user browsers later in the day.

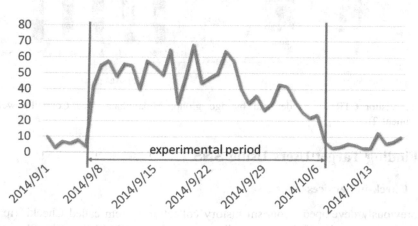

Fig. 4. Visitor numbers: Minamihara Area Council's website (Experiment 2)

Figure 6 compares the visitor CTR by (a) gender and (b) age group for the Minamihata Area Council's website in Experiment 2. The results of both experiments showed that the CTR for females and for the over-45 age group tended to be higher than for the other groups.

We can identify the target users using our proposed method; in this case they are females over the age of 45 living in Tokyo or in Iwate Prefecture.

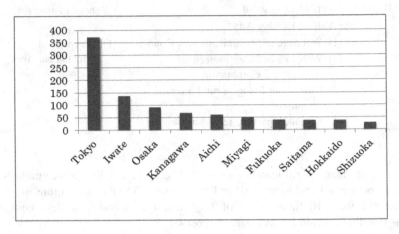

Fig. 5. Total visitor numbers by domicile area: Minamihata Area Council's website (Experiment 2)

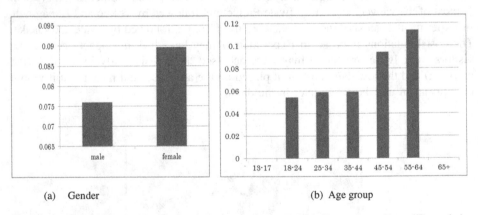

(a)   Gender   (b) Age group

Fig. 6. Visitor CTR by gender and by age group: Minamihata Area Council's website (Experiment 2)

3   Finding Target Users Using SNS

3.1   Check-in Services

We previously developed a tourism history collection system called CheekiTrip that uses a check-in service. This system collaborates with current SNSs such as Facebook and Foursquare and collects check-in and profile date from them. There are many SNSs that visitor data can be collected from. In addition to check-in services, photograph-sharing services are available to find target users and to recommend interesting places to the users. Exact recommendations could be realized by analyzing the photograph data and the check-in data to combine the visiting place data with the user profile data.

Our research approach is shown in Fig. 7. We collected visiting place data and user profile data from SNSs. The data came from photograph data and check-in data that included global positioning system (GPS) information. The user profile data included age, gender and country of residence. We then analyzed the data relationship. Finally, the data were displayed as a weighted recommendation on a map.

We used the photograph data previously collected for a tourism potential map [12].

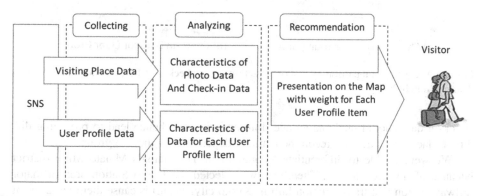

Fig. 7. Recommendation system research approach using SNS check-in data and photograph data

There, the photograph data were collected from Flickr and displayed as a heat map. We collected the check-in data from CheekiTrip.

We assessed the photograph data and check-in data numbers in a 3-km radius of Yokohama city center in Japan: in total, 6,462 photograph data from [12] and 1,071 check-in data from CheekiTrip. We compared the check-in and photograph data distribution and found that the popular (famous) spots have high check-in and photograph levels, the sightseeing (good view) spots have medium check-in levels and high photograph levels and the playing (recreation) spots have high check-in levels and medium photograph levels. We can categorize the spots using this method.

We collected and analyzed the check-in data and profile data from CheekiTrip and created a heat map to confirm the visitors' age and gender spread. Data limitations confined the age comparison to two groups: young (under 29) and mature (30–49).

Figure 8 compares the age groups using check-in data from Yokohama's Minato Mirai district (the central business district in Yokohama city, Japan) in March 2015. It shows that the young group prefers sightseeing in Minato Mirai and at the Red Brick Warehouse and the mature group prefers recreation and eating at the Anpanman Museum, the Cup Noodle Museum and in Chinatown. Analyzing the profiles of

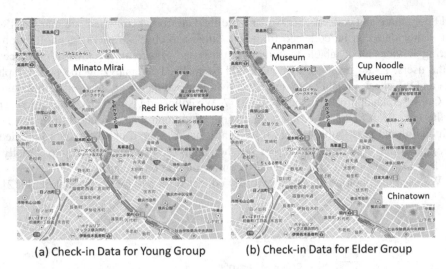

(a) Check-in Data for Young Group   (b) Check-in Data for Elder Group

Fig. 8. Age group comparison by visitor attraction using check-in data for Yokohama's Minato district (March 2015)

check-in data should facilitate an age differentiation and hence lead to providing different place and attraction recommendations depending on the age group.

We were unable to differentiate by gender in Yokohama's Minato Mirai district because of insufficient data. Therefore, we selected the Kyoto Station area (a major railway station and transportation hub in Kyoto city, Japan) because there are a lot of data relating to it, and compared the differences by gender (Fig. 9). This shows that the males focused on Kyoto Station, Kyotogoen and Heian Shrine and that the females focused on eating places such as cafes and restaurants. This result confirms that different visitor attraction recommendations should be made for each gender.

3.2   Photograph Sharing Website

The target users who are interested in regional Japanese areas are both Japanese people and foreign tourists. The Japan National Tourism Organization announced that the number of foreign travelers to Japan was over 10 million for the first time in the fiscal 2013 [12]. However, foreign travelers tend to visit popular places such as Tokyo, Kyoto and Hokkaido and are unlikely to visit the less well-known regions such as Iwate Prefecture. To resolve this, we aim to find those foreign people who are interested in regional Japanese areas. We are further attempting to develop an individually tailored recommendation system that introduces interesting but not well-known spots to foreign travelers.

There are previous recommendation system studies for foreign tourists to Japan, such as [13, 14]. That paper used the GPS data from Flickr photographs uploaded by foreigners and displayed the resulting potential recommendations on a map. However, the study did not analyze the different foreign countries involved.

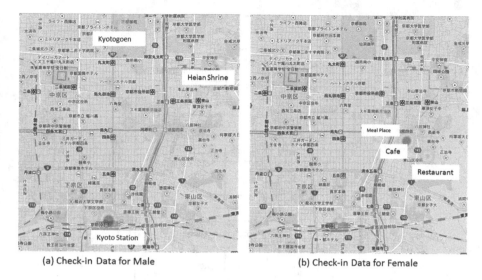

(a) Check-in Data for Male   (b) Check-in Data for Female

Fig. 9. Gender comparison by visitor attraction using check-in data for the Kyoto Station area (March 2015)

We investigated and analyzed the places of interest to foreign visitors and identified the preferences by each visitor country. For this analysis, we selected Iwate Prefecture as a case study. We collected Flickr data and we showed the differences and tendencies by photographer's country and by the photographs taken in each spot.

We are developing a prototype of the recommendation system, as shown in Fig. 10. In the system, photographs and their meta-data—including the photographer's nationality and the photograph location—can be collected from the chosen SNS photograph sharing service and the data are accumulated in the *knowledge base*. Using the knowledge base, recommended spots can be introduced for each visitor individually based on the traveler's nationality and their current location. We selected the Flickr SNS because it is currently the most popular photograph sharing service and we can use the application interface (API) to develop the prototype system. We are developing the *photograph collection and analyzing module* to collect and classify the photographer's country using PHP scripting language. We are developing the *presentation module* to show the recommendation level for each user as a heat map on the Google Maps mapping service using the JavaScript programming language.

To verify any differences between the photographer's country of origin and the number of photographs taken for each location, we manually analyzed the photograph data taken by foreigners in Iwate Prefecture. The results confirm that differences exist. For example, Chinese people took 197 Sakura (cherry blossom) photographs in Morioka Castle Ruins Park and in Kitakami city park, American people took 144 photographs of Sakura and Hiraizumi (a UNESCO World Heritage Site), British people took 35 photographs of temples in Hiraizumi, Canadian people took 87 photographs of autumn leaves in Hachimantai or at Iwate Mountain and Australian people took 40

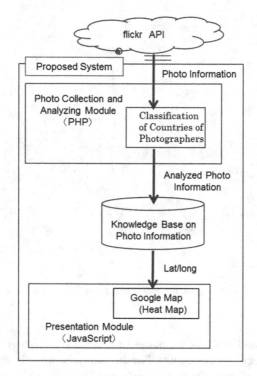

Fig. 10. Prototype recommendation system structure

photographs of ski resorts. Therefore, the proposed recommendation system is expected to be effective.

We have developed a prototype system that can automatically collect photographs from Flickr, that can classify the photographs by the photographer's country and that can display the photograph density at each spot as a heat map on Google Maps. Figure 11 shows an example of the photograph distribution in Iwate Prefecture as taken by American people.

In Iwate Prefecture, we collected over 2,000 Flickr photographs taken in March 2015 by photographer country: 875 American, 808 Chinese, 241 Canadian, 239 Australian and 170 British. We can select the relevant country using the pull down tab at the upper left corner of the display. Combining this system with the previously described methods, we can find the target users by country as well as by gender and age groups. We plan to develop an integrated system to find the target users who are interested in any regional area.

4   Future Study

The previous sections described how to find the target users who are interested in a specific region using online advertising and SNS (photographs and check-ins). We plan to apply this research to a tourism recommendation system and to a tourism strategy

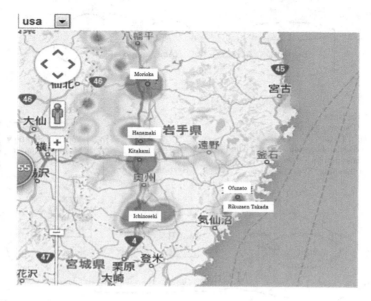

Fig. 11. Iwate Prefecture photograph distribution by American photographers obtained from the prototype system (March 2015).

making support system. Figure 12 illustrates the planned application systems that are outlined as follows.

(1) When a user visits a tour spot (A, B or C), not only the SNS data (photographs and check-in) but also the location and visit time information can be obtained from GPS data on the user's device. Further, the consumption data (such as shopping and event admissions) may also be available. Those data will be amalgamated to form a big data set.

(2) A cloud server can collect the required data from the big data and can analyze the relationship between the user characteristics data (such as gender, birth place and age) and the tour spot data. We call these data sets tourist property (TP) and tour spot property (TSP), respectively.

(3) If the analyzed result is applied to the *recommendation system*, then the system selects and introduces the tour spots from the TSP group that the specific TP group system user prefers.

(4) If the analyzed result is applied to the *tourism strategy making support system* that can be used in a city/town/village tourism office, then the system shows a target TP group who tends to visit each tour spot in the relevant city/town/village. The tourism office can implement an optimal tourism strategy to provide the appropriate services for their target tourists according to the TP groups.

To realize these application systems, the concrete items must be decided and the analyzing system's detailed algorithm must be developed. This forms our future work.

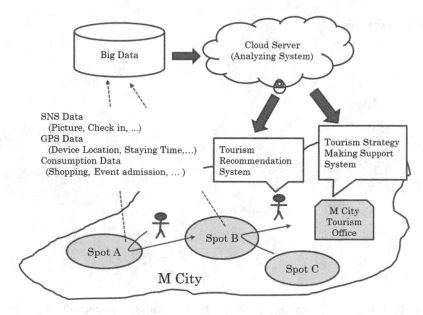

Fig. 12. Planned application systems

5 Conclusions

This paper proposed two methods to find the target users who are interested in regional areas: online advertising and SNS. An online advertisement that promoted staying in Shizukuishi town of Iwate Prefecture showed that the target users were women aged over 45 living in Tokyo or in Iwate Prefecture. This method is effective for finding people who are not strongly interested in regional areas.

To make specific recommendations, we combined the visiting place data (photograph data and check-in data) and the user profile data. This approach differentiated the photograph data distribution and the check-in data distribution. We then analyzed the check-in data from CheekiTrip to confirm the visitors' age and gender spreads. We will be able to recommend different places and attractions depending on the age group.

We developed a prototype system that can automatically collect photographs from Flickr, that can classify the photos by the photographer's country and that can display the photograph density at each spot as a heat map on Google Maps. We collected over 2,000 photos taken by foreign country people visiting Iwate Prefecture in March 2015. An analysis of the photographs showed that the number of photographs taken of specific items depended on the photographer's country.

The experimental results confirm that all of our proposed methods would be effective to find the target users interested in a regional area. As these methods have different features, it is necessary to apply the optimal method on a case-by-case basis. Future studies should investigate how to select or combine these methods and how to use other big data sets to construct a useful target user finding system and a tour recommendation system.

Acknowledgments. We would like to thank the Morioka-wide area Promotion Bureau of Iwate Prefecture, Minamihata Area Council and Shizukuishi Town Office for their cooperation with our research and experiments. We would also like to thank Minamihata Project member Takuya Sakuyama and Yuki Tetsuka of Iwate Prefectural University for their cooperation in the experiments.

References

1. Japan Policy Council. http://www.policycouncil.jp/en/index.html
2. National Governors' Association. http://www.nga.gr.jp/english/index.html
3. Cao, L., Luo, J., Gallagher, A., Jin, X., Han, J., Hauang, T.S.: A worldwide tourism recommendation system based on geotagged web photos. In: 2010 IEEE International Conference on Acoustics Speech and Signal Processing (ICASSP) (2010)
4. Tarui, Y.: Recommendation System of Tourist Site Using Collaborative Filtering Method and Contents Analysis Method. Jobu University Bulletin, vol. 36, pp. 1–14 (2011) (Japanese)
5. Okuzono, M., Hokota, M., Hirano, H., Masuko, S., Hoshino, J.: Recommendation system of sightseeing area for groups. IPSJ SIG Technical report, vol. 2015-HCI-162, No.19 (2015)
6. Togashi, J., Sugimoto, T.: An interactive sightseeing spot recommendation system using Wikipedia and Google maps. In: IPSJ General Conference No. 71, pp. 321–322 (2009)
7. Moreno, A., Valls, A., Isern, D., Marin, L., Borràs, J.: Ontology-based personalized recommendation of tourism and leisure activities. Eng. Appl. Artif. Intell. (Elsevier) **26**(1), 633–651 (2013)
8. Komatsu, I., Takagi, M., Yamada, K., Sasaki, J.: Strategy to activate rural areas using web advertising and social networks. In: The 13th International Conference on New Trends on Intelligent Software Methodologies, Tools, and Techniques (SoMeT2014), pp. 921–935 (2014)
9. Sasaki, J., Komatsu, I., Takagi, M., Yamada, K.: Effect of web advertisement for finding target users interested in rural areas. In: Fujita, H., Selamat, A. (eds.) SoMeT 2014. CCIS, vol. 513, pp. 391–403. Springer, Heidelberg (2015)
10. Komatsu, I., Yamada, K., Takagi, M., Sasaki, J.: A proposal on a tourism history collecting system using check-in services. In: Proceeding of the 2014 IEICE General Conference, D-23-4 (2014) (Japanese)
11. Sasaki, J., Sakuyama, T., Takahashi, S., Komatsu, I., Yamada, K., Takagi, M.: Regional-charm-content delivering model by using web advertisement and SNS. In: The 8th International Conference on Advanced Information Technologies (AIT), No. 221 (2014)
12. Kurata, Y.: Automatic selection of photo in photo-sharing site for making sightseeing potential map. In: 6th Research Conference on Society for Tourism Informatics (2012) (Japanese)
13. Yabe, N., Kurata, Y.: An analysis of the behavior of inbound tourists in the Tokyo Metropolitan Area from the data of IC transit cards. Theory Appl. GIS **21**(1), 35–46 (2013). (Japanese)
14. Kuarta, Y.: Toward more reliable potential maps: development of rules for automated selection of shared photos for a data source. In: 22th GIS General Conference (2013)

Semi-automatic Detection of Sentiment Hashtags in Social Networks

Gajo Petrovic[(⊠)] and Hamido Fujita

Iwate Prefectural University, Takizawa, Iwate, Japan
gajopetrovic@gmail.com, issam@iwate-pu.ac.jp

Abstract. Communication in social networks is often carried in messages of limited size, and in some cases, like Twitter, the limit is imposed by the social network itself. Therefore, it can be hard, even for a human expert, to calculate the correct sentiment based on the message alone. Sentiment hashtags present one way to help determine tweet polarity better. In this paper we present a way to semi-automatically detect sentiment hashtags from initial tweet sentiment analysis and then recalculate tweet polarity and improve accuracy. The methodology presented helps jumpstart sentiment analysis research.

Keywords: Social networks · Twitter · Sentiment analysis · Data mining

1 Introduction

In recent years we have seen an exponential increase in the number of users of social networks such as Facebook, Twitter, Google+ and similar. People have started using these now popular sites in order to share their opinions, sentiments and stories about a wide variety of topics including politics, commercial products, various activities, etc. This also provides researchers with well defined platforms to extract and analyze user sentiments from the content they publish in order to make election predictions, do product popularity tracking, measure rising trends, and similar.

With platforms such as this, a series of new issues become apparent when analyzing the texts that originated from there. In most cases, the content that needs to be processed is written almost exclusively in a natural language and is often completely unstructured. The algorithms that are capable of analyzing such input belong to the family of NLP (Natural Language Processing) algorithms, and the problems that are tackled with them, while usually solvable by human experts (still not trivial) tend to be very hard for machines. Because of this, the accuracy of such methods tends to either be very low, or the problem is reduced to a slightly simplified version, often by only looking at well written text, with correct grammar and very little or no ambiguity, irony or sarcasm.

Thankfully, many of these social networks also contain some semi-structured information present in the format of the messages, which can be of tremendous help for sentiment analysis. Example of such semi-structured data can be seen in emoticons (e.g. "John :feelinghappy:") which are chosen from a limited, predefined set, as well as sentiment hashtags [1] which are popular terms used that contain a certain sentiment towards a specific topic (e.g. "#NoNetNeutrality"). The only drawback of the sentiment

© Springer International Publishing Switzerland 2015
H. Fujita and G. Guizzi (Eds.): SoMeT 2015, CCIS 532, pp. 216–224, 2015.
DOI: 10.1007/978-3-319-22689-7_16

hashtags is that these aren't predefined in the platform, and in order to use them, they must first be identified. The identification is most often done manually, and in this paper we propose a method for a semi-automatic detection of sentiment hashtags, which should help jumpstart sentiment analysis research by automating yet another part of it.

Section 2 presents the related work. In Sect. 3 we present the proposed methodology, while in Sect. 4 we describe the dataset and in Sect. 5 present the results. Lastly, in Sect. 6 we conclude the paper.

2 Related Work

The field of sentiment analysis has been a growing, popular topic since the industry realized the potential for creating automated tools that could collect information from social networks in a cheaper way than by running direct polling, and because of the ability to cover a large and wide part of the population which would otherwise be unfeasible.

The approach to NLP has often involved rule-based methods [2], which while simplistic are often able to provide much more consistent results, as well as machine learning based approaches [3] that tend to offer slightly higher accuracy but are also often significantly more complex and might require manually labeled data.

In this paper we have explored ways of automatically detecting sentiment hashtags. This was motivated by research done in [1], where the authors used manually defined sentiment hashtags in order to track new political trends during the 2013 German elections.

Besides politics, sentiment analysis has also seen use in other domains, such as health care, and one example of this can be seen in [4], where it was used in order to analyze patient feedback, and also presents a case of a dataset that contains mostly well written text.

Recent development has also come to present a view that there is use for NLP tools which are specific to a social network [5, 6], such as is in the case of Twitter NLP [7, 8]. This is due to the slightly different grammar and vocabulary used in each platform, due to the trends and limitations of each platform (e.g. Twitter has a 140 character limit imposed for tweets which results to increased usage of Internet slang and informal abbreviations). These tools are supposed to be configured to better parse text which originates from such networks.

Additionally, there are existing knowledge bases and software libraries that contain lexical and semantic knowledge useful for extracting meaning from texts, such as WordNet [9], ConceptNet [10, 11], SenticNet [12, 13], SentiWordNet [14] and similar. The growing number of freely available tools is useful not only for the industry, but also to researchers as it provides an accessible and meaningful way to benchmark new algorithms against the state of the art.

Cold start is another issue often seen in these systems, where it is hard to make predictions about user sentiments toward specific topics due to the lack of the information available, which is often the case with new users or users that aren't very active.

There have been attempts to tackle this issues in a number of different ways such as it was done in [15, 16].

Topic detection and discovery is also an interesting field of research [1, 6] and often considered a part of the sentiment analysis process itself. The detection of the topic the sentiments are about is not trivial, and can be especially complex when multiple different topics are mentioned in the same text section (e.g. sentence). Topic discovery involves finding new and interesting subtopics related to the main topic of data mining. An example of such research can be seen in [1] where authors followed trends arising during the German election campaign.

The additional difficulty that's present in NLP in general and also sentiment analysis is the case of messages with sarcasm, irony and other ambiguous content, which have been investigated in multiple papers such as [17], but still remain largely unsolved.

3 Methodology

The main goal was to compute tweet (message) sentiments of the extracted Twitter data, and then use that information to discover sentiment hashtags. As a basis for the tweet sentiment calculation, we have used Cambria's SenticNet 3 model [13]. SenticNet introduces a *bag of concepts* model for representing sentiments, where each concept can be a sequence or one or more words. This is seen as an improvement over the basic *bag of words* model, since it can distinguish between word homonyms such as *cloud* in *cloud computing* and *cloud* in *weather cloud*.

The goal of sentiment analysis is to extract sentiment or opinion towards a specific topic from a given text. The sentiment is often described as polarity: a real value in the range [−1, 1], where higher values express positive sentiment, and lower values express the negative. In the *bag of concepts* model, each concept has a predefined sentiment defined in the SenticNet ontology. To calculate the polarity of a sentence, we use the Hourglass model [18], where sentiments are presented as in the following formula:

$$p = \sum_{i=1}^{N} \frac{Pleasantness(c_i) + |Attention(c_i)| - |Sensitivity(c_i)| + Aptitude(c_i)}{3N}$$

The four attributes: *pleasantness*, *attention*, *sensitivity* and *aptitude* are defined in an OWL[1] format in SenticNet3 for each concept, and are used to calculate the resulting polarity p.

The proposed algorithm is displayed in Fig. 1. We compute the initial tweet sentiments using just the concept extraction and sentence sentiment calculation from SenticNet 3 as mentioned above, and as an optimization, we store these results in order to optimize further calculations as the NLP methods computed in this phase take the largest amount of time in the entire process and need not be repeated.

Then, the algorithm proceeds as follows:

---

[1] OWL – Ontology Web Language http://www.w3.org/TR/owl-ref/.

1. Discover new sentiment hashtags based on tweet sentiments. This is done by looking whether certain hashtags tend to appear predominantly in tweets with positive or negative sentiments.
2. (Optional) Manually confirm the validity of the calculated hashtags. This step, while optional, can be useful in certain cases in order to increase accuracy and is what makes the process semi-automated.
3. Recalculate the tweet sentiments, now using the recently obtained sentiment hashtags. In this case, each sentiment hashtag is considered to have an impact to the polarity of the tweet which is equal to +0.5 if positive, or is −0.5 if negative. The algorithm terminates if a stopping criterion has been met (e.g. a predefined number of iterations reached, or the necessary number of sentiment hashtags obtained). Otherwise repeat from step 1.

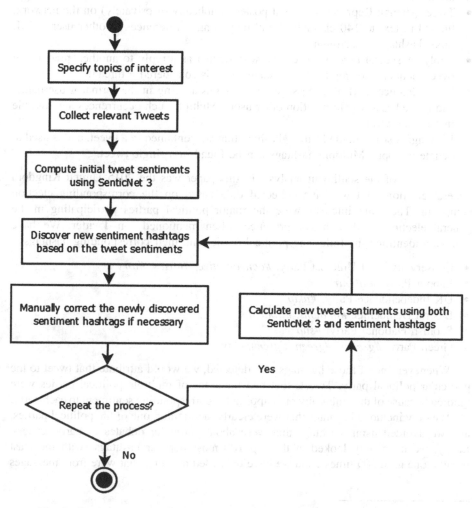

Fig. 1. Sentiment hashtag discovery and tweet sentiment recalculation algorithm

In our case, we have looked at only the 10 most popular hashtags for each topic, and assumed that sentiment hashtags were those hashtags that were predominantly positive or negative using a threshold of 85 %.

4   Dataset

To obtain the data needed for experimental evaluation of the proposed method, we have created software that collects messages posted on Twitter[2].

Firstly, we define the concepts from the Twitter Social Network relevant to this paper:

- User: Entity (human or person) that posts messages and interacts with other users on the network.
- Tweet (status): Represents content posted (publically or privately) on the network, limited in text to 140 characters, and may contain references to other users, URL links, hashtags and similar.
- Reply: A special type of tweet that was written as a reply to another, preexisting tweet. Sequence of replies to the same tweet is considered a thread.
- User reference: Part of a message that contains a string in the format @username, and is used as a way to mention other users. Multiple such occurrences are possible in a single tweet.
- Hashtag: A string in the format #hashtag that are contained in a tweet, and is used to denote its topic. Multiple hashtags can be found in a single tweet.

The topic of the sentiment analysis in this paper was the 2015 United Kingdom general election, and we have collected data based on the corresponding election campaign. The main interests were the major political parties participating in the general elections with a heavy presence (often mentioned) on Twitter. We have manually identified the following political parties and their corresponding hashtags:

- Conservative and Unionist Party: *#conservative, #tories, #tory*
- Labour Party: *#labour*
- UK Independence Party: *#ukip*
- Liberal Democrats: *#libdems, #libdem*
- Scottish National Party: *#snp*
- Green Party: *#greens, #green, #greenparty*

Whenever one of those hashtags was detected, we would attribute that tweet to the particular political party. Tweets that had mentions of multiple political parties were ignored because of the ambiguity on mapping the corresponding sentiment to each party.

We only included hashtags that were clearly mentioning one of the political parties, and we avoided using hashtags that were about particular debates or party leaders. Lastly, we have only looked at the top 100 most popular hashtags (with the least popular one used 209 times), and we have only used hashtags that were from messages

---

[2] Twitter website: https://twitter.com/.

written in English and could be properly identified as such (this is probably why there were no hashtags identified for parties from Wales and Northern Ireland).

Hashtags were considered case insensitive and we also only collected tweets that also contained the string GE2015 (whether as a hashtag: #GE2015, user mention: @GE2015 or just part of the regular text: GE2015). This was done in order to ensure the messages are directly related to the 2015 United Kingdom general elections and not to other subjects (which would likely be the case of hashtags such as #green). This task was accomplished by obtaining tweets posted under the "#GE2015" hashtag during May 2015 in the period from 15th–20th and 22nd–27th by using the Twitter Streaming API[3]. We had a local outage on the 21st and therefore no data was collected that day.

A total number of 241364 tweets have been collected related to the election, which after preprocessing was reduced to 41466. The summary of the collected data with the top 5 most popular hashtags for each topic is shown in Table 1.

Table 1. Sentiment hashtag distribution between topics.

Conservative	Labour	UKIP	Liberal	SNP	Green
voteconservative	labour	ukip	libdems	snp	greens
tories	votelabour	voteukip	ldge2015	votesnp	votegreen2015
conservative	labourdoorstep	bbcdebate	libdemmanifesto	snpout	election2015
tory	bbcdebate	ukipmanifesto	libdem	scotland	london
conservatives	labourmanifesto	farage	bigppcquiz	bbcdebate	greenparty

The distribution of tweets per party can be seen in Table 2.

Table 2. Number of tweets extracted per topic

	Conservative	Labour	UKIP	Liberal	SNP	Green
Tweets	9934	7179	6070	2777	11587	3919

Interestingly, the number of tweets per party was inconsistent with real world popularity in the opinion polls as well as the electoral results, although this is a common discrepancy present in social networks, where parties tend to appear mentioned online more often than the number of votes received on the election.

5 Results

From the 10 most popular hashtags for each topic, we have extracted those that were consistently positive or negative and came up with the following sentiment hashtags as can be seen in Table 3.

---

[3] https://dev.twitter.com/streaming/overview.

Table 3. Extracted sentiment hashtags by topic

Topic	Sentiment hashtag	Achieved threshold(%)
Conservative	VOTECONSERVATIVE	94
Conservative	CONSERVATIVE	85
Conservative	CONSERVATIVEMANIFESTO	84
SNP	SNPMANIFESTO	89
Labour	VOTELABOUR	86
Labour	LABOURDOORSTEP	92
Labour	LABOURMANIFESTO	89
Labour	NHS	87
Liberal	LIBDEMS	87
Liberal	LIBDEMMANIFESTO	87
Liberal	BIGPPCQUIZ	100
Liberal	BBCDEBATE	85
Liberal	MANIFESTO	91
Liberal	NICKCLEGG	85
UKIP	BELIEVEINBRITAIN	92
UKIP	ELECTION2015	88
Green	GREENS	90
Green	VOTEGREEN2015	88
Green	ELECTION2015	97
Green	LONDON	100
Green	GREENPARTY	87
Green	GREENSURGE	87
Green	BBCDEBATE	89
Green	GREEN	94
Green	BIGPPCQUIZ	100
Green	POLICYCHALLENGE	98

Considering the sentiment hashtags, some of them are what we would've expected intuitively, such as the VOTEPARTY hashtags. The MANIFESTO hashtags are also generally positive as they tend to mention a party's political plan. Surprisingly, there were no consistently negative and also popular hashtags detected, although this was in part because sarcasm detection is still rather limited. The green party had a lot of generally positive hashtags, mostly in part because they weren't a major contestants in the election (and thus not attacked as often), but also not particularly radical/controversial as the UKIP for example.

In order to compute the efficiency of our algorithm, we have manually labeled 200 tweets by attributing each with a positive or a negative sentiment. We have calculated the accuracy by comparing whether the sentiment computed by the algorithm matched the manually labeled sentiment. In this case, we only looked if the sign matched (e.g. by both being positive or negative), while the value itself was ignored (there was no difference between a "slightly positive" sentiment and a "greatly positive" one).

We have calculated the efficiency of our proposed solution by comparing the base method (which just calculates the tweet sentiments, ignoring the sentiment hashtags) with the results achieved by also taking the discovered sentiment hashtags into account.

We report an accuracy of **75 %** with a completely automated version, and **78.5 %** with a semi-automated version of the proposed method in comparison to **74 %** achieved by the base method. While not a great improvement, the results are still rather good considering that only some tweets that were tested had sentiment hashtags, and also, more importantly, the sentiment hashtags that have been extracted can now be used to provide an approximation of a tweet sentiment without relying on NLP tools, which are often time consuming. This leads to a significant optimization of the sentiment analysis process, while still providing decent accuracy. The lack of a greater accuracy increase can also be attributed in the generally small number of sentiment hashtags in proportion to the total number of messages, as was mentioned in Sect. 4.

6 Conclusion

In this paper we have presented a method for semi-automatically detecting sentiment hashtags, and displayed the results on a Twitter dataset related to the United Kingdom 2015 general elections. We have also noticed a general disparity between the tweet statistics of the dataset we have collected and the real world election and opinion poll data which is a common characteristic of social networks.

Most of the popular sentiment hashtags have a positive connotation, and the majority of the extracted hashtags can be confirmed valid by the experts. A few of the detected hashtags could have been guessed intuitively (such as the VOTEPARTY ones), but this also provides a way to get addition insight which would otherwise slip undetected if completely manual hashtag selection was to be used.

Besides increasing message sentiment analysis accuracy, the usefulness in extracting sentiment hashtags is also in the insight it provides when analyzing a specific topic, as experts can pay attention to the development of positive or negative trends. It can serve as an optimization method, as NLP is computationally expensive, whereas extracting hashtags is pretty trivial and provides a decent estimate of the tweets sentiment.

For future work, we will consider simultaneous topic and sentiment hashtag discovery, and widen the research from hashtags into topic-specific sentiment value discovery for arbitrary concepts.

References

1. Rill, S., Reinel, D., Scheidt, J., Zicari, R.V.: PoliTwi: early detection of emerging political topics on twitter and the impact on concept-level sentiment analysis. Knowl. Based Syst. **69**, 24–33 (2014)
2. Poria, S., Cambria, E., Winterstein, G., Huang, G.-B.: Sentic patterns: dependency-based rules for concept-level sentiment analysis. Knowl. Based Syst. **69**, 45–63 (2014)

3. Pennacchiotti, M., Popescu, A.-M.: A machine learning approach to twitter user classification. In: ICWSM, vol. 11, pp. 281–288 (2011)

4. Cambria, E., Hussain, A., Eckl, C.: Bridging the gap between structured and unstructured healthcare data through semantics and sentics. In: ACM Web Sci 2011: 3rd International Conference on Web Science, Koblenz, Germany, 14–17 June 2011

5. Lee, W.-J., Oh, K.-J., Lim, C.-G., Choi, H.-J.: User profile extraction from twitter for personalized news recommendation. In: 2014 16th International Conference on Advanced Communication Technology (ICACT), pp. 779–783 (2014)

6. Hong, L., Davison, B.D.: Empirical study of topic modeling in Twitter. In: Proceedings of the First Workshop on Social Media Analytics, pp. 80–88 (2010)

7. Gimpel, K., Schneider, N., O'Connor, B., Das, D., Mills, D., Eisenstein, J., Heilman, M., Yogatama, D., Flanigan, J., Smith, N.A.: Part-of-speech tagging for twitter: annotation, features, and experiments. In: Proceedings of the 49th Annual Meeting of the Association for Computational Linguistics: Human Language Technologies: Short Papers, vol. 2, pp. 42–47 (2011)

8. Owoputi, O., O'Connor, B., Dyer, C., Gimpel, K., Schneider, N., Smith, N.A.: Improved part-of-speech tagging for online conversational text with word clusters. In: HLT-NAACL, pp. 380–390 (2013)

9. Miller, G.A.: WordNet: a lexical database for English. Commun. ACM **38**(11), 39–41 (1995)

10. Havasi, C., Speer, R., Alonso, J.: ConceptNet 3: a flexible, multilingual semantic network for common sense knowledge. In: Recent Advances in Natural Language Processing, pp. 27–29 (2007)

11. Speer, R., Havasi, C.: Representing general relational knowledge in ConceptNet 5. In: LREC, pp. 3679–3686 (2012)

12. Cambria, E., Havasi, C., Hussain, A.: SenticNet 2: a semantic and affective resource for opinion mining and sentiment analysis., In: FLAIRS Conference, pp. 202–207 (2012)

13. Cambria, E., Olsher, D., Rajagopal, D.: SenticNet 3: a common and common-sense knowledge base for cognition-driven sentiment analysis. In: Twenty-Eighth AAAI Conference on Artificial Intelligence (2014)

14. Baccianella, S., Esuli, A., Sebastiani, F.: SentiWordNet 3.0: an enhanced lexical resource for sentiment analysis and opinion mining. In: LREC, vol. 10, pp. 2200–2204 (2010)

15. Lam, X.N., Vu, T., Le, T.D., Duong, A.D.: Addressing cold-start problem in recommendation systems, p. 208 (2008)

16. Zhang, X., Cheng, J., Qiu, S., Zhu, G., Lu, H.: DualDS: a dual discriminative rating elicitation framework for cold start recommendation. Knowl. Based Syst. **73**, 161–172 (2015)

17. Justo, R., Corcoran, T., Lukin, S.M., Walker, M., Torres, M.I.: Extracting relevant knowledge for the detection of sarcasm and nastiness in the social web. Knowl. Based Syst. **69**, 124–133 (2014)

18. Cambria, E., Livingstone, A., Hussain, A.: The hourglass of emotions. In: Esposito, A., Esposito, A.M., Vinciarelli, A., Hoffmann, R., Müller, V.C. (eds.) COST 2102. LNCS, vol. 7403, pp. 144–157. Springer, Heidelberg (2012)

Cloud Computing
and the Semantic Web

Ontology-Based Technology for Development of Intelligent Scientific Internet Resources

Yury Zagorulko[✉] and Galina Zagorulko

A.P. Ershov Institute of Informatics Systems, Siberian Branch of the Russian
Academy of Sciences, Novosibirsk, Russia
{zagor,gal}@iis.nsk.su

Abstract. The paper discusses the main features of a technology for
the development of subject-based Intelligent Scientific Internet Resources
(ISIR) providing content-based access to systematized scientific knowledge and information resources related to a certain knowledge area and
to their intelligent processing facilities. An important merit of ISIR is its
ability to reduce appreciably the time required to access and analyze
information thanks to the accumulation of the semantic descriptions
of the basic entities of a knowledge area being modeled, the Internet
resources relevant to this area, and the information processing facilities (including web-services) used in it directly in the ISIR content. The
specific features of the technology are the use of ontology and semantic network formalisms and orientation to experts, i.e. specialists in the
knowledge areas for which ISIR are built.

Keywords: Intelligent scientific internet resource · Ontology · Semantic
network · Thesaurus · Semantic web service · Technology

1 Introduction

Though a great bulk of information related to various areas of knowledge is available directly on the Internet, the problem of supplying the scientific community
with information on the subjects of interests has no satisfactory solution yet.

This situation is partly attributed to the specifics of scientific knowledge
representation on the Internet, which is weakly formalized, insufficiently systematized and distributed over various Internet sites, electronic libraries, and
archives. In addition, a major portion of the information presented on the Internet is practically inaccessible for users because of unsatisfactory operation of
modern search engines, which use primitive keyword search mechanisms taking
into account neither the semantics of the words contained in the query nor its
context.

Another reason for this situation is that modern information systems use a
rather reduced set of methods for information representation, search, and interpretation. As a rule, data and knowledge are represented in these systems as
text documents (in the Enterprise Document Management System) or a set

© Springer International Publishing Switzerland 2015
H. Fujita and G. Guizzi (Eds.): SoMeT 2015, CCIS 532, pp. 227–241, 2015.
DOI: 10.1007/978-3-319-22689-7_17

of information resources (on the Internet catalogues or portals), though the most human-friendly form of information representation is a network of inter-related facts. Such mode of information interpretation facilitates its perception and allows content-based search and convenient navigation through it.

The problem of a convenient access to information processing means developed in various knowledge areas also remains unsolved. The methods of information processing, even those already implemented and presented on the Internet, remain inaccessible for a wide range of users because of their poor systematization and the absence of semantic information about them.

To solve the problems discussed above, we have suggested a conception of a subject-based Intelligent Scientific Internet Resource (ISIR) intended for the information and analytic support of scientific and production activity in a certain knowledge area. We call the ISIR an intelligent internet resource because not only information representation and systematization, but also all the functionality of this resource are based on the formalisms of ontology [1] and semantic networks [2].

Since the systems of this class are in great demand, we propose a technology for the development and life-cycle maintenance of a subject-based ISIR oriented directly to specialists in the knowledge areas for which such resources are created. This technology is an elaboration of the technology of building scientific knowledge portals that was earlier developed by the authors and successfully used for constructing scientific Internet resources for some knowledge areas [3].

The paper discusses the main features of the technology for the development of subject-based intelligent scientific Internet resources. The rest of the paper is structured as follows: Sect. 2 presents the ISIR conception and architecture; Sect. 3 describes the technology of ISIR development; Sect. 4 gives an example of using the technology; and Sect. 5 discusses some works that are related to the topic of the paper. The main features and merits of the technology, as well as its future evolution, are discussed in the closing section.

2   Conception and Architecture of the Subject-Based ISIR

In accordance with the suggested conception, a subject-based ISIR is an Internet-accessible information system which provides systematization and integration of scientific knowledge and information resources related to a certain knowledge area, gives the content-based access to them, and supports their use for the solution of various research and production tasks supplying proper interfaces and services.

2.1   Knowledge System of ISIR

As previously mentioned, an intelligent scientific Internet resource is based on the ontology and semantic network formalisms. The ontology is the core of the ISIR knowledge system containing, along with a description of various aspects of the modeled knowledge area, a description of the structure and typology of information resources and methods of intelligent information processing facilities associated with this area. As for the semantic network, whose structure is defined by the ontology, in ISIR it plays the role of an intelligent data warehouse storing the information about the basic entities of the modeled knowledge area and relevant scientific information resources and about the web-services implementing information processing methods used in this area.

The ISIR ontology (see Fig. 1) consists of three interrelated ontologies responsible for the representation of the knowledge components mentioned above. They are the ontology of a knowledge area, the ontology of scientific Internet resources and the ontology of tasks and methods.

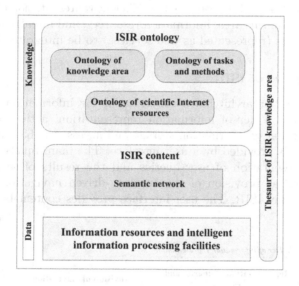

Fig. 1. Knowledge system of ISIR

The ontology of a knowledge area defines the system of concepts and relations intended for a detailed description of the ISIR knowledge area and scientific and research activity performed within the frameworks of this area.

The ontology of scientific Internet resources serves to describe information resources related to the ISIR knowledge area and presented on the Internet.

The ontology of tasks and methods includes the descriptions of tasks to be solved by ISIR and methods for their solution and descriptions of web-services implementing both the methods of task solution and information processing methods elaborated in the modeled knowledge area.

Based on the ontology and semantic network, a convenient navigation through scientific knowledge and information resources and intelligent data processing facilities (methods and web-services implementing them) is implemented, as well as the content-based search for information required.

Apart from the ontology and semantic network, the ISIR knowledge system includes a thesaurus which contains terms of the modeled area, i.e. the words and word combinations used for the representation of the ontology concepts in texts and user queries. Using various semantic relations, the thesaurus also determines the meaning of concepts by giving the correlation between concepts rather than their text definitions. Due to this fact, the thesaurus can be applied both to user queries processing and to searching for and annotating the information resources to be integrated in ISIR.

Thus, the knowledge system of ISIR not only includes a formal description of the knowledge area of ISIR, determines the typology of relevant information resources, tasks to be solved in this area and the methods of their solution (by means of the ontology), describes the meaning of concepts used in this area (by means of the thesaurus), but also provides efficient representation of information about real objects of this area, information resources, and intelligent information processing facilities (represented as web-services) to be integrated in ISIR.

2.2   Architecture of ISIR

ISIR has a three-tier architecture conventional for information systems (see Fig. 2). It includes a tier of information representation, a tier of information processing and a tier of information storage and access (the base tier).

The first tier is provided by a user interface. The main function of the user interface is representation of user queries and the results of search and task solutions, as well as provision of the ontology-driven navigation through the information space of ISIR. The user interface provides content-based access to

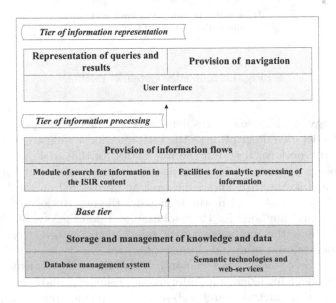

Fig. 2. Architecture of a subject-based ISIR

both the ISIR content and facilities for analytic information processing. In addition, owing to the use of the ontology and thesaurus, the user interface enables a query to be defined in terms of the modeled knowledge area.

At the tier of information processing, various kinds of information search and processing, as well as its transfer between tiers, are provided. For this purpose, the tier includes a module of search for information in the ISIR content and facilities for its analytic processing implemented, among others, as web-services.

The module of search enables one to perform both the information search by keywords and extended semantic search using query representation in terms of concepts and relations of the ontology and constraints imposed on them. These facilities support navigation through the ISIR content by supplying the user interface with a semantic neighborhood of concepts and information objects to be browsed.

The facilities for filtering and visualization of ontology concepts and objects of the semantic network are used as analytic tools.

The base tier ensures the performance of the functions of knowledge (the ontology and thesaurus) and data (the ISIR content) storage and management by means of relational DBMS, Semantic Web technologies and semantic web-services [4].

The platform-independent warehouse Jena Fuseki [5] was selected to be the data warehouse, because it supports the standard query language SPARQL [6], data update and logical inference. In this warehouse, data is represented as a set of triples defining the assertions of "subject-predicate-object" kind corresponding to the well-known RDF model [7]. This data structure is highly flexible in data and knowledge representation, which enables it to store in one place both the ISIR content and specification of the ontology and thesaurus.

Program components of the ISIR base tier providing knowledge and data management are realized with the help of the SPARQL query language. Communication with the data warehouse is performed via SPARQL HTTP client, so the program components are independent of a concrete implementation of the data warehouse. In case of need, the latter can be easily replaced with another data warehouse, more efficient or suitable for a class of tasks to be solved by ISIR.

To store the housekeeping information, in particular, information about administrators and developers of the subject-based ISIR, DBMS MySQL is used.

3   Technology of ISIR Building

A technology for building subject-based ISIRs is under development. Its main feature is orientation to experts, i.e. specialists in a certain knowledge area. It stems from the fact that mass production of ISIR for different knowledge areas can be provided only by involving in the process the specialists from a target area. This technology allows them to collect and systematize, within the frameworks of a unified information space, an extensive knowledge and data on the required knowledge area, as well as intelligent data processing facilities used in this area.

This technology has the following basic components:

1. The methodology of ontology building together with a suit of the base ontologies;
2. The expert interface providing access to program facilities which support the construction of ontologies and thesauri and management of the ISIR content;
3. A subsystem for automatized collecting the ontological information from the Internet;
4. The user interface providing a content-based access to the ISIR content and facilities for analytical information processing;
5. A data warehouse providing universal structures for a consistent storage of the ontology, thesaurus and the ISIR content, as well as program facilities supporting access to them.

The methodology of the ontology building is the most important component of the technology suggested, since the ontology is the basis of the ISIR knowledge system. Let us consider it in detail.

3.1   Methodology of the ISIR Ontology Building

The ontology of a specific ISIR is built by the methodology whose basic principles are as follows:

- Structuring the ISIR ontology by dividing it into a set of relatively independent ontologies;
- Using a suit of the base ontologies including the most general concepts independent of the ISIR knowledge area;
- Building all ISIR ontologies by means of completion and elaboration of the base ontologies.

The use of this methodology considerably simplifies the construction of the ISIR ontology and its maintenance.

As mentioned above, the ISIR ontology consists of three relatively independent but interrelated ontologies: the ontology of the knowledge area, the ontology of scientific Internet resources, and the ontology of tasks and methods. All these ontologies are built from the base ontologies.

The following ontologies are proposed as the base ones: (1) the ontology of research activity, (2) the ontology of scientific knowledge, (3) the base ontology of tasks and methods, (4) the base ontology of scientific information resources, and (5) the thesaurus representation ontology.

The ontology of the knowledge area is built on the basis of the first two ontologies; the ontology of tasks and methods is built on the basis of the third one; the ontology of scientific Internet resources is built using the forth one. The thesaurus representation ontology supplies a set of concepts and relations for building the thesaurus of the ISIR knowledge area. Let us describe these ontologies in detail.

The scientific knowledge ontology contains classes which define the structures for the description of the concepts of specific areas of knowledge, such as

Subdivision of science, Research method, Object of research, Scientific result, etc. The ontology also includes the relations linking the objects of these classes. Using these classes we can extract and describe divisions and subdivisions that are significant for a given knowledge area, determine classification of methods and objects of research, and describe the results of research activity.

The ontology of research activity is based on the ontology suggested in [8] for describing research projects and extended for applying it to a wider class of tasks. The ontology includes classes of concepts relating to the organization of scientific and research activities, such as Person, Organization, Event, Scientific Activity, Project, Publication, etc.

This ontology also contains relations which enable us to link its concepts not only to each other but also to the concepts of the scientific knowledge ontology. Note that the choice of these relations was based on both the completeness of the ISIR knowledge area presentation and the convenience of navigation through the information space of ISIR and information search in it.

The base ontology of scientific information resources includes Information resource as the main class. This class serves to describe the information resources relevant to the ISIR knowledge area (including the resources presented on the Internet). The set of attributes and relations of the Information resource class is based on the Dublin Core standard [9]. It has the following attributes: Title of resource, Language of resource, Subject of resource, Resource type, etc. To represent information about the sources and creator of the resource, as well as events, organizations, persons, publications and other entities associated with it, special relations are included in the ontology.

The base ontology of tasks and methods contains classes, such as Task, Method of solution, and Web-service, as well as the relations linking these classes to each other and to the classes of other base ontologies. Using these classes and relations, we can describe the tasks to be solved by a specific ISIR, methods of their solution, as well as the web-services implementing them. Besides, this ontology also describes the web-services implementing the information processing methods used in the ISIR knowledge area.

The descriptions of web-services are based on the OWL-S ontology [10] intended to describe semantic web-services. Due to this, a web-service is linked not only to the description of its interface in terms of types of input and output data, but also to a description of its semantics, i.e. what the service can do, its subject domain, constraints on the application area and service quality, etc. Besides, all its declarative properties, functionality, and interfaces are encoded in a single-valued form applicable to machine processing.

The presence of a semantic description of web-services not only facilitates their search and correct use (performance), but also makes it possible to compose from them new services in order to obtain the functionality required to solve the user problems. In addition, available semantic descriptions of the web-services predetermine their successful integration into ISIR. Besides, the content-based access to the web-services will be provided not only for software agents, but also for those who want to find intelligent information processing facilities necessary to solve their tasks.

The thesaurus representation ontology is based on the international and Russian standards regulating the structure of monolingual and multilingual information retrieval thesauri, the set and properties of the basic entities and relations between them, therefore it includes a suit of generic concepts and relations which are present in any thesaurus. In particular, it contains classes describing the following thesaurus entities: terms which are divided into descriptors (preferred terms) and ascriptors (text entries which can be replaced by the corresponding descriptors during document indexing and retrieval), sources of terms (web-resources, text documents, and collections of text documents containing terms or their definitions), and subareas of knowledge related to terms. The ontology also includes the relations that link the objects of classes listed above.

The ISIR knowledge area thesaurus is created by supplementing with specific terms the thesaurus core which is built on the basis of the thesaurus representation ontology and contains the set of terms corresponding to the names of classes and relations of the base ontologies.

3.2   Management of the ISIR Knowledge System

To support the process of adjustment and management of the ISIR knowledge system, the technology provides developers with ontologies and data editors. These editors have convenient graphical interfaces implemented as web-applications and provide remote adjustment and management of the ISIR knowledge system by authorized users (experts) via the Internet. To support cooperative development of the ISIR knowledge system by a team of experts, the editors have a procedure for granting privileges to experts of different levels.

The ontology editor serves for ontology building and management. Its design enables it to be used not only by knowledge engineers, but also by experts who are not specialists in computer science and mathematics.

The ontology editor allows an expert to create, modify and delete any elements of the ontology (classes of concepts, relations, and domains). When an expert describes a new class, he/she can select its parent from the set of already created classes which is represented for a user as a tree. Thereby the class inherits from the parent class not only all its attributes, but also its relations; at the same time, the parent class is linked with a new class by a "subclass" relation. For each attribute of the class, its name, the range of values, the number of possible values (one or a set), and the status of value filling (mandatory or not) are defined. When a new relation is created, its arguments are also selected from the tree of classes.

ISIR content management is implemented with the help of the data editor which operates under the control of the ontology. This allows one not only to facilitate considerably the correct insertion of information, but also to provide its logical integrity. The data editor allows one to create, modify, and delete information objects (the objects of classes defined in the ontology) and relations between them.

When a new information object is created, first of all, the expert selects the corresponding class of ontology from the tree of classes. Then, based on the description of this class presented in the ontology, a form for information insertion is automatically generated. This form contains entry fields for the values of attributes of the object and its relations with other objects. If an attribute takes its value from a domain, then the list of its possible values is displayed.

Simultaneously with the object creation, the expert can specify its connection with other objects already existing in the ISIR content. The type of these connections and classes of these objects are defined by the corresponding relations of ontology. The form for their input is automatically generated on the basis of descriptions of these relations. Based on these descriptions and the current state of the ISIR content, the data editor displays for each relation of the created (edited) object a list of objects with whom the object can be linked by a given relation.

The thesaurus building and editing its content are also implemented with the help of the data editor operating under the control of the thesaurus representation ontology. This provides the logical integrity of the thesaurus terminological system.

To be a useful resource, ISIR should have the knowledge system which contains exhaustive information about the modeled knowledge area and the scientific activity performing within its frameworks. Building and maintenance of such resource is a rather complex and labor-intensive problem requiring considerable efforts of developers.

The complexity of the problem is due to a large variety of kinds of the information collected and modes of its representation on the Internet. In particular, information about organizations, persons, projects, conferences and publications is collected from information portals, digital libraries and journals, web-sites of organizations, projects, conferences, etc. The great labour input is attributed to the large volume of information to be collected.

To solve this problem, a subsystem intended to automatize the collection of information about the basic entities of the ISIR knowledge area and Internet resources relevant to it is developed. The subsystem unites the methods of meta-search and information extraction based on ontologies and thesauri.

Information collection for ISIR consists of the following stages: (1) search for Internet resources relevant to the ISIR knowledge area, (2) extraction of information from these resources, and (3) insertion of obtained information into the ISIR content. According to this, a subsystem of information collection includes a module of a search, a module of information extraction, a module of information insertion into the ISIR content, as well as a data base for the storage of links to the Internet resources (DB LIR). Note that when ISIR is adjusted to a knowledge area DB LIR can be filled with the Internet links to the relevant (according to the experts opinion) Internet resources.

At the first stage, the search queries used by the search module for the retrieval of relevant Internet resources are generated on the basis of the ontology and thesaurus. This module addresses the search systems of Google, Yandex and Bing via their program interfaces. It uses meta-search methods to obtain links to the Internet resources. Then this module filters duplicate and irrelevant links and adds relevant links in the DB LIR. (Note that relevance of a resource (Web page) is defined on the basis of the cosine similarity measure calculated between the vectors of weights of the terms of the search query and the Web page downloaded by its link.)

At the second stage, relevant Internet resources are analyzed and information is extracted from them. A feature of the approach to information collection implemented here is that for every type of entities (the ontology class) a specific method of information collection adjustable to the knowledge area and kinds of Internet resources is developed. Each of these methods includes a set of patterns. In these patterns, for every kind of extracted information, markers defining its position are given as well as the engines implementing the algorithm of the analysis of the corresponding fragments of Web pages and extraction of the required information from them. These patterns are also generated on the basis of the ontology. To improve the recall (completeness) of information extraction, the patterns use alternative terms from thesaurus (synonyms and hyponyms) to describe the markers.

At this stage, DB LIR can be also updated with the Internet links found in the Internet resources processed. Subsequently, these links are analyzed by the experts who decide on their relevance.

At the third stage, the information extracted at the previous stage is inserted in the ISIR content.

4   Use Case: ISIR in Decision-Making Support

The technology of ISIR development was used for creating a resource in the area of decision-making support. This resource contains systematized information about the knowledge area "decision support" and methods for solving the problems specific for this area, and provides the content-based access to them.

In accordance with the methodology, the ontology of the resource in question is built from base ontologies. The ontology of the knowledge area has been extended by such concepts as Decision-making process, Decision-making stage, Situation, Problem situation, Alternative, and the relations between them. The base ontology of tasks and methods was supplemented with the entities concretizing the concepts and relations contained in it. For example, for the class Task, the subclasses Structuring of knowledge area, Situation analysis, Objectives formulation, Criteria formulation, Alternatives development, Criteria evaluation, and others were introduced. These subclasses describe the tasks to be solved at different stages of decision-making.

A structured description of the entities of this resource gives an idea about all aspects of decision-making support and the use of specific methods. It allows one to obtain answers to the questions like "What problems are solved at certain stages of decision-making?", "What methods are used to solve this problem?", "What input data are required for this method?", and "What solvers, frameworks or web-services are available for the implementation of the method?".

It is also possible to get both informal and formal descriptions of a method, information about groups and teams developing this method, and links to Internet resources relevant to the method.

Figure 3 shows the user interface of the resource as a page with ontology and description of the interior point method belonging to the class of linear programming methods.

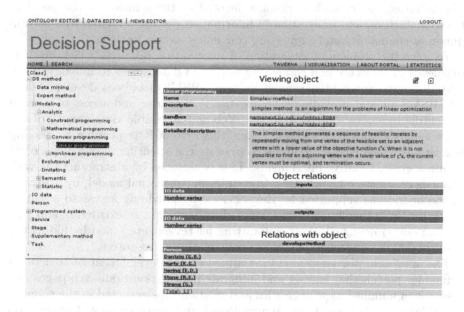

Fig. 3. User interface of the resource on decision-making support

The basic functionality of the resource is implemented using the services described in Sect. 2.2. Let us consider some particular services created specifically for this resource.

Since the description of decision support methods often requires a complex mathematical description, a service has been developed that provides advanced text edition functions including mathematical formulas editing.

The methodology of web-services development was tested on linear programming methods. A web-service was designed in the C# language using the data transfer protocol SOAP running under HTTP protocol and the WSDL language [11]. This web-service can be used in two ways: to explore its work and to embed it into third-party applications. For these purposes, it is supplied with appropriate user interfaces. In the first case, the interface is a kind of a "sandbox" which allows one to set the input data, run the chosen method and look through the results of its work. In the second case, the interface enables one to obtain a method specification, a description of the input data, as well as the examples of requests to the service and its responses.

The user interfaces of the web-service are accessible from the page containing the description of the method. For example, a page with the description of the interior point method shown in Fig. 3 contains a detailed text description of this method, references to the "sandbox" and method specification.

5 Related Work

A large variety of research works are devoted to the solution of the problem of systematization and integration of information resources related to a certain domain or community and supporting convenient access to them.

To solve the problem of integration of information resources which are heterogeneous in structure and content as well as in data access technology, a scientific Resource Space Management System (sRSMS) has been developed [12]. The sRSMS aims at providing a homogeneous view over and access to a space of scientific resources sourced from the Web and accessible via a variety of different heterogeneous technologies. Using this system it is possible to develop applications which enable the users to operate the scientific resource space via domain-specific, intuitive instruments. This is provided by abstracting the various kinds of scientific knowledge into a uniform conceptual model, by abstracting the operations supported by the services, by providing access to scientific knowledge (from merely accessing paper data/metadata to extracting and tagging content, crawling citations, submitting for review, etc.), and by hiding the technical details of accessing heterogeneous platforms/resources.

The approach, discussed in [13], is aimed at the development of structured community portals that extract and integrate information from Web pages and present it in a unified view of entities and relationships accepted in the community. This approach is top-down, compositional, and incremental. At first, experts select a small set of data sources highly relevant to the community. In order to facilitate the selection, a special tool to search a data source and rank it using the PageRank and TF-IDF metrics for measuring their relevance is provided. Next, plans extracting data from these sources and representing them in the form of entities and relationships are composed from a given set of extraction/integration operators. These plans are built for every entity. Executing these plans yields an initial structured portal (in the form of an entity-relationship graph). Then this portal can be incrementally expanded by detecting and adding new sources.

Note that the first approach involves the programmer in the development of applications (for building adapters to the resources integrated in them). In the second approach, only experts (for the selection of relevant data sources) and a knowledge engineer (for the definition of an ER schema and composition of plans extracting information) are needed. Though in outward appearance our approach is similar to the first approach, in spirit it is closer to the second one. In contrast to it, however, our approach provides a more detailed description of the modeled knowledge area, supplying the user with a set of base ontologies containing a wide spectrum of entities for representing research activity.

As for the collection of information from the Internet, many researchers deal with this problem. However, as shown in the survey [14], the majority of such studies are aimed at the extraction of information needed for the solution of the tasks of electronic commerce or analysis of social networks [15], and only a minor part of this research collects information for the needs of research activity [16]. In particular, in the study [16] information about the scientific content of Knowledge-Based Systems journal for the period 1991–2014 extracted from the bibliometric database ISI Web of Science is used to study the knowledge field of the journal and the community formed around it with the help of performance analysis and science mapping methods [17].

6   Conclusion and Future Work

The paper presents the main features of the technology for the development of subject-based intelligent scientific Internet resources (ISIR) providing content-based access to the systematized scientific knowledge and information resources related to a certain knowledge area and to intelligent processing facilities used in this area.

An important merit of ISIR is that it allows the researchers to reduce appreciably the time required to access and analyze information thanks to the accumulation of the semantic descriptions of the basic entities of a knowledge area being modeled, the Internet resources relevant to this area, and the information processing facilities used in it directly in the ISIR content.

The use of ontologies as a conceptual basis of ISIR makes it a convenient and efficient tool for the representation and systematization of all kinds of information necessary for the researcher about the knowledge area modeled.

The use of ontologies also raises the level of the ISIR development technology and creates prerequisites for its use by experts, i.e. specialists in the modeled knowledge area. On the one hand, basing the facilities for development and maintenance of the ISIR knowledge system on ontology makes them available for experts since knowledge representation in the form of objects (classes) and relations between them accepted in the ontology is most natural for humans. On the other hand, ontology is a convenient means to formalize and fix common knowledge, shared by all experts-developers, about the area modeled. In addition, ontology enables knowledge reuse, which simplifies and speeds up the development of new applications. Moreover, the availability of a representative suit of the base ontologies and methodology for building all ISIR ontologies on their basis, together with knowledge and data editors convenient for experts, makes ISIR building much easier and less labour-consuming.

However, our experience of applying the technology suggested has shown that though it provides convenient facilities for building ISIRs, it remains complicated for experts. Therefore, the future development of the technology will aim at eliminating this shortcoming. For this purpose, within the frameworks of the technology specialized program shells oriented to particular classes of knowledge areas and tasks will be built. The shells will differ in base ontologies sets and, possibly, program components. Such shells will be virtually "empty" ISIRs, i.e. they will include all the necessary conceptual and procedural components, but the lower levels of their ontologies will be undeveloped and their contents will be empty. We suppose that the development of such specialized shells will make the technology of ISIR building completely applicable for experts.

Acknowledgments. The authors are grateful to the Russian Foundation for Basic Research (grant No. 13–07–00422) for financial support of this work.

References

1. Guarino, N.: Formal ontology in information systems. In: Proceedings of FOIS 1998, Trento, Italy, pp. 3–15. IOS Press, Amsterdam (1998)
2. Deliyanni, A., Kowalski, R.A.: Logic and Semantic Networks. Comm. ACM **22**(3), 184–192 (1979)
3. Borovikova, O., Globa, L., Novogrudska, R., Ternovoy, M., Zagorulko, G., Yu, Z.: Methodology for knowledge portals development: background, foundations, experience of application, problems and prospects. In: Joint NCC&IIS Bulletin, Series Computer Science, vol. 34, pp. 73–92 (2012)
4. McIlraith, S.A., Son, T.C., Zeng, H.: Semantic web services. IEEE Intell. Syst. **16**(2), 46–53 (2001)
5. Fuseki: serving RDF data over HTTP. http://jena.apache.org/documentation/serving_data/
6. SPARQL Query Language for RDF. W3C Recommendation, 15 January 2008. http://www.w3.org/TR/rdf-sparql-query/
7. Resource Description Framework (RDF). http://www.w3.org/2001/sw/wiki/RDF
8. Benjamins, V.R., Fensel, D.: Community is Knowledge! in (KA)2. In: Proceedings of 11th Banff Knowledge Acquisition for Knowledge-based Systems Workshop, KAW 1998, Banff, Canada, April 1998. SRDG Publications, University of Calgary, Calgary (1998)
9. Hillmann, D.: Using Dublin Core. http://dublincore.org/documents/usageguide/
10. OWL-S: Semantic Markup for Web Services. http://www.w3.org/Submission/OWL-S/
11. Chinnici, R., Moreau, J.-J., Ryman, A., Weerawarana, S.: Web Services Description Language (WSDL) Version 2.0 Part 1: Core Language. http://www.w3.org/TR/wsdl20/
12. Parra, C., Baez, M., Daniel, F., Casati, F., Marchese, M., Cernuzzi, L.: A scientific resource space management system. Technical report DISI-10-013. University of Trento, Ingegneria e Scienza dell'Informazione (2010)
13. DeRose, P., Shen, W., Chen, F., Doan, A.H., Ramakrishnan, R.: Building structured web community portals: a top-down, compositional, and incremental approach. In: VLDB 2007, Vienna, Austria, 23–28 September 2007, pp. 399–410 (2007)
14. Ferrara, E., De Meo, P., Fiumara, G., Baumgartner, R.: Web data extraction, applications and techniques: a survey. Knowl.-Based Syst. **70**, 301–323 (2014)
15. Bernabe-Moreno, J., Tejeda-Lorente, A., Porcel, C., Fujita, H., Herrera-Viedma, E.: CARESOME: a system to enrich marketing customers acquisition and retention campaigns using social media information. Knowl.-Based Syst. **80**, 163–179 (2015)

16. Cobo, M.J., Martinez, M.A., Gutierrez-Salcedo, M., Fujita, H., Herrera-Viedma, E.: 25 years at knowledge-based systems: a bibliometric analysis. Knowl.-Based Syst. **80**, 3–13 (2015)
17. Cobo, M.J., Lopez-Herrera, G., Herrera-Viedma, E., Herrera, F.: Scimat: a new science mapping analysis software tool. J. Am. Soc. Inf. Sci. Technol. **63**(3), 1609–1630 (2012)

A Science Mapping Analysis
of the Literature on Software Product Lines

Ruben Heradio[1], Hector Perez-Morago[1], David Fernandez-Amoros[1],
Francisco Javier Cabrerizo[1], and Enrique Herrera-Viedma[2(✉)]

[1] Departamento de Ingeniería de Software y Sistemas Informáticos,
UNED, 28040 Madrid, Spain
{rheradio,hperez,david,cabrerizo}@issi.uned.es
[2] Departamento de Ciencias de la Computación e Inteligencia Artificial,
Universidad de Granada, 18071 Granada, Spain
viedma@decsai.ugr.es

Abstract. To compete in the global marketplace, manufacturers try to differentiate their products by focusing on individual customer needs. Fulfilling this goal requires companies to shift from mass production to mass customization. In the context of software development, software product line engineering has emerged as a cost effective approach to developing families of similar products by support high levels of mass customization. This paper analyzes the literature on software product lines from its beginnings to 2014. A science mapping approach is applied to identify the most researched topics, and how the interest in those topics has evolved along the way.

Keywords: Software product lines · Bibliometrics · Science mapping

1 Introduction

Mass customization is the new frontier in business competition for both manufacturing and service industries. To improve customer satisfaction, reduce lead-times and shorten costs, families of similar software products, known as *Software Product Lines* (SPLs), are built jointly by combining reusable parts that implement the features demanded by the customers.

The SPL approach brings the benefits of economies of scope to software engineering, since less time and effort are needed to produce a greater variety of products. Many companies have exploited the concept of software product lines to increase the resources that focus on highly differentiating functionality and thus improve their competitiveness with higher quality and reusable products while decreasing the time-to-market condition. For instance, van der Linden et al. [15] summarize experience reports from ten different companies working on diverse domains (e.g., Bosch on Gasoline Systems, Nokia on Mobile Phones, Philips on Consumer Electronics Software for Televisions, Siemens on Medical Solutions, etc.).

© Springer International Publishing Switzerland 2015
H. Fujita and G. Guizzi (Eds.): SoMeT 2015, CCIS 532, pp. 242–251, 2015.
DOI: 10.1007/978-3-319-22689-7_18

Science mapping [6] attempts to display the structural and dynamic aspects of scientific research, delimiting a research field, and identifying, quantifying and visualizing its thematic subfields.

This paper analyzes the literature on SPLs from 1995 to 2014. A science mapping approach is applied to identify the most researched topics, and how the interest in those topics has evolved along the way. In particular, we have used a technique called *co-word analysis*, that measures the association strengths of publication keywords [11], to process 1,338 records retrieved from ISI Web of Science. To the extent of our knowledge, this work is the first attempt to do so using bibliometric techniques. Hence, this paper complements existing literature reviews on SPLs [4,16] using an alternative approach to provide a panoramic view of the field.

The remainder of the paper is structured as follows: Sect. 2 summarizes the methodology used to carry out our work. Section 3 applies co-word analysis to identify the cognitive structure and evolution of the SPL literature. Finally, some concluding remarks are provided in Sect. 4.

2   Materials and Methods

To perform the bibliometric analysis described in this paper, the workflow proposed in [5,9] has been followed, which is composed of the following steps:

1. *Data retrieval.* There are several outstanding bibliographic databases where data can be retrieved, such as ISI Web of Science[1] (ISIWoS), Scopus[2], and Google Scholar[3]. In particular, the data processed in this paper comes from ISIWoS, which offers an impressive collection of over 54 million records covering 5,294 publications in 55 disciplines, more than 760 million of cited references, and 100 years of abstracts. On January 2015, the following query[4] was made on the ISIWoS Core Collection for the time span 1995–2014, obtaining 1,338 records:

```
TOPIC =
  "software product line*" or
  (
    (
      "product line*" or "mass customization" or "product famil*" or
      "program famil*" or "software factor*" or "product platform*"
    ) and
    (
      "domain engineering" or "application engineering" or
      "feature model*" or "feature diagram*" or
      "decision model*" or "decision diagram*" or
      (software and variabilit*)
    )
  )
```

---

[1] http://www.webofknowledge.com/.

[2] http://www.scopus.com.

[3] http://scholar.google.com.

[4] The asterisk pattern character means zero to many characters; it is used in our query to catch the noun plurals.

2. *Preprocessing.* The data retrieved from bibliographic databases usually have errors. For instance, references may be duplicated, authors' names may appear in different ways, etc. So, it is necessary to preprocess the data before carrying out any analysis.

To track the evolution of the SPL research area we have used co-word analysis, which requires analyzing publication keywords and citations. Hence, we have performed a laborious preprocessing procedure to:

(a) Standardize keywords; e.g., the following keywords included in the data: "Product Configuration", "Product Derivation", "Product Derivation Process", and "Derivation" were considered synonyms.
(b) Correct invalid citations; e.g., the technical report [1] appears cited in the raw data gathered from ISIWoS as "Bachman F., 2005, CMUSEI2005 TR012" and "Bachman**n** F., 2005, CMUSEI2005TR012".

3. *Analysis.* Finally, the data preprocessed in the previous step was examined using co-word analysis.

To preprocess and analyze the bibliographic data retrieved from ISIWoS, the open source software tool SciMAT [10] has been used, which is freely available at http://sci2s.ugr.es/scimat/.

3   Science Mapping Analysis of Research on Software Product Lines

In this paper, a particular science mapping approach known as co-word analysis has been used to identify the main topics of a scientific field and their inter-relationship. It measures the association strengths of terms representative of the publications in the field by analyzing the co-occurrence frequency of pairs of keywords. Several measures have been proposed to estimate the association strength between publication keywords. Van Eck et al. [12] performed an analysis of many of those measures, concluding that *equivalence index* [6] is the most appropriate one for normalizing co-occurrence frequencies.

The equivalence index $e_{A \leftrightarrows B}$ of two keywords A and B is defined by Eq. 1, where $c_{A \leftrightarrows B}$ is the number of publications where A and B appear together, and c_A and c_B are the total number of documents that include A and B, respectively.

$$e_{A \leftrightarrows B} = \frac{c_{A \leftrightarrows B}^2}{c_A \cdot c_B} \tag{1}$$

The value of $e_{A \leftrightarrows B}$ falls into the interval $[0, 1]$:

- When there is no publication where A and B appear together as keywords, $c_{A \leftrightarrows B} = 0$, and thus $e_{A \leftrightarrows B} = 0$
- If A and B are keywords that always appear together, $c_A = c_B = c_{A \leftrightarrows B}$, and thus $e_{A \leftrightarrows B} = 1$

A clustering algorithm can use the equivalence index to identify research topics by looking for groups of strongly linked keywords [6,7,13]. In such a way, each detected topic is modeled by a cluster of interrelated keywords known as a *thematic network*. In this paper, the algorithm of *simple centers* [6] has been used to get the clusters, each one representing a topic. This algorithm has been successfully used in a number co-word studies [2,8,11,17] and has the advantage of producing labeled clusters (in contrast to other alternative approaches that generate unlabeled clusters, which need to be revised by an expert to identify the topics they represent). Algorithm 1 summarizes in pseudocode how the approach works.

Algorithm 1. simple_centers

Input $min_{occurrences}$; $min_{co\text{-}occurrences}$; $min_{keywords}$; $max_{keywords}$;
Output *set of clusters;*
begin

Remove all keywords included in less than $min_{occurrences}$ publications;
repeat

Get the link with highest $e_{A\leftrightarrows B}$ from all possible keywords to begin a cluster;
From that link, form other links in a breadth-first manner, until no more links are possible due to $min_{co\text{-}occurrences}$ or $min_{keywords}$ or $max_{keywords}$;
The keyword which participates in more links is considered the cluster center and so it provides the cluster name;
Remove all incorporated keywords from the list of subsequent available keywords;
until *No two remaining keywords co-occur frequently enough to begin a cluster;*

Since the equivalence index has the drawback of being high when keywords appear infrequently but almost always together, a clustering algorithm guided by that index might overestimate the importance of those keywords and create irrelevant clusters [11]. To overcome that problem, the simple center algorithm needs to be adjusted through the following parameters:

- The minimum number of publications where keywords are required to appear ($min_{occurrences}$).
- The minimum number of publications where a pair of keywords need to appear together to be taken into account ($min_{co\text{-}occurrences}$). If this parameter is too high, few links may be formed; if it is too low, an excessive number of links may result. In the former case, subspecialities in a field may not emerge; in the latter case, more representative and well-connected topics will be harder to detect due to the noise of less representative and less well-connected ones [11].
- The minimum and maximum number of keywords a cluster can group ($min_{keywords}$ and $max_{keywords}$). These parameters set the size of the clusters.

Table 1. Parameters for Algorithm 1

Parameter	Period 1 (1995–1999)	Period 2 (2000–2004)	Period 3 (2005–2009)	Period 4 (2010–2014)
$min_{occurrences}$	2	3	4	4
$min_{co\text{-}occurrences}$	2	3	3	3
$min_{keywords}$	2	2	2	2
$max_{keywords}$	5	5	5	5

To analyze the structure and dynamics of the SPL research area, data from ISIWoS was divided into four consecutive periods of time: 1995–1999, 2000–2004, 2005–2009, and 2010–2014. To detect the main topics of each period, the algorithm of simple centers was run using the parameters summarized in Table 1. Out of a total of 1,338 documents, 16 were published in Period 1, 189 in Period 2, 594 in Period 3, and 530 in Period 4. Note that periods 1 and 2 has rather less documents than periods 3 and 4. As recommended by [8,11], parameters $min_{occurrences}$ and $min_{co\text{-}occurrences}$ were reduced for those periods to accommodate the lesser volume of data.

The role that a topic plays in a research area can be characterized using the following measures:

- Cluster's *density*, which estimates its internal coherence by measuring the strength of the links that tie together the keywords of the cluster [6]. Density may be computed with Eq. 2, where A and B are keywords belonging to the cluster, and #cluster is the number of keywords of the cluster.

$$density_{cluster} = \frac{100}{\#cluster} \cdot \sum_{A,B \in cluster} e_{A \leftrightarrows B} \qquad (2)$$

- Cluster's *centrality*, which measures its degree of interaction with other clusters. The greater the number and strength of the links of a topic to other clusters, the more central this topic is in the research field [3]. Centrality may be computed with Eq. 3, where A and B are keywords inside and outside the cluster, respectively [6].

$$centrality_{cluster} = 10 \cdot \sum_{A \in cluster, B \notin cluster} e_{A \leftrightarrows B} \qquad (3)$$

To get a global representation of the role of all topics, a *strategic diagram* can be used [14], which is a two-dimensional layout where the x-axis and y-axis represent cluster's centrality and density, respectively. Figure 1 offers a global representation of the simple center algorithm outcomes using four strategic diagrams. Thematic networks are depicted as nodes whose volume is proportional to the number of publications they have associated.

Tables 2, 3, 4, and 5 summarize the performance of the periods, i.e., the number of publications for each thematic network, the number of citations they received in total and on average, and the H-index for each network.

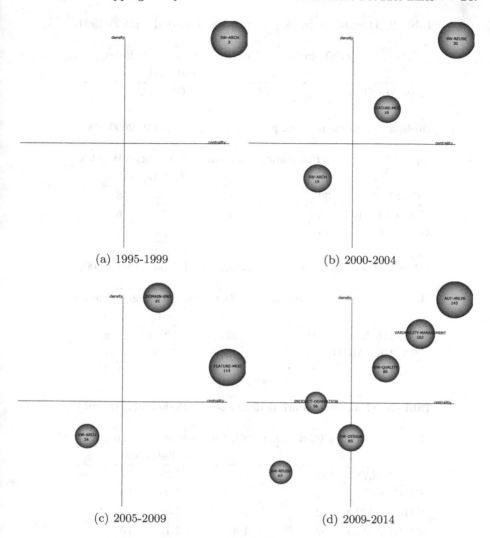

(a) 1995-1999

(b) 2000-2004

(c) 2005-2009

(d) 2009-2014

Fig. 1. Strategic diagrams for periods 1, 2, 3, and 4

Figure 2 describes in detail topic evolution. Thematic networks are depicted as nodes whose volume is proportional to the number of publications they have associated. Nodes are vertically aligned by periods (e.g., the second column includes the topics present in Period 2). The inclusion index [18] of two topics T and T' is represented by the thickness of the edge that links T to T'. Such index is computed by Eq. 4 as the number of common words to both sets divided by the number of words of the smallest set.

$$\text{inclusion index}_{T \rightleftarrows T'} = \frac{\#(T \cap T')}{\min(\#T, \#T')} \qquad (4)$$

Table 2. Thematic network performance for Period 1 (1995–1999)

Topic	#Publications	#Citations	Average citations	H-index
SW-ARCH	5	54	18.06	2

Table 3. Thematic network performance for Period 2 (2000–2004)

Topic	#Publications	#Citations	Average citations	H-index
SW-REUSE	30	184	6.13	8
FEATURE-MOD	18	86	4.78	6
SW-ARCH	19	53	2.79	5

Table 4. Thematic network performance for Period 3 (2005–2009)

Topic	#Publications	#Citations	Average citations	H-index
DOMAIN-ENG	81	221	2.73	8
FEATURE-MOD	114	455	3.99	11
SW-ARCH	54	218	4.04	7

Table 5. Thematic network performance for Period 4 (2010–2014)

Topic	#Publications	#Citations	Average citations	H-index
AUT-ANLYS	145	272	1.88	7
SW-DESIGN	85	92	1.08	4
VARIABILITY	102	112	1.09	5
SW-QUALITY	89	100	1.12	6
PRODUCT DERIVATION	56	80	1.43	5
SW-REUSE	63	84	1.33	5

According to Fig. 2, the evolution of the SPL area has behaved properly, growing smoothly and continuously. The number of publications has increased in each period. Moreover, no topic has abruptly disappeared; on the contrary, original topics have progressively been consolidated and, especially in the last five years, they have been branched out to more specific research themes.

Feature modeling has been the most important topic in the whole SPL research area. It presents the best evolution behavior and the best quality indi-

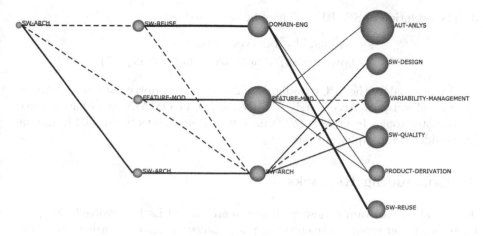

Fig. 2. Detailed view of topic evolution between periods

cators (see the H-index of FEATURE-MOD, AUT-ANLYS, SW-QUALITY, and PRODUCT-DERIVATION in Tables 3, 4, and 5). Research on software architectures and software reuse has also been essential for the development of the area.

Let us name the quadrants of a strategic diagram as:

$$\frac{Q_4 \mid Q_1}{Q_3 \mid Q_2}$$

By doing so, the following conclusions may be drawn from Figs. 1 and 2:

1. The initial motor topic, which inspired research on SPLs, was SW-ARCH. Nevertheless, it moved from the first quadrant in Period 1, to the third quadrant in Periods 2 and 3, becoming a peripheral topic. If we denote $T_i^{Q_j}$ a topic T in period i and placed in quadrant Q_j in the corresponding strategic diagram in Fig. 1, the evolution of SW-ARCH may be described as:

$$\text{SW} - \text{ARCH}_1^{Q1} \rightarrow \text{SW} - \text{ARCH}_2^{Q3} \rightarrow \text{SW} - \text{ARCH}_3^{Q3} \rightarrow \{\text{SW} - \text{DESIGN}_4^{Q2,Q3}, \text{SW} - \text{QUALITY}_4^{Q1}\}$$

2. The evolution of FEATURE-MOD may be described as:

$$\text{FEATURE} - \text{MOD}_2^{Q1} \rightarrow \text{FEATURE} - \text{MOD}_3^{Q1} \rightarrow$$
$$\{\text{AUT} - \text{ANLYS}_4^{Q1}, \text{SW} - \text{QUALITY}_4^{Q1}, \rightarrow \text{PRODUCT} - \text{DERIVATION}_4^{Q3,Q4}\}$$

From Period 2, feature modeling has behaved as an essential motor topic for the development of the SPL field. As the size of the nodes in Fig. 2 shows, the number of publications on this topic has grown dramatically. In the last five years research on feature modeling has spread out to several subareas: AUT-ANLYS, PRODUCT-DERIVATION, and SW-QUALITY (two of them playing a motor role).

3. The evolution of SW-REUSE may be described as:

$$\text{SW} - \text{REUSE}_2^{Q1} \to \text{DOMAIN} - \text{ENG}_3^{Q1} \to$$
$$\to \{\text{SW} - \text{REUSE}_4^{Q3}, \text{PRODUCT} - \text{DERIVATION}_4^{Q3,Q4}\}$$

A main goal for the SPL paradigm is shifting from opportunistic to systematic reuse of software. Accordingly, SW-REUSE and DOMAIN-ENG have worked as motor topics from 2000 to 2009. However, nowadays SW-REUSE may be considered a peripheral topic.

4 Concluding Remarks

To provide a panoramic view on how research on SPLs has evolved along the time, this paper reports a science mapping analysis of 1,338 records corresponding to papers published on SPLs for the time span 1995–2014, and gathered from the ISIWoS Core Collection.

The analysis shows that software architecture was the initial motor of research in SPLs, that work on software systematic reuse has also been essential for the development of the area, and that feature modeling has been the most important topic for the last fifteen years, having the best evolution behavior in terms of number of published papers and received citations.

Acknowledgments. The authors would like to acknowledge FEDER financial support from the Project TIN2013-40658-P, and also the financial support fromthe Andalusian Excellence Project TIC-5991.

References

1. Bachmann, F., Clements, P.C.: Variability in software product lines. Technical report, Software Engineering Institute. CMU/SEI-2005-TR-012 (2005)
2. Bailon-Moreno, R., Jurado-Alameda, E., Ruiz-Baños, R.: The scientific network of surfactants: structural analysis. J. Am. Soc. Inform. Sci. Technol. **57**, 949–960 (2006)
3. Bauin, S., Michelet, B., Schweighoffer, M., Vermeulin, P.: Using bibliometrics in strategic analysis: understanding chemical reactions at the CNRS. Scientometrics **22**(1), 113–137 (1991)
4. Benavides, D., Segura, S., Ruiz-Corts, A.: Automated analysis of feature models 20 years later: a literature review. Inf. Syst. **35**(6), 615–636 (2010)
5. Börner, K., Chen, C., Boyack, K.W.: Visualizing knowledge domains. Annu. Rev. Inf. Sci. Technol. **37**(1), 179–255 (2003)
6. Callon, M., Courtial, J., Laville, F.: Co-word analysis as a tool for describing the network of interactions between basic and technological research: the case of polymer chemsitry. Scientometrics **22**(1), 155–205 (1991)
7. Callon, M., Law, J., Rip, A.: Qualitative scientiometrics. In: Callon, M., Law, J., Rip, A. (eds.) Mapping the Dynamics of Science and Technology, pp. 103–123. Palgrave Macmillan Ltd, New York (1986)

8. Cobo, M., López-Herrera, A., Herrera-Viedma, E., Herrera, F.: An approach for detecting, quantifying, and visualizing the evolution of a research field: a practical application to the fuzzy sets theory field. J. Informetrics 5(1), 146–166 (2011)
9. Cobo, M., Lopez-Herrera, A., Herrera-Viedma, E., Herrera, F.: Science mapping software tools: review, analysis, and cooperative study among tools. J. Am. Soc. Inform. Sci. Technol. 62(7), 1382–1402 (2011)
10. Cobo, M., Lopez-Herrera, A., Herrera-Viedma, E., Herrera, F.: Scimat: a new science mapping analysis software tool. J. Am. Soc. Inform. Sci. Technol. 63(8), 1609–1630 (2012)
11. Coulter, N., Monarch, I., Konda, S.: Software engineering as seen through its research literature: a study in co-word analysis. J. Am. Soc. Inform. Sci. 49(13), 1206–1223 (1998)
12. van Eck, N.J., Waltman, L.: How to normalize cooccurrence data? An analysis of some well-known similarity measures. J. Am. Soc. Inform. Sci. Technol. 60, 1635–1651 (2009)
13. Kandylas, V., Upham, S.P., Ungar, L.H.: Analyzing knowledge communities using foreground and background clusters. ACM Trans. Knowl. Discov. Data 4(2), Article 7, 1–35 (2010)
14. Law, J., Bauin, S., Courtial, J.P., Whittaker, J.: Policy and the mapping of scientific change: a co-word analysis of research into environmental acidification. Scientometrics 14(3–4), 251–264 (1988)
15. van der Linden, F.J., Schmid, K., Rommes, E.: Software Product Lines in Action: The Best Industrial Practice in Product Line Engineering. Springer, Berlin (2007)
16. Lopez-Herrejon, R.E., Linsbauer, L., Egyed, A.: A systematic mapping study of search-based software engineering for software product lines. Inf. Softw. Technol. 61, 33–51 (2015)
17. Lopez-Herrera, A., Cobo, M., Herrera-Viedma, E., Herrera, F., Bailon-Moreno, R., Jimenez-Contreras, E.: Visualization and evolution of the scientific structure of fuzzy sets research in Spain. Inf. Res. 14, 1–23 (2009)
18. Sternitzke, C., Bergmann, I.: Similarity measures for document mapping: a comparative study on the level of an individual scientist. Scientometrics 78(1), 113–130 (2009)

Asymmetry Theory and Asymmetry Based Parsing

Anna Maria Di Sciullo[(⊠)]

UQAM, Montreal, Canada
di_sciullo.anne-marie@uqam.ca

Abstract. We consider the properties of an integrated competence-performance model where the grammar generates the asymmetrical relations underlying linguistic expressions and the parser recovers these asymmetries. This model relates Asymmetry Theory, which is a theory of the Language Faculty, and asymmetry-based parsing, which is a theory of language use. We discuss the derivation and parsing of morphological and syntactic argument structure dependencies under the world level and above in order to show that the grammar generates these dependencies and that the parser recovers them. The integrated competence-performance model is sensitive to the configurational and featural asymmetries underlying linguistic expressions and contributes to reduce the complexity. Lastly, we draw consequences for natural language understanding.

Keywords: Asymmetry · Argument structure · Morphological linking · Syntactic linking · Parsing · Pronominal anaphora resolution

1 Introduction

This paper describes the properties of a model that relates competence, viz. the knowledge of language, and performance, viz. the use of language [1] via asymmetrical relations. We assume that asymmetry is a property of relations R such that if R hold for the pair (x, y) but not hold for the pair (y, x). According to the Asymmetry Theory, [2, 3] asymmetrical relations are core relations of the Language Faculty. Asymmetry Based Parsing, [4], is a model of parsing that implements the operations of the Asymmetry Theory for the analysis of linguistic expressions. In this model, the grammar generates the underlying asymmetrical relations constitutive of linguistic expressions and the parser recovers the asymmetries, both configurational and featural in nature. While the configurational asymmetries rely on the c-command relation[1] [5], featural asymmetries rely on the proper sub-set relation between the set of features of the pairs of nodes in binary branching trees.

We have shown in [6, 7] that Asymmetry Theory provided a morpho-syntactic theory limiting the set of possible derivations for morphological and syntactic derivations. We have shown that Asymmetry based Parsing recovers the morphological

---

[1] *C-command*: X c-commands Y iff X and Y are categories and X excludes Y, and every category that dominates X dominates Y. *Asymmetric c-command*: X asymmetrically c-commands Y, if X c-commands Y and Y does not c-command X.

© Springer International Publishing Switzerland 2015
H. Fujita and G. Guizzi (Eds.): SoMeT 2015, CCIS 532, pp. 252–268, 2015.
DOI: 10.1007/978-3-319-22689-7_19

structure of complex morphological expressions in [8–10], it recovers the syntactic structure of sentences [11] as well as it recovers the antecedents of pronouns, whether they are overt or covert [12]. This paper focuses on the capacity of the integrated model to reduce the complexity brought about by cases where more than one argument structure dependency is possible. We focus on argument linking in morphological and syntactic domains, as well as in the domain of the discourse.

The organization of this paper is the following. In the first section, we discuss core properties of the Asymmetry Theory. In the second section we consider the properties of Asymmetry Based Parsing and show how it recovers the underlying asymmetrical argument structure relations and reduce complexity. Lastly we consider the consequences of the integrated competence-performance model for natural language understanding and raise novel research questions.

2 Asymmetry Theory

The Asymmetry Theory [3] is a theory of the human Language Faculty, according to which the hypothesis in (1) is central. This theory is part of the generative grammar research agenda, including works from [5, 13–18].

(1)   The Asymmetry Hypothesis
        Asymmetric relations are core relations of the Language Faculty.

It has been shown that asymmetry is basic in the description and the explanation of syntactic and phonological phenomena; the Asymmetry Theory points to the centrality of asymmetrical relations to morphological objects. Consequently, the objects generated by the grammar share a basic property of form: asymmetry. These objects however, diverge with respect to other properties of their primitives, operations and interface conditions. In the following section, we describe syntactic derivations according to the Asymmetry Theory.

The generic operations of the grammar, Shift and Link, in (2), may apply to categories as well as to already formed trees in order to derive the structure of linguistic expressions. The operations are subjects to the Agree condition, (3). This condition ensures that the features of the categories that combine one another are in a proper subset relation. Thus, in this theory, configurational and featural asymmetries ensure that the derivations are well formed.

(2)   a. *Shift*(α,β):   Given two objects α,β, Shift (α,β) derived a new object δ
                           projected from α.
        b. *Link*(α, β):   Given two objects α and β, Link (α,β) derives the object
                           (α,β), where α and β are featurally related.
(3)   *Agree* (φ1, φ2): Given two sets of features φ1 and φ2, Agree holds between
                           φ1 and φ2, iff φ1 properly includes φ2.

In the derivation of syntactic expressions, the operations Shift and Link apply to linguistic elements, unanalysed elements or already derived trees, and derive structures where configurational and featural asymmetries hold. The Strict Asymmetry condition, (4) ensures that syntactic derivation at every step relies on asymmetrical relations. The proper inclusion relation must hold between the feature bundles of the elements that are subject to the Shift and Link of the grammar, and the asymmetric c-command relation holds between pairs of elements that are subject to the link operation. Both operations are subject to the asymmetrical Agree relation in (3).

(4)   *Strict Asymmetry:* Every object {head, non-head} introduced in a derivation must be part of an asymmetric relation with another object of the same sort {head, non-head} as early as possible.

Morphological shells, that is, constituent formed with two minimal trees, constitute minimal morphological phases, [19]. They satisfy the interface Legibility condition, according to which only interpretable elements in asymmetric relations are optimally legible by the external systems, semantic and sensorimotor. This is not the case for syntactic phases, which are generally more extended than morphological phases, as illustrated here with the syntactic derivation in (6) derived by the operation of the grammar on the basis of the numeration (MUM) in (5). See [6] for a step-by-step derivation.

(5) NUM= {C, T, {D, Num, N, v, V, D, Num, N}}

(6)

The Asymmetry Theory makes theoretical and empirical predictions for the form and interpretation of morphological and syntactic objects. One theoretical prediction is that configurational symmetry is not part of the properties of morphological relations, whether it can be a property of syntactic relations. An empirical prediction of the theory is that morphological and syntactic objects are subject to different interface semantic and sensorimotor interpretations.

If nothing would restrict the combination and the liking between affixes and roots, non-words can be derived. Asymmetry Theory reduces the complexity in the sense that it excludes derivations that do not lead to grammatical objects. Non-words and non-sentences could be derived if the operations of the grammar would not be subject to the asymmetrical Agree condition.

In this framework, the morphological and the syntactic derivations derive complex trees on the basis of simpler ones. This is the case of the shell structure [20, 21] adopted for the generation of argument structure. In this analysis the derivation of causative verbs is based on two layers of asymmetrical relations relating the lover verbal projection VP including the verb and its logical object and a higher layer including an abstract causative verb small v and its logical subject (vP).

(7)

```
        vP
       /  \
     SU    v
          / \
         v   VP
            /  \
           V
          / \
         V   OB
```

The centrality of the Shell in Morphological and Syntactic derivations suggests that human grammar includes a universal formalism for developing individual grammars and deriving linguistic expressions. This is reminiscent of a central idea in Tree Adjoining Grammar (TAG) [22, 23]. What Asymmetry Theory shares with TAG is that grammar may combine trees based on the application of a small set of formal operations to the trees. See [3] for discussion.

2.1 Summary

We highlighted cores properties of the Asymmetry Theory and showed how this theory restricts the derivation of complex grammatical objects on the basis of operations that are sensitive to the configurational and the feature structure asymmetries. We also identified cores similarities and differences between morphological and syntactic derivations. We compared the Asymmetry Theory to TAG and pointed out to the central role of Minimal trees, in the derivation of morphological and syntactic objects. The next section is devoted to the Asymmetry Based Parsing.

3 Asymmetry Based Parsing

Computational implementations of asymmetric relations are available. The asymmetric c-command relation is part of Marcus's parser [31], as well being part of the framework of Principled Based Parsing [32, 33] and of the more recent works on asymmetry and minimalism [34, 35].

The Asymmetry Based Parsing is a model of language use. It is part of the integrated competence-performance model, as it is related to the Asymmetry Theory. The parser implements a grammar and recovers the underlying structure of the sentences that constitutes its input. We illustrate the recovery of the underlying asymmetrical relations at the syntactic level in the following sections.

3.1 Recovering Syntactic Relations

[11] describes the properties of a syntactic LL(1) parser that implement the Asymmetry Theory and performs a left to right top-down analysis of sentences. The parser interprets the operations of the grammar as applying groups of rules in local domains.

```
(8)    Dom CP
           Proj CmaxP
               Spec  [getw(word, 'cat') == 'WHadj']
                           : shift, link(FPP.Spec);
               H     [word.get_cat() == 'Vaux']
                           : shift, link(FauxP.h);
               Cmpl shift;
               ...
           Grp DP
           (PName <DdefP.h> | Dpron <DpronP.h> ...
           AP <MP.Spec>
```

The trace of the interrogative sentence *who arrived yesterday?* in Fig. 1 below shows that the asymmetrical relations are recovered, be it at the level of argument structure, modification as well as at the level of operator variable structure.

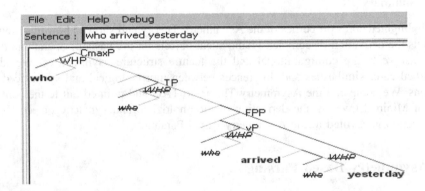

Fig. 1. Trace of the wh-expression *Who arrived yesterday?*

Thus, the wh-word occupies the Specifier of the CmaxP projection, which sister contains the functional modification projection FPP and the verbal argument structure projection (VP). It is copied in the subject position, which is the Specifier of the TP

(Tense phrase) as well as in the Specifier of the verbal projection VP and is located in the complement of the VP. This analysis is correct, as the verb *arrive* is an intransitive verb with only one internal argument, which in this case is the wh word *who*. The temporal modifier yesterday however, is generated in the Specifier of FPP, which is located outside of the argument structure domain of the VP.

The Asymmetry-based parser recovers the configurational asymmetries between argument structure, aspectual modification structure and operator structure in the extended verbal and nominal projections. The configurational asymmetry is described in (9), where the head of each projection is related to the others via asymmetrical c–command (>). Thus, in the extended verbal projection, CmaxP stands for Complemetizer phrase, FP stands for functional phrase, TP stands for Tense phrase, FnegP stands for negation phrase, Faux P stands for auxiliary phrase, FPP stands for functional prepositional phrase, vP and VP stand for verbal phrases. In the extended nominal projection, Dmax stands for determiner phrase, FP stands for functional phrase QP stands for quantifier phrase, NumP stands for numeral phrase, AdjP stands for adjectival phrase, nP and NP stand for nominal phrases.

(9)   a. CmaxP > FP > TP > FnegP > FmodP > FauxP > FPP > vP > VP
       b. DmaxP > FP > QP > NumP > AdjP > nP > NP

Given that it implements the operations of the Asymmetry Theory, the parser recovers the underlying syntactic relations of the sentences it analyses. Computational complexity is reduced as the parser deterministically recovers the asymmetrical relations of the categories that are part of the syntactic expressions it analyses, without the need to eliminates choice points and alternative derivations.

3.2   Recovering the Antecedent of Pronouns

In this section, we show that the competence performance model reduced computational complexity at the discourse level for the identification of the antecedent of pronouns.

The asymmetric c-command has been shown to govern the syntactic properties of constituents, their displacements, the relation between operators and variables, as well as the binding of pronouns by antecedents. Asymmetrical c-command is part of the definition of binding in the Binding Theory [13, 14], which includes the Principle B, (10). While a pronominal is free in its local domain, it must by bound in the domain of the discourse [38].

(10)   Principle A: An anaphor is bound in its local domain.
        Principle B: A pronominal is free in its local domain.

According to Principle B, pronouns are free from feature matching asymmetrically c-commanding antecedents in their local domain. Thus, in (11a), the pronoun *him* cannot be bound by John. This is also the case for *the brother of John* in (11b) and *John's brother* in (11c). These constituents asymmetrically c-command the pronoun him, which, according to Principle B of the Binding Theory is free in its local domain. However, pronouns can be co-referential with feature matching non c-commanding constituents. In (11), *John* does not asymmetrically c-command the pronoun *him*, as is it embedded in the DP, and thus it can be a possible antecedent for the pronoun. This is also the case for (11c).

(11)   a. John likes him.
        b. The brother of John likes him.
        c. John's brother likes him.
        d. John thinks that Mary likes him.
        e. John met Mary. She really likes him.

Furthermore, given that the binding theory applies in local domains, such as the domain of the sentence, *John* can be a possible antecedent for the pronoun *him* in (11d) and (11e) as *John* is not part of the same sentential domain than the pronoun *him*. In such cases co-reference instead of binding applies between the antecedent and its pronominal anaphor. Contrary to binding, which is an operator-variable relation, co-reference is the free assignment of referential indexes to constituents [39]. The pronoun simply happens to pick out a referent, directly, which in turn happens to be the same referent picked out by the name, as in the representations in (12).

(12)   a. the brother of John$_1$ likes him$_2$ (where $1 = 2$)
        b. John$_1$'s brother likes him$_2$.
        c. John$_1$ thinks that Mary likes him$_2$.
        d. John$_1$ met Mary. She really likes him$_2$.

The parser is the input of a pronominal anaphora resolution module, as described in [12]. This module applies to within and between sentences. The trace in Fig. 2 shows that the parser recovers the antecedent of pronouns in cases such as (12a), where the antecedent does not asymmetrically c-commands the pronoun.

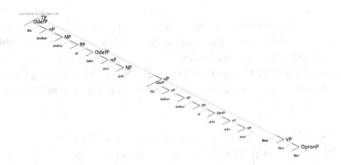

Fig. 2. Trace for the sentence *the brother of John likes him.*

The parse tree in Fig. 2 shows that the nominal constituent *the brother of John* is located in the subject position within the vP as well as in the extended projection of V, in the Specifier of TP. This constituent includes *John*, which does not asymmetrically c-command the pronoun *him*, located in the complement position of V. Co-reference between *John* and *him* is possible since their features are in a proper inclusion relation, as the representation in (13) illustrates. *John* and *him* do not differ in grammatical features of person, gender and number, as will as with respect to the semantic feature of animacy (ani). They do differ with respect to the semantic feature of independent reference (Ir). Proper names, contrary to pronouns, have independent reference. Thus *John* and *him* are in asymmetrical relation with respect to their feature structure, *John* is the superset and *him* is the proper subset. This is also the case in the example in (14) where the pronoun is reflexive. Reflexive pronouns differ from non-reflexive pronouns with respect to whether or not they denote a part-whole relation. This difference is expressed in terms of the feature w in the examples below. The set of semantic features associates with DPs also includes the definite feature (def), differentiating definite from indefinite DPs.

(13)   The brother of John   likes him

                    | |

            { D ; +3p +sg,+msc ;   { D; +3p+ sg +msc

            +Ir, +ani, +w, +def}   -Ir , +ani, +w, +def}

(14)   The brother of John   likes himself

                    | |

            { D ; +3p +sg,+msc ;   { D; +3p+ sg +msc;

            +Ir, +ani, +w}   -Ir , +ani, -w, +def}

We argued in [12] that shallow parsing and dependency parsers are not sufficient to recover the anaphoric relations between pronouns and their antecedents. Deep parsing that recovers the whole CP structure is necessary. Assuming that deep parsing includes the recovery of covert arguments, such as silent pronominals PRO and Pro. The implementation of asymmetry-based principles by the parser provides the means to optimise Pronominal Anaphora Understanding and to recover anaphoric dependencies where either the antecedent or the pronoun is covert. We illustrate this with the example in (15a), where silent pronominals may occupy the subject of infinitives (PRO) and the object of verbs selecting an internal argument with a constant (con) semantic interpretation (Pro_{con}). In (15b) *John* is the antecedent of PRO but not the antecedent of Pro_{con}. Pro may occupies the subject position of imperatives in languages such as English, as well as the subject position of tensed sentences in null subject languages such as Italian, as the example in (15c) from Italian illustrates.

(15)   a. [John wants [PRO to study Pro_{con}]]
        b. [Pro_{you} study Pro_{con}] [It is good for you]
        c. [Gianni dice [Pro volere [PRO studiare Pro_{con}]]] (It)
           'Gianni says (he) wants to study.'

These dependencies cannot be recovered directly by systems using shallow or statistical parsing, and that do not incorporate such principles [40]. The trace in Fig. 3 illustrates that the parser is capable of recovering the antecedent of covert pronouns.

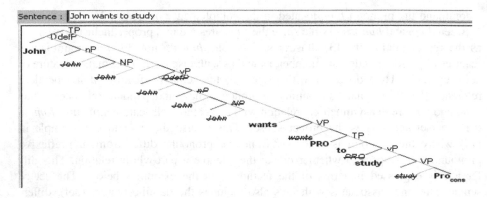

Fig. 3. Trace of the sentence *John wants to study*.

The trace in Fig. 3 shows that there is an anaphoric relation between the null DP subject (PRO) of the embedded verb *study* and the overt subject *John* of the matrix clause, whereas there is no such relation between the null DP object (Pro) of the embedded verb.

Pronominal anaphora resolution relying on Asymmetry Based Parsing and feature asymmetry leads to reduce the complexity brought about by ambiguous anaphoric relations. We consider cases where there is more than one possible compatible antecedent for a pronoun. The complexity is eliminated by the requirement that an asymmetrical proper subset relation must hold between the features of the antecedent and the feature of the anaphor, assuming that the features of pronouns (DPpro) and nominal expressions (DP) include the following, as specified in Table 1.

Table 1. DPpro and DP features

	Formal	Phi			Semantic			
	D	Per	num	gen	Ir	ani	w	def
DPro	+	+	+	+	±	±	±	±
DP	+	3^{rd}pers.	+	+	+	±	±	±

Thus, in addition to their formal (D) and phi-features, DPs and DPros have semantic features that participate in anaphoric relations. In particular, DPs have independent reference [+Ir], whereas DPros are [−Ir]. An anaphoric relation has only one [+Ir] feature, the [−Ir] feature of DPros is linked by the [+Ir] feature of the antecedent DPs. Given the Binding Theory, an anaphoric pronoun, such as *himself*, must be bound by an antecedent in its binding domain, whereas pronouns, such as *him* must be free in their binding domain. However, a pronoun such as *him* must be linked in its discourse domain.

We have shown elsewhere [38] that the proper inclusion relation reduces the complexity of ambiguous pronominal anaphora in the case where the possible antecedents for the pronouns are definite DPs, either proper names or definite descriptions that asserts or presupposes that one and only one entity satisfies the given description, as it is the case in (18).

(16)   [the president] talked to [the members of the company]   today.

              {+Ir, +ani, +w}   {+Ir, +ani, +w}

              {+3pers,+ sing, +masc} {+3pers,+ plur, +masc}

[The reactions of the shareholders] were unequal.

                  {+Ir, -ani, +w }

                 {+3pers,+ plur, +masc}

[The minutes of the meeting] indicate [that [the chief officer] trusts [him]

          {+Ir, -ani, +w}   {+Ir, +ani, +w}   {-Ir , +ani, +w}

          {+3pers, + plur, +neut} {+3pers,+ sing, +masc} {+3pers,+ sing, +masc}

The so-called uniqueness theory of definite descriptions differs from the familiarity theory of these expressions. Example such in (16), from [41], brings support to the familiarity theory, as they do not seem to assert or presuppose uniqueness. In (17), the pronoun *him* takes the indefinite DP *a man* as its antecedent.

(17)   If a man beats a donkey, the donkey kicks him.

There is some evidence that there are actually two kinds of definite expressions, some fitting the uniqueness theory and others fitting the familiarity theory. The definiteness feature is part of the feature structure of DPs and its plays a role in anaphoric relations. The difference between definite and indefinite DPs affects anaphora resolution [42]. While definite DP are easy to identify, indefinite DPs are ambiguous between quantificational and referential interpretations. It has been shown that indefinite antecedents in subject position are harder to process [43] and more costly to refer back [44]. Evidence from eye-tracking indicate that adults are more-likely to fixate the definite NP rather than the indefinite NP 1200 ms after ambiguous pronoun onset [45]. These experimental results indicate that definiteness affects anaphora resolution only in cases of higher ambiguity. If this is the case, the proper identification of definite as opposed to indefinite expressions is a core aspect of natural language processing, including pronominal anaphora resolution. Pronouns lack independent reference and DPs may qualify reference for pronouns. However, definite DPs are preferred to indefinite DPs as possible antecedents of pronouns, as the following example illustrate.

(18)   a. A professor came in. The brother of [John]$_i$ likes him$_i$
        b. [The professor]$_i$ came in. The brother of John likes him$_i$

Thus, in a context where both a definite and an indefinite expression are possible antecedents for a pronoun, viz. they do not asymmetrically c-command that pronoun as in the examples in (18), the definite expression will be preferred to the indefinite expression. Recent psycholinguistic results [46] indicate that this is the case for human processing. Thus, in contexts where more than one possible compatible antecedent is available for anaphora resolution, the feature structure constraint will prevail over the configurational constraint. This indicates that our model can reduce the complexity brought about by the ambiguity of certain anaphoric contexts by eliminating choice points between two possible antecedents for pronouns.

3.3   Evaluation

In this section, I will point to comparative results for pronominal anaphora resolution based on non asymmetry-based parsers on the one and the asymmetry-based parser.

Mitkov's Anaphora Resolution System (MARS) [47] relies on a shallow parser that does not recover the basic argument structures asymmetrical relation. Mars uses the FDG parser [48]. That is, there is no asymmetrical c-command relation between the subject and the object of simple linguistic expressions. In [49], the RAP applies to the syntactic representations generated by McCord's data driven Slot Grammar parser [50], which like the FDG parser, is not oriented by the recovery of asymmetrical relations. We used the implementation of RAP based on Charniak's statistical parser.[2] In [51], MARS and RAP are compared with the aLAD, a pronominal anaphora resolution systems developed at the Interface Asymmetry Lab (LAD) integrating the asymmetry based parser described in Sect. 3 above.

In the first test, we constructed 20 sentences, such as the ones in (19). This set contained 26 pronouns, including an expletive pronoun, and 22 anaphoric relations, including 4 relations with a covert antecedent, such as (19 g) and (19 h), as well as one case of backward anaphora, such as (19). The results are shown in Table 2.

Table 2. Results with 20 constructed examples

	Precision	Recall	F-measure
MARS	46,1	54,5	49,9
RAP	50,0	59,0	54,1
aLAD	96,0	96,0	96,0

---

[2] http://www-appn.comp.nus.edu.sg/~rpnlpir/cgi-bin/JavaRAP/JavaRAPdemo.cgi .

(19) ...

    a. John knows himself.

    b. John likes him.

    c. The brother of John likes him.

    d. The man who came with John likes him.

    e. The children that deserve them will receive the prizes they desire.

    f. John knows the answer and Mary knows it too.

    g. We studied a lot. It seems it was too technical.

    h. We ate a lot. It was too spicy.

While the three systems performed well in simple cases, such as (19a) and (19b). The aLAD outperformed both RAP and MARS in case where the antecedent of a pronoun was in the local domain of that pronoun but did not c-command it, for example in cases (19c) and (19d). RAP did not resolve the anaphoric relation with the referential it pronoun in (19f), contrary to MARS. The backward anaphora case (19e) was not resolved by these systems, including the aLAD.

We conducted a second test, since neither RAP nor MARS covers pronominal anaphora resolution in cases where the antecedent is covert; we excluded such relations from the corpus and considered only the case where the antecedent is overt. The performance scores are the following (Table 3):

Table 3. Results with 16 constructed examples

	Precision	Recall	F-measure
MARS	54.5	57,1	55,7
RAP	59,0	61,9	60,4
aLAD	95,2	95,2	95,2

The results show that the aLAD still outperforms RAP or MARS, neither of which relies on asymmetrical relations.

MARS does not rely on Asymmetrical Agreement between the features of a possible antecedent and a pronoun, as shown in (20), where the system wrongly identified *the country,* which is the first nominal constituent outside of the local domain of the pronoun *him,* as the antecedent of this pronoun.

(20)   The easiest thing would be to sell out to Al Budd and leave the country, but there was a stubborn streak in him that wouldn't allow it .

    MARS : him appears in paragraph 8, sentence 1, from position 24 to position 24. It is singular. The antecedent is indicated to be **the country** in paragraph 8, sentence 1, from position 14 to position 15

RAP does not rely on asymmetrical c-command, which leads the system to wrongly identify the antecedent of the referential pronoun *it* in the imbedded clause to the non-referential pronoun it in the matric clause in the example in (21).

(21)   We studied a lot. It seems it was too technical.

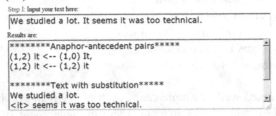

The antecedent of the referential pronoun it is located outside of its asymmetrical c-command domain. In the example in (22) the antecedent of this pronoun is the covert object of the verb *studied* in the first sentence.

The RAP uses Charniak's parser, and MARS uses the FDG parser, neither of which recovers covert arguments, including implicit objects. This is the case however for the LAD parser, as discussed in Di Sciullo et al. (2013). For example, in (22) the covert pronominal *pro* in the matrix clause is the antecedent of the referential pronoun *it*, located in the embedded clause.

(22)   [We studied *pro* a lot] [[It seems [it was too technical]]]
                   |......................|

The expletive pronoun *it*, the subject of the verb *seems* asymmetrically c-commands the referential subject *it* of the embedded clause and thus cannot be its antecedent; whereas the covert pronominal *pro* in the matric clause does not asymmetrically c-command the pronoun and thus can be the antecedent of that pronoun.

3.4   Summary

In this section, we illustrated with simple linguistic expressions le fact that the asymmetry-based parser recovers the underlying asymmetrical domains of linguistic expressions and is capable to identify possible antecedents of pronouns, as it relies on the asymmetric configurations and Agree relation. This requires that grammatical dependencies between constituents be mediated via configurational and featural relations, namely asymmetrical c-command and the proper inclusion relation. In the case of pronominal anaphora resolution, pronouns must be free from compatible c-commanding nominal constituents. They can be co-referential however with non-asymmetrically c-commanding nominal constituents. In which case only the asymmetry in the feature structure of these constituents prevails. We also evaluated the asymmetry-based parser by comparing the aLAD to other pronominal anaphora resolution systems that do not rely on an asymmetry-based parser.

4 Consequences and Further Research

Together, the Asymmetry Theory and the Asymmetry Based Parsing constitute an integrated competence-performance model, where the knowledge of language and the language use are integrated on the basis of the generation and the recovery of asymmetrical relations. We have shown that this model makes the right predictions and reduce the complexity for the generation and the processing of argument structure related dependencies under the word level and above. Further work is needed however to show that the model covers the aspectual and the operator-variable dependencies under the word level and above.

The model has consequences for linguistic theory and parsing theory, as well as for information processing, as it differentiates itself form statistical and probabilistic approaches to morphological and syntactic parsing that do not rely on configurational and featural asymmetries, as well as from pronominal anaphora resolution based on shallow parsing, including dependency parsers, such as Connexor [47, 48], and probabilistic parsers, such as the Stanford Parser [52]. Shallow parsers parse part of syntactic expressions, dependency parsers only analyze the main constituents (subject, verb, object), probabilistic parsers rely on corpus-based training. These parsers neither recover the empty categories (silent copies of the constituents) left by displacements nor do they recover implicit arguments. While the limits of statistical and shallow parsers are already identified in several works including [53] the recovery of fine-grained asymmetrical relations are needed to improve the performance of morphological and syntactic parsers. The integration of asymmetry based parser in natural language technologies aiming to extract precise information from texts is likely to contribute to their optimization. Further work is needed to evaluate the performance of the asymmetry based parsing as opposed to statistical and shallow parsing.

Acknowledgements. This work is supported in part by funding from the Social Sciences and Humanities Research Council of Canada to the Major Collaborative Research on Interface Asymmetries, grant number 214-2003-1003, and by funding from funding from the FQRSC on Dynamic Interfaces, grant number 137253 awarded to professor Anna Maria Di Sciullo, of the Department of Linguistics at the University of Quebec in Montreal. www.interfaceasymmetry. uqam.ca, www.biolinguistics.uqam.ca.

References

1. Chomsky, N.: Reflections on Language. Random House, New York (1975)
2. Di Sciullo, A.M.: Local Asymmetry. Papers from the Upenn/MIT Roundtable on the Lexicon. MIT Working Papers in Linguistics #35, pp. 25–49. The MIT Press, Cambridge (1999)
3. Di Sciullo, A.M.: Asymmetry in Morphology. The MIT Press, Cambridge (2005)
4. Di Sciullo, A.-M.: Parsing asymmetries. In: Christodoulakis, D.N. (ed.) NLP 2000. LNCS (LNAI), vol. 1835, pp. 1–15. Springer, Heidelberg (2000)
5. Kayne, R.: The Antisymmetry of Syntax. The MIT Press, Cambridge (1994)
6. Di Sciullo, A.M., Isac, D.: The asymmetry of merge. Biolinguistics **2**, 260–290 (2008)

7. Di Sciullo, A.M.: Minimalism and I-morphology. In: Kosta, P., Franks, S., Radeva-Bork, T. (eds.) Minimalism and Beyond: Radicalizing the Interfaces, pp. 267–286. John Benjamins, Amsterdam (2014)

8. Di Sciullo, A.M., Fong, S.: Asymmetry, zero morphology and tractability. In: Language, Information and Computation, PACLIC 15, Language Information Sciences Research Center, pp. 61–72. University of Hong Kong (2001)

9. Di Sciullo, A.M., Fong, S.: Efficient parsing for word structure. In: NLPRS 2001, Proceedings of the Sixth Natural Language Processing Pacific Rim Symposium, pp. 741–748 (2001)

10. Di Sciullo, A.M., Fong, S.: Morpho-syntax parsing. In: Di Sciullo, A.M. (ed.) UG and External Systems, pp. 247–248. John Benjamins, Amsterdam (2005)

11. Di Sciullo, A.M., Gabrini, P., Batori, C., Somesfalean, S.: Asymmetry, the Grammar, and the Parser. Linguistica e modelli tecnologici di ricerca, pp. 477–494. Atti del XL Congresso Internazionale di Studi della Società Linguistica Italiana. Monica Mosca, Bulzoni (2010)

12. Di Sciullo, A.M.: Asymmetric agreement in pronominal anaphora. In: Fujita, H., Revetria, R. (eds.) Frontiers in Artificial Intelligence and Applications 246, pp. 395–410. IOS Press, Amsterdam (2012)

13. Chomsky, N.: Lectures on Government and Binding: The Pisa Lectures. Foris, Dordrecht (1981)

14. Chomsky, N.: The Minimalist Program. The MIT Press, Cambridge (1995)

15. Chomsky, N.: Derivation by Phase. In: Kenstowicz, M. (ed.) Ken Hale: A Life in Language, pp. 1–52. MIT Press, Cambridge (2001)

16. Chomsky, N.: Three factors in language design. Linguist. Inquiry 36(1), 1–22 (2005)

17. Chomsky, N.: Problems of Projection. Lingua 130, 33–49 (2013)

18. Moro, A.: Dynamic Antisymmetry. The MIT Press, Cambridge (2000)

19. Di Sciullo, A.M.: Morphological phases. In: The 4th GLOW in Asia 2003, Generative Grammar in a Broader Perspective. The Korean Generative Grammar Circle, pp. 44–45 (2004)

20. Larson, R.: On double object construction. Linguist. Inquiry 19, 335–351 (1988)

21. Hale, K., Keyser, S.J.: Prolegomenon to a Theory of Argument Structure. The MIT Press, Cambridge (2002)

22. Joshi, A.K., Levy, L.S., Takahashi, M.: Tree adjunct grammars. J. Comput. Syst. Sci. 10(1), 136–163 (1975)

23. Joshi, A.K.: How much context-sensitivity is necessary for characterizing structural descriptions - tree adjoining grammars. In: Dowty, D., Karttunen, L., Zwicky, A. (eds.) Natural Language Processing – Theoretical, Computational and Psychological Perspectives. Cambridge University Press, New York (1985)

24. Chomsky, N.: Logical Structure of linguistic theory. Language 31(1), 36–45 (1955)

25. Chomsky, N.: Syntactic Structures. Mouton, The Hague (1957)

26. Frank, R.: Phrase Structure Composition and Syntactic Dependencies. The MIT Press, Cambridge (2002)

27. Lebeaux, D:. Language acquisition and the form of the grammar. Unpublished doctoral dissertation. University of Massachusetts, Amherst (1988)

28. Chomsky, N.: A Minimalist program for linguistic theory. In: Hale, K., Keyser, S.J. (eds.) The View from Building 20: Essays in Linguistics in Honor of Sylvain Bromberger, pp. 1–52. The MIT Press, Cambridge (1993)

29. Frank, S.: Restricting grammatical complexity. Cogn. Sci. 28(5), 669–698 (2004)

30. Chomsky, N.: Language and Problems of Knowledge: The Managua Lectures. The MIT Press, Cambridge (1988)

31. Marcus, M.: A Theory of Syntactic Recognition of Natural Language. The MIT Press, Cambridge (1980)
32. Berwick, R., Abney, S., Tenny, C. (eds.): Principle-Based Parsing: Computation and Psycholinguistics. Studies in Linguistics and Philosophy. Kluwer, Dordrecht (1991)
33. Fong, S.: Computational properties of principle-based grammatical theories. Ph.D. thesis. Artificial Intelligence Laboratory, MIT (1991)
34. Fong, S.: Computation with probes and goals. In: Di Sciullo, A.M. (ed.) UG and External Systems: Language, Brain and Computation, pp. 311–334. John Benjamins, Amsterdam (2005)
35. Harkema, H.: Minimalist languages and the correct prefix property. In: Di Sciullo, A.M. (ed.) UG and External Systems: Language, Brain and Computation, pp. 289–310. John Benjamins, Amsterdam (2005)
36. Knuth, D.E.: On the translation of languages from left to right. Inf. Control **8**(6), 607–639 (1965)
37. Earley, J.: An efficient context-free parsing algorithm. Commun. ACM **13**(2), 94–102 (1970)
38. Di Sciullo, A.M.: Domains of argument structure asymmetries. In: WMSCI 2005, Proceedings from the 9th World Multi-conference on Systemics, Cybernetics and Informatics, pp. 316–320 (2005)
39. Grodzinsky, Y., Reinhart, T.: The innateness of binding and coreference. Linguist. Inquiry **24**, 69–102 (1993)
40. Ge, N., Hale, J., Charniak, E.: A statistical approach to anaphora resolution. In: Proceedings of the Workshop on Very Large Corpora, Montreal, pp. 161–170 (1998)
41. Heim, I.: The semantics of definite and indefinite noun phrases. Doctoral dissertation Available from ProQuest. Paper AAI8229562 (1982). http://scholarworks.umass.edu/dissertations/AAI8229562
42. Hawkins, J.A.: Definiteness and Indefiniteness. Humanities Press, Atlantic Highlands (1978)
43. Gibson, E.: Linguistic complexity: the locality of syntactic dependencies. Cognition **68**, 1–76 (1998)
44. Filiaci, F.: Null and overt subject bias in spanish and italian: a cross-linguistic comparison. In: Borgonovo, C. (ed.) Selected Proceedings of the 12th Hispanic Linguistics Symposium, Cascadilla, Somerville, pp. 171–182 (2010)
45. von Heusinger, K., Chiriacescu, S., Brocher, A., Graf, T.: Definiteness and givenness affect pronoun resolution: evidence from eye fixations. In: Oral presentation at the 27th annual CUNY Conference on Human Sentence Processing. Ohio State University, Columbus, Ohio (2014)
46. Mastropavlou, M., Katsiperi, M., Fotiadou, G., Fleva, E., Peristeri, E., Tsimpli, I.: The role of definiteness in anaphora resolution. In: Experimental Psycholinguistic Conference (ERP), Madrid, Spain (2014)
47. Mitkov, R.: Anaphora Resolution. Pearson Education, Edinburgh-London (2002)
48. Tapanainen, P., Järvinen, T.: A non-projective dependency parser. In: Proceedings of the 5th Conference on Applied Natural Language Processing, Washington, D.C., pp. 64–71 (1997)
49. Lappin, S., Leass, H.L.: An algorithm for pronominal anaphora resolution. Comput. Linguist. **20**(4), 535–561 (1994)
50. McCord, M.: Slot grammar. In: Studer, R. (ed.) Natural Language and Logic. LNCS, vol. 459, pp. 118–145. Springer, Heidelberg (1990)
51. Batori, C.: Optimisation du traitement automatique des relations anaphoriques pronominales par l'utilisation des relations d'asymétrie. Doctoral dissertation. University of Quebec in Montreal, Montreal, Canada (in preparation)

52. Klein D., Manning, C.D.: Accurate unlexicalized parsing. In: Proceedings of the 41st Annual Meeting of Association for Computational Linguistics, Sapporo, Japan, pp. 423–430 (2003)
53. Rimell, L., Clark, S., Steedman, M.: Unbounded dependency recovery for parser evaluation. In: Proceedings of the 2009 Conference on Empirical Methods in Natural Language Processing, Singapore, pp. 813–821 (2009)

Reuse of Rules in a Mapping-Based Integration Tool

Vladimir Dimitrieski[1(✉)], Milan Čeliković[1], Nemanja Igić[1],
Heiko Kern[2], and Fred Stefan[2]

[1] Faculty of Technical Sciences, University of Novi Sad,
Trg Dositeja Obradović 6, 21000 Novi Sad, Serbia
{dimitrieski,milancel,nemanjaigic}@uns.ac.rs
[2] Business Information Systems, University of Leipzig,
Augustusplatz 10, 04109 Leipzig, Germany
{kern,stefan}@informatik.uni-leipzig.de

Abstract. In the Internet of Things scenario, the integration of devices
with business application systems requires bridging the differences in
schemas of transmitted and received data. Further, different device configuration may introduce a variety in a data schema of a single device.
Currently, mitigating this schema variation problem requires a manual
adaptation of data transformations between the devices and business
application systems. In this paper, we propose an algorithm that uses
previously created transformations to automatically adjust the new ones
for schema variations. The algorithm only considers isolated schema element information in order to find possible candidates in a transformation
repository. Schema elements can be compared using multiple comparators, and the result is combined in a final similarity metric. Both, the
algorithm and the repository are implemented as a module of AnyMap –
a mapping-based integration tool. We also present a case study on which
we evaluated the approach.

Keywords: Mapping · Reuse · Integration · Technical space

1 Introduction

With the emergence of Internet of Things (IoT) [1] continuous integration of
devices and business application systems came into the spotlight. One of the
main goals of IoT is to achieve a greater value of the whole system through connecting various devices that exchange data. Manufacturers of application systems
that gather and analyze the data are facing the particular challenge as they need
to integrate their products into the existing customers' device landscapes. The
problem arises as the devices often communicate using different protocols and
send data that belong to different technical spaces. According to the authors
of [2], the notion of the technical space may be defined as a working context
with a set of associated concepts, body of knowledge, tools, required skills, and

© Springer International Publishing Switzerland 2015
H. Fujita and G. Guizzi (Eds.): SoMeT 2015, CCIS 532, pp. 269–281, 2015.
DOI: 10.1007/978-3-319-22689-7_20

possibilities. In order to import data sent by devices, developers of the application system must develop adapters that transform the data from the device technical space to the application system technical space. Such transformations need to be implemented either by using a language specific to the particular combination of technical spaces or by a general purpose language. This makes the creation of these adapters time consuming, costly, and error-prone. Additionally, the schema according to which a device sends the data, may vary based on the device configuration. We name this phenomenon as the intra-space heterogeneity. It introduces more complexity to the manual implementation of the adapters.

In order to provide an uniform way of creating transformations between technical spaces, we have created a declarative language and the tool named AnyMap [6,7]. The tool provides the following functionalities: (i) importing the existing technical space data schemes or automatically deducing a schema from a schema-less data file, (ii) a declarative language for creation of mappings between the schema elements, and (iii) a generation of executable transformations to transform the data. Although having a single language speeds up the process of transformation specification, the intra-space heterogeneity problem still exists. The schema variations have to be resolved manually and the executable transformations need to be generated again. The main goal of the research presented in this paper is to provide a solution to the schema variability problem. The solution comprises reusing the previously created mappings in order to automatize the process of adapting a new mapping to the schema changes. We have developed an algorithm that finds reuse candidates in the saved mappings by discovering the similarities between the new schema elements and the elements in stored mappings. Different comparators have been developed and may be combined to increase the algorithm precision. The result of the algorithm is a set of mappings that may be automatically applied to the new schema. Optionally, the resulting mapping can be manually refined before the application. Both the algorithm and the repository that stores all created mappings comprise the AnyMap reuse module.

In addition to the Introduction and Conclusion sections, this paper is structured as follows. In Sect. 2, we provide a brief overview of the main modules and mechanisms of the AnyMap tool. Next, we provide a detailed description of the reuse algorithm and the mapping rule reuse process in Sect. 3. In Sect. 4, a use case is presented which concerns the integration of sensor devices and manufacturing execution systems. In this example we present the creation of repository rules and the application of the reuse process. Finally, in Sect. 5 we discuss the related work.

2   The AnyMap Tool – A Brief Overview

In this section, we present the overview of the AnyMap tool architecture and its mapping language. More details about the tool and the mapping language can be found in [6,7].

The tool is designed to provide one approach that can be used to integrate various technical spaces. We accomplished this by implementing a generic element tree structure used to represent any technical space specific schema structure in a generic way. Based on this generic structure, mappings between technical spaces can be specified using the mapping language. Instead of learning a new language for each combination of technical spaces, this approach allows users to specify correspondences between technical spaces with a single, declarative, mapping language. Once a mapping is created, an executable transformation between technical space may be generated. The tool handles both importing of different schemes and generation of executable transformation code in a black box manner.

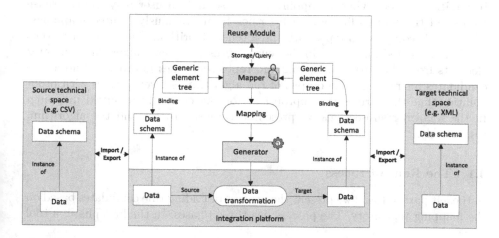

Fig. 1. The AnyMap tool architecture

In Fig. 1 we present the main modules of the AnyMap tool. The tool allows a user to import a data file from a supported technical space into the tool by using an appropriate importer. Importer creates the generic element tree from the data file schema that can be explicitly defined or implicitly contained in the file. The tree is created in the current mapping. By the notion of current mapping, we represent a current working context, i.e., the mapping file currently opened in the tool. Each mapping file comprises the source and target generic element trees and the mapping container with the mapping rules. With the rules, a user may define correspondences between source and target generic tree elements. During the import, the bindings between the created element and the original element from a data schema are created. These bindings are used in the generator module as the generated transformation is executed directly on the data from a specific technical space.

Once both source and target generic element trees have been created, a user may create arbitrary number of rules between the elements. This functionality is provided by the mapper module of the tool. There are five different kinds of rules based on the number of source and target elements: (i) one-to-one, (ii) one-to-many, (iii) many-to-one, (iv) many-to-many, and (v) zero-to-any rules. Rules can be also organized hierarchically with a parent-child relationship.

After a mapping is specified, the generator module may be used to generate executable data transformation programs based on the mapping and its rules. A generator iterates over the rules of the current mapping and creates transformation code.

3   The Reuse Module

In addition to specifying a mapping from a scratch, a user may use the reuse module of the tool to find applicable rules from previously created mappings. The module comprises a repository and a reuse algorithm. The repository stores previously created mappings. In the reuse process, the reuse algorithm compares elements from the current mapping and repository rules in order to find a rule candidates for reusing. The output of the algorithm is a set of rules with probabilities that these rules are appropriate for the currently observed mapping. In the following subsections we present the reuse process and the algorithm, respectively.

3.1   The Reuse Process

In the left part of Fig. 2 we present the process of finding rule candidates based on the mapping repository. The process has three phases. In the first phase, a tool

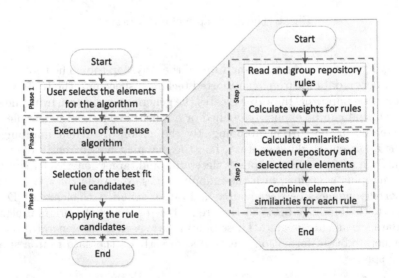

Fig. 2. The AnyMap reuse process (left) and the reuse algorithm steps (right)

user may select one or more source and target elements that represent an input for the reuse algorithm. Once the elements are selected, they are passed to the reuse module which is responsible for the execution of the two algorithm steps presented in Subsect. 3.2. After the execution of the algorithm, list of possible candidate rules for reuse are found. For each candidate a probability of being the appropriate one for the current mapping is calculated.

In the third and final phase of the rule candidate finding process, after all rule probabilities are calculated, they are applied to the current mapping. In the case of manual rule choice, all candidate rules that have a probability above a defined threshold are presented to the user. The user may choose the rules that fit best to the current mapping. In the case of the automatic choice process, rules with the highest probabilities are automatically chosen. In both cases, chosen candidate rules are then applied to the current mapping and represented in the tool.

3.2 The Reuse Algorithm

Based on [3], we may classify reuse algorithms as: (i) reuse algorithms based on isolated element information, (ii) reuse algorithms based on element structure, and (iii) reuse algorithms based on element semantic. Our goal is to create a generic algorithm that may be used in the creation of mappings between any two technical spaces. In such a case, we can only rely on isolated mapping information as we do not know in advance which two technical spaces are being mapped. Therefore, the reuse algorithm presented in this paper belongs to the first category. In addition to just considering isolated element information, presented algorithm also considers past executions and previous user choices in order to improve the accuracy. In the rest of this section we present the reuse algorithm based on isolated mapping information implemented for the AnyMap tool.

The steps of the algorithm are presented in the right part of Fig. 2. The first step of the algorithm is the preprocessing of all repository rules. During this step, a number of occurrences of each repository rule is calculated. Based on the number of occurrences, the probability of a repository rule is calculated as:

$$W_{S_r \to T_r} = \frac{N_{S_r \to T_r}}{N_{S_r \to \forall}}$$

$W_{S_r \to T_r}$ represents the probability of the $S_r \to T_r$ rule being the appropriate repository rule for the reuse algorithm. With $N_{S_r \to T_r}$, we denote the number of occurrences of the $S_r \to T_r$ rule in the repository. S_r and T_r are sets of source and target elements of a repository rule, respectively. With $S_r \to \forall$ we present all repository rules that have S_r as the set of source elements. For example, let us consider a repository containing two instances of the rule: $A \to B$ and one instance of the rule $A \to C, D$. In total, there are 3 rules with the A set of elements as source. Therefore, the initial probability that the element set A should be mapped onto B is $W_{A \to B} = \frac{2}{3} \approx 0.67$ and that A should be mapped onto C, D is $W_{A \to C, D} = \frac{1}{3} \approx 0.33$.

In the second step of the algorithm, user selected elements are matched against the elements from the repository rules. The element comparison is based on element names and done by combining different comparators which take two elements and produce a single number representing a similarity between the element names. Currently, we have implemented several string comparison algorithms such are Levensthein [4] and Jaro-Winkler [5] algorithms. Each pair of elements can be compared with an arbitrary number of comparators. Similarities calculated by different comparators can be combined into a single value by weighted multiplication of produced values. The weights are chosen globally by a user, in the tool settings, and assigned to all comparators. Therefore, the element similarity is calculated as:

$$S_{E,E_r} = \frac{\sum_{i=1}^{n}(S_{E,E_r,C_i} \cdot W_{C_i})}{n}$$

S_{E,E_r} represents the similarity of the selected element (E) and a repository rule element (E_r). With S_{E,E_r,C_i} we denote the similarity of elements E and E_r calculated by the comparator C_i. Comparators produce a normalized similarity that fits the $[0,1]$ interval. Additionally, W_{C_i} is the weight assigned to each comparator by a user and it has a value in the same interval. The sum of all calculated similarities is divided by the number of comparators (n) in order for the final similarity to be also normalized to fit the same interval.

In order to calculate a probability of a repository being an appropriate candidate for reuse, similarities between all repository rule elements and user selected elements must be calculated and combined into a single number specific for the rule. This is calculated as follows:

$$P_{S_r \to T_r} = \left(\frac{\sum_{i=1}^{n} S_{E_{s_i},E_{rs_i}} + \sum_{i=1}^{k} S_{E_{t_i},E_{rt_i}}}{n+k}\right) \cdot W_{S_r \to T_r}$$

$P_{S_r \to T_r}$ represents the probability of a rule $S_r \to T_r$ being a candidate for reuse. With E_s we represent a selected source element, while with $E_r s$ we denote a source element of a repository rule. $S_{E_{s_i},E_{rs_i}}$ represents a similarity between aforementioned source elements. Similarly, $S_{E_{t_i},E_{rt_i}}$ represents the similarity between a selected target element (E_t) and a target element of a repository rule $(E_r t)$. Both user selected element collection and repository rule element collections are ordered in the same way and comprise the same number of source elements (n) and target elements (k). $W_{S_r \to T_r}$ is a weight factor calculated in the first step of the algorithm.

We should note here that the collection of user selected elements may contain zero or more source elements and zero or more target elements. If the user initiated the algorithm without selecting any elements, the algorithm will search for the rule candidates containing any elements from a source or target generic element tree. If a user selects one or more source elements, the algorithm considers only these elements instead of all generic tree elements. In the case when, for example, all selected source elements correspond only to a subset of a repository rule source elements, other rule source elements must be also considered. They are compared to the rest of the unselected generic source tree elements to find a match. Only when a match is found for all of these other rule elements, it can be considered as a candidate. This is due to the fact that we consider a rule to be an atomic semantic unit that is either considered for reuse with all of its elements, or completely ignored. We do not consider rules with just a subset of its elements. The algorithm works in a similar way when the user selected elements comprise zero or more target elements.

In the case where a collection of selected source elements has fewer elements than n or a collection of selected target elements has fewer elements than k, then the following formula may be used to calculate the rule probability for reuse:

$$
P_{S_r \to T_r} = \left(\frac{\sum\limits_{i=1}^{n} S_{E_{s_i}, E_{rs_i}} + \sum\limits_{i=n}^{m} S_{E_{gst_i}, E_{rs_i}} + \sum\limits_{i=1}^{k} S_{E_{t_i}, E_{rt_i}} + \sum\limits_{i=k}^{l} S_{E_{gtt_i}, E_{rt_i}}}{n + m + k + l} \right) \cdot W_{S_r \to T_r}
$$

Two new segments are added to this formula. The $\sum\limits_{i=n}^{m} S_{E_{gts_i}, E_{rs_i}}$ segment represents the calculation of similarities between the repository rule elements that are not paired with any of user selected elements (E_{rs_i}) and one of the elements from the generic element source tree (E_{gts_i}). The number of repository rule elements not paired with the selected source elements is denoted with m. The element from the generic source tree is chosen to have the maximum similarity with the element E_{rs_i}. This maximum similarity must be larger than a user defined threshold. Analogously, $\sum\limits_{i=k}^{l} S_{E_{gtt_i}, E_{rt_i}}$ segment represents a calculation of similarities of the unmatched target elements of the repository rule. The number of unpaired repository rule target elements is denoted with l.

4 A Case Study: Integration of Sensor Devices and Manufacturing Execution Systems

In this section, we present a case study to demonstrate the AnyMap reuse algorithm. The use case concerns transformation of Comma Separated Value (CSV) files to eXtensible Markup Language (XML) files. CSV files represent an output of sensor devices that measure wafer dimensions (radius, weight, and thickness) during the production to ensure the quality of the process. Each CSV file contains measurement data of a sensor over a predefined period of time or defined number of measurements. This data need to be imported into a Manufacturing Execution System (MES) that gathers and analyzes such a data to provide the production information to the manufacturing decision maker. The MES offers data interfaces which allow the import of XML documents conforming to a defined schema. Therefore, CSV files need to be converted to the corresponding XML files in order to be analyzed by the MES. Beside the technical space heterogeneity (between CSV and XML spaces), the import mechanism of the MES

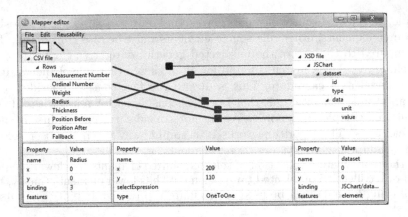

Fig. 3. An example of a mapping in the repository

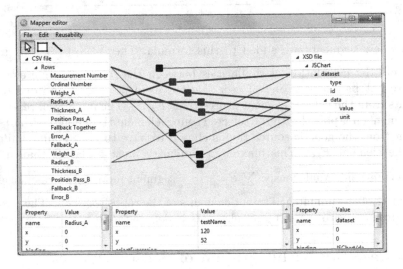

Fig. 4. Rules suggested by the reuse algorithm

needs to overcome the intra-space heterogeneity of source devices. The existence of different measurement methods and different number of sensors lead to a variability in CSV files. For example, a machine may use one sensor to measure radius of a wafer producing a CSV with only one column concerning the radius of a wafer. Such CSV files are called single-layer files. Our approach aims at overcoming the problem of intra-space heterogeneity by automatically creating a new, adapted, transformation between technical spaces based on previously stored transformations. In order to allow easier following and understanding of the use case, we use a simplified XML schema for the MES system. This schema only contains elements and attributes necessary for the visualization of the imported data using the JSChart java script library [8].

In order for the reuse algorithm to function properly, a mapping repository needs to contain at least one mapping. Prior to the experiment, a domain expert has created several sample mappings representing a mapping of *weight* and *radius* columns from a CSV file to appropriate XML elements. A mapping of a wafer radius element to appropriate XML schema elements is presented in the Fig. 3. On the left hand side, the imported schema of the singe-layer CSV document is presented. On the right side of the figure, the imported XML schema is presented. The presented mapping comprises five rules:

- R_1 - zero-to-any rule used for the creation of *JSChart* root element;
- R_2 - a rule for creating the *dataset* element from the *radius* CSV column;
- R_3 - a rule for creating the *data* element for each *row* in CSV file;
- R_4 - a rule for populating data element *unit* (x-axis of the JSChart) based on the value in the *ordinal number* CSV column; and
- R_5 - a rule for populating data element *value* (y-axis of the JSChart) based on the value in the *radius* CSV column.

Several other mappings of single-layer CSV files are created automatically using the reuse algorithm. They have been reviewed by the domain expert and stored in the repository. In total, repository comprises eight mappings of single-layer CSV files.

When a sensor device has multiple sensors for measuring the same wafer dimension, a multi-layer CSV file is obtained. In this section we consider double-layered CSV files. An example of the double-layer CSV is presented on the left side of Fig. 4. In such a file there are two columns for each measured dimensions (e.g., Radius_A and Radius_B). The reuse algorithm considers the repository mapping and calculates similarities presented in Fig. 5.

Rule candidates are produced as the output of the algorithm and grouped by their source elements. Highlighted candidates are the most probable candidates based on the calculated probabilities. In the case of automatic rule application, these highlighted rules would be applied to the current mapping. The similarity for both $Radius\_A \rightarrow dataset$ and $Radius\_A \rightarrow value$ is the same as the Radius element is always mapped to both of these elements in the repository mappings. On the other hand, some of the repository mappings do not have $Weight \rightarrow dataset$ rule and therefore, in the same figure, it can be seen that the reuse algorithm is slightly favoring the $Weight\_A \rightarrow value$ rule. Analogously, probabilities of other rules containing Radius_B, Weight_B, Thickness_A, and Thickness_B are calculated. In Fig. 4, we present the result of the application of the chosen rule candidates for the radius dimension of the wafer. For each radius column, a set of four rules is created based on the single-layer mappings in the repository. Also, a rule for creating the *JSChart* element is applied in order to have a functional mapping. In the case of automatic rule application, rules are chosen for the thickness and weight of the wafers, too. Such a mapping does not require any manual intervention. However, we choose to manually omit these rules due to a large number of lines that hinder the readability of the figure.

In addition to this use case, the reuse algorithm is evaluated on similar problems in the area of machine integration. By introducing the reuse algorithm

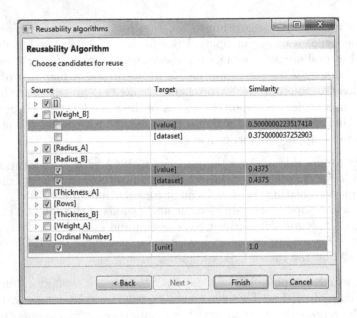

Fig. 5. Reuse algorithm output

and allowing the automatic application of best fit rule candidates, the speed of mapping creation is greatly increased in comparison to a manual creation. By allowing the user to change and improve such mappings and save them to the repository, the algorithm suggestions become more precise thus improving the quality of the process. The automatic derivation of mapping rules also works well in other use cases that we have evaluated and no major weaknesses were found. The finding of mappings in the repository depends on the quality of the stored mappings and the comparison algorithms. The development of other comparison algorithms and the optimal weights for the combination of the comparators is a work in progress.

5   Related Work

Several mapping approaches and environments are proposed in literature. Wimmer proposes in [9] an approach to model-based tool integration in the context of the ModelCVS project. However, this approach heavily depends on the EMF technical space and it is not easily applicable to other technical spaces. In [10,11], authors present the ATLAS Model Management Architecture (AMMA). It provides an extendable core language for specifying platform independent transformations. Authors of the paper argue that for a tool integration process, a specific language should be derived from the core language in order to cover the specific need of that process. However, we feel that this could be burdensome for the users of such a tool as for each integration scenario they need to create new concepts. Our goal is to provide a single and powerful mapping language that can be used regardless of the tools being integrated. Several other mapping approaches can be found in literature, such as Clio [12], Rondo [13], RDFT [14], and the UML-based approach presented in [15]. All of these approaches focus on the integration of certain technical spaces or languages, such as, XML, Relational Databases, or UML. However, none of these approaches allows a single language for the integration of arbitrary technical spaces.

The reuse of transformations is a well-known problem. As it is presented in [16], currently there is a strong focus on the reuse in the implementation phase. However, the reuse across all development phases is not yet acomplished. Our focus is on the design phase. In addition to reuse in transformation languages, our approach is influenced by the ontology alignment approaches. In papers [17–20], multiple ontology alignment scenarios and approaches are proposed. Based on the observations from these papers, we were able to fine tune our algorithm and also see its drawbacks that should be improved in the future.

6   Conclusion

In this paper we presented the reuse process in a mapping based integration framework. All created mappings are stored in the repository that we have developed for our tool. Further, we have developed the reuse algorithm that uses isolated schema element information (e.g. only their names and other properties) in order to find appropriate rule candidates in the repository. A set of string comparators is developed that can be combined to improve the process. Once the rule candidates are calculated by the algorithm, they may be automatically applied. This helps solving the problem of intra-space heterogeneity as it automatizes the process of adjusting the mapping for different schema variations. The reuse module also allows semi-automatic application of the rules. In this mode, rule candidates need to be approved or modified by a user before they are applied. We have also evaluated this algorithm on a case study concerning the integration on sensor devices and the manufacturing execution systems. Based on this example and other use cases, we find this reuse algorithm suitable for automating the process of transformation derivation in the case of intra-space variations.

One of the possible future steps is to develop semantic and structure based reuse algorithms. Instead of relying only on isolated element, structure based algorithm would allow more complex comparisons that consider the parent-child relationships between elements. Semantic algorithm would allow string comparison to be expanded to include not only letter variations but also semantic synonyms for each string. This may be accomplished by using one of the existing online semantic dictionaries such as WordNet [21] for the English language. Creating the new algorithms would allow more precise and better results in the reuse process. Also, a comparison of different reuse algorithms needs to be performed in respect to their performance and accuracy. We also plan to evaluate our tool on more use cases.

Acknowledgments. Research presented in this paper was supported by the German Exchange Service and Ministry of Education, Science and Technological Development of Republic of Serbia as part of the bilateral project "Discovering Effective Methods and Architectures for Integration of Modeling Spaces with Application in Various Problem Domains", 2014 – 2015.

References

1. Weber, R.H., Weber, R.: Internet of Things. Springer, Berlin (2010)
2. Bézivin J., Kurtev I.: Model-based technology integration with the technical space concept. In: Proceedings of the Metainformatics Symposium, pp. 44–49. Springer (2005)
3. Manakanatas, D., Plexousakis, D.: A tool for semi-automated semantic schema mapping: design and implementation. In: DISWEB caise, Luxembourg (2006)
4. Levenshtein, V.I.: Binary codes capable of correcting deletions, insertions, and reversals. Sov. Phys. Doklady **10**(8), 707–710 (1966)
5. Winkler, W.E.: String Comparator Metrics and Enhanced Decision Rules in the Fellegi-Sunter Model of Record Linkage (1990)
6. Kern, H., Stefan, F., Dimitrieski, V., Čeliković, M.: Mapping-based exchange of models between meta-modeling tools. In: Proceedings of the 14th Workshop on Domain-Specific Modeling, SPLASH, pp. 29–34, Oregon, USA (2014)
7. Kern, H., Stefan, F., Fähnrich, K.-P., Dimitrieski, V.: A mapping-based framework for the integration of machine data and information systems. In: Proceedings of 8th International Conference on Information Systems, pp. 113–120, Portugal (2015)
8. JSChart. http://www.jscharts.com. Accessed on 12 April 2015
9. Wimmer, M.: From mining to mapping and roundtrip transformations-a systematic approach to model-based tool integration. Ph.D. Thesis, Vienna University of Technology (2008)
10. Bézivin, J., Jouault, F., Rosenthal, P., Valduriez, P.: Modeling in the large and modeling in the small. In: Aßmann, U., Akşit, M., Rensink, A. (eds.) MDAFA 2003. LNCS, vol. 3599, pp. 33–46. Springer, Heidelberg (2005)
11. Del Fabro, M.D., Bèzivin, J., Jouault, F., Breton, E., Gueltas G.: AMW: a generic model weaver. In Proceedings of the lères Journèes sur l'Ingènierie Dirigèe par les Modèles, vol. 200, pp. 105–114 (2005)
12. Miller, R.J., Hernández, M.A., Haas, L.M., Yan, L.-L., Ho, C.H., Fagin, R., Popa, L.: The Clio project: managing heterogeneity. In: SIGMOD, pp. 78–83 (2001)
13. Melnik, S., Rahm, E., Bernstein, P.A.: Rondo: a programming platform for generic model management. In: Proceedings of the 2003 ACM SIGMOD International Conference on Management of Data, pp. 193–204. ACM (2003)
14. Omelayenko, B.: RDFT: a mapping meta-ontology for business integration, In: Proceedings of the Workshop on Knowledge Transformation for the Semantic Web at the 15th European Conference on Artificial Intelligence, pp. 77–84 (2002)
15. Hausmann, J.H., Kent, S.: Visualizing model mappings in UML. In: Proceedings of the 2003 ACM Symposium on Software Visualization, pp. 169–178, ACM (2003)
16. Kusel, A., Schönböck, J., Wimmer, M., Kappel, G., Retschitzegger, W., Schwinger, W.: Reuse in model-to-model transformation languages: are we there yet? Softw. Syst. Model. **14**, 1–36 (2013)
17. Euzenat, J., Valtchev, P.: Similarity-based ontology alignment in OWL-lite. In: Proceedings 16th European Conference on Artificial Intelligence, pp. 333–337 (2004)

18. Groß, A., Dos Reis, J.C., Hartung, M., Pruski, C., Rahm, E.: Semi-automatic adaptation of mappings between life science ontologies. In: Baker, C.J.O., Butler, G., Jurisica, I. (eds.) DILS 2013. LNCS, vol. 7970, pp. 90–104. Springer, Heidelberg (2013)
19. Jung, J.J.: Reusing ontology mappings for query routing in semantic peer-to-peer environment. Inf. Sci. **180**, 3248–3257 (2010)
20. Kappel, G., Kapsammer, E., Kargl, H., Kramler, G., Reiter, T., Retschitzegger, W., Schwinger, W., Wimmer, M.: Lifting metamodels to ontologies: a step to the semantic integration of modeling languages. In: Wang, J., Whittle, J., Harel, D., Reggio, G. (eds.) MoDELS 2006. LNCS, vol. 4199, pp. 528–542. Springer, Heidelberg (2006)
21. WordNet - a lexical database of English. https://wordnet.princeton.edu/

Artificial Intelligence Techniques and Intelligent System Design

An Arbitrary Heuristic Room Matching Algorithm in Obtaining an Enhanced Initial Seed for the University Course Timetabling Problem

Teoh Chong Keat[1]($\boxtimes$), Habibollah Haron[1], Antoni Wibowo[2], and Mohd. Salihin Ngadiman[1]

[1] Department of Computer Science, Faculty of Computing (FC),
Universiti Teknologi Malaysia, Johor Bahru, Malaysia
christeoh.ck@gmail.com, {habib,salihin}@utm.my
[2] Department of Decision Sciences, School of Quantitative Sciences,
UUM College of Arts and Sciences, Universiti Utara Malaysia, Sintok, Malaysia
antoni@uum.edu.my

Abstract. The curriculum-based course timetabling problem is a subset of the university course timetabling problem which is often regarded as both an NP-hard and NP-complete problem. The nature of the problem concerns with the assignment of lecturers-courses to available teaching space in an academic institution. The curriculum-based course timetabling problem confronts the problem of a multi-dimensional search space and matrices of high conflict-density, thus impeding the task to search for an improved solution. In this paper, the authors propose an arbitrary heuristic room matching algorithm which attempts to improve the initial seed of the curriculum-based course timetabling problem. The objective is to provide a reasonably advantageous search point to perform any subsequent improvement phase and the results obtained indicate that the proposed matching algorithm is able to provide very promising results as the fitness score of the solution is significantly enhanced within a short period of time.

Keywords: University course timetabling problem · Curriculum-based course timetabling problem · Initial seed · Room matching algorithm

1 Introduction

The curriculum-based course timetabling problem (CB-CTT) is a subset of the university course timetabling problem which is often regarded as both an NP-hard and NP-complete problem in which there is no known polynomial time algorithm which guarantees in obtaining the best solution (Bardadym 1996; Ismayilova et al. 2007). The objective of the CB-CTT is to assign a set of available resources which comprises of entities such as lecturers, courses and rooms to available timeslots whilst adhering to the stipulated constraints of a particular institution. Inherently, there are two types of constraints to adhere by which are hard constraints - constraints which cannot be

H. Fujita and G. Guizzi (Eds.): SoMeT 2015, CCIS 532, pp. 285–295, 2015.
DOI: 10.1007/978-3-319-22689-7_21

violated at any time, lest the timetable is rendered infeasible; and soft constraints - constraints which typically determine the quality of the timetable.

Metaheuristic algorithms are stochastic methods which are employed to solve complex optimization problems when either the search space becomes too vast or when there are no known algorithms which are capable of finding the solutions within a polynomial time (Rossi-Doria et al. 2002). However, the parameters of the algorithms often require careful tuning prior to before they could be applied to solve the problem (Brownlee 2011). Therefore one of the main concerns is how to produce an enhanced initial seed before employing the metaheuristic algorithms to further enhance the result. For example, a graph colouring heuristics has been employed to produce an enhanced initial seed in examination timetabling problem by (Burke et al. 1995) and a two-point hybrid evolutionary algorithm is employed by (Rizam and Bakar 2008) to produce an enhanced initial seeding in a similar examination timetabling problem. Nonetheless, in the literature, the CB-CTT has been reported to be solved successfully through various metaheuristic algorithms such as the Genetic Algorithm (Agustín-Blas et al. 2009; Jain et al. 2010; Kohshori and Abadeh 2012; Suyanto 2010), Ant Colony Optimization (Lutuksin and Pongcharoen 2010; Thepphakorn et al. 2009), Particle Swarm Optimization (Qarouni-Fard et al. 2007; Shiau 2011; Tassopoulos and Beligiannis 2012), Simulated Annealing (Aycan and Ayav 2009; Frausto-solís et al. 2008; Zhang et al. 2010) and Tabu Search (Alvarez-Valdes et al. 2002; Lü and Hao 2010) to name a few. Since metaheuristic algorithms are stochastic algorithms, having a quality initial seed will provide a vantage point for the algorithm to search for an optimal solution. In this paper, the authors propose an arbitrary heuristic room matching algorithm (AHRMA) which seeks to improve the initial seed of the solutions.

The rest of the paper is organized as such: Sect. 2 provides the CB-CTT model definition, Sect. 3 details the solution methodology, Sect. 4 presents the results and discussion of the experiment conducted and the paper concludes with some concluding remarks and suggestions for future works.

2   Model Definition

The CB-CTT structure is widely applicable to many universities around the world. The problem essentially deals with the scheduling of a set of lectures to various rooms and timeslots, where conflicts between courses are set according to the curriculums published by the University and not on the basis of enrolment data. In this paper, the dataset of the CB-CTT is adopted from the Track 3 of the International Timetabling Competition 2007 (ITC-2007) and the description of the various entities are described in Sect. 2.1 while the constraints are described in Sect. 2.2. (Gaspero et al. 2007):

2.1   Entities

This section presents the entities involved in the dataset. There is a total of 7 entities namely day (d), timeslots (h), period (p), courses (c), lecturers (tc), rooms (r), curriculums (*Cr*). These entities describe the resources of dataset and form the basis of constraint formulation which is described in Sect. 2.2. The entities are as follow:

1. **Days, Timeslots, and Periods.** A number of *teaching days* are given in the week (typically 5 or 6). Each day is split into a fixed number of *timeslots*, which is equal for all days. A *period* is a pair composed of a day and a timeslot. The total number of scheduling periods is the product of the days times the day timeslots.
2. **Courses and Lecturers.** Each course consists of a fixed *number of lectures* to be scheduled in distinct periods; it is attended by given *number of students*, and is taught by a *lecturer*. For each course there is a minimum number of days that the lectures of the course should be spread in, moreover there are some periods in which the course cannot be scheduled.
3. **Rooms.** Each *room* has a *capacity*, expressed in terms of number of available seats. All rooms are equally suitable for all courses (if large enough).
4. **Curriculums.** A *curriculum* is a group of courses such that any pair of courses in the group has students in common. Based on curriculums, we have the *conflicts* between courses and other soft constraints.

The solution to the problem therein is to assign a period (day and timeslot) and a room to every lecture for each course with respect to the stipulated constraints. The curriculum-based timetabling problem is composed of a set of n courses $C = \{c1,...,cn\}$ to be assigned to a set of m rooms $R = \{r1,...,rm\}$ and a set of p periods $T = \{t1,...,tp\}$. Every course ci consists of li lectures to be scheduled. A period consists of a day and a timeslot. A total of p periods are spread out over h daily timeslots and d days, i.e. $p = h \times d$. In addition, there is a set of w curricula $CR = \{Cr1,...,Crw\}$ in each curriculum Crk is a group of courses that share common students. The nomenclature described in Table 1 is adopted from (Lü and Hao 2010) whilst the properties of the dataset described in Table 2 is adopted from (Abdullah and Turabieh 2012).

2.2 Constraints

The stipulated constraints define the search space of the solution and in this work; the matching algorithm only considers solutions which are already in its feasible form i.e. satisfying all of the hard constraints and only evaluates the penalty of the soft constraints. The hard and soft constraints of the problem are listed as follows:

H_1 (Lectures) – "All lectures of a course must be scheduled, and assigned to distinct periods. A violation occurs if a lecture is not scheduled or two lectures within a course are scheduled in the same period."

H_2 (Conflicts) – "All lectures of courses in the same curriculum or taught by the same lecturer must be scheduled in different periods. Two conflicting lectures in the same period represent one violation. Three conflicting lectures count as 3 violations: one for each pair."

H_3 (Room Occupation) – "Two lectures cannot be assigned to the same room at the same period. Two lectures in the same room at the same period represent one violation. Any extra lecture in the same period and room counts as one more violation."

Table 1. Nomenclature in the curriculum-based university course timetabling problem

Symbols	Description
n_c	Total no of courses
m	Total no of rooms
d	Number of working days per week
h	Number of timeslots per working day
p	Total number of periods, $p = d \times h$
s	Total number of curricula
C	set of courses, $C = \{c_1,...,c_n\}$, $|C| = n$
R	set of rooms, $R = \{r_1,...,r_m\} = m$
T	set of periods, $T = \{t_1,..., t_p\}$, $|T| = p$
CR	set of curricula, $CR = \{Cr_1,...,Cr_w\}$, $|CR| = w$
CR_k	k^{th} curriculum including a set of courses
l_{-i}	number of lectures of course c_i
l	total number of all lectures, $$l = \sum_{1}^{n} l_i$$
std_i	Number of students attending course c_i
tc_i	Lecturer instructing course c_i
md_i	Number of minimum working days of course c_i
cap_j	Capacity of room r_j
$uav_{i,j}$	whether course c_i is unavailable at period t_j. $uav_{i,j} = 1$ if it is unavailable, $uav_{i,j} = 0$ otherwise
$con_{i,j}$	whether course c_i and c_j are conflicting each other; $$con_{i,j} = \begin{cases} 0, & if\left(tc_i \neq tc_j\right) \wedge \left(\forall Cr_q, c_i \notin \right) Cr_q \wedge c_j \notin Cr_q \\ 1, & otherwise \end{cases}$$
$\chi_{i,j}$	The course scheduled at room r_j and period t_i
$nr_i(X)$	Number of rooms occupied by course c_i for a candidate solution X; $$nr_i(X) = \sum_{j=1}^{m} \sigma_{ij}(X)$$ where $$\sigma_{ij}(X) = \begin{cases} 1, & if \forall_{\chi_{kj}} \in X, \chi_{k,j} = c_i \\ 0, & otherwise \end{cases}$$
$nd_i(X)$	Number of working days that course c_i takes place at in candidate solution X, $$nd_i(X) = \sum_{j=1}^{d} \beta_{ij}(X)$$ where $$\beta_{ij}(X) = \begin{cases} 1, & if \forall_{\chi_{u,v}} \in X, \chi_{u,v} = c_i \wedge \left[\frac{u}{h}\right] = j, \\ 0, & otherwise \end{cases}$$
$app_{k,i}(X)$	Whether Cr_k appears at t_i in X; $$app_{k,i}(X) = \begin{cases} 1, & if \forall_{\chi_{i,j}} \in X, \forall_{\chi_{i,j}} = C_u \wedge C_u \in Cr_k, \\ 0, & otherwise \end{cases}$$

Table 2. Properties of the various problem instances featured in Track 3 of the ITC-2007

Instance	Course	Total lectures	Rooms	Period per day	Days	Curricula	Min-Max lectures per day per curriculum
comp01	30	160	6	6	5	14	2–5
comp02	82	283	16	5	5	70	2–4
comp03	72	251	16	5	5	68	2–4
comp04	79	286	18	5	5	57	2–4
comp05	54	152	9	6	6	139	2–4
comp06	108	361	18	5	5	70	2–4
comp07	131	434	20	5	5	77	2–4
comp08	86	324	18	5	5	61	2–4
comp09	76	279	18	5	5	75	2–4
comp10	115	370	18	5	5	67	2–4
comp11	30	162	5	9	5	13	2–6
comp12	88	218	11	6	6	150	2–4
comp13	82	308	19	5	5	66	2–3
comp14	85	275	17	5	5	60	2–4
comp15	72	251	16	5	5	68	2–4
comp16	108	366	20	5	5	71	2–4
comp17	99	339	17	5	5	70	2–4
comp18	47	138	9	6	6	52	2–3
comp19	74	277	16	5	5	66	2–4
comp20	121	390	19	5	5	78	2–4
comp21	94	327	18	5	5	78	2–4

H_4 (Availability) – "If the teacher of the course is not available to teach that course at a given period, then no lecture of the course can be scheduled at that period. Each lecture scheduled in a period unavailable to that course is one violation."

S_1 (Room capacity) - "The number of students that attend the course for each lecture must be less than or equal to the number of seats of the rooms hosting its lectures. Each student above the capacity counts as 1 violation."

S_2 (Minimum working days) - "The lectures of each course must be spread over the given minimum number of days. Each day below the minimum, counts as 1 violation."

S_3 (Isolated lectures) - "Lectures belonging to a curriculum should be adjacent to each other (i.e., in consecutive periods). For a given curriculum we account for a violation every time there is one lecture not adjacent to any other lecture within the same day. Each isolated lecture in a curriculum counts as 1 violation."

S_4 (Room stability) - "All lectures of a course should be delivered in the same room. Each distinct room used for the lectures counts as 1 violation."

A list which details the various properties of the datasets is described in Table 2. It is worth to reiterate that the pre-requisite of the AHRMA is a feasible solution, denoting that constraints H1, H2, H3 and H4 are fully satisfied at the point of initialization. In other words, the objective of the AHRMA is to minimize the violation of the soft constraints, specifically constraint S1 such that it yields an improved initial seed for the subsequent optimization process. As such, the mathematical equation which describes the constraints of the problem is given in Eq. 1 as follow:

$$Min\ G(X) = f_1(x_{i,j}) + f_2(c_i) + f_3(x_{i,j}) + f_4(c_i) \tag{1}$$

where:

$G(x)$ = Fitness value of candidate solution

S_1: Room Capacity: $\forall x_{i,j} = c_k \in X$,

$$f_1(x_{i,j}) = \begin{cases} std_k - cap_j, & if\ std_k > cap_j \\ 0, & otherwise. \end{cases}$$

S_2: Minimum Working Days: $\forall c_i = C$,

$$f_2(c_i) = \begin{cases} md_i - nd_i(X), & if\ nd_i(X) > md_i \\ 0, & otherwise \end{cases}$$

S_3: Isolated Lectures (curriculum compactness): $\forall x_{i,j} = c_k \in X$,

$$f_3(x_{i,j}) = \sum_{Cr_q \in CR} \chi\{c+_k \in Cr_q\}.iso_{q,i}(X),$$

where

$$iso_{q,i}(X) = \begin{cases} 1, & if\ (i\ mod\ h = 1 \vee app_{q,i-1}(X) = 0) \wedge (i\ mod\ h = 0 \vee app_{q,i+1}(X) = 0), \\ 0, & otherwise. \end{cases}$$

S_4: Room Stability: $\forall c_i = C$,

$$f_4(c_i) = nr_i(x) - 1.$$

Based on the mathematical model as stated above, the goal therein is to obtain an enhanced initial seed, X^* which reduces the fitness score of the solution such that $G(X^*) \leq G(X)$ for all X in the feasible search space region. The proposed AHRMA aims to reduce the cost of S1 (Room Capacity) through the reassignment of better rooms to all lectures in order to improve the initial seed of the solution.

3   Solution Methodology

Metaheuristic algorithms are stochastic algorithms which are employed when the size of the search space becomes too vast for exact methods and that no effective heuristic of identifying optimal solution is available (Rossi-Doria et al. 2002). In order to overcome the setback of the algorithm due to the random and stochastic nature, a quality initial seed is required to assist the algorithm to converge to a local or global optimum within a shorter amount of time. Therefore one of the main concerns in the timetabling research community is how to produce a high quality initial seed. For instance (Burke et al. 1995) proposed a graph colouring heuristics to produce an initial seeding of higher quality as compared to randomly generated solutions while (Rizam and Bakar 2008) has employed a two-point hybrid evolutionary algorithm (Tp_HEA) to capture the enhanced initial seed to be used in the sequential evaluation phase. Hence, this paper is motivated by the aforementioned works and proposes an arbitrary heuristic room matching algorithm (AHRMA) which attempts to produce an enhanced initial seed for CB-CTT. This paper omits the procedure in obtaining a feasible timetable solution as it is out of the scope of this paper. However, interested readers may refer to the constructive algorithm proposed by (Chiarandini et al. 2006; Lü and Hao 2010).

3.1   Arbitrary Heuristic Room Matching Algorithm

In this paper, the proposed AHRMA attempts to heuristically reassign the rooms of the solutions with random feasible rooms in order to improve the initial seed of the candidate solution. Since is quite frequent in practice, for simplicity purpose, for rooms to be assigned at the end after the assignment of lectures to periods, the proposed algorithm is invoked after a feasible solution is found and has led to a significant improvement in the overall fitness score (enhanced initial seed). Figure 1 outlines the room matching algorithm pseudocode.

Phase 1: Construction of a feasible solution, X
Output the feasible solution, $X_{feasible}$ to be utilized by the matching algorithm
Phase 2: Arbitrary Heuristic Room Matching Algorithm
  Construct a *MasterTimeslot* matrix, *MT* for each room
  Construct a *course_room* matrix, *crseroom* which matches
  the usable rooms to each courses based on S_{index}
  Invoke Matching Algorithm
      do while (j<no. of courses)
          if $d_j \geq std_k$ AND *period$_j$* == *period$_k$*
              select r_i from *crseroom* assign r_i to c_k
              update the removal of r_i from *MT*
          end
      end

Fig. 1. Pseudocode of room matching algorithm

Upon obtaining a feasible solution, the AHRMA is invoked to reassign random rooms which can cater to the capacity of the students to all courses. The algorithm initializes with the construction of a MasterTimeslot matrix, MT which lists every available timeslots for all rooms. Subsequently, a course_room matrix, crseroom is constructed based on a suitability index, Sindex similar to that to the works of (Caldeira and Rosa 1997) which measures the suitability of each room by subtracting the room capacity, rci from the student enrolment, stdi of a particular course. The assignment is only possible for all negative values of di and the suitability increases for di → 0. In the computation of the Sindex illustrated in Fig. 2, room B with a seating capacity of 200 can be assigned to course c0001 with the enrolment of 130 students with its di value −70. Only negative value of Sindex is accepted as this implies that the room capacity is able to sustain the student enrolment. At the end of each iteration, the MT is updated with the removal of the assigned room to prevent any form of conflict.

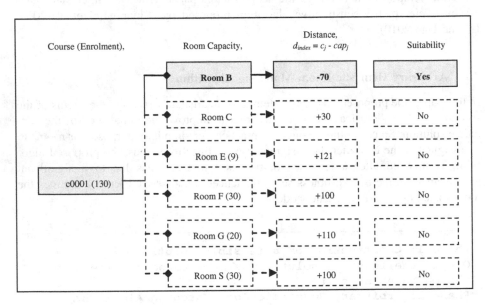

Fig. 2. Computation of suitability index, S_{index}

The proposed algorithm is then implemented on Track 3 of the Second International Timetabling Competition which consists of twenty-one problem instances which comprises the early, middle and late dataset of the curriculum-based course timetabling problem model.

4   Results and Discussion

This section provides the results of the experiment. Table 3 and Fig. 3 depict the soft constraints improvement score of the initial feasible solution for twenty-one problem instances of the curriculum-based course timetabling problem. For each problem instance, the fitness scores obtained from AHRMA is averaged across ten unique initial solutions to demonstrate the efficiency of the algorithm. The table and figure respectively describe the mean initial fitness score, finit, the mean improved fitness score,

Table 3. AHRMA fitness scores

Instance	f_{init}	$f_{improve}$	$f'_{improve}$	σ	$\%_{improvement}$	t (s)
comp01	2157.63	38.67	4	34.67	98.21	0.03
comp02	7974.35	0.00	0	0.00	100.00	0.04
comp03	6609.06	0.00	0	0.00	100.00	0.02
comp04	5672.41	0.00	0	0.00	100.00	0.02
comp05	8052.27	0.00	0	0.00	100.00	0.03
comp06	7197.43	0.00	0	0.00	100.00	0.07
comp07	6412.47	0.00	0	0.00	100.00	0.08
comp08	5668.66	0.00	0	0.00	100.00	0.04
comp09	5588.13	0.00	0	0.00	100.00	0.03
comp10	5699.23	0.00	0	0.00	100.00	0.06
comp 11	826.23	0.00	0	0.00	100.00	0.02
comp 12	2232.19	0.00	0	0.00	100.00	0.04
comp 13	8597.25	0.00	0	0.00	100.00	0.06
comp 14	4308.79	0.00	0	0.00	100.00	0.05
comp 15	6635.81	0.00	0	0.00	100.00	0.04
comp 16	5538.86	0.00	0	0.00	100.00	0.06
comp 17	6653.33	0.00	0	0.00	100.00	0.06
comp 18	648.02	0.00	0	0.00	100.00	0.01
comp 19	4471.74	0.00	0	0.00	100.00	0.05
comp 20	7219.69	0.00	0	0.00	100.00	0.06
comp 21	5436.84	0.00	0	0.00	100.00	0.05

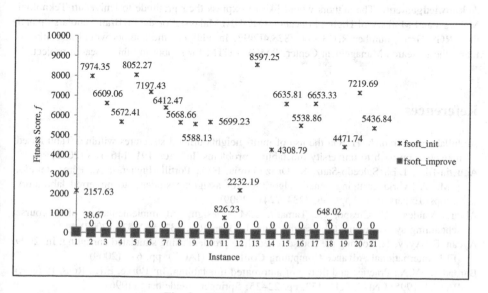

Fig. 3. AHRMA fitness scores

fimprove, the best value of the improved fitness score, f'improve, standard deviation, σ, percentage of improvement, %improvement and the computational time, t measured in seconds.

The reassignment of rooms as demonstrated by the proposed AHRMA is able to enhance the quality of the initial seed significantly. In all of the tested problem instances, the AHRMA exhibits an improvement of at least 98.21 % to 100 % in the fitness score, fsoft_improve in less than one second, which is reflected in column t(s) in Table 2. By simply reassigning a better room to each course lectures, the AHRMA has assisted in any metaheuristic algorithms by providing a considerable advantageous search point for the optimization of soft constraints as the metaheuristic algorithm no longer needs to be concerned with the assignment of a suitable room and is able to focus in other regions of improvement.

5   Conclusion

This paper has presented an alternative method to graph colouring in generating an enhanced initial seed for the CB-CTT which constitutes the Track 3 of the Second International Timetabling Competition. In order to acquire an enhanced initial seed for the CB-CTT, the authors have proposed an algorithm entitled AHRMA which heuristically reassigns better rooms randomly to each course lectures. This approach is simple yet effective as it is able to render significant improvement to the candidate solutions in a very short amount of time and allows any future optimization to negate the aspect of room capacity. To provide some foreseeable future works, the authors intend to incorporate heuristics which take into account other soft constraints collectively to provide even a greater quality initial solution.

Acknowledgement. The authors would like to express their gratitude to Universiti Teknologi Malaysia and Ministry of Higher Education (MOHE) Malaysia for the myBrain scholarship and the FRGS Grant, number R.J130000.7828.4F497. In addition, the authors would also like to thank the Research Management Center (RMC) – UTM for supporting this research project.

References

Abdullah, S., Turabieh, H.: On the use of multi neighbourhood structures within a Tabu-based memetic approach to university timetabling problems. Inf. Sci. **191**, 146–168 (2012)

Agustín-Blas, L.E., Salcedo-Sanz, S., Ortiz-García, E.G., Portilla-Figueras, A., Pérez-Bellido, Á.M.: A hybrid grouping genetic algorithm for assigning students to preferred laboratory groups. Expert Syst. Appl. **36**, 7234–7241 (2009)

Alvarez-Valdes, R., Crespo, E., Tamarit, J.M.: Design and implementation of a course scheduling system using Tabu search. Eur. J. Oper. Res. **137**, 512–523 (2002)

Aycan, E., Ayav, T.: Solving the course scheduling problem using simulated annealing. In: 2009 IEEE International Advance Computing Conference (IACC), pp. 6–7 (2009)

Bardadym, V.A.: Practice and theory of automated timetabling. In: Burke, E.K., Ross, P. (eds.) PATAT 1995. LNCS, vol. 1153, pp. 22–25. Springer, Heidelberg (1996)

Brownlee, J.: Clever Algorithms. Nature-Inspired Programming Recipes, Lulu Enterprises, pp. 401–402 (2011)

Burke, E.K., Elliman, D.G., Weare, R.F.: A hybrid genetic algorithm for highly constrained timetabling problems. In: Proceedings of the Sixth International Conference on Genetic Algorithms, pp. 605–610 (1995)

Caldeira, J.P., Rosa, A.C.: School timetabling using genetic search. In: Proceedings of the 2nd International Conference on the Practice and Theory of Automated Timetabling, Toronto, pp. 115–122 (1997)

Chiarandini, M., Birattari, M., Socha, K., Rossi-Doria, O.: An effective hybrid algorithm for university course timetabling. J. Sched. 9(5), 403–432 (2006)

Frausto-Solís, J., Alonso-Pecina, F., Mora-Vargas, J.: An efficient simulated annealing algorithm for feasible solutions of course timetabling. In: Gelbukh, A., Morales, E.F. (eds.) MICAI 2008. LNCS (LNAI), vol. 5317, pp. 675–685. Springer, Heidelberg (2008)

Gaspero, L., Di Mccollum, B., Schaerf, A.: The Second International Timetabling Competition (ITC-2007): Curriculum-Based Course Timetabling (Track 3), pp. 1–12 (2007)

Ismayilova, N.A., Sağir, M., Gasimov, R.N.: A multiobjective faculty–course–time slot assignment problem with preferences. Math. Comput. Model. 46(7–8), 1017–1029 (2007)

Jain, A., Jain, S., Chande, P.K.: Formulation of genetic algorithm to generate good quality course timetable 1(3), 248–251 (2010)

Kohshori, M., Abadeh, M.: Hybrid genetic algorithms for university course timetabling. Int. J. Comput. Sci. 9(2), 446–455 (2012)

Lü, Z., Hao, J.K.: Adaptive Tabu search for course timetabling. Eur. J. Oper. Res. 200(1), 235–244 (2010)

Lutuksin, T., Pongcharoen, P.: Best-worst ant colony system parameter investigation by using experimental design and analysis for course timetabling problem. In: 2010 Second International Conference on Computer and Network Technology, pp. 467–471 (2010)

Qarouni-Fard, D., Najafi-Ardabili, A., Moeinzadeh, M.-H.: Finding feasible timetables with particle swarm optimization. In: 4th International Conference on Innovations in Information Technology, IIT 2007, pp. 387–391 (2007)

Rizam, M., Bakar, A.: Selecting quality initial random seed for metaheuristic approaches : a case of timetabling problem. Int. J. Comput. Internet Manage. 16(1), 38–45 (2008)

Rossi-Doria, O., et al.: A comparison of the performance of different metaheuristics on the timetabling problem. In: Burke, E.K., De Causmaecker, P. (eds.) PATAT 2002. LNCS, vol. 2740, pp. 329–351. Springer, Heidelberg (2003)

Shiau, D.F.: A hybrid particle swarm optimization for a university course scheduling problem with flexible preferences. Expert Syst. Appl. 38(1), 235–248 (2011)

Suyanto, S.: An informed genetic algorithm for university course and student timetabling problems. In: Rutkowski, L., Scherer, R., Tadeusiewicz, R., Zadeh, L.A., Zurada, J.M. (eds.) ICAISC 2010, Part II. LNCS, vol. 6114, pp. 229–236. Springer, Heidelberg (2010)

Tassopoulos, I.X., Beligiannis, G.N.: Solving effectively the school timetabling problem using particle swarm optimization. Expert Syst. Appl. 39(5), 6029–6040 (2012)

Thepphakorn, T., Hicks, C., Pongcharoen, P.: An ant colony based timetabling tool. Int. J. Prod. Econ. 149, 131–144 (2009)

Zhang, D., Liu, Y., M'Hallah, R., Leung, S.C.H.H.: A Simulated Annealing with a new neighborhood structure based algorithm for high school timetabling problems. Eur. J. Oper. Res. 203(3), 550–558 (2010)

Evaluating Extant Uranium: Linguistic Reasoning by Fuzzy Artificial Neural Networks

M. Reza Mashinchi[1,2,3], Ali Selamat[1,2(✉)], and Suhaimi Ibrahim[3]

[1] UTM-IRDA Center of Excellence, Universiti Teknologi Malaysia,
81310 Johor Baharu, Johor, Malaysia
r_mashinchi@yahoo.com
[2] Faculty of Computing, Universiti Teknologi Malaysia,
81310 Johor Baharu, Johor, Malaysia
aselamat@utm.my
[3] Advanced Informatics School, Universiti Teknologi Malaysia,
81310 Johor Baharu, Johor, Malaysia
suhaimiibrahim@utm.my

Abstract. This paper aims at estimating the extant uranium by soft computing approach. The rising contribution of this resource in the energy cycle is the reason to this research. Untidy relations and uncertain values in geological data increase the complexity of estimating extant uranium, and thus it requires a proper approach. This paper applies artificial neural networks (ANNs), in both crisp and fuzzy concepts, with the exploit of genetic algorithms (GAs). Artificial neural networks (ANNs) trace the untidy relations even though under uncertain circumstances by fuzzy artificial neural networks (FANNs), where GAs can explore the best performance of these networks. We use the type-3 of FANNs against the conventional ANNs to reveal the results, where the Lilliefors and Pearson statistical tests validate them for two geological datasets. The results showed the type-3 of FANNs is preferred for desired outcome with uncertain values, while ANNs are unable to deliver this particular.

Keywords: Inexactness · Mining · Uranium amount · Genetic algorithm

1 Introduction

In this paper, processing the uranium data is studied as a complex problem to estimate the extant amount of this element. Macro planes for future of fuel resources makes this study contributive by providing invaluable information on uranium resources [1]. Therefore, exploring and developing the approaches that support this contribution is considerable. The uranium is used as a fuel resource as well as using for other costs of processing. Therefore, it needs an approach to abate the processing cost of this complexity.

Soft computing techniques solve the complex problems in low-cost approaches [2]. Neural networks (NN) have taken a significant place among soft computing techniques since its proposal. NN based approaches trace the complexities by learning for estimation. In the other hand, fuzzy modeling is another conventional approach to deal

© Springer International Publishing Switzerland 2015
H. Fujita and G. Guizzi (Eds.): SoMeT 2015, CCIS 532, pp. 296–307, 2015.
DOI: 10.1007/978-3-319-22689-7_22

with complex perceptions [3]. It is a strong preprocessing approach to represent the complexities, and particularly, it has been manifested to have better results when hybrid with other mechanisms. As an example, fuzzy artificial neural networks (FANNs) have fascinated many researchers as generalized form of neural networks. They derive the advantages from both fuzzy modeling and neural networks. Regarding hybrid approaches in gamut of soft computing, genetic algorithms are widely used as the other potent soft computing techniques. GA, denotes for genetic algorithm as a model of optimization, has been successfully used in a many applications. Its puissance has been used in hybrid with other methods since the potent of GAs became to notice. For example, the hybridization of GAs with artificial neural networks improves the efficiency of learning. In addition, FANNs that are based on GAs have been improved to support involvement of these networks in application areas [4–17].

This paper constructs a system that estimates the extant amount of uranium element based on geological data. Such system should decrease the processing costs when encounter complexity of environment. ANNs, and a few other approaches, have been engaged in studies related to uranium [18]. However, estimating extant uranium for mining purposes has not been studied by FANNs. Soft computing approaches decrease the processing costs behind the complex problems, where relations between data are difficult to be traced. It is noticeable that they do not guarantee to find the optimal solution as they depend on random functioning; however, it mostly eventuates to suitable results. In this regard, this paper applies FANNs to estimate the extant uranium where GA gives advantages to the performance of FANNs.

To achieve the aim of this paper, Sect. 2 discusses on utilized models; where, Subsect. 2.1 describes fuzzy modeling with respect to uncertainty, followed by Subsect. 2.2 that describes optimization modeling with respect to optimizing the status of estimator by genetic algorithms. Section 3 explains FANNs; where, Subsect. 3.1 reviews GA-based FANNs as the main part of this paper. Section 4 provides the implementation and results of the proposed approach, and, Sect. 5 concludes the findings of the paper.

2 Modeling the Problem

Estimating the extant amount of uranium is a complex problem where tracing the relations of data are difficult. To have a suitable estimation, a proper model is required to cope with this complexity. Otherwise, not only the problem being solved but also it will increase the costs. Here, fuzzy sets and genetic algorithms are used to model the uncertainty of uranium data and to find the optimal status of the estimator as are discussed in Sects. 2.1 and 2.2 respectively.

2.1 Uncertainty Modeling of Uranium Environment

Uncertainty is a concept for complexity, which is intangible with human sense. The true example of uncertainty is inexactness and linguistic terms that are used in datasets of this paper. Uncertainty is the main issue that fuzzy sets theory intends to solve it by a fuzzy model. The fuzzy sets are a generalized form of classical set theory, which intends for a better representation of the real world. In the classical or crisp set the fact that elements of the universe of discourse are either belong or do not belong to a crisp set A indicates that it can be formally represented by the characteristic function of A whose images are dual in perspective. The model of crisp representation is far away from the reality when it is desired to develop the real world. Therefore, fuzzy modeling is aimed at better representation of the concepts particularly for complex situations. Processing based on fuzzy representation is done using fuzzy operations. Common arithmetic operations are those defined on fuzzy triangular numbers due to the simplicity, where this paper use them for the same reason. A fuzzy number $\tilde{A} = (a_1, a_2, a_3)$ is a map $\tilde{A} : R \to [0, 1]$ where its membership function is as follows:

$$
\mu_{\tilde{A}}(x) = \begin{cases} 0 & x \le a_1 \\ (x - a_1)/(a_2 - a_1) & a_1 < x < a_2 \\ (x - a_3)/(a_2 - a_3) & a_2 < x < a_3 \\ 0 & x \ge a_3 \end{cases} \tag{1}
$$

where R is the set of all real numbers and $a_1, a_2, a_3 \in R$. We apply the arithmetic operations of addition and multiplication defined as below:

$$
\tilde{A} + \tilde{B} = (a_1, a_2, a_3) + (b_1, b_2, b_3) = (a_1 + b_1, a_2 + b_2, a_3 + b_3) \tag{2}
$$

$$
\tilde{A} + \tilde{B} = (a_1, a_2, a_3) + (b_1, b_2, b_3) = [\min(a_1.b_1, a_1.b_3), a_2.b_2, \min(a_3.b_1, a_3.b_3)] \tag{3}
$$

There are two reasons to use fuzzy modeling for the current problem. First, fuzzy sets support a good exhibition for continuous boundaries in well-defined semantics to emerge fully meaningful entities. Second, fuzzy models are conventionally attached to the artificial neural networks in the literature. Fuzzy modes have been used to increase the ability of artificial neural networks to deal with fuzzy data and also to generalizing them. Fuzziness is used to aid the learning process of artificial neural networks when the there are unmitigated complexity from using full content of each data. This paper tries to derive the advantages of different models to solve the current problem, by using hybrid methods that are promising better results.

2.2 Optimization Modeling of Estimator

Regardless the nature of problem, whether to be exact or inexact, finding optimum solution has always been an interesting study to abate the computation costs. Soft computing techniques are proven to be suitable approaches in this regard. Genetic algorithms, as soft computing techniques, are widespread among optimization techniques. They perform based on randomly generated populations to find the optimum solution. Evolutionarily obtaining optimal solution in GAs is based on some functions, which are inspired from natural evolutions as selection, crossover and mutation functions. The suitability of obtained solutions from these functions is defined by fitness function known as an important part of GAs.

The selection operator involves choosing members of the population randomly to enter a mating pool. There are several ways for the selection, where one of them is the proportional selection. The roulette wheel selection is the most appealed for the proportional selection. The advantage of using roulette wheel method is that each individual has the chance to be selected, and thus, the weak individuals are not eliminated as in some other methods. Selected members are then mated to produce the offspring which is done using crossover function. Among the crossover functions, uniform crossover is driven to be the most appealed that mates based on a mixing ratio. The decision rate of uniform crossover is known as mixing ratio, which is the allowance of parents in contributing to offspring. Created offspring from mating the parents in the crossover stage are needed to be diversified which is done by mutation. It is a genetic operator maintains genetic diversity through generations. As in uniform mutation, one of the variables of the parents are selected and set equal to a random number, which is uniformly distributed between the lower and upper bounds of a selected variable.

In this paper, we propose a method to benefit from GAs in optimizing the learning mechanism. This has been achieved by hybridized GAs and FANNs.

3   Fuzzy Artificial Neural Networks

ANNs, denotes for artificial neural networks, reason by learnt data. ANNs are inspired from biological neural networks, and, they have positioned themselves in the gamut of soft computing. Afterward observing disabilities of crisp-based approaches to deal with complex data, the ANNs have been hybridized with fuzzy-based approaches to propose fuzzy artificial neural networks. Therefore FANNs, denotes for fuzzy artificial neural networks, have attracted many researches by deriving benefits from hybridization of soft computing techniques. FANNs are categorized in three types based on their weights and biases as $FANN_1$, $FANN_2$ and $FANN_3$. We use $FANN_3$ in this paper as a generalized form of three-layer FANNs as shown in Fig. 1.

In Fig. 1, the input is the first layer with no computational unit. The outcome is caused by the operation in second and third layers as aggregations, multiplications and

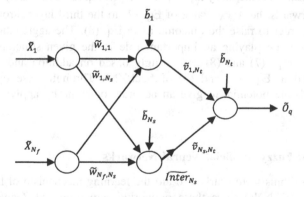

Fig. 1. A three layers FANN.

activation functions. The second layer of network and the matrix of fuzzy weights $\tilde{w}_{N_f,N_s}$ show fuzzy weights connect the neuron N_f in the first layer to the neuron N_s in the next layer. Each input $\tilde{X}_{N_f}$ are multiplied to the connected weights $\tilde{W}_{N_f,N_s}$ and aggregated with the bias in the second layer, where the vector of fuzzy biases $\tilde{b}_{N_s}$ shows fuzzy bias of neuron N_f. Similarly, in the last layer, fuzzy weight matrix $\tilde{v}_{N_s,N_t}$ shows fuzzy weights connects the neuron N_s in the hidden layer to the neuron N_t in the last layer. Here, the activated outcomes from the neurons of the second layer are multiplied to the connected weights $\tilde{v}_{N_s,N_t}$ and aggregated with $\tilde{b}_{N_t}$. The activation functions utilized for the neurons here are the sigmoid function given as below in Eq. (4).

$$f(x) = \frac{1}{1+e^{-x}} \tag{4}$$

Fuzzy outputs of $_{Inter_{N_s}}$ and $\tilde{O}_q$ are given in Eqs. (5) and (6) for the second and third layers of this architecture respectively as below:

$$\tilde{Inter}_{N_s} = f(\tilde{Agg}_{N_s}), N_s = 1, 2, \ldots, n \tag{5}$$

$$\tilde{O}_q = \tilde{Agg}_{N_t}, N_t = 1, 2, \ldots, n \tag{6}$$

where $\tilde{Agg}_{N_s}$ and $\tilde{Agg}_{N_t}$ are defined in Eqs. (7) and (8) for the fuzzy outcomes of second and third layers and N_f and N_s in Eqs. (5)–(8) are the number of neurons in the second and third layers respectively.

$$\tilde{Agg}_{N_s} = \sum_{i=0}^{N_f} \tilde{X}_i \cdot \tilde{w}_{ij} + \tilde{b}_j, j = 1, 2, \ldots, N_s \tag{7}$$

$$\tilde{Agg}_{N_t} = \sum_{j=1}^{N_s} \tilde{Agg}_j \cdot \tilde{V}_{jq} + \tilde{b}_{N_t}, q = 1, 2, \ldots, N_t \tag{8}$$

where $\tilde{X}_i$ in Eq. (7) is the fuzzy input and $\tilde{Agg}_{N_t}$ in Eq. (8) is the fuzzy outcome. The second layer forwards the $\tilde{Agg}_{N_s}$ value of Eq. (7) to the third layer through the fuzzy weight $\tilde{v}_{N_s,N_t}$ in order to raise the outcome as in Eq. (8). The aggregation and multiplication operators are playing an important role in the given structure of FANNs, where the major Eqs. (7) and (8) are strongly based on addition and multiplication operators defined in Eqs. (2) and (3) of Sect. 2.1. Through these operators, well designed FANNs are potential to give an accurate outcome by applying on suitable weights

3.1   GA-Based Fuzzy Artificial Neural Networks

The genetic algorithms were sparked to aid the learning mechanism of fuzzy artificial neural networks (FANNs) since these networks were proposed. Genetic algorithm

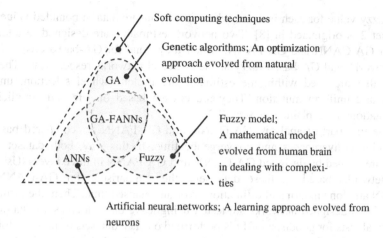

Fig. 2. GA-FANNs proposed in joints of other soft computing techniques.

based FANNs, denoted as GA-FANNs, are the result of using three approaches from soft computing area. Figure 2 illustrates the soft computing techniques that contribute to GA-FANNs. Here, the optimization aspect of GAs gives a suitable learning to ANNs, where fuzzy modeling aids the learning process to track the relations in the complex environments.

The researches on FANNs have been attached to GAs afterward the reveal of GA capabilities in hybrid with other approaches for the applications. Indeed, the optimization ability of GAs is used to improve the learning convergence of FANNs, since the learning mechanism is highly dependent on adjustments of the network weight. In this way, hybridization of GAs and FANNs proffers to attain a suitable reasoning by optimizing network variables. Global optimization in GAs is one aspect that benefits FANNs, where the values of network weights can be found in absolute optimum. Globally found optimal values of the network variables is used to predict the amount of extant uranium based on given input. This is the aim of this research to decrease the cost of estimating the uranium amount by using GA-FANNs as given in Algorithm 1.

Algorithm 1 illustrates the steps of GA-FANNs; where, Steps 5 and 6 are the main parts to take before the reproduction meets the termination conditions. The fitness is assigned by suitability of values to meet the termination, where the intended optimal values are obtained from proper operation of the reproduction explained in Sect. 2.2.

The initialization in Step 2 is based on randomness that causes the algorithm to not guarantee yielding the optimal values. However, it mostly eventuates to the satisfactory results meanwhile suitable reproduction holds an important role in the algorithm.

4   Implementation and Results

This section presents the applicability of GA-ANNs, abbreviated for genetic algorithms based artificial neural networks, to estimate the extant amount of uranium element. We used two datasets to give seven analyses in two parts. Dataset 1 is represented in the form of fuzzy value for each instance where it was unsure data in bounded value [19], and dataset 2 is originated in [8]. Two network estimators are designed to attain the results for GA-CANN and GA-FANN, which they stand for GA-based crisp artificial neural networks and GA-based fuzzy artificial neural networks respectively. The GAs operators that are used within the estimator are roulette wheel selection, uniform crossover and uniform mutation. They are chosen based on rife and simplicity of implementations as explained in Sect. 2.2.

For the first part of analysis, GA-CANN and GA-FANN are compared based on their learning convergences and convergence time. In this way, both dataset 1 and dataset 2 are trained by designed GA-CANN and GA-FANN in three layers. Using the trained networks based on these data sets, the comparisons for GA-CANN and GA-FANN are done in terms of estimation error and elapsed time. Then, the estimation abilities of two designed networks are tested using leave-one-out cross-validation and, the statistical tests for goodness-of-fit is performed on each datasets using Lilliefors and Pearson's tests. For the second part of analysis, the learning behavior of GA-FANN is analyzed in terms of time and generated error for variation of training data and GA population.

In order to do the first analysis, the obtained results for GA-CANN and GA-FANN in terms of generated error and execution time are shown in Figs. 3 and 4. Here, 150 populations and 500 generations are used to learn each dataset. The estimation

```
1 begin
2 initialize ( )
3 x    select ( )
4 while ≠ terminationCriterion (x) do
5 x(x_{new1})    crossover (x)
6 x(x_{new2})    mutate (x_{new1})
7 if f(x_{new2}) < f(x) then    x    x_{new2}
8 return x
9 end
```

Fig. 3. Algorithm1: GA-based FANNs.

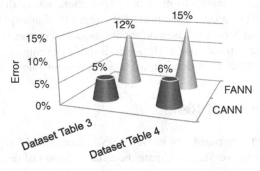

Fig. 4. Comparison for CANN and FANN in terms of generated error.

performances of designed networks are measured by the distance of output and ideal value. In addition, fuzzy outcome has been defuzzified after receiving from trained GA-FANN to be comparable with GA-CANN outcome.

In order to test the networks ability, we used leave-one-out cross-validation. Two networks consisting of 25 neurons in 4 layers were designed, and then each instance was predicted based on others after 500 learning generations by using 150 populations for each generation. The outcomes from trained GA-FANN and GA-CANN have been presented in Table 1. Similarly, the estimation ability of designed GA-FANN was tested using dataset 2. Table 2 gives the test results of trained network using 700 generations and 200 populations.

The presented results for the first part of analysis show the ability of ANNs in predicting uranium element meanwhile CANNs give better results. However, it is worth mentioning that in spite of having less accuracy for GA-FANNs, the fuzzy outcome is more compatible with the data nature of dealt problem to be bounded value. The obtained results are tested for goodness-of-fit to normal density using Lilliefors and Pearson's tests. The tests are performed on each fold of testing stages, and the average of goodness is given in Table 3 based on 5 % of significance level.

Table 1. Estimation of GA-FANN and GA-CANN based on dataset 1 [19].

Input	Outcome		Desire fuzzy value
	GA-FANN	GA-CANN	
$\tilde{X}1$	(7.15, 23.8, 30.9)	24.03	(10.5, 27.1, 43.7)
$\tilde{X}2$	(4.9, 13.26, 23.17)	12.4	(7.4, 13, 18.6)
$\tilde{X}3$	(3.48, 4.02, 5.42)	3.4	(3, 3.8, 4.6)

Table 2. Estimation of GA-FANN based on dataset 2 [8].

Input	GA-FANN outcome	Desired fuzzy value
$\tilde{X}1$	(64.01, 73.54, 76.26)	(64, 75.5, 78)
$\tilde{X}2$	(64.20, 74.8, 77.31)	(64, 75.5, 78)
$\tilde{X}3$	(60.7, 67.32, 74.15)	(62, 64, 73)
$\tilde{X}4$	(65.35, 74.65, 79.17)	(64, 75.5, 78)
$\tilde{X}5$	(60.25, 66.04, 75.21)	(62, 64, 73)
$\tilde{X}6$	(62.57, 65.15, 75.00)	(64, 75.5, 78)
$\tilde{X}7$	(64.24, 74.53, 78.11)	(64, 75.5, 78)
$\tilde{X}8$	(60.64, 73.65, 89.27)	(64, 75.5, 78)
$\tilde{X}9$	(62.31, 70.16, 77.69)	(62, 64, 73)
$\tilde{X}10$	(59.49, 61.56, 81.46)	(62, 64, 73)
$\tilde{X}11$	(60.76, 65.91, 76.35)	(62, 64, 73)
$\tilde{X}12$	(61.40, 66.70, 74.25)	(62, 64, 73)
$\tilde{X}13$	(62.37, 71.42, 76.33)	(64, 75.5, 78)

Table 3. Overall statistical tests for GA-FANN and GA-CANN.

Dataset	GA-FANN		GA-CANN	
	Lilliefors	Pearson	Lilliefors	Pearson
Table 4	71 %	67 %	78 %	73 %
Table 6	61 %	55 %	75 %	68 %

For the second part of analysis, learning behavior of GA-FANN is analyzed in three parts. First, we trained GA-FANN using dataset of dataset 2; to this end, we designed it using 16 neurons in 3 layers. We observed the learning behavior of this network when decreasing the number of data under train (Figs. 5 and 6). The learning behaviors for different numbers of training data in dataset are given by the trend of the percentage that each generated error contributes over the generation. The results are shown in Fig. 5 and trend over time in Fig. 6.

Analyzing Fig. 5; we observe alike behavior near dash line B. Though after that, decreasing the ability of learning in GA-FANN shows it traps in local minima for the larger datasets. Therefore, the more growth of dataset dimension, the more complexity of problem. This causes the search algorithm to trap into local minima. The initial generations affect on learning behavior as shown in Fig. 6; where, the higher

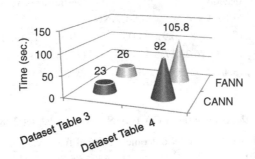

Fig. 5. Comparison for CANN and FANN in terms of execution time.

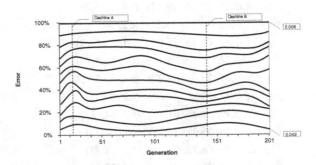

Fig. 6. Effect of increasing the number of training data on GA-FANN in terms of generated error.

convergence rates before dash line, the higher convergence after dash line. The variations around vertical dash line lead to analyze learning behavior based on different populations Fig. 8 .

Analysis on using different population for learning behavior helps to find the effectiveness of the number of population in keeping the learning rate before the last generation. To this end, the learning behaviors of trained network were obtained as shown in Fig. 7, where 50, 100 and 200 populations were used to learn dataset. Here the variations on line C are noticeable, which are based on variation of learning convergence in terms of estimation error. The convergence rate has been decreased by passing dash line C. It happens at almost 10 % of all learning generations – as the same as line A in Fig. 7. This indicates that: first, the general value of solution has been obtained before a threshold, and then after a threshold, more optimized value is obtained. A future work can devise an approach to keep the convergence rate in generations afterward threshold.

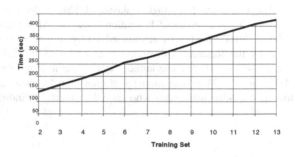

Fig. 7. Effect of increasing the number of training data on GA-FANN in terms of elapsed time.

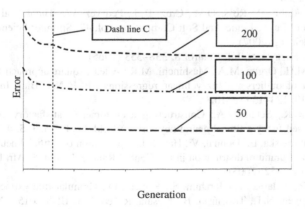

Fig. 8. Effect of different populations to train GA-FANN.

5 Conclusion

This paper establishes an algorithm to predict the amount of extant uranium for mining purposes. The estimation process has been situated as a complex problem and thus dealing with such problem is very costly. Since this study intends to approach it in a low cost level, applying soft computing techniques were put forward. The prediction process was based on learning the extant amount of uranium using artificial neural networks; however GA optimization and fuzzy modeling were aided since the problem complexity hampers suitable learning. Therefore GA-FANNs are utilized as a hybrid system to solve the current problem. To see the performance of the proposed method, two datasets are used and seven analyses are given in two parts. The results of GA-FANNs and GA-based crisp artificial neural networks were compared in terms of estimation error and elapsed time. The ability of artificial neural networks in general, and, the compatibility of fuzzy artificial neural networks with uncertainties of data in particular are revealed in dealing with the studied problem. Finally, some analysis to conduct the future works elucidates the potent of GA-FANNs in dealing with uncertain nature of the studied problem.

Acknowledgements. The Universiti Teknologi Malaysia (UTM) under Research University Funding Scheme (Vot01G72) and Ministry of Education Malaysia (MOE) under Fundamental Research Funding Scheme (FRGS) are hereby acknowledged for supporting this research. Also, this research is funded by the Research University grant of Universiti Teknologi Malaysia (UTM) under the Vot no. 4F238, 4F550. The authors would like to thank the Research Management Centre of UTM and the Malaysian ministry of education for their support and cooperation including students and other individuals who are either directly or indirectly involved in this project.

References

1. Switkowski, Z.: Uranium mining, processing and nuclear energy: opportunities for Australia? (2006)
2. Castillo, O., Melin, P., Ross, O.M., Cruz, R.S., Pedrycz, W.: Theoretical Advances And Applications of Fuzzy Logic And Soft Computing, vol. 42. Springer Science and Business Media, Heidelberg (2007)
3. Zadeh, L.A.: Fuzzy sets. Inf. Control **8**, 338–353 (1965)
4. Mashinchi, M.H., Orgun, M.A., Mashinchi, M.R.: A least square approach for the detection and removal of outliers for fuzzy linear regressions. IEEE Nat. Biol. Inspired Comput. (NaBIC) **2010**, 134–139 (2010)
5. Mashinchi, M.R., Selamat, A.: Constructing a customer's satisfactory evaluator system using GA-based fuzzy artificial neural networks. World Appl. Sci. J. **5**, 432–440 (2008)
6. Tutu, H., Cukrowska, E., Dohnal, V., Havel, J.: Application of artificial neural networks for classification of uranium distribution in the Central Rand goldfield. S. Afr. Environ. Model. Assess. **10**, 143–152 (2005)
7. Mashinchi, R., Selamat, A., Ibrahim, S., Krejcar, O.: Granular-rule extraction to simplify data. In: Nguyen, N.T., Trawiński, B., Kosala, R. (eds.) ACIIDS 2015. LNCS, vol. 9012, pp. 421–429. Springer, Heidelberg (2015)

8. Mashinchi, R., Selamat, A., Ibrahim, S., Krejcar, O., Penhaker, M.: Evaluating customer satisfaction: linguistic reasoning by fuzzy artificial neural networks. In: Barbucha, D., Nguyen, N.T., Batubara, J. (eds.) New Trends in Intelligent Information and Database Systems. SCI, vol. 598, pp. 91–100. Springer, Heidelberg (2015)

9. Mashinchi, M.R., Mashinchi, M.H., Selamat, A.: New approach for language identification based on DNA computing. In: BIOCOMP, pp. 748–752 (2007)

10. Mashinchi, M.H., Mashinchi, M.R., Pedrycz, W.: Genetically tuned fuzzy back-propagation learning method based on derivation of min-max function for fuzzy neural networks, GEM, pp. 213–212. CSREA Press (2007)

11. Mashinchi, M.H., Mashinchi, M.R., Mashaallah, M.: Tabu search solution for fuzzy linear programming. In: ACIS-ICIS, pp. 82–87 (2008)

12. Mashinchi, M.R., Selamat, A., Ibrahim, S., Fujita, H.: Outlier elimination using granular box regression. Info. Fusion, 27, 161–169 (2016)

13. Dastanpour, A., Ibrahim, S., Mashinchi, R.: Using genetic algorithm to supporting artificial neural network for intrusion detection system. In: The Society of Digital Information and Wireless Communication, pp. 1–13

14. Mashinchi, M.R., Selamat, A.: An improvement on genetic-based learning method for fuzzy artificial neural networks. Appl. Soft Comput. 9, 1208–1216 (2009)

15. Mashinchi, M.R., Selamat, A.: Measuring customer service satisfactions using fuzzy artificial neural network with two-phase genetic algorithm. In: Ali, A.-D. (ed.) Computational Intelligence and Modern Heuristics. InTech, Osaka (2010)

16. Mashinchi, M., Shamsuddin, S.M.H.: Three-term fuzzy back-propagation. In: Hassanien, A.-E., Abraham, A., Vasilakos, A.V., Pedrycz, W. (eds.) Foundations of Computational, Intelligence Volume 1: Learning and Approximation. SCI, vol. 201, pp. 143–158. Springer, Heidelberg (2009)

17. Mashinchi, M.H., Mashinchi, M.R., Shamsuddin, S.: A genetic algorithm approach for solving fuzzy linear and quadratic equations. World Acad. Sci. Eng. Technol. 28, 209–213 (2007)

18. Kelly, M., Thorne, M.: An approach to multi-attribute utility analysis under parametric uncertainty. Ann. Nucl. Energy 28, 875–893 (2001)

19. Staudenrausch, S., Kaldorf, M., Renker, C., Luis, P., Buscot, F.: Diversity of the ectomycorrhiza community at a uranium mining heap. Biol. Fertil. Soils 41, 439–446 (2005)

A Method for Class Noise Detection
Based on K-means and SVM Algorithms

Zahra Nematzadeh[1(✉)], Roliana Ibrahim[1], and Ali Selamat[1,2]

[1] Faculty of Computing, Universiti Teknologi Malaysia,
81310 Johor Baharu, Johor, Malaysia
zahra_nematzadeh@yahoo.com, {roliana,aselamat}@utm.my
[2] UTM-IRDA Digital Media Centre of Excellence,
Universiti Teknologi Malaysia, 81310 Johor Baharu, Johor, Malaysia

Abstract. One of the techniques for improving the accuracy of induced classifier is noise filtering. The classifiers prediction performance is affected by the noisy datasets used in the induction of classifiers. Therefore, it is very important to detect and remove the noise in order to increase the classification accuracy. This paper proposed a model for noise detection in the datasets using k-means and support vector machine (SVM) techniques. The proposed model has been tested using the datasets from University of California, Irvine machine learning repository. Experimental results reveal that the proposed model can improve data quality and increase the classification accuracies.

Keywords: Class noise detection · K-means · Support vector machine

1 Introduction

A noise filtering is considered as a process of removing the insignificant data from real data. Although there are many researches have been done to remove the noise through data collection process, it is often impossible to eliminate all the noises. This may happen during the process of selecting, measuring and recording tasks [1] of the datasets. The main advantage of noise handling techniques in machine learning is to improve the classification accuracy of models which are induced from the data [2].

The focus of this research is to remove the noise in the class datasets which occurs due to the subjectivity and errors in the data entry process. There are two kinds of class noises, which are the inconsistent instances and the error in the classification of datasets, respectively. The error based on inconsistent instances refers to the samples with the same feature values that belong to two or more different classes of the dataset. The error in the classification of datasets is referring to the samples that are determined wrongly to a specific class. This kind of error typically occurs when the classes have the same values for the features. Since, the noise in the classes will alter the class boundaries; it makes the algorithm to be difficult to specify them. Therefore, it effects on the classifier performance [3]. Thus, in this paper, we proposed a method of detecting noisy samples in a dataset based on k-means and support vector machines (SVM).

The paper is organized as follows: Sect. 2 explains the related works. Section 3 describes the proposed model to discover the noise in the datasets using k-means and

© Springer International Publishing Switzerland 2015
H. Fujita and G. Guizzi (Eds.): SoMeT 2015, CCIS 532, pp. 308–318, 2015.
DOI: 10.1007/978-3-319-22689-7_23

support vector machines (SVM). In Sect. 4, the experimental datasets and the performance evaluation criteria are presented. In Sect. 5, we benchmarked the proposed model with different datasets from the UCI machine learning repository [4] and we evaluated them based on accuracy, sensitivity and specificity measurements. Finally, we concluded the research findings in Sect. 6.

2 Related Works

Based on the review of the existing studies, there are many research have been done to handle the noise in the datasets using machine learning algorithm [2, 5–7]. For example, Sluban et al. have proposed new variants of class noise detection algorithms including the high agreement random forest filter. The algorithm can identify most of the noisy data in datasets [2]. Li et al. have proposed a fuzzy relevance vector machine (FRVM) model. The algorithm can decrease the unbalanced datasets and diminishing the effects of noises or outliers [8]. Moreover, Daza et al. have proposed a new algorithm based on data quality measure of noise. The algorithm used for detecting noise on supervised classification and the advantage of the algorithm is on decreasing misclassification error rates [3]. Xiong et al. have studied on four algorithms including Local Outlier Factor (LOF) of an object, distance-based, clustering-based, and a new technique which is a hyperclique-based data cleaner (HCleaner). According to this technique data analysis is enhanced with noise removal with unsupervised techniques [9]. Also, Li proposed algorithms contain the Clustering-based Probabilistic Algorithm (CPA), the Probabilistic Fisher (PF), and the Probabilistic Kernel Fisher (PKF). The suggested algorithms allow standard classifiers to reduce the class noise [10]. Zeng et al. have presented a neural network based on automatic noise reduction (ANR) to clean noise in datasets. The performance of ANR has been tested by estimating its capacity of recognizing noise in the datasets. The outcome demonstrates that the ANR can eliminate a large part of noise with a small error of misidentifying of non-noise data [11]. Zhu et al. have proposed a partitioning filter method for noise detection from large and distributed datasets. They have applied various threshold schemes to recognize the noise in the datasets. The results show that their proposed approach is effective in recognizing noisy data [12].

Also, Lawrence et al. have presented an algorithm in order to construct a Kernel Fisher discriminant (KFD) from noisy training samples. The KFD has provided better classifications results on a dataset of construction images taken from The Corel Gallery 1,000,000 Collection [13]. Gamberger et al. have applied a simple compression measure to distinguish noisy training samples where the noise is based on random classification errors. This noise removal technique is used to pre-process data for the machine learning algorithms such as KNN, C4.5 that have been evaluated for medical domains [14]. These approaches do not provide better mechanism to recognize noise in classification procedure. Also, the accuracy evaluations are not reflecting specific consideration using specific experiments with different types of dataset because their proposed techniques could not recognize all the noisy samples.

Thus, this paper is proposing a model using k-means clustering algorithm and SVM to recognize the noisy datasets. For this study, we consider Glass, Ecoli, Pima and Wisconsin original breast cancer datasets related to the classification problems from the UCI repository [4].

3   Methodology

In this study, we proposed a combination of clustering and classification techniques in order to detect the noisy datasets in UCI datasets. The proposed technique is based on K-means support vector machine (K-SVM). There are two steps involved in the classifications as follows:

1. Apply the k-means clustering algorithm to split the dataset into two distinctive and small clusters. This is to find out the misclassified data in each cluster and consider them as noise.
2. Use the SVM to predict the label of each noisy data and produce noise free dataset to enhance the quality of data.

3.1   K-means Clustering Technique

We have selected k-means clustering algorithm to split the data and extract small and distinctive subsets of clusters. When the misclassified data are extracted separately then they are used for the prediction using SVM. Figure 1 shows the steps used for the k-means algorithm. Based on Fig. 1, the C vector refers to the centroids of each cluster, x denotes as a dataset, and b is assigned to the "estimated labels" [15].

```
Algorithm K-means Clustering
1 Initialize Cᵢ i= 1,..,K for example, to K random xᵗ
2: repeat
3:      for all xᵗ in X do
4:              bit ←1 if |xᵗ − mᵢ | = minⱼ |xᵗ − mⱼ |
5:              bit 0 otherwise
6:      end for
7:      for all Cᵢ i= 1,..,K do
8:              Cᵢ  sum over t (bᵢᵗ Xᵗ)
9:      end for
10: until Cᵢ converge
```

Fig. 1. The k-means clustering algorithm [15]

3.2   Support Vector Machine (SVM)

One of the important machine learning technologies is Support Vector Machine which is introduced by Vapnik et al. [16]. SVM has border that divides the group of positive data from negative data set with maximum boundary in the feature space [17]. In this study SVM with RBF kernel is used. The equation is illustrated below:

$$K(xi, xj) = \exp\left(-\gamma\|xi - xj\|^2\right) \tag{1}$$

3.3 The Proposed Model

In this section we have described the proposed noise reduction model to discover the clusters and noisy data in each of the cluster. The general architecture of the proposed model (K-SVM) is shown in Fig. 2. In phase 1, we have prepared the datasets from the UCI repository [4] and have divided them into the test and train sets using 10-fold cross

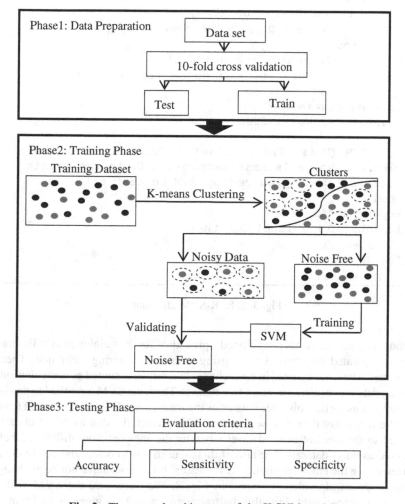

Fig. 2. The general architecture of the K-SVM model

```
Algorithm K-SVM
Input:    Tr //Training dataset
          Ts //Testing dataset
Output:   nf //Noise free dataset
          N  //noisy dataset
Method:
1: D_c = kmeans clustering (Tr)   //Tr is separated into D_c1
and D_c2 clusters
2: if num(D_c11 )< num(D_c12)
      Noise←D_c11;  Noise free← D_c12;
   End
3:      if num(D_c11 )> num(D_c12)
            Noise ← D_c12; Noise free ← D_c11;
         End
4:       If num(D_c21) < num(D_c22)
              Noise ←D_c21; Noise free ← D_c22;
           End
5:         If num(D_c21) > num(D_c22)
                Noise ← D_c22; Noise free ← D_c21;
              End
6: If num(Noise)= 0
   Noise = Ts; Noise free = Tr;
   Else
7: D_n = SVM (Noise free, Noise) // Noise free is training
samples and Noise is test sample and D_n is the matrix
with class labels produced by SVM on test set
     End
8: Repeat until true
   If label(D_c) = label(D_n) then
      nf ← D_n
  else
      N ← Dn
```

Fig. 3. The K-SVM algorithm

validation. In phase 2, we have developed a procedure for the training phase. The training dataset is separated into two clusters using k-means clustering technique. Then, the misclassified data is recognized in each cluster that can be assumed as noisy data and the remaining data is considered as noise free dataset. Then, the SVM is applied to predict the noisy samples using the noise free dataset as the training set. Based on the result from this phase, the real noisy data will be detected. The predicted value by SVM classifier is compared to the label of noisy dataset whereby the samples from different labels are considered as noisy datasets. The aim of this algorithm is to detect and delete the noisy instances, while the class distribution and classes' boundaries have not been changed.

The proposed algorithm is shown in Fig. 3. We have used the SVM with RBF kernel for our experiment. Initially, the training dataset Tr is given as an input to the k-means clustering algorithm. The k-means splits the data and produces D_{c1} and D_{c2} which includes data with class label "1" and "-1". The data in cluster 1 with class label "1" is considered as D_{c11}, and data with class label "−1" is considered as D_{c12}. Also, the data in cluster 2 with class label '1' is considered as D_{c21}, and data with class label '-1' is considered as D_{c22}. Then, the misclassified data in each cluster is recognized and assumed as noisy data which is used as validation set to be predicted using the SVM. The remaining data from each clusters, will be assumed as noise free dataset and it is used as training set for the SVM. Based on the training data (Tr_2), the SVM classifies noisy dataset and produces new label for each data, which are presented as D_{n1} and D_{n2}. Then the produced label is compared with the original label. If the SVM classifier misclassifies the instances, they are considered as noisy data and removed from dataset. In some cases, if the noisy data is not recognised, the algorithm uses SVM to classify the original dataset. Finally, the accuracy of noise free dataset can be increased using the SVM-RBF.

4 Experimental Studies

In this section, the hybrid of clustering and classification techniques are presented and analysed. The aim is to obtain a set of dataset to classify them and detecting noisy data and remove them using the K-SVM algorithm. In the following subsections, we consider the experimental datasets and the performance evaluation criteria used in this study. Finally, we analysed the performance of the proposed model according to the evaluation criteria. We have analysed the effect of the proposed model on several datasets. The datasets are divided into training and testing sets, and 10-fold cross validation is used to train and test a classifier to avoid sample variability which may affect the performance of these classifiers.

4.1 Machine Learning Datasets

In this study, we have considered four machine learning datasets related to classification problems from the UCI repository [4]. Table 1 presents the datasets used in this research and represents their area, number of classes (#class), number of dataset (#dataset), and number of attributes (#Attribute).

Glass datasets [4] which are used in the criminological investigation comprises 214 instances with 9 attributes. We considered two types of glass dataset for classification: that are "float" or "not a float", and "non_float" or "not a non_float" which are illustrated in Table 2.

Table 1. Dataset summary

Dataset	Area	# class	#dataset	# attribute
Glass	Physical	7	214	9
Wisconsin original breast cancer	Life	2	699	9
Ecoli	Life	8	336	8
Pima	Life	2	768	8

Table 2. Glass categories for classification

Glass1 category	Number of dataset	Type of Glass	Glass2 category	Number of dataset	Type of glass
Non_float	76	(builing_windows_non_float_ processed, vehicle_windows_non_ float_processed)	Float	87	(builing_windows_float_ processed, vehicle_windows_ float_processed)
Not a non_ float	138	(building_windows_float_ processed, vehicle_windows_ float_processed, containers, tableware, headlamps)	Not a float	127	(building_windows_non_float_ processed, vehicle_windows_non_float_ processed, containers, tableware, headlamps)

Dataset of ecoli [4] includes protein localization sites and contains 336 samples with 8 features. We used two types of categories for classification as "Cytoplasm, or, Not a Cytoplasm" and "Inner membrane, or, Not an Inner membrane" as presented in Table 3.

Dataset of Breast Cancer Wisconsin (Original) comprises of 699 sets of 9 types of cancer as follows; clump thickness, uniformity of cell size, uniformity of cell shape, marginal adhesion, single epithelial cell size, bare nuclei, bland chromatin, normal nucleoli, and mitoses. The number of missing values is 16 which are eliminated from dataset. Besides, It has two class types "malignant" and "benign" [4].

Pima Indians Diabetes dataset includes 768 samples with 8 attributes which are collected from women over the age of 21. The features contains number of times pregnant, plasma glucose concentration a 2 h in an oral glucose tolerance test, diastolic blood pressure (mm hg), triceps skin fold thickness (mm),2-hour serum insulin (mu u/ml), body mass index (weight in kg/(height in m)2),diabetes pedigree function and age (years). Also, it has two types of classes which are "positive" and "negative" results [4].

4.2   Evaluation Criteria

To evaluate the performance of our proposed model the sensitivity, specificity and accuracy parameters are calculated. Accuracy is calculated by taking the ratio of the truly classified samples (true positive, true negative) to the total number of the samples. As it is shown in Eq. (2), the accuracy which is used to evaluate the overall performance of the model is measured.

$$\text{Accuracy} = \frac{TP + TN}{TP + TN + FP + FN} \tag{2}$$

Sensitivity which is presented in Eq. (3) is calculated by dividing the true positive (TP) samples to the true positive (TP) and false negative (FN) samples. Specificity which is presented in Eq. (4) is calculated by dividing the true negative (TN) samples to the true negative and false positive (FP) samples.

Table 3. Ecoli categories for classification

Ecoli1 category	Number of dataset	Type of ecoli	Ecoli2 category	Number of dataset	Type of ecoli
Cytoplasm	143	Cytoplasm (cp)	Inner membrane	116	Inner membrane without signal sequence (im), inner membrane (imU), inner membrane lipoprotein (imL), inner membrane (imS) 220
Not a cytoplasm	193	(perisplasm (pp), inner membrane without signal sequence (im), inner membrane (imU), inner membrane lipoprotein (imL), inner membrane (imS), outer membrane (om), outer membrane lipoprotein (omL))	Not an inner membrane	220	(cytoplasm (cp), perisplasm (pp), outer membrane (om), outer membrane lipoprotein (omL))

$$\text{Sensitivity} = \frac{TP}{TP + FN} \tag{3}$$

$$\text{Specificity} = \frac{TN}{TN + FP} \tag{4}$$

5 Discussion on the Result

In this section, Table 4 illustrates the results of classification and noise detection on UCI dataset in terms of accuracy, sensitivity and specificity. It can be seen that, K-SVM algorithm can detect most of noise and the results of classification are better

Table 4. Results of noise detection using K-SVM on UCI datasets

Dataset	After noise reduction (K-SVM)		
	Accuracy	Sensitivity	Specificity
Pima	66.84	76.48	49.06
Ecoli1	77.67	64.71	95.24
Ecoli2	90.21	94.13	82.75
Glass1	65.66	78.24	43.23
Glass2	70.43	54.72	93.29
Wisconsin breast cancer (original)	96.24	93.56	97.32

Table 5. Comparative analysis for Glass, Ecoli, Pima and Wisconsin dataset on noise detection

Results of proposed model		Previous results		
Dataset	Accuracy	Model	Accuracy	Ref.
Glass1	**65.66**	Automatic Unsupervised Clustering	77.05	[1]
Glass2	**70.43**	MedSum	69.6±0.104	[18]
Ecoli1	**77.67**	Hyperbox set-based (ecoli1)	70.3960	[19]
Ecoli2	**90.21**	Hyperbox set-based (ecoli2)	79.9999	[19]
Pima	**66.84**	Automatic Unsupervised Clustering	79.77	[1]
		Genetic Algorithm and Prototype Selection (GAPS)	93.4	[20]
Wisconsin breast cancer (original)	**96.24**	Hyperbox set-based	88.226 ± 1.596	[19]
		RILBoost	95.8	[21]

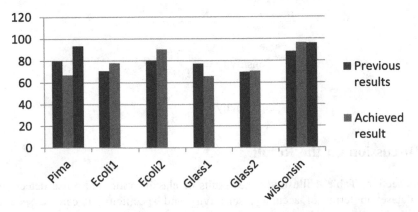

Fig. 4. Comparison on previous results and the result achieved using K-SVM algorithm

than the previous results in some cases. Also, 10-fold cross validation is used to train and test a classifier and the proposed model is run 10 times. The Matlab software is used for implementation.

Moreover, the results of proposed model and previous results are compared in Table 5. In comparison with other techniques, the K-SVM algorithm could not achieve better result for Pima dataset with accuracy 66.84 % while there was an impressive increase in Ecoli dataset with accuracy 90.21 % for Ecoli2 and 77.67 % for Ecoli1. Although, the accuracy of Glass1 dataset did not increase but the accuracy of Glass2 was better than other technique. Also, Wisconsin dataset was better than previous result with accuracy 96.24 %.

According to Fig. 4, the classification result of Ecoli1 and Ecoli2 is superior in terms of accuracy in comparison with other techniques. Also, the proposed technique achieves 96.24 % accuracy for Wisconsin dataset and 70.43 % for Glass2 dataset, which are better than previous results. But the accuracy of Pima and Glass1 dataset is inferior in comparison with other techniques.

6 Conclusion

Since, the noisy data can harm the training data, which cause classifiers not producing accurate models, the proposed model can help the researcher to detect and eliminate noisy data, which therefore will enhance data quality and improves classification accuracy. Our proposed algorithm combines clustering and classification techniques to identify noise and remove them. Also, the performance of K-SVM algorithm is achieved using UCI dataset. Although, the results did not increase so much in some dataset like Pima and Glass1 dataset, but this algorithm can be used as noise reduction technique for other dataset. Furthermore, according to the comparison of accuracy test after noise detection, the efficiency of data classification and data analysis increases.

Acknowledgement. This work is supported by the Ministry of Education and Research Management Centre at the Universiti Teknologi Malaysia under the Research University Grant Scheme (Vote No. Q.J130000.2528.05H84).

References

1. Lowongtrakool, C.: Noise filtering in unsupervised clustering using computation intelligence. Int. J. Math. Anal. **6**, 2911–2920 (2012)
2. Sluban, B., Gamberger, D., Lavra, N.: Advances in class noise detection, pp. 1105–1106 (2010)
3. Daza, L., Acuna, E.: An algorithm for detecting noise on supervised classification (2007)
4. Frank, A., Asuncion, A: UCI machine learning repository (2011). https://archive.ics.uci.edu/ml15:22
5. Hodge, V.J., Austin, J.: A survey of outlier detection methodologies. Artif. Intell. Rev. **22**(2), 1–43 (2004)

6. Van Hulse, J.D., Khoshgoftaar, T.M., Huang, H.: The pairwise attribute noise detection algorithm. Knowl. Inf. Syst. **11**, 171–190 (2006)
7. Miranda, A.L., Garcia, L.P.F., Carvalho, A.C., Lorena, A.C.: Use of classification algorithms in noise detection and elimination. In: Corchado, E., Wu, X., Oja, E., Herrero, Á., Baruque, B. (eds.) HAIS 2009. LNCS, vol. 5572, pp. 417–424. Springer, Heidelberg (2009)
8. Li, D., Hu, W., Xiong, W., Yang, J.: Fuzzy relevance vector machine for learning from unbalanced data and noise. Pattern Recogn. Lett. **29**, 1175–1181 (2008)
9. Xiong, H., Pandey, G., Member, S.: Enhancing data analysis with noise removal. IEEE Trans. Knowl. Data Eng. **18**, 304–319 (2006)
10. Li, Y.: Classification in the presence of class noise. Pattern Recogn. **5**, 1–30 (2003)
11. Zeng, X., Martinez, T.: A noise filtering method using neural networks. In: IEEE International Workshop on Soft Computing Techniques in Instrumentatian, Measurement and Related Application, SCIMA 2003, pp. 26–31. IEEE (2003)
12. Zhu, X., Chen, Q.: eliminating class noise in large datasets, pp. 920–927.(2003)
13. Lawrence, N.D., Schölkopf, B.: Estimating a kernel Fisher discriminant in the presence of label noise. In: ICML, pp. 306–313. Citeseer (2001)
14. Gamberger, D., Lavrac, N.: Noise detection and elimination in data preprocessing: experiments in medical domains. Appl. Artif. Intell. **14**(2), 205–223 (2000)
15. Shah, Z., Mahmood, A.N., Mustafa, A.K.: A hybrid approach to improving clustering accuracy using SVM. In: Industrial Electronics and Applications (ICIEA), pp. 783–788. IEEE (2013)
16. Vapnik, V.N., Vapnik, V.: Statistical Learning Theory. Wiley, New York (1998)
17. Jiang, B., Zhang, X., Cai, T.: Estimating the confidence interval for prediction errors of support vector machine classifiers. J Mach. Learn. Res. **9**, 521–540 (2008)
18. Kordos, M., Rusiecki, A.: Improving MLP neural network performance by noise reduction. In: Dediu, A.-H., Martín-Vide, C., Truthe, B., Vega-Rodríguez, M.A. (eds.) TPNC 2013. LNCS, vol. 8273, pp. 133–144. Springer, Heidelberg (2013)
19. Salehi, S., Selamat, A., Mashinchi, R., Fujita, H.: The synergistic combination of particle swarm optimization and fuzzy sets to design granular classifier. Knowl.-Based Syst. **76**, 200–218 (2015)
20. Byeon, B., Rasheed, K., Doshi, P.: Enhancing the quality of noisy training data using a genetic algorithm and prototype selection. In: IC-AI, pp. 821–827 (2008)
21. Utkin, L.V., Zhuk, Y.A.: Robust boosting classification models with local sets of probability distributions. Knowl.-Based Syst. **61**, 59–75 (2014)

GDM-VieweR: A New Tool in R to Visualize the Evolution of Fuzzy Consensus Processes

Raquel Ureña[1]([⊠]), Francisco Javier Cabrerizo[2], Francisco Chiclana[3], and Enrique Herrera-Viedma[1]

[1] Department of Computer Science and A.I,
University of Granada, Granada, Spain
{raquel,viedma}@decsai.ugr.es
[2] Department of Software Engineering and Computer Systems,
Universidad Nacional de Educación a Distancia (UNED),
28040 Madrid, Spain
[3] Centre for Computational Intelligence, Faculty of Technology,
De Montfort University, Leicester, UK
chiclana@dmu.ac.uk

Abstract. With the incorporation of web 2.0 frameworks the complexity of decision making situations has exponentially increased, involving in many cases many experts, and a pontentially huge number of different alternatives. In the literature we can find a great deal of methodologies to assist multi-person decision making. However these classical approaches are not prepared to deal with huge complexity environments such as the Web 2.0, and there is a lack of tools that support the decision processes providing some graphical information. In this context is where data visualizations plays a key role. Therefore the main objective of this contribution is to present an open source tool developed in R to provide a quick insight of the evolution of the decision making by means of meaningful graphical representations. These tools allows its users to convey ideas effectively, providing insights into a rather sparse and complex data set by communicating its key-aspects in a more intuitive way and contributiong to the decision maker engagement in the process.

Keywords: Group decision making · Fuzzy preference modeling · Software development · R

1 Introduction

Nowadays, new paradigms and ways of making decisions, such as web 2.0 frameworks, social networks and e-democracy, have made the complexity of decision making processes to increase, involving in many cases a huge number of decision makers [4]. In the literature we can find a wide range of Group decision making (GDM) approaches. Generally speaking these approaches consist on multiple decision makers, with different knowledge and points of view, interacting to choose the best option among all the available ones [7,15]. Usually those opinions should be considered to arrive at a consensus solution accepted by the whole group [5].

© Springer International Publishing Switzerland 2015
H. Fujita and G. Guizzi (Eds.): SoMeT 2015, CCIS 532, pp. 319–332, 2015.
DOI: 10.1007/978-3-319-22689-7_24

However these new scenarios require automatic tools not only to combine the information in the best possible way but also to better analyze the whole context, providing a rapid and complete insight about the current state of the process at each stage.

In this sense some initial efforts have been carried out: Alonso et al. in [3], presented a web based consensus support system dealing with different types of incomplete preference relations. This system implements the iterative decision making process proposed in [14], among with the consensus reaching process in [12]. Also Perez-Galvez et al. in [20] present a decision approach designed for dynamic mobile systems whose main novelty was its capability to include or remove new alternatives during the decision process. These authors also proposed in [21], a web based consensus approach aimed to deal with a large set of alternatives by defining a fuzzy ontology which selects an smaller sub-set of the most likely ones. On the other hand Palomares et al. in [19] proposed a Matlab graphical monitoring tool based on Self-Organizing Maps (SOMs). These authors also introduced in [18], a consensus system following a multiagent architecture able to deal with GDM processes involving a large number of decision makers overcoming the problem of the human intervention, presenting a semisupervised operation mode in which there is no need to use a human moderator in the different consensus rounds. The main weaknesses identified in the above tools are twofold:

1. The already available tools are developed as closed systems and therefore they are not aimed to be upgraded or extended by other researchers, since in most of the cases they do not provide the source code or they are based in proprietary software. Besides, they are extremely dependent of the user interface and, therefore, they cannot be adapted to work in other environments such as smart phones.
2. The available DSSs do not provide any type of graphical visualizations or output measures providing and a quick and meaningful insight about the evolution of the consensus process.

In this contribution, we present a new open-source software tool developed in R to graphically asses the evolution of the consensus processes.To that aim it offers powerful visualizations tools to quickly verify the state of the decision process. One the one hand, it allows to quickly recognize those experts which are far from the consensus solution and are more reluctant to change their mind. One the other hand, it also identifies those ones who provide more contradictory or inconsistent opinions. The system also allows to check visually the evolution of the global consensus and consistency during the decision process.

The rest of the paper is set out as follows: In Sect. 2, we introduce the main concepts of a GDM situation. Section 3, presents the proposed system while a practical example to illustrate how the proposed system works, is included in Sect. 4. Finally Sect. 5 closures this work pointing out future research lines and summarizing our conclusions.

2   GDM Problems

A classical GDM problem may be defined as a decision situation where [9]: (i) there exists a group of two or more decision makers, $E = \{e_1, \ldots, e_m\}$ ($m \geq 2$), (ii) there is a problem to solve in which a solution must be chosen among a set of possible alternatives, $X = \{x_1, \ldots, x_n\}$ ($n \geq 2$), and (iii) the decision makers try to achieve a common solution. In a fuzzy context, the objective is to classify the alternatives from best to worst, associating with them some degrees of preference expressed in the $[0, 1]$ interval.

There are various preference representation formats which can be used by decision makers to provide their testimonies. Among them, preference relations are one of the most widely used since it provide the decision makers with more flexibility to enunciate their opinions. Concretely they use of fuzzy preference relations is the most extended in the literature [15,17,24].

Definition 1. *A fuzzy preference relation P^h on a set of alternatives X, given by a decision maker e_h, is a fuzzy set on the Cartesian product $X \times X$, i.e., it is characterized by a membership function $\mu_P \colon X \times X \longrightarrow [0, 1]$.*

A fuzzy preference relation P^h may be represented by the $n \times n$ matrix $P^h = (p_{ik}^h)$, being $p_{ik}^h = \mu_{P^h}(x_i, x_k)$ ($\forall i, k \in \{1, \ldots, n\}$) interpreted as the degree or intensity of preference of alternative x_i over x_k: $p_{ik}^h = 1/2$ indicates indifference between x_i and x_k ($x_i \sim x_k$); $p_{ik}^h = 1$ indicates that x_i is absolutely preferred to x_k; $p_{ik}^h > 1/2$ indicates that x_i is preferred to x_k ($x_i \succ x_k$). Obviously, we have that $p_{ii}^h = 1/2 \ \forall i \in \{1, \ldots, n\}$ ($x_i \sim x_i$).

In what follows, we are going to describe two important aspects which need to be addressed in GDM problems involving fuzzy preference relations.

2.1   Consistency

Consistency can be interpreted as a measure of the self-contradiction expressed in the preference relation and is related to the concept of transitivity. A preference relation is considered consistent when the pairwise comparisons among every three alternatives satisfy a particular transitivity property. For fuzzy preference relations, there exist many properties or conditions that have been suggested as rational conditions to be verified by a consistent relation [8]. Among them we can highlight the additive transitivity [14], for fuzzy preference relations. It can be seen as the parallel concept of Saaty's consistency property for multiplicative preference relations [22].

$$(p_{ij}^h - 0.5) + (p_{jk}^h - 0.5) = p_{ik}^h - 0.5, \quad \forall i, j, k \in \{1, \ldots, n\} \tag{1}$$

Additive transitivity implies additive reciprocity. Indeed, because $p_{ii}^h = 0.5$, $\forall i$, if we make $k = i$ in Eq. (1), then we have: $p_{ij}^h + p_{ji}^h = 1$, $\forall i, j \in \{1, \ldots, n\}$. Equation (1) can be rewritten as follows:

$$p_{ik}^h = p_{ij}^h + p_{jk}^h - 0.5, \quad \forall i, j, k \in \{1, \ldots, n\} \tag{2}$$

A fuzzy preference relation is considered to be "additively consistent" when for every three options encountered in the problem, say x_i, x_j, $x_k \in X$, their associated preference degrees, p_{ij}^h, p_{jk}^h, p_{ik}^h, fulfill Eq. (2).

Given a fuzzy preference relation, Eq. (2) can be used to calculate an estimated value of a preference degree using other preference degrees. Indeed, using an intermediate alternative x_j, the estimated value of p_{ik}^h ($i \neq k$) can be obtained in three different ways (see [14]).

2.2   GDM Steps

The solution for a GDM problem is derived either from the individual preferences provided by the decision makers, without constructing a social opinion, or by computing first a social opinion and then using it to find a solution [15]. Here, we focus on the second one, since we are interested in obtain a solution accepted by the whole group of decision makers (see Fig. 1). In the following, we describe in more details these steps.

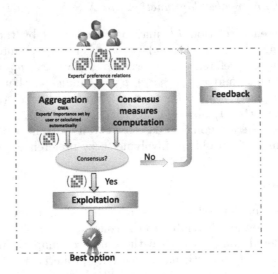

Fig. 1. Steps of a GDM process.

2.2.1   Aggregation Step

In order to obtain a collective fuzzy preference relation, the aggregation step of a GDM problem consists in combining all the preferences given by the decision makers into only one preference structure that summarizes or reflects the properties contained in all the individual preferences. This aggregation can be carried out by means of various aggregation operators [28]. Among them, the Ordered Weighted Averaging (OWA) operator proposed by Yager [26] and the Induced Ordered Weighted Averaging (IOWA) operator [27] are the most widely used.

2.2.2 Exploitation Step

In order to identify the solution set of alternatives, the exploitation step uses the information produced in the aggregation step. Here, some mechanism must be applied to obtain a partial order of the alternatives and thus select the best one(s). There are several ways to do this. A usual one is to associate a certain utility value to each alternative, based on the aggregated information, producing a natural order of the alternatives. To do so, two quantifier-guided choice degrees of alternatives can be used: a dominance and a non-dominance degree [14].

2.2.3 Consensus

In order to avoid that some decision makers disagree with the final solution arguing that their opinions have not been taken into consideration [5], it is preferable to include mechanism to check the agreement among the decision makers before obtaining a solution ensuring that enough agreement have been achieved. Those mechanisms are widely known as consensus processes [13] and they consist on iterative negotiations where the decision makers agree to change their testimonies following the advice given by a moderator, which calculates the agreement or consensus degree at each iteration [6]. If enough agreement have been reached the consensus process stops and the aggregation and the exploitation is carried out. Otherwise, some feedback is given to the decision makers to help them to reach the desired agreement.

3 The Proposed System

The proposed solution is a graphical monitoring tool to support decision makers by providing them with easily understandable visual information about the current status and the evolution of the decision process. This tool eases the analysis of diverse crucial aspects that are common in these problems, among them, we can highlight the following:

- Monitoring the evolution of the global consensus across the whole GDM process.
- Monitoring the decision makers' consistency along the whole GDM process. This is especially important to make sure that they are keeping an acceptable consistency level in their preferences after the recommendation rounds.
- Detection of the alternatives that are posing more controversy in the GDM process.
- Detection of those decision makers or group of them, whose preferences are further from the consensus solution, or those that are more reluctant to change their point of view.
- Detection of those decision makers that are being influenced or manipulated to provide preferences far from the consensus solution.
- Providing information to the decision makers about the GDM process, and showing them how their preferences are located with respect to the consensus one.

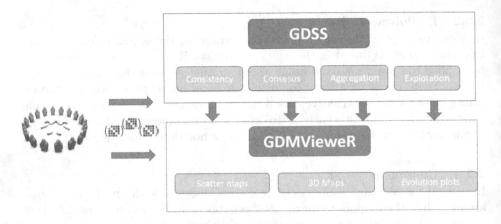

Fig. 2. Working flow

The proposed system is fully developed in R [1]which provides very powerful tools to carry out graphical representations. Among them we can highlight Lattice [23], Scatterplot3D [16] and Rgl3 [2] to be the ones that have been mainly used in the proposed solution.

Due to the fact that our tool is built to work in collaboration with a Group Decision support system, GDSS, in order to ease its integration it has been designed following a Model-View-Controller architectural pattern [10] where the logic is completely separated from the data storage requirements and from the user interface. This design also enables its adaptation to different platforms, such us web or mobile environments. Figure 2 depicts an overview of the proposed tool and its integration with the GDSS. As we can observe the GDMViewR platform receives as input the experts preferences an also the metrics computed in the decision support system, that is, the consistency, and consensus measures, the collective decision matrix and the ranking of the alternatives.

The information that our solution provides can be divided in two wide groups, depending on if they show the evolution among the various consensus rounds, or if they show information related to a single round:

- Evolution across the consensus rounds:
    - *Consistency vs consensus evolution in the GDM process.* This representation shows the evolution of both global consistency and global consensus in each consensus round. The desirable situation is that most of the points or at least the final ones lie over the diagonal line showing a positive tendency. That means that the final solution has reached a high level of agreement and it is consistent. This representation also enables to detect whether the consensus process is not only helping to bring the decision makers' opinions closer but also to keep or increase their consistency.
    - *Decision maker's consistency vs decision maker's consensus in the GDM process.* This representation allows to check how decision makers' consensus and consistency evolves during the GDM process. It also enables

to visually check the different decision makers profiles depending on the shape of the curve for each decision maker. On the one hand, curves with a positive tendency and located over the diagonal represent the desired situation of those decision makers that are more willing to change their opinions in the interest of increasing the global consensus while keeping a highly consistency level. On the other hand, curves parallel to the y-axis represents those decision makers which are reluctant to change their mind during the process, and therefore they may require special attention.

- Consensus and consistency state in each single round:
  - *Barplot of each decision maker's proximity to the aggregated solution.* This representation enables to check who are the decision makers whose opinions are closer to achieve a high degree of consensus, and who are those with highly disagree with the proposed solution.
  - *Barplot of the average consensus achieved for each alternative.* Thanks to this representation, one can identify the alternatives that are posing more controversy in the decision process.
  - *Barplot of the average consistency achieved for each decision maker.* Thanks to this representation, one can identify those decision makers providing more consistent fuzzy preference relations in the decision making process.
  - *2D representation map of the decision makers' fuzzy preference relations and the consensus solution.* This representation provides a quick insight of the current state of the decision process and enables the rapid identification of sub groups of decision makers who share similar opinions. It also eases the detection of conflicts among decision makers. Moreover, it provides the decision makers with a good idea about the status of the consensus process and how far their opinions are from the consensus solution. This 2D representation is obtained after carrying out a classical 2D multidimensional scaling reduction of the decision makers' fuzzy preference relation matrix [11]. In addition, R also offers the possibility of non metric multidimensional scaling.
  - *3D representation of the position of each decision maker with respect to the consensus solution among with their consistency.* This plot easily allows to identify those groups of decision makers that are far from the consensus solution but keep a high degree of consistency, and, therefore, need special attention. To easily visualize this plot, we have also included a interactive representation.

4   Illustrative Example

To analyze the performance of the proposed system we consider a GDM situation involving 20 decision makers and 4 different alternatives, where the minimum consensus threshold that needs to be achieved is 0.8, and the maximum number of consensus rounds is four. Recall that the system can also work indicating only the maximum number of possible rounds or only the desired level of consensus.

Table 1. Evolution of the decision makers' preferences among the consensus rounds.

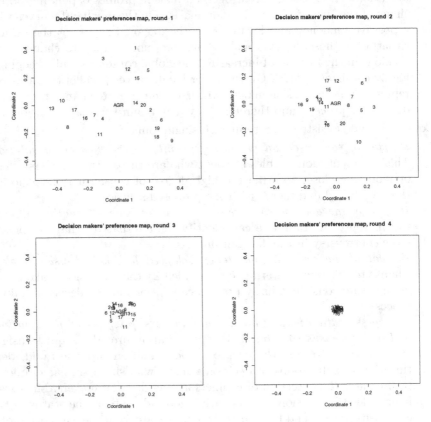

In addition, the initial average level of consistency of the fuzzy preference relations is 0.8 and the initial average level of consensus is 0.6.

First of all, in Table 1, we can visualize a 2D map with the position of each decision maker with respect to the aggregated solution in the different consensus rounds. The global solution is presented always in the center of the plot in order to ease the rapid detection of those decision makers whose opinions are far from the global solution as it is the case, in this example, of decision maker 1. Hence, in real case situations, some especial actions can be taken with these decision makers depending on the characteristics of the process, such as discarding their opinions since they can be considered as outliers. Moreover, we can observe how in the first round, the preferences are in general pretty spread up. However, after each round of recommendations, we observe that the opinions of the decision makers get closer and closer, which able to verify that the decision making process is going in the right direction. Therefore, this type of maps allow to easily recognize those decision makers who are reluctant to change their opinions in order to achieve a solution accepted by the whole group. These maps also are useful to recognize small sub-communities of decision makers that share similar

Table 2. Evolution of the decision makers preferences among the consensus rounds.

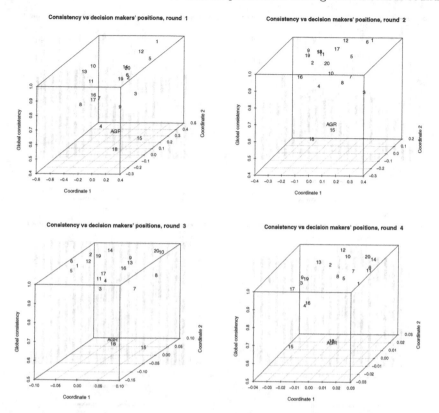

opinions, but whose preferences are far from the global solution, and those who exert a greater influence on their sub-communities.

In Table 2, a 3D map of the decision makers preferences among with the degree of consistency for each decision maker is shown. These maps allow to recognize the decision makers whose preferences are more consistent and how close their opinions are to the global solution. For example, in the very first iteration, for the decision maker number 1, we can observe that even though his/her preferences are far from the consensus solution, his/her consistency level is very high. Therefore, this decision maker's opinions are worth to be taken into consideration. It also allows to quickly recognize communities of decision makers who share the same points of views, and also identify those decision makers who have more influence or more persuasion power over the group. They can be recognized easily since they do not change their opinions with the time, but they attract others forming small clusters in the map that become bigger with the time. Usually, the most influential decision makers also present a high level of consistency.

In Table 3, the system presents a barplot with the decision makers average consensus and consistency degree per round, along with both lines showing the global average consensus and consistency degrees. These plots easily allow to

Table 3. Evolution of the decision makers' consistency and consensus in each round.

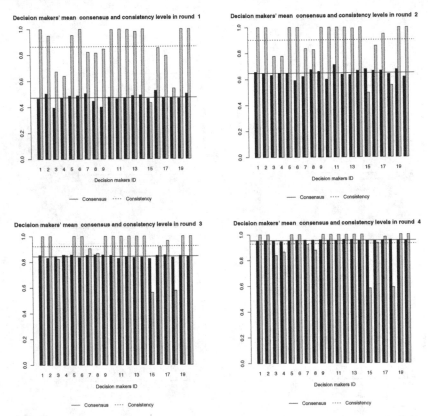

asses the evolution of both consensus and consistency and recognize those decision makers that may present more controvert opinions, or less consistent ones, and take especial actions with those ones.

4.1   Results of the GDM Process

The decision making process finishes when the maximum number of rounds has been overpassed or when the desired consensus degree has been achieved. In Fig. 3, we can observe the evolution of the consensus vs the evolution of the consistency in each round of consensus. Depending on the slope of the line in this plot, we can easily recognize how the decision process has gone. For example, if the line is almost parallel to the x-axis it will mean that the different rounds of the decision process have only contributed to increase the global consistency. That is, in average the decision makers' opinions have become more consistent with the time, but the decision makers had not change their mind to increase the consensus. This type of line allows to recognize that the decision makers are very committed to provide non contradictory solutions to the problem, but they

Table 4. Dominance and non-dominace degrees in the exploitation phase.

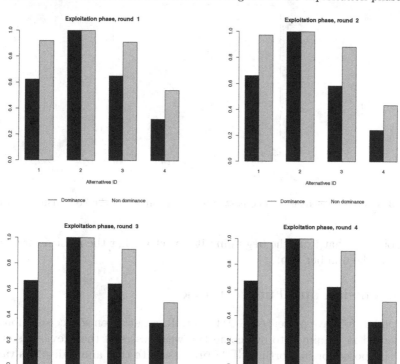

present a non cooperative behavior towards achieving a solution accepted for the whole group.

A similar situation would happen if the line is parallel to the y-axis, but in this case it would mean that the consensus has improved whereas the decision makers consistency has barely changed. This situation means that decision makers are easily manipulated to change their minds, without caring about the quality of the provided solution.

The most desired solution is having a line with positive slope, like the one in Fig. 3, that means that the different rounds have contributed to positive increase both the consensus and the consistency of the decision makers. Also the average slope of this line also provide us with a general measure of how fast the consensus increase vs the consistency, this measurement can be leverage to test the performance of different decision making approaches.

Finally, the system provides a graphical representation with the ranking of the alternatives using both the dominance and the non-dominance degrees as we have explained in previous sections. In Table 4, we can observe the evolution of these degrees during the consensus rounds. More concretely, for this example,

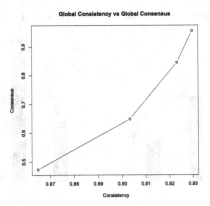

Fig. 3. Global consensus and consistency evolution along the consensus rounds.

we can observe that from the beginning it was clear that the most desired alternative was the number two.

5   Conclusion and Future Work

In this paper, we have presented GDM VieweR, a new open source solution fully implemented in R, aimed to overcome the weaknesses of the previous software systems proposed for supporting GDM processes. To that aim it displays various graphical representations which provide a rapid insight of the state of the GDM process and enable, among them, to identify decision makers whose opinions are far from the group solution and those who are reluctant to change their mind in order to reach an agreement.

As future work, we point out several directions as the extension of this solution to work with different interfaces such as mobile and web based frameworks. Extending the system to carry out GDM processes in environments in which the decision makers can access to the decision process from different platforms and locations. In addition, more complex approaches based on ontologies [21] and trust networks [25] will be included.

Acknowledgments. The authors would like to acknowledge FEDER financial support from the Project TIN2013-40658-P, and also the financial support from the Andalusian Excellence Project TIC-5991.

References

1. The comprehensive R archive network (2015). http://cran.r-project.org/. Accessed 20 February 2015
2. Adler, D., Murdoch, D., Nenadic, O., Urbanek, S., Chen, M., Gebhardt, A., Bolker, B., Csardi, G., Strzelecki, A., Senger, A.: RGL: 3d visualization device system (opengl) (2015). http://cran.r-project.org/web/packages/rgl/index.html. Accessed 20 February 2015

3. Alonso, S., Herrera-Viedma, E., Chiclana, F., Herrera, F.: A web based consensus support system for group decision making problems and incomplete preferences. Inf. Sci. **180**(23), 4477–4495 (2010)
4. Alonso, S., Pérez, I.J., Cabrerizo, F.J., Herrera-Viedma, E.: A linguistic consensus model for web 2.0 communities. Appl. Soft Comput. **13**(1), 149–157 (2013)
5. Butler, C.T., Rothstein, A.: On Conflict and Consensus: A Handbook on Formal Consensus Decision Making. Food Not Bombs Publishing, Takoma Park (2006)
6. Cabrerizo, F.J., Moreno, J.M., Pérez, I.J., Herrera-Viedma, E.: Analyzing consensus approaches in fuzzy group decision making: advantages and drawbacks. Soft. Comput. **14**(5), 451–463 (2010)
7. Cabrerizo, F.J., Ureña, R., Pedrycz, W., Herrera-Viedma, E.: Building consensus in group decision making with an allocation of information granularity. Fuzzy Sets Syst. **255**, 115–127 (2014)
8. Chiclana, F., Herrera-Viedma, E., Alonso, S., Herrera, F.: Cardinal consistency of reciprocal preference relations: a characterization on multiplicative transitivity. IEEE Trans. Fuzzy Syst. **17**(1), 14–23 (2009)
9. Fodor, J.C., Roubens, M.: Fuzzy Preference Modelling and Multicriteria Decision Support. Kluwer Academic Publishers, Dordrecht (1994)
10. Gamma, E., Helm, R., Johnson, R., Vlissides, J.: Design Patterns: Elements of Reusable Object-oriented Software. Addison-Wesley Longman Publishing Co. Inc., Boston (1995)
11. Gower, J.C.: Some distance properties of latent root and vector methods used in multivariate analysis. Biometrika **53**(3–4), 325–328 (1966)
12. Herrera-Viedma, E., Alonso, S., Chiclana, F., Herrera, F.: A consensus model for group decision making with incomplete fuzzy preference relations. IEEE Trans. Fuzzy Syst. **15**(5), 863–877 (2007)
13. Herrera-Viedma, E., Cabrerizo, F.J., Kacprzyk, J., Pedrycz, W.: A review of soft consensus models in a fuzzy environment. Inf. Fusion **17**, 4–13 (2014)
14. Herrera-Viedma, E., Chiclana, F., Herrera, F., Alonso, S.: Group decision-making model with incomplete fuzzy preference relations based on additive consistency. IEEE Trans. Syst. Man Cybern. Part B Cybern. **37**(1), 176–189 (2007)
15. Kacprzyk, J.: Group decision making with a fuzzy linguistic majority. Fuzzy Sets Syst. **18**, 105–118 (1986)
16. Ligges, U., Maechler, M., Schnackenberg, S.: Scatterplot3d: 3d scatter plot (2015). http://cran.r-project.org/web/packages/scatterplot3d/index.html. Accessed 20 February 2015
17. Orlovski, S.A.: Decision-making with fuzzy preference relations. Fuzzy Sets Syst. **1**(3), 155–167 (1978)
18. Palomares, I., Martínez, L.: A semisupervised multiagent system model to support consensus-reaching processes. IEEE Trans. Fuzzy Syst. **22**(4), 762–777 (2014)
19. Palomares, I., Martínez, L., Herrera, F.: MENTOR: a graphical monitoring tool of preferences evolution in large-scale group decision making. Knowl.-Based Syst. **58**, 66–74 (2014)
20. Pérez, I.J., Cabrerizo, F.J., Herrera-Viedma, E.: A mobile decision support system for dynamic group decision-making problems. IEEE Trans. Syst. Man Cybern. Part A Syst. Humans **40**(6), 1244–1256 (2010)
21. Pérez, I.J., Wikstram, R., Mezei, J., Carlsson, C., Herrera-Viedma, E.: A new consensus model for group decision making using fuzzy ontology. Soft. Comput. **17**(9), 1617–1627 (2013)
22. Saaty, T.L.: Fundamentals of Decision Making and Priority Theory with the AHP. RWS Publications, Pittsburg (1994)

23. Deepayan Sarkar. Lattice: Lattice graphics (2015). http://cran.r-project.org/web/packages/lattice/index.html. Accessed 20 February 2015
24. Tanino, T.: Fuzzy preference orderings in group decision making. Fuzzy Sets Syst. **12**(2), 117–131 (1984)
25. Wu, J., Chiclana, F., Herrera-Viedma, E.: Trust based consensus model for social network in an incomplete linguistic information context. Appl. Soft Comput. (2015, in press)
26. Yager, R.R.: On ordered weighted averaging aggregation operators in multicriteria decision making. IEEE Trans. Syst. Man Cybern. **18**(1), 183–190 (1988)
27. Yager, R.R., Filev, D.P.: Induced ordered weighted averaging operators. IEEE Trans. Syst. Man Cybern. Part B Cybern. **29**(2), 141–150 (1999)
28. Yager, R.R., Kacprzyk, J.: The Ordered Weighted Averaging Operators: Theory and Applications. Kluwer Academic, Boston (1997)

Swarm Intelligence in Evacuation Problems: A Review

Guido Guizzi[1](✉), Francesco Gargiulo[1], Liberatina Carmela Santillo[1], and Hamido Fujita[2]

[1] Dipartimento di Ingegneria Chimica, Dei Materiali E Della Produzione Industriale, University of Naples Federico II, P.le Tecchio 80, 80125 Naples, Italy
{g.guizzi,f.gargiulo,santillo}@unina.it
[2] Intelligent Software Systems Laboratory, Iwate Prefectural University, Takizawa, Iwate 020-0193, Japan
issam@soft.iwate-pu.ac.jp

Abstract. In this paper authors introduce swarm intelligence's algorithms (ACO and PSO) to determine the optimum path during an evacuation process. Different PSO algorithms are compared when applied to an evacuation process and results reveal important aspects, as following detailed.

Keywords: Evacuation · FSE · Swarm intelligence · ACO · PSO

1 Introduction

The management of the crowd plays a key role, in order to ensure that most people can reach a safe area [1]. In literature we find several models to analyze the evacuation process characterized by the parameters and each has unique and specific features. The study of evacuation process is based on simulation models in which are considered the building characteristics, the fire characteristics and behavioral models (also called evacuation models), in which a key role is played by occupant characteristics and their interaction with fire [2]. The implementation of swarm-based systems, inspired behavior of social living beings, began from the early nineties [3]. From the early twenty-first century the study was aimed to understand how to assimilate human behavior during an emergency to animal behavior.

This idea led to develop different methods to study the problem such as ACO (Ant Colony Optimization) and PSO (Particle Swarm Optimization). The aim of this work is to identify the most promising lines of research into the phenomenon and implement appropriate preventive action to safeguard human lives.

2 Evacuation

Natural and man-made emergency events can pose a serious threat to humans. Evacuation is a complex problem because of several aspects mainly due to subjective human behaviors, such as different perception of danger, panic in emergency

© Springer International Publishing Switzerland 2015
H. Fujita and G. Guizzi (Eds.): SoMeT 2015, CCIS 532, pp. 333–340, 2015.
DOI: 10.1007/978-3-319-22689-7_25

situations, etc. [4]. In literature are available different algorithms and different solutions to optimization [5,6]. In case of fire, for example, the literature presents some studies concerning the influences of the variables related to human response to evacuations [7]. The results of this studies show that the occupant behavior varies according to three major elements: the occupant, the building and the fire characteristics [8]. The bond between evacuation and human behavior is much studied in literature. However, regardless of the model used, the most crucial aspect of a building's safety in facing fire is the possibility a safe escape. A fundamental role in the evacuation process is played by the wayfinding which is, in most cases, a purposive and motivated activity [9–11]. About the consideration above during the evacuation process the occupiers choice is not always the best one because they are not aware of all the possible alternatives to reach the exit [12]. Therefore it's worth analyzing some optimization algorithms, in particular it will shown how the swarm intelligence could be applied to evacuation process.

3   Swarm Intelligence in Evacuation Field

Swarm intelligence takes inspiration from the social behaviors of insects and other animals [13]. The first studies regarding swarm intelligence date back to early nineties: it's a relatively new approach to problem solving. The most relevant algorithms based on swarm intelligence concept are ACO algorithm (Ant Colony Optimization) and PSO algorithm (Particle Swarm Optimization) [14,15]. ACO algorithm takes inspiration from the behavior of ant when searching food. More specifically on ants' ability to find always the shortest path between their nest and food sources [16,17]. PSO is a population-based stochastic approach and it uses swarm intelligence to solve continuous and discrete problems [18]. The PSO is inspired by the natural behavior of fish schools and birds flocks [19]. Their original idea was to simulate the social behavior of a bird flock trying to reach an unknown destination [4,20]. Due to their flexibility, PSO algorithms were developed as interesting candidates to address complex problems such as the optimization of multi modal functions in various areas of interest. It's fundamental to observe that the modeling of evacuation becomes more complicated when considering some aspects of human behavior, such as the queuing behavior, self-organization, crowd psychology and sub-group phenomena [21]. The understanding of occupants' responses during an evacuation is crucial because our first goal is to determine the optimum evacuation route toward safe areas [19]. The algorithm of standard PSO is described by the following equations:

$$v_i(t+1) = v_i(t) + c_1 r_1(t)(p_i(t) - x_i(t)) + c_2 r_2(t)(p_g(t) - x_i(t)) \tag{1}$$

$$x_i(t+1) = x_i(t) + v_i(t+1) \tag{2}$$

where x_i is the i_{th} particle location in search space, p_i is the best position achieved so far by the i_{th} particle, that is the one with the best fitness value, the location p_g is the best p_{best} among all the particles, also called g_{best}, v_i is the velocity for the i_{th} particle. The basic concept of PSO consists of changing the velocity and the location of each particles towards its p_{best} (cognition part) and g_{best} (social part) location. Starting from standard PSO Cheng et al. [22] modified the algorithm introducing an inertia factor ω to prevent particles' premature convergence (the new model is called "Linear Weight Decreasing Particle Swarm Optimization (LWDPSO)"). Inertia weight ω was implemented as:

$$\omega(t) = 0.9 - \frac{t}{MaxNumber} * 0.5 \tag{3}$$

where ω [0.4, 0.9] and MaxNumber is the maximum number of iterations.

Once that a particle found the exit, its location is supposed to be g_{best} for each exit found, this mean that the other particles should compare all the g_{best} and they should choose the nearest g_{best} as moving target. So LWDPSO have the equation $p_g(t) = Min(distance(p_i, p_g^j))$ where p_g^j is the jth location of exit.

The comparison between LWDPSO model and other models - e.g. "social force" model and CA (Cellular Automata) model - shows that LWDPSO provides better results. Results show that behaviors like avoid impact, queuing and congestion are well performed. LWDPSO model has good efficiency and practicability. Fang et al. [19] suggested, paying attention to jamming and clogging phenomena, a new formula to evaluate the velocity adopted to move to a subsequent location.

$$v_i(t + 1) = \omega_i^t \otimes v_i(t) + c_g^t \otimes (x_g^t - x_i^t) + c_p^t \otimes (x_i^p - x_i^t) \tag{4}$$

where ω_i^t is the motion inertia factor, c_g^t and c_p^t are gain factor whose elements are confined within limits [0,1] and they are sampled from some probability distributions. x_g^t is the best performing particle and is determined by a problem dependent fitness function such that $g = argmin_i \, f(x_{i=1,..N}^t)$ for a minimization problem. x_i^p is the best performing instances of individual particles and is given by $p = argmin_\tau \, f(x_i^{\tau=1,\cdots t})$. Therefore the future location of a particle or its behavior is influenced by its motion inertia, the interaction among swarm and its own past experience. Using the PSO algorithm can be obtained deep observations about evacuation phenomena e.g. embedding the leader following behavior in a crowd of occupants, efficient evacuation results with a linear relationship between the number of individuals and the time for all occupants to leave the room. In 2009 Iziquierdo et al. [23] studied PSO to achieve an optimization by the introduction of a fitness function defined as "the sum of the distances between each occupant and the set of exits". The minimization of such a function is achieved by minimizing each distance of individuals to the set of exit. They proposed some conditions, such as considering continuos movement, taking into account both individual behavior and social interaction, and so on. The evolution of the particles is defined in the following way:

$$newX_i = currentX_i + newV_i \tag{5}$$

$$newV_i = \omega*currentV_i + c_1*rand()*(P_i - currentX_i) + c_2*rand()*(P_a - currentX_i) \tag{6}$$

where: $\omega * currentV_i$ represent particle current trajectory and the formula for inertia is:

$$\omega = 0.5 + \frac{1}{2 * (logk + 1)} \begin{cases} k \text{ is the iteration number} \\ \omega \text{ decrease asymptotically from 1 (k=1) to 0.5(k=∞);} \end{cases}$$

$rand()$ is a function generating uniform pseudo-random numbers between 0 and 1; c_1 and c_2 are the acceleration constants (respectively 3 and 2) and they represent the weight of stochastic acceleration terms that pull each particle simultaneously toward its best-ever reached or desired position and the best global position; P_i associated with the perceived best position for individual i, is calculated taking into account some aspects as "familiarity of the individuals with venue" and "queuing behavior"; P_g directly points to the closest exit for i_{th} individual. It's important to note that: $newV_i$ has an upper bound (maximum velocity) used to prevent excessive roaming and to adapt people movement to reasonable value and if $newX_i$ is occupied by another particle, the direction velocity is changed by a small angle and a new updating attempt is made. If the situation still persists the particle is bounded to a limited movement or even stays at its current position during current iteration. The optimization is obtained through the following, non linear, function (fitness function which measures the distance between a particle to the exit):

$$F(X) = d(X, E) = min(d(X, e), e \in E) \tag{7}$$

Iziquierdo et al. [23] studied also the influence of the door size and door allocation on the evacuation process and, in order to reduce the evacuation time, they studied how to optimize the allocation of people and areas to the different available exits. The PSO-based model presented allows the assessment of behavioral patterns followed by individuals during a rapid evacuation process and the forecast of the time required for evacuation under different conditions. Yusoff et al. [18] implemented two discrete algorithm DPSO (different from canonical PSO at initialization stage as it introduces a new fitness value: pickup best) and improved-DPSO (introduces instead an additional loop required for velocity clamping and updating particle position) aimed to optimize the number of vehicles to be sent to the flooded area. This problem, identified as Vehicle Assignment Problem (VAP), is formulated, subject to some constraints, as follows:

$$maxZ = \sum_{v \in V} \sum_{e, p \in P} Y_{pev} \tag{8}$$

DSPO and improved-DPSO are proposed and experimented to examine their performances. The coefficients used in DPSO are $c_1 = 2.5$ and $c_2 = 1.5$. The study indicates a decreasing trend of g_{best} value for both static weight ($\omega = 0.9$) and dynamic weight (starting from 1.4 to 1) and demonstrates that improved-DPSO gives generally better performance compared to DPSO, but also that both DPSO and improved-DPSO provide solutions near to the optimal.

Zheng et al. in 2012 [20] presented a new pedestrian evacuation model, applying a new PSO-based heterogeneous evacuation model. The concepts of local density and of compressibility were introduced. Both the maximal velocity and the area occupied by a particle are supposed to depend on local density that varies with time and space. Based on Eq. (6) calculated velocity should not exceed certain value: $V_i \leq V_{max}$ and in crowd situations it reduces according to local density. In order to take into account the fact that during a real evacuation process each person has its own area and that the others are forbidden to enter, the authors introduced also a relationship between local density and diameter of the particles (defined as "Compressibility of particles"). The new velocity, calculated according Eq. (6) will be adjusted to avoid conflicts in case the new position of a particles is occupied by another one. In a real emergency situation, movement may cause damages or injuries to the occupants. This is taken into account by introducing in the model two thresholds I_a and I_b which represent respectively the threshold of damage impulse and the threshold of injury impulse. So the maximum speed depend on I_a and I_b. In particular when the impulse is greater than I_b, the particle probably is injured and cannot move after, whereas, when the impulse is greater than I_a but less than I_b, the particle is damaged and its mobility is reduced. If the maximal velocity, for a damaged particle, decreases to zero the particle is regarded as an injured equally. Looking at simulation results we can affirm that the implemented model is more flexible in describing the velocities of individuals since it is not limited to discrete values and directions according to the new updating rule. This gives higher precision and flexibility to the model.

Zheng et al. [24] introduced a multi-objective particle swarm optimization (MOPSO) to achieve an effective method for population classification in fire. The main purpose of population classification is to identify the situation of evacuees and the possible interactions among the evacuees themselves and also between the evacuees and the responders. Two objective functions are used to evaluate the quality of classification rules, their goal, "precision"and "recall". Where precision can be thought as a measure of exactness whereas recall is a measure of completeness. The MOPSO wanted to maximize both functions, although their trends showed an inverse relationship between them. The multi-objective method (MOPSO) is able to optimize the two measures simultaneously. Zheng et al. [24] introduce two new strategies to the MOPSO: the first concerns updating p_{best} and the second describes the updating of particles' velocity. The starting equations are:

$$v_j^{(t+1)} = \chi(v_j^{(t)} + c_1 r_1 (pbest_j^{(t)} - x_j^{(t)}) + c_2 r_2 (gbest_j^{(t)} - x_j^{(t)}) \tag{9}$$

$$x_j^{(t+1)} = x_j^{(t)} + v_j^{(t+1)} \tag{10}$$

where χ is a constriction factor derived from acceleration constants for controlling the velocity:

$$\chi = \frac{2}{\left| 2 - \varphi - \sqrt{\varphi^2 - 4\varphi} \right|} \qquad \varphi = c_1 + c_2$$

c_1 and c_2 are two acceleration constants reflecting the weight of cognitive and social learning, respectively, and r_1 and r_2 are two distinct random numbers in $[0, 1]$. So Eq. (9) has a different expression:

$$v_j^{(t+1)} = \chi(v_j^{(t)} + cr(cbest_j^{(t)} - x_j^{(t)}))$$ (11)

where every particle χ can learn from a different exemplar at each dimension j, increasing the information shared by the particles. Comparative experiments have shown that the proposed algorithm performs better than some state-of-the-art methods and it has high ductility and can be extended to many multi-objective rule mining problems. Li et al. [25] present a simulation model based on PSO by setting the following criteria: people may choose different escape strategies in emergencies and two behaviors are simulated by familiar-coefficient and following-coefficient. The effect of both, smoke and heat and their influences on human behavior, are considered. Each particle is represented in a two-dimensional space through a set of vectors. A hazard model is used to simulate the influences of fire and its secondary factors. It is used a Fractional Effective Dose (FED) model to consider the physiological effect of fire hazards on moving speed of the occupants.

$$FED_{FIRE} = FED_{HEAT} + FED_{GAS} + FED_{SMOKE}$$

$$V_x^t = (1 - FED_{FIRE})(v_o + r * \Delta v_0) * C_x^t; V_y^t = (1 - FED_{FIRE})(v_o + r * \Delta v_0) * C_y^t$$

The model is based on the hypothesis that during an emergency only three escape strategies are possible: shortest-path, backtracking and following-up. The model assumes that half of pedestrians are familiar with the site and the other half follows the crowd in the process of evacuation, i.e. $familiar - coefficient = following - coefficient = 0.5$. The study of results of the extended particle swarm optimization (E-PSO) model reveals that the general pattern of evacuation consists of two phases: an efficient evacuation (graphically a steep part) and an inefficient evacuation (graphically a flat part). Sharper is the slope with the higher density of occupants, better the evacuation efficiency is. The results indicate also that adding a new exit is better than widening its size in order to minimize evacuation time.

Zong et al. [21] presented an evacuation model for mixed traffic flow based on temporal-spatial conflict and congestion. To solve this mixed evacuation problem they proposed a novel discrete particle swarm optimization with learning factor (DPSONLF). In this problem more than one objective need to be optimized simultaneously, such as minimal total evacuation time, minimal pedestrian-vehicle temporal-spatial conflict degree and minimal temporal-spatial congestion degree. The conflict-congestion model for pedestrian-vehicle mixed evacuation is described below:

$$minF_1 = \sum_{k=1}^{M} \sum_{(i,j) \in P_k} t_{ij}^k$$

$$minF_2 = \sum_{i \in N} \sum_{t=0}^{T} Conflict_i(t) \cdot \Delta t; minF_3 = \sum_{i \in N} \sum_{t=0}^{T} Congestion_i(t) \cdot \Delta t$$

To improve the effectiveness of the DPSO algorithm it has been introduced a neighborhood learning factor. The velocity update function is modified as:

$$v(t+1) = \omega \cdot v(t) + c_1 r_1 (P_{pbest} - X(t)) + c_2 r_2 (P_{nbest} - X(t)) + c_3 r_3 (P_{gbest} - X(t))$$

The results of this paper indicate that DPSONLF has better performance in the control of conflict and congestion both in time and in space during the evacuation process for mixed pedestrian and vehicles.

4 Conclusions

In this paper has been compared several algorithms and the study pointed out interesting results. PSO algorithms best performs the optimization in case of evacuation, the reason is inside the following statement "the information exchange take place locally in a dynamic way". It means that in PSO-based algorithms the evaluation process is based on real time information exchanged continuously in response to changing environmental conditions. The literature shows different approaches to the PSO algorithms: discrete or continuos, with or without inertia factor, different value assigned to the inertia factor, the use of two learning factor c_1 and c_2 or adding c_3. Starting from this assessment, the future development will be the comparison of PSO-based models and the implementation of a new PSO-based model taking into account additional factors, not yet considered. This study will identify the appropriate design solutions that enable interaction between "environment" and "population" in order to "drive" evacuees' behavior. In this sense, computers and extensively the Internet of Things can certainly be an important aid in the implementation of considered design solutions.

References

1. Fang, Z., Zong, X., Li, Q., Li, Q., Xiong, S.: Hierarchical multi-objective evacuation routing in stadium using ant colony optimization. J. Transp. Geogr. **19**, 443–451 (2011)
2. Guizzi G., Santillo L.C., Zoppoli P.: On methods for cost optimization of condition based maintenance systems. In: Proceedings - 13th ISSAT International Conference on Reliability and Quality in Design, pp. 117–121 (2007)
3. Parpinelli, R.S., Lopes, H.S.: New inspirations in swarm intelligence: a survey. Int. J. Bio-inspired Comput. **3**(1), 1–16 (2011)
4. Izquierdo, J., Montalvo, I., Perez, R., Fuertes, V.S.: Forecasting pedestrian evacuation times by using particle swarm intelligence. Phys. A **388**, 1213–1220 (2009)
5. Goerigk, M., Grün, B., Heßler, P.: Branch and bound algorithms for the bus evacuation problem. Comput. Oper. Res. **40**, 3010–3020 (2013)
6. Goerigk, M., Deghdak, H.P.: A comprehensive evacuation planning model and genetic solution algorithm. Transp. Res. Part E **71**, 82–97 (2014)
7. Caliendo, C., Ciambelli, P., De Guglielmo, M.L., Meo, M.G., Russo, P.: Simulation of people evacuation in the event of a road tunnel fire. In: SIIV "5th International Congress" Sustainability of road infrastructures. Social and Behavioral Sciences 53, pp. 178–188 (2012)

8. Proulx, G.: Occupant behaviour and evacuation. In: 9th International Fire Protection Symposium, pp. 219–232, Munich (2001)
9. Rahman, A., Mahmood, A.K., Schneider, E.: Using agent-based simulation of human behavior to reduce evacuation time. In: Bui, T.D., Ho, T.V., Ha, Q.T. (eds.) PRIMA 2008. LNCS (LNAI), vol. 5357, pp. 357–369. Springer, Heidelberg (2008)
10. Hajibabai, L., Delavar, M.R., Malek, M.R., Frank, A.U.: Agent-Based Simulation of Spatial Cognition and Wayfinding in Building Fire Emergency Evacuation. Lecture Notes in Geoinformation and Cartography, pp. 255–270. Springer, Berlin (2007)
11. Shiwakoti, N., Sarvi, M., Rose, G., Burd, M.: Enhancing the safety of pedestrians during emergency egress. Transp. Res. Record: J. Transp. Res. Board **2137**, 31–37 (2010)
12. Bryan, J.L.: Human behavior and fire. In: NFPA Handbook, Sect. 7, NFPA, Quincy, MA, (Chap. 1) (1992)
13. Filippi, S., Giribone, P., Revetria, R., Testa, A., Guizzi, G., Romano, E.: Design Support System of Fishing Vessel Through Simulation Approach. Transactions on Engineering Technologies, pp. 615–629. Springer, Netherlands (2014). ISBN 978-94-017-9114-4
14. Tran, D.-H., Cheng, M.-Y., Cao, M.-T.: Hybrid multiple objective artificial bee colony with differential evolution for the time-cost-quality tradeoff problem. Knowl.-Based Syst. **74**(1), 176–186 (2015)
15. Salehi, S., Selamat, A., Mashinchi, M.R., Fujita, H.: The synergistic combination of particle swarm optimization and fuzzy sets to design granular classifier. Knowl.-Based Syst. **76**, 200–218 (2015)
16. Blum, C.: Ant colony optimization: introduction and recent trends. Phys. Life Rev. **2**, 353–373 (2005)
17. Dorigo, M., Birattari, M., Stulze, T.: Ant colony optimization: artificial ants as a computational intelligence technique. IEEE Comput. Intell. Mag. **1**, 28–39 (2006)
18. Yusoff, M., Ariffin, J., Mohamed, A.: An improved discrete particle swarm optimization in evacuating planning. In: International Conference of Soft Computing and Pattern Recognition, pp. 49–53 (2009)
19. Fang, G., Kwok, N.M., Ha, Q.P.: Swarm interaction-based simulation of occupant evacuation. In: 2008 IEEE Pacific-Asia Workshop on Computational Intelligence and Industrial Application, pp. 329–333 (2008)
20. Zheng, Y., Chen, J., Wei, J., Guo, X.: Modeling of pedestrian evacuation based on the particle swarm optimization algorithm. Phys. A **391**, 4225–4233 (2012)
21. Zong, X., Xiong, S., Fang, Z.: A conflict congestion model for pedestrian vehicle mixed evacuation based on discrete particle swarm optimization algorithm. Comput. Oper. Res. **44**, 1–12 (2014)
22. Cheng, W., Bo, Y., Lijun, L., Hua, H.: A modified particle swarm optimization-based human behavior modeling for emergency evacuation simulation system. In: 2008 IEEE International Conference on information and Automation, pp. 23–28, China (2008)
23. Izquierdo, J., Montalvo, I., Pérez, R., Fuertes, V.S.: Forecasting pedestrian evacuation times by using swarm intelligence. Phys. A **388**, 1213–1220 (2009)
24. Zheng, Y.J., Ling, H.F., Xue, J.Y., Chen, S.Y.: Population classification in fire evacuation: a multiobjective particle swarm optimization approach. IEEE Transact. Evol. Comput. **18**(1), 70–81 (2014)
25. Li, L., Yu, Z., Chen, Y.: Evacuation dynamic and exit optimization of a supermarket based on particle swarm optimization. Phys. A **416**, 157–172 (2014)

A Framework for a Decision Tree Learning Algorithm with Rough Set Theory

Masaki Kurematsu[✉], Jun Hakura, and Hamido Fujita

Faculty of Software and Information,
Iwate Prefectual University, Takizawa, Japan
{kure,hakura,issam}@iwate-pu.ac.jp

Abstract. In this paper, we improve the conventional decision tree learning algorithm using rough set theory. First, our approach gets the upper approximate for each class. Next, it generates the decision tree from each upper approximate. Each decision tree shows whether the data item is in this class or not. Our approach classifies the unlabeled data item using every decision trees and integrates the outputs of these decision trees to decide the class of unlabeled data item. We evaluated our method using mechanically-prepared datasets whose the proportion of overlap of classes in datasets differs. Experimental result shows our approach is better than the conventional approach when the dataset has the high proportion of overlap of classes and few data items which have the same set of attributes. We guess it is possible to get better classification rules from uncertain and dispersed datasets using our approach. However, we don't use enough datasets to show this advantage in this experiment. In order to evaluate and enhance our approach, we analyze various and big datasets by our approach.

Keywords: Decision tree learning algorithm · Rough set theory · Future reduction

1 Introduction

A decision tree learning algorithm [1] is one of well-known supervised machine learning algorithms. We use this algorithm to make a decision tree from the transaction dataset and predict a class label of the unlabeled data item using the decision tree. A decision tree shows the set of classification rules which show how to decide a class label of each data item based on attribute values. Though there are some statistical methods or machine learning algorithms to make classifiers from dataset, for example, SVM (support vector machine [2]), ANN (Artificial Neural networks [3]), analysts and researchers use this algorithm to make rules from dataset and predict a class of a unlabeled data item. One of reasons for using this algorithm is that it is easy to understand a decision tree made by this algorithm. The other reason is that there are some tools based on this algorithm, for example, Weka [4], R [5] and SPSS [6]. So this algorithm is used in many research filed, such as marketing, psychology and medical [7,8].

Though there are many researches using decision tree type algorithms, this algorithm has some weak points. One of well-known weak points is that this algorithm has the impact of the training dataset. The quality of a decision tree made by this algorithm

© Springer International Publishing Switzerland 2015
H. Fujita and G. Guizzi (Eds.): SoMeT 2015, CCIS 532, pp. 341–352, 2015.
DOI: 10.1007/978-3-319-22689-7_26

depends on the quality and the quantity of the training dataset. If the training dataset demonstrates the area most clearly, we can make the good decision tree. It is not easy to make a good decision tree from small training dataset. If the training dataset has ambiguity, for example, there is a data item in one class which has same attribute values as other data item in the other class. We have to prepare good a training dataset in advance, however, it is difficult to do. So we have to manage the impact of the training dataset.

In order to solve this issue, we make decision trees which predict whether a data item is in the target class or not and predict the class label by voting every decision trees [9]. Before making a decision tree, we make the dataset for each class label. There are two class labels in each dataset. One class label shows the target class label and the other class label shows remaining class labels. We make a decision tree from each dataset. We predict a class label of the unlabeled data item by these decision trees and select the class label which has the maximum predict score. Experimental results said this approach was better than a conventional decision tree, however, this approach has some issues, for example, this approach does not make a good decision tree when the training dataset is small or ambiguity. We have to enhance this approach.

On the other hand, the research about Rough set theory is actively pursued. Rough set theory is a mathematical approach to vague and uncertain data analysis and imperfect knowledge proposed by Zdzisław I. Pawlak [10]. This approach has the some advantages, for example, it provides efficient algorithms for finding hidden patterns in data, it finds reduced sets of data and it identifies relationships that would not be found using statistical methods. So, this theory has possibilities to improve our approach.

In this paper, we propose a new approach to improve a decision tree learning algorithm with rough set theory. In this approach, we make some training datasets form an original training dataset by rough set theory and make some decision trees from each datasets. We predict unlabeled data item's class by voting these decision trees.

Next section gives an outline of related works. We describes our approach in Sect. 3 and the experiment for evaluation our research in Sect. 4. We also describe discussion about our approach according to the experimental result and future works in Sect. 4. Finally, we conclude this paper in Sect. 5.

2 Related Works

2.1 Overview of Enhancing a Decision Tree Learning Algorithm

As we mentioned in Sect. 1, a decision tree learning algorithm is considered to be appropriate if the tree can classify the unlabeled data items accurately and the size of the tree is small. We need good training dataset in order to make an appropriate decision tree because the performance of a decision tree depends on training dataset. However, it is not easy to prepare good training dataset in advance. So we need to improve a decision tree learning algorithm to manage the impact of the training dataset. There are some researches to improve a decision tree learning algorithm. There are two big streams, one is to make a multitude of trees and the other is to preprocess dataset.

First approach makes some difference decision trees and predicts using them. Random Forest [11] is one well-known method in first approach. Random forests are an ensemble learning method for classification that operate by constructing a multitude of decision trees at training time and outputting the class that is the mode of the classes output by individual trees. The training algorithm for random forests repeatedly selects a random sample with replacement of the training dataset and makes a decision tree for each sample. After training, predictions for unseen samples can be made by averaging the predictions from all the individual regression trees.

Second approach adds extra information to dataset before learning. For example, Treabe et al. proposed a novel approach that the knowledge on attributes relevant to the class is extracted as association rules from the training data [12]. The new attributes and the values are generated from the association rules among the originally given attributes. They elaborate on the method and investigate its feature. The effectiveness of their approach is demonstrated through some experiments. Liang focused on the current automotive maintenance industry and combining K-means method and decision tree theory to analyze customer value and thus promote customer value [13]. This investigation first applies the K-means method to establish a customer value analysis model for analyzing customer value. By the results of the K-means method, the customers are divided into high, middle and low value groups. Moreover, further analysis is conducted for clustering variables using the LSD and Turkey HSD tests. Subsequently, decision tree theory is utilized to mine the characteristics of each customer segment. Gaddam et al. presented "*K-Means + ID3*," a method to cascade k-Means clustering and the *ID3* decision tree learning methods [14] for classifying anomalous and normal activities in a computer network, an active electronic circuit, and a mechanical mass-beam system [15]. The *K-Means* clustering method partitions the training instances into k clusters using Euclidean distance similarity. On each cluster, representing a density region of normal or anomaly instances, they build an *ID3* decision tree. The decision tree on each cluster refines the decision boundaries by learning the subgroups within the cluster. To obtain a final decision on classification, the decisions of the *K-Means* and ID3 methods are combined using two rules: the Nearest-neighbor rule and the Nearest-consensus rule.

Though there are some approaches to try to improve a decision tree learning algorithm, they have advantage and disadvantage. One of big disadvantage is that these algorithms make the comprehensibility of a decision tree worse. Some algorithms use additional attributes made by them. Users don't know these additional attributes. So it becomes difficult for users to understand these decision trees. Other algorithms make multiple decision trees. That is, users have to understand more than one decision tree. Understanding multiple decision trees need more time than understanding a decision tree. So we should continue to improve a decision tree learning algorithm.

2.2   Overview of Rough Set Theory

Rough set theory is a mathematical approach to vague and uncertain data analysis and imperfect knowledge proposed by Zdzisław I. Pawlak. This approach has the some advantages, for example, it provides efficient algorithms for finding hidden patterns in data, it finds reduced sets of data and it identifies relationships that would not be found using statistical methods. We can use rough set theory for many real-life applications in various domains.

The basic concept of rough set theory is reduct. A reduct is a set of attributes that preserves partition. It means that a reduct is the minimal subset of attributes that enables the same classification of elements of the original data as the whole set of attributes. In other words, attributes that do not belong to a reduct are superfluous with regard to classification of elements of the original data. We can reduce superfluous attributes for classification using rough set theory.

Other basic concepts of rough set theory are the lower and the upper approximation. They are used to draw conclusions from data. Informal definition of the lower approximation of a set X with respect to data D is the set of all facts that can be for certain classified as X in view of the data D and informal definition of the upper approximation of a set X with respect to data D is the set of all facts that can be possibly classified as X in view of the data D. We use the lower and the under approximations to understand and manipulate uncertainty. Table 1 shows the example of rough set theory. In Table 1, A_i means i-th attribute and C means class label. Now, we consider the set of items with the class label Y. The correct set is {#1, #4, #6}. Item #2 and item #6 have same attributes but belong to difference class. It is important to manage such items. The lower approximate for class label Y is {#1, #4}, i.e., it removes {#6} from the correct set. All items in the lower approximate should belong to class Y. On the other hand, the upper approximate for the class label Y is {#1, #2, #4, #6}, i.e., it includes {#2} which doesn't belong to class Y.

Table 1. Example of rough set theory

ID	A_0	A_1	A_2	A_3	C
#1	V_1	V_3	V_5	V_7	Y
#2	V_1	V_4	V_5	V_8	N
#3	V_2	V_4	V_6	V_9	N
#4	V_2	V_3	V_6	V_7	Y
#5	V_2	V_4	V_6	V_7	N
#6	V_1	V_4	V_5	V_8	Y

2.3 Overview of a Decision Tree Learning Algorithm with Rough Set Theory

There are some researches about a decision tree learning algorithm with rough set theory, because it is possible to manage the uncertainty of dataset using rough set theory. We show some existing works in as the following;

Longjun Huang et al. [16] proposed the degree of dependency of decision attribute on condition attribute is used as a heuristic for selecting the attribute based on rough set theory. One of the keys to constructing decision tree model is to choose standard for testing attribute, for the criteria of selecting test attributes influences the classification accuracy of the tree. There exists diversity choosing standards for testing attribute based on entropy, Bayesian, and so on. They proposed the degree of dependency of decision attribute on condition attribute, based on rough set theory, is used as a heuristic for selecting the attribute that will best separate the samples into individual classes. The results of example and experiments showed that compared with the entropy-based approach, their approach were a better way to select nodes for constructing decision tree.

Chang-Sik Son et al. [17] proposed the decision-making model for early diagnosis of congestive heart failure using rough set and decision tree approaches. The accurate diagnosis of heart failure in emergency room patients is quite important, but can also be quite difficult due to their insufficient understanding of the characteristics of heart failure. The purpose of their study was to design a decision-making model that provides critical factors and knowledge associated with congestive heart failure (CHF) using an approach that makes use of rough sets (RSs) and decision trees. Among 72 laboratory findings, it was determined that two subsets (RBC, EOS, Protein, O2SAT, Pro BNP) in an RS-based model, and one subset (Gender, MCHC, Direct bilirubin, and Pro BNP) in a logistic regression (LR)-based model were indispensable factors for differentiating CHF patients from those with dyspnea, and the risk factor Pro BNP was particularly so. To demonstrate the usefulness of the proposed model, they compared the discriminatory power of decision-making models that utilize RS- and LR-based decision models by conducting 10-fold cross-validation. The experimental results showed that the RS-based decision-making model (accuracy: 97.5 %, sensitivity: 97.2 %, specificity: 97.7 %, positive predictive value: 97.2 %, negative predictive value: 97.7 %, and area under ROC curve: 97.5 %) consistently outperformed the LR-based decision-making model (accuracy: 88.7 %, sensitivity: 90.1 %, specificity: 87.5 %, positive predictive value: 85.3 %, negative predictive value: 91.7 %, and area under ROC curve: 88.8 %). In addition, a pairwise comparison of the ROC curves of the two models showed a statistically significant difference ($p < 0.01$; 95 % CI: 2.63–14.6).

Jin-Mao Wei et al. [18] proposed rough set based approach for inducing decision trees. In their research, they proposed a new approach for inducing decision trees based on Variable Precision Rough Set Model. The presented approach was aimed at handling uncertain information during the process of inducing decision trees and generalizes the rough set based approach to decision tree construction by allowing some extent misclassification when classifying objects. In their research, two concepts, i.e. variable precision explicit region, variable precision implicit region, and the process for inducing decision trees are introduced. They discussed the differences between the rough set based approaches and the fundamental entropy based method. The comparison between the presented approach and the rough set based approach and the fundamental entropy based method on some data sets from the UCI Machine Learning Repository [19] were also reported.

There are some researches about improving a decision tree learning algorithm with rough set theory. Most approaches reduce attributes by using reduction of rough set theory to get a good decision tree.

3   A Framework for a Decision Tree Learning Algorithm with Rough Set Theory

3.1   Overview of Our Approach

There are some datasets which some data items have same attributes but belong to the different class. There are some reasons that we make such a dataset. One is that we take some mistake at making dataset and the other is that we miss some necessary attributes. We can say such a dataset is uncertainty dataset. It is difficult to divide data items into each class, so the decision tree learning algorithm cannot make a good decision tree. So we have to manage the uncertainty.

There are some proposed methods to manage the uncertain data. We focus on the rough set theory, because, we can modify class information of datasets by using the upper and lower approximates. We show it is possible that modified class information is useful to enhance the decision tree in previous research. We decide to use the rough set theory. Our approach makes the decision tree from the upper approximate of each class and it classifies new data items by integrating the prediction results by using these trees. Basically, our approach uses ID3 algorithm to generate the decision tree, however, our approach predict an unlabeled data item using the different method.

In next subsection, we will explain our approach in detail.

3.2   The Algorithm of Our Approach

First, we explain how to generate a decision tree and extract classification rules from this tree.

Our approach collects class labels from the given dataset and does the following steps for each class label.

(1) It makes the upper approximate for a class label C_i from the given dataset, where C_i is one of class labels in the given dataset.

(2) It redefines a class label of all data items in the given dataset. If a data item in the given dataset is the member of the upper approximate for the selected class label C_i, our approach modifies the class label of this data item to "the class label $C_i = Y$". Otherwise, it modifies the class label of this data item to "the class label $C_i = N$". After that, it makes a new dataset based on the new dataset. So, there are only two class labels in the new dataset.

(3) Our approach generates a decision tree from the new dataset using the conventional decision tree learning algorithm. It extracts every paths of the decision tree as classification rules. These rules consist of conditions and the class information. Leaf node shows the class information and other nodes and brunches show conditions. There are one or two class labels with proportion in each leaf node. The proportion equals the number of data items in one class divided by the number of nodes in the leaf node. When there is one class label, it extracts a path as a classification rule for the class. Otherwise, our approach extracts a path as a classification rule for the class whose proportion is higher than other's one. If proportion of each class label is

same, it extracts classification rules for each class label. Moreover, it uses the proportion as the weight of a classification rule.

Next, we explain how to predict an unlabeled data item's class label using classification rules.

Our approach compares an unlabeled data item's attributes and each classification rule's conditions. If the unlabeled data item matches all conditions of the classification rule, our approach multiplies the weight of this rule by the number of the classification rule's conditions and adds this value to the point of the class label in the classification rule.

After comparing an unlabeled data item and all classification rules, our approach lets the point of "the class label $C_i = Y$" as Zero, if the point of "the class label $C_i = Y$" is smaller than the point of "the class label $C_i = N$".

Next, our approach calculates the sum of the point of "the class label $C_i = Y$" and divides the point of "the class label $C_i = Y$" by it. This value is the final point of "the class label $C_i = Y$".

Finally, our approach selects the class label which has the maximum value of the final point as an answer and it returns the class label with its point.

4 Experiments

4.1 Overview of Our Experiments

In order to evaluate our approach, we do experiments using some datasets. According to the algorithm, our method may not be effective in all cases. So, we use some datasets to find the good condition for our approach. We will explain the overview of our experiments next.

First, we explain about dataset. Each data item in the dataset has four attributes and one class label. These attributes are categorical data. We define four class labels and make the subset for each class label. We control the overlapping region among some subsets. We make datasets to show in Table 2 using a program. In Table 2, # of data items shows the number of data items in each dataset and the size of each class is same. Overlapping ratio means the percentage of data items whose attributes equals other data item belongs to other class. If overlapping rate is more than zero, the data set is uncertain dataset. We use these datasets except #A4, #B4 and #C4 to generate classification rules and to predict #A4, #B4 and #C4 using these classification rules.

In order to generate classification rules, we use our approach and the conventional decision tree learning algorithm. When we use the conventional decision tree learning algorithm, we select the path of the decision tree whose proportion is more than 0.5 as the classification rule. We can run our approach using the lower approximate or the

Table 2. The outline of datasets

Dataset ID	#A1	#A2	#A3	#A4	#B1	#B2	#B3	#B4	#C1	#C2	#C3	#C4
# of data items	40	200	400	800	40	200	400	800	40	200	400	800
Overlapping Ratio	0.0	0.0	0.0	0.0	0.3	0.3	0.3	0.3	0.7	0.7	0.7	0.7

original class, instead of the upper approximate. In order to indicate the upper approximate is the best training sets for our approach, we generate classification rules with the lower approximate or the original class.

There are two points for evaluation the decision tree, one is the simplicity of the decision tree and the other is the accuracy of them. Our approach is weaker than the conventional approach about the simplicity of the tree, because our approach makes more than one decision trees. So we evaluate about the accuracy of them and focus on the number of data items which has the extracted class label is same as the given class label, the number of data items which has the extracted class label is not same as the given label, the number of data items which doesn't have the extracted class label.

4.2 The Result of Experiments

Table 3 shows the outline of experiments. In Table 3, RS shows the set of classification rules by each method. DT means the set of rules generated by the conventional decision tree learning algorithm. UA means the set of rules generated by the proposed approach with the upper approximate. LA means the set of rules generated by the proposed approach with the lower approximate. OS means the set of rules generated by our approach with original class and this rule set is same as the set of rules generated by our previous approach. Every columns show the result of predication the data items in a test dataset. When we use #A1, #A2 and #A3 to generate classification rules, #A4 is a test dataset. When #B1, #B2 and #B3 are training datasets, #B4 is a test dataset. We use #C4 as the test dataset when we use #C1, #C2 and #C3 as training dataset. The column whose label is OK shows the number of data items predicted correctly. NG means the number of data items predicted in wrong class and MISS means the number of data

Table 3. The outline of experiments

RS	ID	OK	NG	MISS	ID	OK	NG	MISS	ID	OK	NG	MISS
DT	#A1	800	0	0	#B1	420	180	200	#C1	0	600	200
UA	#A1	800	0	0	#B1	210	340	250	#C1	60	690	50
OS	#A1	800	0	0	#B1	420	180	200	#C1	0	600	200
LA	#A1	800	0	0	#B1	140	60	600	#C1	0	200	600
DT	#A2	800	0	0	#B2	560	240	0	#C2	0	800	0
UA	#A2	800	0	0	#B2	140	660	0	#C2	60	740	0
OS	#A2	800	0	0	#B2	560	240	0	#C2	0	800	0
LA	#A2	800	0	0	#B2	0	0	800	#C2	0	0	800
DT	#A3	800	0	0	#B3	560	240	0	#C3	560	240	0
UA	#A3	800	0	0	#B3	400	400	0	#C3	400	400	0
OS	#A3	800	0	0	#B3	560	240	0	#C3	560	240	0
LA	#A3	800	0	0	#B3	0	0	800	#C3	0	0	800

items not predicted using classification rules, i.e., the system cannot classify data items. We judge a approach is better than others, if this approach has the biggest number of OK.

When we use #A1, #A2 and #A3 as training dataset and #A4 as a test dataset, there are no different among each method. When we use #B1, #B2 and #B3 as a training dataset and #B4 as a test dataset, the conventional algorithm is better than our approach with the upper approximate. In #C1 and #C2, our approach is better than other. However, the conventional approach is better than our approach in #C3.

5 Discussion

According to the experimental results, our approach is better than others when the overlapping region between classes is big and most data items differ each other, where the overlapping region between classes means data items which has same attribute patterns but belongs to the different class. On the other words, the dataset is uncertain and few data items in the dataset has same attributes set as others one. It is difficult for the decision tree learning algorithm to divide data items which have same attributes set but belong to the different class, because this algorithm tries to divide data items based on the attribute sets. Our approach changes the class of data items using the upper approximate from the rough set theory before classification, so, it can divide these data items. The decision tree learning algorithm, however, can divide such data items when the number of data items is high, because, it can use the proportion of data items in one class as a means of supplementing for processing these data items. This method is same as a means of supplementing for noise. We don't use some classification rule with low weight, i.e., the proportion of data items in a class is low, so, it is possible to enhance the accuracy of classification using the decision tree by using all classification rules.

In order to identify the feature of our approach, we compare classification rules generated by four approaches. Table 4 shows the result of comparing. In Table 4, #P means the number of positive classification rules and #N means the number of negative classification rules. Positive classification rules for a class judge an unlabeled data item as a member of the class. On the other hand, negative classification rules for a class judge an unlabeled data item as a not member of the class. The conventional decision tree learning algorithm doesn't generate negative classification rules and generating these rules is one of main points for our approach. According to result, the number of classifications generated by the conventional algorithm is smaller than our approach with the upper approximate and the number of positive rules is smaller than the number of negatives, because, the number of data items belonging negative class is bigger than the number of data items belonging the class. When the number of data items is low, the number of rules seems to be proportionate to the ratio of overlapping. However, the number of rules doesn't increase when the number of data items increases. When the number of data items, these algorithm can integrate some rules based on the proportion of classes in a leaf nodes, i.e., cut off rules with low probability. So, the number of rules doesn't increase when the number of data is high. Moreover, $P shows the mean of the weight of positive classification rules and $N shows the mean of the weight of negative

Table 4. The result of comparing of rules generated by approaches

		Number		Weight			Number		Weight			Number		Weight	
RS	ID	#P	#N	$P	$N	ID	#P	#N	$P	$N	ID	#P	#N	$P	$N
DT	#A1	9	0	1		#B1	20	0	0.67		#C1	20	0	0.67	
UA	#A1	9	15	1	1	#B1	14	18	1	1	#C1	18	22	1	1
EA	#A1	9	15	1	1	#B1	20	34	0.67	0.8	#C1	20	34	0.67	0.8
LA	#A1	9	15	1	1	#B1	4	16	1	1	#C1	4	16	1	1
DT	#A2	9	0	1		#B2	16	0	0.7		#C2	16	0	0.7	
UA	#A2	9	15	1	1	#B2	19	19	1	1	#C2	19	19	1	1
EA	#A2	9	15	1	1	#B2	15	32	0.7	0.85	#C2	16	30	0.7	0.84
LA	#A2	9	15	1	1	#B2	0	0			#C2	0	0		
DT	#A3	9	0	1		#B3	16	0	0.7		#C3	16	0	0.7	
UA	#A3	9	15	1	1	#B3	17	17	0.93	0.93	#C3	17	17	0.93	0.93
EA	#A3	9	15	1	1	#B3	10	30	0.7	0.84	#C3	16	28	0.7	0.85
LA	#A3	9	15	1	1	#B3	0	0			#C3	0	0		

classification rules in Table 4. $N of our approach with the upper approximation is same as $P of one.

In addition to, we compare rules generated by each approach and show the result in Table 5. The denominator shows the total number of classification rules and the numerator shows the number of common classification rules. When there is not the overlapping region between each class, the classification rules generated by each approach are same. Fewer than half of classification rules generated by our approach are same as the classification rules generated by the conventional decision tree algorithm. Table 5 shows the accuracy of classification rules generated by the conventional approach is better than the accuracy of our approach. The classification rules generated by our approach are worse than rules generated by the conventional rules.

According to the experimental results, it is difficult to say our approach is better than the conventional approach. Our approach, however, is better than others in a few cases. So, it is worth using the rough set theory to generate the decision tree. Selecting our approach and the conventional approach is possible to enhance the accuracy of the

Table 5. The result of comparing between DT and UA

RS#1:RS#2	#A1	#A2	#A3	#B1	#B2	#B3	#C1	#C2	#C3
DT:UA (P)	9/9	9/9	9/9	1/20	2/16	2/16	9/20	10/16	6/16
DT:OS (P)	9/9	9/9	9/9	5/20	8/16	2/16	7/20	6/16	8/16
DT:LA (P)				1/20			1/20		
UA:OS (P)	9/9	9/9	9/9	0/14	1/19	2/17	2/18	4/19	4/17
UA:OS (N)	15/15	15/15	15/15	11/18	7/19	3/17	2/22	3/19	4/17

decision tree. Our future works are as follow. We continue experiments with other datasets which have more attributes and patterns in order to identify the feature of datasets for using our approach. After that, we select the conventional approach or our approach based on the feature of given datasets. We also consider to use our idea when we generate child nodes, because the decision tree learning algorithm is implemented as the recurrence function and the dataset changes on recurrence process. Moreover, we can cut out conflicted data items which have same attributes set but belong to different class using the lower approximate, so, we reconsider the lower approximate, too. Alongside of modification our approach, we evaluate our modified approach with some open datasets and real-world datasets.

6 Conclusion

In this paper, we proposed a modified decision tree learning algorithm. We have improved the conventional decision tree learning algorithm using rough set theory. Our approach generates the decision tree as follows. First, our approach gets the upper approximate for each class. Next, it generates the decision tree from each upper approximate. Each decision tree shows whether the data item is in this class or not. Our approach classifies the unlabeled data item using every decision trees and integrates the outputs of these decision trees to decide the class of unlabeled data item. We evaluated our method using mechanically-prepared datasets whose the proportion of overlap of classes in datasets differs. Experimental result shows our approach is better than the conventional approach when the dataset has the high proportion of overlap of classes and few data items which have the same set of attributes, i.e., the dataset is uncertain and small. So, we guess it is possible to get better classification rules from uncertain and dispersed datasets using our approach, such as medical datasets. However, we don't use enough datasets to show this advantage in this experiment. In order to evaluate and enhance our approach, we prepare various and big datasets and analyze them by our approach. After improving our approach based on experimental results, we analyze some open and real-world datasets using our approach and the other approaches and evaluate our approach based on the results.

Acknowledgment. We would like to thank Mr. Yasutomo FUKADA who graduated Iwate Prefectural University in March, 2015 and Ms. Saori AMANUMA who has completed a master's course of the graduate school of Iwate Prefectural University.

References

1. Breiman, L., Friedman, J.H., Olshen, R.A., Stone, C.J.: Classification and Regression Trees (Wadsworth Statistics/ Probability). CRC-Press, Boca Raton (1984)
2. Corinna, C., Vladimir, N.V.: Support-vector networks. Mach. Learn. **20**(3), 237–297 (1995). Kluwer Academic Publishers, Hingham
3. Rosenblatt, F.: Principles of Neurodynamics: Perceptrons and the Theory of Brain Mechanisms. Spartan Books, Michigan (1962)

4. Weka 3 - Data Mining with Open Source Machine Learning Software in Java. http://www.cs.waikato.ac.nz/ml/weka/. Accessed 12 March 2015
5. The R Project for Statistical Computing. http://www.r-project.org/. Accessed 12 March 2015
6. IBM SPSS software. http://www-01.ibm.com/software/analytics/spss/. Accessed 12 March 2015
7. Bach, M.P., Ćosić, D.: Data mining usage in health care management: literature survey and decision tree application. Medicinski Glasnik 5(1), 57–64 (2008). Bosnia and Herzegovina
8. MacQueen, J.B.: Some methods for classification and analysis of multivariate observations. In: Proceedings of 5th Berkeley Symposium on Mathematical Statistics and Probability, pp. 281–297. University of California Press, Berkley (1967)
9. Kurematu, M., Hakura, J., Fujita, H.: An extraction of emotion in human speech using speech synthesize and each classifier for each emotion. WSEAS Trans. Inf. Sci. Appl. 3(5), 246–251 (2008). World Scientific and Engineering Academy and Society, Greece
10. Pawlak, Z.: Rough sets. Int. J. Parallel Program. 11(5), 341–356 (1982). Springer, Heidelberg
11. Breiman, L.: Random forests. Mach. Learn. 45(1), 5–32 (2001). Academic Publishers, Hingham
12. Terabe, M., Katai, O., Sawaragi, T., Washio, T., Motoda, H.: Attribute generation based on association rules. Knowl. Inf. Syst. 4(3), 329–349 (2002). Springer, Heidelberg
13. Liang, Y.-H.: Combining the K-means and decision tree methods to promote customer value for the automotive maintenance industry. In: IEEE International Conference on Industrial Engineering and Engineering Management 2009, pp. 1337–1341. IEEE, Hong-Kong (2009)
14. Quinlan, J.R.: Induction of decision trees. Mach. Learn. 1(1), 81–106 (1986). Springer, Heidelberg
15. Gaddam, S.R., Phoha, V.V., Balagani, K.S.: K-Means + ID3: a novel method for supervised anomaly detection by cascading k-means clustering and ID3 decision tree learning methods. IEEE Trans. Knowl. Data Eng. 9(3), 345–354 (2007). IEEE, Washington
16. Huang, L., Huang, M., Guo, B., Zhang, Z.: A new method for constructing decision tree based on rough set theory. In: Granular Computing, GRC 2007, p. 241. IEEE, Washington (2007)
17. Son, C.-S., Kim, Y.-N., Kim, H.-S., Park, H.-S., Kim, M.-S.: Decision-making model for early diagnosis of congestive heart failure using rough set and decision tree approaches. J. Biomed. Inf. 45(5), 999–1008 (2012). Elsevier, NewYork
18. Wei, J.-M., Wang, S.-Q., Wang, M.-Y., You, J.-P., Liu, D.-Y.: Rough set based approach for inducing decision trees. Knowl.-Based Syst. 20(8), 695–702 (2007). Elsevier, NewYork
19. UCI Machine Learning Repository. http://archive.ics.uci.edu/ml/datasets/. Accessed 29 March 2015

Software Development
and Integration

Description and Implementation of Business Logic for End-User-Initiative Development

Takeshi Chusho[(✉)] and Jie Xu

Department of Computer Science, Meiji University, Kawasaki, Japan
chusho@cs.meiji.ac.jp

Abstract. The development of Web applications should be supported by business professionals since Web applications must be modified frequently based on their needs. In our recent studies utilizing the three-tier architecture of user interfaces, business logic and databases, Web applications are developed using a domain-specific application framework and visual modeling technologies. Description and implementation of business logic is a key technology. In this paper, an approach that business logic is implemented in stored procedures within database is introduced. The four basic stored procedures {select, insert, update and delete} for each table of a reuse support system are prepared. The other stored procedures are generated by modifying these basic stored procedures.

Keywords: Web application · Stored procedure · Business logic · End-user

1 Introduction

The number of Web applications for business professionals has been increasing in recent years. Most of these applications are developed by IT professionals. Thus, attempting to achieve automation is limited to highly specific tasks which calculate profit over the development cost. Furthermore, it is difficult to develop applications quickly. Primarily, Web applications should be supported by business professionals since Web applications must be modified frequently based on users' needs. Therefore, end-user-initiative development has become important for the automation of end-users' fulfilling their own needs [5].

There are several approaches for end-user-initiative development. The UI-driven approach makes it possible to easily develop applications for the UI-centered front-end systems. It is strengthened by using domain-specific framework technologies. The model-driven approach makes it possible to easily develop applications for workflow-centered back-end systems. It is strengthened by using a visual modeling tool. End-user software engineering research for end-user programmers and domain experts has also appeared [4]. Recently, agile software development has been coming popular and end-users are expected to participate in the development team with IT professionals.

The target of our research is that business professionals with domain expertise develop Web applications for their own tasks without strong support by IT professionals. Furthermore, the popular three-tier architecture of the user interfaces, business logic and databases for Web applications is assumed. In our studies [1], domain-specific application frameworks and visual modeling tools based on components were developed for

© Springer International Publishing Switzerland 2015
H. Fujita and G. Guizzi (Eds.): SoMeT 2015, CCIS 532, pp. 355–366, 2015.
DOI: 10.1007/978-3-319-22689-7_27

this purpose. They support the construction of a graphical user interface and a simple database system.

It is, however, difficult to support business logic because there are various kinds of business logic. For end-user-initiative development, business logic should be expressed from the view of the service providers or support systems instead of the view of the clients. In this paper, an approach that business logic is implemented in stored procedures within database is introduced [9].

This paper presents basic approaches in Sect. 2, business logic for matching in Sect. 3, the development process in Sect. 4 and description and implementation of business logic in stored procedures in Sect. 5.

2 Basic Approaches

2.1 Domain-Specific Technologies

Our approach to Web application development is explained in the following layers:

- The business level {Business models}
- The service level {Domain models}
- The software level {Components}

A business model at the business level is proposed by those end-users who are business professionals and domain experts. Then, at the service level, the domain model is constructed and the required services are specified as the requirement specification. At the software level, the domain model is implemented using components. In this approach, the granularity gap between components and the domain model is bridged by business objects [6], patterns and application frameworks. On the other hand, the semantic gap between the domain model and the business model should be bridged by domain-specific technologies with domain knowledge [7].

Approaches to end-user-initiative Web application development based on the three-tier architecture are classified into the three categories of UI-driven, model-driven and data-driven processes by first focusing on either the UI (user interface), the model (business logic) or DB. Recently, as Web applications have been increasing sharply, a UI-driven approach has emerged. In our UI-driven approach, visual forms were defined first and the framework was used. The business logic dependent on the application was included in form definitions. The other business logic was embedded into the framework.

End-users can get application software by visual modeling which defines forms and form-to-form transformations. A model which is defined by end-users is finally transformed into the Java codes of the Web application. One of the main problems for end-user-initiative development is how to describe business logic.

2.2 The Template for Business Logic Definition

The analysis of business logic is indispensable to support that end-users describe the various kinds of business logic. Therefore, first, many types of business logic were gathered by a survey on the Internet and classified into several categories in our previous work [2]. The five types of business rules, {Facts, Constraints, Action Enablers, Inferences, Computations} [8], were adopted. In this classification, there was one problem that many rules were represented from the view of service clients. For the software requirement specifications, however, rules are represented from the view of the service providers or the support system. Consequently, business logic is defined from the view of service providers or the support system in this paper because the end-users imply the service providers. Then the business logic at the requirement specifications level is mapped into the combination of user interfaces (UI), business logic (BL) and databases (DB) based on the typical three-tier architecture. The following template, named UtoU, is introduced because the UI-driven approach is suitable for the end-user-initiative development:

(1) UI: The system gets a request from a client.
(2) BL: The system processes the request.
(3) DB: The system accesses the database.
(4) BL: The system processes the results.
(5) UI: The system displays the results.

It is easy for an end-user to understand this process because the end-user is familiar with the following typical work flow such as getting a resident's card:

(1) A client fills out an application for the card and hands it to the service counter at a city office.
(2) A clerk at the service counter checks the application and passes it to a computer operator in the back.
(3) The operator inputs the information about the client and gets the resident's card.
(4) The clerk receives it and confirms the contents.
(5) The clerk finally hands it to the client.

3 Business Logic for Matching

3.1 Domains of Web Applications

In our studies, the application domains such as lending books or equipment, the reservation of meeting rooms and the reuse of second-hand articles were selected. All of them required at least two DB tables for services. One is for member registration and the other is for object registration. The member implies a system user, including a system administrator. The object is a book, a piece of equipment, a room or an article. The basic operations are CRUD (create, read, update and delete). Although the columns of a record are dependent on the object, these differences are unified by the concept of "matching" between an object provider and an object requester. Figure 1 shows the basic behavior of system users in the use cases of UML.

The practical naming of the selection may be different for each application. Furthermore, business logic must be different for each application. There are many kinds of applications in the domain of matching services. It is difficult to develop an application framework that can be used for all kinds of matching services because such

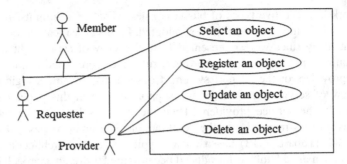

Fig. 1. A use case diagram for a matching service

a framework requires a lot of customization and the merit of easy development of an application is lost. Therefore, it is necessary to focus our research target on a limited subdomain. For this purpose, we analyzed and classified matching services [3].

A typical website for a matching service is modeled as the following three factors:

- WHO: providers and requesters.
- WHAT: things and services.
- HOW: algorithms for matching decision.

For the WHO factor, providers and requesters are limited to ordinary users. Such business activities as online shopping and hotel reservations are not our research target because the requirements for Web applications are too complex. Reuse promotion services supported by local governments, however, are our target because these services are operated at actual counters, instead of websites, and often face a shortage of talents or funds. Our research product will solve this problem effectively.

Regarding the WHAT factor, our research targets are such things which are reused or are lent as well as services such as volunteers work for snow shoveling or the repair of houses damaged by floods.

As for the HOW factor, our research target is limited to domains with simple algorithms and applications with complicated algorithms are omitted because it is difficult for end-users to define business logic.

3.2 Analysis for Matching Service

For the analysis of many kinds of matching domains, the following two criteria were introduced:

- Request for the trustworthiness of participants.
- Request for quality of things or services.

There are three kinds of participants in a matching site, namely providers, requesters, and website administrators. In particular, the request for trustworthiness of providers and requesters is considered as the essential criterion. For example, a babysitter assigned by a website may mistreat the baby. The request for quality of things or services is also considered as the essential criterion for matching domains.

Let's give some examples based on these two criteria. The reuse support service that an article to be reused is given free to a requester by a provider is characterized by (low, low) as values of two criteria. Another reuse support service that an article to be reused is sold to a requester by a provider is characterized by (high, high). In this case, there may be troubles with payment. The other reuse support service that the requester pays to the provider via the website is characterized by (low, high) because the risk of trouble in payment is reduced. Finally, a voluntary snow shoveling that a volunteer may visit a house in which an old person lives alone is characterized by (high, low).

The classification with these two criteria is based on the user view. The end-user-initiative development, however, requires the system view instead of the user view. Therefore, the following other two criteria were introduced:

- Algorithmic complexity.
- Quantity of business rules.

The possibility of end-user-initiative development depends on these criteria. If the business logic which the end-users define requires complex algorithm, the automatic generation of the corresponding source codes will become difficult. If the number of business rules increase too much, it may be difficult for end-users to define the business logic consistently.

The evaluation of three reuse support services and the voluntary snow shoveling mentioned above, are characterized by (low, low), (low, high), (high, low) and (low, low) based on these two criteria. Strictly speaking, the characteristics of each application depend on the preconditions. Our research target is limited to the domain in which the algorithm is simple and the business rules are not too many.

3.3 Case Study of Business Logic Definition

In this paper, we focus our attention on reuse support service only for free articles which is characterized by (low, low) as values of two criteria based on a system view. Reuse support systems are expected that information technology contributes to saving resources and environmental preservation for a sustainable society. Many local governments in Japan support reuse promotion activities for ecological movements. Most of them use Web sites for announcements of activities, but do not use them for practical operations. Practical operations are executed at the actual counters. These services deal limited articles to limited customers in a local area. The number of articles and the number of customers will increase if business professionals develop an application for the web site in which customers can easily register articles to be reused or search the list of registered articles for their own use.

There are, however, regulations which are dependent on each local government's policy. For example, the following business rules of items are given:

1. The donor must declare that the article has been used in domestic life.
2. Large pieces of furniture registered must be kept at home.

The second rule is not necessary on a website service because it is assumed that every article will be kept at home. The main process is defined as follows:

(1) UI: The system displays a form for registration and gets a request from a client.
(2) BL: The system checks the request according to the business rules.
(3) DB: The system accesses the database for registration.
(4) BL: The system gets the results from the database.
(5) UI: The system displays the results including the registration number.

In this process, some details are omitted such as error handling, and registration number generation. The displayed form includes the check box for the declaration. Although there are a lot of variations in business logic, it is confirmed that the template is useful for defining the requirements.

4 Development Process Based on Three-Tier Architecture

As a result of the case studies, the Web application generation process by end-users, named the ABC development model, is expressed as "Application = Business logic + CRUD" and is shown as follows:

(1) The user interface is defined at the logical level.
(2) The DB table is also defined at the logical level.
(3) The business logic is defined based on (1) and (2).

The CRUD definition tool is used at the step (1) and (2) and the business logic definition tool is used at the step (3). It is important to describe these three steps at the same abstraction level. Finally, the business logic which is defined based on the results of the first two steps is transformed to program codes with SQL statements for DB access although the first and second steps may be performed simultaneously or the DB table may be defined prior to the UI definition.

Let's consider the previous example for the registration of an article and apply this process to it. At the step (1), the first user interface of the template, {*UI* > BL > DB > BL > UI}, is defined by listing all input columns, {the name of the donor, the member identification number, the name of the article, the details, the check box for a declaration that the article has been used in domestic life}, at the logical level. Then, the last user interface of the template, {UI > BL > DB > BL > *UI*}, is defined by listing all output columns, {the name of a donor, the article registration number}, at the logical level.

During the step (2), the DB table of the template, {UI > BL > *DB* > BL > UI}, is defined by listing all columns, {the article registration number, the name of the article, the details, the member identification number of the donor, the registration date, the status of "registration", "requested" or "deletion"}, at the logical level.

At the step (3), the first business logic of the template, {UI > *BL* > DB > BL > UI}, is defined by listing all processes checking input values as follows:

- All input columns are filled in.
- All input data are valid.
- The identification of the registration date.
- The generation of the article registration number.

Then, the last business logic of the template, {<u>UI > BL > DB > *BL* > UI</u>}, is defined by listing all processes checking output values as follows:

- The name of the donor.
- The article registration number.

As a result, it is possible that end-users of business professionals define requirement specifications of a Web application. One of the problems in building domain-specific framework is determining which components should be prepared. The range of applications is dependent on a related library of components.

5   Development Process Based on Stored Procedure

5.1   Basic Design for Case Study

In the development process based on stored procedure, the basic precondition that web applications are developed using the three-tier architecture is the same. The significant feature is the implementation of business logic that the main part of procedures for business logic is included in the database.

The functions of the reuse support system for a case study were defined as follows:

(1)   The user registration and modification of the user information.
(2)   The user identification by using the mail address.
(3)   The article registration and update of the article information.
(4)   The search and request for articles.
(5)   The process for making a decision of the receiver.

The items (1) and (2) relate to the WHO factors mentioned in Sect. 3.1. The items (3) and (4) relate to the WHAT factors. The item (5) relates to the HOW factor. The system was developed based on ASP.NET MVC model. The system configuration is shown in Fig. 2.

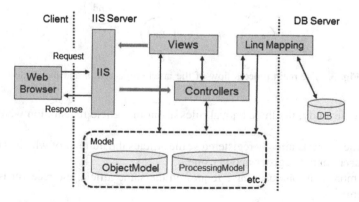

Fig. 2. The configuration of a reuse support system based on ASP.NET MVC

The object model includes a user model and an article model. The processing model includes a user registration model and a mail address registration model. The DB server was implemented by using the SQL server. The six DB tables were introduced. The information of users is stored in USER_TBL. The information of articles is stored in GOODS_TBL. The information of requests for registered articles is stored in APPLY_TBL and modified frequently. Furthermore, TYPE_TBL for the kind of an article, DELIVER_TBL for methods for passing articles, and APPLY_STATE_TBL for management of matching state transition are introduced.

5.2   Description of Business Logic

Let's consider the article registration and the request as an example of business logic. The main process flow is shown in Fig. 3. The algorithm becomes complicated if a set of business rules increase.

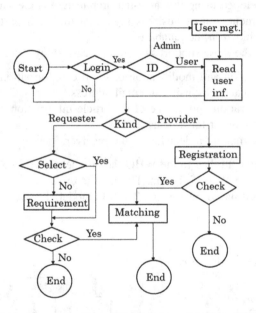

Fig. 3. The main process flow of the article registration and the request

In this case study, the three typical rules about the article registration were selected as follows:

(r1) If the user has already registered some articles the number of which is the upper limit, the user cannot register another one.

(r2) If more than one user have requested the same article, the receiver is selected among them.

(r3) If the pre-defined time has passed after the articles were registered, the articles which have not been requested are deleted.

These rules require the database access. The first rule will be processed as follows:

(1) The information about the registered articles by the user is retrieved from the database.
(2) The number of registered articles is counted.
(3) If the number is less than the upper limit, the article is registered.
(4) If the number is the upper limit, the article is not registered.

The second rule will be processed as follows:

(1) The requesters are listed.
(2) The receiver is decided by using a random function.
(3) The requesters were informed of the decision.
(4) The information of the receiver is modified and the information of other requesters is deleted.

The third rule will be processed as follows:

(1) The registration date about every article is checked.
(2) If the pre-defined time has passed after an article was registered, it is listed.
(3) The providers were informed of the decision.
(4) The listed articles are deleted.

Almost all processes execute database access. Then a conventional method that the program modules such as Java classes require database access by using SQL statements will increase the frequency of database access as the business rules become complicated.

The one solution of this problem is stored procedure technologies. The first rule is implemented in a stored procedure as follows:

```
ALTER PROCEDURE
  [dbo].[ap_CheckNumberGoodsbyUser]
  @count INT = 0
  @user_No varchar(50)
  @IsAllowed Bit OUTPUT
AS
BEGIN
SET NOCOUNT ON;
  select @count = COUNT(*)
  from dbo.User_Tbl u, dbo.Goods_Tbl g
  where g.User_No = u.User_No
  And u.User_No = @user_No
  if  @count >= 5
  begin  set @IsAllowed = 0
    select * from dbo.Goods_Tbl
    where user_no = @user_No
  end
  else  set @IsAlowed = 1
END
```

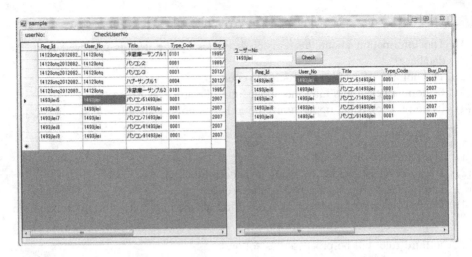

Fig. 4. An example of a window for article registration

In the first five lines, the variable of @count implies the total number of registered articles, the variable of @user_No implies the user identification number and the variable of @IsAllowed implies the result of "true" or "false." In the four lines from the select-statement, the total number of registered articles is calculated and the result is stored in @count. In the six lines from the if-statement, if the total number of registered articles is greater than or equal to five, the new article cannot be registered and the list of registered articles is returned. If not, the new article is registered. The left part in the Fig. 4 displays a list of all registered articles and highlights the current user identification number. The right part displays the list of articles which the current user has registered.

For this implementation, the SQL Server is used and database objects are created in CLR (Common Language Runtime). Stored procedures are executed in this environment. The business logic in stored procedures will be executed easily. The maintainability is improved for frequent business rule modification.

5.3   End-User-Initiative Development Support

End-users are not familiar with coding of the stored procedures although they are business professionals of business rule processing. Therefore, they require some tools. The description of business rules which end-users input by using a visual tool should be transformed into the stored procedures by an automatic code generation tool. Furthermore, the stored procedure should be customized by end-users. These are domain-specific tools. The four basic stored procedures {select, insert, update and delete} for each table of a reuse support system are prepared. The other stored procedures are generated by modifying these basic stored procedures.

Let's consider the first rule of "If the user has already registered some articles the number of which is the upper limit, the user cannot register another one" mentioned in

Sect. 5.2. It is supposed that the upper limit is five. The required parameters are listed first. The parameter of @sEntity is introduced for the entity of the user. The parameter of @sRelatedEntity is introduced for the entity of an article. Then, the parameters of @nSign and @nLimit are introduced for the condition. The @nSign implies the comparison operator such as "greater than" and @nLimit implies the upper limit. The parameter of @IsChk is introduced for the result of checking of "true" or "false." As a result, the following codes are defined:

```
select @count = COUNT(*)
from @sEntity , @sRelatedEntity
where @sEntity .fnTablePrimaryKey(@sEntity)
       = @sRelatedEntity. fnTablePrimaryKey(@sEntity)
and @sEntity. fnTablePrimaryKey(@sEntity) = @user_no

if @count fnSign(@nSign) @nLimit
  begin
   set @IsAllowed = 0
   if @IsChk = 0
     select * from @sRelatedEntity
     where @sEntity. fnTablePrimaryKey( @sEntity)
           = @user_no
  end
else
  begin
    set @IsAlowed = 1
    if @IsChk = 1
       select * from @sRelatedEntity
       where @sEntity. fnTablePrimaryKey( @sEntity)
             = @user_No
  end
end
```

6   Conclusion

This paper described the approach to the end-user-initiative development of Web applications and description and implementation of business logic by using matching applications. When Web applications were constructed based on the three-tier archi-tecture, the business logic was defined after the user interface and DB tables were defined. There were two methods for the business logic implementation. One method was that the business logic was transformed to program codes with SQL statements. The other was that it was transformed to stored procedures in DB. The latter method was studied and the domain-specific tool for reuse support systems were proposed. The tool provided four basic stored procedures {select, insert, update and delete} for each table. The other stored procedures were generated by modifying these basic stored procedures.

References

1. Chusho, T., Zhou, F., Yagi, N.: End-user-initiative development with domain-specific frameworks and visual modeling. In: 10th International Conference on Software Methodologies, Tools and Techniques (SoMeT 2011), pp. 57–71. IOS Press (2011)
2. Chusho, T.: Classification and definitions of business logic for end-user-initiative development. In: 11th International Conference on Software Methodologies, Tools and Techniques (SoMeT 2012), pp. 41–56. IOS Press (2012)
3. Chusho, T.: The classification of matching applications for end-user-initiative development. In: 2015 IAENG International Conference on Software Engineering (ICSE 2015), pp. 476–481. IAENG (2015)
4. Fischer, G., Nakakoji, K., Ye, Y.: Metadesign guidelines for supporting domain experts in software development. IEEE Softw. **26**(5), 37–44 (2009). IEEE
5. Ko, A.J., Abraham, R., Burnett, M.M., Myers, B.A.: Guest editors' introduction: end-user software engineering. IEEE Softw. **26**(5), 16–17 (2009). IEEE
6. Sinha, A.P., Jain, H.: Ease of reuse: an empirical comparison of components and objects. IEEE Softw. **30**(5), 70–75 (2013). IEEE
7. Sprinkle, J., Mernik, M., Tolvanen, J., Spinellis, D.: Guest editors' introduction: what kinds of nails need a domain-specific hammer? IEEE Softw. **26**(4), 15–18 (2009). IEEE
8. Wiegers, K.E.: Software Requirements, 2nd edn. Microsoft Press, Redmond (2003)
9. Xu, J., Chusho, T.: End-user-initiative development for web application. (in Japanese) IEICE SIG - KBSE (Knowledge-based Software Engineering), KBSE2013-81, pp. 13–18. IEICE (2014)

Combining of Kanban and Scrum Means with Programmable Queues in Designing of Software Intensive Systems

Petr Sosnin[✉]

Ulyanovsk State Technical University,
Severny Venetc str. 32, 432027 Ulyanovsk, Russia
sosnin@ulstu.ru

Abstract. The existing problem of the extremely low level of the success in developments of software intensive systems (SISs) is a reason for the ongoing search for innovations in software engineering. One of the promising areas of the search is a continuous improvement of agile methods of the project management the most popular of which are bound with Kanban and Scrum approaches. The paper presents the way of combining the Kanban and Scrum means with the programmable queues of project tasks that are implementing by designers in the real-time. In any queue, its elements present the states of the corresponding tasks in their conceptually-algorithmic solutions. Interactions of designers with queues provide the parallel and pseudo parallel work with tasks. Such way-of-working promotes increasing the reliability of operational planning. The specialized toolkit WIQA (Working In Questions and Answers) supports the offered version of the project management.

Keywords: Automated designing · Ontology · Precedent · Question-answering · Software intensive system

1 Introduction

The extremely low degree of the success in designing of SISs is an important reason [1] for searching the new approaches to the collaborative work in this subject area. Perspective ways of the search are opened by the initiative called SEMAT (Software Engineering Methods and Theory) where the necessity of reshaping the basis of software engineering is declared [2].

In normative documents of SEMAT, a way-of-working used by designers is marked as a crucial essence. There, "way-of-working" is defined as "the tailored set of practices and tools used by the team to guide and support their work [2]." Therefore, ways-of-working are very perspective objects of scientific investigations aimed at increasing the successfulness in designing the SISs.

The essential part of any successful way-of-working is an efficient management. In designing of SISs, the effective management should use agile means (but not only). For example, in explanations of SEMAT essence, Scrum-means [2] are applied.

It should be noted that nowadays Scrum approach is widely used in software engineering [3]. Another popular Agile technology is Kanban [4], means of which

© Springer International Publishing Switzerland 2015
H. Fujita and G. Guizzi (Eds.): SoMeT 2015, CCIS 532, pp. 367–377, 2015.
DOI: 10.1007/978-3-319-22689-7_28

useful combine with Scrum-means. The central feature of the Scrum approach is the use of a series of fixed-length iterations called sprints while the specificity of Kanban is usually bound with visualizing of workflows on card-index board.

Scrum teams tend to categorize work items into two types, User Stories and Bugs. It should be noted that examples of such types can be decomposed into project tasks that are usually combined in workflows. A similar possibility is open for Kanban work items that can be, for example, Requirements, User Stories, Use Cases, Bugs, Defects or Improvement Activities. Below, work items and their compositions will be considered from the viewpoint of workflows and their tasks.

The paper presents the way of combining the Kanban and Scrum means with the programmable queues of project tasks that are implementing by designers in the real-time. In any queue, its elements present the states of the corresponding tasks in their conceptually-algorithmic descriptions. The choice of such forms for modeling the states of tasks is caused by the intent to express the behavioral feature of designer actions. For example, technological practices usually describe in the occupationally-natural language with using the numbering of steps and keys of algorithmic relations. Any of such practices is fulfilled by the designer who works similarly to the processor that executes the definite "program."

A division of the work with tasks on algorithmic steps opens the possibility for the management of parallel and pseudo parallel solutions of tasks that are registered in Kanban or Scrum queues. This kind of the management is additional for the Kanban or Scrum-management, and such addition promotes increasing the adequacy of estimations for Kanban and Scrum metrics [5].

In the offered approach, conceptually algorithmic modeling of the work with project tasks is based on mapping of the used way-of-working on a semantic memory of the toolkit WIQA [6]. By the other words, in the work with tasks, the toolkit supports the conceptually-algorithmic programming the feature of which is its implementing in the semantic memory of the question-answer type.

The remainder of the paper is structured as follows. Section 2 discusses the brief works related to the designer model. Section 3 specifies the reflection of the way-of-working on the semantic memory. In Sect. 4, we introduce combining the means of agile management with programmable queues and multitasking behavior. Finally, Sect. 5 makes conclusions.

2 Related Works

The offered version of instrumental means that support combining Kanban and Scrum means with programmable queues is coordinated with fundamental principles of the SEMAT Kernel, which is described in [2]. "The process is what the team does. Such processes can be formed dynamically from appropriate practices in accordance with current situations. The informational cards and queue mechanisms are useful for managing in ways-of-working."

As told above, interests of the paper are bound with designing of SIS for the creation of which a team of designers should solve the huge amount of tasks. Also, the greater part of tasks arises in front of designers in the real-time in accordance with the flow of unexpected and unpredictable situations. Therefore, there exists the problem of flexible management in the work of designers who should solve tasks in parallel with using the collaboration and coordination. Kanban and Scrum support such version of the project management [7]. In addition, they help the use of metrics for increasing the adequacy of planning [8] and for adjusting the team on the collaborative work [9]. Moreover, values of metrics reflect personified characteristics of the corresponding team.

Another way of increasing the adequateness of planning and personified productivity of the team is bound with the use of managing the queues [10] of work items that are processed in Kanban or Scrum or their composition. The use of rational human-computer interruptions [11] that support multitasking processes [12] in the work of designers is a prospective way of additional effects in the management of tasks' queues. In the offered approach, such composition occupies the central place.

All of the indicated studies were taken into account in the proposed approach. They were used as sources of requirements for the study described in this paper. We note that the combination of Kanban and Scrum means with conceptually-algorithmic programming of multitasking processes is not covered in the above references and other related studies that we have found in acceptable informational sources.

3 Mapping the Way-of-Working on the Semantic Memory

The feature of the offered version of the agile management defined by mapping the used way-of-working on the semantic memory of the toolkit WIQA [6]. Rules of mapping help to create interactive objects the simplest version of which is presented in Fig. 1.

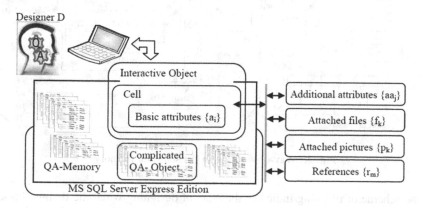

Fig. 1. The cell structure of the semantic memory

The semantic memory has the specialized type that allows modeling any unit of uploading with the use of question-answering. A pair of a question (Q) and corresponding answer (A) helps to build the simplest QA-model (or QA-object) of the uploading unit. But, as it is shown in Fig. 1, a description of such simplest object can have a rich semantic expression. It inherits essential attributes of the memory cell (for example, the textual description, index label, type of objects in the semantic memory, name of a responsible person and the time of last modifying). Also, the designer has the possibility for useful expanding the set of attributes. Necessary files (including the files of graphical types) and useful references can be also attached to the QA-object.

It should be noted that a complicated QA-object combines a set of QA-object as components. To underline the feature of the described memory, it is designated as QA-memory. Thus, QA-memory with its cells is intended for registering the conceptual content of reflected units with taking into account the semantics of their textual descriptions. Available expressivity of QA-memory semantics allows for designers to model any component of the used way-of-working. This possibility extends to the way proposed in Fig. 2.

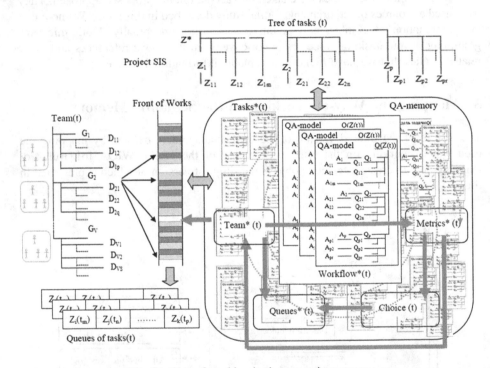

Fig. 2. Way-of-working in the semantic memory

The scheme of mapping indicates the state of designing when the definite backlog of works (front of works) is extracted from the tree of project task for their solving by the team of designers. In this state, any of called essences is a dynamic construct because the awaited step of work can demand or lead to changing this construct. For example, additional members will require to include in a definite working group of the team or some tasks will be demanded to solve additionally. Therefore, the management of processes at any planned step of works should be flexible.

The scheme also demonstrates the presence of tasks' queues with which the designers should interact in their work at the current step of designing. In described study, all called essences (and not only they) are mapped to their models on QA-memory. Results of mapping are marked by symbol "*", for example, team*(t) or workflow*(t). Any of these models is stored in the definite area of memory cells.

It should be noted that the necessity of works with models in QA-memory has led to the development of the specialized conceptually-algorithmic language of programming that is oriented to the features of this memory [6]. This language has the pseudo code type. The toolkit WIQA includes means of programming at the called language that is designated as L^{WIQA}. The presence and accessibility of L^{WIQA} for designers essentially evolve for them the possibilities of mapping the used "units". For example, it opens the possibility of mapping the constructs in QA-memory on their models in this memory.

There are three types of models for corresponding constructs:

- declarative models that are mapped constructs from the viewpoint of their static (their states or their nature);
- imperative models that can be used as computer programs;
- behavioral models that reflect human (in our case, designer) actions in the computerized environment.

Different models of these types can be mapped on QA-memory, but, for this paper, the models of the behavioral type are especially important. For example, any occupational practice of any technology has a behavioral nature. The use of conceptually-algorithmic modeling of behavioral actions can lead to useful innovations in the flexible project management.

4 Combination of Kanban and Scrum Means with Programmable Queues of Tasks

4.1 The Workspace of the Flexible Management

As it is known [4], queues of tasks lie in the basis of the Kanban approach to the management of designers' actions in software engineering. Traditionally, queues consist of visualized cards that are located in thematic columns of the board. The number of cards in any column is limited in accordance with agreed norms of Works in Progress (WIP), or tasks in progress, the works with which are not finished in a current state of queues.

There is a set of rules that helps to manage the parallel work in the team by interactions of designers with queues. When the number of tasks in all queues greater the number of team members, while some of them or all designers should work in the pseudo parallel manner, switching among the appointed tasks. In this case, any designer interacts with personal queues that are allocated on the common board.

The necessity of work in parallel and pseudo parallel exists in Scrum and Scrum-ban where cards of tasks are allocated to the visualized board also, but rules for cards in queues and rules of interactions with queues differ from rules in Kanban. In the offered approach, the way-of-working is mapped onto QA-memory, and that leads to a number of positive effects caused by pseudocode programming the rules for queues of tasks in applying of Kanban or Scrum or Scram-ban. The workspace for the use of developed means is shown in Fig. 3.

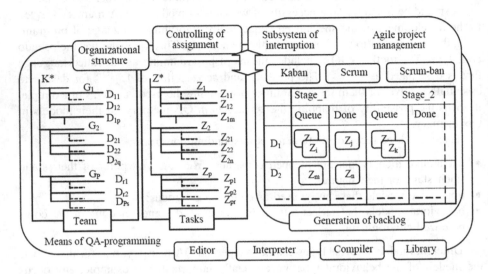

Fig. 3. The workspace of the flexible management

The scheme of the workspace consists of following parts:

- the organizational structure that reflects relations among team K^*, its groups $\{G_p(\{D_{ps}\})\}$, their members $\{D_{ps}\}$ and project tasks $\{Z_i\}$ in real-time;
- a number of means that can be fitted on agile project management in Kanban or Scrum or Scrum-ban version;
- a number of means, including Editor, Interpreter, Compiler and Library, which support QA-programming the work with queues of tasks;
- subsystem "Controlling of assignment" that allows appointing the estimated characteristics of time for planned work with each task Z_i included to the front of tasks (backlog of Kanban or Scrum or Scrum-ban);
- subsystem of interruption that supports the work with tasks in parallel and in pseudo parallel mode.

The scheme also demonstrates two dimensions of the work with cards of tasks and their queues. The first dimension is bound with an organization and specifications of "columns" of cards and "vertical" queues that should correspond to rules of the chosen version of the flexible management (Kanban or Scrum or Scrum-ban). This dimension has features for each of management versions any of which can be assembled and configured for the team and project with using of QA-programming.

The second dimension reflects the personal work for each member of any group of the team. This dimension helps to assemble "horizontal" queues the tasks of which must solved in pseudo parallel mode. Interactions of designers with such queues can be also programmed in QA-memory.

It should be noted, the main innovation of the offered approach is the inclusion of additional managing for behavioral actions of designers when they work with steps of tasks (operators of any task in its pseudo-code description). It opens the possibility, for example, for planned or situational interruptions on steps of any task, analysis of current situation, useful non-planned actions in points of interruptions and the choice of rational subsequent actions. These behavioral actions are absent in traditional practices of Kanban, Scrum and Scrum-ban technologies that specify any task as a wholeness.

4.2   Interactions with Programmable Queues of Tasks

As told above, the use of mapping the offered way-of-working on QA-memory opens the possibility for pseudocode programming the rules in Kanban or Scrum or Scram-ban.

Programmed rules of interactions must be implemented by the designer who should rationally choose the preferable card from the personal queue of tasks for continuing the work after processing of any interruption. The choice of the preferred task Z_x must take into account in the real-time:

- the condition (C^1, Z_x, t) of relations among the tasks of workflows that are processed in queues;
- the condition (C^2, Z_x, t) of relations among the tasks any of which can be activated to continue with the interruption point.

As it is schematically shown in Fig. 4, the choice can be interpreted as two-step execution of V^1-program and V^2-program by the designer fulfilling the role of an intellectual processor (I-processor).

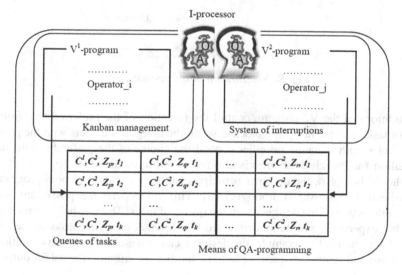

Fig. 4. Two faces of the designer

In Fig. 4, any row consists of a set of conditions any of which should be checked before the designer chooses the preferable task from the personal queue of tasks. Any condition is extracted from the corresponding card that models the definite task as the queue element.

Checking begins with conditions that forbid the work with tasks in accordance with real-time restrictions of workflows. These conditions compose the V^1-program that blocks the extraction of a number of tasks (if there are) from the queue of tasks. The following subsequence of if-operators demonstrates the typical structure of V-programs:

A value of any condition TaskFinished(&ZX&) is a result of computing the function TaskFinished(&ZX&) the pseudo code of which is written in the special area of the corresponding card. But values of processed data are registered on other cards of the corresponding workflow in variables &TaskEnabled&.

For any designer, the current state of the personal work is visualized as it is shown in Fig. 5 where some positions are marked by labels because the screenshot is in Russian. The designer can open the necessary card for the access to normative information registered on the face and back sides of the card. Codes of function TaskFinished(&ZX&) and variable &TaskEnabled& are located on the back side of the card. The content of these components can be edited in real-time.

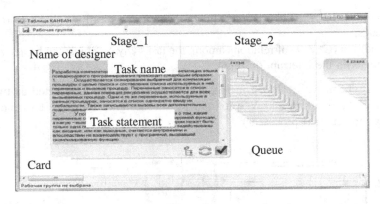

Fig. 5. Visualization of queues and cards

Conditions of the V2-program control the selection of the preferred task from the queue of tasks that are not being blocked when the designer interacts with the personal queue. Rules with dynamic priorities control the choice of the preferable card (task). Information for checking the rules is also registered in cards.

It should be noted, the designer participates in the execution of both programs as the intellectual processor (I-processor) [6]. This role opens the possibility for the creative interaction of the designer with the queue of tasks. The role helps to refer to the accessible experience and its models when the designer estimates tasks at the preferability of the choice. For example, the designer can make changes to the conditions of the program and re-execute them or initiate another interruption for useful purposes.

4.3   Retrospective Analysis

The major advantage of the described management mechanisms is their empirical nature, which are based on the calculated metrics and charts. For Kanban, a set of used metrics usually includes Cycle Time, Average Lead, Wasted Time, Effectiveness, and Throughput. The Cumulative Chart often demonstrates the integrated picture of the process. In the offered approach, all of these characteristics are calculated and drawn by service functions and procedures written in L^{WIQA}.

The following function demonstrates elements of L^{WIQA}-syntax and the example of the code for calculating Cycle Time:

For Scrum, designers usually use such metrics as Team Velocity, Individual Velocity, Value Delivered, and On-time Delivery. For the integral estimation of results and continuous improvement of collaboration, they use burndown charts. In our case, the form of visualized Burndown Charts is shown in Fig. 5. These charts have been build in the actual project, and they use have allowed to improve planning the collective work (Fig. 6, with labels because screenshots in Russian).

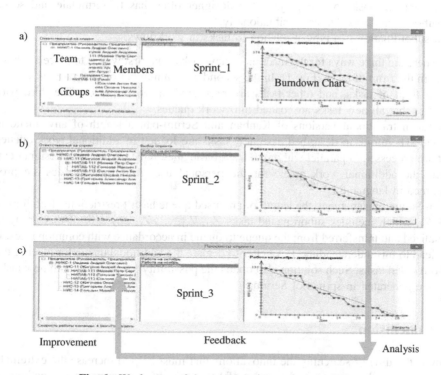

Fig. 6. Workspace of the retrospective analysis in Scrum

It should be noted that used metrics are calculated with taking into account conceptually-algorithmic structures of tasks implemented in multitasking processes. Therefore, any metrics reflects additional parallelism in the activity of designers.

Scram applications have a rich empirical history of using the different metrics that can be combined in such groups as Scrum Team & Process Metrics, Release Metrics, Product Metrics, Code & Technical Metrics, Team & People Metrics. For example, for Team metrics can be defined Happiness Metrics, Frequency of effective team retrospectives, Frequency of completed team improvement experiments, Team Tenure, Staffing Changes. The toolkit WIQA provides programming and experimenting with useful metrics for the agile management.

Scrum-ban as well as Kanban uses Average Lead and Cycle Time metrics for performance. The Cumulative Chart is the typical form for the integral estimation of the collaborative works.

4.4   The Use of Additional Queues

One more specificity of programmable queues is bound with their dynamics that is to take into account the following features of designing:

- solving the tasks of the project, the designer often has to formulate and solve subordinate tasks that arose situationally;
- a subordination is a typical relation to tasks in workflows.

There are three ways for the reaction to new tasks. The first way is to place all these tasks in the front of tasks (Fig. 1). In the second way, a number of new tasks is located in the front of tasks, and other tasks are registered in work queues. The third way assumes that all new tasks are loaded into work queues.

But in traditional versions of Kanban and Scrum-ban a length of any queue is limited. Therefore, in described case new tasks are loaded in additional work queues that are processed in parallel with tasks from basic queues. Moreover, any designer can create the additional work queue for the personal use. Additional queues are programmed in language L^{WIQA}.

In Scrum management, the length of any used queue hasn't restrictions. But, for the task Z_i, which includes subordinated tasks Z_{i1}, Z_{i1}, ..., Z_{i1} any task of this group is visualized and transferred from the queue to queue in accordance with common rules. It can lead to misunderstanding. It is better to declare the additional queue for placing the subordinated tasks. Such solution also opens the possibility for working with new tasks that are generated in sprints of Scrum.

5   Conclusion

Now is the time of searching the innovations that must help to increase the extremely low degree of the success in designing of SISs. One of the prospective directions to solve this problem is the search for innovations in the flexible management based on means of Kanban, Scrum and Scrum-ban technologies. The described approach evolves these means by the use of their mapping on the semantic memory that opens the possibility for (pseudo code) programming the rules of the work of designers with queues of tasks in the real-time.

The offered means help to structure the work with the task till step by step actions of the designer at the operator level of task solution. It is especially important at the conceptual stage when the designer tries to build such solution with the use of experimenting.

The features of collective and personal activities of designers require making changes to the structure of queues and rules of interaction with them. Developed changes concern possibilities of parallel in pseudo parallel works of designers with tasks in queues in conditions of generating the new tasks that are arisen situationally. Changes also concern rational taking into account the subordination of tasks in workflows. In addition, changes support adjusting the developed means on the use of Kanban or Scrum or Scrum-ban version of the flexible project management. The usefulness of the offered approach was tested and confirmed in developments of the simulation system for laser cutting of parts from the steel sheet.

References

1. Reports of the Standish Group. https://secure.standishgroup.com/reports
2. Jacobson, I., Ng, P.-W., McMahon, P., Spence, I., Lidman, S.: The essence of software engineering: the SEMAT kernel. Queue **10**(10), 1–12 (2012)
3. The State of Scrum: Benchmarks and Guidelines. Scrum Alliance (2013). http://www.scrumalliance.org/scrum/media/ScrumAllianceMedia/Files%20and%20PDFs/State%20of%20Scrum/2013-State-of-Scrum-Report_062713_final.pdf
4. Wang, J.X.: Lean manufacturing business bottom-line based. In: Kanban: Align Manufacturing Flow with Demand Pull, pp. 185–204. CRC Press (2010)
5. Ladas, C.: Scrumban: Essays on Kanban Systems for Lean Software Development. Modus Cooperandi Press, Seattle (2009)
6. Sosnin, P.: Scientifically experimental way-of-working in conceptual designing of software intensive systems. In: Proceedings of the IEEE 12th International Conference on Intelligent Software Methodologies, Tools and Techniques, pp. 43–51 (2013)
7. Anderson, D.J., Concas, G., Lunesu, M.I., Marchesi, M., Zhang, H.: A comparative study of Scrum and Kanban approaches on a real case study using simulation. In: Wohlin, C. (ed.) XP 2012. LNBIP, vol. 111, pp. 123–137. Springer, Heidelberg (2012)
8. Sjoberg, D.I.K., Dyba, T., Jorgensen, M.: The future of empirical methods in software engineering research. In: Proceeding of the Workshop Future of Software Engineering (FOSE 2007), pp. 358–378 (2007)
9. Dyba, T., Dingsoyr, T.: Empirical studies of agile software development: a systematic review. Inf. Softw. Technol. **50**(9–10), 833–859 (2008)
10. Downey, S., Sutherland, J.: Scrum metrics for hyperproductive teams: how they fly like fighter aircraft. In: HICS, pp. 4870–4878 (2013)
11. Adamczyk, P.D., Iqbal, S.T., Bailey, B.P.: A method, system, and tools for intelligent interruption management. In: Proceedings of the 4th International Workshop on Task Models and Diagrams, pp. 123–126. ACM Press, New York (2005)
12. Benbunan-Fich, R., Adler, R.F., Mavlanova, T.: Measuring multitasking behavior with activity-based metrics. ACM Trans. Comput. Hum. Interact. **18**(2), 1–22 (2011)

Efficient Supply Chain Management via Federation-Based Integration of Legacy ERP Systems

Luigi Coppolino[1]([✉]), Salvatore D'Antonio[1], Carmine Massei[2], and Luigi Romano[1]

[1] Department of Engineering, University of Naples "Parthenope", Naples, Italy
{luigi.coppolino,salvatore.dantonio,luigi.romano}@uniparthenope.it
[2] CeRICT, Centro Regionale Information Communication Technology, Naples, Italy
carmine.massei@gmail.com

Abstract. The development of SCM systems is a difficult activity, since it involves integrating critical business flows both within and among participating companies. The inherently difficulty of the problem is exacerbated by the business constraint (that almost invariably applies in the real world) that the investments made by individual companies throughout the years must be preserved. This maps to major design constraints, since SCM systems must be built around the pre-existing ICT infrastructures of the individual companies and – also importantly – without affecting the local policies. We propose a federation-based approach to seamless and effective integration of legacy enterprise information systems into a unified SCM system. The proposed solution is implemented using a combination of Open Source BPM and ERP products, and validated with respect to a real world use case taken from a research activity (namely: the GLOB-ID project) conducted cooperatively by academic and industrial parties.

1 Rationale and Contribution

Supply Chain Management (SCM) – i.e. the oversight of materials, information, and finances as they move in a process from supplier to manufacturer to wholesaler to retailer to consumer - is an inherently difficult activity, since it involves coordinating and integrating the aforementioned flows both within and among companies. In a Supply Chain (SC), the processes of each company are interconnected, to form an integrated system where the final element is the consumer [4]. Failure of even just one of the processes that make up the SC affects all the downstream processes. In the recent years, growing attention is being paid in the industry to developing efficient techniques and tools for accurate and timely SCM support. Below is given a brief overview of some of the "best-of-breed" products. In this paper, we describe the results of a research activity conducted cooperatively by academic and industrial parties, within the context of an applied research project – namely: the GLOB-ID project – funded by the Italian Ministry of Economic Development. The objective of the project

© Springer International Publishing Switzerland 2015
H. Fujita and G. Guizzi (Eds.): SoMeT 2015, CCIS 532, pp. 378–387, 2015.
DOI: 10.1007/978-3-319-22689-7_29

was to develop a flexible SCM environment, that could be customized to meet the requirements of a real world SCM scenario from the agro-food domain.

The production processes of agro-food companies are becoming more and more complex, since they are handled by multiple companies, each one operating in a different product area. The agro food sector – and particularly in the areas of interest of the project, namely: Abruzzo, Campania, Apulia, and Sicily – suffers for a high degree of fragmentation, also due to the prevalence of Small and Medium Enterprises (SMEs) in the production process, that limits the ability to work together in an integrated SC. The GLOB-ID project aimed at innovating the logistics system connected to the processes of the supply chains of the agro-food sector through the use of advanced technology solutions.

The proposed solution consists in the development of an ICT platform implementing an organizational and management model that enables tracking, traceability, and real time monitoring of activities and products. The platform can be easily configured, so to accomodate the specific requirements of a generic SC of the agro food sector. The ICT platform includes a system for modeling, from an informational point of view, the internal logistics of each company, as well as the interconnections among them in the SC. The platform provides a decision support tool that extracts relevant information – particularly related to tracking – from the chain, thus ultimately enabling optimization of the logistics and production processes, both at the level of the SC as a whole and at the level of individual actors. The traceability module handles traceability information from the first to the last actor in the supply chain. Also importantly, to ensure safety of the final consumer, it provides fast and efficient product recall functionalities.

The basic principle is to clearly identify the information that is needed to correctly identify a product, namely: trade name, scientific name, ingredients, manufacturer's identification (including the address of the production plant), indication of the raw materials, area of origin, indications about how to preserve the product, lot, net weight, packaging date, and expiration date. In addition to this information, which is required by law, the developed system also handles information on primary and secondary packaging, to support intelligent packaging solutions. Also importantly, our case study had some additional requirements and design constraints (which by the way is typically the case for most SCM scenarios from the real world).

Each of the companies involved in the GLOB-ID project already had its own management system, that was based on one or more of the various enterprise systems available on the market. The first design step was then to develop a supply chain organizational model, that could enable the harmonization and the integration of processes and information flows of the individual manufacturing units involved, from raw material acquisition to the delivery of finished products to the final customers. The second step was to design an ICT platform for the acquisition and sharing of information about the logistics of the companies belonging to the food and agricultural industry that could implement the aforementioned organizational model in a flexible and extensible SCM tool. The rest of the paper is organized as follows. In Sect. 2 we provide an overview of the state of the art of the technology. In Sect. 3 we present the conceptual architecture of our solution, and in Sect. 4 we describe its implementation. Section 5 describes how to configure the system for the operational phase. Finally, Sect. 6 draws the conclusions of the work done so far.

2 State-of-the-Art Analysis

In this section, we provide a brief – yet right to the point – analysis of the three main categories of products that can be used to build Enterprise Systems (ES), namely: Enterprise Resource Planning (ERP), Customer Relationship Management (CRM), and Supply Chain Management (SCM).

Enterprise Resource Planning (ERP) is a generic term for an integrated enterprise computing system. Studies are demonstrating that, since ERP technology is an effective tool for implementing company strategies, it has a positive impact in terms of improvement of the competitiveness of an enterprise [11]. The ERP software market is dominated by commercial solutions offered by well-known enterprise software vendors such as SAP, Oracle, and Microsoft. Besides these (quite expensive, indeed) offerings, there are several Open Source products that have features that make them as complete as their closed source counterparts [7]. These include Apache OFBiz [15], Odoo (formerly known as OpenErp) [14], and Openbravo ERP [13].

Customer Relationship Management (CRM) methodology enables an organization to understand customers' needs and behaviour better. It introduces reliable processes and procedures for interacting with customers and develops stronger relationships with them. This process helps organizations to assimilate information (about customers, sales, marketing effectiveness, responsiveness, and market trends), which is then used to get insight into behaviour of customers, and thus facilitates retaining those customers. The ultimate goal is to reduce costs and to increase profitability by holding on to customers' loyalty. CRM technologies enable greater customer insight, increased customer access, more effective customer interactions, and integration between customer channels and back-office enterprise functions. The basic steps are: attracting present and new customers, acquiring new customers, serving the customers, and finally retaining the customers [9]. Again, we focus on CRM software solutions that are available as Open Source. Open Source CRM software is a great opportunity for SMEs, since they can help to improve their competitiveness, thanks to the possibility of adapting the software to the specific business needs of the company, and of adding new modules that can be developed according to the specific requirements of the company [10]. Some of the most widely used Open Source CRM solutions are: SugarCRM [18], and SuiteCRM [19].

Supply Chain Management (SCM) can be defined as follows: *"SCM is the integrated planning, implementation, coordination and control of all business processes and activities necessary to produce and deliver, as efficiently as* *possible, products that satisfy market requirements.*" Here a *business process* is a structured, measured set of activities designed to produce a specified output for a particular customer or market [2]. Open source supply chain systems aren't yet seeing the market growth of open source ERP or CRM software, but they are integrated in the form of modules in several ERP products that are currently available, e.g. Openbravo, Odoo, ApacheOFBiz, opentaps, and Dolibar. For example, Openbravo ERP has a SCM module for procurement management, warehouses, and distribution centres management.

3   Proposed Solution: Conceptual Architecture

The organizational model of the supply chain that we have developed allows harmonization and integration of processes and information flows of individual companies, while preserving the pre-existing management procedures for the stages of the production process that are not meant to be exposed to the external world. The initial design phase consisted in a detailed analysis of the logical (and logistical) organization of the specific supply chains of the companies participating in the GLOB-ID project. The analysis focused on the logical operation of the supply chain as a whole, as well as on the role played by individual systems. This has been achieved by (i) defining a model for inbound and outbound logistics, and (ii) establishing rules and standard management protocols for the different processes and products.

For the purpose of the analysis of production processes, we represent a supply chain as a sequence of processes of transformation of a product, each one executed by an individual subject, that we call transformer. A transformer receives a lot, transforms it, and then sends it to the next transformer. At each stage, the output lot becomes the input for the next processing step. All actors in the processing chain must be able to manage the data of their interest, as well as to share with the whole organization the information that is of general interest. This is typically done by setting up data bases and (intermediate) services that are easily accessible to all transformers involved. In this flow, some of the exchanges are internal to a company, some happen across the boundaries between distinct enterprises. To accommodate this, we propose a federation-based distributed architecture.

Thus, the conceptual architecture of the GLOB-ID SCM system, represented in Fig. 1, has a federation-based distributed structure. The edge of the system is formed by the pre-existing IT systems of the individual companies. The core of the system is represented by the GLOB-ID SCM Engine. Individual companies preserve their pre-existing ICT infrastructure, and – importantly– their organizational and management policies. The exchange of information and the coordination of activities is done by the GLOB-ID SCM Engine, which is the core element of the architecture (it is responsible for deploying the process definitions, starting the various business processes, and executing the tasks). Interactions between the central engine and the peripheral IT systems are enabled by a set of custom adapters, i.e. information gateways whose structure and operation

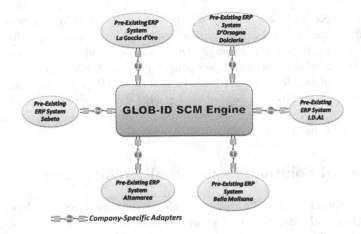

Fig. 1. GLOB-ID conceptual architecture, in the center, the GLOB-ID SCM Engine, and in the edge the pre-existing IT systems of the individual companies.

depends on the peculiar characteristics of the pre-existing ICT infrastructure of the specific company to which they provide connection. It is worth noting that considered the multi-tenancy nature of the application it is of paramout importance to be able to monitor the QoS of the provided Service [5] but this is outside the scope of this paper.

4   Proposed Solution: Implementation Details

The implementation of the GLOB-ID SCM Engine heavily relies on an existing Commercial-Off-The-Shelf (COTS) Business Process Management (BPM) solution, namely Activiti. In the GLOB-ID SCM Engine, a business process is a set of one or more linked procedures or activities which collectively implement a business function within the context of an organizational structure where functional roles and relationships are clearly defined. The Activiti BPM platform [8] is used for automating the business processes and integrating them with other software products that are used within individual companies. By using Activiti BPM, we were able to federate the pre-existing technologies of the partner companies, and combine them to form the complex technology stack of the GLOB-ID SCM. Also importantly, this implementation choice resulted in a dramatic reduction of the development costs of the GLOB-ID SCM, since we were able to reuse many functions that are provided by Activiti.

Activiti is a light-weight workflow and Business Process Management (BPM) Platform. Its core is a process engine written in Java. It addresses important Business Process Management (BPM) issues, ranging from non-technical aspects (such as analysis, modelling, and optimization of business processes) to technical ones (e.g. creating software support for business processes) [12]. We preferred Activiti over other alternatives (such as jBPM [17] and BonitaSoft [16]), based on the results of a comparative evaluation which is not reported here,

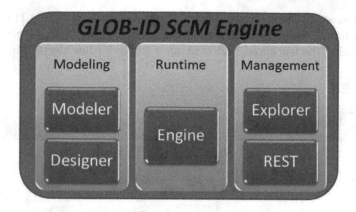

Fig. 2. An overview of the GLOB-ID SCM Engine: in the center, the process engine, and on the right and left sides, the modeling, and management tools.

due to lack of space (it will be included in an extended version of this article). The architecture of the GLOB-ID SCM Engine is represented in Fig. 2. The GLOB-ID SCM engine is a Java process engine that runs BPM processes, i.e. it is responsible for deploying process definitions, starting business process instances, and executing tasks. For modelling business processes, we have two options:

- Modeler: it is a web-based tool for modelling business processes and for deploying them in the server.
- Designer: it is an Eclipse plug-in which allows modelling the business processes from within the Eclipse environment. It is used to add technical details (such as Java classes) to the business process model, to access the process Engine.

For the management of the platform we can use:

- Explorer: it is a web-based application that provides access to the process engine to all system users. It includes task management, process instance inspection, management features, and reporting features.
- REST: it provides a REST API to access the Engine (a REST API is an integration method that provides a way for data to be sent from one system to another).

As to the adapters, these were implemented using Openbravo, an Open Source ERP that supports integration with Activiti. This decision was taken based on the results of a comparative analysis that we performed in the first stages of the project, aimed at finding an ERP software that would integrate easily with the Activiti BPM platform. Among the several software products that we have analysed, we chose Openbravo ERP because it uses open standards and it can thus be easily integrated with external software tools [1]; in general case, if any non standard data adaptation could be needed, more general approaches should be applied [3]. As far as we are concerned, the element of major interest is that OpenBravo ERP has a module that integrates Activiti BPM. This module has several useful features, including: running the Engine, managing users and groups, defining the workflow, and starting workflows from alerts (Fig. 3).

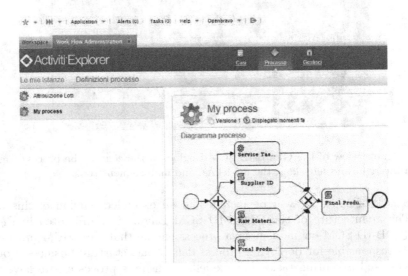

Fig. 3. A screenshot showing Activiti BPM integrated in Openbravo ERP

5   System Set-up and Operation

The chosen approach involves two phases: a design phase and a modelling phase. The design phase mainly consists in the identification of: (i) the processes that are relevant to the problem, (ii) the relations between these processes, and (iii) the actors involved. The result of this preliminary study is a general view of the architecture that provides an overall view of the processes in an organization and their relationships. To limit the intrusiveness of this activity on the operational capability of the company, one possibility is to extract this information from existing documentation (as opposed to interviewing the company personnel). In our case, we used the Hazard Analysis and Critical Control Points (HACCP) plans, which list the critical points for traceability for the company.

In the design phase the theoretical design is prepared, whereas in the modelling phase the theoretical business process is designed using the Business Process Model and Notation (BPMN) standard [6]. BPMN is a standard designed to cover many types of modelling and allows the creation of end-to-end business processes and is based on a flowcharting technique very similar to the activity diagram from the Unified Modelling Language (UML).

The GLOB-ID SCM Engine must be configured with the processes of the specific SC that it must manage. We developed a number of diagrams. An example of a BPMN diagram that models the production process is given in Fig. 4.

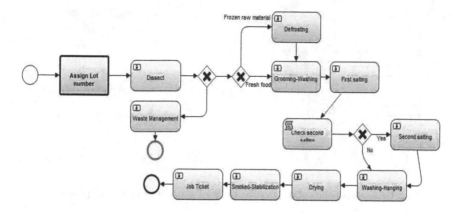

Fig. 4. An overview of the production process designed in the Modeler

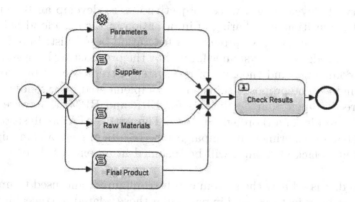

Fig. 5. An overview of the traceability process designed in the Modeler

Other types of diagrams are available, which describe specific system activities (e.g. traceability in Fig. 5). These are not reported in this paper, due to lack of space (they will be included in an extended version of this paper).

Once the system has been configured, it is possible to automate the execution of the business process. This is done via the business process management facilities of the GLOB-ID SCM Engine. Figure 6 shows the Explorer window, that is used to start processes.

6   Summary and Conclusions

In this paper we presented a design approach and an architecture that allow harmonization and integration of processes and information flows of the companies participating in a given Supply Chain, while preserving the pre-existing management procedures for the stages of the production process that are not meant to be exposed to the external (to the enterprise) world. The approach and the

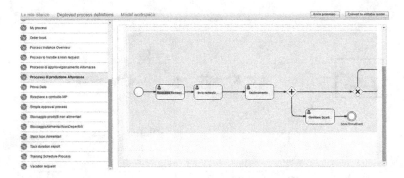

Fig. 6. A screenshot showing the start of a process in the Explorer

architecture were implemented and validated with respect to a real world case study, taken from the GLOB-ID project, a research program funded by the Italian Ministry of Development, whose objective was to develop an ICT platform for efficient acquisition and sharing of information in the agro-food SC domain.

To achieve these goals, we proposed a federation-based distributed architecture, where the edge of the system is formed by the pre-existing IT systems of the individual companies and the core of the system is represented by the GLOB-ID SCM Engine. The proposed solution was implemented by extending existing "best of breed" Open Source solutions for ERP and BPM, that were selected based on the results of a thorough State Of The Art (SOTA) analysis of current offerings, plus an experimental campaign (the results of such a campaign – not reported due to lack of room – will be included in an extended version of this paper).

We also discussed how the system can be configured, and used to implement important business features (and in particular those related to traceability), thus ultimately improving the efficiency of the SC.

Acknowledgements. This work has been supported by the GLOB-ID project funded by the National Operational Programme (NOP) for Research and Competitiveness 2007–2013, co-funded with the European Regional Development Fund (ERDF), and by the TENACE PRIN Project (no. 20103P34XC) funded by the Italian Ministry of Education, University and Research.

References

1. Bhardwaj, B.R.: Sustainable supply chain management through enterprise resource planning (ERP): a model of sustainable computing. In: International Conference on Computing for Sustainable Global Development (INDIACom) (2014)
2. Brown, W.: Agribusiness cases in supply chain management. In: International Farm Management Association (2002)
3. Campanile, F., Cilardo, A., Coppolino, L., Romano, L.: Adaptable parsing of real-time data streams. In: PDP 2007, 15th EUROMICRO International Conference on Parallel, Distributed and Network-Based Processing (2007)

4. Christopher, M.: Logistics and Supply Chain Management. Pearson, London (2012)
5. Cicotti, G., Coppolino, L., Cristaldi, R., D'Antonio, S., Romano, L.: QoS monitoring in a cloud services environment: the SRT-15 approach. In: Alexander, M., D'Ambra, P., Belloum, A., Bosilca, G., Cannataro, M., Danelutto, M., Di Martino, B., Gerndt, M., et al. (eds.) Euro-Par 2011, Part I. LNCS, vol. 7155, pp. 15–24. Springer, Heidelberg (2012)
6. Dumas, M., La Rosa, M., Mendling, J., Reijers, H.: Fundamentals of Business Process Management. Springer, Heidelberg (2013)
7. Huynh, M.: Exploring the open-source ERP alternative for teaching business process integration in supply chain management. Academy of Information and Management Sciences (2010)
8. Rademakers, T.: Activiti in Action: Executable Business Processes in BPMN 2.0. Manning Publications Co., Shelter Island (2012)
9. Robson, A.: CRM: The concept and the technology. Perfect Image White Paper (2005)
10. Tereso, M., Bernardino, J.: Open Source CRM Systems for SMEs. arXiv (2011)
11. Wailgum, T.: ERP Definition and Solutions. CIO (2012)
12. Activiti BPM Platform. http://www.activiti.org/
13. Openbravo ERP. http://www.openbravo.com/
14. Odoo. https://www.odoo.com/
15. Apache OFBiz. http://ofbiz.apache.org/
16. Bonita BPM. http://www.bonitasoft.com/
17. jBPM. http://www.jbpm.org/
18. Sugar CRM. http://www.sugarcrm.com/
19. SuiteCRM. https://suitecrm.com/

BizDevOps: Because DevOps is Not the End of the Story

Volker Gruhn[1] and Clemens Schäfer[2]([⊠])

[1] paluno - The Ruhr Institute for Software Technology,
University of Duisburg-Essen, Gerlingstraße 16, 45127 Essen, Germany
volker.gruhn@uni-due.de
[2] it factum GmbH, Arnulfstraße 37, 80636 Munich, Germany
schaefer@it-factum.de

Abstract. DevOps, the common service responsibility of software development and IT operation within the IT department, promises faster delivery and less conflicts of competence within software development processes and is currently being implemented by many companies. However, the increasing business responsibility of IT, the increasing IT competence in the departments and the standardization of IT operations require a restructuring that goes beyond the boundaries of the IT department.

The logical consequence is the BizDevOps concept: Business, Development and Operations work together in software development and operations, creating a consistent responsibility from business over development to operations.

In this paper we draft a BizDevOps approach by extending the existing DevOps approach with techniques from the area of End User Software Engineering. We present a software platform to support this approach. Based on a case study at a large reinsurance company we share our experiences from using both approach and platform in practice.

Keywords: Software engineering · Software processes · Information systems · Value-orientation · DevOps · End user software engineering

1 Introduction

Development of proprietary software applications for companies is challenging, especially if the competitive power of a company depends on the delivered software in terms of time to market and software quality. Hence companies are looking into possibilities to speed-up the application development process by re-aligning the cooperation between business and IT departments. Current approaches, which (like DevOps) aim at breaking down the silo structures between software development and IT operations, are one possibility to increase speed of the application development process and to improve the process outcome. However, these approaches stay within the boundaries of the IT department and do not address the gap between the business departments

© Springer International Publishing Switzerland 2015
H. Fujita and G. Guizzi (Eds.): SoMeT 2015, CCIS 532, pp. 388–398, 2015.
DOI: 10.1007/978-3-319-22689-7_30

(where requirements arise and the actual money is earned in a company) and IT department, where software is created. Addressing and narrowing this gap promises speeding up the application development process even more.

The BizDevOps approach addresses the boundary between the two distinct disciplines: it aims at redistributing responsibilities between IT (who are professionals in rendering stable and reliable IT systems) and business departments (who understand the rationale of IT systems from business perspective).

- A BizDevOps approach allows people in the business departments to express and review requirements in a hands-on manner and thus reduces the necessary knowledge transfer from business to IT and provides fastest possible feedback cycles (the "Biz" in BizDevOps).
- A BizDevOps approach allows IT departments to govern the whole application development process to ensure high quality of the software artifacts (the "Dev" in BizDevOps).
- A BizDevOps approach provides an integrated and automated tool chain integration to allow as much automation and thus development pace (the "Ops" in BizDevOps).

Current approaches for improving software processes either focus solely on the IT side (like DevOps) or the business side (like End User Software Engineering), but mostly leave the separation between these two sides untouched. Organizational approaches like Agile Methods try to improve communication and interaction at the boundary between IT and business, but they also do not address the boundary itself.

With the BizDevOps approach we present an approach that makes a change to this boundary by providing business departments with an active possibility of creating parts of the final application software. This means, people from the business department become programmers to a certain extent and within certain boundaries. This empowerment of business departments is supported by a conceptual framework which allows IT to mitigate the risks of non-professional programmers. The approach is operationalized by a platform, which is used to create applications following the BizDevOps approach.

The remainder of this paper is structured as follows. We first outline the class of applications that can be realized by the BizDevOps approach. Then we depict the conceptual baseline of our BizDevOps approach as well as the actual platform to develop projects based on the approach. Then we present a case study where we show the implementation of our approach at a large reinsurance company. Finally a conclusion is drawn.

2   Related Work

Approaches like agile software development [1] or best-of-breed-approaches like No-Frills Software Engineering [4] aim at delivering software faster and with better reflection of business goals, i.e. they aim at a deep and widespread understanding of business rationales to deliver software artifacts that generate the best possible business value. All these approaches still require a transition from the business domain (problem space) to the software engineering domain (solution space), since the actual construction of software is always regarded as part of the IT department, and thus consequently the business departments are only allowed to present requirements and review final software but not to actively participate in the actual creation of the software. This is–from our perspective–mostly due to a mindset that larger software applications (as typical for business information systems) require well educated and highly skilled software engineering professionals to ensure long-term stability and scalability of the final software application. Hence these approaches tend to refrain from handing over too much control to the business departments.

The idea of letting users in business department perform substantial part of the coding of applications can be found in literature long time ago, like in the works of Martin [7], where he discusses how business users can create applications without IT involvement. It is common knowledge in IT industry that business departments actually perform software development tasks, often under terms as "Shadow IT" and the like. Precise insights on how far these development activities go can be found in the works of Panko and Port [8]. Actual software engineering performed by non-professional developers is a own field of research on its own, and a good reflection of the status quo can be found in the works of Burnett and Myers [2].

The DevOps concept, which lays the groundwork for our approach, is described by Hüttermann [6] and–being a Continuous Delivery approach–aims at breaking down separations between software development and software operation; compared to our approach it is focusing on a IT-perspective and in its pure form not suitable to include business users as intended by our approach.

3   The BizDevOps Approach

With our BizDevOps approach we address the boundary between IT and business departments in order to allow business departments to participate hands-on in the development of parts of the system and at the same time having measures in place that allow IT to safeguard the development process. Such an approach cannot be a general-purpose approach for all kinds of software projects, but will be beneficial for a certain type of applications. In the following we will detail out the subset of business information systems we deem suitable for the BizDevOps approach.

3.1   BizDevOps for Innovative Systems

An active role for business departments makes sense for systems that reflect business innovations. In literature there are different types of IT systems with different needs for innovation and realization. Gartner [3] proposes a classification scheme with the categories *Systems of Record*, *Systems of Differentiation*, and *Systems of Innovation*.

Systems of Record are the foundation of all organizational IT services. They have a long lifetime and their changes are slow-paced. Systems of Differentiation address the differentiating core of the organization; their changes are medium-paced. At last, Systems of Innovation are subject to fast-paced changes since they are highly opportunistic and aim at following agile market situations.

For our BizDevOps approach we concentrate on applications from the areas Systems of Differentiation and Systems of Innovation, since systems from these two classes need to be individually created for an organization and their success is directly related to how fast and how exact business requirements are reflected by the IT systems.

3.2   Characteristics of Applications for BizDevOps Approach

For these innovative systems the following characteristics allow us to identify applications that are suitable, relevant and will benefit from our approach:

- Time to Market is an issue for the application domain. This means, a company requires fast reflection of requirement changes in the final software product.
- Requirements are rather uncertain and unstable. This means, requirements are evolving (as it is the case for new business fields) or subject to frequent changes (e.g. in marketing/sales-related fields).
- Requirements reflect a high level of business complexity. This means, extensive knowledge about the business domain is required in order to build the applications, leading to an extensive knowledge transfer from business to IT in traditional processes.

Besides these criteria, there are also limiting factors, which result from our aim to allow business departments participate hands-on in the software development:

- The application part to be developed by business departments needs to keep an overall low IT complexity, i.e. the application can be implemented by tech-savvy business people in a straight forward manner once an appropriate overall architecture has been devised.
- The application to be created by the business department can be isolated in the overall system landscape such that side-effects can be effectively controlled and mitigated.

A business value perspective adds the following criteria for assessing the relevance of a system whether it should be realized by the BizDevOps approach or not:

- The intended application has a decent level of criticality, i.e. impact on the company: it either produces numbers that directly go into the books of the company or it affects the way the company presents itself to other companies, competitors or customers.
- The intended application is to be integrated with other systems in an application landscape and is not isolated, hence integration of the application is required.

3.3 Rationale for Direct User Involvement

One aspect of our BizDevOps approach is that we provide business departments with a hands-on participation in the software development process by including End User Software Development principles. This is motivated by observations in the field: Since most Systems of Innovation and Systems of Differentiation are characterized more by their deep business domain involvement than their need for sophisticated software design, business users often already play an active role in creating or at least drafting these applications using well-known office tools as Excel or Access (and thus demonstrate their technical literacy when it comes to implementing parts of business applications). The reasons for this are obvious: tools as Excel and the like are readily available and the application problems are of limited IT-complexity such that business users can implement the solutions themselves. And most important: by implementing such applications themselves, business users completely avoid time lags and functional gaps, which makes this approach intuitively appropriate for innovative systems.

The downside of this approach becomes apparent, when these departmental applications are to be integrated with existing systems or used for business critical processes. Such "home-grown" applications cannot be integrated with business processes, they usually do not scale well, and–most importantly–they lack any compliance with the regulatory settings that any mission critical IT service provision has to adhere to.

This means, to solve this dilemma, a BizDevOps approach needs to aim at allowing business users to create their own applications independently and outside the scope of IT, while at the same time fostering integration in compliance frameworks and existing IT landscapes. Through this, the creative and innovative power of business users is preserved while at the same time the resulting IT applications fulfill the needs of professional IT service provision.

4 BizDevOps Platform

In the following we depict a software development platform which allows to carry out a BizDevOps approach as shown before.

4.1 Conceptual Groundwork

Central element of the platform (see Fig. 1) is a so-called sandbox in which the tech-savvy people from the business department can create the business logic hands-on (by means of a domain specific language), the data models and the user interfaces of the so-called apps.

As mentioned earlier, IT needs to safeguard the application development process outcome. For this reason the platform provides so-called managed resources. These are software components which are under full control of the IT department and hence can be put under IT compliance frameworks. These managed resources are the only connection possibility of the apps in the sandbox with the outer world, i.e. the remainder system landscape.

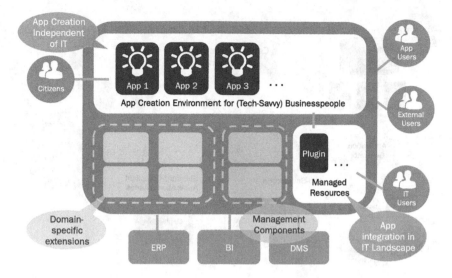

Fig. 1. Elements of a BizDevOps platform

The advantage of this combination is twofold: On the one hand we can provide full flexibility to the business department in terms of development of the apps, and on the other hand IT can retain full control over quality of the outcome, since they safeguard how the parts developed by the business departments interact with the rest of the IT system landscape.

For technical reasons, the platform needs management components (to govern the development workflows) and can make use of domain specific extensions.

4.2   Automated Artifact Generation

The apps generated by the business department in the sandbox need to be transferred into (binary) artifacts which can be deployed in the target IT landscape. Therefore, our platform provides an automated process for generating artifacts (see Fig. 2).

The process of generating, building and deploying applications from business-generated artifacts is highly customizable due to the use of templates. This allows the IT to fully control the final architecture of the applications to be put into operation while at the same time freeing developers in the business departments from the need to know about the final target architecture.

Automated deployment processes allow the business departments to see their apps "in action" during the development and debugging process. These automated workflows can be extended by automated regressions tests and also sign-off processes to further automate release processes with the possibility of automated deployments into different target platforms.

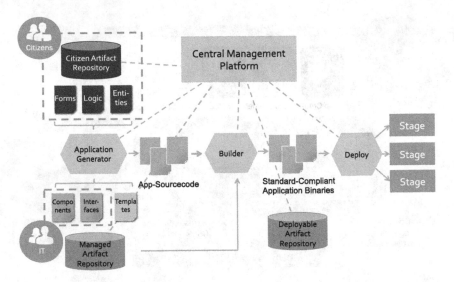

Fig. 2. Software artifact generation in BizDevOps approach

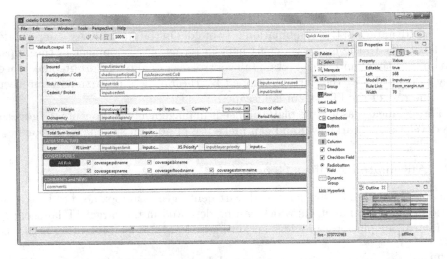

Fig. 3. User interface composition for developers in business department

4.3   Platform Realization

Our realization of the BizDevOps platform consists of three major elements:

- The *Integrated Development Environment*–IDE (see Fig. 3)–is especially targeted towards the needs of developers in the business departments. It allows them to independently create, preview, debug, test and refine their business applications. Graphical editors allow the creation of data models and user interfaces; for business logic there is a coding environment with optimized

Fig. 4. Easy to use deployment workflows for business users

editing and debugging support. All artifacts created in the IDE are automatically subject to version control, which is also optimized in order to reduce complexity to fit the needs of non-IT users.

- An *Execution Component* provides a seamless integration of the applications created by the Citizen Developers into the application landscape of the company and ensures scalability when applications are to be used by a larger number of users.
- A *Central Management* (see Fig. 4) is the main component containing the actual logic how artifacts developed by the developers in the business department and IT-provided resources are stored in version control repositories and later combined in order to create runnable applications. It handles the relations and dependencies between the artifacts, manages the versioning, and ensures compliance by imposing workflows for quality assurance and application deployment.

5 Case Study: BizDevOps at Reinsurance Company

5.1 Facultative Pricing Portal Realized as BizDevOps Project

Over the last years, we were able to work with Hannover Re, the world's third-largest reinsurance company, on an application of our BizDevOps platform for the pricing of facultative insurance risks [5]. These are risks that need to be assessed (i.e. an insurance premium needs to be calculated on a larger number of properties of the risk) on an individual basis with a highly heterogeneous underlying portfolio, ranging from power plants over satellites to fine art. Needless to say, business domain knowledge is at the heart of the pricing process to be supported, especially when all these different risks are to be processed by one single system. Furthermore, the way these risks are assessed may require almost instantaneous changes when reacting to unforeseen events (like an outbreak of an epidemic) is necessary.

With our platform Hannover Re give their reinsurance specialists the possibility of creating pricing tools solely within the business departments, i.e. without IT involvement. The platform itself is integrated with Hannover Re's ERP system (SAP) and linked to other systems like Document Management and the like.

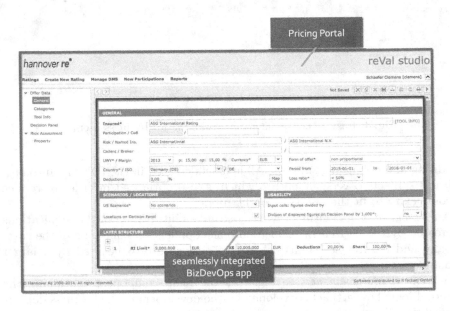

Fig. 5. Final outcome at case study: Pricing portal with integrated calculator app

Today, a yearly premium volume of approximately one billion USD is processed via BizDevOps-created applications by a user-base of several hundred concurrent users worldwide. As shown in Fig. 5, the overall application has been created by IT; the actual pricing tools (right part of the screen) are completely developed in the business departments (as apps in the sandbox). The final platform integrates these apps in a seamless manner to provide a unique user experience. The users claim that they are especially fond of the fact that the applications are built to their actual needs–in a way which would not have been possible –or only with huge IT investments and spending much more time compared to BizDevOps approach– when such solutions would have been created by IT following traditional process models.

5.2 Lessons Learned

The software system for pricing reinsurance risks at Hannover Re is now in productive use for several years. This extensive period of usage together with the fact that the system is used on a world-wide basis 24/7 with a significant number of concurrent users for a decent number of business decisions each year, allows us to derive the following lessons learned:

- *Expressive power of the approach:* It shows that the application of a BizDevOps platform for rendering the various pricing tools produces valid results, since the restrictions imposed by the sandbox-nature of the platform do not negatively affect the expressiveness of the platform with regard to the intended purpose.
- *Development pace:* Although it was not obvious in the very beginning of the platform, it became clear that the developers in the business departments–although tech-savvy but without formal computer-science education–did very well and also very fast in creating the applications; realizing timely adoptions to the applications over the course of time due to market demands was also no problem.
- *Fully functional cooperation between business and IT:* It turned out that cooperation between business and IT along the boundaries which are clearly defined and enforced by the architecture of the platform worked out very well. Experience shows that the separation of work between business department and IT along the lines of the BizDevOps platform allows effective decoupling of the overall development and integration of the platform (by IT) and the actual business logic captured in the apps (by business).
- *Scalability:* Experience shows that the platform provides enough scalability to fulfill the requirements of a mission critical system, even though the usage has grown significantly over the years.
- *Loose coupling:* The loose coupling of the apps to the managed resources also turned out to be an effective means for decoupling development activities.

6 Conclusion and Further Work

For many companies nowadays it is an important task to speed up the software development process for innovative systems which make up the competitive advantage of the companies. By addressing the traditional boundaries between IT and business departments and by handing over control over certain parts of the application from IT to business while at the same time ensuring that IT can safeguard the overall quality of the system, the application development process for innovative systems can be improved.

We have shown how a platform can make a BizDevOps approach operational, where a classical DevOps-approach is extended by elements of End User Software Engineering. As our case study shows, such approach and platform are powerful enough to realize a mission-critical pricing system at a leading insurance company.

Further work lies in the area of applying the approach to other application domains. Currently we are working on tariff calculators presented to end-users in the web. With the approach we hope to provide one possible direction how software development can evolve in the next year under the light of increasing technical literacy of the digital natives, the business departments people of today and tomorrow.

References

1. Beck, K., Beedle, M., Bennekum, A.V., Cockburn, A., Cunningham, W., Fowler, M., Grenning, J., Highsmith, J., Hunt, A., Jeffries, R., Kern, J., Marick, B., Martin, R.C., Mellor, S., Schwaber, K., Sutherland, J., Thomas, D.: Manifesto for Agile Software Development (2001). www.agilemanifesto.org
2. Burnett, M.M., Myers, B.A.: Future of end-user software engineering: beyond the Silos. In: Proceedings of the on Future of Software Engineering, FOSE 2014, pp. 201–211. ACM, New York (2014). http://doi.acm.org/10.1145/2593882.2593896
3. Genovese, Y.: Accelerating Innovation by Adopting a Pace-Layered Application Strategy. Gartner Inc. (2012)
4. Gruhn, V., Schäfer, C.: No-frills software engineering for business information systems. In: New Trends in Software Methodologies, Tools and Techniques - Proceedings of the 9th SoMeT 2010, Prague (2009)
5. Hemstedt, F., Schäfer, C.: Lass den Fachbereich entwickeln: Wie die Entwicklung von Businesslogik im Fachbereich gelingt. OBJEKTspektrum 2015(2), pp. 16–21 (2015) (in German). www.objektspektrum.de
6. Hüttermann, M.: DevOps for Developers. Apress, New York (2012)
7. Martin, J.: Application Development Without Programmers. Longman Higher Education, London (1981)
8. Panko, R.R., Port, D.N.: End user computing: the dark matter (and dark energy) of corporate IT. In: 47th Hawaii International Conference on System Sciences, pp. 4603–4612 (2012)

Modeling Tools for Social Coding

Mirai Watanabe[⊠], Yutaka Watanobe, and Alexander Vazhenin

Department of Information Systems, University of Aizu,
Aizu-Wakamatsu 965-8580, Japan
{d8161105,yutaka,vazhenin}@u-aizu.ac.jp

Abstract. In recent years, the social coding paradigm has become commonly used in software development, taking advantage of version control systems and tracking functions. However, most social coding platforms do not provide modeling tools which support the creation of documents for corresponding products. In the present paper, we propose modeling tools for social coding. The tools are based on hybrid editors, where different experts on a project team can use the correct input methods to modify some features of software components. These editors allow users to manipulate both a visual construct in a high-level representation and the corresponding texts in the low-level format. Some advantages of these approaches are also discussed through a case study and its evaluation.

Keywords: Social coding · Visual and textual coding · Collaborative programming

1 Introduction

In recent years, because of rapid transitions in software needs and related technologies, the life cycle of the software development is getting shorter. In addition, there is a growing trend toward open-source software development to improve software quality based on observation by numerous users and contributors. For short-term developments, a number of paradigms, frameworks, and development strategies have been promoted. Agile software development is a group of software development strategies that emphasizes close collaboration between programmer teams and business experts for small- or middle-scale projects [1,2]. Most agile methods break a task into small incremental phases with minimal planning and do not directly involve long-term planning. Each iteration involves a cross-functional team working in all phases related to planning, requirements analysis, design, coding, unit testing, and acceptance testing.

On the other hand, social coding is an open, collaborative approach to software development, where hundreds of team developers can work remotely, yet in real time, to build or improve software code. For example, GitHub [3] is an open source software hosting service with collaboration among a huge number of users. GitHub provides a set of social coding tools built around a Git version control system and incorporates social functionality that makes a developer's identity and activities visible to other users [4,5].

© Springer International Publishing Switzerland 2015
H. Fujita and G. Guizzi (Eds.): SoMeT 2015, CCIS 532, pp. 399–410, 2015.
DOI: 10.1007/978-3-319-22689-7_31

Some agile methods are promising for use in short-term projects. However, in the case of open software development, the agile methods are not always the best strategy, because they give higher priority to team communication and prototype programs, despite the fact that open-source software development emphasizes documentation. In addition, for a project team, in which different experts such as designers, programmers, and UI designers, as well as customers, are involved, special tools which allow each expert to understand and modify certain features of the software in appropriate ways are required.

We propose a development methodology and the tools that preserve the productivity with the advantages of social coding platforms as well as the documentation. The goal here is to solve the above-mentioned problems by means of visual modeling tools based on hybrid editors for social coding. Using hybrid editors, the end users can manipulate both texts in YAML [6] and operable UML [7] diagrams. The tools automatically generate UML diagrams and the corresponding product template codes of classes and packages in several programming languages, such as Java. These products are generated from intermediate data in the abstract syntax tree (AST), which can be transformed into text in YAML and operable UML diagrams and vice versa. Since the modeling tools use the specifications of Executable UML (xUML) [8] within the transformation process, the produced UML diagrams can be both documents and sources of the product template code. In the present paper, the architecture of hybrid editors and the internal representation of the models are presented. A case study demonstrated that the tools of hybrid editors enable higher productivity, taking advantage of both text and GUI editors.

The remainder of the present paper is organized as follows. In Sect. 2, related research is described. In Sect. 3, the modeling tools and their advantages are described. Section 4 describes the proposed modeling tools and their algorithms are described in detail. In Sect. 5, the proposed approach is evaluated through a case study. Finally, conclusions and future research are discussed.

2   Related Work

The proposed approach has relations with many trends in research and development, aimed to exploit visual languages applied for developing software components as well as for visual programming editors to create them [9,10]. Here, we focus on modeling tools which support to generate diagrams and the corresponding codes.

In short-term development, it is important to reduce the cost of the model generation and implementation for the productivity. There are three different approaches to increasing productivity: (1) generating UML diagrams from texts, (2) generating UML diagrams from source codes, and (3) generating source codes from executable UMLs.

The TextUML Toolkit [11] and yUML [12] are related to the first approach. The TextUML Toolkit is an open-source eclipse plugin for UML. A textual notation is used for an inner representation of a class diagram. This can represent packages, classes, and relations of attributes, associations, operations, and generalizations in class diagrams. The advantages of the text notations of these tools are the simplicity and functionality of their text editors. However, such tools cannot generate the corresponding executable codes, and it is difficult for non-software engineers to manipulate texts in the low-level format.

AmaterasUML [13] and Class Visualizer [14] are related to the second approach. AmaterasUML is an eclipse plugin which can create UML diagrams, including class diagrams, sequence diagrams, and use case diagrams. Among these tools, class diagrams can be automatically generated from source codes in Java. The advantage of these tools is that users can directly generate UML diagrams without cost. On the other hand, it is difficult for non-programmers to manipulate the models within these tools.

The Visual Paradigm [15], the xuml-tools [16] and the Action Language for the Foundational UML (ALF) [17] are related to the third approach, which is based on the model-driven architecture (MDA) approach [21–24]. The MDA approach is important not only for generating source code based on models, but also for involving non-programmers in the system design. The xuml-tools is a web application for xUML which includes a class diagram viewer. A class diagram created within the viewer is compiled to the corresponding source codes in Java. The advantage of these tools is that users can directly generate executable codes from the model and vice versa. On the other hand, because of its tight-coupled models and codes, it is impossible to modify the products within the perfect MDA approach. Although there are many visual tools with rather powerful functionality, it is difficult to find systems which provide users with the ability to work in texts and then switch to diagrams (and vise versa) based on their synchronization.

The creation of software languages and tools is becoming pervasive. Examples include general-purpose programming languages, domain-specific languages and modeling languages. Some of these languages are textual, some are visual, and some are both textual and visual. We will use the term hybrid languages [18–20] for languages that have both textual and visual syntax. Visual languages can benefit from having an alternative textual syntax, for example, to provide a concise standardized file representation, to be able to use existing general text-based development tools, and allowing users with different learning strategies (visual or textual) to use the language in the way they like.

In terms of the development of software languages and tools including general-purpose programming languages, domain-specific languages and modeling languages, there is an approach of hybrid languages that have both textual and visual syntax. In this approach, visual languages can benefit from having an alternative textual representations to be able to use existing general text-based development tools as well as to allow users with different learning strategies (visual or textual) to use the language in the way they like (see for example [18–20]).

3   Modeling Tools with Hybrid Editors

The proposed modeling tools are designed as a graphical user interface (GUI) application. Figure 1 shows the system architecture and the interfaces of the tools, as well as the relations between the tools and products. The tools support text editors and UML editors (viewers) for manipulating codes/models in the inner representation and the corresponding UML diagram, respectively. The text editor is also used to edit product template codes in some programming languages, which are the final products.

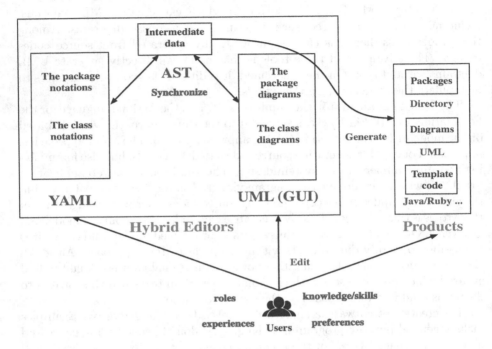

Fig. 1. Architecture of the proposed tools

The tools are supported by YAML for representing the corresponding UML diagrams. YAML is a human-friendly data serialization standard for all programming languages, such as XML and JSON. YAML has a hierarchical structure which is represented by indents, and so is suitable for representing both class and package diagrams, which consist of hierarchical structures. The codes in YAML and UML diagrams are synchronized by intermediate data. The role of the intermediate data is to generate the product template codes and packages of the products in some programming languages. This mechanism has three advantages. First, it is possible to generate a UML diagram by a specification in YAML. Second, users can intuitively manipulate a visual construct in UML. Third, users can generate product template codes and packages at the same time in the process of generating the UML diagram. The hybrid mechanism of each language makes up for the disadvantages of the other while maintaining their advantages. The advantages of editing in YAML for generating UML diagrams are as follows:

- The learning cost is low because YAML is a lightweight markup language.
- The users can use any text editor and benefit from library functions related to replacement, regular expression, and other language support tools, as well as from key binding.
- Using a version control system to manage the differences between different versions of products is easy.

The advantages of the UML representation are as follows:

- It is easy to understand the hierarchical structures and the relationship between components because of visual notations and constructs.
- It is easy even for non-programmers to directly manipulate components through mouse operations.
- A UML representation is easy to extend because it is a subset of UML.

One of advantages of the tools is that users from a team who have different roles, experiences, knowledge/skills as well as preferences can understand and manipulate component features in appropriate ways. In addition, the tools provide a user with interfaces where he/she can switch between the text and diagram editor depending on the situation.

4 YAML for Generating UML Diagrams

In this section, we present details of the text representation in YAML for the corresponding UML diagram.

Figure 2 shows package diagrams and the corresponding inner representation in YAML. A package and a class are represented by a rectangle in the diagram. A package can include packages or classes. YAML has hash and list as data structures. In the YAML representation, a package or a class is represented by its hash, which has *package* or *class* key respectively. A *package* hash has its own *name* and *in* key which consists of a list of *packages* and *classes*. A *class* hash has a list of names of *classes*.

Figure 3 shows a class diagram and the corresponding inner representation in YAML. In the inner representation, a class hash has keys of *name*, *package*, *attributes* and *operations*.

Class diagrams generated by the visual modeling tools support the representation of *association*, *aggregation*, *composition*, *dependency*, *generalization* and *realization* in UML. Figure 4 shows a class diagram which has a relationship of *aggregation* and the corresponding inner representation. In order to include a relationship, the corresponding hash can be defined in the YAML representation. The hash of a relationship has a list of *classes* as a value. Each class has a multiplicity hash as a value which represents its multiplicity.

Figure 5 shows a class diagram which has relationships of *generalization* and the corresponding inner representation. In order to include such a relationship, the corresponding hash can be defined in the YAML representation. The hash of a relationship has a list of *classes* as a value.

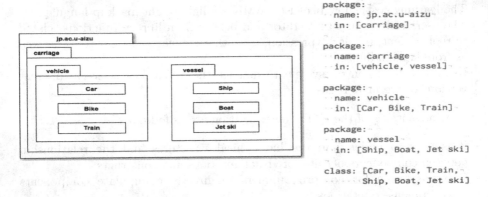

Fig. 2. Package diagram generated by description in YAML

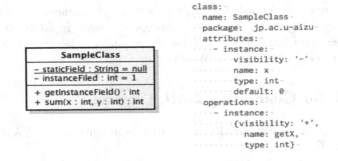

Fig. 3. Class diagram generated by description in YAML

As an experimental system, algorithms to automatically generate the corresponding product packages and classes in Java have been developed and implemented in order to construct the visual modeling tools. Here, some details of the algorithms are presented. The algorithms generate products based on the intermediate representation in an AST. The intermediate representation in the AST is represented in a tree structure. A node of the tree structure corresponds to a package hash or a class hash in YAML for generating UML diagrams. We developed a special parser to transform texts in YAML into a tree structure, where a package hash with a non-empty hash becomes an internal node and a class hash (and a package hash with an empty hash) becomes a leaf. A pre-order traversal scheme generates the corresponding directory structure.

In order to generate a class diagram from an intermediate representation, we use an approach of template programs so that the generator can create products in different programming languages. Figure 6 shows an example of a pair consisting of a template program and a product template code. The template program includes formal keywords enclosed by angle brackets to be replaced with real values defined in the internal representation.

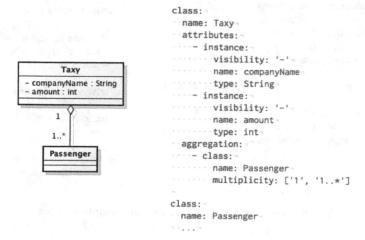

```
class:
  name: Taxy
  attributes:
    - instance:
        visibility: '-'
        name: companyName
        type: String
    - instance:
        visibility: '-'
        name: amount
        type: int
  aggregation:
    - class:
        name: Passenger
        multiplicity: ['1', '1..*']

class:
  name: Passenger
    ...
```

Fig. 4. Class diagram with an aggregation relationship

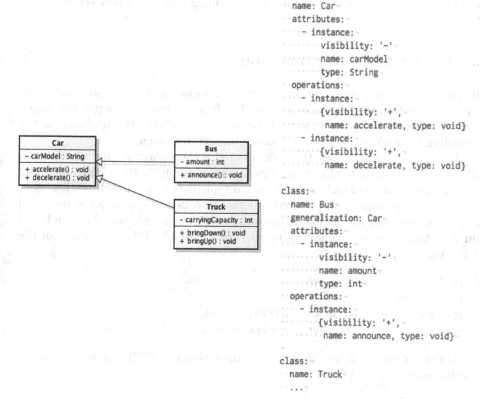

```
class:
  name: Car
  attributes:
    - instance:
        visibility: '-'
        name: carModel
        type: String
  operations:
    - instance:
        {visibility: '+',
         name: accelerate, type: void}
    - instance:
        {visibility: '+',
         name: decelerate, type: void}

class:
  name: Bus
  generalization: Car
  attributes:
    - instance:
        visibility: '-'
        name: amount
        type: int
  operations:
    - instance:
        {visibility: '+',
         name: announce, type: void}

class:
  name: Truck
    ...
```

Fig. 5. Class diagram with an generalization relationship

```
package <class.package.name>;                  package jp.ac.u-aizu

<visibility> class <name>                      public class SampleClass
 extentds <name>                                extends FooClass
 implements <name>{                             implements BarInterface{

  <visibility> <(static)> <type> <name> = <default>;   private static int x = 0

  <visibility> <(static)> <type>               public int getX(){
   <name>(<arguments> ...){                      return x;
    return <type default value>;               }
  }                                              ...
  ...                                          }
}
```

Fig. 6. Template program and product template code

Figure 6 shows an example of template programs in Java. The important thing is that the modeling tools support template programs in different languages including Scala, C++, Ruby, and JavaScript. Beside, users can customize the template programs based on environment, coding rules, and preferences of the team.

5 Case Study and Evaluation

In this section, we present a case study and its evaluation. The purpose of the case study is to develop a package related to fundamental data structures which consist of several types and their relations. We evaluate the usability of the modeling tools to create a package based on a certain scenario.

For evaluation and case study we selected a class diagram that can be considered as a medium level complexity. As shown in Fig. 7, the package includes the fundamental constructions of stack and queue (Fig. 8) as well as their generalization, realization, and related objects. In order to evaluate the proposed approach, we count the number of operations needed to create the diagram based on a certain scenario. We define an operation in an YAML text as any of the following:

– Add, change or delete a word.
– Replace words.
– Replace words based on a regular expression.
– Reset the state of document based on a version control system.

On the other hand, we also define an operation in a UML diagram as any of the following:

– Add or delete a construct.
– Add, change, or delete a parameter.

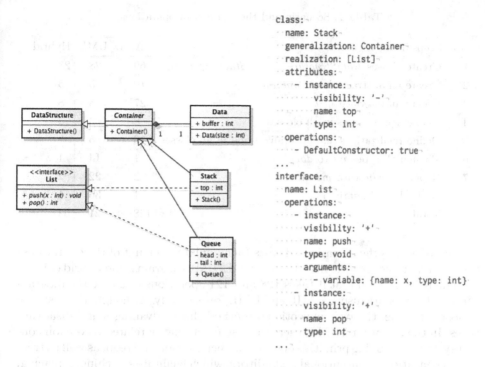

```
class:
  name: Stack
  generalization: Container
  realization: [List]
  attributes:
    - instance:
        visibility: '-'
        name: top
        type: int
  operations:
    - DefaultConstructor: true
...
interface:
  name: List
  operations:
    - instance:
        visibility: '+'
        name: push
        type: void
        arguments:
          - variable: {name: x, type: int}
    - instance:
        visibility: '+'
        name: pop
        type: int
...
```

Fig. 7. Class diagram for stack and queue and related objects

```
/* Stack */
public class Stack extends
Container implements List{
  public int top;

  public Stack(){}

  public void push(int x){}

  public int pop(){
    return 0;
  }
}
```

```
/* Queue */
public class Queue
  extends Container implements List{
  public int head;
  public int tail;

  public Queue(){}

  public void push(int x){}

  public int pop(){
    return 0;
  }
}
```

Fig. 8. Parts of the template code of the stack and queue program

- Add or delete a relation of constructs.
- Switch the input device from keyboard to mouse within the UML diagram, or vice versa.

Table 1. Scenario and the number of operations.

No.	Steps in the scenario	YAML	UML	Hybrid
1	Create classes *DataStructure, Data, Stack, Queue*	69	28	28
2	Create an abstract class *Container*	10	5	5
3	Create an interface *List*	27	8	8
4	Define aggregations in all classes	8	3	3
5	Define relalizations and generalizations in all classes	10	5	5
6	Change all types *int* to *double*	1	14	1
7	Replace *public* with *private*	2	22	2
8	Go back to Scenario 5	1	36	1
	Total	128	121	53

Table 1 shows the scenario and costs (accumulated amount of the operations) of each step in the scenario in terms of YAML, UML diagrams, and hybrid editors.

The results reveal that it takes 128 and 121 operations to create the diagram through the scenario using YAML and UML, respectively. Although, the costs are almost the same, the two conventional methods have advantages and disadvantages. In the editor for YAML, users can use functionality related to version control systems, including primitive operations such as undo and redo, as well as tracers. The utilities of conventional text editors, which facilitate searching, replacing, and copying based on regular expressions as well as cursor movement, are also available. The important thing is that all such operations can be performed by only a keyboard with the key binding setting. On the other hand, in the editor for diagrams, users can manipulate the codes much more intuitively through visual objects, based on visual editors, where drag and drop operations and other functions which are available in conventional drawing tools can be used.

In contrast, 53 operations are required in order to create the same diagram and the scenario using hybrid editors. The important thing is that the users can switch editors according to their preference and to roles in the team. Thus, the operation cost can be decreased further based on optimum usage. The proposed modeling tools are aimed at supporting documentation in the short term development based on agile methods. Since the modeling tools generate both the documents and the corresponding product template codes, the project team can decrease the cost for documentation. Besides, the approach facilitates communication within the agile team because both programmers and non-programmers can involve in documentation through the manipulation in both texts and diagrams. The proposed modeling tools can support social coding combining advantages of the MDA approaches and the agile software development.

6   Conclusion

Visual modeling tools based on hybrid editors for social coding and their usability in short-term projects related to agile software development have been presented.

The editors allow users, including both non-programmers and programmers, as well as other project members, to have different roles. The editors allow users to manipulate both a visual construct in a high-level representation based on UML and the corresponding texts in the low-level format based on YAML. The modeling tools automatically generate template codes in different languages as products based on the intermediate data, which synchronize the representations in UML and YAML. The preliminary experiment on the tool has demonstrated that hybrid editors can decrease the number of operations needed to create a class diagram and the corresponding product codes compared to other types of editors. Hybrid editors also have advantages over version control systems in managing products. Our results show that the tools can be applied to short-term software development based on social coding. Future research will include the development of a generator, which converts the source codes to the corresponding models, as well as an evaluation based on comparison with other development strategies and modeling tools.

References

1. Martin, R.C.: Agile Software Development, Principles, Patterns, and Practices. Prentice Hall, Upper Saddle River (2012)
2. Bergmann, R., Gessinger, S., Gorg, S., Muller, G.: The collaborative agile knowledge engine CAKE. In: GROUP 2014 Proceedings of the 18th International Conference on Supporting Group Work (2014)
3. Github. https://github.com
4. Git. http://git-scm.com
5. Spinelis, D.: Version control systems, Software, Software, IEEE (2005)
6. YAML. http://yaml.org
7. UML. http://www.uml.org
8. Mellor, S.J., Balcer, M.J.: Executable UML: A Foundation for Model-driven Architecture. Addison-Wesley Professional, Reading (2002)
9. Ford, J.L.: Scratch Programming for Teens, 1st edn. Course Technology Press, Boston (2008)
10. Bitter, R., Mohiuddin, T., Nawrocki, M.: LabView: Advanced Programming Techniques, 2nd edn. CRC Press, New York (2007)
11. TextUML. http://abstratt.github.io/textuml/readme.html
12. yUML. http://yuml.me
13. AmaterasUML.   http://amateras.sourceforge.jp/cgi-bin/fswiki/wiki.cgi?page= AmaterasUML
14. Class Visualizer. http://class-visualizer.net
15. Visual Paradigm. http://www.visual-paradigm.com
16. xuml-tools. https://github.com/davidmoten/xuml-tools/blob/master/README. md
17. Seidewitz, E.: UML with meaning: executable modeling in foundational UML and the Alf action language. In: HILT 2014 Proceedings of the 2014 ACM SIGAda Annual Conference on High Integrity Language Technology (2014)
18. Niklas, F., Hedin, G.: Using refactoring techniques for visual editing of hybrid languages. In: Workshop on Refactoring Tools (WRT 2013) (2013)

19. Koitz, R., Slany, W.: Empirical comparison of visual to hybrid formula manipulation in educational programming languages for teenagers. In: PLATEAU 2014 Proceedings of the 5th Workshop on Evaluation and Usability of Programming Languages and Tools (2014)

20. Maciaszek, L.A., Zhang, K.: Structure editors: old hat or future vision? Evaluation of Novel Approaches to Software Engineering (2011)

21. Mellor, S.J., Scotto, K., Uhi, A.: MDA Distilled: Principles of Model-Driven Architecture. Addison-Wesley Professional, Reading (2004)

22. Hailpern, B., Tarr, P.: Model-driven development: the good, the bad, and the ugly. IBM Syst. J. **45**, 451–461 (2006)

23. Brown, A.B., Iyengar, S., Johnston, S.: A rational approach to model-driven development. IBM Syst. J. (2007)

24. Marth, K., Ren, S.: Model-driven development with eUML-ARC. In: Proceedings of the 27th Annual ACM Symposium on Applied Computing (2012)

Security and Software Methodologies for Reliable Software Design

A Change Impact Analysis Tool: Integration Between Static and Dynamic Analysis Techniques

Nazri Kama[1(✉)], Saiful Adli Ismail[1], Kamilia Kamardin[1],
Norziha Megat Zainuddin[1], Azri Azmi[1,2],
and Wan Shafiuddin Zainuddin[2]

[1] Advanced Informatics School, Universiti Teknologi Malaysia,
54100 Kuala Lumpur, Malaysia
{mdnazri,saifuladli,kamilia,norziha.kl,
azriazmi}@utm.my
[2] CyberSecurity Malaysia, Sapura@Mines, 43300 Seri Kembangan
Selangor, Malaysia
wanshafi@cybersecurity.my

Abstract. Accepting too many software change requests could contribute to expense and delay in project delivery. On the other hand rejecting the changes may increase customer dissatisfaction. Software project management might use a reliable estimation on potential impacted artifacts to decide whether to accept or reject the changes. In software development phase, an assumption that all classes in the class artifact are completely developed is impractical compared to software maintenance phase. This is due to some classes in the class artifact are still under development or partially developed. This paper is a continuous effort from our previous work on combining between static and dynamic analysis techniques for impact analysis. We have converted the approach to an automated tool and call it a CIAT (Change Impact Analysis Tool). The significant achievements of the tool are demonstrated through an extensive experimental validation using several case studies. The experimental analysis shows improvement in the accuracy over current impact analysis results.

Keywords: Software development · Change impact analysis · Impact analysis

1 Introduction

Managing software changes is crucial in meeting the evolving needs of customers and later, satisfying their requirements [1]. On one hand taking risk by accepting huge number of changes will lead to delay in delivering project deadline. On the other hand, rejecting the changes contribute to customers unsatisfactory. Looking at this scenario, it is a challenge for software project manager to make a decision when software changes occur during software development. One type of inputs that can assist the software project manager to make an effective decision is through an early prediction on the number of impacted artifacts (or classes) by the changes. The prediction can be done by performing impact analysis or change impact analysis [2].

© Springer International Publishing Switzerland 2015
H. Fujita and G. Guizzi (Eds.): SoMeT 2015, CCIS 532, pp. 413–424, 2015.
DOI: 10.1007/978-3-319-22689-7_32

Referring to [3–5], impact analysis is defined as a process of investigating potential consequences of making a change, or estimating what are the artifacts that will be affected to accomplish a change. In other words, the impact analysis is an activity of identifying software artifacts that are potentially to be affected by a change. Impact analysis has been widely used in software maintenance phase rather than software development phase [6–9]. This is because the current developed impact analysis solutions assume that all classes or class artifacts are completely developed. Most solutions use dynamic analysis techniques [10–13] for their impact analysis implementation.

Our previous works [6–9] have shown that there is a clear difference on change impact analysis implementation between software maintenance and software development phases. This is due to the existence of partially developed classes in the software development phase. This existence causes the current implementation of dynamic analysis techniques are impractical to be implemented in the software development phase. The dynamic analysis technique uses method execution path model as a source of analysis. This model is developed through reverse engineering from source code [10–13]. The technique tends to produce inaccurate results because some method execution paths that involve partially developed classes [7, 8] are not visible due to they have yet to be implemented. This will led to inaccuracy of the generated results.

This paper is a continuous works on change impact analysis approach to support software development activity [6–9]. To note, this paper has close related to our newly published work in [8]. The difference is that this paper focuses on our experiment in automating the previously developed manual impact analysis approach whereas in [8] we extend the automated approach to support change effort estimation. In few recent studies [14, 15], the combination of static and dynamic approaches has indicated some noticeable advantages from both worlds. In this paper, we have extended our work to developing a prototype tool to support the previously developed approach. This paper will give more explanation on the developed tool rather than the concept of change impact analysis approach itself. Details explanation on the approach can be found in [6–9].

This paper is presented: Sect. 2 related work, Sect. 3 explanation on the prototype tool main screen, Sect. 4 and Sect. 5 provide explanation on evaluation procedure and its results. Lastly, Sect. 6 concludes and position our future works.

2 Related Work

Based on our literature, impact analysis has two categories that are static analysis technique and dynamic analysis technique. Our previous definitions have said that the static analysis technique generates a set of potential impacted classes from software artifacts. The dynamic analysis technique conversely builds a set of potential impacted classes through source code execution.

2.1 Static Analysis

Two most related existing static analysis techniques are selected as comparative to the new proposed approach which are the Use Case Maps (UCM) technique [16] and the class interactions prediction with impact prediction filters (CIP-IPF) technique [17, 18].

The UCM technique perform impact analysis on the functional requirements and the high level design models when all the functional requirements have been completely identified and the high level design models have been fully developed. Nevertheless, the main limitation of this technique is there is no traceability link between the functional requirements and the high level design models to the actual source codes. This technique only makes an assumption that the content of these two artifacts are reflected to the class artifacts in which any affected elements in the UCM models are indirectly reflected to the affected class artifacts.

Next, CIP-IPF technique [17, 18] uses the class interactions prediction model in order to define the impacted class artifacts. The advantage of the technique over the UCM technique is that it has a traceability link between the requirements artifacts and the class artifacts. Impact of changes at the requirement level to the class artifacts can be performed based on this traceability link.

In these two techniques, there is a tendency of missing some actual impacted class due to inconsideration of actual source code analysis. This is based on the precept that some of the effect of a change from a class to other classes may only be visible through dynamic or behavior analysis of the changed class [19, 20].

2.2 Dynamic Analysis

Two most related dynamic analysis works are identified in our research which are the Influence Mechanism technique [11, 13] and the Path Impact technique [12]. These two techniques analyzing the actual source code in order to predict the impact set which consists of classes or methods.

The Influence Mechanism technique [11, 13] introduces the Influence Graph (IG) as a model to identify the impacted classes. However, this technique only analyze the class artifacts as the only source of analysis with the condition that the source code are completely developed.

Next, the Path Impact technique [12] uses the Whole Path DAG (Directed Acyclic Graph) model as a model to identify the impacted classes. The technique is almost similar to the Influence Mechanism technique as this technique also uses the class artifacts as a source of analysis and assumes that the class artifacts are completely developed. In addition to that, this technique also performs a preliminary analysis prior to performing a detail analysis. The main limitation of this technique is the implementation is time consuming as the technique opens to a huge number of data when the analysis goes to a large application.

The main similarity of both techniques in terms of its limitation is there is no traceability process or formal mapping from requirements artifacts or design models to the class artifacts. This process is crucial in impact analysis process as changes not only come from class artifacts but it may also come from design and/or requirements artifacts. Since design and requirements artifacts do interact among them vertically (between two different artifacts of a same type) and horizontally (between requirement and design artifacts), changes that happen to them could contribute to different affected class artifacts. In some circumstances, focusing on the source code analysis may not able to detect those affected classes.

3 The CIAT

There are two main modules in the Change Impact Analysis Tool (will called "CIAT" henceforth). The modules are Class Interaction Prediction (CIP) Module and Impact Analysis Module as in Fig. 1.

Fig. 1. System overview

The CIP model is a traceability model that shows interactions of all the software artifacts. This model will be used for static change impact analysis implementation. This model can be developed in any format, but for the purpose of this project we developed it for a consistent xml format. It consists of two sections, first section contains the project information and the second section contains the artifacts information.

For the impact analysis module, the process begins with performing static impact analysis to identify direct and indirect impacted classes. The process starts with the static impact analysis identify direct impacted classes which are the first layer of classes affected by a particular changes requirement. To note, this layer has yet included vertical traceability analysis. Later, the identification of indirect impacted classes are executed by performing the vertical traceability analysis.

Due to space limitation, this paper concentrates on impact analysis module only. Basically, the interaction between these two modules is done through an interface file named CIP. This file will be exported from Class Interactions Prediction Module and imported by Impact Analysis Module. In other words the output of the first CIP Module acts as an input for impact analysis module.

Overall functionalities of this tool are: (1) To import the CIP file to the system database; (2) To acquire the change request information; and (3) To perform static and dynamic impact analysis. See Fig. 2:

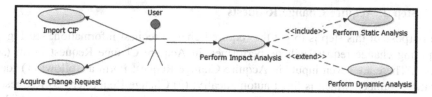

Fig. 2. Overall functionalities of CIAT

The following sub-sections explain briefly the implementation steps of this tool as shown in Fig. 3:

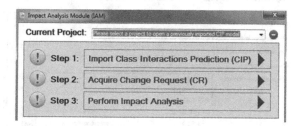

Fig. 3. Main page form

3.1   Step 1: Import CIP

The purpose of this procedure is to import the generated CIP model file. The CIP model file can be an XML (.xml) file or a CIP (.cip) file. Both should have been developed according to the CIP descriptions in XML format. The tool will extracts the software artifacts: (1) requirement, (2) design and (3) class information in the CIP model file as in Fig. 4 below.

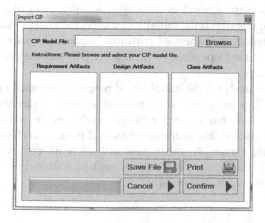

Fig. 4. Import CIP form

3.2   Step 2: Acquire Change Requests

The purpose of this step is to get the required change request information, see Fig. 5. Acquiring change request will be performed in Acquire Change Request Form (see Fig. 7). There are seven inputs in Acquire Change Request Form as follow: (1) Identification Number, which is filled automatically; (2) Change Requester; (3) Requested Change; (4) Change Priority; (5) Affected Requirements; and (6) Comments, which is optional.

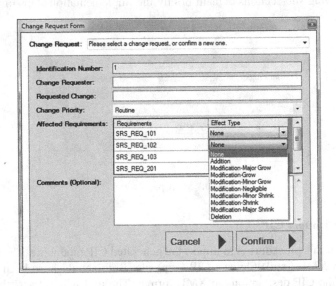

Fig. 5. Change request form

3.3   Step 3: Impact Analysis Implementation

This step analyses change request document to identify a set of potential impacted classes. The result of this step is the initial set of impacted classes. After identifying the initial set of impacted classes, the tool performs impact analysis using two filtration levels and they are Class Dependency Filtration (CDF) and the Method Dependency Filtration (MDF) levels.

In brief, the CDF analyzes the initial set of potential impacted classes using static analysis technique. This analysis is implemented in order to identify the existence of any interaction links that has no change impact value in the initial set of potential impacted classes. We define this interaction link as if there is no change happens to one side of two interacting classes, the other class will not be affected because the opposite class does not require the changed class for its implementation. For the MDF level, the following section gives explanation on it.

Static Analysis – Class Dependency Filtration Level. In this level, the class dependency filtration (CDF) will be performed on the static impact analysis results as in Fig. 6. The process begins with performing static impact analysis to identify direct and indirect affected classes; the static impact analysis will firstly find the direct impacted classes which are the first layer of classes affected by a particular changes requirement without vertical traceability relations consideration. Then indirect impacted classes will be identified by complete traceability search through the CIP interactions to find all related classes to the changed requirement.

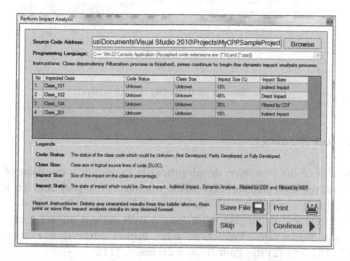

Fig. 6. Sample of CDF filtration on impact analysis

Dynamic Analysis – Method Dependency Filtration (MDF). The MDF conducts another layer of filtration on the CDF level outcomes or results. All method execution paths from the CDF level results will be extracted and analyzed to remove any false detected impacted classes. We have selected the backward and forward analysis technique [13].

There is one main challenge of the current dynamic impact analysis approaches from the software development phase perspective which is they do not consider partially developed class in their process. This is happening due to the nature of classes in the software maintenance phase have been fully developed.

We claim that the inclusion of partially developed class analysis plays significant role in impact analysis from software development perspective. A situation might exist in the software development phase where of some classes are still under development. Figure 7 shows the dynamic impact analysis form.

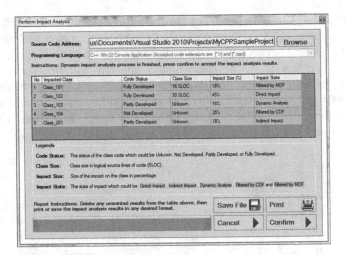

Fig. 7. Sample of dynamic impact analysis

4   Evaluation Strategy

The ultimate aim of the prototype development is to answer a question of "does the developed prototype tool gives an acceptable accuracy of impact analysis results than the selected current impact analysis techniques? To answer this question, we have compared the accuracy of the prototype results with current impact analysis approaches: (1) Class Interactions Prediction with Impact Prediction Filters (CIP-IPF) approach [17, 18]; and (2) the Path Impact approach [11].

We constructed four evaluation attributes: (1) case study; (2) development process; (3) evaluation metrics; and (4) hypothesis.

4.1   Case Study

We have selected three groups of masters student that is currently undertaking master of software engineering course. There are five to seven members of each group that performing various roles in software development activity. We issued several change request to each group and asked them to perform impact analysis at several specific phases. Three impact analysis approaches are used: CIP-IPF approach [17, 18], the Path-Impact approach [11] and the newly developed prototype tool.

4.2   Development Process

Several change requests were issued during the development of a software i.e., requirement phase, design phase, coding phase. Waterfall kinds of development structure were selected [21]. For future evaluation, Agile model kinds of development structure will be taken into consideration.

4.3 Evaluation Metrics

We used the evaluation metrics as described in [19]. Each prediction results on the impacted classes were grouped according to:

- Not Predicting and Not Changing (NP-NC): number of pairs of classes correctly predicted to not be changing;
- Predicting and Not Changing (P-NC): number of pairs incorrectly predicted to be changing;
- Not Predicting and Changing (NP-C): number of classes incorrectly predicted to not be changing; and
- Predicting and Changing (P-C): number of classes correctly predicted to be changing.

Based on the groups, the following values were then calculated [20, 22]: (1) Completeness value: The ratio of the actual class interactions or impacted classes that were predicted; (2) Correctness value: The ratio of the predicted class interactions that were actually interacting or impacted classes that were actually impacted; and (3) Kappa value [19]: This value reflects the accuracy or the prediction (0 is no better than random chance, 0.4–0.6 is moderate agreement, 0.6–0.8 is substantial agreement, and 0.8–1 is almost perfect agreement [16, 20]).

4.4 Hypotheses

- H_0: CIAT does not give higher accuracy of impact analysis results than the selected current techniques results
- H_a: CIAT gives higher accuracy of impact analysis results than the selected current evaluation Results

To validate the hypothesis, an Independent T-Test statistical analysis was used. At the first stage, we compared Means results between the CIP-IPF approach and the CIAT whereas the second stage is between Means results of Path Impact technique and CIAT.

5 Evaluation Results

Table 1 below shows the impact analysis results produced by all selected impact analysis techniques (CIP-IPF, Path Impact and CIAT).

Table 1. Impact analysis results produced by all techniques

CR ID	CIP-IPF			Path Impact			CIAT		
	Com (%)	Corr (%)	Kappa value	Com (%)	Corr (%)	Kappa value	Com (%)	Corr (%)	Kappa value
CR1	80	100	0.785	66.7	100	0.652	86.7	100	0.876
CR2	81.3	100	0.821	78.6	100	0.789	92.9	100	0.935
CR3	76.9	100	0.768	80	92.3	0.752	100	93.8	0.944
CR4	83	94	0.795	88.7	94.1	0.85	94.4	94.4	0.903
CR5	83	91	0.767	91.7	91.7	0.852	91.7	91.7	0.852
CR6	82.4	100	0.832	76.5	92.9	0.721	94.1	94.1	0.842
CR7	81.8	90	0.734	80	94.1	0.764	95	95	0.912
CR8	80	100	0.806	78.6	100	0.787	92.9	100	0.935
CR9	75	100	0.752	87.5	100	0.884	87.5	100	0.884
CR10	76	100	0.77	88.2	100	0.892	94.1	100	0.947
CR11	85.7	100	0.863	73.7	93.3	0.695	94.7	94.7	0.908
CR12	80	100	0.773	68.8	100	0.676	87.5	100	0.884
CR13	90.9	90.9	0.83	76.5	100	0.769	94.1	100	0.947
CR14	83	100	0.843	77.8	100	0.784	94.4	100	0.95
CR15	80	92	0.749	80	100	0.804	86.7	100	0.874

Key: Com- Completeness; Corr- Correctness

Table 2 below shows the summary of T-Test results.

Table 2. T-Test results

Stage Analysis	Technique	Means Results
Stage 1	CIP-IPF	0.7927
	CIAT	0.9060
Stage 2	Path Impact	0.7773
	CIAT	0.9060

5.1   Stage 1 Analysis: The CIP-IPF Technique Vs. CIAT

Table 2 shows the CIAT means value is 0.9060 and CIP-IPF approach value is 0.7927. This indicates that CIAT value is higher than the CIP-IPF approach. Thus, the values reject the null hypothesis (H_0: CIAT does not improve on the CIP-IPF approach results) and accept the alternate hypothesis (H_a: CIAT approach gives higher accuracy of impact analysis results than the CIP-IPF approach).

5.2   Stage 2 Analysis: The Path Impact Technique Vs. CIAT

The results show CIAT value is 0.9060 and the Path Impact approach value is 0.7773. This shows that the CIAT value is higher than the Path Impact approach. Thus, the values reject the null hypothesis (H_0: CIAT does not give higher accuracy of impact analysis results than the Path Impact approach) and accept the alternate hypothesis (H_a: CIAT gives higher accuracy of impact analysis results than the Path Impact approach).

6 Conclusion and Future Work

Our contribution on this paper is an automated prototype tool. This tool implements our previously developed change impact analysis approach. The uniqueness of the approach or the prototype tool is the introduction of Class Dependency Filtration (CDF) and Method Dependency Filtration (MDF) in impact analysis implementation, The MDF is used to handle the partially developed class analysis issues. For the future works, we plan to extend the tool implementation from agile methodology perspective instead of waterfall methodology.

Acknowledgements. The research is financially supported by Ministry of Education Malaysia and Universiti Teknologi Malaysia under Prototype Research Grant Scheme (PRGS), Vot No: 4L617.

References

1. Pfleeger, S.L., Bohner, S.A.: A framework for software maintenance metrics. In: Proceedings of the International Conference on Software Maintenance, pp. 320–327 (1990)
2. Bennet K.H., Rajlich, V.T.: Software maintenance and evolution: a roadmap. In: Proceedings of the International Conference on the Future of Sofware Engineering, pp. 75–87 (2000)
3. Kotonya, G., Somerville, I.: Requirements Engineering: Processes and Techniques. Wiley, Chichester (1998)
4. Arnold, R.S., Bohner, S.A.: Impact analysis-towards a framework for comparison. In: CSM-93, Proceedings Conference on Software Maintenance, pp. 292–301, 27–30 September 1993 (1993)
5. Antoniol, G., Canfora, G., Casazza, G.: Information retrieval models for recovering traceability links between source code and documentation. In: Proceedings of the International Conference on Software Maintenance, pp. 40–44 (2000)
6. Kama, N.: A change impact analysis approach for the software development phase: evaluating an integration approach. Int. J. Soft. Eng. Appl. **7**(2), 293304 (2013)
7. Kama, N.: Integrated change impact analysis approach for the software development phase. Int. J. Soft. Eng. Appl. **7**(2), 293–304 (2013)
8. Basri, S., Kama, N., Ibrahim, R.: A novel estimation approach for requirement changes during software development. Int. J. Softw. Eng. Appl. **9**(1), 237–252 (2015)
9. Kama, N., Basri, S.: Considering partially developed artifacts in change impact analysis implementation. J. Softw. **9**(8), 2174–2179 (2014)
10. Breech, B., Tegtmeyer, M., Pollock, L.: Integrating influence mechanisms into impact analysis for increased precision. In: Proceedings of the 22nd International Conference on Software Maintenance, pp. 55–65 (2006)

11. Law, J., Rothermal, G.: Whole program path-based dynamic impact analysis. In: Proceedings of the 25th International Conference on Software Engineering (ICSE 2003), pp. 308–318 (2003)
12. Breech, B., Danalis, A., Shindo, S., Pollock, L.: Online impact analysis via dynamic compilation technology. In: Proceeding of the 20th IEEE International Conference on Software Maintenance, Washington, US, 11–17 September 2004
13. Law, J., Rothermel. G.: Incremental dynamic impact analysis for evolving software systems. In: Proceeding of the 14th International Symposium on Software Reliability Engineering, Washington, US, 17–20 November 2003
14. Tartler, R., Lohmann, D., Scheler, F., Spinczyk, O.: AspectC++: an integrated approach for static and dynamic adaptation of system software. Knowl.-Based Syst. 23(7), 704–720 (2010)
15. Abaei, G., Selamat, A., Fujita, H.: An empirical study based on semi-supervised hybrid self-organizing map for software fault prediction. Knowl.-Based Syst. 74, 28–39 (2015)
16. Hassine, J., Rilling, J., Hewitt, J., Dssouli, R.: Change impact analysis for requirement evolution using use case maps. In: Proceeding of the 8th International Workshop on Principles of Software Evolution, Washington, US, 5 September 2005
17. Kama, N., French, T., Reynolds, M.: Design patterns consideration in class interactions prediction development. Int. J. Adv. Sci. Technol. 28, 6 (2011)
18. Kama, N., Azli, F.: Requirement level impact analysis with impact prediction filter. In: Proceeding of the 4th International Conference on Software Technology and Engineering, Phuket Thailand, 1–2 September 2012
19. Lindvall, M., Sandahl, K.: How well do experienced software developers predict software changes. J. Syst. Softw. 43, 1 (1998)
20. Cohen, J.: A coefficient of agreement for nominal scales. J. Educ. Psychol. Measur. 20, 1 (1960)
21. Sommerville, I.: Software Engineering, 7th edn. Pearson Education, New Jersey (2008)
22. Landis, J.R., Koch, G.G.: The measurement of observer agreement for categorical data. J. Biometrics 33, 1 (1977)

On the Probabilistic Verification of Time Constrained SysML State Machines

Abdelhakim Baouya[1](✉), Djamal Bennouar[2], Otmane Ait Mohamed[3], and Samir Ouchani[4]

[1] CS Department, Saad Dahlab University, Blida, Algeria
baouya.abdelhakim@gmail.com
[2] CS Department, University of Bouira, Bouria, Algeria
dbennouar@gmail.com
[3] ECE Department, Concordia University, Montreal, Canada
otmane.aitmohamed@concordia.ca
[4] SnT Center, University of Luxembourg, Walferdange, Luxembourg
samir_ouchani@yahoo.com

Abstract. Software and hardware design of complex systems is becoming difficult to maintain and more time and effort are spent on verification than on construction. One of the reason is the number of constraints that must be hold by the system. Recently, Formal methods such as probabilistic approaches gain a great importance in real-time systems verification including avionic systems and industrial process controllers. In this paper, we propose a probabilistic verification framework of SysML state machine diagrams extended with time and probability features. The approach consists of mapping a SysML state machine diagrams to PRISM input language. To ensure the correctness of proposed approach, we capture the semantics of both SysML state machine diagrams and their generated PRISM code. We demonstrate the approach efficiency by analyzing PCTL temporal logic on ATM case study.

Keywords: Sysml state machine diagram · MARTE · Probability · Time

1 Introduction

Constraints on system design in terms of functionality, performance, availability, reliability and time to market are becoming more stringent. Therefore, the design and implementation of successful systems, represents the prime concerns of systems engineering (SE) but reveals several challenges [9]. Indeed, from one side the systems are becoming increasingly complex, in the other side the market pressure for rapid development of these systems makes the task of their designs a challenge. Thus, the evaluation and the correctness of systems at early stage of design reduces the design cost such as maintenance time and effort. Recently, the need of automated verification techniques to cope with errors is imminent, especially when *time* and *probability* are incorporated.

© Springer International Publishing Switzerland 2015
H. Fujita and G. Guizzi (Eds.): SoMeT 2015, CCIS 532, pp. 425–441, 2015.
DOI: 10.1007/978-3-319-22689-7_33

The *probabilistic verification* is used to verify systems whose behavior is unpredictable, unreliable, especially stochastic in nature. The verification of such systems can be focused on either qualitative or quantitative properties [4]. Quantitative properties puts the constraints on a certain event, e.g. the probability of processor failure in the next 3 hours is at least 0.88, while qualitative properties assert that certain event will happen surely (i.e. Probability=1).

In this paper, we are interested in the formal verification of probabilistic systems under time constraints modeled as SysML state machine diagram extended with probability and time features of MARTE profile [13]. The overview of our framework is depicted in Fig. 1. It takes State machine diagrams and PCTL properties as input. Our approach is based on representing state machine diagram to an equivalent PRISM model (*Probabilistic Timed Automata*). The PRISM model checker verifies PCTL properties on the resulting model. We extract the adequate semantics model related to state machine diagram then, we present the underling semantics related to the produced PRISM model. Furthermore, we show tht the relation between both semantic preserves the satisfiability of PCTL properties.

The remainder of this paper is structured as follows: Sect. 2 discusses the related work. Section 3 describes SysML state machine diagram. Sections 4 and 5 provide syntax and semantic meaning of probabilistic and timed state machine diagrams. The syntax and semantics of PRISM Model Checker is presented in Sect. 6. Section 7 provides a mapping mechanism from state machine diagram into the input language of the probabilistic model checker PRISM. The approach soundness is proved in Sect. 8. Section 9 illustrates the application of our mapping rules on Automatic Teller Machine (ATM) case study. Section 10 draws conclusions and lays out the future works.

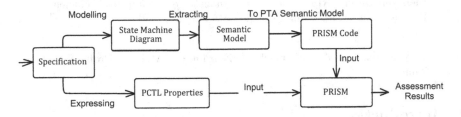

Fig. 1. A SysML State machine diagram verification approach

2   Related Work

In this section, we present the recent works related to the verification of behavioral models then we compare them with our proposed approach.

Doligalski and Adamski [8] propose a verification and simulation of UML State Machine. For this purpose, two mapping mechanisms are defined. The first consists on mapping the original model to Petri network for verification according the requirements. However, probability and time verification are not considered. When the requirements are satisfied, the second mapping occurs to generate VHDL or Verilog description for simulation. Huang et al. [11] propose a verification of SysML State Machine Diagram by extending the model with MARTE [13] features to express the execution time. The tool has as input the State Machine Diagram and as output timed automata expressed in UPPAAL syntax [5]. UPPAAL uses Computational Tree Logic (CTL) properties to check if the model is satisfied with liveness and safety properties. Ouchani et al. [17] propose a verification framework of SysML activity diagram. The authors address a subset of SysML activity diagram artifacts with control flow. The different artifacts have been formalized and mapping algorithm has been proposed to translate these artifacts to PRISM input language. The transformation result is a probabilistic automata to be checked by PRISM. Timing verification is not considered. Kaliappan et al. [12] propose a verification approach for system work-flow especially in communication protocol. The approach takes as input three UML diagrams: state machine diagram, activity diagram and sequence diagram. State machine diagram or activity diagram is converted into PROMELA code as a protocol model and its properties are derived from the sequence diagram as Linear Temporal Logic (LTL). Pajic et al. [18] develop a framework for verification and generation of real time applications either in C/C++code for software or in Hardware description language (HDL) like VHDL or Verilog. The focus of the work is a development of model translation tool from UPPAAL [5] to Stateflow (UPP2SF). The checked UPPAAL model is translated to Stateflow using Simulink which provides full support for C/C++ and HDLs. Ando et al. [3] propose a verification approach of SysML state machine diagram. The diagrams are translated to communication sequential process description (CSP) and they apply the PAT [20] model checker to check the CSP models against the LTL properties. The paper proposes a mapping rules of different state machine artifacts. However, time and probability are not addressed.

Compared to the existing works Table 1, our contribution improves the verification of SysML State Machine diagram by extending state machine with elements of UML MARTE profile to support time and probability. From the comparison, we observe that few of them formalize the behavioral model and prove the soundness of their proposed verification approaches. Moreover, our verification framework is efficient as it preserves all properties.

Table 1. Comparison with the related work.

Approach	Formalization	Probability	Time	Soundness	Automation
[8], [3], [12]					√
[11], [18]		√			√
[17]	√	√		√	√
Our	√	√	√	√	√

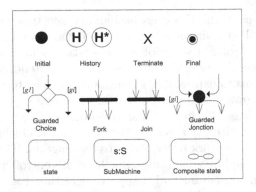

Fig. 2. A subset of State machine diagram artifacts

3   SysML State Machine Diagram

SysML State Machine diagram (SMD) is a graph-based diagram where states nodes are connected by states edges (i.e.transition)[1]. Figure 2 shows the set of interesting artifacts used for verification in this paper. The behavior of a state machine is specified by a set of regions, each of which defines its own set of states. The states in any one region are exclusive; that is, when the region is active, exactly one of its substates is active. A region starts (resp. stops) executing when it initial (resp. final) pseudo-state becomes active. When a state is entered, an (optional) *entry* behavior is executed. Similarly on exit, an optional *exit* behavior is executed. While in a state, a state machine can execute a *do* behavior. Transitions are defined by triggers, guards, and effects. The trigger cause a transition from the source state when the guard is valid, and the effect is a behavior executed once the transition is triggered (opac behavior). In addition, the control nodes supports a junction, choice, join, fork, terminate and history pseudo-state node. A junction splits an incoming transition into multiple outgoing transitions realizes a static conditional branch, as opposed to a choice pseudo-state which realizes a dynamic conditional branch. To illustrate how a probability value is specified, the transition leaving choice nodes are annotated with the ≪ *GaStep* ≫ stereotype using the element *prob* of MARTE profile [13]. The time is specified by applying the stereotype ≪ *resourceUsage* ≫ with element *execTime* to specify the maximum and the minimum value of the time duration written as (value, unit, min/max), where *min, max* are integer values. We present in Definition 1, the formal definition of Probabilistic and timed SMD. Then, we propose a property that explains the state transition in SMD.

Definition 1. Probabilistic and timed SysML state machine diagrams is a tuple $S = (i, fin, \mathcal{N}, X, E, Inv, Enab, Prob)$, where:

- i is the initial node,
- $fin = \{\odot, \times\}$ is the set final nodes,
- $\mathcal{N}$ is a finite set of state machine nodes,

- X is a set of clocks,
- E is a set of events,
- $Inv : \mathcal{N} \rightarrow \mathbb{N}$ is the invariant constraint that represents the maximum clock value supported by state clock,
- Enab: $\mathcal{N} \rightarrow \mathbb{N}$ is an enabling condition that represent the minimum clock value for state transition,
- Prob : $(\{i\} \cup \mathcal{N}) \times E \rightarrow Dist(\mathcal{N} \times 2^X)$ is a probabilistic transition function that assigns for each state $s \in \mathcal{N}$ and $\alpha \in E$ a discrete probability distribution $\mu \in Dist(2^x \times \mathcal{N})$.

Property 1. There are two possible ways in which a SMD can proceed by taking a transition (State transition) or by letting time progress while remaining in a state (Delay transition):

- State transition : for $s, s', \in \mathcal{N}$, $\alpha \in E$ $s \xrightarrow{\alpha,t}_p s'$ when $Enab(s) \leq t \leq Inv(s)$.
- Delay transition : for $s \in \mathcal{N}$, $\alpha \in E$ $s \xrightarrow{\alpha,t} s$ when $t \leq Inv(s)$.

$$
\begin{array}{l}
S ::= \epsilon \mid l : \overline{i}^n \rightarrowtail \mathcal{N} \\
\mathcal{N} ::= \overline{\mathcal{N}} \mid l : F(\mathcal{N},\mathcal{N}) \mid l : D(p, g, \mathcal{N}, \mathcal{N}) \mid \overline{\mathcal{O}}^n \rightarrowtail \mathcal{N} \mid \mathcal{H}(S) \mid l : \odot \mid l : \times \\
\mathcal{O} ::= sB \mid s(S_{entry}, S_{sub}, S_{exit}) \mid s(S_{entry}, S_{do}, S_{exit}) \mid \mathcal{J}(x_1, x_2) \mid M(x_1, g_1, \mathcal{N}) \\
B ::= \uparrow S \mid \epsilon
\end{array}
$$

Fig. 3. Syntax of State Machine Calculus (SMC).

4   Syntax

Based on the SysML textual specification standard [1], we formalize SysML state machine diagrams by developing a calculus called *State Machine Calculus* (SMC) which is proposed in Fig. 3 that offers more flexibility than the graphical notation defined in the standard. In Table 2, each state machine diagram artifact is represented formally by its related SMC term. In SMC syntax, two main syntactic concepts are defined: marked and unmarked terms. A marked term is typically used to denote a reachable configuration. A configuration is characterized by the set of tokens locations in a given term. An unmarked SMC term corresponds to the static structure of the diagram.

To support tokens we augment the "Over bar" operator with integer value n such that the $\overline{\mathcal{N}}^n$ denotes the term $\mathcal{N}$ marked with n tokens. Furthermore, we use a prefix label $l :$ for each node to uniquely reference it in the case of a backward flow connection. Particularly, labels are useful for connecting multiple incoming flows towards junction and join nodes. Let $\mathcal{L}$ be a collection of labels ranged over by $l; l_0; l_1,..$ and $\mathcal{N}$ be any node (except initial) in the SMD. We write $l : \mathcal{N}$ to denote a l-labeled state $\mathcal{N}$. It is important to note that nodes with multiple incoming edges (e.g. join and junction) are visited as many times as

Table 2. Formal Notation of SysML state Machine Artifacts

Artifact	Formal notation	Description
●→(N)	$l : i \rightarrowtail \mathcal{N}$	Initial node is activated when a diagram is invoked.
◉	$l : \odot$	Final node stops the diagram execution
✕	$l : \times$	Terminate node kills only the related token
S Entry/S_{entry} Do/S_o Exit/S_{exit} →(N)	$l : s(S_{entry}, S_{do}, S_{exit}) \rightarrowtail \mathcal{N}$	State with entry/do/exit behavior defines a state represented by a sequence of events
s:S →(N)	$l : s \uparrow S \rightarrowtail \mathcal{N}$	Call behavior state invokes a new behavior related to the state.
s Entry/S_{entry} Exit/S_{exit} →(N)	$l : s(S_{entry}, S_{sub}, S_{exit}) \rightarrowtail \mathcal{N}$	Composite State calls the set of substates that can be parallel
◇[g]{1-p}→(N) ↓[¬g]{p} (N)	$l : \mathcal{D}(p, g, \mathcal{N}, \mathcal{N})$	Choice node with convex distribution p, 1-p and guarded edges g, ¬ g
→●[g]→(N) [g₁] (N)	$l : \mathcal{M}(x, g_1, \mathcal{N}_1, y, g_2, \mathcal{N}_2)$	Junction node with static conditional branch g1, g2
▬ ↓ ↓ (N) (N)	$l : \mathcal{F}(\mathcal{N}_1, \mathcal{N}_2)$	When an incoming transition is taken to the fork pseudo-state, all the outgoing transitions are taken
▮→(N)	$l : \mathcal{J}(x) \rightarrowtail \mathcal{N}$	Join node presents the synchronization, And x is the set of input pins x= {xl, x2}.
s →(H)(N) (N)	$l : \mathcal{H}(\mathcal{N}^*, \mathcal{N})$	History pseudo-states allow a state to be interrupted and then subsequently resume its previously active state or states.

they have incoming edges. Thus, as a syntactic convention we use only a label (i.e. l) to express a SMC term if its related node is encountered already. We denote by $D(g, \mathcal{N}, \mathcal{N})$ and $D(p, g, \mathcal{N}, \mathcal{N})$ to express a non-probabilistic and a probabilistic choices, respectively.

5   Semantics

For the workflow observation on SMD, we use structural operational semantics [14] and [15] to formally describe how the computation steps of SMC atomic terms take place. An element α is the label of the event triggering state transition, x(y) inputs an object name on x and stores it in y to represent the effects of transition and τ represents a silent event. An element **t** is the time for state transition and p is a probability value such that $p \in]0, 1[$. The general form of a transition is $S \xrightarrow{t, \alpha/b(y)}_p S'$. The probability value specifies the likelihood of a given transition to occur and it is denoted by $P(S, t, \alpha, S')$ where $min \leq t \leq max$ $(max, min \in \mathbb{N})$. The case of p = 1 presents a non-probabilistic transition and it is denoted simply by $S \xrightarrow{t, \alpha} S'$. For simplicity, we denote by $S[\mathcal{N}]$ to specify $\mathcal{N}$ as a sub-term of S and by $|S|$ to denote a term S without tokens. For the call behavior case of $s \uparrow \mathcal{N}$, we denote $\mathcal{S}[s \uparrow \mathcal{N}]$ by $\mathcal{S} \uparrow_s \mathcal{N}$ and "*" is used to refers to the recent active substate in the state in case of shallow history. In the sequel, we describe the operational semantic rules of the SMC calculus.

Ax-1 $l : i \rightarrowtail \mathcal{N} \xrightarrow{L}_1 l : \bar{i} \rightarrowtail \mathcal{N}$. This axiom introduces the execution of $\mathcal{S}$ by putting a token on i.

Ax-2 $l : \bar{i} \rightarrowtail \mathcal{N} \xrightarrow{L}_1 l : i \rightarrowtail \overline{\mathcal{N}}$. This axiom propagates the token in the marked term i into its outgoing $\mathcal{N}$.

Ax-3 $\forall n > 0, m \geq 0$ $l : \overline{s^m} \rightarrowtail \mathcal{N}^n \xrightarrow{L}_1 l : \overline{s^{m+1}} \rightarrowtail \mathcal{N}^{n-1}$. This axiom propagates the token from the global marked term to s.

Ax-4 $l : \overline{s^{m+1}} \rightarrowtail \mathcal{N}^n \xrightarrow{t,\alpha/b(y)}_1 l : \overline{s^m} \rightarrowtail \overline{\mathcal{N}}^n$. When event occurs; this axiom propagates the token from the marked term s to $\mathcal{N}$ after t time units and the effect $b(y)$ inputs a name on b and stores it in y.

Ax-5 $\forall n > 0$ $l : \overline{s \uparrow \mathcal{S}^n} \rightarrowtail \mathcal{N} \xrightarrow{L}_1 l : \overline{s \uparrow \mathcal{S}^{n-1}} \rightarrowtail \mathcal{N}$. This axiom propagates the token from the global marked term to s.

Ax-6 $\dfrac{\mathcal{S}[\overline{l':\odot}] \xrightarrow{l'}_1 |\mathcal{S}|}{l : s \uparrow \mathcal{S}^n \rightarrowtail \mathcal{N} \xrightarrow{l'}_1 l : s \uparrow |\mathcal{S}|^n \rightarrowtail \overline{\mathcal{N}}}$. The derivation rule Ax-6 finishes the execution of a call behavior and moves the token to the succeeding term $\mathcal{N}$.

Ax-7 $\dfrac{s \xrightarrow{t,\alpha}_p \mathcal{S}'}{l : s \uparrow \mathcal{S}^n \rightarrowtail \mathcal{N} \xrightarrow{t,\alpha}_p l : \overline{s} \uparrow \mathcal{S'^n} \rightarrowtail \mathcal{N}}$. The derivation rules Ax-7 and Ax-8 present the effect on $\overline{s} \uparrow \mathcal{S}^n$ when $\mathcal{S}$ or $\mathcal{N}$ executes an action a with a probability p.

Ax-8 $\dfrac{\mathcal{N} \xrightarrow{t,\alpha}_1 \mathcal{N}'}{l : s \uparrow \mathcal{S}^n \rightarrowtail \mathcal{N} \xrightarrow{t,\alpha}_p l : s \uparrow \mathcal{S}^n \rightarrowtail \mathcal{N}'}$.

Ax-SUB $\dfrac{\mathcal{S}_{sub}[\overline{l':\odot}] \xrightarrow{l'}_1 |\mathcal{S}_{sub}|}{l : s(\mathcal{S}_{entry}, \overline{\mathcal{S}_{sub}}, \mathcal{S}_{exit}) \rightarrowtail \mathcal{N} \xrightarrow{l'}_1 l : s(\mathcal{S}_{entry}, |\mathcal{S}_{sub}|, \overline{\mathcal{S}_{exit}}) \rightarrowtail \mathcal{N}}$. The derivation rule Ax-SUB finishes the execution of "Sub" behavior and moves the token to the EXIT behavior.

Ax-HIST $l : \overline{\mathcal{N}} \rightarrowtail l' : \mathcal{H}(\mathcal{S}^*, \mathcal{S})^n \xrightarrow{L}_1 l : \mathcal{N} \rightarrowtail l' : \mathcal{H}(\overline{\mathcal{S}}, \mathcal{S})^n$. Ax-HIST is a shallow history; backs to the most recent active substate of its containing state.

FRK-1 $\forall n > 0$ $l : \overline{F(\mathcal{N}_1, \mathcal{N}_2)}^n \xrightarrow{L}_1 l : \overline{F(\mathcal{N}_1, \mathcal{N}_2)}^{n-1}$. The FRK-1 axiom shows the multiplicity of the arriving tokens according to the outgoing sub-terms.

FRK-2 $\dfrac{\mathcal{N}_1 \xrightarrow{t,\alpha} \mathcal{N}_1'}{l : F(\mathcal{N}_1, \mathcal{N}_2) \xrightarrow{t,\alpha} l : F(\mathcal{N}_1', \mathcal{N}_2)}$. The FRK-2 derivation rule illustrates the changes on a fork term when its outgoing trigger a state.

CHOICE-1 $\forall n > 0$ $l : \overline{D(g, \mathcal{N}_1, \mathcal{N}_2)}^n \xrightarrow{g,\alpha} l : \overline{D(g, \overline{\mathcal{N}_1}, \mathcal{N}_2)}^{n-1}$. The axiom CHOICE-1 describes a non-probabilistic choice where a token flows through the edge satisfying its guard.

CHOICE-2 $\forall n > 0$ $l : \overline{D(p, g, \mathcal{N}_1, \mathcal{N}_2)}^n \xrightarrow{g,\alpha}_p l : \overline{D(p, g, \overline{\mathcal{N}_1}, \mathcal{N}_2)}^{n-1}$. The axiom CHOICE-2 describes a probabilistic decision where a token flows through the edge satisfying its guard with probability p.

MRG-1 $l : \overline{\mathcal{N}} \rightarrowtail l' : M(x, g_1, \mathcal{N}_1, y, g_2, \mathcal{N}_2)^n \xrightarrow{L}_1 l : \mathcal{N} \rightarrowtail l' : M(\overline{x}, g_1, \mathcal{N}_1, y, g_2, \mathcal{N}_2)^n$. MRG-1 is a transition with a probability of value 1 to put a token coming from the sub-term $\mathcal{N}$ on a junction labeled by l.

MRG-2 $l : \overline{l' : M(\overline{x}, g_1, \mathcal{N}_1, \overline{y}, g_2, \mathcal{N}_2)}^n \xrightarrow{l,g_1}_1 l : \overline{l' : M(x, g_1, \overline{\mathcal{N}_1}, \overline{y}, g_2, \mathcal{N}_2)}^n$. MRG-2 is a transition with a probability of value 1 to present a token flowing from a junction labeled by l to the sub-term $\mathcal{N}_1$ an the guard g_1 is true.

MRG-3 $l : \mathcal{S}[l' : M(x, g_1, \mathcal{N}_1, y, g_2, \mathcal{N}_2), \overline{l_x}] \xrightarrow{L} l : \mathcal{S}[l' : M(\overline{x}, g_1, \mathcal{N}_1, y, g_2, \mathcal{N}_2), l_x]$. MRG-3 shows the junction enabled when token arrived at one of its pins.

JOIN-1 $l : \overline{\mathcal{N} \rightarrowtail l' : J(x,y)}^n \xrightarrow{l}_1 l : \overline{\mathcal{N} \rightarrowtail l' : J(\overline{x},y)}^n$. JOIN-1 represents a transition with a probability of value 1 to activate the pin x in a join labeled by l'.

JOIN-2 $l : \overline{l' : J(\overline{x},\overline{y}) \rightarrowtail \mathcal{N}}^n \xrightarrow{\tau} l : \overline{l' : J(x,y) \rightarrowtail \mathcal{N}}^n$. JOIN-2 represents a transition with a probability of value 1 to move a token in join to the sub-term $\mathcal{N}$.

JOIN-3 $l : \mathcal{S}[l' : J(x,y) \rightarrowtail \mathcal{N}, \overline{l_x}] \xrightarrow{\tau} l : \mathcal{S}[l' : J(\overline{x},y) \rightarrowtail \mathcal{N}, l_x]$. JOIN-3 shows the join input enabled when token arrived at one of its pins.

FFIN $\mathcal{S}[l : \overline{\times}] \xrightarrow{l} \mathcal{S}[l : \times]$. This axiom states that if the sub-term $l : \times$ is reached in $\mathcal{S}$ then a transition of probability one is enabled to produce a term describing the termination of a flow.

AFIN $\mathcal{S}[l : \overline{\odot}] \xrightarrow{l} |\mathcal{A}|$. This axiom states that if the sub-term $l : \odot$ is reached then no action is taken later by destroying all tokens.

6   PRISM Formalization

In this section, our formalization focus on probabilistic timed automata (PTA) that extends the standard probabilistic automata (PA). The PRISM model checker supports the PTA with the ability to model real-time behavior by adding real-valued clocks (i.e. clocks variable) which increases with time and can be reset (i.e. updated).

A Timed Probabilistic System (TPS) that represents a PRISM program (P) is composed of a set of "m" modules ($m > 0$). The state of each module is defined by the evaluation of its local variables V_L. The global state of the system is defined as the evaluation of local and global variables: $V = V_L \cup V_G$. The behavior of each module is described as a set of statements in the form of: $[act]guard \rightarrow p_1 : u_1.. + p_n : u_n$, which means, for the action act if the guard g is true, then, an update u_i is enabled with a probability p_i. The update u_i is a set of evaluated variables expressed as conjunction of assignments ($V'_j = val_j$)&..&($V'_k = val_k$) where $V_j \in V_L \cup V_G$ and val_j are values evaluated via expressions denoted by $eval$, eval: $V \rightarrow \mathbb{R} \cup \{True, False\}$. The formal definition of a command is given in Definition 2.

Definition 2. A PRISM command is a tuple c $= < $ a, g, u $>$.

- act is an action label.
- guard is a predicate over V.
- u $= \{(p_i, u_i)\}$ $\exists m > 1, i < m,$ $0 < p_i < 1, \sum_i^m p_i = 1$ and u $= \{(v, eval(v)) : v \in V_l\}$.

The set of commands are associated with modules that are parts of a system and it definition is given in Definition 3.

Definition 3. A PRISM module is tuple M $= <V_l, I_l, Inv, C>$, where:

- V_l is a set of local variable associated with a module,
- Inv is a time constraint of the form $v_l \bowtie d\backslash \bowtie \in \{\leq, \geq\}$ and $d \in \mathbb{N}$,
- I_l is the initial value of V_l.
- C$= \{c_i, 0 < i \leq k\}$ is a set of commands that define the module behavior.

To describe the composition between different modules, PRISM uses CSP communication sequential process operators [10] such as Synchronization, Interleaving, Parallel Interface, Hiding and Renaming. Definition 4 provides a formal definition of PRISM system.

Definition 4. A PRISM system is tuple P = <V, I_g, exp, M, CSPexp>, where:

- V = $V_g \coprod_{(i=1)}^{m} V_{li}$ is the union of a set local and global variables.
- I_g is initial values of global variables.
- exp is a set of global logic operators: - , $*, /, +, -, <, <=, >=, >, =, ! =, !, \&,$ | , <=> , => , ? (condition evaluation: condition ? a : b means "if condition is true then a else b").
- M is a set of modules composing a System.
- CSPexp is CSP algebraic expression:
  - M1 || M2 : alphabetised parallel composition of modules M1 and M2 (synchronising on only actions appearing in both M1 and M2)
  - M1 ||| M2 : asynchronous parallel composition of M1 and M2 (fully interleaved, no synchronisation)
  - M1 |[a,b,...]| M2 : restricted parallel composition of modules M1 and M2 (synchronising only on actions from the set a, b,...)
  - M $/\{a, b, ...\}$: hiding of actions a, b, ... in module M
  - M $\{a \leftarrow b, c \leftarrow d, ...\}$: renaming of actions a to b, c to d, etc.

6.1 PRISM Semantics

The probabilistic timed automata of a PRISM program $\mathscr{P}$ is based on the atomic semantics of a command C denoted by [[c]]. The latter is a set of transitions defined as follows: $[[c]] = \{(s, a, \mu) | s \models g\}$ where μ is a distribution over S such that $\mu(s, v_t) = \{|0 \le p_i \le 1, v \in V, s'(v) = eval(V)|\}$. The stepwise behavior of PRISM is described by the operational semantic as follows:

INIT $\langle V_i, init(V_i) \rangle \rightarrow \langle V_i([[init(V_i)]]), -\rangle$INIT initializes variables. For a module M_i, init returns the initial value of the local variable $v_i \in V_i$.

LOOP $\langle V_i, -\rangle \rightarrow \langle V_i \rangle$ This axiom presents a loop in a state without changing variables evaluations. It can be applied to avoid a deadlock.

UPDATE $\langle V_i, v_i' = eval(V) \rangle \rightarrow \langle V_i([[v_i]]) \rangle$ UPDATE axiom describes the execution of a simple assignment for a given variable v_i. Its evaluation is updated in V_i of M_i.

CNJ-UPD $\langle V, v_i' = eval(V) \wedge v_j' = eval(V) \rangle \rightarrow \langle V([[v_i]], [[v_j]]) \rangle$ CNJ-UPD implements the conjunction of a set of assignments.

PRB-UPD1 $\langle V_i, p : v_i' = eval(V) \rangle \rightarrow_p \langle V_i([[v_i]]) \rangle$ $0 < p < 1$.

PRB-UPD2 $\langle V, p : v_i' = eval(V) \wedge v_j' = eval(V) \rangle \rightarrow_p \langle V([[v_i]], [[v_j]]) \rangle$ $0 < p < 1$ PRB-UPD1 and PRB-UPD2 describe probabilistic updates.

ENB-CMD1 $\dfrac{V \models g, Inv(V)}{\langle V, M([a]g \rightarrow p_i:u_i)) \rangle \rightarrow \mu}$ ENB-CMD1 enables the execution of a probabilistic command.

ENB-CMD2 $\dfrac{V \models g, Inv(V) \quad V \not\models g', Inv'(V)}{\langle V, [a]g \rightarrow u; [a']g' \rightarrow u' \rangle \xrightarrow{a} \langle V([[u]]), [a']g' \rightarrow u' \rangle}$ ENB-CMD2 enables the execution of a command in a module.

ENB-CMD3 $\dfrac{V\models g, Inv(V) \quad V\models g', Inv'(V)}{\langle V,[a]g\rightarrow u;[a']g'\rightarrow u'\rangle \xrightarrow{a} \langle V([[u]]),[a']g'\rightarrow u'\rangle}$ ENB-CMD3 solves the non-determinism in a module by following a policy.

SYNC $\dfrac{\langle V_i, c_i\rangle \xrightarrow{a} \mu_i \quad \langle V_j, c_j\rangle \xrightarrow{a} \mu_j}{\langle V_i \cup V_j, M_i || M_j\rangle \xrightarrow{a} \mu_i \cdot \mu_j}$ SYNC derivation rule permits the synchronization between modules on a given action a.

INTERL $\dfrac{\langle V_i, M_i(c_i)\rangle \xrightarrow{a_j} \mu}{\langle V, M_i || \ | M_j\rangle \xrightarrow{a_j} \mu}$ INTERL derivation rule describes the interleaving between modules.

6.2 Property Specification in PRISM

In order to perform model-checking, a property should be specified. We selected PCTL to express such property. Formally, its syntax is given by the following BNF grammar:

$\varphi ::= true \mid ap \mid \varphi \wedge \varphi \mid \neg\varphi \mid P_{\bowtie p}[\psi]$,

$\psi ::= \varphi \cup^{\leq k} \varphi \mid \varphi \cup \varphi$,

Where "ap" is an atomic proposition, P is a probabilistic operator. $p \in [0, 1]$ and "$\bowtie$"$\in <, \leq, >, \geq$. Bound until means that a state satisfying $\varphi 2$ is eventually reached and that, at every time-instant prior to that, $\varphi 1$ is satisfied. The time-bounded variant has the same meaning, where the occurrence of $\varphi 2$ occur within time k. To specify the satisfaction relation of a PCTL formula a class of adversaries (Adv) has been defined [16] to solve the nondeterminism decision.

7 The Verification Approach

This section describes the transformation of SysML state machine diagrams S into a PTA written in PRISM input language. Listing. 1 propose a mapping function Γ that takes as input the SMC terms defined in Table 2 to produce a PRISM commands. The action label of a command is the label of its related term n. The guard of this command depends on how the term is activated and minimal clock valuation. The flag related to the term is its label l that is initialized to false except for the initial node it is true which conforms to the premise of the SMC rule **Ax-1**. The updates of the command deactivate the propositions of the term, activate that ones related to its successors, reset the clock variable of its successors. The functions $L(n)$, $Start(S_i)$ and $E(S_i)$, return the label of the initial term n , the initial and final term of S_i, respectively. Each PRISM code generated for each state machine diagram starts from module S_i and terminates with *endmodule*. The call of substates transitions (line 30 and 31) *synchronize* with the initial (line 42) and the final (line 44) transition, respectively to enable the internal transitions of substate. The final transition (line- 38) reset the local variables to false. However, the PTA model in PRISM model checker does not support the shared variables. To overcome, we use the implication operator to set the proposition to true as shown in line 31 and line 42. The clock variable x is used as guarded condition for state successors activation. In line 34, the next node is activated when the clock $x >= min$ and $x <= max$ defined in the invariant clause within the module as follows:

$$\textbf{invariant} \quad (l = true) \Rightarrow (x \leq max) \quad \textbf{endinvariant}$$

```
1   Γ : S → 𝒫
2   Γ(S) = ∀n ∈ S, L(n == i) = true, L(n ≠ i) = false,  Case n of
3   [l : i → 𝒩] ⇒  // the clock x is reset to 0
4   in  {[l]l → (l' = false)&(L(𝒩)' = true)&(x' = 0)}∪Γ(𝒩);  end
5   [l : M(x, y, g₁, N₁, g₂, N₂)] ⇒
6   in  {[lₓ]lₓ → (l'ₓ = false)&(l_{g1})' = true)}∪ Γ(𝒩₁) ∪ Γ(𝒩₂)∪
7   {[l_y]l_y → (l'_y = false)&(l'_{g2} = true)}∪
8   {[l_{g1}]l_{g1} & g1 → (l'_{g1} = false)&L(𝒩₁)' = true) & (x' = 0)}∪
9   {[l_{g2}]l_{g2} & g2 → (l'_{g2} = false) & L(𝒩₂)' = true) & (x' = 0)}
10  end
11  [l : J(x, y) → 𝒩] ⇒
12  in  {[l]lₓ ∧ l_y → (l'ₓ = false)&(l'_y = false)&(L(𝒩)' = true)&(x' = 0)}  end
13  [l : F(𝒩₁, 𝒩₂)] ⇒
14  in  {[l]l → (l' = false)&(L(𝒩₁)' = true)&(L(𝒩₂)' = true)&(x'₁ = 0)&(x'₂ = 0)}∪Γ(𝒩₁) ∪ Γ(𝒩₂)
15  end
16  [l : D(p, g, 𝒩₁, 𝒩₂)] ⇒
17  Case(p) of
18  ]0, 1[  ⇒
19  in  {[l]l → p : (l' = false)&(l'_g = true) + (1 − p) : (l' = false)&(l'_{¬g} = false)}∪Γ(𝒩₁) ∪ Γ(𝒩₂)∪
20  {[l_g]l_g → (l'_g = false) & (L(𝒩₁)' = true) & (x'₁ = 0)}
21  {[l_{¬g}]l_{¬g} → (l'_{¬g} = false)& (L(𝒩₂)' = true) & (x'₂ = 0)}  end
22  Otherwise ⇒
23  in  {[l]l → (l' = false)&(l'_g = true)}∪{ [l]l → (l' = false) & (l'_{¬g} = true)}∪Γ(𝒩₁) ∪ Γ(𝒩₂)∪
24  {[l_g]l_g → (l'_g = false) & L(𝒩₁)' = true)&(x'₁ = 0)}∪
25  {[l_{¬g}]l_{¬g} → (l'_{¬g} = false)& L(𝒩₂)' = true)&(x'₂ = 0)}  end
26  [l : sB →ᵗ 𝒩] ⇒
27  Case(B) of
28  ↑ Sᵢ  ⇒
29  in
30  {[l]l → (l' = false)}∪Γ(𝒩)∪
31  {[L(E(Sᵢ))]((L(𝒩) = false) ⇒ true) → (L(𝒩)' = true)&(x' = 0)}∪Γ'(Sᵢ)
32  end
33  ε ⇒  // minimal time for state transition
34  in  {[l]l & (t >= min) → (l' = false) & (L(𝒩)' = true) & (x' = 0)}end
35  [l : ×] ⇒
36  in  [l]l → (l' = false)  ;  end
37  [l : ⊙] ⇒
38  in  [l]l → & _{l∈ℒ}(L(𝒩)' = false);  end
39  Γ' : S → P
40  Γ(Sᵢ) = ∀m ∈ Sᵢ, L(m) = false,
41  [l : i → 𝒩] ⇒
42  in  {[l] ((L(Start(Sᵢ)) = false) => true) → (L(Start(Sᵢ))' = true)} ∪
43  {[L(Start(Sᵢ))]  L(Start(Sᵢ)) → (L(Start(Sᵢ))' = false) & (L(𝒩)' = true) }∪Γ(𝒩);  end
44  [l : ⊙] ⇒ in  [L(E(Sᵢ))]L(E(Sᵢ)) → (L(E(Sᵢ))' = false);  end
```

Listing 1. PRSIM Commands Generation

8   The Transformation Soundness

Our aim is to prove the soundness of the transformation algorithm Γ by showing that the proposed algorithm preserves the satisfiability of PCTL properties. Let S be a SMC term and M_S is its corresponding PTA constructed by the SMD operational semantics denoted by S such that $\mathcal{X}(S) = M_S$. For the program $\mathscr{P}$ resulting after transformation rules, Let M_p its corresponding PTA constructed

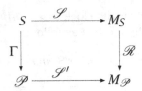

Fig. 4. The transformation soundness.

by PRISM operational semantics denoted $\mathcal{X}'$ such that $\mathcal{X}'(\mathscr{P}) = M_{\mathscr{P}}$. As illustrated in Fig. 4, proving the soundness of $\varGamma$ algorithm is to find the adequate relation $\mathcal{R}$ between M_S and $M_{\mathscr{P}}$.

To define the relation $M_S \mathcal{R} M_{\mathscr{P}}$, we have to establish a step by step correspondence between M_S and $M_{\mathscr{P}}$. First, we introduce the notion of the timed probabilistic bisimulation relation [6,19] in Definitions 6 and 7. This relation is based on the probabilistic equivalence relation $\mathcal{R}$ defined in Definition 5 where $\delta/\mathcal{R}$ denotes the quotient space of δ with respect to $\mathcal{R}$ and $\equiv_{\mathcal{R}}$ is the lifting of $\mathcal{R}$ to a probabilistic space.

Definition 5 (The equivalence $\equiv_{\mathcal{R}}$). If $\mathcal{R}$ is an equivalence on δ, then the induced equivalence $\equiv_{\mathcal{R}}$ on $\mathrm{Dist}(\delta \times 2^x)$ is given by: $\mu_{\equiv_{\mathcal{R}}} \mu'$ iff $\mu(\delta, d) \equiv_{\mathcal{R}} \mu(\delta, d')$.

Definition 6 (Timed Probabilistic Bisimulation Relation). A binary relation $\mathcal{R}$ over the set of states of PTAs is timed bisimulation iff whenever $s_1 \mathcal{R} s_2$, α is an event and d is a delay:

- if $s_1 \xrightarrow{d,\alpha} \mu(s_1, d)$ there is a transition $s_2 \xrightarrow{d',\alpha} \mu(s_2, d')$, such that $s_1 \mathcal{R} s_2$. The delay d can be different from d';
- two states s, s' are time probabilistic bisimilar, written $s \sim s'$, iff there is a timed probabilistic bisimulation related to them.

Definition 7 (Timed Probabilistic Bisimulation of PTAs). Probabilistic Timed automata A_1 and A_2 are timed probabilistic bisimilar denoted $(A \sim A')$ iff their initial states in the union of the probabilistic timed transition systems $\mathrm{T}(A_1)$ and $\mathrm{T}(A_2)$ generated by A_1 and A_2 are timed probabilistic bisimilar.

For our proof, we stipulate herein the mapping relation $\mathcal{R}$ denoted by $M_S \mathcal{R} M_P$ between a SMC term $\mathcal{S}$ and its corresponding PRISM term $\mathscr{P}$.

Definition 11 (Mapping Relation). The relation $M_S \mathcal{R} M_{\mathscr{P}}$ between a SMC term $\mathcal{S}$ and a PRISM term $\mathscr{P}$ such that $\varGamma(\mathcal{S}) = \mathscr{P}$ is a timed probabilistic bisimulation relation.

Finally, proving that $\varGamma$ is sound means showing the existence of a timed probabilistic bisimulation between M_S and $M_{\mathscr{P}}$.

Lemma 1 (Soundness). The mapping algorithm $\varGamma$ is sound, i.e. $M_S \sim M_{\mathscr{P}}$.

Proof 1: We prove $M_S \sim M_{\mathscr{P}}$ by following a structural induction on SMC terms and their related PRISM terms. For that, let $e_1, e_1' \in \mathcal{X}_S$ and $e_2, e_2' \in \mathcal{X}_{\mathscr{P}}$. We distinguish the following cases where $L(s)$ takes different values:

1. $L(e_1) = l : \overline{x} \rightarrowtail \mathcal{N}$ such as $x = \{i, s\} \Longrightarrow \exists e_1 \xrightarrow{d,\alpha}_1 e_1'$, $L(e_1') = l : x \rightarrowtail \overline{\mathcal{N}}$.
   For $L(e_2) = \Gamma(L(e_1))$, we have $L(e_2) = \langle L(x), \neg L(\mathcal{N}) \rangle$ then $\exists e_2 \xrightarrow{d',\alpha}_1 e_2'$ where $L(e_2') = \langle \neg L(x), L(\mathcal{N}) \rangle$.

2. $L(e_1) = l : \overline{D(g_1, \mathcal{N}_1, \mathcal{N}_2)}^n$ then $\exists e_1 \xrightarrow{g_1,\alpha}_1 e_1'$, $L(e_1') = l : \overline{D(g_1, \mathcal{N}_1, \mathcal{N}_2)}^{n-1}$.
   For $L(e_2) = \Gamma(L(e_1))$, we have $L(e_2) = \langle l, \neg l_{\mathcal{N}_1}, \neg l_{\mathcal{N}_2} \rangle$ then $\exists e_2 \xrightarrow{g_1,\alpha}_1 s_2'$ where $L(e_2') = \langle \neg l, l_{\mathcal{N}_1}, \neg l_{\mathcal{N}_2} \rangle$.

3. $L(e_1) = l : \overline{\odot}$ then $\exists e_1 \xrightarrow{\alpha}_1 e_1'$, $L(e_1') = l : \odot$. For $L(e_2) = \Gamma(L(e_1))$, we have $L(e_2) = \langle l \rangle$ then $\exists e_2 \xrightarrow{\alpha}_1 e_2'$ where $\forall l_i \in \mathcal{L} : L(e_2') = \langle \neg l_i \rangle$.

From the obtained results, we found that $\mu(e_1, d) = \mu(e_2, d') = 1$ then $e_1 \sim e_2$. In addition, the unique initial state of M_S is always corresponding to the unique initial state in $M_{\mathscr{P}}$. By studying all SMC terms, we find that $M_S \sim M_{\mathscr{P}}$, which confirms that Lemma 1 holds.

In the following, we show that the mapping relation preserves the satisfiability of PCTL properties. This means, if a PCTL property is satisfied in the resulting model by a mapped function Γ then it is satisfied by the original one.

Proposition 1 (PCTL Preservation). For two PTAs M_S and $M_{\mathscr{P}}$ such that $\Gamma(S) = \mathscr{P}$ where $M_S \sim M_{\mathscr{P}}$. For a PCTL property ϕ, then: $(M_S \vDash \phi) \iff (M_{\mathscr{P}} \vDash \phi)$.

Proof 2: The preservation of PCTL properties is proved by induction on the PCTL structure and its semantics. Since $M_S \sim M_{\mathscr{P}}$ and by relying to the semantics of each PCTL operator $\zeta \in \{U, U^{\leq k}, F, P_{\bowtie p}\}$, we find that $(M_S \vDash \zeta) \iff (M_{\mathscr{P}} \vDash \zeta)$ which means: $(M_S \vDash \phi) \iff (M_{\mathscr{P}} \vDash \phi)$.

9   Case Study

In the following, we present a case study [7] describing an automated teller machine (ATM). We perform the verification of this design with respect to predefined properties including time constraints and [2] is the corresponding generated code.

The ATM interacts with a potential customer (user) via a specific interface and communicates with the bank over an appropriate communication link. A user that requests a service from the ATM has to insert an ATM card and enter a personal identification number (PIN). The card number and the PIN need to be sent to the bank for validation. If the credentials of the customer are not valid, the card will be ejected. Otherwise, the customer will be able to carry out one or more transactions (e.g., cash advance or bill payment). The card will be retained in the ATM machine

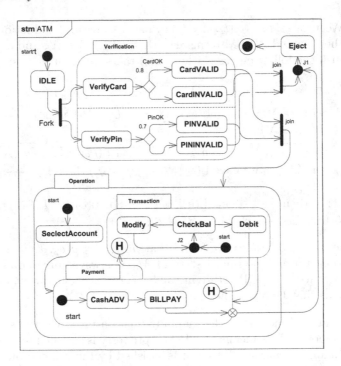

Fig. 5. ATM state machine diagram

during the customers interaction until the customer wishes for no further service. Figure 5 shows the SysML state machine diagram of the ATM system.

ATM state machine encloses four substates: IDLE, Verification, Eject, and Operation. The IDLE is the default initial substate of the top state. The Verification state represents the verification of the cards validness and authorization. VerifiyCard and VerifyPin substates have interval time]3s, 5s[,]4s, 5s[respectively (s for seconds). The SMD could let time progress while remaining in VerifiyCard and VerifyPin states until 5 seconds and the transition is triggered or the transition is triggered just after both states minimal time is attained (after time progress). The probability to get pin and card validated is 0.7 and 0.8, respectively. The Eject state depicts the phase of termination of the users transaction. The Operation state is a composite state that capture several functions related to banking operations. These are the *Selectaccount*, *Payment*, and *Transaction*. When Selectaccount is active, and the user selects an account, the next transition is enabled and the *Payment* is entered. The Payment state has two substates; for cash advancing and bill payment. It represents a two-item menu. Finally, the Transaction state captures the transaction phase and includes three substates: *CheckBal* for checking the balance, *Modify* for modifying the amount, if necessary, and *Debit* for debiting the account. Each one of the Payment and Transaction states contains a shallow history pseudostate. If a transition targeting a shallow history pseudostate is fired, the most recently active sub-state in the composite state containing the history connector is activated.

In order to check the correctness of the ATM system, we propose to verify two functional requirements at specific time or at different time stamps k. They are expressed in PCTL as follows:

1. The maximum probability value that the modification occurs during the Bill Payment after k=5 time units: $Pmax =?[F^{\leq k}(BillPAY \ \& \ Modify))]$.
2. The maximum probability value to get the card and pin validated after k time units: $Pmax =?[F^{\leq k}(CardVALID \ \& \ PinVALID \ )]$.

The maximum probability value for the modification that occurs during the Bill payment is equal to 0.3 when k equal to 5 (time units). The verification results of the second property are shown in Fig. 6. After 4 time units (seconds), the verification results converge to 0.3. However, the verification time for the first property took 246.3 s due to the state explosion during the model checking.

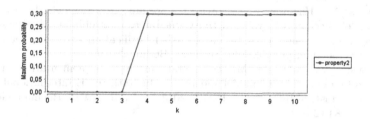

Fig. 6. Property2

10   Conclusion

In this paper, we presented a formal verification approach of probabilistic systems modeled by using SysML state machine diagram. For this purpose, the approach maps state machine into the input language of the probabilistic model checker PRISM. We proposed a calculus dedicated to this diagram that captures precisely their underlying semantics. In addition, we formalized PRISM language by showing its semantics. Thus, we proved the soundness of our proposed approach by defining adequately the relation between the semantics of the mapped diagrams and the resulting PRISM models. In addition, we proved the preservation of the satisfiability of PCTL properties. Finally, we have shown the effectiveness of our approach by applying it on a case study representing an ATM state machine diagram where time and probability are evaluated using PCTL properties. The presented work can be extended in the following two directions. First, we want to transform our behavioral diagram to its equivalent HDL (hardware description language) code for RTL verification. Second, we want to validate our approach on different real case studies.

References

1. OMG Systems Modeling Language (Object Management Group SysML). O. M. Group (Ed.) (2012)
2. Abdelhakim, B.: State machine diagram verification (2015). https://github.com/ gitmodelcheking/ATM/blob/master/ATM.nm
3. Ando, T., Yatsu, H., Kong, W., Hisazumi, K., Fukuda, A.: Formalization and model checking of SysML state machine diagrams by CSP#. In: Murgante, B., Misra, S., Carlini, M., Torre, C.M., Nguyen, H.-Q., Taniar, D., Apduhan, B.O., Gervasi, O. (eds.) ICCSA 2013, Part III. LNCS, vol. 7973, pp. 114–127. Springer, Heidelberg (2013)
4. Baier, C., Katoen, J.P.: Principles of Model Checking (Representation and Mind Series). The MIT Press, Cambridge (2008)
5. Behrmann, G., David, A., Larsen, K.G.: A tutorial on UPPAAL. In: Bernardo, M., Corradini, F. (eds.) SFM-RT 2004. LNCS, vol. 3185, pp. 200–236. Springer, Heidelberg (2004)
6. Ben-Menachem, M.: Reactive systems: modelling, specification and verification. SIGSOFT Softw. Eng. Notes 35(4), 34–35 (2010)
7. Debbabi, M., Hassane, F., Jarraya, Y., Soeanu, A., Alawneh, L.: Probabilistic model checking of SysML activity diagrams. In: Debbabi, M., Hassane, F., Jarraya, Y., Soeanu, A., Alawneh, L. (eds.) Verification and Validation in Systems Engineering, pp. 153–166. Springer, Berlin (2010)
8. Doligalski, M., Adamski, M.: UML state machine implementation in FPGA devices by means of dual model and verilog. In: 11th IEEE International Conference on Industrial Informatics, INDIN 2013, 29–31 July 2013, Bochum, Germany, pp. 177–184 (2013)
9. Gajski, D.D., Abdi, S., Gerstlauer, A., Schirner, G.: Embedded System Design: Modeling, Synthesis and Verification, 1st edn. Springer Publishing Company Incorporated, New York (2009)
10. Hoare, C.A.R.: Communicating Sequential Processes. Prentice-Hall Inc., Upper Saddle River (1985)
11. Huang, X., Sun, Q., Li, J., Pan, M., Zhang, T.: An MDE-based approach to the verification of SysML state machine diagram. In: Proceedings of the Fourth Asia-Pacific Symposium on Internetware, Internetware 2012, pp. 9:1–9:7. ACM, New York (2012)
12. Kaliappan, P.S., König, H., Kaliappan, V.K.: Designing and verifying communication protocols using model driven architecture and spin model checker. In: International Conference on Computer Science and Software Engineering, CSSE 2008, Volume 2: Software Engineering, 12–14 December 2008, Wuhan, China, pp. 227–230 (2008)
13. Mallet, F., de Simone, R.: MARTE: a profile for RT/E systems modeling, analysis and simulation? In: Proceedings of the 1st International Conference on Simulation Tools and Techniques for Communications, Networks and Systems & Workshops, SimuTools 2008, 3–7 March 2008, Marseille, France, p. 43 (2008)
14. Milner, R.: Communicating and Mobile Systems: The π-calculus. Cambridge University Press, New York (1999)
15. Norman, G., Palamidessi, C., Parker, D., Wu, P.: Model checking the probabilistic π-calculus. In: Proceedings of the 4th International Conference on Quantitative Evaluation of Systems (QEST 2007), pp. 169–178. IEEE Computer Society (2007)

16. Norman, G., Parker, D., Sproston, J.: Model checking for probabilistic timed automata. Form. Methods Syst. Des. **43**(2), 164–190 (2013)
17. Ouchani, S., Mohamed, O., Debbabi, M.: A probabilistic verification framework of sysml activity diagrams. In: IEEE 12th International Conference on Intelligent Software Methodologies, Tools and Techniques (SoMeT), vol. 246, pp. 165–170, September 2013
18. Pajic, M., Jiang, Z., Lee, I., Sokolsky, O., Mangharam, R.: From verification to implementation: a model translation tool and a pacemaker case study, pp. 173–184 (2012)
19. Segala, R.: A compositional trace-based semantics for probabilistic automata. In: Lee, I., Smolka, S. (eds.) CONCUR '95: Concurrency Theory. Lecture Notes in Computer Science, vol. 962, pp. 234–248. Springer, Heidelberg (1995)
20. Sun, J., Liu, Y., Dong, J.: Model checking CSP revisited: introducing a process analysis toolkit. In: Margaria, T., Steffen, B. (eds.) ISoLA 2008. Communications in Computer and Information Science, vol. 17, pp. 307–322. Springer, Heidelberg (2008)

HMAC Authentication Mechanisms in a Grid Computing Environment Using Gridsim Toolkit

Saiful Adli Ismail[1(✉)], Md Asri Ngadi[2], Johan Mohd Sharif[2], Nazri Kama[1], and Othman Mohd Yusop[1]

[1] Advanced Informatics School, Universiti Teknologi Malaysia,
Jalan Sultan Yahya Petra, 54100 Kuala Lumpur, Malaysia
{saifuladli,mdnazri,othmanyusop}@utm.my
[2] Faculty of Computing, Universiti Teknologi Malaysia,
81310 UTM Skudai, Johor, Malaysia
{dr.asri,johan}@utm.my

Abstract. Recently the authentication of grid computing environment has been to secure the security of local and remote entities in the surrounding. The existing authentication mechanisms mostly use public key infrastructure (PKI), but the potential PKI vulnerability and implementation constraints are still cannot be a void. In order to satisfy the security needs of grid computing environment, this paper proposes an authentication mechanism using HMAC (a hash, MAC) to secure the user identification that bears the characteristic of public key replacement attack resistance, which run the experiment in the GridSim toolkit simulator.

Keywords: HMAC · Authentication · GridSim

1 Introduction

The authentication protocols based on symmetric cryptography need to store pre-shared keys between the communication entities. Most Certificate authority (CA) in a traditional public key cryptosystem (PKC) has to store large amounts of public key certificates, real-time public key certificate has to be transmitted and stored in the signature verifying process, which will raise unnecessary waste of bandwidth and time delay. In addition, identity-based authentication protocol does not demand to store big quantities of public key credentials, but key escrow becomes an inevitable problem, because the user's private key is generated by the key generation center (KGC).

To defeat the aforesaid problem, Al-Riyami et al. [1] proposed certificateless public key cryptosystem (CL-PKC) in 2003. The KGC generates user's partial private key instead of whole private keys. Many certificateless signature schemes [2–8] have been proposed, but some of them [2–8] suffer from the public key replacement attack, the other certificate signature schemes have short signature length and can provide higher computational efficiency [9]. Grounded along the design idea of little signature, we propose an authentication mechanism that bears the characteristics of public key

© Springer International Publishing Switzerland 2015
H. Fujita and G. Guizzi (Eds.): SoMeT 2015, CCIS 532, pp. 442–452, 2015.
DOI: 10.1007/978-3-319-22689-7_34

replacement attack resistance as well as high computational efficiency. The new mechanisms provide mutual authentication and non-repudiation.

2   Related Work

In 1984 Adi Shamir [10] introduced the concept of Identity based Cryptography (IBC) and offered a signature scheme. After 17 years, Boneh and Fanklin [11] in 2001 have proposed IBE from the Weil pairing which is more secure and practical. In 2002 Gentry and Silverberg [12] proposed hierarchical IBC scheme and signature schemes. By default, authentication of users in the architecture of grid computing is using PKI certificates where weaknesses in the single point of CA server failure or compromise, verification process, change and confirms the validity of the certificate that the certificate is required, and the cost is very high. Certificate management is very complex and throws a poor scalability, which determines the number of sessions of protocol 2 in GSI [13, 14]. Thus, the evolution of the use of IBC/PKI in a grid computing architecture is introduced by Lim, H.W. [15] in 2004 as an appropriate hierarchical IBC in grid environment. In the same year Moa, W. [16] introduced the Identity-based non-interactive authentication framework for grid computing where, this framework is a certificate-free and show significant performance improvement.

   In 2005, Lim, H.W., and Robshaw [16] propose hybrid approach combining IBC at the user level and PKI above the user level. This approach resolves the key escrow, but lose non-interactive authentication and certificate-free. In 2007 Chen, L., et al. [11] revisit grid security infrastructure (GSI) in the GT2 and improved the GSI architecture and protocol by proposing an alternative authentication framework. The framework proposes by Chen, L., is still using certificate to do the authentication. Again in 2007 Li, H., et al. [7] has proposed identity-based architecture for grid (IBAG) and identity- based authentication protocol. Later in 2008 Wenbo, Z., et al. [12] proposed identity-based signcryption scheme to meet cross-domain authentication. However, the architecture proposed and authentication mechanism is still not clear on how it to be implemented and the certificate authority (CA) is still not disappear thoroughly. In this paper, we present our work on introducing HMAC authentication mechanisms to secured user identification into the Gridsim simulation toolkit.

3   GridSim Architecture and Component

The GridSim architecture with a new DataGrid layer has been mentioned by Sulistio in [17] is shown in Fig. 1. GridSim is based on SimJava2 [18], a general-purpose discrete-event simulation software system implemented in Java. Therefore, SimJava2 manages the first layer at the bottom of Fig. 1 for handling the interaction or events among GridSim component.

   All components in GridSim communicate with each other through message-passing operations defined by SimJava. The second layer models the core elements of the distributed infrastructure, namely Grid resources such as clusters, storage repositories, and network links. These core components are utterly indispensable to create

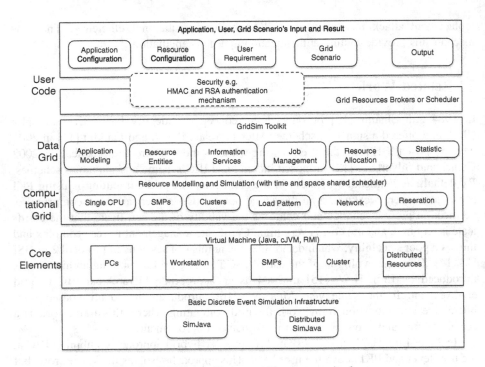

Fig. 1. GridSim architecture with new security layer

simulations in GridSim. The third and fourth layers are concerned with modeling and simulation of services specific to computational and data Grids, respectively. Some of the services provide functions common to both types of Grids, such as data about available resources and managing job submission.

In the event of data Grids, job management also incorporates managing data transfers between computational and storage resources. Replica Catalogs (RCs), information services for files and data, are also specifically implemented for data Grids. The fifth layer contains components that assist users in following out their own schedulers and resource brokers so that they can prove their own algorithms, security and strategies. The layer above this helps users define their own scenarios and configurations for validating their algorithms.

4   Methodology

This part begins by making an operational framework and an overview of the methodology selected for network grid security performance evaluation as presented in Fig. 2.

There are three major phases that compose to three major milestones of the task:

Phase1: Reviewing current Grid Computing authentication mechanism implementation.

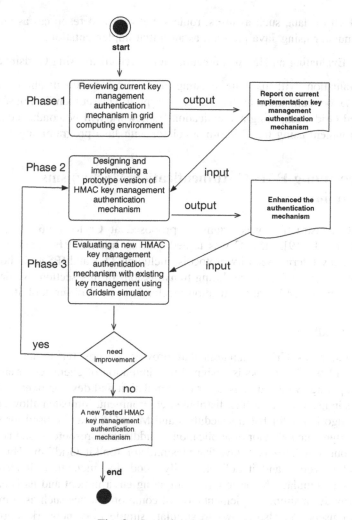

Fig. 2. Operational framework

This phase analyses current implementation of Grid Computing authentication mechanism. After that, an analysis of current practice of implementation of Grid Computing authentication mechanism development phase is then conducted. In this phase, focused on authentication time for users to authentication server (e.g., broker, certificate authority (CA) and single-sign on server), waiting time and respond time. A matrix will be developed to match or tailor between the security and performance of existing and current authentication mechanism.

Phase2: Designing and implementing a prototype version of HMAC authentication mechanism.

Based on the list of existing and current authentication framework mechanisms, a new authentication framework will then be designed and implemented. This phase will use a small set of data, such as users, routers, network and resources as an input for Gridsim simulator using Java program as an initial implementation.

Phase3: Evaluating an HMAC authentication mechanism using Gridsim simulator.

The evaluation will use the existing and current authentication mechanism parameter to be compared to the developed prototype authentication framework. A controlled Grid Computing authentication framework will be conducted in a simulation environment using the GridSim simulator with Java programming.

5   Implementing HMAC Authentication Mechanisms in GridSim

The HMAC construction was originally proposed at Cryto 1996 conferences by Bellare, M., et al. [19]. HMAC was turned into an Internet RFC, and was quickly adopted in many Internet security protocols, including TLS and IPSec. In both cases it protects the integrity of message during transmission. In this section, we describe the implementation of HMAC authentication mechanisms in GridSim toolkit.

5.1   Why GridSim?

There are numerous Grid simulators that provide various functionality. Based on [20, 21] articulated that Bricks is designed for simulation of client server architectures in Grid computing, SimGrid is used for the simulation and development of distributed applications in heterogeneous and distributed environment. Simbatch allows evaluating scheduling algorithms for batch schedulers and MicroGrid can be used for systematic study of the dynamic behavior of applications, middleware, resources, and networks. In this work, our simulator is a Java based simulator toolkit GridSim. This toolkit is flexible and universal and it delivers really good documentation. It also provides functionality to simulate the basic Grid computing environment and its behavior. The GridSim provides a simple implementation of common entities such as computational resources or users and also allows to simulate simple jobs, network topology, data storage and others useful functionalities.

5.2   HMAC Authentication Network Architecture

In this section, we briefly describe HMAC authentication mechanism network architecture. From the Fig. 3, we can see that HMAC authentication network architecture is composed of three entities, which are users, broker server and resources. The authentication occurred, as depicted in Fig. 3 are users get the secret key from the database server through secure communication such as Diffie Hellman key mechanisms. The users then encrypted the username and password using HMAC and secret key, SK and send it to broker server. Server broker request to database regarding username, Ui and database server will respond to the broker server with a secret key, SK. When the broker retrieves user secret key SK, broker will generate HMAC to compute cipher text and c-length. The next broker server does verification by testing

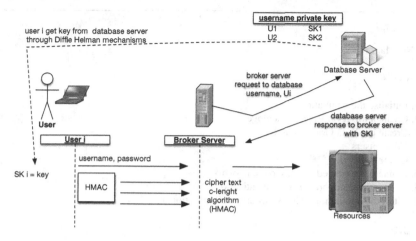

Fig. 3. HMAC authentication mechanisms

to compare the recalculated MAC should be equal, if the answer is yes, then the user can access the resources otherwise can't.

5.3 Finding

The platform for simulation experiment is GridSim, which is based on Java. Since GridSim is based on SimJava which is a discrete event simulation tool, and simulates various entities by multiple thread. This aligns well with the grid computing environment. In the simulation environment special users and resources can be generated by reconfiguring these interfaces and connected the network connection through two routers as describe in Fig. 4. In Fig. 5 shows the step to generate all the entities and process to run the simulation in pseudo code.

```
//create network
Router r1 = new RIPRouter("router1", trace_flag);   // router 1
Router r2 = new RIPRouter("router2", trace_flag);   // router 2
.
.
.
.
// attach r2 to r1
r1.attachRouter(r2, link, r1Sched, r2Sched);
```

Fig. 4. Link the network between the router

The experiments were performed on Intel Core i7 2.9 GHz machine with 8 GB 1600 MHz DDR3 RAM. The tests were run for a different number of available machines with different CPU ratings. We have run tests for 100 jobs with release dates,

```
FUNC Main ( )

 BEGIN

 1. Initialise the simulation
 2. Create a top level Replica Cataloge
 3. Create the Data Grid resources
 4. Create users
 5. Create network
 6. Connect the created entities to the network
 8. Connect users to broker for authentication
 7.  Start the simulation - GridSim.startGridSimulation();


 END
```

Fig. 5. Simulation framework

HMAC authentication time, computation time, communication time and authentication time. All the data are generated into log file using log4j in Java after running the simulation. The output file is depicted in Fig. 6.

```
2014-04-27 23:32:50,890  - Starting Log
2014-04-27 23:32:54,642  - (type,usr,compcost,simtime),HMAC,33,5.0,70.0
2014-04-27 23:32:54,642  - (type,usr,authcost,simtime),HMAC,33,1.0,70.0
2014-04-27 23:32:54,642  - (type,usr,commcost,simtime),HMAC,33,2.0,70.0
2014-04-27 23:32:54,643  - (type,usr,compcost,simtime),HMAC,29,5.0,70.0
2014-04-27 23:32:54,643  - (type,usr,authcost,simtime),HMAC,29,0.0,70.0
2014-04-27 23:32:54,643  - (type,usr,commcost,simtime),HMAC,29,2.0,70.0
2014-04-27 23:32:54,644  - (type,usr,compcost,simtime),HMAC,25,5.0,70.0
2014-04-27 23:32:54,644  - (type,usr,authcost,simtime),HMAC,25,1.0,70.0
```

Fig. 6. HMAC log file

In this experiment we create one scenario where the total grid users are 5 to simulate the concurrent request and uniformly distributed them among the two trust resources. In our simulation setup, some parameters are set identically for all network elements, such as the maximum transfer unit (MTU) of a link and the latency. The detail parameter of the simulation in the experiment is shown in Table 1 below.

Table 1. Simulation parameter

Parameter	Value
Number of users	5
Number of resources	2
Number of gridlet	100
Baud rate	1000 bits/s
Propagation delay	10 ms
MTU	1500 bytes

5.4 Analysis and Simulation

In this section, analysis, comparison of HMAC communication cost performance with RSA communication cost is firstly discussed. Secondly, computation time and lastly authentication time comparison will be discussed. Then simulation experiment gives precise result.

5.4.1 Communication Cost

Based on Fig. 7, it was found that the HMAC average communication cost for the user to the resource would take around 2 ms per simulation time compared to RSA mechanism, which take around 4 ms per simulation time. We can see that the result shown in the simulation is significantly fast.

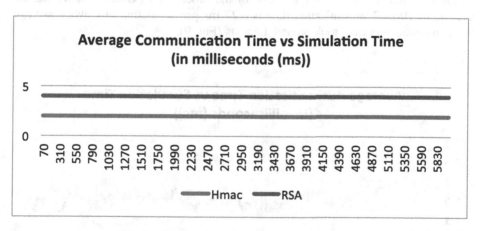

Fig. 7. Communication cost per simulation time

5.4.2 Computation Cost

Execution computation cost time; the average for the HMAC computation time for job on each 5 users is plotted in Fig. 8. We can see that, the average for the HMAC computation time is 5 ms per simulation time during the performance. On the other hand, RSA computation time is 25 ms per simulation time. It shows that the RSA algorithm calculation needs more processing time compared to HMAC mechanism.

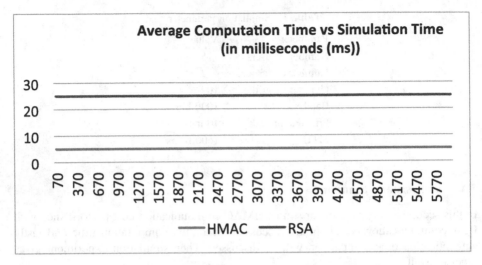

Fig. 8. Computation cost per simulation time

5.4.3 Authentication Cost

For this experiment, the execution of authenticated user from the user to the resources through broker node has been done. At the beginning, the result shows that HMAC authentication starts at 0.4 ms to 0.6 ms. However, RSA authentications start at 2.8 ms to 1.6 ms. This is due to the fluctuation of the processor CPU time. After that, the average of HMAC authentication time is 0.22 ms per simulation time while average RSA authentication time took around 1.55 ms (Fig. 9).

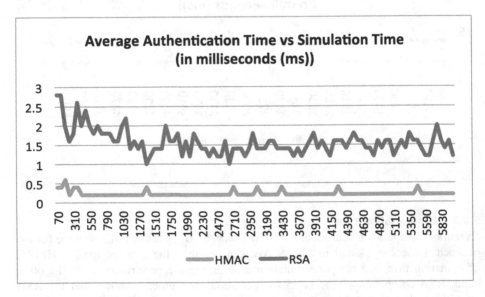

Fig. 9. Authentication cost per simulation time

6 Conclusion and Future Work

Security is significant in a grid computing network environment. In this work we present a security grid simulation as an extension to GridSim, a well-known computational Grid simulator. With the addition of this extension, GridSim has the ability to handle basic Grid security functionality, such as user authentication to data grid resources via broker node. In summation, we tested the average authentication time from the server, computation time in the server and communication time between users on the authentication server. The most obvious finding to emerge from this experiment is that the HMAC authentication mechanism performs better than RSA authentication mechanism. Nevertheless, the describe simulation was used in the experiment as an example of the different functionality of the simulator. We think that this study can help researchers make important finding and help solve problems arising in data grid security. In the time to come, we are contriving to look at the other authentication mechanisms such as using IBI, DSA and ECC. We are also intending to include comparison of implementation, testing and analyze the result using GridSim simulator.

Acknowledgements. We would like to thank to Universiti Teknologi Malaysia (UTM) and Ministry of Higher Education (MoHE) Malaysia for their financial support. Also to Advanced Informatics, School staff, Universiti Teknologi Malaysia who have been involved in the study.

References

1. Al-Riyami, S.S., Paterson, K.G.: Certificateless public key cryptography. In: Laih, C.-S. (ed.) ASIACRYPT 2003. LNCS, vol. 2894, pp. 452–473. Springer, Heidelberg (2003)
2. Zhang, Z., Wong, D.S., Xu, J., Feng, D.: Certificateless public-key signature: security model and efficient construction. In: Zhou, J., Yung, M., Bao, F. (eds.) ACNS 2006. LNCS, vol. 3989, pp. 293–308. Springer, Heidelberg (2006)
3. Gorantla, M.C., Saxena, A.: An efficient certificateless signature scheme. In: Hao, Y., Liu, J., Wang, Y.-P., Cheung, Y., Yin, H., Jiao, L., Ma, J., Jiao, Y.-C. (eds.) CIS 2005. LNCS (LNAI), vol. 3802, pp. 110–116. Springer, Heidelberg (2005)
4. Yap, W.-S., Heng, S.-H., Goi, B.-M.: An efficient certificateless signature scheme. In: Zhou, X., Sokolsky, O., Yan, L., Jung, E.-S., Shao, Z., Mu, Y., Lee, D.C., Kim, D.Y., Jeong, Y.-S., Xu, C.-Z. (eds.) Emerging Directions in Embedded and Ubiquitous Computing, pp. 322–331. Springer, Heidelberg (2006)
5. Zhang, J., Mao, J.: An efficient RSA-based certificateless signature scheme. J. Syst. Softw. **85**(3), 638–642 (2012)
6. Li, X., Chen, K., Sun, L.: Certificateless signature and proxy signature schemes from bilinear pairings. Lith. Math. J. **45**(1), 76–83 (2005)
7. Liu, J.K., Au, M.H., Susilo, W.: Self-generated-certificate public key cryptography and certificateless signature/encryption scheme in the standard model: extended abstract. In: Proceedings of the 2nd ACM Symposium on Information, Computer and Communications Security, New York, NY, USA, pp. 273–283 (2007)
8. Xiong, H., Qin, Z., Li, F.: An improved certificateless signature scheme secure in the standard model. Fundam. Informaticae **88**(1), 193–206 (2008)

9. Zhang, M., Yao, J., Wang, C., Takagi, T.: Public key replacement and universal forgery of SCLS scheme. Int. J. Netw. Secur. **15**(1), 115–120 (2013)
10. Shamir, A.: Identity-based cryptosystems and signature schemes. In: Blakely, G.R., Chaum, D. (eds.) CRYPTO 1984. LNCS, vol. 196, pp. 47–53. Springer, Heidelberg (1985)
11. Boneh, D., Franklin, M.: Identity-based encryption from the weil pairing. In: Kilian, J. (ed.) CRYPTO 2001. LNCS, vol. 2139, pp. 213–229. Springer, Heidelberg (2001)
12. Gentry, C., Silverberg, A.: Hierarchical ID-based cryptography. In: Zheng, Y. (ed.) ASIACRYPT 2002. LNCS, vol. 2501, pp. 548–566. Springer, Heidelberg (2002)
13. Li, H., Sun, S.: Identity-based cryptography for grid. In: Eighth ACIS International Conference on Software Engineering, Artificial Intelligence, Networking, and Parallel/Distributed Computing, SNPD 2007, vol. 2 (2007)
14. Mao, W.: An identity-based non-interactive authentication framework for computational grids. Hewlett-Packard Lab. Technical report, HPL-2004-96 (2004)
15. Lim, H.W., Robshaw, M.J.B.: On identity-based cryptography and grid computing. In: Computational Science - ICCS 2004, pp. 474–477 (2004)
16. Lim, H.W., Robshaw, M.J.B.: A dynamic key infrastructure for Grid. In: Sloot, P.M., Hoekstra, A.G., Priol, T., Reinefeld, A., Bubak, M. (eds.) EGC 2005. LNCS, vol. 3470, pp. 255–264. Springer, Heidelberg (2005)
17. Sulistio, A., Cibej, U., Venugopal, S., Robic, B., Buyya, R.: A toolkit for modelling and simulating data Grids: an extension to GridSim. Concurr. Comput. Pract. Exp. **20**(13), 1591–1609 (2008)
18. Simatos, C.: Making simjava count. MSc Proj. Rep. Univ. Edinb. (2002)
19. Bellare, M., Canetti, R., Krawczyk, H.: Keying hash functions for message authentication. In: Koblitz, N. (ed.) CRYPTO 1996. LNCS, vol. 1109, pp. 1–15. Springer, Heidelberg (1996)
20. Klusáček, D., Rudová, H.: Alea 2: job scheduling simulator. In: Proceedings of the 3rd International ICST Conference on Simulation Tools and Techniques, p. 61 (2010)
21. Klusáček, D., Matyska, L., Rudová, H.: Alea – Grid scheduling simulation environment. In: Wyrzykowski, R., Dongarra, J., Karczewski, K., Wasniewski, J. (eds.) PPAM 2007. LNCS, vol. 4967, pp. 1029–1038. Springer, Heidelberg (2008)

Hermes: A Targeted Fuzz Testing Framework

Caleb Shortt[✉] and Jens Weber

University of Victoria, Victoria, Canada
{cshortt,jens}@uvic.ca

Abstract. Security assurance cases (security cases) are used to represent claims for evidence-based assurance of security properties in software. A security case uses evidence to argue that a particular claim is true, e.g., buffer overflows cannot happen. Evidence may be generated with a variety of methods. Random negative testing (fuzz testing) has become a popular method for creating evidence for the security of software. However, traditional fuzz testing is undirected and provides only weak evidence for specific assurance concerns, unless significant resources are allocated for extensive testing. This paper presents a method to apply fuzz testing in a targeted way to more economically support the creation of evidence for specific security assurance cases. Our experiments produced results with target code coverage comparable to an exhaustive fuzz test run while significantly reducing the test execution time when compared to exhaustive methods. These results provide specific evidence for security cases and provide improved assurance.

Keywords: Security · Assurance · Fuzzing · Testing · Genetic-algorithms · Evidence

1 Introduction

Assurance is confidence that an entity meets its requirements based on evidence provided by the application of assurance techniques [2]. *Security assurance* narrows this scope to focus on security claims or requirements. Security assurance cases (security cases) are used to argue the assurance of specific claims. They provide a series of evidence-argument-claim structures that, when combined, provide assurance on the original claim.

A popular tool in security assurance is fuzz testing [6,8–10]. Fuzz testing is an automated type of random, or semi-random, negative testing that attempts to cause a target system to crash, hang, or otherwise fail in an unexpected manner [4–7]. It takes a dynamic analysis approach and tracks the attempted input and the resulting response from the system − whether or not it fails and, in some cases, includes the type of failure. In essence, it is a black-box "scattergun" approach where the accuracy of the "gun" is determined by the fuzzer utilized.

Due to the undirected nature of traditional fuzz testing methods, the evidence provided by fuzz tests is not specific to particular types of defects and thus fuzz testing results are only weakly linked to specific security claims. Traditional fuzz testing tools encounter difficulties, and become ineffective, if most generated

© Springer International Publishing Switzerland 2015
H. Fujita and G. Guizzi (Eds.): SoMeT 2015, CCIS 532, pp. 453–468, 2015.
DOI: 10.1007/978-3-319-22689-7_35

inputs are rejected early in the execution of the target program [12]. Random testing usually provides low code coverage [13]. While it is possible to afford a large amount of resources (time and/or computational) increase the coverage of fuzz tests, it would be more economically feasible to be able to target the fuzzer to particular security concerns in order to provide stronger evidence for specific assurance cases.

Directed fuzz testing approaches exist and include solutions that rely on taint analysis, symbolic execution, and constraint-solvers to provide a certain level of introspection [12,14,15]. These approaches are certainly an improvement over undirected fuzz testing in the quality of evidence provided, but the issues of performance, complexity, and uncertainty of application in "real world" systems leave much to be desired. It is an open question if symbolic execution fuzz testing can consistently achieve high code coverage on "real world" applications [14], and the symbolic execution "is limited in practice by the imprecision of static analysis and theorem provers" [13]. Finally, fuzz testing is executed for a certain amount of time to be considered "good enough". However "good enough" is a subjective term and lacks the quantitative properties required to be reviewed as evidence.

In this paper, we present a method for targeted fuzz testing that combines the input of static code analysis with an optimization function (based on Genetic Algorithms) that utilizes dynamic code coverage analysis. Our method has been implemented in a tool prototype (called Hermes) and evaluated in a case study using a real-world software system (Crawler4j) [31].

The purpose of our research is to investigate the questions: "Is it possible to use targeted fuzz testing to provide targeted evidence for security assurance cases? Is it also possible to reduce the computation time required while achieving the same code coverage as a full fuzz test run?".

Our evaluative analysis of software (the Crawler4j Java library [31]) using Hermes produced promising results and achieved near-parity code coverage when compared to an exhaustive, undirected, fuzz test – or full fuzz test, but each evaluation was able to do so in reduced execution time.

There rest of this paper is structured as follows. The next section discusses background and related work. We introduce Hermes in Sect. 3 and discuss our evaluation method in Sect. 4. Section 5 present the results of our evaluation experiment. Finally, we close with concluding remarks and pointers to future work in Sect. 7.

2   Related Work

2.1   Security Assurance Cases

"Assurance is confidence that an entity meets its requirements based on evidence provided by the application of assurance techniques" [2]. *Security assurance* narrows this scope to focus on security claims or requirements. Security assurance cases (security cases) are used to argue the assurance of specific claims. They provide a series of evidence-argument-claim structures that, when combined, provide assurance on the original claim.

For example, the claim "the REST API is secure against attack" may not be provable directly. Therefore the main claim will have to be decomposed into a set of *subclaims* that must be assured to assure the main claim. Once the subclaims are assured, the main claim can be considered assured. These subclaims would include statements such as "The use of the REST API cannot cause a buffer overflow". This subclaim would require either more subclaims that must be assured, or it must provide evidence that sufficiently support the claim.

The types of evidence vary widely depending on design and environment of a system, however some common types of evidence for security cases include black-box testing results, white-box testing results, model checking, standards compliance check lists, fuzz test results, and penetration-test reports.

2.2 Fuzz Testing

Fuzz testing is an automated type of random, or semi-random, negative testing that attempts to cause a target system to crash, hang, or otherwise fail in an unexpected manner [4–7]. It takes a dynamic analysis approach and tracks the attempted input and the resulting response from the system – whether or not it fails and, in some cases, includes the type of failure. In its traditional form, it is a black-box scattergun approach where the accuracy of the "scattergun" is determined by the fuzzer utilized.

Fuzz testing has proved to be a valuable addition to current software security techniques and has caught the attention of industry leaders such as Microsoft who have incorporated it into the Security Development Lifecycle (SDL) [9,10]. It is particularly well-suited to discover finite-state machine edge cases via semi-malformed inputs [6,8]. The partially-correct inputs are able to penetrate the initial layers of verification in a system and test the bounds of areas that may have not been considered by the developers or design team. These partially-correct inputs can be generated from inputs provided to the fuzzer at runtime where it uses it as a template, or they can be "mutated" from capturing input information that is known to be correct. These two methods define the two categories of fuzzers: "Mutation-based" and "generation-based" [6,8].

Generation-based fuzzers use random or brute-force input creation and are usually customized to generate variations of a particular protocol model or application data format that an application uses. Once the fuzzer is connected to the target it can generate its inputs and track the responses returned [8].

Mutation-based fuzzers do not incorporate a model for generating inputs but rather use random mutations on a library of known valid inputs [32]. The mutation process may include checksum calculation and other more advanced methods to penetrate the application's primary level of input validation [32]. Mutation-based fuzzers are considered "generic fuzzers" as the need to customize them to a particular target application is minimal [29]. Limited customization is possible to target specific parts of the input data format (or protocol) by using a "block-based approach" that segments the input into separate blocks [33]. Each block can either be fuzzed or left in its original state. With a block-based approach, additional information blocks can be created and reused to construct various protocol definitions, file formats, or validation techniques such as checksums [34].

Directed Fuzzers and Optimization. Directed fuzz testing utilizes methods to optimize the mutation or generation of inputs, and include solutions that rely on taint analysis to provide a certain level of introspection [12,15]. Taint analysis relies on a "clean" run to provide a baseline execution pattern for the target application. It then compares all subsequent executions to the baseline in an attempt to find discrepancies. Further approaches include the addition of symbolic execution and constraint solvers to take full advantage of the introspective properties of the taint analysis approach [14].

Various techniques can be used for optimizing directed fuzzers with respect to a defined utility function, such as code coverage. Genetic Algorithms (GA) are one particularly well suited optimization technique in this context as the concept of a "genetic information string" defining a vector of features that are switched on and off during the generation or mutation of fuzzed input provides a natural fit. The idea behind GA's is modelled after the natural evolutionary process [17,18]. A GA is used to simulate the evolutionary progress of a population towards a certain "fitness" goal [19,36]. A "population", in this case, can be any group of features (called a feature string, individual, genotype, or chromosome) that are evaluated to provide a "fitness value" [20]. An evaluation function must be defined which provides one, or many, performance measures for a given feature string. The fitness function then determines which feature strings are most "fit" and should be used for creating the next-generation population [19,20]. Once a subset of feature strings is selected the next generation is created by mutation and crossover (also called "mating") [17,40,41]. An important advantage of a GA is that it is able to manipulate numerous strings simultaneously. This greatly reduces the chances of the optimization becoming stuck in a local minima [17].

3   The Hermes Approach

3.1   Overview

The approach we have implemented within Hermes falls under the category of directed, generation-based fuzzing and combines static and dynamic code analysis along with an optimization process that utilizes Genetic Algorithms. We will first provide an overview on our method and then discuss its elements in more detail. It is assumed that our fuzz testing method is used to generate evidence for security assurance cases, e.g., the ability of a software component to resist exploitation of certain types of security vulnerabilities. Once the vulnerabilities to target have been defined, our method starts with applying a static code analyzer to identify source code locations that may be vulnerable to specific types of security threats. The goal of our smart fuzzer is then to optimize test case generation to maximize coverage of the code that contains the potential vulnerabilities. Since our fuzzer is generation-based, it has a model of the input data (or protocol) of the software to be tested. Specific features in this model may be switched on or off depending on a binary string that controls the random test case generation process. A first set of such feature strings are randomly generated and referred to as the *first generation* of tests. Consequently, the fuzz testing framework runs the target software with the test cases generated for the first generation of tests. The code coverage of the vulnerable target areas (determined by the static analyzer) is analyzed for these initial test runs. The feature strings that yield the highest code coverage are selected and used for producing of the next generation of feature strings, using a GA.

3.2 Design

The design of Hermes is based on a client-server architecture which facilitates both remote and local testing of targets, cf. Fig. 1. The processing for both the genetic algorithm and the fuzz test generation (using Sulley [43]) happens on the server side while the client is a thin wrapper that includes the code coverage tool (EMMA [44]). The client monitors the target and sends the coverage metrics to the server to complete the asynchronous loop of test, measure, and revise.

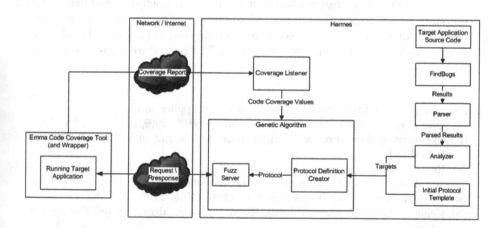

Fig. 1. A view of Hermes' architecture

Hermes relies on static analysis to find the initial sections of code with potential defects. It then parses, sorts, and identifies the target code that the framework will focus on. The list of targets and a protocol definition that specifies how to dynamically generate a language-specific protocol are passed to the genetic algorithm to begin the analysis. Hermes is able to dynamically generate a protocol for a specific language, with certain features included or excluded, start or stop the fuzz server, and revise the protocol based on code coverage feedback and the genetic algorithm's suggestions.

Protocol generation is achieved by using a protocol template that specifies a language's syntax in the Sulley protocol language [43]. Each feature is defined using the language's syntax as building blocks. This allows Hermes to select which features to include or exclude to create a new protocol. A feature string determines the inclusion or exclusion of a protocol. The feature strings specified in Hermes include seven unique features for the target language – in our evaluation, HTML. The HTML features are anchor tags, image tags, div tags, iframe tags, object tags, javascript tags, and applet tags. Thus a feature string with all features included would look like the following: (1, 1, 1, 1, 1, 1, 1).

4   Evaluation

Our evaluation procedure is divided into two sections: the undirected fuzz testing baseline and the directed fuzz testing using Hermes.

We first established a baseline for the metrics specified in Sect. 4.2. This is achieved by executing the undirected fuzz testing method on the target application and logging both the code coverage and the number of mutations for the configured target area percentage.

Once a baseline is established, the evaluation of the directed fuzz testing method is executed with respect to the same metrics. Each directed evaluation is compared to its associated undirected counterpart for the given target area percentage. For example, the directed and undirected evaluations for the top 10 % of offending code are compared, and so on. The procedure steps are outlined in Fig. 2.

1. Execute undirected fuzz testing method on target application.
   (a) Configure method for target area percentage (10%, 20%, ...).
   (b) Exhaustively fuzz test target application with a full protocol (All features turned on).
   (c) Record metrics
2. Execute directed fuzz testing method on target application.
   (a) Configure method for target area percentage (10%, 20%, ...).
   (b) Generate targeted protocol using Hermes' genetic algorithm (3600-mutation "tracer round").
   (c) Exhaustively fuzz test target application using targeted protocol.
   (d) Record metrics.
3. Compare results.

Fig. 2. Evaluation procedure

"Offending code" in these evaluations are the lines of code contained in the method where a potential defect is found. For example, the top 10 % of the offending code will reflect the lines of code for each of the top 10 % most-severe potential defects – based on the FindBugs bugrank metric.

Our evaluation includes ten variations in the percentage of the offending code in increments of 10 % from 10 % to 100 %. We chose to include these increments in an attempt to identify possible "sweet-spots" where coverage or performance would perform exceptionally-well compared to other results.

Both the undirected and directed methods were executed and their code coverage of the target areas measured. The protocol for the baseline calculation was kept constant (a full protocol with all features available) and EMMA was configured to track the code coverage for a given target area. This baseline code coverage was then compared to the calculated values of Hermes' directed fuzz approach.

Directed protocols were generated by Hermes' genetic algorithm with specific targets (in this case percentage of most severe offending code) in mind. The resulting best-fit protocol was then exhaustively evaluated to produce code coverage and number-of-mutation metrics for that target range.

4.1 Target Application

The target application selected for evaluation is the Crawler4J [31] library. To fuzz test this library a simple crawler was developed using Crawler4J and configured to connect to the Hermes fuzz test server.

The Crawler4J library was selected for evaluation because it is a Java-based application with its most recent revision being downloaded just under 15,000 times, it is designed to be extended, and it is open-source. The fact that Crawler4J is open-source allowed Hermes to provide full introspection and utilize its white-box features to their fullest extent.

4.2 Measurement

We designed our experiment to evaluate code coverage and performance. Code coverage was used as the fitness criteria for the genetic algorithm while performance was used to supplement the comparison of results. Thus performance was a secondary goal to maximizing code coverage of the target code.

Code Coverage. Code coverage is a measure of the amount of source code a specific test suite is able to evaluate.

There are three common forms of code coverage: function coverage, path coverage, and statement coverage [46]. Function coverage is the number of functions that are called by a given test suite. Statement coverage is the total number of individual statements executed by the test suite. Path coverage measures the coverage of all possible routes through the executed code. These values are compared to the total number of functions, statements, or paths in the target application to produce a code coverage percentage.

In addition the the general definition of code coverage, Sutton [6] defines code coverage within the context of fuzz testing to be "the amount of process state a fuzzer induces a target's process to reach and execute".

Code coverage was chosen as a metric for Hermes because, although it is "well-known that random testing usually provides low code coverage, and performs poorly overall [in that respect]" [13,14], code coverage has been extensively used as a metric to measure the performance of fuzz testing [5,16,29,32,46–48], additionally, there is a general "lack of measurable parameters that describe fuzz test completeness" to draw from [29]. Specifically, we chose line coverage for the entire method where a target bug type was identified as the metric used for our analysis.

Performance. The evaluation of Hermes requires a performance metric. We chose to evaluate Hermes based on the number of mutations that the fuzzer generates to achieve a target code coverage. A baseline performance metric is set by executing an undirected and exhaustive fuzz test on the target while logging the number of mutations and code coverage achieved.

In the context of the Crawler4J crawler, the number of mutations equals the number of crawler requests to the server as each request included a single mutation of the protocol.

Previous research has utilized a variety of performance metrics including number of fuzzed inputs, total errors found, errors found per hour, and number of distinct errors found per hour [5,15,16,47].

The number of fuzzed inputs (mutations) was chosen because it is less subjective than a pure time comparison. A time comparison could be improved by simply increasing the CPU power of the host machine and would introduce a subjective aspect to our analysis.

4.3   Configuration

The default selection criteria for Hermes' analyser was set to use the FindBugs internal "bugrank" metric. Bugrank is calculated by FindBugs using a combination of the potential defect's category type and the type of potential defect found. The bugrank metric represents an overall severity metric for the potential defect.

The genetic algorithm was configured to be more aggressive in its mutation capabilities. This allows for more features to be brought back into the "gene pool" if there is an early, dominating, feature string that does not converge to a maximum later in the analysis, or if the population size is small. The initial configuration of the genetic algorithm is detailed in Fig. 3.

High growth ratios and increased mutation rates allow for quicker convergence in simple problems but suffer with more complex problems. These issues

P(Crossover) = 0.5
P(Mutation) = 0.05
Number of Generations = 30
Feature Strings per Generation = 10
Selection Algorithm = Tournament Selection (size=3)
Mutation Limit = 3600

Fig. 3. Initial configuration of Hermes' genetic algorithm

can be mitigated partially by increased population sizes and multiple populations with varying success [37]. In the configuration detailed in Fig. 3, a small population is used with a higher mutation, and lower crossover, probability. A higher population increases variability within the population, which will include more feature strings with high fitness, but it will slow the convergence to a maximum. For the purposes of time we chose a small population size of 10 for 30 generations. The mutation limit of 3600 was chosen to limit the amount of time required to evaluate a single feature string in the genetic algorithm. This initial mutation limit of 3600 will be used as a "tracer round" to target the full fuzz testing capabilities.

Typical crossover probabilities lie in the 0.5 to 1.0 range, while typical mutation probabilities are in the 0.005 to 0.05 range [41]. Tournament selection was used because "ranking and tournament selection are shown to maintain strong growth under normal conditions, while proportionate selection without scaling is shown to be less effective in keeping a steady pressure towards convergence" [37].

We configured Hermes to act as a "honeypot" server where it captures HTTP requests by providing non-repeating and self-directed links back to itself. Once an HTTP client, such as a crawler, is captured the server responds with mutated HTML mixed with valid HTML and begins the fuzz test process. The use of valid HTML within the server's response ensures that HTTP clients have a valid HTML link back to the server so that it may continue to be captured.

5 Results

5.1 Baseline: Undirected Fuzz Testing with Code Coverage

We calculated the baseline by executing a full-fuzz test (brute-force) on the full protocol definition. By brute-forcing the protocol we are able to produce the worst-case values for number of mutations, mean code coverage, the standard deviation for the mean code coverage, the mean code coverage of the targeted code's complement, and the standard deviation for the complement's mean code coverage. These results are detailed in Table 1. The mean code coverage is used with the standard deviation to provide an overall value for all of the sections of targeted code. The target code complement represents the code coverage that is *not* part of the target scope. The total number of possible unique mutations for the full target protocol is 67788. The baseline exhaustively evaluates the protocol which explains the constant number in the "Mutations" column.

The data in Table 1 follows an expected behaviour where the code coverage is high and the standard deviation is low when only looking at small sections of the code, but as the amount of target code increases so does the standard deviation and the mean coverage decreases.

For the baseline, we observed that a noticeable drop in code coverage and increase in standard deviation when the target code reaches 40%. This may signal that a defect with little or no code coverage was added that was not in the previous set. In fact, observation of the detailed baseline results for 30%

and 40 % showed that *two* defects are added with little code coverage. This would cause the drop in coverage we observed. The discrepancy between 30 % and 40 % is most prevalent in the standard deviation values where we observe a jump from a standard deviation of 0.1575 to 0.3606 – more than double.

Table 1. Baseline results from an undirected and exhaustive fuzz test with a full protocol

Targeted % of Code	Mutations	Mean Coverage	Standard Deviation	Complement Mean Coverage	Complement Std. Deviation
10	67788	0.8625	0.1304	0.4343	0.4664
20	67788	0.79	0.1485	0.4339	0.4663
30	67788	0.8425	0.1575	0.4334	0.4663
40	67788	0.7036	0.3606	0.4343	0.4664
50	67788	0.7283	0.3548	0.4337	0.4662
60	67788	0.785	0.3145	0.4337	0.4664
70	67788	0.8148	0.2901	0.433	0.4662
80	67788	0.7834	0.3248	0.4334	0.4663
90	67788	0.7493	0.3339	0.433	0.4663
100	67788	0.7415	0.3315	0.4328	0.4663

5.2   Directed Fuzz Testing with Code Coverage

Our evaluation analyzes the target application in two steps:

1. Find the best-fit candidate protocol that performs best under a restricted number of mutations – in this case 3600 mutations. This is the "tracer round" that directs the full-fuzz test evaluation. Table 2 details the results for each best-fit candidate.
2. Exhaustively fuzz test the best-fit protocol to fully evaluate the target application with respect to the given target code. Table 3 details the results of exhaustively fuzzing the best-fit protocols.

The results in Table 2 were surprisingly similar to the baseline detailed in Table 1 – with a significant reduction in mutations. Most of the mean coverage results for the best-fit protocols were within 3 % of their baseline counterparts. This is true for all values except the 80 % evaluation which differed by 5.58 %. After further investigation it was revealed that this drop in accuracy was due to a significantly-lower code coverage in a single section of offending code. As with the baseline, we observe the jump in standard deviation at the 30 % to 40 % mark. Finally, these values do not represent the entire best-fit protocol and

Table 2. Results from the best-fit candidates produced by Hermes

Targeted % of Code	Mutations	Mean Coverage	Standard Deviation	Complement Mean Coverage	Complement Std. Deviation
10	3600	0.8425	0.1622	0.4116	0.4624
20	3600	0.775	0.1636	0.412	0.4625
30	3600	0.8312	0.172	0.4116	0.4624
40	3600	0.6954	0.3623	0.4115	0.4624
50	3600	0.7208	0.3569	0.4115	0.4624
60	3600	0.752	0.3131	0.4094	0.4619
70	3600	0.8064	0.2962	0.4102	0.4622
80	3600	0.7276	0.3472	0.41	0.4621
90	3600	0.7441	0.3343	0.4097	0.4622
100	3600	0.7365	0.3318	0.4108	0.4624

they must be exhaustively evaluated to assure that the results are not simply "surface" matches.

The results from an exhaustive evaluation of the best-fit protocols are detailed in Table 3. Here, we observe fluctuations in the number of mutations, and thus the computation time, of the evaluations. This is the result of Hermes tailoring each protocol to attack the specified set of potential defects while pruning any redundant or useless features to minimize the total number of mutations. Furthermore, 8 of the 10 evaluations achieve parity with their baseline counterparts

Table 3. Results from exhaustively evaluating the generated best-fit protocols

Targeted % of Code	Mutations	Mean Coverage	Standard Deviation	Complement Mean Coverage	Complement Std. Deviation
10	41964	0.8625	0.1304	0.4171	0.4637
20	51648	0.79	0.146	0.4307	0.4656
30	41964	0.8425	0.1575	0.4347	0.4662
40	35508	0.7027	0.3607	0.4161	0.4635
50	51648	0.7283	0.3548	0.432	0.4657
60	50185	0.785	0.3145	0.4311	0.4658
70	41964	0.81	0.2939	0.4162	0.4638
80	23672	0.7834	0.3248	0.4147	0.4634
90	49162	0.7493	0.3339	0.4316	0.4659
100	49981	0.7415	0.3315	0.4319	0.4658

on mean code coverage, and the other 2 evaluations are within 0.5 % of *their* baseline counterparts.

The standard deviation results followed a similar trend set by the mean coverage. Seven of the ten evaluations achieved parity with their baseline counterparts with the other 3 evaluations within 0.4 % of their baseline counterparts. In one case, the 20 % evaluation, we observed a *decrease* in the standard deviation of the mean coverage while continuing to maintain mean coverage parity.

6   Analysis

6.1   Best-Fit Protocols and Their Accuracy

The best-fit protocols generated by Hermes were produced by selecting the best-performing protocol in a 3600-mutation evaluation (detailed in Table 2). The resulting protocols were then exhaustively evaluated (fuzzed) to produce the values shown in Table 3.

Our analysis compared the code coverage for the 3600-mutation best-fit protocol and its exhaustively-fuzzed counterpart. We observed that although the full evaluation achieves better code coverage in every evaluation it does not deviate from the initial best-fit evaluation with 3600 mutations in a significant manner. The two major discrepancies are at the 60 % and 80 % evaluations with a difference of 3.3 % and 5.58 % respectively. Additionally, the full evaluation achieves a lower or equivalent standard deviation compared to the initial evaluation. The notable anomalies are at the lower percentage targets (10 %, 20 %, and 30 %) and at the 80 % evaluation. At these areas we see a lower standard deviation than the initial best-fit evaluations.

Table 4. A comparison of the baseline and the full evaluations of best-fit protocols

Targeted % of Code	Difference in Mean Coverage (%)	Difference in Std Deviation	Baseline # Mutations	Full Best-Fit # Mutations	Difference in # Mutations
10	0	0	67788	41964	25824
20	0	0.0025	67788	51648	16140
30	0	0	67788	41964	25824
40	0.0009	0.0001	67788	35508	32280
50	0	0	67788	51648	16140
60	0	0	67788	50185	17603
70	0.0048	0.0038	67788	41964	25824
80	0	0	67788	23672	44116
90	0	0	67788	49162	18626
100	0	0	67788	49981	17807

The similarity between the initial and full best-fit evaluations may be due to the size of the target application or the size of the feature string used in the genetic algorithm. The deviation between the initial and full evaluations may increase with a change in either of these two factors.

6.2 Comparing Directed and Undirected Approaches

The directed (full best-fit) evaluations and the undirected (baseline) evaluations are compared in Table 4. In this table we observe that the full best-fit mean coverage and standard deviation results achieve near-parity with their baseline counterparts. Additionally, the areas that *did not* achieve parity were within 0.5 % of their targets.

We observe from Table 4 that *every* evaluation was able to reduce the number of mutations (and thus computation time as described in Sect. 4.2) required. In the case of the 80 % evaluation Hermes was able to reduce the number of mutations by 65 % from 67788 to 23672 mutations while achieving complete parity in both mean code coverage *and* standard deviation. The minimum improvement observed from our evaluations is a decrease in the number of mutations by 23.8 % (from 67788 to 51648 mutations) while maintaining parity within 0.5 % of mean code coverage and standard deviation.

7   Conclusion

Evidence in security assurance cases must be definitive, convincing, and accurate. The more specific the evidence the stronger the associated assurance argument. Fuzz testing is has become a popular tool for software security assurance but in its traditional (undirected) form, it provides only weak evidence for specific security cases. We have presented a method, tool implementation and experimental results for a directed fuzzer, which can be used to target specific potential code vulnerabilities. Our experimental results indicate that the method shows promise in reducing resources needed for covering code that is of interest from a security perspective (as indicated by static code analysis). We were able to achieve reductions in execution time (ranging from 23.8 % to 65 %), while targeting specific bug types (in this evaluation we chose the most-severe defects), and achieving near-equivalent code coverage to an exhaustive fuzz test (within 0.5 %) Clearly, our evaluation to date is limited, since we have only studied one real-world target software system. Additional experiments are needed to confirm the generalizability of our results.

References

1. Lipner, S.: The trustworthy computing security development lifecycle. In: 20th IEEE Computer Security Applications Conference, pp. 2–13. IEEE (2004)

2. Agudo, I., Vivas, J., Lopez, J.: Security assurance during the software development cycle. In: International Conference on Computer Systems and Technologies and Workshop for PhD Students in Computing, p. 20. ACM (2009)

3. Kelly, T., Weaver, R.: The goal structuring notation-a safety argument notation. In: Dependable Systems and Networks 2004 Workshop on Assurance Cases. Citeseer (2004)

4. Godefroid, P., Levin, M., Molnar, D.: Automated whitebox fuzz testing. In: NDSS, vol. 8 (2008)

5. Takanen, A., Demott, J., Miller, C.: Fuzzing for software security testing and quality assurance. Artech House (2008)

6. Sutton, M., Greene, A., Amini, P.: Fuzzing: brute force vulnerability discovery. Addison-Wesley Professional (2007)

7. Miller, B.P., Fredriksen, L., So, B.: An empirical study of the reliability of UNIX utilities. Commun. ACM **33**(12), 32–44 (1990)

8. DeMott, J.: The evolving art of fuzzing. Technical report, DEF CON, vol. 14 (2006)

9. Marshall, A., Howard, M., Bugher, G., et al.: Security best practices for developing windows azure applications. Technical report, Microsoft Corporation (2010)

10. Howard, M., Lipner, S.: The security development lifecycle, vol. 11. Microsoft Press (2009)

11. Goertzel, K.M., Winograd, T., McKinley, H.L., et al.: Software security assurance: a State-of-Art Report (SAR). DTIC Document (2007)

12. Wang, T., Wei, T., Gu, G., Zou, W.: TaintScope: A checksum-aware directed fuzzing tool for automatic software vulnerability detection. In: IEEE Symposium on Security and Privacy (SP), pp. 497–512. IEEE (2010)

13. Godefroid, P., Klarlund, N., Sen, K.: DART: directed automated random testing. ACM Sigplan Not. **40**(6), 213–223 (2005)

14. Cadar, C., Dunbar, D., Engler, D.R.: KLEE: unassisted and automatic generation of high-coverage tests for complex systems programs. OSDI **8**, 209–224 (2008)

15. Ganesh, V., Leek, T., Rinard, M.: Taint-based directed whitebox fuzzing. In: IEEE 31st International Conference on Software Engineering, pp. 474–484. IEEE (2009)

16. Wu, Z., Atwood, J.W., Zhu, X.: A new fuzzing technique for software vulnerability mining. In: IEEE CONSEG, vol. 9. IEEE (2009)

17. Jain, L.C., Karr, C.L.: Introduction to evolutionary computing techniques. In: Electronic Technology Directions, pp. 122–127 (1995)

18. Holland, J.H.: Adaptation in natural and artificial systems: an introductory analysis with applications to biology, control, and artificial intelligence. U. Michigan Press (1975)

19. Belew, R.K., McInerney, J., Schraudolph, N.N.: Evolving networks: using the genetic algorithm with connectionist learning. Citeseer (1990)

20. Whitley, D.: A genetic algorithm tutorial. Stat. Comput. **4**(2), 65–85 (1994)

21. Eiben, A.E., Smith, J.E.: Introduction to Evolutionary Computing. Springer, Berlin (2010)

22. Chess, B., McGraw, G.: Static analysis for security. Secur. Priv. **2**(6), 76–79 (2004). IEEE

23. Ayewah, N., Hovemeyer, D., Morgenthaler, J.D., et al.: Using static analysis to find bugs. Software **25**(5), 22–29 (2008). IEEE

24. Nagappan, N., Ball, T.: Static analysis tools as early indicators of pre-release defect density. In: ACM 27th International Conference on Software Engineering, pp. 580–586. ACM (2005)
25. Zitser, M., Lippmann, R., Leek, T.: Testing static analysis tools using exploitable buffer overflows from open source code. ACM SIGSOFT Softw. Eng. Not. **29**(6), 97–106 (2004). ACM
26. Ball, T.: The concept of dynamic analysis. In: Wang, J., Lemoine, M. (eds.) ESEC 1999 and ESEC-FSE 1999. LNCS, vol. 1687, pp. 216–234. Springer, Heidelberg (1999)
27. Mock, M.: Dynamic analysis from the bottom up. In: WODA 2003 ICSE Workshop on Dynamic Analysis, p. 13 (2003)
28. Ernst, M.D.: Static and dynamic analysis: synergy and duality. In: WODA 2003: ICSE Workshop on Dynamic Analysis, pp. 24–27 (2003)
29. Clarke, T.: Fuzzing for software vulnerability discovery. Department of Mathematic, Royal Holloway, University of London. Technical report. RHUL-MA-2009-4 (2009)
30. Yang, Q., Li, J.J., Weiss, D.M.: A survey of coverage-based testing tools. Comput. J. **52**(5), 589–597 (2005)
31. Crawler4j - Open Source Web Crawler for Java. https://github.com/yasserg/crawler4j
32. Oehlert, P.: Violating assumptions with fuzzing. IEEE Secur. Priv. **3**(2), 58–62 (2005)
33. Clarke, T., Crampton, J.: Fuzzing or how to help computers cope with the unexpected. Technical report, Royal Holloway University of London (2009)
34. Aitel, D.: The advantages of block-based protocol analysis for security testing. Technical report, Immunity Inc. (2002)
35. Juranic, L.: Using fuzzing to detect security vulnerabilities. Technical report, Infigo Information Security (2006)
36. Goodman, E.D.: Introduction to genetic algorithms. In: GECCO Conference Companion on Genetic and Evolutionary Computation, pp. 3205–3224. GECCO (2007)
37. Goldberg, D.E., Deb, K.: A comparative analysis of selection schemes used in genetic algorithms. In: Foundations of Genetic Algorithms, pp. 69–93 (1991)
38. Gen, M., Cheng, R.: Genetic Algorithms and Engineering Optimization. Wiley, New York (2000)
39. Deep, K., Mebrahtu, H.: Combined mutation operators of genetic algorithm for the travelling salesman problem. Int. J. Comb. Opt. Prob. Inf. **2**(3), 1–23 (2011)
40. Srinivas, M., Patnaik, L.M.: Genetic algorithms: a survey. IEEE Comput. **27**, 17–26 (1994). IEEE
41. Srinivas, M., Patnaik, L.M.: Adaptive probabilities of crossover and mutation in genetic algorithms. IEEE Trans. Syst. Man Cybern. **24**(4), 656–667 (1994). IEEE
42. Fortin, F., De Rainville, F., et al.: DEAP: evolutionary algorithms made easy. J. Mach. Learn. Res. **13**(1), 2171–2175 (2012)
43. Sulley: A Pure Python Fully-Automated and Unattended Fuzzing Framework. https://github.com/OpenRCE/sulley
44. Emma, A Free Java Code Coverage Tool. http://emma.sourceforge.net/
45. FindBugs - Find Bugs in Java Programs. http://findbugs.sourceforge.net/

46. Marovic, B., Wrzos, M., Lewandowski, M., et al.: GN3 quality assurance best practice guide 4.0. Technical report (2012)
47. Guang-Hong, L., Gang, W., Tao, Z., et al.: Vulnerability analysis for x86 executables using genetic algorithm and fuzzing. In: Third International Conference on Convergence and Hybrid Information Technology, IEEE ICCIT 2008, vol. 2, pp. 491–497 (2008)
48. Iozzo, V.: 0-knowledge fuzzing. Technical report, Black Hat DC (2010)

New Middleware for Secured Reconfigurable Real-Time Systems

Rim Idriss[✉], Adlen Loukil, and Mohamed Khalgui

LISI Laboratory, INSAT Institute, University of Carthage, Carthage, Tunisia
{rym.driss,khalgui.mohamed}@gmail.com,
adlen.loukil@insat.rnu.tn

Abstract. The paper deals with secured reconfigurable real-time embedded systems that should be adapted to their environment according to user requirements. For various reasons, a reconfiguration scenario is a run-time automatic operation that allows the addition-removal-update of Operating System tasks. These tasks are secured and should meet real-time constraints. In this case, security mechanisms are assumed to be executed to protect them. Nevertheless, when a reconfiguration is applied to add new tasks and their related mechanisms, some deadlines can be violated. We propose a new middleware that constructs a new execution model of the system after reconfiguration scenarios. It proposes to reduce the execution number of mechanisms that share the security of several tasks, or also reduces the security level of others. The middleware is based on a multi-agent model, is composed of Reconfiguration Agent that controls reconfigurations, Security Agent that controls the security of the system, Scheduling Agent that constructs the new execution model, and Execution Agent that applies the new model. The paper's contribution is implemented and applied to a case study.

Keywords: Software security · Embedded real-time system · Reconfiguration and adaptation · Multi-agent system · Real-time scheduling · Evaluation

1 Introduction

Dynamic reconfigurable embedded systems [1] offer potential opportunities for higher performance as well as adaptability to change their system requirements. Real-time constraints [2,3] are common bases for most of those systems, since they have many time requirements imposed on their activities. These systems follow a well-defined classification [4]. The functions performed by the real-time systems are executed by a fixed number of tasks. Reconfiguration scenarios [1] are assumed to be off-line or run-time concurrent operations, allowing additions-removals-updates of those tasks to improve the performance or save the system on the occurrence of software faults. The reconfiguration is generally a solution that adapt the system to its environment when some conditions are satisfied. However, the security issue presents a serious risk and attacks against these

© Springer International Publishing Switzerland 2015
H. Fujita and G. Guizzi (Eds.): SoMeT 2015, CCIS 532, pp. 469–483, 2015.
DOI: 10.1007/978-3-319-22689-7_36

systems become more critical and sophisticated [5].The modification of the system behavior at run-time can be a way to run attacks. We aimed to resolve this problem in the work [17] published in the 28th European Simulation and Modelling Conference (ESM 2014), where we proposed a new software solution based on a multi-agent architecture to allow feasible secured reconfigurations of embedded control systems. Nevertheless, in real-time embedded systems, where timing requirements are critical, choice of security mechanisms is important in terms of satisfaction of temporal requirements. Any added security solution may cause deadline misses or unacceptable security level degradation. So, our problem is not the scheduling itself but the feasible scheduling while guaranteeing an acceptable security level after any reconfiguration scenario (after any added mechanism). Although security and real-time systems have been well-studied separately, a short list of works has been done to meet both timing and security requirements and to address particular cases of dynamic reconfigurations. To address this problem, we formulate the security support in Real-Time system as a Security level optimization problem where the constraints of real-time and security are treated together. We propose a novel adaptive approach in which an adaptive real-time system is based on a multi-agent architecture to control the system's security and temporal constraints after each reconfiguration scenario. As a matter of fact, the particularity of the work that we propose in this paper lies, essentially, in the possibility of reconfiguring the security mechanisms as well as the set of real-time tasks, optimizing the security level and also the processor utilization after each scenario of reconfiguration in order to meet their deadlines. For this reason, we have proposed a middleware to be based on a model of execution of security mechanisms and tasks while meeting the deadline, and at the same time we keep an optimum level of safety. This model is based on two parameters (β, α) in order to control the execution and the occurrence of each security mechanism. A security mechanism can be executed many times, which may lead to deadline misses that can produce catastrophic failures. So, we propose to determine the number of occurence of this mechanisms denoted by β in order to stabilize the system. Nevertheless, it can be executed only once for various tasks by determining the α. So, the proposed middleware is composed of: (i) Reconfiguration Agent handles automatic reconfigurations, (ii) Security Agent is defined to guarantee safe reconfiguration, (iii) Scheduling Agent is defined to verify real-time constraints and finally Execution Agent which is responsible for the memory management of the system.

The remainder of the paper is organized as follows. Section 1 gives an overview on the different axes that create the context of the work. The scope of the work is described by discussing the basic assumptions and formulating the problem of security and real-time performance management. In Sect. 2, we present the formalization of a real-time system and also the case study that takes an example of reconfigurable tasks in order to explain the problematic. Section 3 describes the proposed architecture. Then, we explain our contribution by presenting the proposed algorithms and exposing the simulation in Sect. 4. Finally, Sect. 5 concludes the paper and discusses the future work.

2   Background

We describe in this section some related works of reconfigurable real-time embedded systems and security.

2.1   Reconfiguration and Real-Time Systems

Nowadays, several interesting studies have been proposed to develop reconfigurable real-time embedded systems. Those systems encode several tasks under classically functional and extra-functional (e.g. QoS and temporal) constraints. Reconfiguration scenarios [1] are assumed to be off-line or run-time concurrent operations, allowing additions-removals-updates of tasks or services to improve the performance or save the system on the occurrence of software faults. The work in [8] proposes a static reconfiguration technique for the reuse of the tasks that implement a broad range of systems. Each task is statically reconfigured without any reprogramming. The proposed methodology in [9] is based on the human intervention to dynamically reconfigure the tasks of the considered systems. Besides, an ontology-based agent is proposed in [10] in order to perform system's reconfigurations according to user requirements and the evolution of the environment. However, only the work in [11] is reported to address the problem of dynamic reconfiguration under real-time constraints. We are interested in this original research in dynamic secured reconfigurations of real-time embedded systems.

2.2   Security Issues in Reconfigurable Real-Time Systems

Although existing dynamic real-time scheduling algorithms are effective in enhancing the performance of systems, security requirements posed by scheduled tasks are even not factored in [11]. Several interesting results have been proposed for security in real-time scheduling. In [12], Palis proposes a task-scheduling algorithm that provides quality of service guarantees in the context of reservation-based real-time systems. The work in [13] proposes novel dynamic scheduling algorithms with security awareness. The scheduling techniques are based on security-aware of making use of a Security Level controller. Our task model in this paper assumes that each task has multiple acceptable security levels, which is similar to the concept of Security level introduced in [13]. Recently, Tao Xie, XiaoQin et al. have proposed a security-aware scheduling strategy, or SAREC, and scheduling algorithm SAREC-EDF, which integrates security requirements into scheduling for real-time applications [13].

Although all these related studies are interesting, we are interested in the security while meeting real-time constraints. We propose a new solution for the execution of real-time tasks when a new reconfiguration scenario is applied. Some tasks can be added and also related mechanisms are added too. In this case, some corresponding deadlines can be violated. So, we propose an execution model in order to allow secured reconfiguration scenarios while meeting real-time constraints. After any scenario, the execution model reduces the execution of mechanisms or also the security level of tasks. We developed in this paper a middleware which is based on a multi-agent model (Reconfiguration, security, real-time).

3   Methods

We describe in this section the formalization of a Reconfigurable Real-Time System and present also a case study to expose the paper's problem.

3.1   Formalization of Reconfigurable Real-Time Systems

A real-time task [4], designated in this paper as τ_i, is essentially characterized by its: (i) Computation time C known as Worst Case Execution Time (WCET), this parameter has to be determined previously, (ii) Deadline D is the time limit by which τ_i must be accomplished, (iii) Starting time S is the moment when the system decides to start τ_i, (iv) Period T which serves as a duration of one cycle on a repeating execution of a periodic task and represents the interval between two consecutive activations. It is important to mention that in the case of an aperiodic task, the concept of period is utterly missing and finally (v) response time R is the length of time from the moment of release to the instant when the task completes its execution.

The processor utilization, U, of a periodic task is expressed by:

$$U_i = \frac{C_i}{T_i} \tag{1}$$

The processor utilization of n tasks is given by:

$$U = \sum_{i=1}^{n} \frac{C_i}{T_i} \tag{2}$$

Based on the M/M/1 model [15] that is widely used in uniprocessor schedule, the aperiodic tasks arrive according to the Poisson process with a Poisson distribution which is characterized by rate λ_r. The WCETs of all the tasks are exponentially distributed with λ_c. So, the processor utilization U_{api} is formalized by: $U_{api} = \frac{\lambda_r}{\lambda_c}$.

A mechanism can be considered as a real-time task which is based on security goals which are presented by different services : confidentiality, availability and integrity [7]. Indeed, a security service for a particular security requirement can be implemented by one or more mechanisms, so, only the quality differs. According to [7], we assume a set of security services denoted by $Set_{Ser} = \{C, I, A\}$ where each one presents respectively (i) confidentiality protection service, (ii) integrity protection service and (iii) availability protection service. We assume for each security mechanism a range of security requirement levels where a security level is a predefined combination of transport and message security mechanisms. This value may be: low, high or medium.

$$M_i = \begin{pmatrix} SL_{iC} \\ SL_{iI} \\ SL_{iA} \end{pmatrix} \tag{3}$$

3.2 Case Study

Let us consider an embedded system Sys to be reconfigured automatically. A reconfiguration scenario is assumed to be run-time additions-removals or updates of tasks. Sys is characterized by a superset of OS tasks that offer all its number of services, but it is implemented at a particular time by a subset of tasks. Regarding memory constraints in many embedded systems, it is generally useful to load subsets of tasks to perform the system's services at a particular time. Therefore, the reconfiguration is a modification of the current system's subset. We define the following seven tasks to offer all the required services ($Number_{services} = 7$):(i) τ_1 is based on an input event to activate a key on the embedded keyboard, (ii) τ_2 blocks any undesired communication from remote well-known devices, (iii) τ_3 is the software task allowing to send a well-known file via bluetooth, (iv) τ_4 is a financial task that allows a secured communication with banks for a required payement service,(v) τ_5 is a software task allowing a secured remote payement of bills, (vi) τ_6 is an access secured task to a remote website for consulting and (vii) τ_7 is an update secured task.

To handle secured reconfigurations, we assume a set of security mechanisms denoted by $SetM = \{M_1, ..., M_{10}\}$ that present respectivily:(i) spam filter (calls and emails from unwanted users), (ii) selective permission,(iii) authentication, (iv) firewall, (v) intrusion detection system, (vii) dynamic resource allocation, (viii) access control, (ix) sandboxing, (x) encryption and (xi) application certification. These mechanisms are based on security goals which are presented by different services : confidentiality, availability and integrity. Each security service can be implemented by one or more mechanisms.

The details related to the intial system Sys are given by Table 1. The task τ_2 for example is periodically executed each 55 time units, and uses the security mechanism M_2 for 2 time units. According to the simulator Cheddar [14], the system Sys is feasible since all the tasks meet the related deadlines and capacity as shown in Fig. 1.

Table 1. Parameters of the initial tasks

Tasks	Security Level	Mechanisms	Computation times (Ci)	Periods
τ_1	0,2	M_1	5	60
τ_2	0,8	M_2	2	55
τ_3	1,3	-	3	45
τ_4	1,1	-	2	40
τ_5	0,3	-	3	50
τ_{a1}	0,1	M_3	8	-

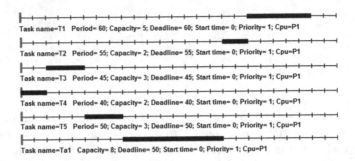

Task name=T1   Period= 60; Capacity= 5; Deadline= 60; Start time= 0; Priority= 1; Cpu=P1

Task name=T2   Period= 55; Capacity= 2; Deadline= 55; Start time= 0; Priority= 1; Cpu=P1

Task name=T3   Period= 45; Capacity= 3; Deadline= 45; Start time= 0; Priority= 1; Cpu=P1

Task name=T4   Period= 40; Capacity= 2; Deadline= 40; Start time= 0; Priority= 1; Cpu=P1

Task name=T5   Period= 50; Capacity= 3; Deadline= 50; Start time= 0; Priority= 1; Cpu=P1

Task name=Ta1   Capacity= 8; Deadline= 50; Start time= 0; Priority= 1; Cpu=P1

Fig. 1. Execution graph of the tasks

Table 2. Parameter of the tasks after reconfiguration.

Tasks	Security Level	Mechanisms	Computation times (Ci)	Periods
τ_1	0,2	-	10	20
τ_2	0,8	M_1	5	50
τ_3	1,3	M_3	5	15
τ_6	1,1	M_3	7	20
		M_{11}	15	
τ_7	2	M_6	10	35
		M_8	8	
		M_{10}	5	

Task name=T1   Period= 20; Capacity= 10; Deadline= 20; Start time= 0; Priority= 5; Cpu=P1

Task name=T2   Period= 50; Capacity= 5; Deadline= 10; Start time= 8; Priority= 4; Cpu=P1

Task name=T3   Period= 15; Capacity= 5; Deadline= 5; Start time= 1; Priority= 3; Cpu=P1

Task name=T6   Period=20 ; Capacity= 15; Deadline= 20; Start time= 0; Priority= 1; Cpu=P1

Task name=T7   Period= 35; Capacity= 10; Deadline= 15; Start time= 0; Priority= 1; Cpu=P1

Task name=Ta1   Capacity= 5; Deadline= 50; Start time= 0; Priority= 1; Cpu=P1

Fig. 2. Execution graph of the tasks after reconfigurations

Let we assume the following reconfiguration that adds the tasks τ_6 and τ_7 and removes τ_4 and τ_5 under well-defined conditions.

The application of the reconfiguration adds new tasks and related mechanisms and allows the violation of real-time constraints leading automatically to the violation of the feasibility conditions as shown in Fig. 2.

4 Design of the Proposed Middleware

In this section, we describe the proposed middleware and also the formalization of the multi-agent architecture.

4.1 Proposed Architecture

The proposed approach is explained in (Fig. 3). This architecture is based on a middleware containing four agents: Reconfiguration Agent (RA), Security Agent (SA), Scheduling Agent (SchA) and Execution Agent (ExA). In order to obtain a feasible reconfigurable system, we propose those layers to control the real-time and security constraints. Nevertheless, the control of this reconfiguration at the level of **(RA)** is extremely important because any uncontrolled automatic reconfiguration applied in the device can lead to critical security problems. So, we propose the second layer that controls and defines the useful solutions that meet the security constraints, this layer is denoted by Security Agent **(SA)**. To meet real-time constraints, we propose another agent **(ScA)** in order to control the scheduling of the software tasks. This approach allows to handle secured reconfiguration scenarios while guaranteeing secured behaviors of the system after each scenario. Finally, the last layer **(ExA)** interacts with the system in order to execute the final solution.

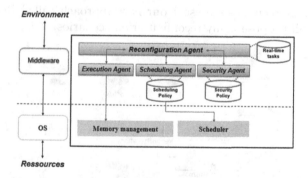

Fig. 3. Architecture of the proposed approach

4.2 Reconfiguration and Security Control

In the paper [17], the Reconfiguration Agent is modeled by nested state machines to handle automatic reconfigurations, and the Security Agent is defined by state machines to guarantee safe reconfigurations.

4.3 Dynamic Scheduling Control and Execution

In reconfigurable systems with shared resources and security mechanisms, it is required to not only meet real-time constraints but also support the data integrity, confidentiality, and authenticity. So, we consider that the Scheduling Agent is a component that provides run-time solutions in order to get a real-time feasibility of the system while meeting security constraints. The ScA ensures the execution of various tasks and mechanisms by applying the constraints and conditions defined in the database (ScDB).

The Execution Agent (ExA) allocates an exclusive space memory to each new software task or mechanism received by the Scheduling Agent. In this case, the latter should propose useful functional (removal of tasks) or temporal (change their parameters) solutions for the minimization of the processor utilization (deadlines, periods...): (i) Modification of the periods and the deadlines of tasks and (ii) removal of some tasks (including security mechanisms). Applying security services to a system incurs overhead to the system including more CPU and memory usage. For this reason, we define a new concept defined by a quantitative notion Risk of Security (RoS) (presented in [17]). This concept presents an adaptive security policy in which the value of RoS can be degraded by decreasing the number of security mechanisms or their characteristics. So, for each security mechanisms, we can modify the proposed solution of the Security Agent that can be:

- Stabilizing or Minimizing CPU usage (U): this technique can be achieved by the modification of WCET, period or deadline values.
- Minimizing the storage in the memory (removal of some tasks).

Those different techniques present our new approach called Reconfigurable Security that will propose many reconfiguration scenarios.

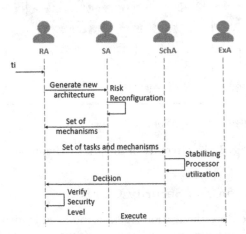

Fig. 4. Intercommunication between agents

We define the agent communication protocol in Fig. 4, where the SA handles the different requests to access to the resources of the system and takes the appropriate decision (Authorized request, denied request or other). When the

RA checks the environment evolution, it takes into account the user requirements to apply automatic reconfiguration scenarios at the different levels (architecture, structure or data). For each scenario, the RA should send a request to the SA in order to: (i) verify each set of tasks with the different blocks in its database, (ii) based on the component of security policy, determine the criteria to be secured (Integrity, confidentiality or availability) and the security level of the system in the case of this reconfiguration form, (iii) determine the appropriate mechanisms and (iv) finally send the decision to the RA with a new set of tasks. But, the response of the agents is controlled by the Scheduling Agent.

Formalization: Scheduling Agent: The Scheduling Agent receives the new set of tasks including the set of security mechanisms considered as a simple task: $Sys^{(0)} = \{\tau_1...\tau_n, M_1...M_{nm}\}$, where n presents the number of tasks and n_m presents the number of mechanisms. When a reconfiguration scenario is dynamically applied at run-time to add new tasks or new security mechanisms, we can reach the conclusion that U_{aft} is greater than or equal to U_{bef}, with:

$$U = \sum_{k=1}^{n} \frac{C_k}{T_k} + \sum_{m=1}^{n_m} \frac{C_m}{T_m} \qquad (4)$$

The formula (4) calculates the processor utilization (U) of the system that is the amount of real-time tasks (n) and mechanisms (n_m).

Running Example 1: *The system $Sys^{(1)}$ after reconfiguration is illustrated through the Figure 2 shown by Table 2. It contains periodic and aperiodic tasks with the distributions $\lambda_c = 0, 5$ and $\lambda_r = 0, 1$. The processor utilization of the new set of tasks is equal to $U_T = 0, 57$. The processor utilization of mechanisms is $U_M = 0, 60$. After their addition to the system, the new processor utilization $U_{sys} = 1, 2 > 1$, the system is infeasible.*

The objective of the Scheduling Agent (ScA) is to adapt the security mechanisms with the system in compliance with real-time constraints. So, we present two solutions:

First Solution: Occurrence of Mechanisms: Each mechanism can be executed many times, which may lead to deadline misses that can produce catastrophic failures in safety critical systems. So, we propose to determine the number of occurrences denoted by β of each mechanism in order to stabilize the processor utilization U_{sys} (the formula 5).

$$U_{sys} = \sum_{i=1}^{n} \frac{C_i}{T_i} + \sum_{j=1}^{k} \frac{\beta C_j}{T_j} \qquad (5)$$

where the parameter $\beta(1 \leq \beta(j) \leq n(M_j))$ presents a factor for the execution of security mechanisms: $\beta(j) = \sum_{j=1}^{k} \beta$

Running Example 2: *Taking the mechanism M_1, it will be executed for three tasks $\{\tau_1, \tau_3, \tau_6\}$. The mechanism is presented by three security services $\{SS_a, SS_i, SS_C\}$ that correspond respectively to authentication, integrity* and confidentiality. If $(SS_a > 0)$ then β *may be higher than 1. In our run-ning example, we have* $SS_a > 0$, *so, the* M_1 *is a mechanism of authentication. It can be concluded that* $\beta = 3$.

$$\text{So, we have } \beta(j) = \begin{pmatrix} \beta(1) = 3 \\ \beta(2) = 1 \\ \beta(3) = 1 \end{pmatrix}$$

By computing the processor utilization of the system, we found that U_{sys} becomes $0,95 \leq 1$.

Second Solution: Period Modification of Mechanisms: The periodicity of security mechanisms can be adjusted by a scaling factor $\alpha[\alpha_{min}, \alpha_{max}]$ in order to define a new period αT_j. So, the new processor utilization U_{sys} is presented by (6).

$$U_{sys} = \sum_{i=1}^{n} \frac{C_i}{T_i} + \sum_{j=1}^{k} \frac{\beta C_j}{\alpha T_j} \tag{6}$$

Assume that the mechanism can be executed for each task $\tau_i \in Sys^{(t)}$ in different time.

Case 1: $\alpha = 1$: The period of mechanism M_i. We note: $T_{jm} = \alpha T_j = T_j$

Case 2: $\alpha \in [\alpha_{min}, \alpha_{max}]$: The actual period of mechanism M_i when it will call only one time: $T_j = \frac{T_{jm}}{\alpha}$. The system uses the earliest deadline first (EDF) algorithm [14] as the underlying scheduling policy. Accordingly, the upper bound of schedulable CPU utilization is 100 %, and the schedulability condition is:

$U_{Sys} \leq 1 \leftrightarrow U_T + U_M \leq 1 \leftrightarrow U_T + \sum_{j=1}^{k} \frac{C_j}{\alpha T_j} \leq 1$

For $\alpha > 1$, $\frac{U_j}{\alpha} \leq 1 - U_T \leftrightarrow \alpha \geq \frac{U_m}{1-U_T}$.

$$\alpha_{min} = \frac{U_m}{1 - U_T}$$

We have $T_j \geq \alpha \leftrightarrow \frac{C_j}{T_j} \leq \frac{C_j}{\alpha} \leftrightarrow U_m \leq \sum_{m=1}^{k} \frac{C_m}{\alpha} \leftrightarrow \alpha \leq \frac{1}{U_m} \sum_{j=1}^{k} C_j$

$$\alpha_{max} = \frac{1}{U_m} \sum_{j=1}^{k} C_j$$

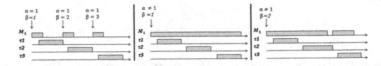

Fig. 5. Execution graph(the proposed solution)

Running Example 3: *In this example, we will modify the period of mechanisms. So, it is possible that a periodic mechanism becomes aperiodic. And also, it is* *possible that the concept of task parallelism is achieved. The mechanism can be executed for two tasks or more (according to the priorities). And also it can be launched 2 times or more. Determining α and β ? For M_1 and M_2, the value of α is 1 and for the M_3, we have $\alpha T_3 = 69$. By computing the processor utilization of the system, we found that U_{sys} becomes $0,89 \leq 1$. According to the simulator Cheddar [14], the system is feasible compared to the other solutions Fig. 5.*

5   Implementation and Evaluation

The algorithm and implementation of the reconfiguration and security agents are presented in the paper [17]. The algorithm of the scheduling agent is presented in Fig. 6. It is based on two classes: (i) The Interpreter-based agent scheduling loads the tasks according to their mechanisms and their parameters and (ii) the generator-based agent scheduling is started by the "Interpreter" in order to calculate the parameters of mechanisms (α, β) based on the formulas described previously (5 and 6). We present in Fig. 7 the behaviors's cycle of this algorithm.

```
Algorithm : Scheduling Agent

1  T ← Tasks , M ← Mechanisms, i ←1, j←1
2  While ( i < N(Tasks)) do
3      If ( Interpreter ( T(i), M) = NULL) Else Execute(T(i))
4      Else If (Interpreter ( T(i), M) = (Mext))
5          While ( j < N(Mext)) do
6              α(j), β(j) ← generate(α, β ); // calculate α et β
7              If (α(j)=1) && (β(j)=1) then Execute(M(j),T(i))
8              Else If (α(j)=1) && (β(j) > 1) then
9                  Tj = Correspond(M(j))
10                 Usys // Calculate the CPU utilization (formula 6)
11                 FaisibilityTest();
12                 Execute(M(j), T(i), Tj);
13             Else If (β(j)≥ 1) && (α(j) > 1) then
14                 update(M(j)); // update period of mechanism.
15                 Tj = Correspond(M(j))
16                 Usys // U after the addition of mechanisms and tasks.
17                 FaisibilityTest();
18                 Execute(M(j), T(i), Tj);
19             End If
20         End While
21     End If
22 End While
```

Fig. 6. Algorithm of the Scheduling Agent

We developed a plugin at LISI Laboratory of INSAT Institute that allows to build analyzable and predictable systems that meet their real-time and security requirements by ensuring secured reconfiguration scenarios (Figs. 8 and 9): (i) evaluates the security level of tasks of the initial system, (ii) evaluates the security level of any reconfiguration scenario after the addition-removal task, (iii) tests the processor utilization and (vi) allows or denies the system to execute this scenario.

Any reconfiguration scenario is based on the decision of the proposed agents (SA and SchA). Moreover, in order to meet all the real-time and security constraints, the relative deadline D_i and the priority of each task is configured by the intelligent control agent SchA. According to Eq. (5), U_{bef} of Sys is calculated by functions of the WCETs and the periods of tasks. This indicates that

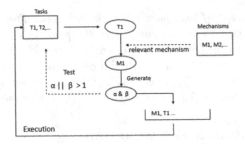

Fig. 7. Cycle of agents's behaviors(SchA and ExA)

WCETs and periods play important roles in the reconfigurations. In this case, we are not interested in the initial relative deadline of each task. The goal is to improve the security level while respecting the real-time constraints to minimize the processor utilization and to meet their relative deadlines. All the initial and new tasks are represented as follows: (i) The initial and added tasks of Sys are shown in Fig. 8 and (ii) All the added mechanisms are added by the Security Agent that is shown in Fig. 9.

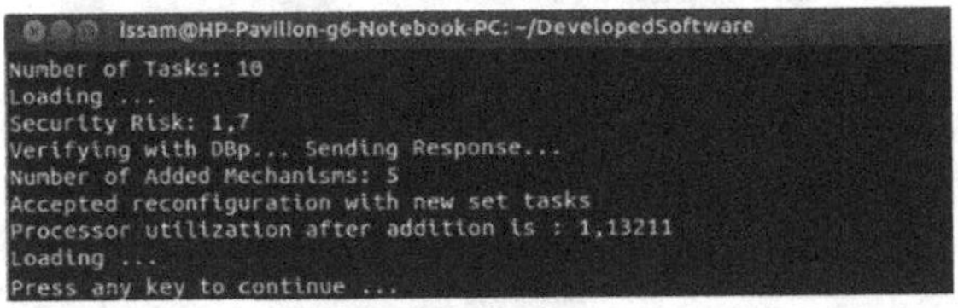

Fig. 8. Developped intelligent control agent: SA

The developed agent SchA can configure all the parameters and evaluate the CPU utilization. This latter presents a key performance metric. It can be used to track CPU performance regressions or improvements, and is a useful datapoint for performance problem investigations. Moreover, according to the results suggested by SchA, the developed agent ExA must allocate and set the proper memory protection attributes in order to execute the added tasks or mechanisms.

Evaluation and Comparative Study: we run the example, displayed in Sect. 3, with different forms of reconfigurations presented in Table 3 for 30 days such as the addition of a new task for 3 times in one day etc.

The testing of the system's behavior after the application of our approach is shown in Fig. 10. We can notice that the control of the Security Level and the CPU utilization for each added task helps the system to proceed a correct execution. Then, according to SL_{sys} and U_{sys} (6), it is clear that the risk of the system without the intervention of the Scheduling and Security Agent U_{bef} and

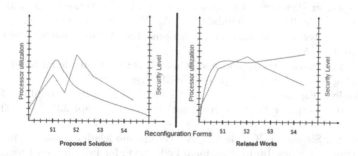

Fig. 9. Developped intelligent control agent: SchA

Table 3. Reconfiguration Scenarios Test

Reconfiguration Form	Execution Time	Reconfiguration number
S1	5	3 times
S2	15	5 times
S3	5	2 times
S4	3	1 times

$Risk_{bef}$ is more than U_{aft} and $Risk_{aft}$. Unlike our solution, the related works's solution (Fig. 10) can allow the violation of security properties and destroy the whole system in some situations.

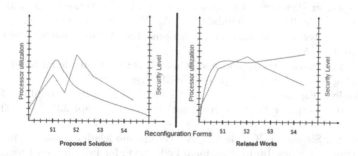

Fig. 10. Safety critical systems analysis

6   Conclusion

Although the applicability of related works in security and reconfigurable real-time systems is various and clear, we believe in this article in their security limitations when automatic reconfiguration scenarios are applied at run-time to add-remove-update OS tasks for the adaptation of the system. Therefore, this paper gives a new strategy to allow useful regulations of secured reconfigurable systems. The goal is to run secured software reconfigurations that adapt the system to its environment while meeting real-time and security constraints. This idea is performed by adding an autonomous plugin to be used at run-time for checking real-time and security constraints. For this reason, we have defined in this paper a middleware which is based on four agents: Reconfiguration Agent handles automatic reconfigurations, Security Agent is defined to guarantee safe reconfiguration, Scheduling Agent is defined to verify real-time constraints. In this paper, we present the simulation of the proposed approach with the testing of the relevant formulas, and the next step will be the experimentation.

We plan in our future work to study secured reconfigurable hardware components as well as networked distributed embedded systems. A real case study will be applied also for the evaluation of the paper's contribution.

References

1. Gharbi, A., Gharsellaoui, H., Khalgui, M., Valentini, A.: Safety reconfiguration of embedded control systems. In: Embedded Computing Systems: Applications, Optimization, and Advanced Design, pp. 184–210 (2013)
2. Shyamasundar, R.K., Aghav, J.V.: Validating real-time constraints in embedded systems. In: Pacific Rim International Symposium, pp. 347–355. IEEE Press (2001)
3. Dave, B.P.: CRUSADE: hardware/software co-synthesis of dynamically reconfigurable heterogeneous real-time distributed embedded systems. In: Design, Automation and Test in Europe Conference and Exhibition, pp. 97–104. IEEE Press (1999)
4. Rammig, F., Ditze, M., Janacik, P., Heimfarth, T., Kerstan, T., Oberthuer, S., Stahl, K.: Basic Concepts of Real Time Operating Systems. In: Ecker, W., Mller, W., Dmer, R. (eds.) Hardware-dependent Software, Principles and Practice, pp. 15–45. Springer (Science + Business Media B.V), The Netherlands (2009)
5. Khelladi, L., Challal, Y., Bouabdallah, A., Badache, N.: On security issues in embedded systems: challenges and solutions. Int. J. Inf. Comput. Secur. IJICS 2(2), 140–174 (2008)
6. Singh, B.: Network security and management. In: Computational Intelligence and Computing Research ICCIC, pp. 1–6. IEEE Press (2010)
7. Spyropoulou, E., Levin, T., Irvine, C.: Calculating costs for quality of security service. In: Computer Security Applications ACSAC, pp. 334–343. IEEE Press (2000)
8. Angelov, C., Sierszecki, K., Marian, N.: Design models for reusable and reconfigurable state machines. In: International Federation for Information Processing, pp. 152–163. IEEE Press (2005)
9. Gehin, A.L., Staroswiecki, M.: Reconfiguration analysis using generic component models. IEEE Trans. Syst. Mach. Cybern. 38(3), 575–583 (2008)
10. Al-Safi, Y., Vyatkin, V.: An ontology-based reconfiguration agent for intelligent mechatronic systems. In: Proceedings 4th International Conference Holonic and Multi-Agent System Manufacturing, pp. 114–126, Regensburg, Germany (2007)
11. Wang, X., Khalgui, M., Li, Z.W.: Dynamic low power reconfigurations of real-time embedded systems. In: Proceedings 1st Pervasive and Embedded Computing and Communication Systems, Algarve, Portugal (2011)
12. Palis, M.A.: Online real-time job scheduling with rate of progress guarantees. In: Parallel Architectures, Algorithms, and Networks, pp. 65–70 (2002)

13. Xie, T., Qin, X., Sung, A.: SAREC: a security-aware scheduling strategy for real-time applications on clusters. In: Parallel Processing ICPP, pp. 5–12. IEEE Press (2005)
14. Singhoff, F., Legrand, J., Nana, L., Marc, L.: Cheddar: a flexible real time scheduling framework. ACM SIGAda Ada Letters **24**(4), 1–8 (2004)
15. Bhat, U.N.: An Introduction to Queueing Theory. Birkhäuser Boston, IEEE Press, Boston (2008)
16. El-Hoiydi, A.: Soft deadline bounds for two-way transactions in bluetooth piconets under co-channel interference. In: Emerging Technologies and Factory Automation, pp. 143–150. IEEE Press (2001)
17. Idriss, R., Loukil, A., Khalgui, M.: New solutions for feasible secured reconfiguration of embedded control systems. In: The European Simulation and Modelling Conference (2014)

New Software Techniques in Image Processing and Computer Graphics

Real-Time Light Shaft Generation for Indoor Rendering

Hoshang Kolivand$^{(\boxtimes)}$, Mohd Shahrizal Sunar, and Ali Selamat

MaGIC-X (Media and Games Innovation Centre of Excellence),
UTM-IRDA Digital Media Centre Universiti Teknologi Malaysia,
81310 Skudai, Johor, Malaysia
kolivand@magicx.my, {shahrizal,aselamat}@utm.my

Abstract. Realistic natural phenomena such as light shaft for indoor and outdoor environments are used in various applications. The main issue with the existing light shaft algorithms is not sufficient quality in real-time rendering. In this paper, we address this issue by proposing a hybrid technique based on the widely used shadow generation techniques. Shadow maps are used to recognize the silhouette of the occluders geometrically. Then, shadow volume is employed to generate the volume of the light shaft. This volume is the volume between occluder and shadow receivers. Finally, light scattering is employed to create light shaft in real-time rendering. The results are convenient for any indoor rendering environments.

Keywords: Light shaft rendering · Shadows · Illumination · Indoor rendering

1 Introduction

Natural illumination is the most important part of outdoor rendering [21, 24], which is lit with the sun with sky color creating shadows correctly. The main problem with natural illumination is how to deal with all natural light sources such as the sun, the moon, and the sky. A salient part of natural illumination deals with lighting and shadows. Although various tools are used to illuminate scenes in 3D Studio Max, May and Lightwave, they are patch-oriented and unsuitable for real-time rendering.

Many issues influence the realism of generated 3D objects in computer graphics such as lighting, shadowing and illumination. In general, illumination refers to both the light that comes from light source directly and light from other surfaces or objects which is called indirect lighting. Illumination has been studied as an attractive subject especially since the advent of computer graphics. Applying illumination on virtual objects such as light-shaft may increase the realism in combination of outdoor and indoor environments.

The process of light-shaft rendering in virtual environments is approximated by physical based lighting. In this collision (light with surface), many complicated dynamic processes occur that determine pixel's color of light-shaft.

© Springer International Publishing Switzerland 2015
H. Fujita and G. Guizzi (Eds.): SoMeT 2015, CCIS 532, pp. 487–495, 2015.
DOI: 10.1007/978-3-319-22689-7_37

Many methods [9,21] have been proposed to generate light shaft based on Ray-tracing. Although, they create realistic light shafts their rendering is a time-consuming process.

This paper introduces a method whereby image based and geometrically based techniques are combined to create volume between occluders and shadow receivers applying different illuminations on the volume to produce a light shaft whose lighting depends on the location, date and time.

In addition to enhancing the realism of outdoor and indoor integration and recognizing the best direction of building to save the energy, building design industries can use the final software to overcome this issue. The amount of light passing through windows in any specific location, date and time can be visualised during a day. This leads building designers to find the best suited orientation of any building in any specific location.

2   Research Background

More than 30 years has passed since the first computer game was invented (3D Monster Maze 1981); many prominent researchers have focused on improving the quality of virtual environments and making virtual scenes realistic, i.e. similar to what meets the eyes. Nowadays, large companies, e.g. NVIDIA, Maya and 3D Studio Max spend exorbitant amounts on improving the quality of various fields of computer games. Although speed is crucial in real-time applications, visual quality is also a very significant factor [2,7,12,27,28].

Many different methods have been proposed for generating images based on scattering and absorption [1,4,5,11,13]. Nishita et al. [22] focused on multiple scattering to generate a realistic sky color.

Earlier works on light shaft generation can be found in [9,10,18,19] while other works show light shaft is still opened in the case of qualitative and quantitative [20]. Reference [17] proposed unified volumes representation for light shaft and shadow, which is an efficient method for simulating natural light shafts and shadows with atmospheric scattering effect. Reference [25] presented a model for temporal color changes exploring its use for the analysis of outdoor scenes from time-lapse video data.

Most real-time rendering has focused on indoor rendering but the real ability of computer graphics can be demonstrated in outdoor rendering taking the sky illumination into account [23,24]. It is because, the sky usually illuminates a point from almost all directions. A realistic sky scene will greatly improve the reality of not only outdoor virtual environments [26] but also indoor light-shaft which comes from outdoor. Generating sky color as a background for each outdoor scene is an essential factor for making it realistic. Displaying the sky has become critical, as many buildings are designed, so that the sky or a surrounding scene is reflected in the windows [3].

Lighting rendering includes outdoor, indoor and a combination which is a very extensive topic in video games. The main problem when dealing with the combination of outdoor and indoor scenes is the visual realism of sky illumination, light-shaft and shadows [24]. The sun moves over time and light-shafts are often soft. The light comes from a wide area like the sky or the entire sphere of influence around a point contributing to the illumination. The illumination at the points is very important for the realistic light-shaft in outdoor-indoor scenes.

In real-time rendering, realism can be achieved only through combination of sophisticated modellings such as daylight, reflection, absorption and shadows [8]. Most real-time rendering has focused on indoor rendering due to the complexity of outdoor rendering [23,24] all of which motivate us to focus on integration of outdoor and indoor rendering taking outdoor illumination, light-shaft and shadows into account.

Kolivand et al. [15] proposed a technique to apply the effect of sky color on virtual objects in augmented reality in any specific location, date and time for flat shadow receivers and extended the work for different shadow receivers in 2014 [16].

3   Methods

In this section some of the techniques that have been taken into consideration for generating light shafts are discussed. A simple framework is illustrated in Fig. 1.

4   Light Shaft Components in Indoor Environments

4.1   Lighting

The process of light rendering in virtual environments involves approximation of physical based lighting. Further analysis requires knowledge of photons or the study of electromagnetic wave modeling under the physics of light. In this case the brightness and the color of light can be controlled by the number of photons, and energy contained in photons, respectively.

In indoor rendering the effect of sky can be taken into consideration but to simplify the case we have not considered outdoor environments. To demonstrate the ability, light shaft with different types of color is employed as illustrated in the result section.

4.2   Light Scattering in Indoor Scenes

Direct illumination arrives at the object directly from light of sources; while indirect illumination reaches the point through reflection of lighting from other objects. The main direct light source is the sun and sky, but indirect illumination can be obtained from $n - 1$ objects where the number of objects in the scene is n.

In the case of direct illumination, although the sun is distant it cannot be considered as a point light source (about 0.5 degree angular diameter). This is the main reason why shadows' silhouettes in outdoor rendering are almost soft. However, the skylight is the result of sun illumination and it should be considered as an independent light source in outdoor rendering. Thus, indirect illumination more subtly exerts effect in making scenes realistic.

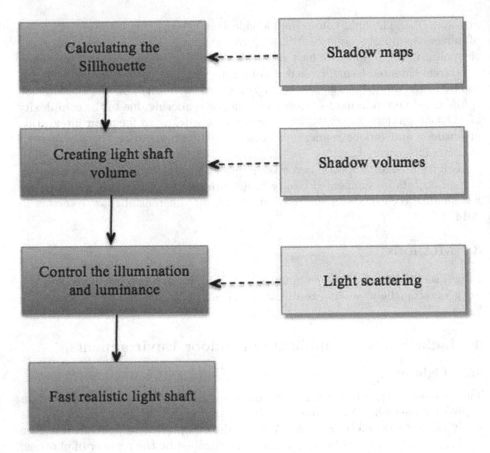

Fig. 1. A framework for realistic indoor light shaft

4.3   Indoor Light Shaft

For indoor light shaft rendering the integration of shadow volume and shadow
maps [14] involves consideration of a light scattering. Shadow maps are used
to recognize the silhouette of the occluders image based. Applying this idea no
more action is needed to detect the silhouette of occluders geometrically. Then,
shadow volume is employed to generate the volume of light shaft. This volume
is the volume between occluders and shadow receivers as shown in Fig. 2.

Multiplying the luminance from a light source by a factor w is equivalent to
multiplying the intensity of the light source by w. In general, luminance of sky
light can be calculated using the following formula:

$$I_{skylight} = \int_{\Omega} \pounds(s)\kappa(s)ds \qquad (1)$$

where

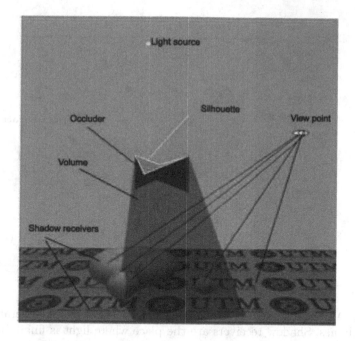

Fig. 2. Shadow volumes and silhouettes

Ω is the hemispherical integral domain above the surface.

S is a unit vector toward an arbitrary direction in the hemisphere above the surface.

$\mathcal{L}(s)$ represents the intensity distribution of the sky.

$\kappa(s)$ is a factor determined by the reflectance function of the calculation point.

The main idea of ray marching is based on epipolar sampling that has been employed by [6]. Figure 3 shows the idea of epipolar sampling.

Theory of light shaft generation using shadow volumes and shadow maps is illustrated in Fig. 4 where light is shown to originate from outside through

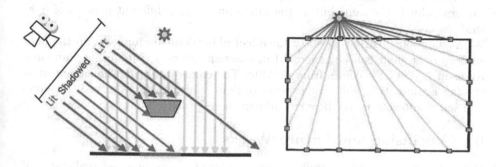

Fig. 3. Idea of epipolar sampling to be applied in indoor rendering

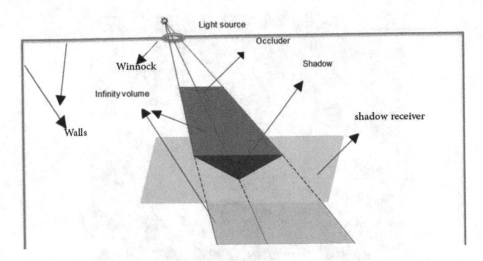

Fig. 4. Theory of light shaft

a winnock. An occluder blocks the light. Light shaft volume is generated using shadow volumes. Shadow receivers are the place where light is finally received.

5   Implementation and Results

Firstly, we need to clear color-buffer and z-buffer. The scene is rendered with only ambient and emissive lighting. The stencil-buffer is disabled for writing in color-buffer and z-buffer, Then, the z-buffer test is used. Finally, the scene is rendered with only diffuse and secular lighting.

Figure 5 shows an indoor environment where light comes from outside. The light effects some occluders as a fan. The fan is turning effecting light shaft. The difference between the left side and the right side figures lies in the different light shaft colors. No shadows exist in these figures except for those from the direct lighting. The scenes are not realistic due to the lack of shadowing.

Figure 6 shows a different environment where light comes from outside. The camera point is the same but as the fan is animating, different aspects of light shaft can be observed.

As mentioned earlier, to show the effect of outdoor illumination on the light shaft, a light shaft can be generated in different colors. Figure 7 shows an environment where light comes from outside. The camera point is the same but as the fan is animating, different aspects of light shaft can be observed. Shadows and self shadowing make the environment more realistic.

6   Conclusion and Future Works

Here, shadow generation techniques are employed to create a fast realistic light shaft for indoor environments. The combined method makes use of hardware-accelerated volume rendering technique. The realistic light shaft is generated

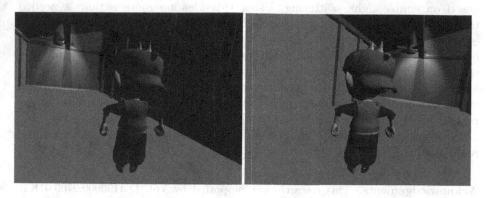

Fig. 5. An indoor environment with different light shaft colors without shadows

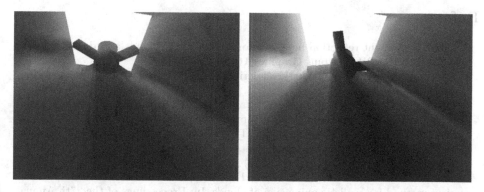

Fig. 6. An indoor environment from single view point with shadows and self shadowing

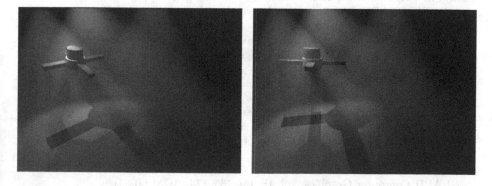

Fig. 7. An indoor environment from a single view point in some different light shaft colors with different situation of light shaft including shadows and self shadowing

based on simple light scattering. Using this idea no more action is needed to detect the silhouette of occluders geometrically. Then, shadow volume is employed to generate the volume of light shaft. This volume is the volume between occluders and shadow receivers. Finally, light scattering is employed to create light shaft in real-time rendering.

Future works may involve outdoor environments. The effect of sky color and sun position on the light shaft forms the future work that the authors of the present paper are going to address. Other natural phenomena such as fog, haze and rainbow could also exert effects on both virtual environments and augmented realities.

Acknowledgements. This research was supported by Vot. Q.J130000.2709.01K26 PAS grant at the MaGIC-X (Media and Games Innovation Centre of Excellence) UTM-IRDA Digital Media Centre Universiti Teknologi Malaysia

References

1. Blinn, J.F.: Light reflection functions for simulation of clouds and dusty surfaces. ACM SIGGRAPH Comput. Graphics **16**(3), 21–29 (1982)
2. Boulanger, K.: Real-time realistic rendering of nature scenes with dynamic lighting. Ph.D Thesis (2008), proQuest
3. Dobashi, Y., Nishita, T., Kaneda, K., Yamashita, H.: A fast display method of sky colour using basis functions. J. Vis. Comput. Anim. **8**, 115–127 (1997)
4. Dobashi, Y., Kaneda, K., Nakashima, T., Yamashita, H., Nishita, T., Tadamura, K.: Skylight for interior lighting design. In: Computer Graphics Forum, vol. 13, pp. 85–96. Wiley Online Library (1994)
5. Dobashi, Y., Kaneda, K., Yamashita, H., Okita, T., Nishita, T.: A simple, efficient method for realistic animation of clouds. In: Proceedings of the 27th Annual Conference on Computer Graphics and Interactive Techniques, pp. 19–28. ACM Press/Addison-Wesley Publishing Co. (2000)
6. Engelhardt, T., Dachsbacher, C.: Epipolar sampling for shadows and crepuscular rays in participating media with single scattering. In: Proceedings of the 2010 ACM SIGGRAPH Symposium on Interactive 3D Graphics and Games, pp. 119–125. ACM (2010)
7. Feng, Y.: Estimation of light source environment for illumination consistency of augmented reality. In: Congress on Image and Signal Processing 2008, CISP 2008, vol. 3, pp. 771–775. IEEE(2008)
8. Jansen, F.W., Chalmers, A.: Casting shadows in real time. In: Cohen, M.F., Puech, C., Sillion, F.(eds.) Fourth Eurographics Workshop on Rendering, pp. 27–46 (1993)
9. Jensen, H.W., Christensen, P.H.: Efficient simulation of light transport in scences with participating media using photon maps. In: Proceedings of the 25th Annual Conference on Computer Graphics and Interactive Techniques, pp. 311–320. ACM (1998)
10. Kajiya, J.T., Von Herzen, B.P.: Ray tracing volume densities. In: ACM SIGGRAPH Computer Graphics, vol. 18, pp. 165–174. ACM (1984)
11. Kaneda, K., Okamoto, T., Nakamae, E., Nishita, T.: Photorealistic image synthesis for outdoor scenery under various atmospheric conditions. Vis. Comput. **7**, 247–258 (1991)

12. Kim, Y.: Augmented reality of flexible surface with realistic lighting. In: 2010 Proceedings of the 5th International Conference on Ubiquitous Information Technologies and Applications (CUTE), pp. 1–5. IEEE (2010)
13. Klassen, R.: Modeling the effect of the atmosphere on light. ACM Trans. Graphics **6**, 215–237 (1987)
14. Kolivand, H., Sunar, M.: An overview on based real-time shadow techniques in virtual environment. TELKOMNIKA **10**(1), 171–178 (2012)
15. Kolivand, H., Sunar, M.: Covering photometric properties of outdoor components with the effects of sky color in mixed reality. Multimed. Tools Appl. pp. 1–20, 26 May 2013
16. Kolivand, H., Sunar, M.S.: Realistic real-time outdoor rendering in augmented reality. PloS one **9**(9), e108334 (2014)
17. Li, S., Wang, G., Wu, E.: Unified volumes for light shaft and shadow with scattering. In: 2007 10th IEEE International Conference on Computer-Aided Design and Computer Graphics, pp. 161–166. IEEE (2007)
18. Max, N.L.: Atmospheric illumination and shadows. In: ACM SIGGRAPH Computer Graphics, vol. 20, pp. 117–124. ACM (1986)
19. Max, N.L.: Light diffusion through clouds and haze. Comput. Vis. Graphics Image Process. **33**(3), 280–292 (1986)
20. McGuire, M., Enderton, E.: Colored stochastic shadow maps. In: Symposium on Interactive 3D Graphics and Games, pp. 89–96. ACM (2011)
21. Moro, Y., Miyazaki, R., Dobashi, Y., Nishita, T.: A fast rendering method for shafts of light in outdoor scene
22. Nishita, T., Dobashi, Y., Kaneda, K., Yamashita, H.: Display method of the sky color taking into account multiple scattering. In: Pacific Graphics, vol. 96, pp. 117–132 (1996)
23. Preetham, A., Shirley, P., Smith, B.: A practical analytic model for daylight. In: computer Graphics, (SIGGRAPH 1999 Proceedings), pp. 91–10 (1999)
24. Rönnberg, S.: Real-time rendering of natural illumination. citeseer (2004)
25. Sunkavalli, K., Matusik, W., Pfister, H., Rusinkiewicz, S.: Factored time-lapse video. ACM Trans. Graphics **26**, 1–10 (2007)
26. Wang, C.: Real-time rendering of daylight sky scene for virtual environment. In: Ma, L., Rauterberg, M., Nakatsu, R. (eds.) ICEC 2007. LNCS, vol. 4740, pp. 294–303. Springer, Heidelberg (2007)
27. Xing, G., Liu, Y., Qin, X., Peng, Q.: On-line illumination estimation of outdoor scenes based on area selection for augmented reality. In: 2011 12th International Conference on Computer-Aided Design and Computer Graphics (CAD/Graphics), pp. 43–442. IEEE (2011)
28. Xing, G., Liu, Y., Qin, X., Peng, Q.: A practical approach for real-time illumination estimation of outdoor videos. Comput. Graphics **36**, 857–865 (2012)

Motif Correlogram for Texture Image Retrieval

Atoany Nazareth Fierro-Radilla, Gustavo Calderon-Auza,
Mariko Nakano-Miyatake, and Héctor Manuel Pérez-Meana[✉]

Postgraduate Section of ESIME Culhuacán, Instituto Politecnico Nacional,
Av. Santa Ana no. 1000 Col. San Francisco Culhuacan, Mexico City, Mexico
afierror1300@alumno.ipn.mx, {mnakano,hmperezm}@ipn.mx

Abstract. In this paper we present a novel, compact and effective method for extracting texture information from an image. We denominate this method as Motif Correlogram (MC), which computes the correlation between motif pairs of the same type. The proposed method was evaluated using different metrics commonly used in image retrieval, such as ARP (Average Retrieval Precision), ARR (Average Retrieval Rate) and ANMRR (Average Normalized Retrieval Rank). Also, the proposed scheme was compared with other texture descriptors, such as Steerable FIltres, Edge Histogram Descriptor (EHD) and two Co-occurrence Matrix-based algorithms: Motif Co-Occurrence Matrix (MCM) and Directional Local Motif XoR Patterns (DLMXoRP). The performance of the proposed method was evaluated using the *Kylberg Dataset*. The evaluation results show the proposed texture descriptor improves the texture image retrieval performance.

Keywords: Motif correlogram matrix · Texture · Image retrieval · Co-occurrence matrix

1 Introduction

There are a great amount of works related to the Content-Based Image Retrieval (CBIR), which aims to describe an image using visual content such as color, shape and texture in order to retrieve, index or classify multimedia data. The traditional process of retrieving, indexing and classifying multimedia data relies on using textual descriptions about the visual content. This is done manually and as a consequence, it is time-consuming process. Also, the traditional manner is subjective and ambiguous, because it depends on the person who is describing the visual content using text information. Unlike the traditional manner mentioned above, the CBIR offers a more adequate description of images. Considering that the digital images play an important role in different fields of study, such as biology, medicine, tourism and commerce, the CBIR has become an important and urgent research topic. Despite many proposals of the CBIR, there are still some shortcomings that can be overcome.

Texture is considered as one of the most important low-level features in the CBIR [1, 2], because surface of each object in natural images presents its unique texture. Texture can be defined as repetitive patterns of pixels found in the image [3].

© Springer International Publishing Switzerland 2015
H. Fujita and G. Guizzi (Eds.): SoMeT 2015, CCIS 532, pp. 496–505, 2015.
DOI: 10.1007/978-3-319-22689-7_38

The Steerable Filter is one of the most important texture descriptor, which is used in many vision and image processing task, such as texture analysis, edge detection, image compression, motion analysis, and image enhancement [2]. The MPEG-7 standard has proposed a scheme for texture information extraction called as Edge Histogram Descriptor (EHD) [4]. The EHD computes the histogram of edges oriented at 5 different directions. The shortcoming of this scheme is the large length of the feature vector, since the image is divided into 4×4 blocks, and for each block, a 5-bin histogram is computed. Finally the histograms generated for all 16 blocks are concatenated, generating a feature vector with 5×16 elements. The schemes based on co-occurrence matrix [5, 6] are alternative methods to describe texture features. In [5], six types of Motifs are obtained, and using Co-occurrence Matrix (MCM), the texture information is extracted. On the other hand, in [6], authors proposed the Directional Local Motif XoR Patterns (DLMXoRP), which relies on using the XoR operation at four different orientations of the motif co-occurrence matrix.

In this paper, we proposed an effective and compact scheme called Motif Correlogram (MC), which computes the correlation of motif pairs in the image. This method is based on the principle of the color correlogram proposed in [7]. The proposed method is evaluated using the common metrics for the CBIR systems, such as ARP (Average Retrieval Precision), ARR (Average Retrieval Rate) and ANMRR (Average Normalized Retrieval Rank) [8, 9], and it was compared with the conventional texture descriptors mentioned above. The experiments were done using 1500 texture images from the Kylberg texture database [10]. The experimental results show that the proposed descriptor provides better performance compared with other texture descriptors [3–6].

The rest of this paper is organized as follows: in Sect. 2, we present the proposed texture descriptor. In Sect. 3 the similarity measurement is explained. In Sect. 4, the experimental results are shown. Finally, in Sect. 5 we conclude this work.

2 Proposed Method

The proposed method computes the correlation between same types of motif in an input image to obtain a texture descriptor. The process is composed by two stages, which are Motif transformation of the image and computation of Motif correlogram. Each stage is described in detail.

2.1 Motif Transformation of the Image

Motif can be defined as a pattern of intensity of gray-level pixel values in an image and, in order to extract them, we used 2×2 grids. In general, it is possible to extract 24 motifs from a grid of 2×2. However, as in [5], we only consider six motifs which start from the position (1,1) of the grid. These six motifs are given by Fig. 1.

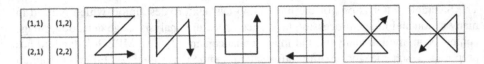

Fig. 1. Motif extraction

Table 1. Motif label

Motif	Label
Z	1
N	2
U	3
C	4
Gamma	5
Alfa	6

202	53	149	54	255	255	255	124
78	55	84	52	57	190	186	250
129	68	35	128	160	38	36	255
183	29	140	68	54	31	144	182
176	52	47	43	47	53	145	156
145	38	61	45	40	62	140	176
150	186	95	188	220	211	87	167
99	196	189	174	155	159	151	106

3	2	4	5
2	6	2	3
2	6	2	2
4	6	4	5

a)   b)   c)

Fig. 2. Motif Extraction, (a) Gray-level pixel values, (b) Motif scan and (c) Motif transformed image

The motif transformation of the image relies on scanning the whole image using non-overlapping 2×2 grids and replacing each grid by the label of corresponding motif of the grid, as shown in the Table 1. And the Fig. 2 shows an example of the motif transformation.

The size of the motif transformed image is $\frac{M}{2} \times \frac{N}{2}$, being $M \times N$ the size of the original image.

2.2 Motif Correlogram Extraction

The Motif Correlogram (MC) is based on the basis of the Color Correlogram proposed in [7]. The MC can be defined as the probability of finding a motif of type i in the position $m_1 = (x_1, y_1)$ away from a motif of the same type in the position $m_2 = (x_2, y_2)$ with a distance of k in the motif transformed image I.

$$MC_{ii}^{(k)}(I) \triangleq Pr_{m_1 \in I_i, m_2 \in I_i}[m_2 \in I_i \| m_1 - m_2 \| = k] \tag{1}$$

where the distance $|m_1 - m_2| \equiv max\{|x_1 - x_2|, |y_1 - y_2|\}$.

In order to compute the MC, we used a $((2k + 1) \times (2k + 1))$ overlapping grid, which scans the whole motif transformed image, as in Fig. 2.

2	5	3	4	2
5	1	2	1	4
2	5	1	4	4
6	3	2	6	3
6	1	6	1	6
4	4	2	6	3

Fig. 3. An example of Motif Correlogram with $k = 1$, here motif type Z labeled as 1 is analyzed.

Figure 3 shows an example of the Motif correlogram computation of the motif type Z labeled as 1. Let m_c be the total number of motif type Z in the image. In this example, we can observe that $m_c = 5$. In the Fig. 3, there is one single motif type Z away from the central motif (circle in red). Let m_n be the total number of motif type Z away from the central motif at each position of the grid. In this example, $m_n = 4$ motifs type Z away from a same type Z at a distance of $k = 1$. So, the probability of finding a motif type Z away from another motif type Z at a distance of $k = 1$ is computed as follows:

$$MT(i) = \frac{m_n}{m_c \times 8 \times k} \tag{2}$$

where k is the distance ($k = 1$), 8 is the number of neighbor motifs in a 3×3 grid and i indicates label of motif type ($i = 1$). The process is the same for the rest of the motifs. In this paper we computed MC at four different distances, $k = 1, 3, 5, 7$. The feature vector contains the probability of every type of motif at four different distances. As a result, the size of the feature vector is (number of motif types) × (number of distances k), which is $6 \times 4 = 24$.

3 Similarity Measurement

A similarity measurement is normally defined as a metric distance [11]. In this paper we used the Minkowski-form distance, which is defined as:

$$d_p(\boldsymbol{Q}, \boldsymbol{T}) = \left(\sum_{t=0}^{N-1} (Q_i - T_i)^p \right)^{\frac{1}{p}} \tag{3}$$

where $\boldsymbol{Q} = \{Q_0, Q_1, \ldots, Q_{N-1}\}$ and $\boldsymbol{T} = \{T_0, T_1, \ldots, T_{N-1}\}$ are the query and the target feature vectors, respectively [11]. In this paper we set $p = 1$ and $p = 2$, the Eq. 3 with $p = 1$ can be written as:

$$d_1(\boldsymbol{Q}, \boldsymbol{T}) = \sum_{i=0}^{N-1} |Q_i - T_i| \tag{4}$$

The Normalized *City Block distance* or *Manhattan Distance* from (4) is defined as:

$$d_1(\boldsymbol{Q}, \boldsymbol{T}) = \sum_{i=0}^{M-1} \frac{|Q_i - T_i|}{1 + Q_i + T_1} \tag{5}$$

The Euclidian distance *(p = 2)* is defined as:

$$d_2(\boldsymbol{Q}, \boldsymbol{T}) = \left(\sum_{i=0}^{N-1} (Q_i - T_i)^2 \right)^{\frac{1}{2}} \tag{6}$$

The value of the distance computation is in the range [0, 1], where 0 means the images are the same and 1 means the images are completely different.

4 Experimental Results

In this paper, we used 1500 texture images from Kylberg Dataset [10]. The set of images used in this paper is divided into 15 categories, with 100 ground truth images per class. The classes and the images were selected randomly. In the Fig. 4 we present images belong to 15 categories of the Kylberg dataset.

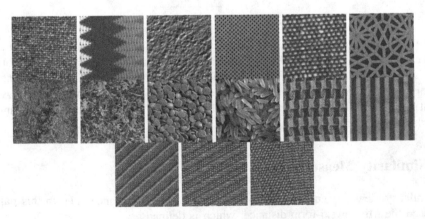

Fig. 4. 15 classes of Kylberg Dataset [10] used in this paper

In order to evaluate the proposed algorithm, we use metrics commonly used in the CBIR systems, such as ARP, ARR and ANMRR [8, 9]. The ARP can be defined as:

$$ARP = \frac{1}{N_Q} \sum_{q=1}^{N_Q} RP(q) \tag{7}$$

$$RP(q) = \frac{N_s(q)}{N_R(\alpha, q)} \tag{8}$$

where $N_s(q)$ is the number of relevant retrieved images for q-th query image within the first $N_R(\alpha, q)$ retrieved images and N_Q is the number of query images used for evaluation. On the other hand, the ARR is defined as:

$$ARR = \frac{1}{N_Q} \sum_{q=1}^{N_Q} RR(q) \leq 1 \tag{9}$$

$$RR(q) = \frac{N_R(\alpha, q)}{N_G(q)} \leq 1 \tag{10}$$

where $N_R(\alpha, q)$ indicates the number of relevant retrieved images found in the first $\alpha \times N_G(q)$ and $N_G(q)$ is the number of ground truth images of the class where the q-th query image belongs to. In this paper, we set $\alpha = [0.25, 0.5, 1]$ for the ARP metric and $\alpha = [1, 2]$ for the ARR. The ANMRR is considered as one of the most accurate metric which is defined as:

$$ANMRR = \frac{1}{N_Q} \sum_{q=1}^{N_Q} NMRR(q) \leq 1 \tag{11}$$

$$NMRR(q) = \frac{2 \times AVR(q) - N_G(q) - 1}{2 \times W - N_G(q) + 1} \tag{12}$$

$$AVR(q) = \frac{1}{N_G(q)} \sum_{r=1}^{N_G(q)} R(r) \tag{13}$$

where $N_G(q)$ is the number of ground truth images of the q-th query, W is a window size of retrieved images which is obtained as $2 \times N_G(q)$. $R(r)$ is the rank of r-th ground truth image. For the r-th ground truth image retrieved in the first W images, a rank $R(r) \leq W$ is assigned. The ground truth images which do not appear in the first W images, $R(r)$ is penalized as $R(r) = W + 1$. The range of ANMRR is $[0, 1]$ and 0 means that whole ground truth images were found, indicating a perfect performance of the CBIR, while 1 means that any ground truth image was not found, indicating the worst performance of the CBIR. The experimental results are obtained using two different distance metrics d_1 and d_2 between query and target images under different distances k between motifs. In the Tables 2 and 3 the results are presented.

We can observe that using d_1 distance metric and computing the proposed Motif correlation (MC) at four different distances k, the images can be described and retrieved

Table 2. Results of using d_1 distance metric at different distances between motifs

Distance Metric	Distance	ANMRR	ARR $\alpha = 1$	ARR $\alpha = 2$	ARP $\alpha = 0.5$	ARP $\alpha = 0.25$
d_1	$k = 1$	0.23	0.66	0.82	0.83	0.88
d_1	$k = 3$	0.24	065	0.80	0.83	0.93
d_1	$k = 5$	0.24	0.65	0.83	0.81	0.88
d_1	$k = 7$	0.26	0.61	0.80	0.79	0.91
d_1	$k = 1, 3, 5, 7$	**0.15**	**0.74**	**0.89**	**0.92**	**0.97**

Table 3. Results of using d_2 distance metric at different distances between motifs

Distance Metric	Distance	ANMRR	ARR $\alpha = 1$	ARR $\alpha = 2$	ARP $\alpha = 0.5$	ARP $\alpha = 0.25$
d_2	$k = 1$	0.26	0.63	0.81	0.78	0.83
d_2	$k = 3$	0.29	0.60	0.75	0.78	0.90
d_2	$k = 5$	0.29	0.60	0.76	0.78	0.90
d_2	$k = 7$	0.31	0.58	0.74	0.75	0.88
d_2	$k = 1, 3, 5, 7$	**0.19**	**0.70**	**0.86**	**0.91**	**0.98**

better than using d_2 distance metric. Therefore for the comparison and evaluation of proposed method, we used the Manhattan distance d_1 given by (5).

The proposed scheme was compared with other texture descriptors proposed in the literature, such as Steerable Filters [3], EHD [4], MCM [5] and DLMXoRP [6]. The results of the evaluation and comparisons are shown in the Table 4.

Table 4. Evaluation and comparison results

Method	ANMRR	ARR $\alpha = 1$	ARR $\alpha = 2$	ARR $\alpha = 0.5$	ARR $\alpha = 0.25$
Steerable Filters [3]	0.27	0.60	0.81	0.78	0.87
EHD [4]	0.40	0.50	0.66	0.65	0.73
MCM [5]	0.22	0.68	0.83	0.83	0.87
DLMXoRP [6]	0.21	0.69	0.82	0.88	0.96
MC (Proposed)	**0.15**	**0.74**	**0.89**	**0.92**	**0.97**

The comparison results show that the proposed texture descriptor provides better performance for texture image retrieval than four texture descriptors proposed in the literature [3–6]. The performance of the proposed scheme and the DLMXoRP in ARP with $\alpha = 0.25$ is very similar; however, our algorithm describes the texture images using only 24 elements, being 42 times smaller than the DLMXoRP. In the Table 5, the dimensions of feature vectors of every method evaluated in this paper are presented.

Two examples of the retrieved images by the proposed MC method are presented in Figs. 5 and 6. Both figures show first 20 most similar images to a given query image,

Table 5. Feature vector sizes

Method	Feature vector dimensions
Steerable filters [3]	8
EHD [4]	80
MCM [5]	36
DLMXoRP [6]	1024
MC (Proposed)	24

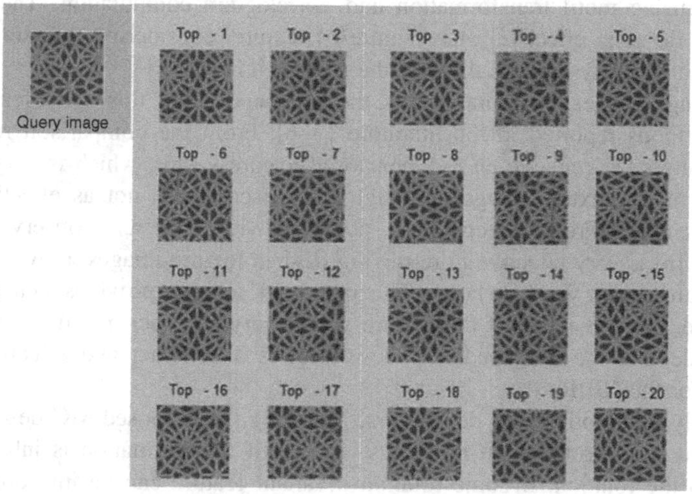

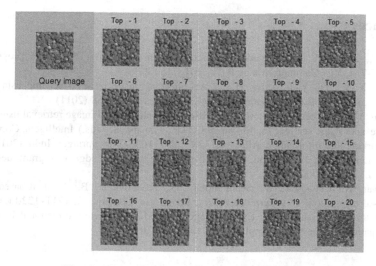

Fig. 5. Retrieved images of class floor using MC

Fig. 6. Retrieved images of class lentils using MC

retrieved from 1500 texture images in dataset. Figure 5 shows a perfect retrieval, in which 20 retrieved images belong to the same category with the query image, while in Fig. 6 the first 19 images are retrieved correctly, although the last image is incorrectly retrieved.

5 Conclusions

In this paper, we proposed a texture descriptor called Motif Correlogram (MC), which is obtained using motif transformation and correlogram computation. The MC was designed to describe effectively the feature of texture, considering that some unique patterns are iteratively appears through the texture image.

According to the experimental results, the MC can describe this visual feature better than the methods reported in the literature [3–6]. From the comparison results, the Steerable Filters [3] generate an 8-dimensional feature vector, which is very compact description of the texture image, although this descriptor is not as effective as the proposed scheme. From effectiveness point of view, we can observe that the DLMXoRP [6] is very effective in retrieving desired texture images; however the size of the feature vector is very large. The proposed scheme provides better retrieval performance, being the size of the feature vector very compact. From the results, we can conclude that the proposed MC descriptor is a compact and effective texture descriptor for the CBIR.

Generally, the motif-based descriptors, including the proposed MC descriptor, are not invariant to the rotation. It is because the motif transformation is inherently not invariant to the rotation. If some rotation-invariant feature can be introduced to the proposed MC descriptor, the retrieval performance may be improved firthermore. It is a principal feature work that we consider.

References

1. Xu, F., Zhang, Y.-J.: Evaluation and comparison of texture descriptors proposed in MPEG-7. J. Vis. Commun. Image R **17**, 701–716 (2006)
2. Wang, X.-Y., Yu, Y.-J., Yang, H.-Y.: An effective image retrieval scheme using color, texture and shape features. Comput. Stand. Interfaces **33**, 59–68 (2011)
3. Milind, V.L., Praveen, B., Pritesh, J.: An efective content-based image retrieval using color, texture and shape feature. In: Mohapatra, D.P., Patnaik, S. (eds.) Intelligent Computing, Networking and Informatics. AISC, vol. 243, pp. 1163–1170. Springer, India (2014)
4. Park, D.K., Jeon, S.Y., Won, C.S.: Efficient use of local edge histogram descriptor. ETRI J. **24**, 23–30 (2002)
5. Jhanwar, N., Chaudhuri, S., Seetharaman, G., Zavidovique, B.: Content-based image retrieval using motif co-occurrence matrix. Image Vis. Comput. **22**, 1211–1220 (2004)
6. Vipparthi, S.K., Nagar, S.K.: Expert image retrieval system using directional local motif XoR patterns. Expert Syst. Appl. **41**, 8016–8026 (2014)

7. Huang, J., Kumar, S.R., Mitra, M., Wei-Jing, Z., Zabih, R.: Image indexing using color correlograms. In: IEEE International Conference on Computer Vision and Pattern Recognition, pp. 762–768 (1997)
8. Manjunath, B.S., Ohm, J.-R., Vasudevan, V.V., Yamada, A.: Color and texture descriptors. IEEE Trans. on Circuit Syst. Video Technol. **24**, 345–360 (2001)
9. Ahmed, T., Massudi, M., Husniza, H., Loay, G.: A weighted dominant color descriptor for content-based image retrieval. J. Vis. Commun. Image Represent. **24**, 345–360 (2013)
10. Kylberg, G.: The Kylberg Texture Dataset v. 1.0. Centre for Image Analysis, Swedish University of Agricultural Science and Uppsala University, External report (Blue Series) No. 35. http://www.cb.uu.se/~gustaf/texture/
11. Zhang, D., Lu, G.: Evaluation of similarity measurement for image retrieval. In: IEEE International Conference on Neural Networks and Signal Processing, pp. 14–17 (2003)

Face Recognition Under Bad Illumination Conditions

Daniel Toledo de los Santos, Mariko Nakano-Miyatake,
Karina Toscano-Medina, Gabriel Sanchez-Perez,
and Hector Perez-Meana[✉]

Instituto Politecnico Nacional,
Av. Santa Ana 1000, 04430 Mexico, D. F., Mexico
{mnakano,hmperezm}@ipn.mx,
http://www.posgrados.esimecu.ipn.mx

Abstract. Accurate face recognition in variable illumination environments has attracted the attention of the researchers in recent years, because there are many applications in which these systems must operate under uncontrolled lighting conditions. To this end, several face recognition algorithms have been proposed which include an image enhancement stage before performing the recognition task. However, although the image enhancement stage may improve the performance, it also increases the computational complexity of face recognition algorithms. Because this fact may limit their use in some practical applications, recently some algorithms have been developed that intend to provide enough robustness under variable illumination conditions without requiring an image enhancement stage. Among them, the local binary pattern and eigenphases-based schemes are two of the most successful ones. This paper presents an analysis of the recognition performance of these approaches under varying illumination conditions, with and without image enhancement preprocessing stages. Evaluation results show the robustness of both approaches when they are required to operate in illumination varying environments.

Keywords: Face recognition · Retinex theory · Image analysis · Filters

1 Introduction

Face recognition is one of the most widely used biometric technologies because the data acquisition approach is non-intrusive, because the data acquisition is performed by taking a picture that can be performed with or without the cooperation of the person under analysis.

Variable illumination, pose, facial expressions and occlusions are some of the most important problems in face recognition because these factors alter the perception of face images, thereby significantly decreasing the accuracy of face recognition algorithms. Among these factors, changes in lighting conditions occur not only between indoor and outdoor environments but also within indoor environments due to the 3D shape of the face, which produces shadows depending on the direction of illumination; this issue has received significant attention [1]. Accordingly, several approaches have been proposed

© Springer International Publishing Switzerland 2015
H. Fujita and G. Guizzi (Eds.): SoMeT 2015, CCIS 532, pp. 506–516, 2015.
DOI: 10.1007/978-3-319-22689-7_39

in recent years to reduce the effect of variable illumination problems, which can be divided into two groups. The first group processes the input image to reduce the illumination changes and improve the quality of the input face image before performing the face recognition task. Among them we have illumination plane subtraction [1], histogram equalization [2], pixel normalization and contrast-limited adaptive histogram equalization (CLAHE) [3]. A second approach to addressing variable illumination conditions is the development of face recognition algorithms that have the ability to provide robust performance under such conditions because the effectiveness of a face recognition system depends heavily on the accuracy of the feature extraction algorithm. Thus, several methods have been proposed that are designed to provide simultaneously small intra-person and significant interpersonal variability under varying illumination conditions [5−15]. Among them, two of the most successful approaches are the eigenphase [4−6] and local binary patterns (LBP) approaches that, under certain conditions, provides recognition rates of over 95 %. Although these schemes intend to avoid the use of the image enhancement stage, a proper choice of an image enhancement scheme may improve performance of such face recognition systems [1 −3]. This paper analyzes the recognition performance of eigenphases and LBP-based face recognition method under bad illumination conditions, with and without image enhancement preprocessing stage and show that these methods present enough robustness to varying illumination conditions without requiring a preprocessing stage. From the evaluation results we can conclude that their recognition performance may be improved only if the preprocessing scheme is properly chosen.

The rest of the paper is organized as follows: Sect. 2 provides a description of the face recognition systems used to obtain the evaluation results, which are provided in Sect. 3. Finally, Sect. 4 provides the conclusion of this work.

2 Face Recognition Scheme

A face recognition system, whose block diagram is shown in Fig. 1, receives the face image of the person to be identified which is then inserted into a preprocessing stage for enhancement, resizing or noise reduction, etc. Next, the resulting image is inserted into the feature extraction stage that estimates a set of near invariant parameters that minimize the intraclass and maximize the interclass differences. Finally, the estimated feature vector is inserted into the recognition stage, which during training estimates the optimal parameters of the classifier and during testing performs the identification task. Next sub-sections present a description each one of the above mentioned stages.

2.1 Preprocessing Stage

The preprocessing stage in the face recognition system, shown in Fig. 1, performs an image enhancement operation to improve the input signal contrast and then the feature extraction operation. To this end several algorithms have been proposed, among them the retinex scheme, histogram equalization and pixels normalization appears to be some desirable approaches. Next sections provide a brief description of each of them.

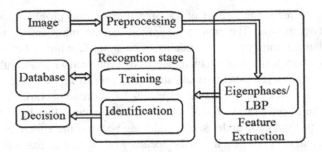

Fig. 1. General structure of a face recognition system

Retinex Approach The image enhancement approach based on the retinex theory [16], shown in Fig. 2 assumes that the input image is given by the product of the luminance $L(x,y)$ and reflectance $R(x,y)$ components, that is $f(x,y) = R(x,y)L(x,y)$. Then to improve the image quality, the system estimates and process both of them separately and finally multiply the resulting components to obtain the enhanced images. To this end, firstly the system estimates the luminance as follows:

$$\hat{L}(x,y) = \frac{N_1 + N_2}{S_v + S_o + 1} \tag{1}$$

Where

$$S_o = \frac{H}{\left(\ln\frac{1+f(x,y-1)}{1+f(x,y+1)}\right)^2 + \delta} \tag{2}$$

$$S_v = \frac{H}{\left(\ln\frac{1+f(x-1,y)}{1+f(x+1,y)}\right)^2 + \delta} \tag{3}$$

$N_1 = \alpha(f(x-1,y)s_v + f(x,y-1)s_0)$, $N_2 = ((s_v + s_o)(1-\alpha) + 1)f(x,y)$, $H = 0.01$, $\alpha = 0.75$ and δ is a constant used to avoid the division by zero. Ones the luminance is estimated, the system estimates the logarithm of the reflectance dividing, pixel by pixel, the input image by the estimated luminance, that is $R'(x,y) = \ln(f(x,y)/\hat{L}(x,y))$. Next using $R'(x,y)$ the processed reflectance is estimated as follows

$$R(x,y) = 2\left(\frac{1}{1 + \exp(-cR')} - \frac{1}{2}\right) \tag{4}$$

After the reflectance has been processed, the system estimates the processed luminance as follows

$$L_p(x,y) = \Gamma(\hat{L}) = 255\left(\frac{\hat{\Gamma}(x,y)}{255}\right)^{0.3\frac{\hat{\Gamma}(x,y)}{255}+0.3} \tag{5}$$

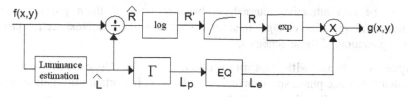

Fig. 2. Retinex method for image enhancement

$$c = \begin{cases} h_1 + \dfrac{h_2 - h_1}{d} |R'| & si\ |R'| < d \\ h_2 & otherwise \end{cases} \qquad (6)$$

where d = 0.4, h_1 = 0.3, h_2 = 0.2. Then the histogram of $L_p(x,\ y)$ is equalized, as described below, to further enhance the luminance of the input image $f(x,\ y)$. Finally the equalized luminance $L_e(x,\ y)$ is combined with $R'(x,\ y)$ to synthesize the enhanced image which is given by $g(x,\ y) = exp(R'(x,\ y))L_e(x,\ y)$.

Histogram Equalization Consider the normalized histogram of a given image which is given by $p_r(r_k) = n_k/MN$, $k = 0,1,2,...,L\text{-}1$, where n_k is the number of pixels whose intensity is equal to r_k. Because the intensities distribution determines the image contrast, a suitable form is to modify the values of n_k such that $p_r(r_k)$ becomes approximately constant. This goal in achieved using the histogram equalization in which the pixels values are modified as follows [2]

$$s_k = (L-1)\sum_{j=0}^{k} p_r(r_j), \quad k = 0,1,2,...,L-1 \qquad (7)$$

Pixel Normalization Other method that can be used to reduce the effect of varying illumination environment consists on normalizing the pixels amplitude, such that the $(m,n)\text{-}th$ pixel of processed image is given by [5]

$$I_{n,m}(x,y) = \frac{I_{n,m}(x_k,y_k)}{\left(\sum_{x_k=1}^{N_k}\sum_{y_k=1}^{M_k} I_{n,m}^2(x_k,y_k)\right)^{1/2}} \qquad (8)$$

2.2   Feature Extraction

The feature extraction stage is a fundamental part of any pattern recognition scheme whose purpose is, simultaneously, to maximize the differences between patterns belonging to difference classes while minimizing the differences between patterns belonging to the same class. That is to maximize the interclass differences while minimizing the intraclass differences. Because the importance of this stage several approaches have been proposed, among them he eigenphases and LBP approaches appear to be two attractive alternatives because both of them provides enough robustness to illumination changes in several practical situations. Next section provides a brief explanation of these schemes.

Eigenphases Scheme with Optimum Block Size The Oppenheim's experiment shows that the image phase spectrum contains the most important information required for face recognition. Based on this result, the eigenphases method was proposed [5 – 7] in which the image phase spectrum is estimated and used together with the principal component analysis (PCA) algorithm [17] to obtain the image features vector. This features vector is then used together with some suitable classification method to carry out the recognition task. This method performs fairly well, although the recognition performance degrades in the presence of illumination variations and partial facial occlusions. To improve the performance of the eigenphases method with different illumination conditions, in Ref [6] the input image with $N \times M$ pixels is firstly segmented in $(N/2) \times (M/2)$ blocks of 2×2 pixels. Next, the phase spectrum of each block is estimated whose components are concatenated to estimate the feature vector of the face image under analysis. This process is illustrated in Fig. 3.

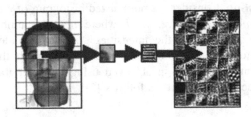

Fig. 3. Feature extraction using the eigenphases method.

One important advantage of this block segmentation before phase spectrum estimation is that when the input image is divided in block of 2×2 pixels, the difference between two images of the same person with different illumination conditions is negligible, and then the performance of eigenphases algorithm with blocks of 2×2 pixels is almost the same independently of illumination conditions [6]. Figure 4 shows the phase spectrum of two face images with different illumination conditions when the phase spectrums are estimated using blocks of 2×2.

Because the feature vector size is in general large, the principal component analysis is used for dimensionality reduction [17]. To this end, firstly, the phase spectrums of the training images, estimated as described above, are represented as a one dimensional vector $X = [x_0, x_1, ..., x_r, x_{N-1,M-1}]^T$, where $r = j+2k + 2mN + 4n$, $j = 0,1$, $k = 0,1$, $m = 0,1$, ..., $M/2-1$, $n = 0,1,...,N/2-1$, of size MN, where $M \times N$ is the image size. Next a matrix W of size $(NM) \times Q$ is constructed concatenating the all vectors X contained in the training set, where (NM) is the dimensionality of X, and $Q = TS < NM$, where T is the number of classes and S the number of training images for each class. Next, the eigenvectors and eigenvalues of the covariance matrix given by W^TW are estimated and used to generate a dominant feature matrix Φ of size $L \times NM$, where

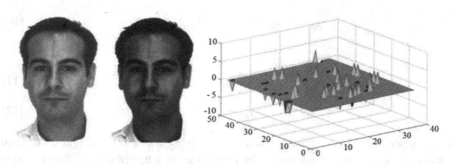

Fig. 4. Difference between the phase spectrum of the images with different lighting conditions when the input image is segmented in blocks of 2 × 2 pixels.

$L = Q$ corresponds to the number of most representative eigenvectors contained in the original image [44]. Finally, the feature vector of each image is given by

$$Y = \Phi X \qquad (9)$$

where Y is the resulting feature vector of size $L \times 1$, Φ is the dominant matrix, and X is the vector containing the phase spectrum of the image under analysis described above.

Local Binary Patterns The LBP algorithm introduced by Ojala et al. [18] is one of the most efficient methods for describing texture. The original method, called hLBPI, uses masks of 3 × 3 pixels, called the "texture spectrum", to represent a neighborhood around a central pixel, as shown in Fig. 5a, where the values of the neighboring pixels are compared with the central pixel, taking that pixel value as the threshold. Pixels are labeled as 0 if values are smaller than the threshold; otherwise, they are labeled as 1, as shown in Fig. 5b. Next, the pixel labels are multiplied by 2^p, where $0 \le p \le 7$ is the position of each pixel in the neighborhood, as shown in Fig. 5c. Finally, the resulting values are added to obtain the label of the central pixel in that neighborhood, yielding Fig. 5d. This method produces 128 possible values for the central pixel label. This process is repeated for the entire image, producing a LBP labeling matrix (with the same size as the input images), which is used to estimate the vector for the face image features. Therefore, this method obtains information about local spatial structures.

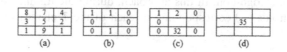

(a)   (b)   (c)   (d)

Fig. 5. LBP estimation process

Consider the gray level, g_c, of the central pixel (x_c, y_c) of a given neighborhood of an image $I(x,y)$, whose pixels are in a circular neighborhood of radio 1 with 8 equally spaced pixels with gray levels, g_p, defined by

$$g_p = I(x_p, y_p), \quad p = 01, 2, \ldots, 7 \tag{10}$$

Where

$$x_p = x_c, \tag{11}$$

$$y_p = y_c, \tag{12}$$

are the neighborhood coordinates. Then, by assigning a binomial weight 2^P to each component $s(g_p\text{-}g_c)$ and transforming the differences in a neighborhood into a unique LBP code around g_c, it follows that

$$LBP_{8,1}(g_c) = \sum_{p=0}^{7} s(g_p - g_c)2^P \tag{13}$$

where $s(g_p\text{-}g_c) = 0$ if $g_p < g_c$ and 1 otherwise. This equation means that the signs of the differences in a neighborhood are interpreted as a 8-bit binary number, resulting in 2^P different values for the LBP code. This process is illustrated in Fig. 5.

Next the principal component analysis describe above is used to estimate de features vector. Figure 6 shows the block diagram of feature extraction scheme using the LBP algorithm.

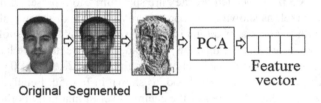

Original Segmented   LBP

Fig. 6. Block diagram of LBP based feature extraction method.

2.3   Classification Stage

The k-means algorithm is one of the most commonly and simplest used classification methods in pattern recognition. In this approach, during the training stage, the system estimates the centroids (y_t) corresponding to each of the T classes to be identified as follows:

$$y_t = \frac{1}{S}\sum_{k=0}^{S-1} I_{t,k}(x, y), \qquad t = 1, 2, \ldots, T \tag{14}$$

where S is the number of training images belonging to the class t. Next, to perform the identification task, the system estimates the distance between the features vector of the image under analysis x_s and the T centroids stored in the database. Finally, the system determines that the image under analysis belongs to the class with the smallest distance. In this paper the cosine distance is used which given by:

$$dst_{\cos} = 1 - \frac{x_s y_t^T}{\sqrt{(x_s x_s^T)(y_t y_t^T)}} \qquad (15)$$

3   Evaluation Results

Several experiments, using the AR face data base [19] together a data base built for this purpose with several illumination conditions (Fig. 7) were carried out to evaluate the recognition performance of LBP and eigenphases-based approaches under illumination varying conditions described in Sect. 2.1. Figure 8 show the recognition performance of LBP and eigenphases-based face recognition schemes, using the image enhancement schemes described above when they operate under good and poor illumination conditions. The recognition performance without using any image enhancement scheme is

Fig. 7. Examples of face images with several illumination conditions used for evaluation of face recognition system

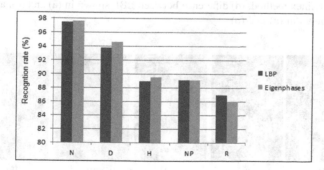

Fig. 8. Recognition performance of LBP and eigenphases-based face recognition schemes using and without using image enhancement preprocessing stage, Here N means good quality image, D means a dark image, H enhanced using histogram equalization, NP normalized pixels and R image enhanced using retinex method.

also shown for comparison. Figure 8 shows that both systems are robust enough to illumination varying and in most cases perform better without using any of the image enhancement scheme methods describe above. This fact is illustrated in Figs. 10 and 11 which show the estimated LBP and eigenphases matrices of the faces images shown in Fig. 9, where Fig. 9(a) is a face image with good illumination condition, Fig. 9(b) shows a darker version of Fig. 9(a) and (c) shows the enhanced version of Fig. 9(b) using the retinex method. Figures 10 and 11 shows that, although the image enhancement method performs fairly well improving the visual quality, as shown on Fig. 9(c), the LBP and eigenphases with a block size of 2 × 2 provides features matrices that more closely resembles to that obtained from images with good illumination

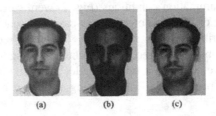

(a)   (b)   (c)

Fig. 9. (a) Good quality image, (b) dark image, (c) enhanced image using retinex method

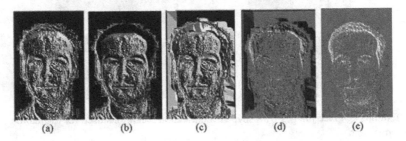

(a)   (b)   (c)   (d)   (e)

Fig. 10. LBP matrices estimated from (a) good quality image, (b) dark image, (c) image enhanced using retinex method, (d) difference between LBP shown in (a) and (c); and difference between LBP shown in (a) and (b).

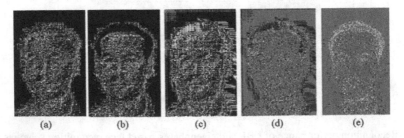

(a)   (b)   (c)   (d)   (e)

Fig. 11. Eigenphases matrices estimated from (a) good quality image, (b) dark image, (c) image enhanced using retinex method, (d) difference between eigenphases matrices shown in (a) and (c); and difference eigenphases shown in (a) and (b).

conditions when using images without preprocessing. This can also be observed comparing Figs. 9(d) with Fig. 9(e) and Fig. 10(d) with Fig. 10(e). Evaluation results show that when illumination changes are uniform, the use and image enhancement schemes may distort the features matrix, resulting in a degradation of the performance of face recognition system.

4 Conclusions

This paper presented and analysis of the recognition performance of LBP and eigen-phases based methods when required to operate under bad illumination conditions, using or without using an image enhancement method. Evaluation results show that both schemes are robust enough to handle bad and relative uniform, illumination changes without using any image enhancement method. Evaluation results show that under uniform illumination changes, the use of image enhancement schemes may reduce the recognition rate instead of increasing it. Thus in such situations it is better do not use it.

Acknowledgements. We thank the National Science and Technology Council (CONACYT) and the National Polytechnic Institute for the financial support for the realization of this research.

References

1. Ruiz-del-Solar, J., Quinteros, J.: Illumination compensation and normalization in eigenspace-based face recognition: a comparative study of different pre-processing approaches. Pattern Recogn. Lett. **29**, 1966–1979 (2008)
2. Ramirez-Gutierrez, K., Cruz-Perez, D., Olivares-Mercado, J., Nakano-Miyatake, M., Perez-Meana, H.: A face recognition algorithm using eigenphases and histogram equalization. Int. J. Comput. **5**, 34–41 (2011)
3. Benitez-Garcia, G., Olivares-Mercado, J., Aguilar-Torres, G., Sanchez-Perez, G., Perez-Meana, H.: Face identification based on contrast limited adaptive histogram equalization (CLAHE). In: International Conference on Image Processing, Computer Vision and Pattern Recognition. http://www.worldacademyofscience.org/worldcomp11/ws/conferences/ipcv11
4. Zaeri, N.: Eigenphases for corrupted images. In: Proceedings of the International Conference on Advances in Computational Tools for Engineering Applications, pp. 537–540 (2009)
5. Olivares-Mercado, J., Hotta, K., Takahashi, H., Nakano-Miyatake, M., Toscano-Medina, K., Perez-Meana, H.: Improving the eigenphase method for face recognition. IEICE Electron. Express **6**, 1112–1117 (2009)
6. Benitez-Garcia, G., Olivares-Mercado, J., Sanchez-Perez, G., Nakano-Miyatake, M., Perez-Meana, H.: A sub-block-based eigenphases algorithm with optimum sub-block size. Knowl.-Based Syst. **37**(1), 415–426 (2012)
7. Olivares-Mercado, J., Sanchez-Perez, G., Nakano-Miyatake, M., Perez-Meana, H.: Feature extraction and face verification using gabor and gaussian mixture models. Adv. Artif. Intell. **4827**, 769–778 (2007)

8. Hu, H.: Variable lighting face recognition using discrete wavelet transform. Pattern Recogn. Lett. **32**, 1526–1534 (2011)
9. Arandjelović, O., Cipolla, R.: A methodology for rapid illumination-invariant face recognition using image processing filters. Comput. Vis. Image Underst. **113**(1), 159–171 (2009)
10. Hotta, K.: Robust face recognition under partial occlusion based on support vector machine with local gaussian summation kernel. Image Vis. Comput. **26**, 1490–1498 (2008)
11. Ahonen, T., Hadid, A., Pietikainen, M.: Face description with local binary patterns: application to face recognition. IEEE Trans. Pattern Anal. Mach. Intell. **28**, 2037–2041 (2006)
12. Ahonen, T., Hadid, A., Pietikäinen, M.: Face recognition with local binary patterns. In: Pajdla, T., Matas, J(. (eds.) ECCV 2004. LNCS, vol. 3021, pp. 469–481. Springer, Heidelberg (2004)
13. Xia, W., Yin, S., Ouyang, P.: A high precision feature based on lbp and gabor theory for face recognition. Sensors **13**, 4499–4513 (2013)
14. Maturana, D., Mery, D., Soto, A.: Face recognition with decision tree-based local binary patterns. In: Kimmel, R., Klette, R., Sugimoto, A. (eds.) ACCV 2010, Part IV. LNCS, vol. 6495, pp. 618–629. Springer, Heidelberg (2011)
15. Yang, B., Chen, S.: A comparative study on local binary pattern (LBP) based face recognition: LBP histogram versus LBP image. Neurocomputing **120**, 365–379 (2013)
16. Marsi, S., Ramponi, G., Carrato, S.: Image contrast enhancement using recursive rational filter. In: International Workshop on Imaging Systems and Techniques, pp. 29–34 (2004)
17. Shlens, J.: A tutorial on principal component analysis. arXiv preprint arXiv:1404.1100 (2014)
18. Ojala, T., Pietikainen, M., Harwood, D.: Performance evaluation of texture measures with classification based on kullback discrimination of distributions. In: Proceedings of the IAPR International Conference on Computer Vision and Image Processing, pp. 582–585 (1994)
19. Martinez, A.: The AR face database. CVC Technical report 24 (1998)

A Prototype for Anomaly Detection in Video Surveillance Context

F. Persia[1]([⊠]), D. D'Auria[1], G. Sperlí[1], and A. Tufano[2]

[1] Dipartimento di Ingegneria Elettrica e Tecnologie dell'Informazione,
University of Naples Federico II, Via Claudio 21, 80125 Naples, Italy
{fabio.persia,daniela.dauria4,giancarlo.sperli}@unina.it
[2] Universitá Telematica Pegaso, Naples, Italy
antonio.tufano@unipegaso.it

Abstract. Security has been raised at major public buildings in the most famous and crowded cities all over the world following the terrorist attacks of the last years, the latest one at the Bardo museum in the centre of Tunis. For that reason, video surveillance systems have become more and more essential for detecting and hopefully even prevent dangerous events in public areas. In this paper, we present a prototype for anomaly detection in video surveillance context. The whole process is described, starting from the video frames captured by sensors/cameras till at the end some well-known reasoning algorithms for finding potentially dangerous activities are applied. The conducted experiments confirm the efficiency and the effectiveness achieved by our prototype.

Keywords: Video surveillance · Anomaly detection · Activity detection · Unexplained activities

1 Introduction

In latest years modern world's needs of safety caused a speed spreading of video surveillance systems; these systems are collocated especially in the most crowded places. The main purpose of a video surveillance system is to create some automatic tools, which can extend the faculties of human perception, allowing collection and real time analysis of data coming from lots of electronic "viewers" (sensors, cameras, etc.).

One of the main limits of modern security systems is that most of them have been designed for specific functionalities and contexts: they generally use an only kind of sensors (such as cameras, motes, scanners) which cannot notice all the possible important phenomena connected to the observation context. A second and not negligible limit is that the "semantics" of the phenomena (events) that such systems can notice is quite limited and, as well, these systems are not very flexible when we want to introduce new events to be identified. For example, a typical video surveillance system at a tunnel mouth uses a set of cameras monitoring train transit and the possible presence of objects in the

© Springer International Publishing Switzerland 2015
H. Fujita and G. Guizzi (Eds.): SoMeT 2015, CCIS 532, pp. 517–528, 2015.
DOI: 10.1007/978-3-319-22689-7_40

scene. When a person transits on the tracks, we want the system automatically to identify the anomalous event and to signal it to a keeper. The commonest "Image Processing" algorithms (that can be directly implemented on a camera processor or can be stored on a dedicated server that can process information sent by a camera) can quite precisely identify the changes between a frame and the next one and, in this way, discover the eventual presence of anomalies (train transit, presence of a person,...) in the scene. In the scene analysis, a system does not consider all the environmental parameters, such as brightness, temperature and so on, and how these parameters can modify the surveys (the identification of a small object in the scene is more complex in the night); as well, this system cannot identify semantic higher level events (such as a package left near a track) with the same precision and reliability. Similarly, a traditional video surveillance system can discover, in a bank, the presence of objects near the safe, but cannot automatically notify an event interesting for the context, such as a "bank robbery" (every time that an object is near the safe, an alarm should be generated: in this way, nevertheless, false alarms could be generated also when the bank clerk goes into the safe room to take some money).

In the end, we want a modern video surveillance system to attain the following points: it is to integrate heterogeneous information coming from different kinds of sensors, to be flexible in capability to discover all possible events that can happen in the monitored environment and to be adaptable to the context features of the observed scene. From a technological point of view, the main requirements of this kind of systems are: heterogeneity of the adopted surveying systems, heterogeneity of noticed data and of those to be processed, wiring of devices and communication with servers dedicated to processing.

In this paper, we present a prototype of framework for anomaly detection in video surveillance context. The whole process is described: thus, we start from the video frames captured by sensors/cameras and then, after several steps, we apply some well-known reasoning algorithms [1,2] for finding high-level *unexplained* activities in time-stamped observation data.

The paper is organized as in the following. Section 2 deals with the evolution and the basic architecture of video surveillance systems. Section 3 describes in detail the proposed prototype for anomaly detection in video surveillance context. Section 4 presents some experiments using real-world datasets. Eventually, Sect. 5 discusses some conclusions and possible future improvements.

2   State of the Art

The video surveillance systems proposed in literature can be classified into three categories (or generations [3,4]), from a technological point of view. The three proposed generations, in fact, have followed the evolution of the communication techniques of the image processing and of the data storing and they have been evolving with the same rapidity as these techniques.

2.1   Evolution of Surveillance Systems

First Generation Surveillance Systems (1GSS) extend human perception capability from a spatial point of view: a set of cameras (*sensor layer*) are used to capture visual signals from different positions set in a monitored environment. Such signals are then sent and visualized by operators, after an analogical transmission, in an only location (control room). 1GSS most considerable disadvantages are due to the operators' short duration of attention, which is responsible for a high rate of missed recording of important events [5].

From the early 80's, because of the increasing interest of research in video processing and in order to improve the basic technologies in this area, scientists obtained a sensible improvement in camera resolution and, at the same time, a reduction of hardware (computers, memories, ...) costs. Most of the researches made during Second Generation Surveillance System (2GSS) period have improved the development of automatic techniques called *automated event detection*. These techniques have made monitoring of very large areas easier, because they act as pre-filters of defined events [4]. Nevertheless, the 2GSS systems are characterized by a good level of digitalization about signal transmission and processing, in the sense that systems include digital components in some parts of their architecture.

The main goal of Third Generation Surveillance Systems (3GSS) is to obtain, to manage and to efficiently transmit real time noticed video events, from a large set of sensors, through a *full digital* approach; this approach uses digital components in all layers of the system architecture, from *sensor layer* till visual and codified presentation of information to operators [3]. In a 3GSS system cameras communicate with some processing and transmission devices: in this way *intelligent cameras* are built. A network layer, whose principal component is an *intelligent hub*, has the purpose to assemble data coming from different cameras. So, we can say that the automatic video surveillance system goal is to act as a *pre-filter* for human validation of suspicious events. Such *pre-filtering* is generally based on video processing and gives some important parameters for object localization and for tracking of their trajectories, while they are in the monitored environment (Fig. 1). The following is a first schematization of a 3GSS video surveillance system logical architecture:

Sensor Layer. The *sensor layer* is composed of one or more fixed or mobile cameras: their purpose is to collect images, to be sent to *image processing* system.

Image Processing Layer. Images captured by cameras are stored in a specific video database (*VideoRepository*); then, they are sent in input to IPS system, that processes them. Such module extracts low-level information (such as the presence of new objects in the scene, their position, and so on...) through *image processing* algorithms; it also converts this information into a format conformable to a syntax used by higher layers. For what *image processing algorithms* concern, Dung et all. [12] propose an approach for object detection based on local

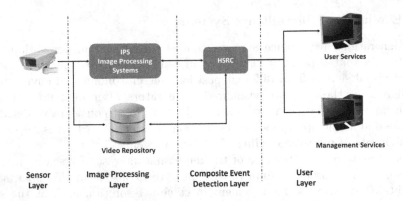

Fig. 1. Video surveillance system architecture

invariant features, exploiting binary features, which allows to meet the requirements of a real time system, and color information as well. Moreover, in order to overcome the object segmentation problem without prior knowledge of the objects, Chaudhary et al. [13] present a method which allows to estimate the same objects through sequential back-tracking via exploitation of affine relationships of consecutive frames. In [14], the authors develop a human detection approach based on a stereo vision system able to extract range images from the foreground, on which there are applied some human detection techniques based on local features in order to improve the detection performance for the occluded humans.

Then, an *Event Description Language* has been defined on the basis of Image Processing algorithms; through this language, it is possible to formalize a complex event in a strict way. The data, organized in this way, are stored in a specific area of Database (*Data Collection*).

Composite Event Detection Layer. A post-processing framework, called HSRC (*High Semantic Reasoning Center*) is the part of the system responsible of complex events' occurrences surveying, through the processing of low-level data made available by IPS. We can classify the following components:

- *Event Repository*: it is the part of Database in which predicates and complex events definitions are stored; as well, information about event occurrence surveying in the video are stored in it, too.
- *Data Collection*: it is the part of Database that collects framework IPS output, organized according to EDL language syntax.
- *Agent Based Processor (ABP)*: its main aims are to capture the interesting event definition, composed of the Event Repository, to capture the observation, that is, the video description in terms of predicates, from Data Collection and to verify the event occurrence during the observation.
- *Subvideo Extractor*: when an event is detected, this framework extracts from the video the interesting frame sequence and saves it in the Video Repository

as a new file; in this way, the sequence is made available for *on-line* and *off-line* visualizations.

– *Query Builder*: the framework assigned to client service creation organizes parameters which the attitude of ABP processor bases on. Management services are built on language capability and on algorithms ability available in IPS.

User Layer. The system presents a set of services to final clients through *user-friendly* interfaces. Such services can be classified into two different categories:

1. *Management services*: the system manager can define new kinds of primitive and complex events and can extend the image processing algorithm suite of IPS framework.
2. *Client services*: the client can specify the working system parameters, based for example on the alert mode. He can visualize *on-line* and *off-line* video sequences corresponding to alarms detected by the system; he can also visualize whole stored videos and make some statistics on detected event occurrences.

2.2 Related Work

In these years many framework have been developed to identify anomalies or suspicious events in video sequences. In [15] the authors present a framework for detecting complex events through inferrencing process based on Markow Logic Network (MLNs) and rule-based event models. Another approach has been employed by Zin et al. [16], which propose an integrated framework for detecting suspicious behaviors in video surveillance systems exploiting multiple background modeling techniques, high-level motion feature extraction methods and embedded Markow chain models.

3 The Proposed Prototype

In this Section, we describe the prototype designed and developed for finding anomalous activities in video surveillance context. The architecture of the proposed prototype (Fig. 2) consists of the following layers: an *Image Processing Library*, a *Video Labeler*, an *Activity Detection Engine* and the *Unexplained Activities Problem (UAP) Engine*, implementing the algorithms for video anomaly detection.

In particular, the *Image Processing Library* analyzes the video captured by sensors/cameras and returns the low level annotations for each video frame as output; the *Video Labeler* fills the semantic gap between the low level annotations captured for each frame and the high level annotations, representing high level events that can be associated to the video frames; then, we used an *Activity Detection Engine* to find activity occurrences matching the well-known models, that can be classified into *good* and *bad* ones: thus, such a module takes as

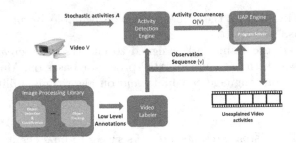

Fig. 2. The prototype architecture

Fig. 3. A video frame from ITEA-CANDELA dataset

inputs the *high level annotations* previously caught by the *Video Labeler* and the stochastic activity models; eventually, the *UAP (Unexplained Activity Problem) Engine* described in [1,2] takes as input the activity occurrences previously found with the associated probabilities and the high level annotations and discovers the *Unexplained Video Activities*.

3.1   The Image Processing Library

The Image Processing Library used in our prototype implementation is the *Reading People Tracker (RPT)* [6,7], that achieves a good accuracy in object detection and tracking. RPT takes the frame sequence of the video as input and returns an XML file describing the low level annotations caught in each frame, according to a standard schema defined in an *XML Schema*. We have only made some few updates to the RPT's source code, in order to be able to get more easily the type of each object detected in a frame (person, package, car). For instance, Fig. 4 shows the low level annotations associated to the frame number 18 (Fig. 3) of a video belonging to the *ITEA - CANDELA* dataset[1], which has been used to carry out some preliminary experiments.

---

[1] http://www.multitel.be/~va/candela/abandon.html.

```
177   <frame xmlns="http://www.cvg.cs.reading.ac.uk/ADVISOR/people"
178         xmlns:xsi="http://www.wr.org/2001/XMLSchema-instance"
179         xsi:schemaLocation="http://www.cvg.reading.ac.uk/ADVISOR
180                             http://www.cvg.cs.reading.ac.uk/~nts/ADVISOR/people tracker-multi.xsd"
181                             id="18" pc_name="fabio-desktop" num_cameras="1">
182     <camera id="2002" time="3600">
183       <mobile id="5" start_time="3400">
184         <track id="5" type="5">
185           <info2d xmin="314" xmax="357" ymin="126" ymax="277" xcog="335" ycog="195" />
186           <info3d x="0" y="0" z="0" width="0" height="0" />
187           <occlusion left="0" right="0" bottom="0" top="0" />
188         </track>
189         <track id="100" type="6">
190           <info2d xmin="314" xmax="357" ymin="126" ymax="277" xcog="333" ycog="197" />
191           <info3d x="0" y="0" z="0" width="0" height="0" />
192           <occlusion left="0" right="0" bottom="0" top="0" />
193         </track>
194       </mobile>
195     </camera>
196   </frame>
```

Fig. 4. The related low level annotations

As we can see in Fig. 4, the RPT correctly identifies two objects (represented by the XML elements called *track*) into the frame shown in Fig. 3: the former, identified by $ID = 5$, is a person (*type* = 5), while the latter, identified by $ID = 100$, is a package (*type* = 6). The XML attribute *type* of the element *track* denotes the type of the detected object.

3.2   The Video Labeler

As we mentioned before, the *Video Labeler* fills the semantic gap between the low level annotations captured for each frame and the high level annotations. So, through the Video Labeler, some high level events, called *action symbols*, with the related *timestamps* are detected; thus, the output of the Video Labeler is the list of *action symbols* related to the considered video source. The Video Labeler has been implemented in *Java* programming language: it uses the *DOM libraries* to parse the XML file containing the output of the *Image Processing Library*. The Video Library defines the rules that have to be checked to verify the presence of each interested *high level atomic event* in the video. So, a Java method for each action symbol we want to detect, containing the related rules, has been defined. There are listed below some examples of rules defined to detect some *atomic events* (action symbols) in a video belonging to the *ITEA-CANDELA* dataset.

Action Symbol *A*: **A person** *P* **goes into the central zone with the package**

- There are at least two objects in the current frame
- At least one of the objects is a person
- At least one of the objects is a package
- The person identified appears on the scene for the first time
- The distance between the person's barycenter and the package one is smaller than an apposite distance threshold

Action Symbol *B*: **A person** *P* **drops off the package**

- There are at least two objects in the current frame

- At least one of the objects is a person
- At least one of the objects is a package
- The person was previously holding a package
- The distance between the person's barycenter and the package one is smaller than an apposite distance threshold

Action Symbol C: A person P goes into the central zone

- There is at least one object in the current frame
- At least one of the objects is a person
- The person identified appears on the scene for the first time
- If there are also some packages on the scene, their distances are greater than an apposite distance threshold

Action Symbol D: A person P picks up the package

- There are at least two objects in the current frame
- At least one of the objects is a person
- At least one of the objects is a package
- The distance between the person's barycenter and the package one is smaller than an apposite distance threshold
- The person was not previously holding a package

Action Symbol E: A person $P1$ gives the package to another person $P2$

- There are at least three objects in the current frame
- At least two of the objects are persons
- At least one of the objects is a package
- P1 was previously holding a package
- In the current frame, both the distances of P1 and P2's barycenters from the package are smaller than an apposite distance threshold
- In the next frames, P1's distance from the package is greater than the threshold, while P2's one is smaller (it means that P2 has got the package and P1 is not holding it anymore)

Action Symbol F: A person P goes out of the central zone with the package

- This symbol is detected when a person holding a package does not appear anymore on the scene for a specified TTL

3.3   The Activity Detection Engine

An *Activity Detection Engine* is able to find activity occurrences matching the well-known models: thus, such a module takes as inputs the list of *action symbols* previously caught by the *Video Labeler* and the *stochastic activity models* and finally returns the list of the discovered activity occurrences with the related probabilities. To reach this goal, a specific software called *tMAGIC*, which is the implementation of a theoretical model presented in [8] has been used.

As a matter of fact, the [8] approach addresses the problem of efficiently detecting occurrences of high-level activities from such interleaved data streams. In this approach, there has been proposed a temporal probabilistic graph so that the elapsed time between observations also plays a role in defining whether a sequence of observations constitutes an activity. First, a data structure called *temporal multiactivity graph* to store multiple activities that need to be concurrently monitored has been proposed. Then, there has been defined an index called *Temporal Multi-Activity Graph Index Creation* (tMAGIC) that, based on this data structure, examines and links observations as they occur. There are also defined some algorithms for insertion and bulk insertion into the tMAGIC index showing that this can be efficiently accomplished. In this approach, the algorithms are basically defined to solve two problems: the *evidence problem* that tries to find all occurrences of an activity (with probability over a threshold) within a given sequence of observations, and the *identification problem* that tries to find the activity that best matches a sequence of observations. There are introduced some complexity reducing restrictions and pruning strategies to make the problem, which is intrinsically exponential, linear to the number of observations. It is demonstrated that *tMAGIC* has time and space complexity linear to the size of the input, and can efficiently retrieve instances of the monitored activities. Moreover, this Activity Detection Engine has been also exploited in other works belonging to different contexts, such as [9–11].

3.4   The UAP Engine

The *UAP (Unexplained Activity Problem) Engine* takes as input the *activity occurrences* previously found by the *Activity Detection Engine* with the associated probabilities and the list of the detected *action symbols* and finally discovers the *Unexplained Video Activities*, that are subsequences of the video source which are not sufficiently explained with a certain confidence by the activity models and that could thus be potentially dangerous. Such module is based on the concept of *possible worlds*, has been developed in Java programming language and provides the implementations of the theoretical algorithms FindTUA, FindPUA [1,2].

4   Experimental Evaluation

We generated a video by concatenating multiple videos from the ITEA - CANDELA dataset, a publicly available dataset depicting a number of staged package exchanges and object drop-offs and pick-ups. We evaluated precision and recall against a ground truth provided by human annotators. Annotators were informed about known activities by providing them with a graphical representation of the activity models (see Fig. 5). They were asked to watch the video and identify video segments where totally (resp. partially) unexplained activities occurred.

Figure 6 shows the processing time of *FindTUA* and *FindPUA* as a function of the length of the video. Note that both axes are on a logarithmic scale.

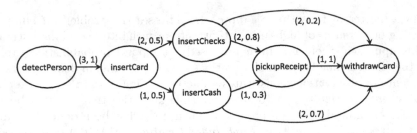

Fig. 5. Example of stochastic activity: ATM deposit

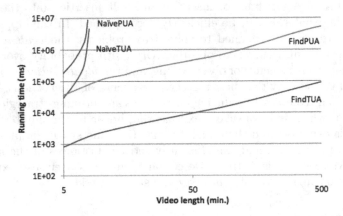

Fig. 6. Processing times

It is clear that both algorithms run in time linear in the length of the video, and significantly outperform naive algorithms that do not use some optimization properties [1].

In order to assess accuracy, we compared the output of our algorithms against ground truth provided by 8 human annotators who were taught the meaning of graphical representations of activities in A (the set of graphs representing our knowledge base) (e.g., Fig. 5). They were asked to identify the totally and partially unexplained activities w.r.t. A. We ran FindTUA and FindPUA with values of the probability threshold τ ranging from 0.4 to 0.8, looking for *all* totally and partially unexplained activities (the minimum length L of an unexplained sequence was set to 200). We use $\{S_i^a\}_{i\in[1,m]}$ to denote the unexplained sequences returned by our algorithms and $\{S_j^h\}_{j\in[1,n]}$ to denote the sequences flagged as unexplained by human annotators. Precision and recall were computed as follows:

$$P = \frac{|\{S_i^a | \exists S_j^h \ s.t. \ S_i^a \approx S_j^h\}|}{m} \tag{1}$$

and

$$R = \frac{|\{S_j^h | \exists S_i^a \ s.t. \ S_i^a \approx S_j^h\}|}{n} \tag{2}$$

where $S_i^a \approx_p S_j^h$ means that S_i^a and S_j^h overlap by a percentage no smaller than 75 %.

Precision and recall when $\tau = 0.4, 0.6, 0.8$ are shown in Table 1a and b: we can easily notice that, the higher is the probability threshold value, the higher is the precision, the lower is the recall and vice versa. That is exactly what we reasonably expected. In summary, we can say that our framework achieved a good accuracy.

Table 1. Precision and recall values

τ	Precision	Recall
0.4	62.5	89.17
0.6	66.67	82.5
0.8	72.22	71.67

(a) FindTUA

τ	Precision	Recall
0.4	59.65	77.38
0.6	64.91	74.6
0.8	70.18	71.83

(b) FindPUA

5   Conclusions and Future Work

This work presented a framework for anomaly detection in video surveillance context. More in details, we started from describing how the video frames are captured by sensors/cameras and thus analyzed, then we showed the different steps applied in order to finally discover some high-level activities which are not sufficiently explained by the well-known activity models and that could be potentially dangerous in the video surveillance context.

Future work will be devoted to compare this framework with other ones which can be built for instance by replacing the components used at each layer with others either already well-known in literature or specifically designed and developed following innovative approaches. For instance, we planned to try also to use another *Image Processing Library* which would hopefully improve the overall effectiveness of the framework and allow the whole process to work as much as possible automatically. Moreover, we can try to exploit a different *UAP Engine* for discovering unexplained activities in video surveillance context, which would be no longer based on the concept of *possible worlds*, but on *game theory*.

References

1. Albanese, M., Molinaro, C., Persia, F., Picariello, A., Subrahmanian, V.S.: Discovering the Top-k unexplained sequences in time-stamped observation data. IEEE Trans. Knowl. Data Eng. (TKDE) **26**(3), 577–594 (2014)
2. Albanese, M., Molinaro, C., Persia, F., Picariello, A., Subrahmanian, V.S.: Finding unexplained activities in video. In: International Joint Conference on Artificial Intelligence (IJCAI), pp. 1628–1634 (2011)
3. Petersen, J.K.: Understanding Surveillance Technologies. CRC Press, Boca Raton (2001)

4. Collins, R., Lipton, A., Kanade, T.K.: Introduction to the special section on video surveillance. IEEE Trans. Patt. Anal. Mach. Intell. **22**(8), 745–746 (2000)
5. Regazzoni, C., Ramesh, V.: Scanning the Issue/Technology Special Issue on Video Communications, Processing, and Understanding for Third Generation Surveillance Systems, University of Genoa, Siemens Corporate Research Inc., University of Udine, IEEE (2001)
6. Siebel, N.T., Maybank, S.J.: Fusion of multiple tracking algorithms for robust people tracking. In: Heyden, A., Sparr, G., Nielsen, M., Johansen, P. (eds.) ECCV 2002, Part IV. LNCS, vol. 2353, pp. 373–387. Springer, Heidelberg (2002)
7. Siebel, N.T., Maybank, S.: The advisor visual surveillance system. In: ECCV 2004 Workshop Applications of Computer Vision (ACV 2004) (2004)
8. Albanese, M., Pugliese, A., Subrahmanian, V.S.: Fast activity detection: indexing for temporal stochastic automaton based activity models. IEEE Trans. Knowl. Data Eng. (TKDE) **25**, 360–373 (2013)
9. Persia, F., D'Auria, D.: An application for finding expected activities in medial context scientific databases. In: SEBD 2014, pp. 77–88 (2014)
10. D'Auria, D., Persia, F.: Automatic evaluation of medical doctors' performances while using a cricothyrotomy simulator. In: IRI 2014, pp. 514–519 (2014)
11. D'Auria, D., Persia, F.: Discovering expected activities in medical context scientific databases. In: DATA 2014, pp. 446–453 (2014)
12. Dung, P., Chi-Min, O., Soo-Hyung, K., In-Seop, N., Chil-Woo, L.: Object recognition by combining binary local invariant features and color histogram. In: 2013 2nd IAPR Asian Conference on Pattern Recognition (ACPR), pp. 466–470 (2013)
13. Chaudhary, K., Mae, Y., Kojima, M., Arai, T.: Autonomous acquisition of generic handheld objects in unstructured environments via sequential back-tracking for object recognition. In: 2014 IEEE International Conference on Robotics and Automation (ICRA), pp. 4953–4958 (2014)
14. Ubukata, T., Shibata, M., Terabayashi, K., Mora, A., Kawashita, T., Masuyama, G., Umeda, K.: Fast human detection combining range image segmentation and local feature based detection. In: 22nd International Conference on Pattern Recognition (ICPR), pp. 4281–4286 (2014)
15. Onal, I., Kardas, K., Rezaeitabar, Y., Bayram, U., Bal, M., Ulusoy, I., Cicekli, N.K.: A framework for detecting complex events in surveillance videos. In: 2013 IEEE International Conference on Multimedia and Expo Workshops (ICMEW), pp. 1–6 (2013)
16. Zin, T.T., Tin, P., Hama, H., Toriu, T.: An integrated framework for detecting suspicious behaviors in video surveillance. In: Society of Photo-Optical Instrumentation Engineers (SPIE) Conference Series (2014)

A Facial Expression Recognition
with Automatic Segmentation
of Face Regions

Andres Hernandez-Matamoros[1], Andrea Bonarini[2],
Enrique Escamilla-Hernandez[1], Mariko Nakano-Miyatake[1],
and Hector Perez-Meana[1(⊠)]

[1] Instituto Politecnico Nacional,
Av. Santa Ana 1000, Mexico D.F. 04430, Mexico
{mnakano,hmperezm}@ipn.mx
[2] Politecnico Di Milano, Via Ponzio 34/5, 20133 Milan, Italy
http://www.posgrados.esimecu.ipn.mx

Abstract. This paper proposes a facial expression recognition algorithm, which automatically detects and segments the face regions of interest (ROI) such as the forehead, eyes and mouth, etc. Proposed scheme initially detects the image face and segments it in two regions: forehead/eyes and mouth. Next each of these regions is segmented into $N \times M$ blocks which are characterized using 54 Gabor functions that are correlated with each one of the $N \times M$ blocks. Next the principal component analysis (PCA) is used for dimensionality reduction. Finally, the resulting feature vectors are inserted in a proposed classifier based on clustering techniques which provides recognition results closed to those provided by the support vector machine (SVM) with much less computational complexity. The experimental results show that proposed system provides a recognition rate of about 98 % when only one ROI is used. This recognition rate increases to about 99 % when the feature vectors of all ROIs are concatenated. This fact allows achieving recognition rates higher than 97 %, even when one of the two ROI are totally occluded.

Keywords: Facial expression recognition · Gabor functions · PCA · Classifier methods · Face detection · Facial ROI segmentation

1 Introduction

The use of smart devices in the solution of several problems has increased recently given as a result the development of very efficient systems that can be used in many practical applications. Among them the facial expression recognition (FER) systems have been used to recognize the mood. This is because several problems can be avoided if it is possible to accurate detect the mood of a person, i.e., if a given person has a nervous breakdown, if he is tired, angry or happiness, etc. For this reason, during the last several years the interest for developing these kinds of systems has increased [1–4]. A very important part of such systems is the detection of face regions because an accurate detection of such regions may improve the performance of FER. Currently, in the literature exists some algorithms able to detect faces in an image and even smiles

© Springer International Publishing Switzerland 2015
H. Fujita and G. Guizzi (Eds.): SoMeT 2015, CCIS 532, pp. 529–540, 2015.
DOI: 10.1007/978-3-319-22689-7_41

must of them based on Viola-Jones [5] algorithm. Unfortunately these schemes are not enough accurate to detect the facial expression and thereby to achieve accurate mood detection. This happens because when someone does a mood a expression, it could be strong or not, some movement of the face muscles is done involuntarily. This movement is, in general, different in each facial expression doing it possible to determine the regions of interest of the face in each case. Several problems are present in facial expression recognition; some of them are related with the face orientation related to the camera, because if the person isn't looking straightforward to the camera partial occlusion of the face may occur [6], or the presence of shadows due to poor illumination conditions. Then it is necessary that the FER system be able to achieve a recognition rate higher than 95 % even if only one of the available regions of interest remains without occlusion. For this reason, we propose a FER algorithm that is able to segment the face ROI under different illumination conditions which does it possible to take accurate decisions even if one of the two ROI of the face has a partial or even total occlusion. In proposed system, after the ROI estimation, each region is segmented in a set of N × M blocks which are correlated with a set of Gabor functions. The resulting factures matrix is then applied to a PCA for dimensionality reduction. We also propose a classifier with low computational cost which provides recognition rates similar to those provided by other high performance classifiers such as the SVM and ANN. This fact allows implementing the proposed scheme even in smart devices with low computation power that require an immediate response. The proposed algorithm was evaluated with kdef data base [7] which consists of 490 images which are divided into seven facial expressions of 70 people which are used to carry out different evaluations. In the first one the FER system was evaluated using only one ROI, assuming that the other one was occluded, while in the second one both ROI were concatenated. Evaluation results show that using one ROI the proposed system provides a recognition rate of 98 %, while using both ROI the recognition rate increase to 99 %. The rest of the paper is organized as follows: Sect. 2 describes the system framework, the experimental results are shown in Sects. 3 and 4 provides the conclusion of this work.

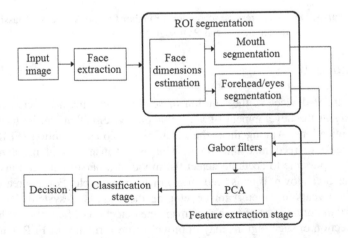

Fig. 1. Proposed facial expression recognition system

2 Proposed System

The System framework of proposed facial expression recognition system (FER) is shown in Fig. 1. Here, firstly the received face image is fed into the face extraction stage, which extracts the face image using the Viola-Jones algorithm [5]. Next the detected face region is inserted into the region of interest (ROI) detection stage, which firstly estimates the face dimensions. Then using this information the ROIs are automatically segmented to get the mouth and Forehead/Eyes using the image moments and projective integrals. These ROIs are then segmented in N × M no overlapping blocks which are then cross-correlated, as mentioned above, with a set of 54 Gabor functions. Next the first value of each estimated cross correlation mentioned above is used for the feature extraction of each ROI, which are then concatenated in 3 different vectors: mouth, forehead/eyes, mouth + front/eyes. Next the feature vectors are independently process by a PCA stage for dimensionality reduction. Finally, the resulting vectors are fed in to the proposed a classifier stage to take the final decision. Next sections provide a description of all stages of proposed system.

2.1 ROI Segmentation

The image received by the FER is firstly processed by the Viola Jones algorithm to segment the face from the background. However, the detected face image may contain noise, such as the hair or ears, which does not contain relevant information for the facial expressions; or the background where the photograph was taken. In order to eliminate this problem that may decrease the recognition rate of the proposed face expression recognition system, a more accurate estimation for face dimension is carried out as shown in Fig. 3.

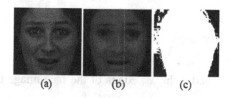

     (a)   (b)   (c)

Fig. 2. (a) Original image, (b) Image obtained by the subtraction, (c) binarized image.

Adjustment of face dimension. To adjust the face dimension parameters, firstly the color face image is divided into its three color components: Red, Green and Blue channels. Next the red and green channels are subtracted from them to highlight the skin as shown in Fig. 2b. Finally, the resulting image is binarized using the equation

$$I(x,y) = \begin{cases} 0 & I(x,y) < 1 \\ 255 & I(x,y) \geq 1 \end{cases} \tag{1}$$

After the image binarization, shown in Fig. 2c, the moments of the resulting image are estimated as follows [8]

$$M_{pq} = \sum_{x=1}^{N} \sum_{y=1}^{M} x^p y^q I(x, y) \tag{2}$$

where $I(x,y)$ is the image intensity at position (x,y), N is the number of columns and M is the number of rows in the image; while p and q define the moment of the image. Next using the Eq. (2) the centriod can be estimated as follows:

$$x_c = M_{1,0}/M_{0,0} \tag{3}$$

$$M = M_{0,1}/M_{0,0} \tag{4}$$

Next, using (3) and (4) the following variables are defined

$$a = \frac{M_{2,0}}{M_{0,0}} - x_c^2 \tag{5}$$

$$b = 2\left(\frac{M_{1,1}}{M_{0,0}} - x_c y_c\right) \tag{6}$$

$$c = \frac{M_{0,2}}{M_{0,0}} - y_c^2 \tag{7}$$

Next using (5)–(7) the face image width can be estimated as follows:

$$W = 2\sqrt{\frac{(a+b) - \sqrt{b^2 + (a-c)^2}}{2}} \tag{8}$$

Using W, the left, x_l, and right, x_r, edges of the face image can be estimated as

$$x_l = \lceil x_c \rceil - \left\lceil \frac{W}{2} \right\rceil \tag{9}$$

$$x_r = \lceil x_c \rceil - \left\lceil \frac{W}{2} \right\rceil + \lceil W \rceil \tag{10}$$

Next, using W the upper edge of the face image can be estimates as follows

$$y_u = \lceil y_c \rceil - 0.84 \left\lceil \frac{W}{2} \right\rceil \tag{11}$$

From (9)–(11) the face image can be segmented as follows

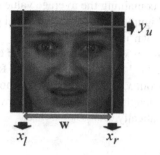

Fig. 3. Segmented face region

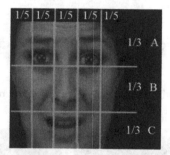

Fig. 4. Symmetrical relationship of the face

Forehead/eye segmentation. A very important part of proposed face expression recognition system is the forehead/face segmentation. To this end, the segmented face region is divided into three regions from the top (A, B and C) as shown in Fig. 4, where the region A is the ROI in the case of the Forehead/eyes segmentation task.

Mouth segmentation. To perform the segmentation of the mouth region, consider the segmented face region which is divided into three regions, of same high, and take the C region of Fig. 4 as our ROI, but unlike the Forehead/eyes region, in this case it is necessary to segment only the mouth region. To this end, the Red and Green image's channels are subtracted among them, then a histogram equalization was performed [9] of image obtained above, obtaining an image as shown in Fig. 5.

Fig. 5. Equalized version of the image obtained from the subtraction of red and green planes.

The next step for the automatic segmentation of the mouth region is the estimation of the horizontal projective integral [10] which is the average of the pixel values of each column. This is a vector containing the average value of the pixels in each column of the image inside the ROI. Figure 6 shows the horizontal projective integral estimated using the equalized image shown in Fig. 5.

Next we obtain the maximum value of the projective error, which will be denoted as "D". Then using the value "D" the left border of the ROI containing the mouth is estimating by subtracting D from x_c, i.e. while the right border is obtained adding it to x_c, keeping the original image height, as shown in Fig. 7, with this procedure the region of interest is extracted automatically.

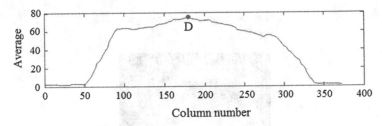

Fig. 6. Horizontal projective integral of the mouth ROI

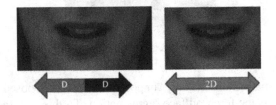

Fig. 7. Detection of mouth ROI.

2.2   Feature Extraction

To perform the feature extraction, each one of the detected ROIs is divided in N × M blocks which are characterized by the average of the first term of the cross correlations between such block and 54 Gabor functions. Next the resulting features vector of each training ROI, with N × M elements, are arranged in a matrix form and applied to a PCA stage for dimensionality reduction. Next sections provide a brief description of these stages.

Gabor functions. The Gabor functions are widely used in many image processing applications such as texture analysis and face recognition tasks [11], because they are robust to luminescence changes. These functions have frequency responses with specific orientations, frequency-selective properties and joint optimum resolution in both spatial and frequency domains. The 2D Gabor functions are given by

$$h(x, y, i, k) = g(x'y') \exp(j2\pi F_i x') \tag{12}$$

where the parameters (x, y) expressed its location in the spatial domain, $F_i = \pi/2^{(i+1)}$, $i = 1,2,..,N_F$ is the spatial frequency, $\phi_k = k\pi/N_\phi$, $k = 1,2,...,N_\phi$ is the rotation angle and $g(x',y')$ is the 2D Gaussian function given by

$$g(x', y') = \frac{1}{2\pi\sigma^2} \exp\left(-\frac{x'^2 + y'^2}{2\sigma^2}\right) \tag{13}$$

where $\sigma = N/2$ and N is the number of blocks in the x axis.

$$(x', y') = x \cos\phi_k + y \sin\phi_k - x \sin\phi_k + y \cos\phi_k. \tag{14}$$

Thus using the Gabor functions given by (12)–(14), the (n,m)-th block of the ROI can be characterized

$$W_{mn} = \frac{1}{N_F N_\phi} \sum_{i=0}^{N_F} \sum_{k=0}^{N_\phi} W(m, n, i, k) \tag{15}$$

Where

$$W(m, n, i, k) = \left| \sum_{x=0}^{R-1} \sum_{y=0}^{Q-1} f(Rn + x, Qn + y)h(x, y, i, k) \right| \tag{16}$$

Principal component analysis. The principal component analysis is one of the most widely used dimensionality reduction methods [12]. To this end, firstly, the feature vectors given by (15) are represented as a one-dimensional vector $\mathbf{W} = [w_0, w_1, .., w_r, w_{NM}]^T$, where $r = nM + m$, $m = 0,1,...,M-1$, $n = 0,1,...,N-1$, where $M \times N$ is the ROI size. Next a matrix $\mathbf{G}$ of size $(NM) \times Q$ is constructed concatenating the all vectors $\mathbf{W}$ contained in the training set, where (NM) is the dimensionality of $\mathbf{W}$, and $Q = TS < NM$, where T is the number of classes and S the number of training images for each class. Next, the eigenvectors and eigenvalues of the covariance matrix given by $\mathbf{G}^T\mathbf{G}$ are estimated and used to generate a dominant feature matrix $\mathbf{\Phi}$ of size $L \times NM$, where $L = Q$ corresponds to the number of the most representative eigenvectors contained in the original image [12]. Finally, the feature vector of each image is given by

$$\mathbf{Y} = \mathbf{\Phi}\mathbf{W} \tag{17}$$

where Y is the resulting feature vector of size $L \times 1$, $\mathbf{\Phi}$ is the dominant matrix, and $\mathbf{W}$ is the vector containing the characteristics of the ROI under analysis given by (15).

2.3   Classification Stage

A low computational complexity classification method is proposed which uses a supervised training approach, like the ANN or SVM approaches, with the characteristic that if a new class must be added, it is not necessary to train the system with all patterns again but only with the patterns belonging to the new class [14].

Training. To develop the proposed classifier consider the set of training patterns

$$
\mathbf{Y} = \begin{bmatrix} y_{1,1} & y_{1,2} & \cdots & y_{1,B} \\ y_{2,1} & y_{2,2} & \cdots & y_{2,B} \\ \cdots & \cdots & \cdots & \cdots \\ y_{L,1} & y_{L,2} & \cdots & y_{L,B} \end{bmatrix} = \begin{bmatrix} \mathbf{Y}_0^T \\ \mathbf{Y}_1^T \\ . \\ \mathbf{Y}_L^T \end{bmatrix}, \tag{18}
$$

and the centroid matrix that is initialized as follows

$$
\mathbf{C} = \begin{bmatrix} y_{1,1} & y_{1,2} & \cdots & y_{1,B} \\ c_{2,1} & c_{2,2} & \cdots & c_{2,B} \\ \cdots & \cdots & \cdots & \cdots \\ c_{P,1} & c_{P,2} & \cdots & c_{P,B} \end{bmatrix} = \begin{bmatrix} y_{1,1} & y_{1,2} & \cdots & y_{1,B} \\ 0 & 0 & \cdots & 0 \\ 0 & 0 & \cdots & 0 \\ 0 & 0 & \cdots & 0 \end{bmatrix} = \begin{bmatrix} \mathbf{Y}_1^T \\ \mathbf{C}_2^T \\ . \\ \mathbf{C}_P^T \end{bmatrix}, \tag{19}
$$

where L is equal to the total number training patterns, and the initial centroids number is et equal to one. Next, the remaining $P-1$ centroids are estimated as follows:

i. While L > 0, compute

$$
\delta_{q,r} = \left| \mathbf{Y}_q - \mathbf{C}_{r_k} \right| \quad q = 1, 2, \dots, L; \quad , r_k = N_{k-1} + j_k; \quad 1 \leq j_k \leq (N_k - N_{k-1}) \tag{20}
$$

$$
\delta_{\min} = \min\left(\delta_{q,r_k}\right) = \delta_{m,r_n} \tag{21}
$$

$$
\delta_{\max} = \max\left(\delta_{q,r_k}\right) = \delta_{M,r_N} \tag{22}
$$

$$
\mathbf{C}_{r_N+1} = \mathbf{Y}_M, \tag{23}
$$

$$
\text{Next for } \mathbf{Y}_m, \text{ update } \mathbf{C}_{r_n} = (\mathbf{C}_{r_n} + \mathbf{Y}_m)/2 \tag{24}
$$

set $L = L - 1$, $P = P + 1$ and $N_j = N_j + 1$.

Finally the resulting clusters are arranged into N_p classes with M_k clusters per class as follows

$$G = \begin{bmatrix} C_1^T, \ldots, C_{N_1+1}^T, C_{N_1+2}^T, \ldots, C_{N_2}^T, C_{N_2+1}^T, \ldots, C_{N_3}^T, \ldots, C_{N_{p-1}}^T, \ldots, C_{N_p}^T \end{bmatrix}^T \quad (25)$$

Testing. For a given input pattern Z, compute

$$\delta_{min} = \left| Z - C_{N_{k-1}+j_k} \right|_{min} \quad (26)$$

Then, if $N_{k-1} < j_k \leq N_k$, where $1 < N_k \leq N_p$, the pattern under analysis belongs to the N_k-*th* class.

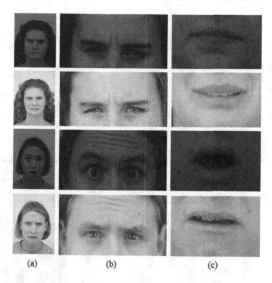

(a)   (b)   (c)

Fig. 8. Performance of face region segmentation stage, (a) original images, (b) eyes/forehead, segmentation, (c) and (f) mouth segmentation.

3 Evaluation Results

An important task of proposed algorithm is the face regions segmentation in order to allow an accurate feature extraction. Figure 8 shows the face region segmentation performance of proposed scheme with different illumination conditions. Evaluation results show that the illumination conditions do not affect the automatic extraction of facial regions.

To carry out the recognition performance of proposed algorithm, after the face region detection, the mouth is reduced to 180 pixels wide and 90 high, while the Front/eyes regions were resized to 300 pixels wide and 150 high. Starting with the goal of find the optimal windows sizes of Gabor filters, different window sizes were analyzed in both face regions, using 50 images for training and 20 testing. Figure 9 shows that for the mouth region a recognition rate of about 97.85 % was obtained when Gabor windows whose sizes where from 10×10 to 30×30; while for Front/Eyes regions the recognition's rates is 99.28 %. Thus a suitable window size is 30×30 pixels because the computational cost is lower. The same experiment was performed using the ANN as classifier, given as results for the mouth 97.14 % recognition, training with 50 images and using windows for Gabor filters 30×30, while for the Forehead/Eyes region was obtained a recognition rate of 91.42 % with 50 training images and windows size of 50×50. Both the recognition's percentage is lower than that obtained using the proposed classifier.

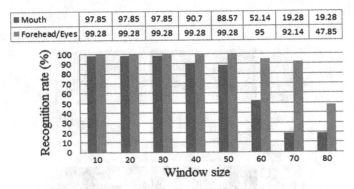

■ Mouth	97.85	97.85	97.85	90.7	88.57	52.14	19.28	19.28
■ Forehead/Eyes	99.28	99.28	99.28	99.28	99.28	95	92.14	47.85

Fig. 9. Average Recognition with different size of windows

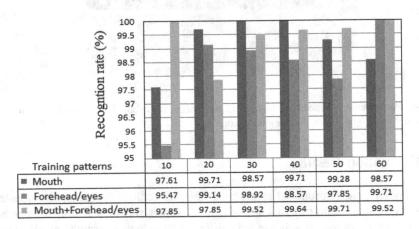

Training patterns	10	20	30	40	50	60
■ Mouth	97.61	99.71	98.57	99.71	99.28	98.57
■ Forehead/eyes	95.47	99.14	98.92	98.57	97.85	99.71
■ Mouth+Forehead/eyes	97.85	97.85	99.52	99.64	99.71	99.52

Fig. 10. Average Recognition with different training's patterns

Figure 10 shows the evaluation results obtained with a different number of training patterns. It is important to mention that for the 3 cases under analysis (mouth region using windows 30×30, Forehead/Eyes region using windows 50×50, mouth region using windows of 30×30 + Region Forehead/Eyes using windows 50×50) the recognition rates are higher than 97 %, when both regions of mouth and front/eyes are used. Evaluation results show that the highest recognition rate is obtained when both, the mouth and forehead regions are jointly used providing a recognition rate of about 99 %.

Figure 11 shows the comparison of recognition performance of proposed facial expression recognition scheme and other recently proposed schemes, [6, 13] reports global recognition rates using the whole face, while [2] reports the recognition performance using the mouth region and the forehead/eyes regions. Evaluation results show that proposed scheme performs better than other previously proposed methods [2, 6] and quite close to that reported in [13], with less computational complexity.

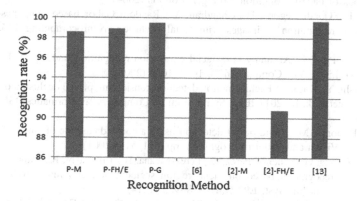

Fig. 11. Recognition performance of proposed scheme using the mouth region P-M, the forehead/eyes P-FH/E and both of them P-G. The performance of other previously proposed schemes are [2, 6] and [13] are also shown for comparison.

4 Conclusions

This paper presents an algorithm for recognizing facial expressions, performing an automatic segmentation of facial regions of interest to achieve this, first what is proposed is a segmentation of the face image obtained through the algorithm Viola Jones, then based on the symmetry of the face and using the integral projective automatically remove the 2 regions of interest, the first region is the Forehead/Eye and the second the Mouth, here is important that adequate extraction of regions even with different luminescence is achieved, this one of the main problems that present for facial expression recognition, moreover a classifier is proposed with low computational cost which performs better than an ANN, in both the percentage of recognition, as in training time. When making a comparison with the literature we can conclude that the proposed system performs better than [6] and [2], because a higher percentage of recognition in all possible cases was obtained and also a facial expression is recognized more accurately. Proposed system provides similar performance that [13] which use the whole image. Thus, it is possible to conclude that our system is able to recognize adequately the facial expressions with a percentage higher than 97 %, either taking the whole face, which in our case consists of regions of interest concatenated, or with partial occlusion, that is only considering one of the regions of interest proposals.

Acknowledgements. We thank the National Science and Technology Council of Mexico (CONACYT) and to the Instituto Politecnico Nacional for the financial support during the realization of this research.

References

1. Tian, Y., Kanade, T., Cohn, J.F.: Facial expressions analysis. In: Li, S.Z., Jain, A.K. (eds.) Handbook of Face Recognition. Springer, London (2004)
2. Zhang, L., Tjondronegoro, D., Chandran, V.: Random Gabor based templates for facial expression recognition in images with facial occlusion. Neurocomputing **145**, 451–464 (2014)
3. Buciu, K., Pitas, I.: An analysis of facial expression recognition under partial face image occlusion. Image Vis. Comput. **26**(7), 1052–1067 (2008)
4. Miyakoshi, Y., Kato, S.: Facial emotion detection considering partial occlusion of face using Bayesian network. In: 2011 IEEE Symposium on Computers & Informatics (ISCI), pp. 96–101 (2011)
5. Viola, P., Jones, M.: Rapid object detection using a boosted cascade of simple features. In: Computer Vision and Pattern Recognition, pp. 511–518 (2001)
6. Benitez-Garcia, G., Sanchez-Perez, G., Perez-Meana, H., Takahashi, K., Kaneko, M.: Facial expression recognition based on facial region segmentation and modal value approach. IEICE Trans. on Inf. Syst. **E97-D(4)**, 928–935 (2014)
7. Lundqvist, D., Flykt, A., Öhman, A.: The Karolinska Directed Emotional Faces - KDEF, CD ROM from Department of Clinical Neuroscience, Psychology section, Karolinska Institutet (1998). ISBN 91-630-7164-9
8. Freeman, W., Tanaka, K., Ohta, J., Kyuma, K.: Computer vision for computer games. In: International Conference on Automatic Face and Gesture Recognition, pp. 100–105 (2008)
9. Pizer, M.: Adaptive histogram equalization and its variations. Comput. Vis. Graph. Image Process. **39**, 355–368 (1987)
10. Li, W., Mao, K., Zhang, H., Chai, T.: Selection of Gabor filters for improved texture feature extraction. In: IEEE International Conference on Image Processing, pp. 361–364 (2010)
11. Pakdel, M., Tajeripour, F.: Texture classification using optimal Gabor filters. In: International Conference on Computer and Knowledge Engineering, pp. 208–213 (2011)
12. Jolliffe, I.: Principal Component Analysis, 2nd edn. Springer, New York (2002)
13. Hasimah, A., Muthusamy, H., Yaacob, S., Adom, A.: Expert Syst. Appl. **42**, 1261–1277 (2015)
14. Hernandez-Matamoros, A., Escamilla-Hernandez, E., Perez-Daniel, K., Nakano-Miyatake, K.M., Perez-Meana, H.: A supervised classifier scheme based on clustering algorithms. In: IEEE Central America and Panama Convention (CONCAPAN XXXIV), pp. 1–5 (2014)

Automatic Estimation of Illumination Features for Indoor Photorealistic Rendering in Augmented Reality

Hasan Alhajhamad[✉], Mohd Shahrizal Sunar, and Hoshang Kolivand

Media and Game Innovation Centre of Excellence (MaGIC-X) UTM-IRDA,
Universiti Teknologi Malaysia, 81310 Johor Bahru, Malaysia
{hzhamad,kolivand}@magicx.my, shahrizal@utm.my
http://magicx.utm.my

Abstract. In this paper, a fast and practical algorithm is presented to estimate the multiple number of lights from every single indoor scene image in Augmented Reality environmet. This algorithm provides a way to accurately estimate the position, directions, and intensities properties of the light sources in a scene. Unlike other state-of-the-art algorithms, it is able to give accurate results without any essential analysis on the objects in the scene. It uses the analysis of the saturation channel HSV data. The evaluation is done by testing a ground truth dataset of synthetic and real images with known properties of lights and then comparing the results with other studies in the field.

Keywords: Illumination estimation · Shadow detection · Photorealistic augmented reality · Indoor spatial images · Computer vision

1 Introduction

Undoubtedly, the estimation of light illumination is one of the trickiest tasks in computer vision especially for indoor scenes. Presence of multiple light sources of different sizes and shapes, intensities and spectral features is a typical condition for such environments. The image based lighting is relatively the latest advanced approach for modeling light which achieves high quality results yet at the cost of processing time [1]. However, the requirements of complex hardware setup with additional cameras and/or light probes based on highly dynamic and superior image resolution are the main shortcoming of this approach.

Currently, the demands in the context of augmented reality applications are exponentially growing, where researchers and engineers have dedicated enormous efforts. Lately, the feasibility to augment real scenes with arbitrary objects and animations opened up broad prospects in the areas of design, entertainment, and human-computer interaction. Therefore, correct estimation of lighting conditions such as 3D positions and colors inside the scene appears to be a crucial step in creating the rendering highly realistic and convincing.

© Springer International Publishing Switzerland 2015
H. Fujita and G. Guizzi (Eds.): SoMeT 2015, CCIS 532, pp. 541–554, 2015.
DOI: 10.1007/978-3-319-22689-7_42

A modified approach that allows direct estimation of the positions of light sources is proposed but it also uses cumbersome hardware [2]. The most popular alternatives to image-based lighting approaches usually aim on the detection and direct analysis of shadings. Generally, these techniques are more suitable for outdoor environments with strong casts, directed light sources, and simple geometry. An exhaustive survey of the cast detection methods is provided in [3], while the possibility of their integration in real-time augmented reality systems is reviewed in [4,5].

Emergent technologies and vision-based robotics for fine-tuning the digital images suffer from lighting factors in real images [6,7]. Information regarding the light source distribution in an image facilitates in analyzing the objects, shadows, and noises present in the scene. Initial dismissal of detailed information related to light sources results inherent difficulty in analyzing the scene in the indoor environments [8].

Appearances of various lighting sources are found to be the major difficulties in real-time image processing. Detection of light sources permits one to estimate their position, direction, and intensity [9–11]. Figure 1 illustrates the background setting of indoor and outdoor scene illumination.

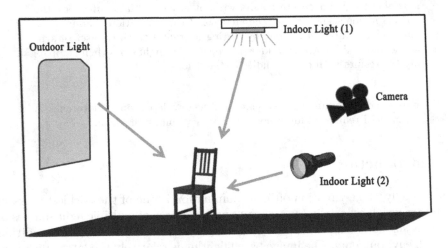

Fig. 1. Setting of indoor and outdoor scene illumination.

In this work, we generate the information on the localization of light sources in real scenes. Light source detection involves different techniques including probe detection which extracts the light properties from a known 3D object. Nevertheless, these techniques are not applicable to multiple lights and require the proper understanding of all 3D objects present in the real scene. Thus, we obtain the information on lighting without accessing any object in the scene itself. Indoor digital images possess varying numbers and directions of light. Researchers aim to estimate the approximate number of light sources to recognize the actual cause of occlusion which may appear from an object, shadow or noise [7, 12–15]. Therefore, the nine directions constriction of every light source in a 2D image is considered.

The presence of high diffuse sunlight in outdoor scenes makes their geometry much wider with less disparity lighting levels. Alternatively, indoor scenes suffer from limited geometry and higher disparity lighting levels due to the presence of multiple lights with different properties and influences. In fact, clear differentiation between these lights and their properties in the scene are extremely difficult. Consequently, we focus only on the color, intensity, position, and direction of each light source.

The algorithm is evaluated based on its accuracy and performance. The accuracy is tested using Lopez-Moreno evaluation where the results are compared with Light Source Detection (LSD) algorithm and synthetic image of known lights. Meanwhile, the performance of LSD algorithm is based on the number of frames per second. It is hoped that our systematic assessment on the automatic estimation of illumination characteristics may improve the performance of sundry applications including real-time digital photography editing, interactive photorealistic augmented reality, vision-based robotics, medical images, or New Media Art.

2   Related Work

Previous researches on the light detection are mostly based on 2D images in Computer Vision. They concerned with the object based and statistical based techniques. Recently, many methods are introduced [13, 15–17] since the founding work of Pentland [6]. Majority of them either focused on extracting the properties of light by receiving information on the image objects or on extorting one direction of light. Fewer methods exploring the shadow detection obtain information on the light sources [18, 19].

Strong assumptions on the background environment are needed for light source detection. Some of them analyze the objects and others estimate the geometry. Recovery of the light via object contours analysis is developed. Light sources illumination are estimated by inserting a hemisphere to the environment and analyzing the reflectance of light on it [20]. Many of them are based on the analyses of the reflectance of lights on real objects' contours in the image [16]. Shadow detection techniques are proven to be satisfactory in tackling the illumination issues [21–24]. Furthermore, recent works on the object analysis methods achieved relatively accurate results. Despite intensive efforts the precise detection of objects in the scene requiring the information of light sources is far from being achieved.

In the Augmented Reality, the first illumination estimation model was based on a simple point light source without ambient light assuming uniformly colored objects. The distant point light source is defined by an illumination direction [13]. Then, Kanbara [25] used a marker with a mirror ball to resolve geometric and photometric registration. Two methods rely on the illuminated geometry with no requirement for knowledge of a specific calibration object, one method was proposed by Sato from shadows [26] and another from Shading by Wang [17]. Then, Wang [20] integrated the above two methods and proposed a new method for multiple directional source estimation. The model came after had used omni-directional stereo cameras to capture environment illumination and to model the distant parts of the environment [26]. Stumpfel [27] introduced other approach by photographed mirror spheres to capture the illuminants in the scene. This paper discusses another way to realize the illuminants in real scene in real-time.

From the get-go, most of the mentioned methods either force constraints on the scene, require more information for detection like depth sensors, or non real-time like in image relighting,

3   Light Source Detection Method

This paper attempts to extract multiple light sources from a single indoor scene image in the absence of any constraint on object detection. The information is directly acquired from the scene to develop a constraint free detection method. It is customary to introduce the structure of the light source estimation step-by-step as shown in Fig. 2. Firstly, a camera is placed in the indoor environment. Then, the light image is extracted from a single RGB image to extract the lighted areas of the scene. Synchronously, a shadow image is extracted from the same image to detect the shadowed areas of the scene. Finally, the calculation of the illumination properties is performed based on the relation between the lighted and shadowed areas as described in the following sections.

3.1   Illustration of Light Image

Even though indoor RGB images are captured by high quality cameras, however the presence of light, noise and scene variations remain a problem to be solved.

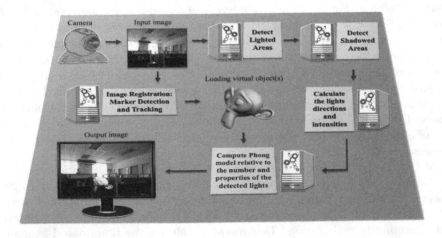

Fig. 2. The pipeline of the illumination sources detection model.

Consequently, the user must extract less noise and get more illumination stability while capturing. The first objective is therefore to control the illumination in the image. Supposing that the output is a single channel light image, one in interested to extract lightness levels of each pixel in the RGB image. Let I_{RGB} be the input of 8-bits RGB image, n is the total number of pixels in the image and ξ_{lights} is the set of the resulted lights. Here each light represents the area of the direct or indirect real light in I_{RGB}. Then, I_{RGB} and ξ_{lights} can be defined as,

$$I_{RGB} = \begin{pmatrix} R_1, G_1, B_1 \\ \cdot \\ \cdot \\ \cdot \\ R_n, G_n, B_n \end{pmatrix}$$

$$\xi_{lights} = \begin{pmatrix} C_0 \\ C_1 \\ C_2 \\ \dots \\ C_{nl} \end{pmatrix}$$

where, R_i, G_i and B_i are the ith red, green and blue channels, respectively. C_i consists of the area $C_i(area)$ of a detected light in some position $C_i(pos)$, direction $C_i(dir)$, and intensity $C_i(int)$, and nl is the number of detected lights. C_i is expressed as,

$$C_i = \begin{pmatrix} area \\ pos \\ dir \\ int \end{pmatrix}$$

To compute each element C_i, the following algorithm comprised of six major steps is proposed:

Algorithm 1. Light Source Detection

1: Convert I_{RGB} to HSL format image I_{hsl}
2: Split I_{hsl} to its Hue, Saturation, and Lightness
3: Calculate Otsu's threshold on the Saturation channel using look-up table
4: Filter the I_{hsl} using Gaussian blur
5: Extract the set of contours ξ_{lights} for the detected spots in I_{hsl}
6: Represent the position $C(pos)$ of each element of ξ_{lights} as the center of the contour C

The red-green-blue (RGB) to Hue-saturation-lightness (HSL) conversion formula is common. The RGB values of one pixel range from 0 to 255 for each channel. Similarly, the value of each channel in one HSL pixel lies in the range of 0 to 1. Consequently, the conversion value of the result is measured by dividing the I_{RGB} channel value by 255 as hereunder:

Let us assume,

$$I_{HSL} = \begin{pmatrix} Hue_1, Sat_1, Lig_1 \\ \cdot \\ \cdot \\ \cdot \\ Hue_n, Sat_n, Lig_n \end{pmatrix}$$

then,

$$R' \leftarrow R/255$$
$$G' \leftarrow G/255$$
$$B' \leftarrow B/255$$

Assuming that C_{min} and C_{max} are the minimum and maximum value of each channel in one pixel, then the difference $diff$ is calculated from,

$$C_{max} = \max(R', G', B')$$
$$C_{min} = \min(R', G', B')$$
$$diff = C_{max} - C_{min}$$

Accordingly,

$$H = \begin{cases} 60° \times (\frac{G'-B'}{diff} \bmod 6), & C_{max} = R' \\ 60° \times (\frac{B'-R'}{diff} + 2), & C_{max} = G' \\ 60° \times (\frac{R'-G'}{diff} + 4), & C_{max} = B' \end{cases}$$

$$L = \frac{C_{max} + C_{min}}{2}$$

$$S = \begin{cases} 0, & 0 \\ \frac{diff}{1-|(2 \times Lightness)-1|}, & otherwise \end{cases}$$

Look-up table is calculated and the optimal performance is obtained to achieve the values of each pixel. Applying Otsu's thresholding [28] on the Saturation channel image a binary image is obtained. The lighted areas of the scene is represented by white spots in the binary image and remained black elsewhere (Fig. 3). By blurring the extracted binary image, the contours of the lighted areas enhanced the smoothness approximation of light which provided better detection quality.

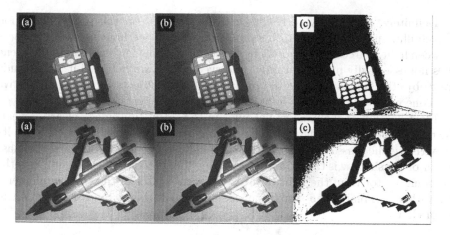

Fig. 3. (a) Original images (b) single channel saturation images (c) lighted areas in binary images.eps

3.2 Shadows Detection

After identifying the albedo spaces, contour detection is implemented to extract the covered areas of the light sources from the binary image. In this case filled closed contours representing each light source area are drawn. Contours are measured by following Suzuki and Abe algorithm [29]. Subsequently, the resulted contour areas are stored in moments. Each moment M_i consists of contour area and its mass center (C_i). In case a moment area covers a small scale in the image (e.g. 30 pixels), the moment is discarded. If the moment is in large-scale area (e.g. $\frac{n}{2}$ or more) then it is segmented into fixed or automatic number of moments. The division processes fixed by 2 moments yields,

$$M_i = \begin{cases} discard, & M_{area} < 30 \\ <M_{area}, C_i>, & \frac{n}{2} > M_{area} \geq 30 \\ Segment(M_i, 2), & M_{area} \geq \frac{n}{2} \end{cases}$$

Thus, the achieved result is a set of moments represented by their mass centers C_i each to behave like a source or a reflection of light as displayed in Fig. 3.

Algorithm 2. Shadows Detection

1: Calculate Otsu's threshold of the dark colors from the Saturation channel using look-up table
2: Filter the I_{hsl} using Gaussian blur
3: Extract the set of contours $\xi_{shadows}$ for the detected spots in I_{hsl}
4: Represent each element of $\xi_{shadows}$ as the center of the contour D

Definitely, the quality of results entirely depends on the proper detection of each illuminant. Illuminant direction is detected by estimating the differences between light sources and shadows in the scene. Estimating shadows in the scene does not essentially mean that only shadowed spaces are detected it also include dark objects. This is because the presence of dark objects in the scene behave the same way as shadows vis-à-vis its reflectance properties.

Identification of the shadow behavior in the saturation image clearly reveals the relation between the light source position, occlusion, and shadow. The results show that if the mass center of the detected light source is obtained and the mass center of the shadow is taken in the same way, the direction of the light forms the marching vector from the light towards the mass center of the shadow moment. Algorithm 2 explains the steps that are adopted in Light Source Detection in Algorithm 1.

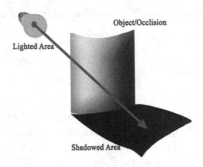

Fig. 4. Direction of the light source starting from its mass center to that of shadow centre for the occluded object.

Figure 4 shows the method to resolve the direction of one light source to one detected shadow. The problem remains in the detection of large number of lights and shadows in the scene. The distribution of lights and the relation between them and other shadows in the scene can lead to approximate both the direction and intensity of each light.

3.3   Light Source Direction and Intensity Detection

This problem is overcome by taking each light and calculating the average distance between its mass center and all other mass centers shadows in the scene. The near and far angles for each shadow are considered. In case some angles are close to each other, the intensity of the light towards this direction must be less than the farther ones. For some far angles the intensity of the light is higher. Algorithm 3 shows the steps for computing the multiple light intensities and light directions.

The algorithm simply considers each of the detected light sources and analyzes the distances between them and other shadows in the scene. Only the close lights and shadows are included.

Algorithm 3. Calculation of multiple lights directions and intensities

1: Define $C_i(int)$ as 0.5 for all C_i in ξ_{lights}.

2: For each light mass center C_i in ξ_{lights} , execute step 2.

3: For each shadow mass center D_j in $\xi_{shadows}$, execute step 3 and 4.

4: calculate the average distance between C_i and D_j.

5: calculate the C_i angle between each shadow. If some shadows are have nearly equal angles, reduce the intensity value of C_i otherwise increase the value.

4   Implementation

A data set of several images is gathered to test the accuracy and performance of the proposed algorithm. Multi-camera Multi-lighting Dome (MCML) Data Sets are used in [30]. These datasets are image sequences captured in a studio for 20 views evenly paced on a ring inside a lighting dome. All images in the dataset are captured from a single PC camera that supports HD quality images.

The experiments are performed in three different scenarios. The first scenario uses a single light source in a known position, direction, and intensity placed in the dark area. Figure 5 depicts the steps to estimate the illumination of a single light source. The lighted areas image in Fig. 5 shows the light and the reflection of it as dark spots which reveals the mass center of them as a white marker based on Algorithm 1.

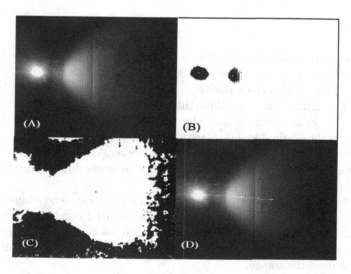

Fig. 5. Scenarios of (a) original image (b) lighted areas image (c) shadowed areas image (d) resulted image.

The shadowed areas image displays the shadow spaces in the image based on Algorithm 2 by considering the measurement of the mass centers of each detected shadow area. Each estimated light is exemplified by a white arrow to represent the accuracy of the data. The single arrow's starting point represents the position of the light source where its length signifies the intensity of the light and the head of the arrow indicates its direction.

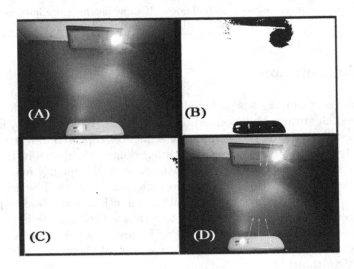

Fig. 6. (a) Original image (b) lighted areas image (c) shadowed areas image (d) resulted image.

In the second scenario, two light sources were placed in a dark space. Figure 6 illustrates the same steps as performed in the first experiment. The results successfully prove the correct position, direction, and intensities of both light sources. The original image exhibits that the two light sources are situated to face each other in a dark area and the lighted areas image estimated total six elements from the original image. Each light is represented as a dark spot, where only two shadowed elements are detected. However, the arrows in the resulted image outnumbered the actual number of light sources due to the existence of reflections.

Figure 7 illustrates the snapshot of an arbitrary indoor scene where the size of the room is considered to be quite large. The estimated number of light sources is nine and the number of detected shadowed areas is fifty four. The resulted image shows that the algorithm had successfully obtained the real light sources in the scene from the image.

Accurately, speed improvement is a major contribution of this paper. For 1024×768 image, the mean processing time is found to vary between 40–60 ms on a laptop with Intel® Core™ i7-4702MQ CPU at 2.20 GHz (8 cores) and 4 GB RAM. The algorithm implementation is administered under in-hand system specifications.

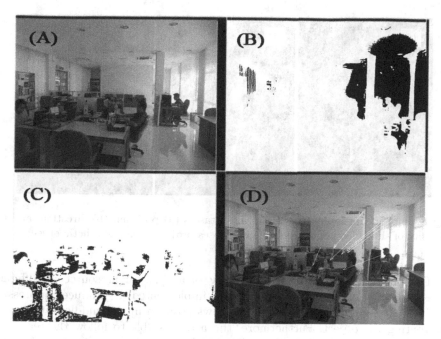

Fig. 7. (a) Original image (b) lighted areas image (c) shadowed areas image (d) resulted image.

Table 1 summarizes the speed of the algorithm in each of the previously described experiments. The estimated performances for each experiment do not exhibit as such big difference between single, two, or multiple light sources.

Table 1. Performance of the algorithm.

Experiment	Frame rate	
	Minimum	Maximum
Single light source	45	54
Two light sources	42	50
Complete indoor scene	40	49

Our results show an improvement from the Multi View Stereo (MVS) algorithms perspective when compared with the work of Wu et al. [30]. This algorithm is advantageous because it overcomes the case of non-Lambertian objects compare to Wu et al. Furthermore, their method requires the access of the scene and the construction of a mesh which leads to slow performance.

Figure 8 depicts the use of similar dataset on the virtual model data with the difference in results.

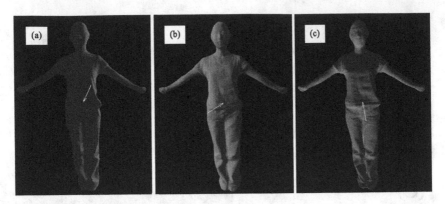

Fig. 8. Implementation on the Wu et al. datasets (a) position, (b) direction, and (c) intensity of single light source in different poses projected on a synthetic object.

The position, direction, and intensity of a single light source in different poses projected on a synthetic object are implemented. It produces impressive results with high level accuracy. The arrows position in the middle of the scene confronting the object. Furthermore, the arrow is able to follow the real light direction and for its intensity immediately after changing the direction. In comparison to our method the earlier one [30] is unable to detect the real light source, and only useful for implementing the relighting on the scene. We assert that the proposed method is efficiently capable in achieving information instantly with the frequent change of the light position, direction, or intensity.

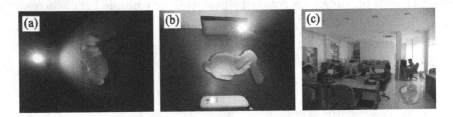

Fig. 9. Implementation of the results of the algorithm in AR scene (a) positioning a single light source, (b) two lights, and (c) complex scene with multiple light source and their projection on a synthetic object.eps

As a result of our previous experiments, Fig. 9 shows an AR scene where a composition of the real scene and a virtual object in real-time after performing the steps in Fig. 3. The provided images where captured in three illumination states; with a single light source, two lights, and complex scene with multiple lights.

5 Conclusions

From the previous work, a novel algorithm for detecting illumination in a scene was described. The algorithm estimates the lights and the reflected lights without going into detailed analysis. Experiments were done by comparing real and synthetic datasets. Real time experiments were done using a conventional camera. The comparability of the performance was found less complex than other image processing techniques. The algorithm has two advantages: it measures the illumination in the scene without access to the analysis of the scene and it provides information about the positions, directions and intensities of the detected illuminants. The confidence of the algorithm's results can vary dependently on the size of the room.

Acknowledgments. This research was undertaken as part of the Research Management Center (RMC) of Universiti Teknologi Malaysia (UTM) via Science Fund grant Vot. R.J13000.7282.4S078.

References

1. Debevec, P.: Image-based lighting. IEEE Comput. Graph. Appl. **22**(2), 26–34 (2002)
2. Frahm, J.-M., Koeser, K., Grest, D.: Markerless augmented reality with light source estimation for direct illumination. In: Conference on Visual Media Production CVMP, London, pp. 211–220. IET (2005)
3. Al-Najdawi, N., Bez, H.: A survey of cast shadow detection algorithms. Pattern Recogn. Lett. **33**(6), 752–764 (2012)
4. Jacobs, K., Loscos, C.: Classification of illumination methods for mixed reality. Comput. Graph. Forum **25**(1), 29–51 (2004)
5. Neverova, N., Muselet, D., Trémeau, A.: Lighting estimation in indoor environments from low-quality images. In: ECCV 2012 Proceedings of the 12th International Conference on Computer Vision, pp. 380–389 (2012)
6. Pentland, A.P.: Finding the illuminant direction. J. Opt. Soc. Am. **72**(4), 448–455 (1982)
7. Yeoh, R.C., Zhou, S.Z.: Consistent real-time lighting for virtual objects in augmented reality. In: 8th IEEE International Symposium on Mixed and Augmented Reality, pp. 223–224. IEEE (2009)
8. Bingham, M.: An Interest Point Based Illumination Condition Matching Approach to Photometric Registration Within Augmented Reality Worlds (2011)
9. Bouganis, C.S., Brookes, M.: Statistical multiple light source detection. IET Comput. Vis. **1**(2), 79–91 (2007)
10. Lopez-moreno, J., Hadap, S., Reinhard, E., Gutierrez, D.: Light source detection in photographs. In: Andujar, C., Lluch, J. (eds.) Congreso Espanol de Informatica Grafica, vol. 11, pp. 161–168. Eurographics S.E. (2009)
11. Wei, J.: Robust recovery of multiple light source based on local light source constant constraint. Pattern Recogn. Lett. **24**(1–3), 159–172 (2003)
12. Agusanto, K., Li, L., Chuangui, Z., Sing, N.W.: Photorealistic rendering for augmented reality using environment illumination. In: The Second IEEE and ACM International Symposium on Mixed and Augmented Reality 2003 Proceedings, vol. 3, pp. 208–216. IEEE Computer Society (2003)

13. Zheng, Q., Chellappa, R.: Estimation of illuminant direction, albedo, and shape from shading. IEEE Trans. Pattern Anal. Mach. Intell. **13**(7), 680–702 (1991)

14. Zhang, Y., Yang, Y.-H.: Multiple illuminant direction detection with application to image synthesis. IEEE Trans. Pattern Anal. Mach. Intell. **23**(8), 915–920 (2001)

15. Lopez-Moreno, J., Hadap, S., Reinhard, E., Gutierrez, D.: Compositing images through light source detection. Comput. Graph. **34**(6), 698–707 (2010)

16. Lopez-Moreno, J., Garces, E., Hadap, S., Reinhard, E., Gutierrez, D.: Multiple light source estimation in a single image. Comput. Graph. Forum **32**(8), 170–182 (2013)

17. Wang, Y., Samaras, D.: Estimation of multiple illuminants from a single image of arbitrary known geometry. In: Heyden, A., Sparr, G., Nielsen, M., Johansen, P. (eds.) ECCV 2002, Part III. LNCS, vol. 2352, pp. 272–288. Springer, Heidelberg (2002)

18. Noh, Z., Sunar, M.S.: Soft shadow rendering based on real light source estimation in augmented reality. Adv. Multimedia - Int. J. **1**(2), 26–36 (2010)

19. Noh, Z., Sunar, M.S.: A review of shadow techniques in augmented reality. In: Second International Conference on Machine Vision, pp. 320–324. IEEE (2009)

20. Wang, Y., Samaras, D.: Estimation of multiple directional light sources for synthesis of augmented reality images. Graph. Models **65**(4), 185–205 (2003)

21. Panagopoulos, A., Wang, C., Samaras, D., Paragios, N.: Illumination estimation and cast shadow detection through a higher-order graphical model. In: IEEE Conference on Computer Vision and Pattern Recognition (CVPR), 2011, pp. 673–680. Image Analysis Lab, Computer Science Dept., Stony Brook University, IEEE, NY, USA (2011)

22. Mei, X., Ling, H., Jacobs, D.W.: Illumination recovery from image with cast shadows via sparse representation. IEEE Trans. Image Process. : Publ. IEEE Signal Process. Soci. **20**(8), 2366–2377 (2011)

23. Sato, I., Sato, Y., Ikeuchi, K.: Illumination from shadows. IEEE Trans. Pattern Anal. Mach. Intell. **25**(3), 290–300 (2003)

24. Panagopoulos, A., Wang, C., Samaras, D., Paragios, N.: Estimating shadows with the bright channel cue. In: Kutulakos, K.N. (ed.) ECCV 2010 Workshops, Part II. LNCS, vol. 6554, pp. 1–12. Springer, Heidelberg (2012)

25. Kanbara, M., Yokoya, N.: Real-time estimation of light source environment for photorealistic augmented reality. In: Proceedings of the 17th International Conference on Pattern Recognition, ICPR 2004, vol. 2, pp. 911–914. IEEE (2004)

26. Sato, I., Sato, Y., Ikeuchi, K.: Acquiring a radiance distribution to superimpose virtual objects onto a real scene. IEEE Trans. Visual Comput. Graphics **5**(1), 1–12 (1999)

27. Stumpfel, J., Jones, A., Wenger, A., Tchou, C., Hawkins, T., Debevec, P.: Direct HDR capture of the sun and sky. In: ACM SIGGRAPH 2006 Courses on - SIGGRAPH 2006. AFRIGRAPH 2004, vol. 1, p. 5. ACM Press (2006)

28. Otsu, N.: A threshold selection method from gray-level histograms. IEEE Trans. Syst., Man, Cybern. **9**(1), 62–66 (1979)

29. Suzuki, S., Be, K.: Topological structural analysis of digitized binary images by border following. Comput. Vis., Graph., Image Process. **30**(1), 32–46 (1985)

30. Wu, C., Liu, Y., Dai, Q., Wilburn, B.: Fusing multiview and photometric stereo for 3D reconstruction under uncalibrated illumination. IEEE Trans. Vis. Comput. Graph. **17**(8), 1082–1095 (2011)

Improving the Efficiency of a Hospital ED According to Lean Management Principles Through System Dynamics and Discrete Event Simulation Combined with Quantitative Methods

Ilaria Bendato[✉], Lucia Cassettari, Roberto Mosca,
and Fabio Rolando

DIME, Genoa University, via Magliotto 2, 17100 Savona, SV, Italy
{bendato,cassettari,mosca,rolando}@dime.unige.it

Abstract. The Emergency Department of a Hospital has both exogenous and endogenous management problems. The first ones are about the relationship with the other Departments, for which the Emergency Department is a noise element on the planned activities, as it generates an unplanned beds occupation. The second ones strictly depend on the Department organizational model.

After an intensive study on the Emergency Department of a medium size Italian Hospital, the Authors illustrate how, through the use of Lean Management philosophy combined with quantitative methods, the current situation can be analyzed and they propose a set of corrective actions. These allow to increase the system efficiency and to reduce both the number of the waiting patients and their stay. At the same time, the activities are reallocated to the staff, improving their utilization coefficient. So the Management can assess the validity of the proposed strategies before their eventual implementation in the field.

Keywords: Emergency Department · Lean Management · System Dynamic · Discrete Event Simulation · Design of Experiment

1 Introduction

The Emergency Departments (EDs) in Hospital structures may have two critical elements from a managerial viewpoint. The first element is given by the fact that the ED may cause a negative impact on the planning of the other Hospital Departments. Indeed the ED represents a significant disturbance, often generating unexpected occupation of beds allocated to specialist activities with a reduction or even blockage of other already planned activities (e.g. surgery). This event occurs more frequently as a consequence of peaks of requests of Hospital admission like those generated above all in winter as a result of flu viruses, worsening of chronic pathologies connected to the climate and so on. The second critical element, on the other hand, is the crowding problem inside the ED [1]. The users are often forced to spend hours waiting in the Department waiting rooms. Both problems can be analysed first and tackled later by using quantitative

© Springer International Publishing Switzerland 2015
H. Fujita and G. Guizzi (Eds.): SoMeT 2015, CCIS 532, pp. 555–572, 2015.
DOI: 10.1007/978-3-319-22689-7_43

methods combined with the modern philosophy of Lean Management. Using these instruments, the consequences of the possible solutions determined can be assessed *a priori*, that is before practical implementation. The Authors of this paper have attempted to tackle both critical elements, by firstly studying the impact of an ED on the Hospital connected to it, a study already illustrated in a previous paper [2], and, now, by analysing the problem of the Department optimised management with a view to Lean Management.

The aim of this paper is to provide an overview of the problems tackled, of the adopted analysis methods and of the solutions found. The approach adopted allowed us to provide the decision makers with a complete framework of the solutions to help ED efficiency and also to assess the benefits to be obtained from the different solutions adopted thanks to quantitative methods application.

2 Theoretical Framework

The main problem considered in this paper can be defined "the crowding problem". Hoot and Aronsky [3] approve the American College of Emergency Physician's definition: "Crowding occurs when the identified need for emergency services exceeds available resources for patient care in the ED, Hospital, or both" [4]. The problem first became apparent in the 1980s, and was thought to be of crisis proportions by the end of that decade. The American College of Emergency Physicians issued several policy recommendations, but the problem just went on growing [5–8]. The topic was also taken into consideration by the Academic Emergency Medicine review in different papers [9–16] but, despite this attention, crowding got worse in the subsequent years [17, 18] culminating in a total breakdown [19]. Crowding has multiple and complex causes and many 'obvious' causes have been discredited [5]. A lot of papers tend to naturally fall into two separate areas, one concerned with long term trends and conditions, and the other with more specific triggering factors. While not denying the influence of the general causal factors, the work on specific factors has introduced issues such as the ones related to internal ED operating efficiency. It could be thought that ED crowding is due to increased number of patients with relatively trivial, non-emergent problems while [1], although not dismissing the concern about non-urgent ED use as a policy issue, it shows that diverting low urgency patients away from the ED will not have a significant impact on crowding.

One of the main observations about the crowding problem is its persistence despite general agreement that it hurts both patients and health care organizations [20, 21]. This seems to be a case of "policy resistance", arising from an incomplete understanding of the problem. Researchers have been "looking in the wrong place" for insights into the crowding problem [22].

A lot of different approaches have been studied to face the crowding problem like the, so called, "4 h mandate". This is a National Health Service (NHS) regulation that patients in the ED must be either admitted, transferred or discharged within 4 h from the time they first signed in to the Department [23]. An analysis of the effect of this mandate shows a sharp peak in Hospital admissions and ED discharges just at 4 h [24]. In literature some System Dynamic (SD) studies over EDs can be found: Lattimer et al.

Table 1. Number of Hospital admissions

Admission sources	Hospital admissions
From E.D.	9361
Ordinary admissions	7944
TOTAL	17305

[25] built an SD model to investigate the patients flow through EDs and how system capacity could be improved; Morrison and Wears [1] evaluated the crowding phenomenon affecting emergency rooms.

3 Methodology

3.1 The Case Study

The ED concerned in this study represents the main source of patients admitted to this Hospital (over 55 %) as shown in Table 1.

There follows a negative impact on the activity of the medical/nursing staff, a serious disservice for the patients on the waiting list, but also, last but not least, the significant economic damage for the Hospital caused by the lack of use of the structures (e.g. operating rooms) generated by the ED.

3.2 Phase 1: Impact of the ED on the Hospital Departments

As mentioned in Sect. 1, the subject of the impact of the ED on the surgical activity and on ordinary Hospital admissions of the other Departments in an Italian Hospital has already been considered by the Authors in a previous paper. The objective of this paper was to specifically assess the influence of those patients who were attributed Yellow code in the phase of triage, on Hospital admissions [2]. The method used by the Authors for this part of the study was System Dynamics, a particularly suitable simulation technique for studying management policies. According to the methodological precepts of SD, the three fundamental elements of the system were considered (ED, Short Stay Observation and Hospital) and the flows of patients into and out of them. With 397 Hospital beds available along with 13 "crisis" beds addressed to face possible emergency situations, two initial management hypotheses to cope with the possible higher loads on the Hospital, generated by the ED, were first determined and then studied. The strategies determined by the Authors in the first analysis were those regarding a reduction of the patients mean stay inside the Hospital Departments and the increase of the beds number. The second hypothesis, while still being a valid one, was rejected from the outset due to the current Italian policies of reducing healthcare costs and, as a consequence, it was not tested on the simulation model.

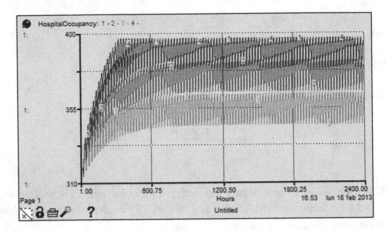

Fig. 1. Hospital occupancy (Color figure online)

The first solution, on the other hand, was implemented on the SD model, producing the following results (Fig. 1):

- if the Hospital mean stay remains at the current levels (9.6 days) the system is critical. It can be seen that there is an oscillation zone (blue zone) which constantly borders on the maximum number of available beds, which is normally reached with a 10 days stay (green zone);
- if the Hospital mean stay drops to even just 0.6 days, the system is more reactive to the critical events as it has not only crisis beds, but also around twenty ordinary beds available (red zone);
- if, finally, the Hospital mean stay is reduced by a whole day, bringing it to 8.5 days, the system, with a reserve of about 40 beds as well as the 13 crisis beds already mentioned, would be capable of coping with the great majority of critical situations (purple zone).

In assessing the feasibility of this possible strategy, the Authors still clashed with the opinions of the clinicians. According to them the shorter Hospital stays lead to an increase of requests to the ED with subsequent new admissions. As a consequence, the Authors have studied another possible solution to the problem. In particular, with further consideration of the data about ED admissions, the Authors identified chronic illness patients (diabetes, heart disease, lung disease) who enter the acute phase as an important component of occupancy of Hospital beds by the ED. It has, therefore, been proposed to establish special monitoring rooms inside the ED dedicated to this kind of pathology typical of elderly patients in order to drastically reduce admissions (chronic patients actually count for approximately 5,000 days/year with an overall cost in the range of 4,000,000€). Further investigations carried out recently on this have enabled the Authors to make a fourth suggestion for chronic patients: online, real time monitoring obtained by using body sensors, which are easy to find on the market nowadays at a limited cost, with data transmission to special supervision centres and specific interventions in order to limit their entry to the acute phase.

3.3   Phase 2: Reengineering of the ED by Means of Discrete Event Simulation

Having come to these conclusions, the Authors set the aim of assessing the need to make the ED more efficient, with a view to Lean Management, by re-engineering the internal processes of the ED itself. This study phase had the aim of reducing the waiting time of the patients and of allowing the emergency medicine specialists to concentrate on the true emergencies (life threatening red and Yellow codes), leaving patients who do not have life threatening problems (Green and White codes) to clinicians without specific emergency skills. All this while respecting the need to safeguard the economic budget of the Department without introducing additional costs to the planned budget, but on the contrary by trying to reduce it.

Mapping, Data Collection and Statistical Analysis of Admission to the ED. In order to better understand the operation of the ED studied, an initial analysis was carried out in order to map the main activities which characterise the inflow of Patients passing through the ED, as shown in Fig. 2.

Subsequently a meticulous campaign of data collection was carried out. It aimed at finding all the information necessary to be able to start up the research. The data collection phase was particularly complex as it was necessary to integrate the information coming from the Hospital information systems with the data collected directly on the field 24/7 (24 h per day and 7 days per week). In this phase the Patient's colour code and the admissions distribution were both taken into account. The admissions distribution varied according both to the time of the day and to the day of the year, with significant differences compared to the mean values. In particular, admissions to the ED were first determined for the year, amounting to 54,141, of which 77.4 % with non-life threatening codes (White or Green), 20.1 % with yellow life threatening codes and the remaining 2.5 % with red life threatening code. Then, the Patients daily admissions were studied, also by colour code, to understand whether affluence trends and/or

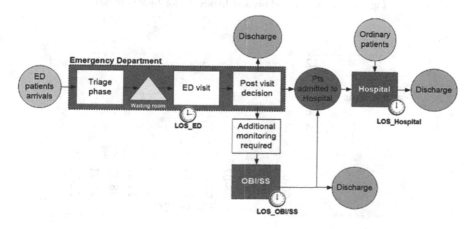

Fig. 2. Flow of the Patients in the ED

regular distribution flows could be found. In Fig. 3 the analysis for the Yellow codes is shown (the other codes analysis are not shown for reasons of space).

By analysing Figs. 3 it can be seen how there are no seasonal trends for any of the three colour codes: the trend is totally random and there are no repeated trends in time.

Analysing the data in more detail, the Authors then studied the admissions distribution during the different hours of the day. To this aim, 30 sample days were chosen and the mean number of Patient admissions was calculated for each time range, as reported in Fig. 4.

Observing the bar chart concerning Patient admissions with Green/White and Yellow codes the presence of a peak demand during the central hours of the day (from 8 am to 3 pm) can be seen, with a mean number of patients found, for about 330 days a year, of 115 for the Green/White codes and of 30 for the Yellow codes. The phenomenon of the White and Green codes high affluence in Italy is accentuated by the lack of day Hospital assistance in the country, which is why people are obliged to go to the ED even for problems not requiring emergency treatment.

Considering the Red code trend, on the other hand, it can be seen how the admission of this type of Patient is totally random. A further analysis was then carried out to identify the days of maximum inflow and the admissions distribution within

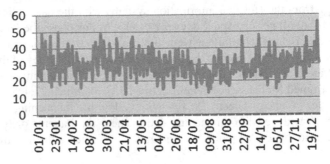

Fig. 3. Yellow code admission trends (Color figure online)

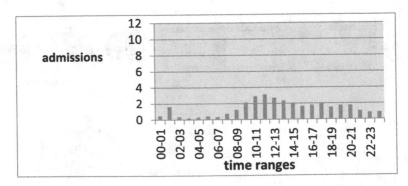

Fig. 4. Distribution of Patient admissions with Yellow code (Color figure online)

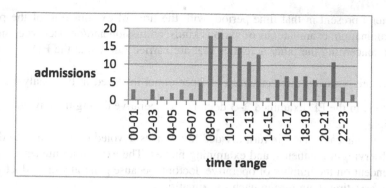

Fig. 5. Green/White code admissions in a maximum load day (Color figure online)

them. This was necessary because, with a view to carrying out simulation tests on the operation of the processes within the ED, the Authors considered it worthwhile assessing the response of the system in conditions of usual staffing, not only with "normal" workloads but also in conditions of maximum service request. Figures 5 and 6 show the admissions bar charts in two sample days of maximum inflow for Green/White codes and for Yellow codes respectively.

It can be seen that, as far as the Green/White codes are concerned, an inflow of more than 140 units occurred on 29 days with peaks of up to 169 patients. For Yellow codes, on the other hand, there were 28 days with a number of patients exceeding 40 and with peaks of up to 56. The maximum load of Red codes has not been illustrated as it was insignificant due to the intrinsic admissions randomness. In the day of maximum inflow, 14 admissions of Red codes was recorded. Indeed, in a typical year, only on 38 days did the number of Red code admissions exceed 6 units. From this it can be seen that the critical period in which the ED response to the work load must be assessed is from 8 am to 3 pm.

Data Collection and Statistical Analysis of the Medical Examination Time. In order to carry out the tests on the simulation model, along with the data previously collected, it was also necessary to document the data about the staff (doctors, nurses

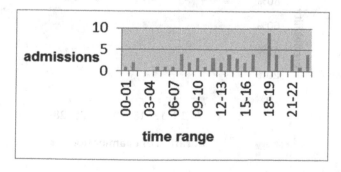

Fig. 6. Yellow code admissions in a maximum load day (Color figure online)

and porters) present in that time period, with the time of examination of the patients (first examination, examinations of various kinds, admission and/or discharge) and with the data concerning the other activities that are carried out inside the ED.

There are basically three categories of personnel involved in this analysis:

- Doctors: in the ED examined 2–3 doctors are operative during the day and just one at night;
- Nurses: this category is in turn divided into nurses devoted to triage and to the area of observing the Patients, and examining nurses. The examining nurses are strictly dependent on the number of operative doctors, because generally each doctor has a nurse assisting them during each examination;
- Porters: there are generally 2 of these members of staff per shift.

As far as the first examination time is concerned, Fig. 7 shows the examination duration distribution for Green codes. By observing the graph in Fig. 7 it can be seen that the duration of the examination is equal to or less than 5 min for 65 % of the Patients. In the event of Yellow codes very similar first examination times were also found.

As regards the post examination flows, whose determination is fundamental to ensure that the simulation model complies to the reality of the ED, it was found that, after the first examination, 61 % of the Patients were directed towards the diagnostic areas (e.g. radiology Department), while the other 39 % remained under observation inside the structure (with periodical re-assessment of the health condition). Once the observation period is over, a doctor may order admission or discharge.

Construction of the Model. It has been shown, from the data collection phase, how the prevalent inflow of White or Green codes involve the Emergency Medicine specialists in uncharacteristic activity, force the Patients to wait a long time and the Hospital authorities to overestimate the needed number of doctors and nurses.

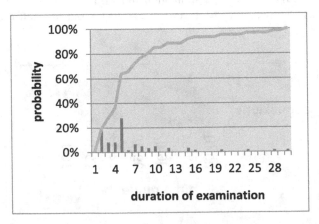

Fig. 7. Distribution of the first examination times of Green codes (Color figure online)

In order to be able to cope with the indicated problems in terms of numbers, the Authors have deemed it necessary to use suitable models. This was done to assess both the efficiency level of the management strategies currently actuated and to determine possible actions of improvement for the overall ED performance. Considering the random nature of the data characterising the various activities and the presence of appointment problems amongst the various actors present in the ED (for example the patient is examined if a doctor is free, the patient is transferred if there is a stretcher free, etc.), the model choice could only be that of Discrete Event Simulation (DES) [26]. In particular, considering the high descriptive capability, also in terms of three-dimensional graphics (which allows the so-called "visual management" to be activated), and for the possibility of presenting the results in an effective and easily understandable manner, the Authors have chosen the DES "FLEXSIM HEALTH-CARE" shell of FLEXSIM SOFTWARE PRODUCTS for the modelling. The result of the modelling is the construction of a true "virtual copy" of the investigated ED: library elements of the programme indeed permit a detailed construction of both the individual activities performed and the possibility of inserting the internal elements of the ED like the instruments and all the process actors (doctors, nurses, porters, nursing assistants and Patients). The software also allows the layout of the investigated system to be easily represented, so as to take the real distances and measurements into precise account. Figure 8 shows Green code examination room.

Using the data collected on the field and from the Hospital databases, the Authors thus constructed, using FLEXSIM HEALTHCARE, a DES model capable of providing a faithful reproduction of the activity, which the assistance service inside the ED is broken down into, from the Patient admission to his discharge from the structure. The aim of the modelling is that of permitting a first phase analysis of the performance of the individual resources involved and then, on the basis of the obtained results, to assess the need to make managerial modifications in order to improve the Department efficiency (e.g. more doctors, more nurses, more porters, lower mean patient waiting time). The first phase was to define the AS IS and then to determine and implement special variants on the basis of the results highlighted by the experimentation.

Fig. 8. View of the model: Green code examination room (Color figure online)

4   Results

4.1   Study of the AS IS Situation

It should be considered that the evolution of the ED in time must be studied on distinct daily time slots according to the different statistical distributions of the patient admissions. As a consequence, each time block in the different load conditions (standard day, day of maximum request), must be replicated several times in order to correctly reproduce the reality of the ED. The number of repeated simulation runs must be such that the investigated sample becomes representative of the population. The first step of the experimentation was, therefore, that of determining a suitable number of replications (size of the sample) to permit the correct inference on the parameters of the population (mean and variance). This was performed by analysing the trend on a standard day of the statistical measurements of Mean Square Pure Error of the mean (MSPE$_{MED}$) and Mean Square Pure Error of the standard deviation (MSPE$_{STDEV}$) (see Appendix A and B) according to the number of repeated simulation runs (Fig. 9).

Both the curves reach settlement after about 200 launches. On reaching the value, the simulation provides stable responses under a known error.

The confidence interval on the mean value of the result obtained by FLEX-SIM HEALTHCARE model, using a level of trust of 95 %, is contained within the interval indicated below:

$$\bar{y} - t_{\frac{\alpha}{2}, n-1}\left(\sqrt{\frac{MSPE_{MED}}{n}}\right) \quad \leq \bar{y} \leq \bar{y} + t_{\frac{\alpha}{2}, n-1}\left(\sqrt{\frac{MSPE_{MED}}{n}}\right) \tag{1}$$

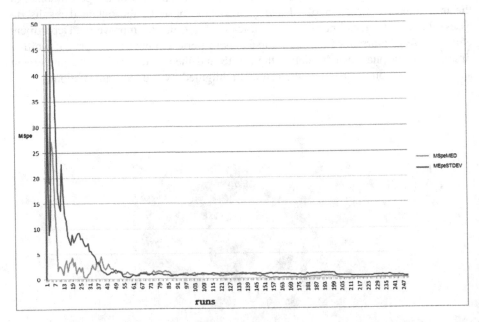

Fig. 9. MSPE$_{MED}$ and MSPE$_{STDEV}$ curves in the standard work day load

where:

n = number of experimental replications (4 in the case studied);

$\bar{y}$ = mean waiting time;

$t_{\frac{\alpha}{2},n-1}$ = value obtained from a t-student distribution with n − 1 degrees of freedom;

$\dot{\alpha}$ = significance level.

Therefore the mean waiting time will be contained, with a 95 % probability, within the following interval:

$$94' \leq \bar{y} \leq 98' \tag{2}$$

The error interval on the mean value of the result corresponds, on the other hand, to the interval:

$$\bar{y} - 3\sqrt{MSPE_{MED}} - 3\sqrt{VAR + MSPE_{STDEV}} \leq y^* \leq \bar{y} + 3\sqrt{MSPE_{MED}} + \\ + 3\sqrt{VAR + MSPE_{STDEV}} \tag{3}$$

where:

VAR = is the square of standard deviation.

Therefore, the real mean waiting time will be contained, with a 99.98 % probability, within the following interval:

$$78' \leq y^* \leq 114' \tag{4}$$

The same analysis of the curves of the MSPE was carried out for the work day at the maximum load.

This was necessary because the probability distributions which regulate the inter-arrival of the patients are different from the previous ones. The two curves, which are omitted for reasons of space, highlighted the need to increase the number of simulation runs replicated from 200 to 250 in order to stabilise the error to acceptable levels.

In this second scenario the bounds of the confidence interval at 95 % and of the error interval are respectively:

$$101' \leq \bar{y} \leq 105' \tag{5}$$

and:

$$83' \leq y^* \leq 123' \tag{6}$$

Whereas the coefficients of use of the doctors are:

- 80 % for the day at standard load
- 85 % for the day at maximum load.

4.2 Sensitivity Analysis

Once the AS IS configuration has been analysed, the stability of the system must be controlled to assess its reaction ability in the event of changes to the set parameters (TO BE scenario). The analysis basically includes two aspects:

1. sustainability of the system in case of absence of a key resource (doctor)
2. reaction ability of the system against the increase of a key resource (doctor).

In the first configuration, in which a single doctor is considered to be present, the bounds of the confidence interval at 95 % and of the error interval are respectively:

$$131' \leq \bar{y} \leq 132' \tag{7}$$

and:

$$106' \leq y^* \leq 157' \tag{8}$$

whereas the doctors utilization coefficient is 83 %.

In the event of the maximum load days, the presence of a single doctor, after some simulation launches, was revealed to be unsustainable, so it was not taken into consideration in view of a possible implementation on the field in the 8 am to 3 pm time slot.

With reference to the second configuration, with 3 doctors present, the bounds of the confidence interval at 95 % and of the error interval were respectively:

$$55' \leq \bar{y} \leq 57' \tag{9}$$

and:

$$43' \leq y^* \leq 69' \tag{10}$$

with a consistent reduction of the mean waiting time.

A similar improvement can be found in the day of maximum load in which the bounds of the confidence interval at 95 % and of the error interval are respectively:

$$87' \leq \bar{y} \leq 90' \tag{11}$$

and:

$$64' \leq y^* \leq 113' \tag{12}$$

whereas the doctors utilization coefficients are:

- 75 % for the standard load day
- 82 % for the maximum load day.

In spite of the substantial improvements that the Authors have determined in the increase from 2 to 3 doctors, the addition of a highly qualified resource is economically and organisationally extremely complex, as also confirmed by the Managers of the ED themselves.

As a consequence the Authors have found an alternative solution which considers a separation of the path of the Yellow/Red codes and Green/White ones. Separation of the paths means a diversification of the two process lines that become almost independent. Indeed, each line will have a pre-assigned number of dedicated doctors. The new configuration would give rise to a "virtual" splitting of the ED by increasing the speed of response of the real emergencies and by creating a structure, suitable for promptly providing care to less critical patients. This was done without affecting the performances of the main function of the ED. In this scenario, in the days of medium load work, the bounds of the confidence interval at 95 % and of the error interval are respectively:

$$31' \leq \bar{y} \leq 34' \tag{13}$$

and:

$$18' \leq y^* \leq 48' \tag{14}$$

In the event of maximum workload the bounds of the confidence interval at 95 % and of the error interval are respectively:

$$86' \leq \bar{y} \leq 91' \tag{15}$$

and:

$$64' \leq y^* \leq 114' \tag{16}$$

whereas the doctors utilization coefficients are:

- 70 % for Yellow and Red codes for the day at standard load
- 76 % for Green and White codes for the day at standard load
- 70 % for Yellow and Red codes for the day at maximum load.
- 79 % for Green and White codes for the day at maximum load

Following the indications of possible organisational configurations of the ED system in terms of assigned personnel, the Authors wanted to investigate further the ED reaction ability with changes in the number of doctors (and thus of nurses) employed in the day at standard loads. For this reason it was analysed whether there are statistically significant differences on the mean waiting time of patients, with changes in the number of ED doctors, by using a statistical analysis technique called One-Way ANOVA and belonging to the Design of Experiments [27]. The experimental campaign is shown in Table 2 whereas the ANOVA table is shown in Table 3.

From the ANOVA table (Table 3) it can be seen how, with changes of the number of doctors present, there are effectively significant differences between the mean waiting times.

Table 2. Experimental campaign

Number of doctors	n_1	n_2	n_3	n_4
1	132.1	128.24	132.89	132.33
2	96.33	96.73	97.37	93.97
3	56.4	55.44	55.9	55.76

Table 3. Variance analysis

Source	DOF	Sum of the quadrates	Mean of the quadrates	Pr > F
Model	1	7.974	7.974	<0.0001
Error	10	0.026	0.003	
Corrected total	11	8.000		

Application of the Tuckey test also confirms that the mean waiting times resulting from the comparisons between the three levels of doctors involved all differ statistically significantly from one another.

By applying a linear regression model to the Table 2 data, we find the analytical relation existing between the independent variable X_1 (doctors) and the dependent variable Y_1 (mean patient waiting time):

$$Y_1 = 4,49 - 2,64E - 02 * X_1 \qquad (17)$$

the trend of this is shown in Fig. 10, along with the relevant confidence and prediction intervals.

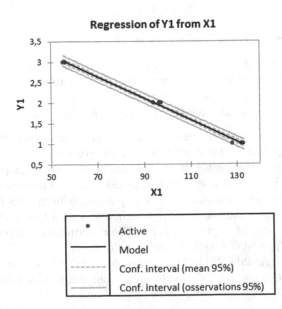

Fig. 10. Regression model

Having established the maximum waiting time required, the regression model obtained thus enables the decision makers to determine the number of doctors necessary and vice versa.

5 Discussion

The Authors' aim, on request of the Management of an average-sized Italian Hospital, was that of analysing the behaviour of the ED in its dual function, on the one hand of connecting element of the Hospital with the outside world (55 % of admissions actually come from the ED) and on the other, of Hospital Department with its relevant internal organisational and management problems. The first aspect mentioned above, already analysed partially in a previous paper, is a source of continuous dispute between the ED and the other Hospital Departments. Indeed the ED is considered by them as a serious disturbing element for their planning, due to the random admissions, a negative element capable of partially paralysing some characteristic activities with the consequent inevitable waste of resources. In order to cope with this situation, the Authors, having dismissed the idea of increasing the number of beds for economic reasons, had highlighted the advantages deriving from reducing the mean Hospital stay from the current 9.6 to 9 and 8.5 days. This was done through the use of an ED model in System Dynamics that allowed to point out to the Clinicians the existence of this possibility, but leaving the final decision to them. As a further solution, the Authors had also determined a second possibility based on the creation, inside the ED, of specific day Hospitals where chronic patients can be monitored (heart disease, lung disease, diabetes) in order to prevent them from entering in the acute phase. This because, if they enter in the acute phase they need for an unspecified Hospital stay, since they are frequently elderly, alone and not self-sufficient (incidence of 5000 days/year and 4000 k€ of relevant cost).

A further possible alternative, which nowadays becomes increasingly possible, thanks to technological improvement and a reduction in the cost of the equipment, is currently undergoing investigation by the Authors. It consists of remotely monitoring chronic patients, on line in real time 24/7, through body sensors which send measurements to specially equipped control centres, which can act in a timely manner with suitable care to prevent a worsening of the condition.

As regards the second aspect of the study, that is, the analysis of the existing organisational model in the ED, considering the discrete and random nature of the activity carried out in it, the Authors have used a DES simulation model.

After a careful phase of observing the ED examined, the flow diagram was firstly drawn up in order to better assess the relations between the different actors and the efficiency of the flow. At the same time a careful and accurate data collection campaign was carried out, divided by colour code, by time period and by day of the year, in order to distinguish the data regarding the days of normal load from those of maximum load. Then a DES model was built combined with a powerful three-dimensional graphic layout. After a careful validation phase, simulation campaigns were set up by using the model to test the Key Performance Indicators chosen as a measure of the ED efficiency (doctors utilization coefficient, patients waiting time, number of patients waiting, etc.)

in the existing AS IS managerial conditions. In the subsequent phase, three hypotheses (TO BE scenarios) were tested through the appropriately modified simulator. One to verify the system reactivity in case of a single doctor and in case of two potential improvements regarding the aim of reducing the patients' stay inside the ED. One was based on the increase of the doctors by one unit, the other on splitting the admitted patients flow. Inspired by the fundamental principles of Lean management, the idea of splitting, in the critical part of the day (8am-3 pm), has the dual purpose of:

1. assigning only the characteristic cases (Yellow and Red codes) to the emergency medicine specialists, thus preventing the waste of professional skills and energies on the most trivial cases (White and Green codes)
2. assigning the Green and White codes to the doctors from the internal Departments who are made available by effect of other Lean Management reorganisations carried out by the Authors in the Hospital itself (e.g. parallel operating rooms and rede-signing the route of the surgical patient).

A direct consequence of the flows splitting is a reduction of the patients' waiting time, the recover of hours from doctors and nurses in the Hospital Departments, who would otherwise be underused, less pressure on the emergency medicine specialists, as well as less need for their simultaneous presence.

Concluding, the Authors point out that:

1. the use of quantitative methods and models combined with the Lean Management philosophy allows the Health Managers to test possible solutions of improving the system. The use of these quantitative instruments means that the impact of the different solutions on the Hospital system is already known before they are implemented and this makes it possible to concentrate only on the solutions with a truly significant impact. All this contributes to improving the process of Decision Making, otherwise based exclusively on experience, on common sense, on the intuition of the decision makers and, as a consequence, with obvious limits in seeking possible solutions;
2. by effect of the results obtained on the ED studied in this paper, the Manager of the ED of another large Hospital has begun an active collaboration with the Authors to carry out a similar streamlining study in his Department. The study performed was considered extremely positive, also in relation to the possibility of pooling the reciprocal skills of doctors and process engineers in a constructive and respectful relationship.

References

1. Morrison, J.B., Wears, R.L.: ED crowding: vicious cycles in the ED. In: 4th Mayo Clinic Conference on Systems Engineering & Operations Research in Health Care Proceedings 2011, Rochester, MN (2011)
2. Cassettari, L., Morrison, J.B., Mosca, R., Orfeo, A., Revetria, R., Rolando, F.: A system dynamics study of an ED impact on the management of Hospital surgery activities. In:

SIMULTECH 2013 - Proceedings of the 3rd International Conference on Simulation and Modeling Methodologies, Technologies and Applications, Reykjavík, Iceland, 29–31 July 2013

3. Hoot, N.R., Aronsky, D.: Systematic review of ED crowding: causes, effects, and solutions. Ann. Emerg. Med. **52**, 126–136 (2008)

4. American College of Emergency Physicians: Hospital and ED overcrowding. Ann. Emerg. Med. **19**, 336 (1990)

5. Derlet, R.W., Richards, J.R.: Overcrowding in the nation's EDs: complex causes and disturbing effects. Ann. Emerg. Med. **35**, 63–68 (2000)

6. Goldberg, C.: Emergency Crews Worry as Hospitals Say, 'No vacancy', p. 27. New York Times, NY (2000). Sect. 1

7. Kellermann, A.L.: Déjà vu. Ann. Emerg. Med. **35**, 83–85 (2000)

8. Zwemer, F.L.: ED overcrowding. Ann. Emerg. Med. **36**, 279 (2000)

9. Adams, J.G., Biros, M.H.: The endangered safety net: establishing a measure of control. Acad. Emerg. Med. **8**, 1013–1015 (2001)

10. Baer, R.B., Pasternack, J.S., Zwemer, F.L.: Recently discharged inpatients as a source of ED overcrowding. Acad. Emerg. Med. **8**, 1091–1094 (2001)

11. Derlet, R., Richards, J., Kravits, R.L.: Frequent overcrowding in U.S. EDs. Acad. Emerg. Med. **8**, 151–155 (2001)

12. Gordon, J.A., Billings, J., Asplin, B.R., Rhodes, K.V.: Safety net research in emergency medicine. In: Proceedings of the Academic Emergency Medicine Consensus Conference on "The Unraveling Safety Net". Acad. Emerg. Med. **8**, 1024–1029 (2001)

13. Kelen, G.D., Scheulen, J.J., Hill, P.M.: Effect of an ED (ED) managed acute care unit on ED overcrowding and emergency medical services diversion. Acad. Emerg. Med. **8**, 1095–1100 (2001)

14. Reeder, T.J., Garrison, H.G.: When the safety net is unsafe: real-time assessment of the overcrowded ED. Acad. Emerg. Med. **8**, 1070–1074 (2001)

15. Schneider, S., Zwemer, F., Doniger, A., Dick, R., Czapranski, T., Devis, E.: Rochester, New York: a decade of ED overcrowding. Acad. Emerg. Med. **8**, 1044–1050 (2001)

16. Schull, M.J., Szalai, J.P., Schwartz, B., Redelmeier, D.A.: ED Overcrowding following systematic Hospital restructuring: trends at twenty Hospitals over ten years. Acad. Emerg. Med. **8**, 1037–1043 (2001)

17. Kellermann, A.L.: Crisis in the ED. N. Engl. J. Med. **355**, 1300–1303 (2006)

18. US General Accounting Office: Hospital EDs: Crowded Conditions Vary Among Hospitals and Communities. Washington, DC, US General Accounting Office: 71 (2003)

19. Institute of Medicine: Hospital-Based Emergency Care at the Breaking Point. T. N. A. Press, Washington, DC (2006). Institution of Medicine of the National Academies

20. Bayley, M.D., Schwartz, J.S., Shofer, F.S., Weiner, M., Sites, F.D., Traber, K.B., Hollander, J.E.: The financial burden of ED congestion and Hospital crowding for chest pain patients awaiting admission. Ann. Emerg. Med. **45**, 110–117 (2005)

21. Falvo, T., Grove, L., Stachura, R., Vega, D., Stike, R., Schlenker, M., Zirkin, W.: The opportunity loss of boarding admitted patients in the ED. Acad. Emerg. Med. **14**, 332–337 (2007)

22. Lane, D.C., Monefeldt, C., Rosenhead, J.V.: Looking in the wrong place for healthcare improvements: a system dynamics study of an accident and ED. J. Oper. Res. Soc. **51**, 518–531 (2000)

23. Department of Health: The NHS Plan: A Plan for Investment, a Plan for Reform. The Stationery Office, London (2000)

24. Locker, T.E., Mason, S.M.: Analysis of the distribution of time that patients spend in EDs. Br. Med. J. **330**, 1188–1189 (2005)

25. Lattimer, V., Brailsford, S., Turnbull, J., Tarnaras, P., Smith, H., George, S., Gerard, K., Maslin-Prothero, S.: Reviewing emergency care systems I: insights from system dynamics modelling. Emerg Med. J. **21**, 685–691 (2004)
26. Cassettari, L., Mosca, R., Revetria, R.: Handbook of Research on Discrete Event Simulation Environments: Technologies and Applications. Information Science Reference, 1st edn., vol. 6, pp. 92–141 (2009)
27. Montgomery, D.C.: Design and Analysis of Experiments. Wiley, New York (2005)

Software Applications Systems
for Medical Health Care

Robust Psychiatric Decision Support Using Surrogate Numbers

Mats Danielson[1], Love Ekenberg[1,2(✉)], and Kristina Sygel[3,4]

[1] Department of Computer and Systems Sciences,
Stockholm University, Stockholm, Sweden
{mad,lovek}@dsv.su.se
[2] International Institute of Applied Systems Analysis, IIASA,
Laxenburg, Austria
[3] Division of Social and Forensic Psychiatry,
Department of Clinical Neuroscience, Karolinska Institutet,
Solna, Sweden
Kristina.Sygel@rmv.se
[4] Department of Forensic Psychiatry,
Swedish National Board of Forensic Medicine, Stockholm, Sweden

Abstract. Decision analytical methods have been utilized and demonstrated to be of use for a broad range of applications in medical contexts, from regular diagnostic strategies and treatment to the evaluation of diagnostic tests and prediction models and benefit-risk assessments. However, a number of issues still remain to be clarified, for instance ease of use, realism of the input data, long-term outcomes and integration into routine clinical work. In particular, many people are unaccustomed or unwilling to express input information with the preciseness and correctness most methods require, i.e., the values need to be "true" in some sense. The common lack of complete information naturally increases this problem significantly and several attempts have been made to resolve this issue. This is not least the case within psychiatric emergency care where the information available often is of a highly qualitative nature. In this article we suggest the use of so called surrogate numbers that have proliferated for a while in the form of ordinal ranking methods for multi-criteria and show how they can be adapted for use in probability elicitation.

1 Introduction

There are a multitude of medical decision support systems and in these contexts, numerous different technologies have been applied, such as rule-based expert systems, fuzzy logics, artificial intelligence, neural networks, probabilistic reasoning, heuristic reasoning, Bayesian networks, and more (Sygel et al. 2015). Nevertheless, these have hitherto been of limited use in actual clinical settings, in particular when clinical subjective estimates are necessary for the decision making and there is very often an empirical lack of complete and precise information. In psychiatric emergency care, this

© Springer International Publishing Switzerland 2015
H. Fujita and G. Guizzi (Eds.): SoMeT 2015, CCIS 532, pp. 575–585, 2015.
DOI: 10.1007/978-3-319-22689-7_44

is typical, and judgments regarding mental conditions and their diagnoses and treatment and practical management are typically based on more subjective estimates and there are often vague beliefs about probabilities and qualitative preferences among the consequences of the various alternatives involved. Decision methodologies in general do not take adequate account of such uncertainties in background information. Even if we have procedures to handle this, one major issue remains how this vague information can be elicited.

Elicitation of subjective beliefs has been applied in numerous areas, such as game and decision theory (Rey-Biel 2009) and various disciplines of economy (Delavande et al. 2011), and many methods have been designed for elicitation purposes. It is in these contexts not seldom assumed that at least experts in the various areas are capable of providing reliable information and acting rationally if the information is elicited in a sensitive way, disregarding that even expert estimates may differ significantly from the true probabilities and that there are still no generally accepted elicitation methods available and the process of eliciting adequate quantitative information is one of the large challenges within decision analysis. In a classical framework, numerical probabilities are assigned to the different events in tree representations of decision problems after the process of identifying which aspects of a problem (parameters) to elicit, and whom to choose for providing the estimates, such as domain experts having to express their beliefs in probabilistic form during the extraction. Many people are, however, unaccustomed to expressing knowledge and in order for an elicitation process to be successful, the values need not be "true" in an objectivist sense (and cannot be judged that way) but should be a perceived representation of the present knowledge in a subjective fashion. The elicitation of probabilities (and utilities) has been extensively studied, and there are several handbooks and recommendations for how to make such assessments and the corresponding problems using direct elicitation, gamble and lottery techniques, as well as more elaborate methods to, as far as possible, reduce biases, aversions and multitudes of other causes for errors when producing as reliable estimates as possible, c.f., e.g., (Corner and Corner 1995; Hogarth 1975; Morgan and Henrion 1990; Wallsten and Budescu 1983; Johnson and Huber 1977). It is here usually assumed that procedures for elicitation should give rise to adequate preference orders, but this assumption is nevertheless often violated in empirical studies, see for example, (Tversky and Kahneman 1981; Lenert and Treadwell 1999; Lichtenstein and Slovic 2006). One approach to elicitation within multi-criteria decision making (MCDM) is to use surrogate numbers, which are derived from ordinal importance information. This approach can be adapted to the elicitation of probabilities as well. While the actual application in MCDA differs, the need to elicit information under a normalisation constraint is similar. Using such methods in MCDA, a decision-maker supplies ordinal information on importance. Thereafter, this information is transformed into surrogate numbers consistent with the extracted ordinal information. Several proposals on how to convert the rankings into such numbers exist for handling criteria weights in MCDM. However, even there, the use of only ordinal information is sometimes perceived as being too vague or imprecise, resulting in a lack of confidence in the alternatives' final values or a too large class of non-dominated alternatives.

In this article, we suggest a decision theoretical framework for elicitation in psychiatric healthcare decision making where detailed data is not normally available. We propose a set of methods for increasing the expressive power in the elicitation of user probability statements, with a particular aim at how the weight function(s) still can be reasonably elicited while preserving the comparative simplicity and correctness of ranking approaches. Below we discuss and compare some important aspects of a number of extensions to a set of ranking methods for weights as well as their relevance and correctness. After having briefly recapitulated and adapted some ordinal ranking methods in the following section, we continue with cardinal ranking methods taking strength into account and discuss a set of interesting candidates for probability elicitation. Thereafter, using simulations, we investigate some properties of the methods and conclude with pointing out, according to the results, a particularly attractive method for weight elicitation.

2 Ranking Methods

Different elicitation formalisms have been proposed, such as based on scoring points, as in point allocation (PA) or direct rating (DR) methods. In PA, the decision-maker is given a point sum, e.g. 100, to distribute and there are N–1 degrees of freedom (DoF) for N criteria or consequences depending of the type of decision. DR, on the other hand, puts no limit to the number of points to be allocated and the points are subsequently normalized by dividing by the sum of points allocated, i.e., there are N degrees of freedom for N criteria. Regardless of elicitation method, the assumption is that all elicitation is made relative to a distribution held by the decision-maker.[1]

Surrogate methods are utilised by many for handling such problems, in particular in MCDM. The crucial issue is, however, to obtain surrogates while losing as little information as possible and preserving the "correctness" when assigning values of various types. Stillwell et al. (1981) discuss rank sum (RS) and rank reciprocal (RR) methods. They are suggested in the context of maximum discrimination power. The rank sum is based on the idea that the rank order should be reflected directly in the assignments. Assume a simplex S_w generated by $w_1 > w_2 > ... > w_N$, $\Sigma w_i = 1$ and $0 \leq w_i$.[2] Assign an ordinal number to each item ranked, starting with the highest ranked item as number 1. Denote the ranking number i among N items to rank. Then the RS surrogates for all $i = 1,...,N$ are defined by

$$w_i^{RS} = \frac{N + 1 - i}{\sum_{j=1}^{N}(N + 1 - j)}$$

---

[1] For various cognitive and methodological aspects of imprecision in decision making, see, e.g., (Danielson et al. 2007, 2013) and various others by the same authors.

[2] We will, unless otherwise stated, presume that decision problems are modelled as simplexes S_x generated by $x_1 > x_2 > ... > x_N$, $\Sigma x_i = 1$, and $0 \leq x_i$.

RR is based on the inverted numbers of the rank order for each item ranked, obtained by assigning an ordinal number to each item ranked. Denote the ranking number i among N items to rank. Then the RR surrogates become

$$w_i^{RR} = \frac{1/i}{\sum_{j=1}^{N} \frac{1}{j}}$$

(Barron 1992) suggested a method based on vertices of the simplex of the feasible space. The ROC (rank order centroid) weights are the centroid vector components of the simplex S_w,

$$w_i^{ROC} = 1/N \sum_{j=i}^{N} \frac{1}{j}$$

The RS model is tailored to the assumption of N degrees of freedom and the RR and ROC models are tailored to the N–1 DoF assumption. A crucial issue here is thus whether a decision-maker does keep the linear dependence in mind when allocating values (N–1 DoF) or whether this is not an actual constraint since normalisation can be perceived to be possible to carry out after the criteria assessments (N DoF). Since the models RS and RR are in this sense opposites, a function combining the properties of RS and RR was proposed in (Danielson and Ekenberg 2014). The SR method is an additive combination of the Sum and the Reciprocal functions:

$$w_i^{SR} = \frac{1/i + \frac{N+1-i}{N}}{\sum_{j=1}^{N} \left(1/j + \frac{N+1-j}{N}\right)}$$

Of the above methods, SR was found to be the most robust. Next, we adapt these MCDM methods to probability elicitation and extend them with cardinal information, i.e. information on the differences in strength between rankings. The decision model we use is a one-level probabilistic tree with M alternatives having N consequences each (same number of consequences but different consequences for each alternative). For use in probability elicitation, the ordering is asked of the decision-maker, but this time in reference to how probable events are as outcomes of a chosen alternative of action.[3]

---

[3] We assume a standard one-level probability tree with a decision node followed by alternatives of action. For each alternative, there is a set of exhaustive and mutually exclusive events which the decision-maker is asked to rank with respect to the probabilities of occurrence. The results are easy to generalise to multi-level trees.

From this basis, more discriminative methods can be defined. Instead of using a pre-determined conversion method to obtain surrogates from an ordinal ranking, the decision-maker will be able to express and utilise more information available.

In this paper, we will use the notations equally probable ($>_0$), slightly more probable ($>_1$), more probable ($>_2$) and much more probable ($>_3$) for the strength of the rankings between consequences on a probability scale as well as some suggestions for a verbal interpretation of these:[4] Let the total number of probability scale positions be Q. Each consequence i has the position $t(i) \in \{1,\dots,Q\}$ on this probability scale, such that for every two consequences c_i and c_j, whenever $p_i >_{s_i} p_{i+1}$, $s_i = |t(i) - t(j)|$. The position $t(i)$ then denotes the relation as stated by the decision-maker.[5] Then the corresponding RS type probabilities (called CRS) and the corresponding rank reciprocal probabilities (CRR) are obtained as

$$p_i^{CRS} = \frac{Q + 1 - t(i)}{\sum_{j=1}^{N}(Q + 1 - t(j))}, \qquad p_i^{CRR} = \frac{\frac{1}{t(i)}}{\sum_{j=1}^{N}\frac{1}{t(j)}}$$

ROC and SR are generalised in the same way and the corresponding strength rank order centroid probabilities (CRC and CSR) are obtained as

$$p_i^{CRC} = \frac{\sum_{j=t(i)}^{Q}\frac{1}{j}}{\sum_{k=1}^{N}\left(\sum_{j=t(k)}^{Q}\frac{1}{j}\right)}, \qquad p_i^{CSR} = \frac{1/t(i) + \frac{Q+1-t(i)}{Q}}{\sum_{j=1}^{N}\left(1/t(j) + \frac{Q+1-t(j)}{Q}\right)}$$

3 Validating Models for Cardinal Relations

Given that we have a set of cardinal methods as in the previous section, how can they be validated? The modelling assumptions regarding decision-makers' mind-sets above are mirrored in the generation of decision problem vectors by a random generator. Thus, following an $N-1$ DoF model, a vector is generated in which the components sum to 100 %, i.e., a process with $N-1$ degrees of freedom. For probability elicitation, the procedure is as follows:[6]

---

[4] Note that these are only suggestions for illustrative purposes. This paper does not intend to discuss problems with eliciting verbal probability statements and their conversion to numerical data. The cardinal information is rather in an actual implementation of the method considered to be input using graphical sliders in a software tool.

[5] In order to simplify the presentation, we use p_i to represent the probability $p(c_i)$.

[6] For simplicity in generation procedures, but without loss of generality, assume that the events in all alternatives have the same number of consequences, N.

1. For an elicitation with N consequences for each event node problem, generate M random probability vectors with N components each. These are called the TRUE probability vectors. Determine the order between the probabilities in each vector. For each elicitation method μ', use those orders to generate vectors $x_j^{\mu'}$.

2. Given M alternatives, generate $M \times N$ random values with value v_{ij} belonging to consequence i in alternative j.

3. Let p_{ij}^{μ} be the probability from method μ for consequence i in alternative j (where μ is either μ' or TRUE). For each method μ, calculate $V_j^{\mu} = \sum_i p_{ij}^{\mu} v_{ij}$. Each method produces a preferred alternative, i.e. the one with the highest V_j^{μ}.

Table 1. The simulation results under various settings

Combined DoF	Symbols	ROC/CRC	RS/CRS	RR/CRR	SR/CSR
3 consequences and 3 alternatives	0	86.9	86.8	86.7	87.0
	1	88.8	87.7	87.9	88.0
	2	89.3	90.1	89.4	90.3
	3	89.5	91.2	90.2	91.3
3 consequences and 15 alternatives	0	70.9	69.2	69.1	69.5
	1	73.9	71.2	70.7	71.0
	2	74.6	76.1	74.4	76.2
	3	74.6	77.7	76.5	78.6
6 consequences and 6 alternatives	0	79.4	79.8	78.0	80.8
	1	83.5	80.8	81.0	82.4
	2	84.0	83.9	80.5	85.4
	3	83.8	85.3	79.3	86.4
6 consequences and 12 alternatives	0	75.0	73.8	72.3	75.1
	1	78.6	75.6	75.3	77.2
	2	78.3	78.3	74.1	78.4
	3	77.6	79.6	72.9	80.9
9 consequences and 9 alternatives	0	76.7	76.5	72.2	78.3
	1	81.0	77.2	76.8	79.8
	2	80.1	78.7	73.3	81.3
	3	78.5	79.7	70.2	81.6
12 consequences and 6 alternatives	0	80.1	80.5	73.2	82.2
	1	83.6	79.9	78.3	82.5
	2	81.9	81.1	73.3	83.5
	3	80.2	81.7	70.0	83.3
12 consequences and 12 alternatives	0	74.8	74.4	67.9	76.3
	1	78.5	73.8	72.3	76.8
	2	77.0	75.7	67.3	78.2
	3	74.8	77.2	62.0	78.7

4. For each method μ', assess whether μ' yielded the same decision (i.e. the same preferred alternative) as TRUE. If so, record a hit.

The hit rate (or frequency) is defined as the number of times a method made the same decision as TRUE. Our simulations were carried out with a varying number of alternatives and consequences. There were four numbers of consequences to each alternative $N = \{3, 6, 9, 12\}$ and five numbers of alternatives $M = \{3, 6, 9, 12, 15\}$ creating a total of 20 simulation scenarios. Each scenario was run 10 times, each time with 10,000 trials, yielding a total of 2,000,000 decision situations generated. An N-variate joint Dirichlet distribution was employed to generate the random probability vectors for the $N-1$ DoF simulations and a standard round-robin normalised random probability generator for the N DoF simulations. Similar to MCDM simulations, unscaled value vectors were generated uniformly, and no significant differences were observed with other value distributions. In addition to the four cardinal methods on test (CRC, CRS, CRR, and CSR), we included two ordinal methods (ROC and SR) for reference. The results of the simulations are shown in Table 1 below, where we show a subset of the results with a selection of pairs (N,M). The measure of success utilised below is the hit ratio as in previous studies ("winner"), i.e. the number of times the highest evaluated alternative using a particular method coincides with the true highest alternative.[7] Table 1 below show the winner frequency utilising a 50 % combination of the simulation methods $N-1$ DoF and N DoF.

The simulations were run with a varying number of cardinal symbols to investigate the marginal utility of using varying cardinal expressibility. In the symbols column, the number of '>' symbols is shown, i.e. *in addition* to the '=' symbol. Thus, 1 means the use of symbols '=' and '$>_1$', 2 means the use of symbols '=', '$>_1$', and '$>_2$', and so on. A 0 in the symbols column denotes the corresponding ordinal elicitation method. This was done using two generators of different DoF and the results were then combined into one measure putting equal emphasis on both cases. The tables show results from quite small to rather large simulations. All hit ratios in all tables are given in per cent and are mean values of the scenario runs.[8] As can be seen from the tables, there are clearly diminishing returns evident in adding more symbols in all simulations. At the same time, there is a clear advantage in introducing the '=' symbol, i.e. for all simulations with a number > 0 in the symbols column. Since additional symbols put a greater demand on decision-makers, two symbols seem therefore to be a balanced and suitable expressional power for most elicitations, i.e. cardinal probability elicitation with '=', '$>_1$' and '$>_2$'. Further, there can be seen a diminishing return on the number of

---

[7] A second success measure we used is the matching of the three highest ranked alternatives ("podium"), the number of times the three highest evaluated alternatives using a particular method all coincide with the true three highest alternatives. A third set generated is the matching of all ranked alternatives ("overall"), the number of times all evaluated alternatives using a particular method coincide with the true ranking of the alternatives. The two latter sets correlated strongly with the first and are not shown in this paper.

[8] The standard deviations between sets of 10 runs were around 0.2–0.3 per cent.

Table 2. The probability and value assessments in the decision tree. $p(e)$ and $p(c)$ and $v(c)$ denote the probabilities and values of the respective nodes

$p(c_{14}) >_0 p(c_{15})$	$p(e_{16}) >_1 p(c_{22})$	$p(c_9) >_2 p(c_{10})$	$p(c_{13}) >_3 p(c_{16})$	$v(c_6) >_1$
$p(c_{19}) >_0 p(c_{20})$	$p(c_{22}) >_1 p(c_{23})$	$p(e_{17}) >_2 p(c_{21})$	$p(e_3) >_3 p(c_5)$	$\{v(c_2),v(c_4),v(c_{13}),v(c_{15}),v(c_{18}),v(c_{20})\} >_1$
$p(c_{12}) >_0 p(c_{13})$	$p(e_{19}) >_1 p(e_{10})$	$p(e_8) >_2 p(c_{11})$	$p(e_9) >_3 p(c_{12})$	$\{v(c_1),v(c_3),v(c_{12}),v(c_{14}),v(c_{17}),v(c_{19})\} >_1$
$p(c_{17}) >_0 p(c_{18})$		$p(e_{11}) >_2 p(e_{14})$		$v(c_7) >_1$
$p(c_3) >_0 p(c_4)$		$p(e_{15}) >_2 p(e_{18})$		$\{v(c_5),v(c_8),v(c_{16}),v(c_{21})\} >_1$
$p(c_6) >_0 p(c_7)$		$p(e_5) >_2 p(c_8)$		$v(c_9) >_1$
$p(c_1) >_0 p(c_2)$		$p(e_1) >_2 p(e_4)$		$\{v(c_{10}),v(c_{11})\} >_1$
		$p(e_6) >_2 p(e_{19})$		$v(c_{22}) >_1 v(c_{23})$

symbols used at a higher number of consequences to each alternative. At 9 or more consequences, cardinal probability elicitation with only '=' and '$>_1$' is to prefer for CRC. It is clear from the results above that the best cardinal elicitation is superior to ordinal. Of the cardinal methods, CRC and CSR outperform the others. The differences between them lies within the margin of error of the investigation but both clearly outperform the other two cardinal as well as all ordinal probability elicitation methods.

4   Decision Support for Emergency Psychiatric Care

Anna is a young woman who pulled out a kitchen knife to defend herself against demons, but her mother managed to calm her down and bring her to the psychiatric emergency department. Obviously, in cases such as Anna's, estimates cannot be made with precision and a reasonably realistic support system for managing such cases must have the capacity to accommodate the imprecise probabilities and value functions involved.

The modelled scenario thus contains an initial decision when Anna presents at the psychiatric emergency department with psychotic symptoms. The question is whether or not Anna should be admitted into compulsory inpatient psychiatric care, against her will (alternative 1) or be permitted to leave and return to the outpatient department the following day, as she and her family wish (alternative 2). Depending on the action taken, this decision is followed by a number of consequences which are all are dependent on this initial decision. For example, if admitted into compulsory inpatient psychiatric care, Anna may remain in inpatient care, or she may appeal to the administrative court, which could order her to be released. If she is permitted to leave the emergency department, she may contact the outpatient clinic and comply with treatment, which is the most favourable outcome. She could also, for example, choose not to comply with outpatient treatment, be lost to follow-up, commit a violent act or attempt suicide. These consequences could in turn lead to custody within forensic psychiatry/the prison service, injury requiring somatic care or even death by suicide.

Figure 1 (in the Appendix) shows the decision model and Table 2 shows the subjective estimates involved in this decision, where the probability and value assessments, p(e) and p(c) and v(c), denote the various probabilities and values. These are given surrogate weights according to the algorithms described above and the expected alternative values can then straightforwardly be calculated as 0.797 and 0.598 respectively, meaning that Alternative 1 is significantly better than alternative 2.

5 Conclusions

Decision analytical methods have been utilized within healthcare for various purposes, but their use has been limited for a number of reasons, not the least of which is weak realism regarding the input data because of difficulties in providing the specific and high-quality input data which most models require. We have therefore focused pragmatically on providing a method trying to balance between the need of simplicity and the requirement for accuracy, i.e. providing a more useful method with reasonable elicitation components, which would reduce some of the applicability issues with existing, more elaborate methods, be able to capture more information than pure ordinal approaches, and be sufficiently robust and cover a broad set of decision situation prerequisites. We have extended some well-known ordinal scale approaches commonly used for criteria weights as well as a newly proposed one with the possibility to supply cardinal information as well and applied this to probabilities. We have furthermore compared the approaches in various ways by carrying out a large set of simulations of the methods and have found some interesting simulation results. We have also discussed some new results regarding a mixed model of decision-maker behaviour and which degree of freedom that is adequate. From the above, it is seems that imprecise cardinal information should be used when available. Furthermore, the proposed CRC and CSR methods have turned out to be particularly appealing. CSR generalises the MCDM weighting procedure SR from (Danielson and Ekenberg 2014) by also taking cardinal relation information of the probabilities into account in a more straightforward way than, e.g., (Danielson et al. 2014). We found that in decision problems with up to 12 consequences to each alternative, CRC and CSR with two '>' symbols are the most efficient methods. Above this, the diminishing return of using a more fine-grained set of expressions is evident and only one '>' symbol is preferred. Thus, while avoiding more complicated methods that we and others have previously suggested for handling imprecision in decision situations (see, e.g., Danielson and Ekenberg 2007), which have turned out to be difficult to understand for normal decision-makers, the methods suggested in this paper give significantly better results than their competitors. It seems that in particular the CRC and CSR methods have some appealing features and give a decent decision quality, better than straightforwardly adapted ordinal MCDM methods, while at the same time solving some of the elicitation problems with either requiring too precise information or neglecting available information.

Appendix

See Fig. 1

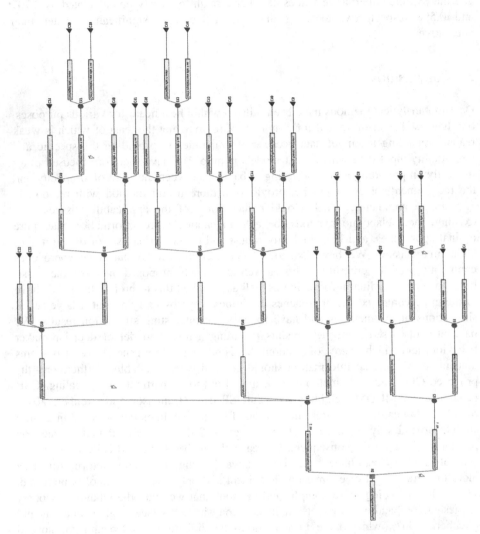

Fig. 1. The complete decision model of the Anna case

References

Sygel, K., Danielson, M., Ekenberg, L., Fors, U.: Handling imprecise information in emergency psychiatric care. In: Proceedings of ICSSE IEEE International Conference on System Science and Engineering (2015)

Barron, F.H.: Selecting a best multiattribute alternative with partial information about attribute weights. Acta Psychol. **80**(1–3), 91–103 (1992)

Corner, J.L., Corner, P.D.: Characteristics of decisions in decision analysis practice. J. Oper. Res. Soc. **46**(3), 304–314 (1995)

Danielson, M., Ekenberg, L.: Rank ordering methods for multi-criteria decisions. In: Zaraté, P., Kersten, G.E., Hernández, J.E. (eds.) GDN 2014. LNBIP, vol. 180, pp. 128–135. Springer, Heidelberg (2014)

Danielson, M., Ekenberg, L., Larsson, A.: Distribution of belief in decision trees. Int. J. Approximate Reasoning **46**(2), 387–407 (2007)

Danielson, M., Ekenberg, L., Larsson, A., Riabacke, M.: Weighting under ambiguous preferences and imprecise differences in a cardinal rank ordering process. Int. J. Comput. Intell. Syst. **7**, 105–112 (2013)

Danielson, M., Ekenberg, L., He, Y.: Augmenting ordinal methods of attribute weight approximation. Decis. Anal. **11**(1), 21–26 (2014)

Delavande, A., Gine, X., McKenzie, D.: Measuring subjective expectations in developing countries: a critical review and new evidence. J. Dev. Econ. **94**, 151–163 (2011)

Hogarth, R.M.: Cognitive processes and the assessment of subjective probability distributions. J. Am. Stat. Assoc. **70**, 271–289 (1975)

Johnson, E.M., Huber, G.P.: The technology of Utility Assessment. IEEE Trans. Syst. Man Cybern. **7**(5), 311–325 (1977)

Lenert, L.A., Treadwell, J.R.: Effects on preferences of violations of procedural invariance. Med. Decis. Making **19**(4), 473–481 (1999)

Lichtenstein, S., Slovic, P. (eds.): The Construction of Preference. Cambridge University Press, New York (2006)

Morgan, M.G., Henrion, M.: Uncertainty—A Guide to Dealing with Uncertainty in Quantitative Risk and Policy Analysis. Cambridge University Press, New York (1990)

Rey-Biel, P.: Equilibrium play and best response to (stated) beliefs in normal form games. Games Econ. Behav. **65**, 572–585 (2009)

Stillwell, W., Seaver, D., Edwards, W.: A comparison of weight approximation techniques in multiattribute utility decision making. Organ. Behav. Hum. Perform. **28**(1), 62–77 (1981)

Tversky, A., Kahneman, D.: The framing of decisions and the psychology of choice. Science **211** (4481), 453–458 (1981)

Wallsten, T.S., Budescu, D.V.: Encoding subjective probabilities: a psychological and psychometric review. Manage. Sci. **29**(2), 151–173 (1983)

Supporting Active and Healthy Ageing by Exploiting a Telepresence Robot and Personalized Delivery of Information

Amedeo Cesta, Gabriella Cortellessa, Riccardo De Benedictis [✉],
and Domenico M. Pisanelli

ISTC, Institute for Cognitive Sciences and Technologies,
CNR, Italian National Research Council, Rome, Italy
{amedeo.cesta,gabriella.cortellessa,riccardo.debenedictis,
domenico.pisanelli}@istc.cnr.it, gabriella.cortellessa@gmail.com

Abstract. Supporting active and healthy ageing represents an opportunity for improving the quality of life of older citizens while reducing the unsustainable pressure on health systems. The GIRAFFPLUS project aims at improving health quality by offering personalized services for end users on top of a non-invasive state-of-the-art continuous data-gathering infrastructure. Specifically, the system collects elderly daily behaviour and physiological measures from distributed sensors in living environments. In addition, GIRAFFPLUS organizes the gathered information so as to provide customizable visualization and monitoring services to the different users of the system. This paper describes the latest results achieved within the project specifically focusing on the interactive services toward the users.

1 Introduction

Most elderly people wish to remain in their homes as long as possible as this gives a richer social life and allows them to maintain their habits. This is also positive from an economic perspective as the cost of care at home is almost always much less than the cost of residential care.

In recent years there is an increasing attention on the topic of "prolonging independent living". Several heterogeneous efforts have focused on the problem of helping aging population with ICT technology (see, for example, [4,13]). A number of R&D programs have been triggered by funding agencies, as an example the European Commission has promoted, the Ambient Assisted Living (AAL) joint program, the area of "ageing well" within the FP7 research program and the topic of "Active and Healthy Ageing" within the Horizon 2020 program. Attention has also been dedicated to the use of robotic devices for helping older users at home and projects and initiatives have promoted their use (see for example [2,8]).

The GIRAFFPLUS[1] aimed to combine technologies for social interaction and long term monitoring to promote independent and healthy living. Among the

---

[1] FP7 #288173 – http://www.giraffplus.eu.

© Springer International Publishing Switzerland 2015
H. Fujita and G. Guizzi (Eds.): SoMeT 2015, CCIS 532, pp. 586–597, 2015.
DOI: 10.1007/978-3-319-22689-7_45

issues addressed in the project are the typical needs taken into account for prolonging independent living:

- Early detection of possible deterioration of health and timely involvement of health care and family need to be assured.
- Adaptive support is needed which can offer services to assist in coping with age-related impairments.
- Ways of supporting preventive medicine must be found to promote a healthy lifestyle and delay the onset of age-related illnesses.

This paper introduces the general ideas of intelligent environment pursued withing the GIRAFFPLUS project, then specifically describes the work done for better serving the users and their need for information, touching upon the issues of visualizing data and personalizing interaction services. The GIRAFFPLUS system has been developed and tested in 15 real homes in three different European Countries.

(a) The Giraff telepresence robot   (b) GiraffPlus in a real setting

Fig. 1. The telepresence robot used in GIRAFFPLUS for social interaction

2   The GIRAFFPLUS Architecture

The general idea underlying the project is given in Fig. 2 (a general description of the project is given in [5] while technical aspects are broadened in [11]). The figure offers a conceptual schematization of the components of the system and allows to identify some key concepts constant reference in our work and also for the current paper.

A first distinction worth being captured concerns the different GIRAFFPLUS users. The intelligent environment, indeed, offers services to different people involved in a single use case. More specifically, the different human actors can be divided into: (a) *primary users*, the older adults living at home, mostly alone, that the system is supposed to actively support and (b) *secondary users*, the network of people who participate in the support of the older adult from outside his/her home. Such users can be further subdivided into formal caregivers (a doctor, the nurse, etc.), informal caregivers (a son, generic relatives, etc.) or simply friends that want to maintain a contact with the old person.

Once we have distinguished the users, we introduce the basic ingredients of the system at design time: (1) a *network of sensors* deployed in the home that continuously gathers data; (2) a *data management infrastructure* that guarantees data gathering in a permanent data store or directly to some external user in real time; (3) a *telepresence robot* (the Giraff, see Fig. 1 a) that guarantees communication between people outside the house and the primary user in the house, enriching the dialogue with the possibility of moving in the home environment and performing visual monitoring through a camera connected to it; (4) a *personalizable interaction front-end* that allows to visualize data from the house and, also, to call the robot from outside the house. On top of these, a set of services deliver personalized information to both primary and secondary users.

It is worth highlighting the two paths implicitly existing in the figure: from inside the house to outside, and vice versa. Different needs and services are associated to the two paths. If we consider the *from-inside-to-outside* path we can say that mainly we are: (a) exporting data for a long term

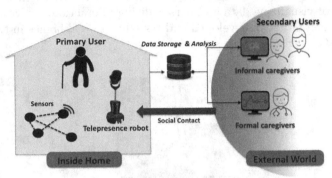

Fig. 2. The GIRAFFPLUS complete system

data analysis (storing them first in a data storage service). Notice that the secondary users usually are heterogeneous people having different "social goals" toward the old person, hence a doctor may be interested in physiological data and general information on the daily activities connected to health, an informal caregiver may be interested in a daily summary that says "everything is OK", "the windows were left open", etc. (b) exporting data for a real time use (hence, for example, for issuing alarms). In fact, the system can rise alarms and/or send warnings, for instance, in case of falls or in case of abnormal physiological parameters. Here a problem exists of delivering them timely and to the right person.

If we explore the *from-outside-to-inside* path, we can say that: (c) the communication through the telepresence robot is the basic media for social communication; additionally (d) having such a general setup, the system offers now a channel from secondary to the primary for messages and reminders created through the visualization front-end and delivered on the robot screen (also other media are possible but here we are focusing on the basic GIRAFFPLUS components). This information exchange is stored by the data storage service for subsequent analysis. In addition, it is worth underscoring how there are also other services that are possible given our infrastructure: (e) long term data from the home sensor network are available in the data storage and can be also shown, with some attention, to the primary user.

3   Visualization and Personalization Services

The rest of the paper is dedicated to describe the work done to realize the *personalizable interaction front-end* introduced in the previous section. In particular we have synthesized a module called Data Visualization, Personalization and Interaction Service (DVPIS) as the system component responsible for the interaction with the users in the large. This is the system part that directly has in charge the user services, bringing data in the right form to each category of users. The basic benefit pursued by the GIRAFFPLUS system is twofold: secondary users are supported by a flexible and efficient monitoring tool; primary users can access the information on their own health condition, enabling them to better manage their health and lifestyle. Both these modules are composed of a **back-end** part, devoted to organize the content of the information to be shown to the users and to offer different services tailored to classes of users, and a **front-end** part, responsible for presenting the information and services to the different categories of users. Figure 3 gives the general idea of the DVPIS.

The DVPIS back end is responsible for preparing "personalized information to the users' and to offer support for different types of services like *reminders*, *reports* and *alarms* (and also the *proactive suggestions* and *warnings*). The **front-end** part is responsible for presenting the information and services to the different categories of users. It has been a natural distinction to introduce two different clients for interacting with the users: (a) one for the broad class of secondary users called DVPIS@Office to be used in the outside world, (b) one from the primary user called DVPIS@Home that we have developed as an

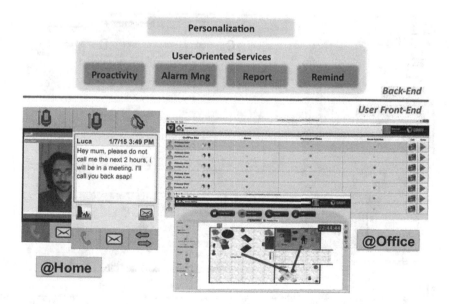

Fig. 3. A representation of the whole Data Visualization and Personalization Service

additional tool to run on the robot at home and deliver additional information to the assisted person in the home environment.

3.1 DVPIS@Office

After an intense phase of user requirements elicitation with potential users of the system, a number of services and parameters to monitor have been identified and selected as the most relevant to be shown through the DVPIS@Office.

This DVPIS@Office allows to a generic secondary user to follow a list of homes and consequently primary users, who have the GIRAFFPLUS system installed in their apartment (Fig. 4 A). Specifically the list of followed user contains a brief and immediate information on the status of the assisted person in terms of three main indicators: **Alarms**, **Physiological** and **Social** aspects. For each of this dimension an immediate feedback is given with a judgment on the level of each indicator: *green = good*; *yellow = warning*; *red = risk* (see also the @Office part in Fig. 3). In this way a secondary user can easily judge if he/she needs to urgently intervene on some specific situations and in general he/she can modulate and prioritize the visit to the different patients thanks to an immediate feedback without the need to entering into the details of each home.

For each of these people the secondary users can observe the real time view of the house on a map depicting sensors installed in the house (Fig. 4 B); the physiological data specific for the patient (Fig. 4 C); can also ask *daily/weekly* or *monthly report* for the main activities in order to observe possible deviations from routines (Fig. 4 D).

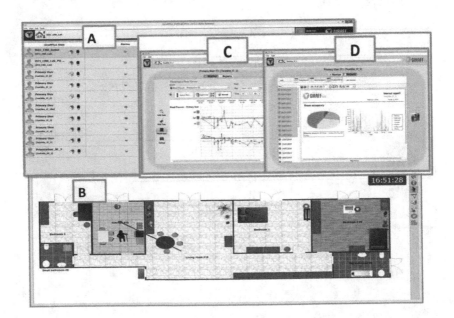

Fig. 4. Example of visualization services for secondary users

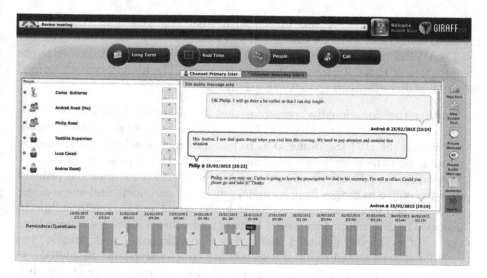

Fig. 5. A screenshot from the DVPIS@Office panel for the message board among secondary users

Another relevant service of the DVPIS@Office is the implementation of a new panel dedicated to foster the discussion among the *network of people* related to a primary user. Specifically, a new environment has been added where the different actors involved in the care of a primary user can exchange information and opinions so as to maximize the overall care for the old person at home. In Fig. 5 an interaction among secondary users is shown. In general this functionality allow also secondary and a primary to interact through text message delivery (see also the @Home example in the lower part of Fig. 3).

This environment is an example of a dialogue space to allow the social networking of people who assist the same primary user. Through these functionalities it is possible to exchange messages among a group of people or in a peer to peer modality. Additionally it is possible to send messages and/or set reminders to the primary users at home that will be delivered through the Giraff telepresence robot as we will show in the next section. Indeed the same social panel is now used to send messages to the primary user and to set reminders over time through a specific dialogue box.

3.2   DVPIS@Home

As mentioned before, the data gathered from the environmental and physiological sensors are also shown to the old user at home. This is done according to the ethical principle that the primary user as "data producer" should maintain a level of understanding on the GIRAFFPLUS operations. Such functionality is currently obtained enlarging the capabilities of the telepresence robot. In fact, we decided to use the telepresence robot as a means to provide services to the primary users and this is also in line with what emerged from the feedback gathered during the iterative evaluation sessions.

The DVPIS module has been endowed with a sub-component dedicated to the visualization of this data toward the primary users. The main services provided to primary users through the DVPIS@Home are:

- **Avatar:** this functionality preserves the "traditional telepresence" service that the Giraff robot provides. The Giraff application has been indeed embedded within the DVPIS@Home so as to maintain the possibility for secondary users to visit the older user's apartment through the telepresence robot.
- **Messages:** an additional environment has been added to allow the primary user to receive messages from secondary users or reminders and suggestions. Messages and reminders are provided in both textual and spoken form. Specifically we have developed a message listener that collects messages coming from the middleware and gathered them with a specific panel that "mimic" the functionality of a mail client or a messenger on a smartphone. In addition to adapting the font size to the user we have decided to integrate an off-the-shelf text-to-speech translator to give the user the possibility to "reading aloud" the messages and re-reading them again and again (most older adult have sight problems).
- **Shared Data:** one of the comment from the evaluation session with users was related to the need to show personal data to the primary user (e.g., physiological measures), and to endow the system with a shared space between the primary user and the secondary users that could foster a discussion on the health status and habits of the old person. The general aim is to improve his/her awareness and also to encourage responsible behaviors for increasing his/her well being. In this light the DVPIS@Home includes an environment that allows such a dialog. The idea is that a secondary user (e.g., an Health Professional) calls a primary user via the Giraff robot and then uses this environment to discuss about the health related data to both explain them to the assisted person and possibly deepen the understanding of them through questions to the old person.

The next two sections provides some additional services which are enabled by the @Home functionalities.

4 Sending Text and Media

The @Home part of the system aims at enriching the features already provided by the standard Giraff robot exposing some additional services to the primary user.

While maintaining the main objective of keeping a pleasant quality of life for the primary users, the GIRAFFPLUS system represents a valid opportunity for connecting the different actors through the same infrastructure. More specifically, secondary users can exchange text and recorded messages with primary users (see Fig. 6(a) for an example of text messages). Since most of the elderly

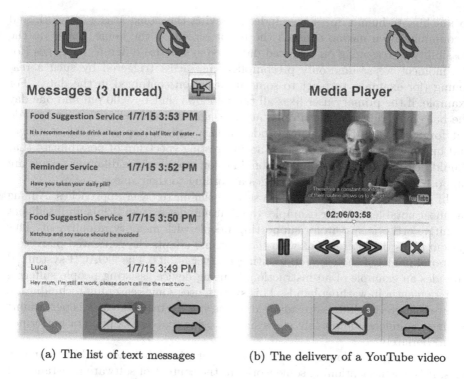

(a) The list of text messages   (b) The delivery of a YouTube video

Fig. 6. Screenshots from the DVPIS@Home

suffer from sight problems, we have endowed the Giraff robot with the possibility of vocally synthesizing the received text messages. Primary users can thus listen to the received messages and, possibly, vocally reply to them. In addition, caregivers can exchange messages both among themselves about, for example, everyday life, as well as with connected doctors, nurses, and other professionals involved in the care of the older people living alone about, for example, some specific health problem of their loved ones. Users can thus send asynchronous messages, allowing a better organization of their time.

An interesting feature that has emerged through the interaction with the real users, during the evaluation phase, is the possibility for the secondary users of sending media files to the primary users. Specifically, secondary users have the possibility to send photo albums to their relative through the telepresence robot and, possibly, YouTube videos that might be reproduced remotely for the pleasure of their elderly relatives and/or friends (see Fig. 6(b) for an example of YouTube video reproduced on the DVPIS@Home).

5   Personalizing Communication

As already mentioned in the previous sections, the GIRAFFPLUS system provides a broad spectrum of communication channels ranging from human-to-human to machine-to-human messages. Indeed, having the home sensor network and a communication media, through the robot screen, in the home, opens up the possibility of reasoning on collected data and synthesize different messages (for the moment we assume only precompiled messages) triggered by such a reasoning (for example, to react to some information contained in the data). For example, if the primary user likes all the windows shut by 9:00 pm and one day the balcony windows are still open at 9:30 pm we could deliver a message "do not forget to close the balcony windows, they are still open". Both messages and information deliveries open up an interesting spectrum of possibilities that should be coordinated by some personalization module since different people are supposed to receive different messages according to their role.

In pursuing our task, we follow a setting similar to other approaches. Among the most notable ones, for example, the Autominder system [12] is an intelligent cognitive orthotic system for supporting people with memory impairment. This system plans the interactions with the user and adapts the generated plans to a temporal model of the user representing his/her habits. The COACH system [1] provides an example of an instructional cueing device assisting people suffering from dementia in washing hands. This system uses some reasoning techniques to ensure that the reminders are adapted to the specific tasks the user is performing issuing reminders if important steps such as using soap are skipped or performed inappropriately.

Even though the domain is slightly different, given their adaptability capabilities, it is worth mentioning some works in the context of software assistance for the office domain. The CybreMinder project [7], for example, provides a Context Toolkit for the definition of arbitrary complex situations describing the context that would trigger the reminder. By doing so, the system is able to manage the timing of a reminder based on a user's context. Still related to the workplace domain, yet very prolific from the point of view of the reminding systems, the CALO project [10] is intended to support a busy knowledge worker with problems of information and task overload. The CALO system is able to provide proactive behaviour automatically initiating reminders for future tasks by applying BDI reasoning [9] and/or by reasoning on digital to-do lists [3].

By reasoning on updated features of the primary user we pursue a "proactive messaging" service modulated by the user model information. The broad idea is to create a proactive service at home, by reasoning on user personal data and modulating system messages, directed to primary users. The possibility to deliver "system generated" messages to the primary user through the @Home interface is a basic enabler.

Specifically, the monitored features are a combination of: (a) a *static user profile*, considered immutable during the care process, describing not only general data (e.g., his/her age), medical condition (a chronic disease), bust also his/her attitude toward interaction and toward technology (these are used for example to avoid flooding a person with undesired information or recommendations he/she is not willing to accept); (b) a *dynamic user profile*, with a higher rate of change with respect to the static parameters, whose components are extracted from the physiological monitoring and other continuous data flows. (c) an *internal status* which, acting on such information, determines the user internal status by performing a classification process and triggers the planning of stimuli toward the involved users. This classification, for example, identifies the set the "colour based" indicators previously shown in Fig. 4 A. The status of such indicators is again a trigger to a strategy to decide which messages and which frequency of messages to select for the users. For example observing value transitions (es., when the physiological status change from good to warning) we can send simple questions like "have you taken your daily pill?", or issuing dietary suggestions like "avoid salt while cooking". These alerting messages can be sent, more or less often, both inside the house, to reassure or advise the primary user through the telepresence robot, and outside the house, to send an alerting message to a designated care person, etc.

6   Interacting with Older Adults at Home

As already mentioned, possible interactions with the primary users, within GIRAFFPLUS, are not limited to sensor data retrieving and/or telepresence robot calls. We have incrementally added the possibility to send messages, and also the possibility to automatically sinthesize reminding or warnings triggered by data analysis [6].

The idea pursued is the one that different GIRAFFPLUS installations can be equipped with interactive services that can be exploited to provide personalized services to the associated primary users. Through the use of multiple-choice questions, proposed by the robot to the primary users, the system is able to build and maintain an updated model of the older person. The GIRAFFPLUS system can thus take into account the input from both environmental and physiological sensors, together with the updated user model, so as to automatically synthesize reminders as well as Health & Wellness suggestions for improving lifestyle.

A functionality we have build starting from this feature is the one of creating suggestions programs for the old person. Suggestions can be of different nature ranging from context independent, such as "tips of the day", valid for everyone, to context dependent messages, such as recommendations on season fruits and vegetables and recommendations based on vital signs. An example of such recommendations is the daily diet suggestions integrated into the system. Context independent messages such as "It is recommended to drink at least one and a half liter of water a day" or "By using herbs and spices, you add flavour and you can reduce consumption of salt" can be sent to the primary users through the robot on a daily basis. In addition to these, context dependent messages such as "Ketchup and soy sauce should be avoided", in case of hypertension, or "Drink only low-fat milk", for overweight people, and also "Prefer oranges, bananas, kiwis, apples, spinaches, cauliflowers, beetroots" when in Winter, are sent to the users only in case some specific related conditions are met.

7   Conclusions

Different people would like different delivery of the information to each of the human actors connected to the dialogue with the GIRAFFPLUS system. Information and messages exchanged open up an interesting spectrum of possibilities that should be coordinated by a personalization infrastructure.

The current trend of common health is to focus more on wellness for stay healthier rather than on mere healthcare. For this reason, a proper nutrition is fundamental for a healthy lifestyle. This is even more relevant for elderly people. In addition to the data visualization services, an interesting aspect of the GIRAFFPLUS system is the idea to provide personalized and proactive interaction services. The system back end is indeed responsible for preparing the "personalized information to the users" and for offering support for different types of services like reminders, reports, proactive suggestions warnings and alarms.

Acknowledgments. Authors work was partially funded by the EU FP7 under the GIRAFFPLUS project (contract #288173). Authors would like to thank all members of the GIRAFFPLUS consortium and particularly Giulio Bernardi, Luca Coraci, Francesca Fracasso and Andrea Orlandini for joint work.

References

1. Boger, J., Poupart, P., Hoey, J., Boutilier, C., Fernie, G., Mihailidis, A.: A decision-theoretic approach to task assistance for persons with dementia. In: Kaelbling, L.P., Saffiotti, A. (eds.) IJCAI, pp. 1293–1299. Professional Book Center (2005)
2. Cesta, A., Coradeschi, S., Cortellessa, C., Gonzalez, J., Tiberio, L., Von Rump, S.: Enabling social interaction through embodiment in ExCITE. In: Second Italian forum on Ambient Assisted Living, Trento, Italy (2010)
3. Conley, K., Carpenter, J.: Towel: towards an intelligent To-Do list. In: AAAI Spring Symposium: Interaction Challenges for Intelligent Assistants, pp. 26–32. AAAI (2007)
4. Connelly, K., Siek, K.A., Mulder, I., Neely, S., Stevenson, G., Kray, C.: Evaluating pervasive and ubiquitous systems. IEEE Pervasive Comput. 7(3), 85–88 (2008)
5. Coradeschi, S., Cesta, A., Cortellessa, G., Coraci, L., Gonzalez, J., Karlsson, L., Furfari, F., Loutfi, A., Orlandini, A., Palumbo, F., Pecora, F., von Rump, S., Stimec, A., Ullberg, J., Ostlund, B.: GiraffPlus: combining social interaction and long term monitoring for promoting independent living. In: HSI: 6th International Conference on Human System Interaction (2013)
6. De Benedictis, R., Cesta, A., Coraci, L., Cortellessa, G., Orlandini, A.: A user-adaptive reminding service. In: Intelligent Environments (Workshops) (2014)
7. Dey, A.K., Abowd, G.D.: CybreMinder: a context-aware system for supporting reminders. In: Thomas, P., Gellersen, H.-W. (eds.) HUC 2000. LNCS, vol. 1927, pp. 172–186. Springer, Heidelberg (2000)
8. Mitzner, T.L., Kemp, C.C., Rogers, W., Tiberio, L.: Investigating healthcare providers' acceptance of personal robots for assisting with daily caregiving tasks. In: CHI 2013 Extended Abstracts on Human Factors in Computing Systems, CHI EA 2013, pp. 499–504. ACM, New York (2013)

9. Myers, K.L., Yorke-Smith, N.: Proactive behavior of a personal assistive agent. In: Proceedings of the AAMAS Workshop on Metareasoning in Agent-Based Systems, Honolulu, HI, pp. 31–45, May 2007
10. Myers, K., Berry, P., Blythe, J., Conley, K., Gervasio, M., McGuinness, D., Morley, D., Pfeffer, A., Pollack, M., Tambe, M.: An intelligent personal assistant for task and time management. AI Mag. **28**(2), 47–61 (2007)
11. Palumbo, F., Ullberg, J., Štimec, A., Furfari, F., Karlsson, L., Coradeschi, S.: Sensor network infrastructure for a home care monitoring system. Sensors **14**(3), 3833–3860 (2014)
12. Pollack, M.E., Brown, L., Colbry, D., McCarthy, C.E., Orosz, C., Peintner, B., Ramakrishnan, S., Tsamardinos, I.: Autominder: an intelligent cognitive orthotic system for people with memory impairment. Robot. Autom. Syst. **44**, 273–282 (2003)
13. Pollack, M.: Intelligent technology for an aging population: the use of AI to assist elders with cognitive impairment. AI Mag. **26**(2), 9–24 (2005)

A Conceptual Model of Human Behaviour in Socio-technical Systems

Mario Di Nardo[1], Mosè Gallo[1], Marianna Madonna[2(✉)],
and Liberatina Carmela Santillo[1]

[1] Department of Chemical, Materials and Industrial Production Engineering,
Naples, Italy
{mario.dinardo,mose.gallo,santillo}@unina.it
[2] INAIL - Operational Territorial Unit of Naples - Research,
Certification and Verification Area, Naples, Italy
m.madonna@inail.it

Abstract. The growing percentage of incidents connected with human error in several industries has led to investigate the factors influencing failures, so that many methods, the so-called Human Reliability Analysis methods, have been developed in order to quantify the human error probabilities. According to the needs of the last generation of the above mentioned methods (i.e. dynamic HRA methods), in order to overcome the lack into modelling the dynamic nature of human performance, this paper focuses on System Dynamics approach to highlight the relationships among the factors that influence human performance. Starting from a literature review on human error taxonomy, a Causal Loop Diagram is proposed to represent in a graphical fashion the interrelations between the variables which most influence and are influenced by human behaviour within a socio-technical system.

Keywords: Human error · Human reliability analysis · Human factors · Performance shaping factors · System dynamics · Causal loop diagram

1 Introduction

In the last decade, valid estimates concur in attributing to human errors 60–80 % of accidents and only the remainder is due to technical failures. According to Reason, considering human error the main cause of accidents, estimating human reliability leading to estimate the reliability of the whole system, even if the uncertainties that still exist when choosing this type of approach to the human factor is in estimating human error probability at the same level as estimating failure probability [1]. The efficiency and effectiveness of the system depend on the reliability of its each component individually and on the interaction between them.

In the field of human behaviour within socio-technical systems and organizations, the scientific research has evolved with the development of many methods, so called Human Reliability Analysis methods, based on human cognitive processes and functions, to quantify the human error probabilities. Therefore, in order to prevent accidents in a complex system, it is important to predict human error and causes and factors that influence it.

© Springer International Publishing Switzerland 2015
H. Fujita and G. Guizzi (Eds.): SoMeT 2015, CCIS 532, pp. 598–609, 2015.
DOI: 10.1007/978-3-319-22689-7_46

According to the last generation of dynamic HRA, the aim of this paper is to use the System Dynamic (SD) approach to model and assess human error in socio-technical systems, by highlighting relations and dependencies of human performance factor. After examining the framework of human reliability analysis methods (Sect. 2) and a brief background on System Dynamics (Sect. 3), a graphical model, by means of Causal loop diagrams, is developed and discussed (Sect. 4). The impact of factors within a socio-technical system on human error is evaluated, by taking into account taxonomy, cognitive model and contextual factors used in some HRA methods. In Sect. 5 some conclusions and future developments are outlined.

2 Background on Human Reliability Analysis (HRA)

In the literature many methods have been developed to assess human reliability in order to quantify the reliability of the whole system. These methods, named human reliability analysis methods, meet the needs of Probabilistic Risk Assessment (PRA) in order to quantify the contribution of human error to the occurrence of an accident, for example HRA approach may be seen as a specialization of PRA [2]. A probabilistic risk assessment identifies all the risks, including human errors, to which the system is exposed, and provides their quantitative estimate including this information in a fault or event tree.

The development of HRA methods has been closely linked to nuclear industry where the contribution of human error to the occurrence on accident could have severe and catastrophic consequences.

In order to quantify the reliability of a whole system the probability of human error should be evaluated. To this purpose a number of different methods have been developed to quantify human error probability in performing an assigned task. These methods mainly differ in the way they estimate the *human error probability* (HEP) and how the *performance shaping factors* (PSFs) influence it.

A number of HRA methods have been developed which differ in their scope, in the cognitive model assumed, in taxonomy of erroneous actions and in the factors influencing the error probability. There are three generation of HRA methods. First generation methods (such as THERP, HCR, HEART etc.) treat human failure in the same way as equipment failure. Human actions are considered in a binary fashion, i.e. as success or failure to achieve the required result from a task. Tasks and subtasks are considered to have an inherent failure probability which is then modified by performance shaping factors depending on the evaluation of the context. The criticism of this generation of methods lies in fact that they ignore the cognitive processes that lead to human error. They are also criticized for not considering the impact of the context factors on error mode.

The second generation of human reliability methods (such as CREAM, SPARH etc.) aims at evaluating the human contribution to incidental event by taking into account the role of the context. They are based on a cognitive model more appropriate to describe human behaviour, so that the focus shifted on the interaction of the contextual factors that increase the human error probability. The lack of the second generation methods lies on the use of a qualitative assessment of the operator' behaviour, in fact, while first generation methods has been validated, the second ones still needs to be empirically validated for the lack of empirical data and the lack of reproducibility being the parameters strongly dependent on the methodology used.

The third generation of HRA methods (NARA and BAYESIAN network) focuses on relations and dependencies of human performance factor [5]. They aim to overcome the second generation methods and, in particular, to model the mutual influence among performance shaping factors in terms of their impact on human performance and their mutual interaction. These methods are called *dynamic methods* as they take into account the dynamic evolution of human behaviour leading up to human error. On a methodological point of view they intend to create a database of human failure to limit the uncertainties linked to human reliability assessment [3–5].

2.1 Framework of Human Reliability Analysis

The development of a HRA method requires the combination of the following elements [2]:

- the development and/or application of a reference cognitive model for human behaviour;
- the development and/or application of a *taxonomy* for a structured representation of human errors;
- the *data collection* on human reliability that are qualitatively and quantitatively significant;
- the description of a *method* where the steps to be followed in applying the analysis are set out;
- the evaluation of the influence of *performance shaping factors* on human error.

2.1.1 Cognitive Model and Taxonomy

In the human reliability analysis there is the need to formalize a model of human behaviour that describe the cognitive process of human beings and its link with human performance [6].

A cognitive model is supported by a corresponding taxonomy that describe formally the human behaviour and performance in a structured manner. A taxonomy is a classification, applied to associate the manifestations of human errors with their relevant causes. Harwood and Sanderson observed that there is a compelling need for an interdisciplinary vocabulary to communicate on the role of humans [7].

In order to model human behaviour various classifications of incorrect actions have been proposed in the literature but the most commonly used in the field of human reliability is Rasmussen's skill-rule-knowledge(SRK) framework with the associated error taxonomy [8]. Rasmussen classified human behaviour into three different types:

- Skill-based behaviour: routine behaviour based on learnt skills. The cognitive commitment required is very low and reasoning is unconscious (automatically activity).
- Rule-based behaviour: behaviour guided by rules that the operator has to follow to carry out well done task. It is a matter of recognizing the situation and applying the

appropriate procedure to carry out the task. The cognitive commitment is higher of skill based behaviour, since it implies a certain level of reasoning.

- *Knowledge-based behaviour*: behaviour aimed at solving problems in no routine or unknown situations (new or unexpected) for which there are no specific rules or procedures. This type of behaviour is defined as knowledge-based as it requires a high cognitive commitment in seeking an effective solution.

The cognitive process, which is stimulus to action, is structured on three different pathways of increasing complexity that require increasing levels of attention and cognitive resources (Fig. 1).

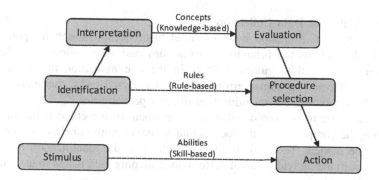

Fig. 1. Rasmussen's skill-rule-knowledge model

At the base of the model there is the skill-based behaviour by which the operator, stimulated by an event(input: signal, noise, etc.), reacts almost instantaneously by carrying out an action linked to a procedure that has been thoroughly internalized. At the intermediate level there is rule-based behaviour by which the operator, on the basis of the information received orders a series of actions through the use of procedures and carries them out. At a higher level there is the knowledge-based behaviour in which the operator is required to creatively and independently use the available information and his/her knowledge (i.e. without using procedures or instinctive behaviour), in order to assess and decide which will be the appropriate actions to undertake. Errors can occur at any step of this cognitive process, and the potential for error can be identified by considering each cognitive step, in order to locate where problems might occur. This Rasmussen's classification leads to identify three different types of error:

- *Slips:* failures in execution that occur at the skill-based level. The operator performs in the wrong way a well-known and routine tasks automatically with little mental processing.
- *Lapses:* failures in execution caused by memory failure. In this case the action achieves a different result from that expected due to a memory failure or accidentally following a well-known procedure instead of a required new one. Unlike slips, lapses cannot be observed directly.

- *Mistakes:* errors not committed during the actual execution of the action. In this case it is the plan itself that is not valid, despite the actions are carried out as planned. They can be of two types: rule-based and knowledge-based.
- *Rule-based mistakes:* errors caused by application of the wrong rule or the misapplication of good rules.
- *Knowledge-based mistakes:* errors due to the lack of knowledge or its incorrect application. The negative outcome of the action resides in the incorrect knowledge that determined it. This type of error is inherent in limited rationality or in any case in the difficulty of responding to problems that have a broad range of possible answers [2, 8].

2.1.2 Methods and Data Collection

The formalization of a method is an essential methodological step for putting into practice models of human behaviour, taxonomies and data collected in the work environment. The method guides analysts in the decomposition of the tasks, the identification of potential human errors related to analysed tasks, the analysis of the performance contexts and in quantification of error probabilities [2].

A characteristic to be considered in the assessment of a method is its ability into reproducing the complexity of the factors that influence human behaviour within relatively simple models. The method gives guidelines in the identification of potential human errors, in the individuation of performance shaping factors and in quantification of error probabilities.

In order to produce valid results, a human reliability method requires significant input data on human error probability that can be obtained from historical statistics, from empirical data or from judgments of experts in the sector [9].

2.1.3 Human Performance Shaping Factors

Human performance reliability within a socio-technical system depends on many influencing factors that describe the necessary preconditions for errors. These factors, influencing the reliability of the operator in performing a task, are called performance shaping factors. Almost all the HRA methods try to take into account the so-called contextual factors, at a varying level of detail, by introducing coefficients that weigh the influence of each factor on human performance.

According to the THERP method, the PSFs could be subdivided into three main categories [10]:

- *External factors*. These are the result of organizational and physical characteristics of the work environment. Organizational characteristics indicate the procedures, information, communication, hierarchy levels, organizational structures, workflows, work planning and execution. Physical characteristics affecting people, and, hence, system reliability, include light, noise, mechanical vibrations, man-machine interface, climate, dirt, humidity, air pressure, toxic gas and radiation.
- *Internal factors*. These factors include human characteristics and limitations which indicate the personal characteristics of the operator (skills, experience, training, knowledge, motivation and expectations), his/her physical characteristics (anthropometric and biomechanical) and his/her psychological characteristics (physical and

mental fatigue and boredom). Other features as leadership behaviour, participation, safety culture and climate can also influence human motivate on and behaviour.

- **Stress factors**. These include the type and number of stressful elements that may be found in various situations.

3 Background on System Dynamics and Its Applications to HRA

System dynamics is the theory of system structures, a theory that deals with the study of the causal interactions between the components which constitute the structure of a complex system. It is a modelling methodology for understanding and representing complex systems and analysing their dynamic behaviour.

System dynamics is a modelling method that allows a system to be represented in terms of feedback. It is founded on the original work of Forrester, who defined it as *"the investigation of the information-feedback character of industrial systems and the use of models for the design of improved organizational form and guiding policy"* [14]. System dynamics deals with the study of how the behaviour of a complex system changes over time.

Looking for the cause of a particular phenomenon (i.e. an accidental event), this one cannot be considered out of its context but it is necessary to adopt a systemic point of view: we must consider it as a set or a group of interacting and interdependent elements which forms a unique entity and act as such. The tool used to evaluate system behaviour is causal loop diagrams (CLDs). They highlight the interrelations between system variables and the feedback and complex interactions between them in an intuitive graphical representation. They are developed by gathering system's variables, and then correlating the variables into cause-effect relationship, where each connection, sketched as an arrow connecting the cause to the effect, could have a positive polarity if the two linked variables are subjected to the same variation (if the cause increases/decrease, the effect increases/decreases) or a negative one in the other case.

Feedback loops are the characteristic elements of Causal Loop Diagram and System Dynamic. Feedback could be defined as the transmission and return process of information: in Engineering it is the counterforce effect of a specific action used to control, improve or adjust system's behaviour; in other words, it is a cause-effect closed loop [15].

In System Dynamics, there are two kinds of feedback loops: *positive* or *reinforcing loop*, that reinforces the change in a specific variable, and *negative* or *balancing loop*, that balances its variation.

Furthermore, in a Causal Loop Diagram it is possible to represent the temporary phase shift between cause and effect using the delay operator. In conclusion, the use of System Dynamics is well suited to a system analysis since it makes possible to capture the circular nature and the dynamics of the cause-effect relationship through the construction of a Causal Loop Diagram.

The third generation of HRA, which is still in progress, focuses on human performance factors relations and dependencies. One of the so called dynamic HRA is the Bayesian networks that attempt to overcome some of the limitations of previous methods through qualitative analysis, which emphasises the importance of representing interactions between human actions and the dynamics between them [5].

The dynamic HRA is the last generation for HRA. Cacciabue [11] has outlined the importance of simulation and modelling of human performance for the field of human reliability. In particular, Bayesian Belief Networks BBNs are considered available to capture the "uncertain nature of the relation between human performance and its organizational context" [12]. BBNs have been used to understand and capture the relationships among PFSs and the quantitative impact of PSFs configurations on the error probability.

However, from the comparison of these two methodologies, Bayesian Belief Networks and System Dynamics, conducted by Gregoriades [13], it can be argued that SD is a more favourite methodology in modelling and assessing the effect of human error on reliability of socio-technical systems in future. This is due to the fact that these systems are composed of elements that are dynamically changing, in the time, according to various conditions (influences). Humans as agents in such systems are influenced dynamically by the changing system's environment. Since human error is an attribute of humans (the most dynamic element in any socio-technical systems) which is continuously altered according to the system's state, the most appropriate methodology to model the dynamic nature of such systems, is the system dynamics [13].

According to the advantages of SD highlighted by Gregoriades, this study uses the System Dynamic approach to model dynamically human error and, thus, to try to overcome the lack of the second generation HRA methods.

4   Causal Loop Diagrams (CLD) of Human Error

The casual loop diagram, proposed in this work, tries to represent the dynamics of human error in socio-technical systems (Fig. 2). The developed CLD highlights the variables which most influence the human behaviour within a socio-technical system.

The groups of factors that mainly influence human error are described in the followings.

Organizational factors. These factors are defined as external performance shaping factors that are the result of organizational prerequisites and can often be described qualitatively. Organizational characteristics involve the procedures, information, communication, hierarchy levels, organizational structures, workflows, work planning and execution. The organizational process refers to corporate decisions and rules that govern the everyday activities within an organization, including the establishment and the use of standardized operating procedures. The latter, in particular, should be written in clearly manner in order to ensure operator's compliance with them. Other features as safety culture and climate can also influence human motivation and behaviour. Culture refers to the unofficial or unspoken rules, values, attitudes, beliefs, and customs of an organization, while organizational climate refers to a broad class of organizational variables that influence worker performance. In general, however, organizational climate can be viewed as the working atmosphere within the organization [3].

Physical environment. Generally the workstation should be designed to ensure acceptable levels of mental comfort, so that the negative effects of all physical factors

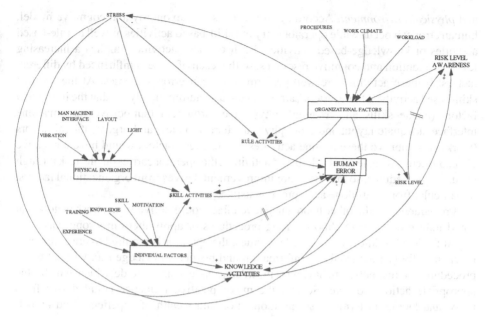

Fig. 2. Causal effect diagram for human performance model

(light, noise, mechanical vibrations, climate, dirt, humidity, air pressure, toxic gas and radiation) that affect operators should be minimized. The man–machine interface should be designed taking into account physical characteristics (anthropometric and biomechanical) and psychological characteristics (mental fatigue and boredom) of the human beings. This interface should improve machine usability in order to achieve performance efficiency and effectiveness [3].

Individual factors. These factors include training, skill, experience, knowledge and motivational factors which, if are appropriate, will enable operator to work more effectively. Motivation is an important behavioural factor that directly influences the decision to act.

Stress factors. The workplace remains a major source of psychological stress [16]. Stress is one of the factors studied to analyse the behaviour of the human factor in the work. For psychologists, stress is the result of any emotional, physical, social, economic or other which requires a response or change in a specific situation. In [17] the authors presented stress as a process in three major conceptual phases, themselves influenced by personal factors, social and environmental. These phases are: stressors, stress and consequences [18]. Stressors are the source of stress existing in the work environment. Stress, the second phase of the stress process, can be long or short term depending on the nature of stressors. This second phase constitutes psychological interpretation and experience of events seen as stressful by an individual. Finally, the consequences, which are behavioural manifestations, psychological, physiological and organizational events, results the prolonged stress.

The causal loop diagram developed in this work highlights how human error is affected by three main groups of variables: *organizational factors, individual characteristics* and *physical environment*. According to Rasmussen's taxonomy and cognitive model, human error can occur while operator carry out skill-based activities as well as rule-based activities or knowledge-based activities. Each of these activities implies a increasing levels of attention and cognitive resources, so that each of these is influenced by different factors. If these activities are well performed, human error decreases. At the level of skill-based activities, the operator carries out the task automatically, so that the individual factors (innate skills and training), physical environment (supportive man-machine interface, adequate layout and other physical characteristics) and organizational factors (workload) improve these routine activities, while stress factors would have a negative effect on them. At the level of rule-based activities, the operator carries out the task through the use of procedures, so that the major improvement derives from organizational factors, in particular from well-done and comprehensible.

Procedures. On the other hand a negative effect could derive from stress factors that could induce operator to choose wrong procedures or apply them in wrong way.

At the level of knowledge-based activities, the operator is required to creatively and independently use the available information and his/her knowledge (i.e. without using procedures or instinctive behaviour), in order to assess and decide which will be the appropriate actions to take. So that the major positive influence could derive from individual factors in terms of strong motivation and wealth of experience and knowledge. Also organizational factors increases knowledge activities mainly due to work climate. A negative impact on knowledge based performance derives from stress factors.

Skill activities, rule activities, knowledge activities, individual factors and stress contribute to the dynamic event that gives rise to human error and indirectly increases the risk level.

The main feedback loop of this model incorporates human error, risk level, risk level awareness, organizational factors and stress. The loop is initiated by the occurrence of human error which subsequently increases risk level, which in turn increases the risk level awareness, which in turn improves organizational factors which increase the level of stress. However stress has a negative effect on human error occurrence; this constitute a reinforcing loop.

5   Case Study

A case study, about a storage LPG distribution plant, is proposed. The causal loop diagram, derived from the conducted analysis (Fig. 3) has some differences with one previously developed. The production activity considered begins with the arrival and weighing of the LPG tankers. Tankers, hooked to a grounding system to avoid electrostatic discharges, are connected to two tanks through two pipes connectors, one for the liquid phase and the other for the gas phase. In order to unload, the tank driver is forced to get down from the vehicle and turn off it in order to open the compartment attachment of pipes and grounding system. These operations are to be carried out each time and require the driver remembering to perform them. These are mnemonic and routine activities so that they are within "skill activities", such the operator performs well-known and routine tasks automatically with little mental processing.

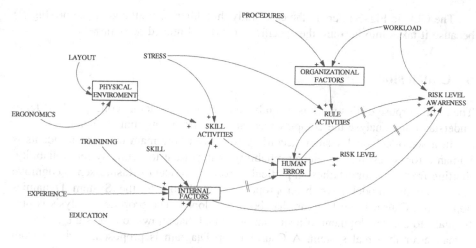

Fig. 3. Causal effect diagram for human performance related to case study

It should be considered that routine and mnemonic tasks could induce the operator in making errors. Therefore, the aim is to understand, in this specific context, what are the variables that come into play and their relationships to assess their impacts on human error and risk level. Training, experience and skills, acquired in carrying out the routine tasks, are the main individual factors which positively affect the variable "skill activities". An element of stress that negatively affects routine tasks of drivers is the workload in terms of hours driving which increases the probability of human error.

Moreover, as the workers of the company must connect the pipes to empty the tanks; in the CLD is stressed the variable "ergonomics" and "layout". A positive relationship between ergonomics and skill activities is expected in terms of appropriate man-system interface and a well-designed layout improves them so as to minimize human error.

The load of the tanks is carried out by pressurizing the contents of the tank. The liquid, under pressure, moves in the conduits till the tank, which will be filled by bubbling. After the load, the valves that connect the arms to the tank are closed and the arms are detached from the connectors. After having described of the loading phase of the LPG, it is passed to the discharge phase. During this phase, they load the tanks for the home delivery of LPG for domestic use, or load the cylinders to be used for food of hobs or stoves for heating of small rooms.

In this scenario, well known and written procedures influence positively "rule activities" by reducing human error, while also the "risk level awareness" play an important role in terms of risk perceived by the operator. According to this analysis it is clear the positive relationship between risk level awareness and individual factors such as education and experience. But on the other hand, the occurrence of human error increases the level of risk and consequently increases objectively the risk awareness that, in this highlighted relationship, does not depend only on individual factors related to risk perception.

The CLD in Fig. 3 refers to the case study that differs from the generic one (Fig. 2) because it takes into account the specific context and related activities.

6   Conclusion

The main purpose of this work is to study and develop a systemic conceptual model to understand and analyse the complex mechanism surrounding human factor.

In a socio-technical system, according to Reason, the main cause of accidents is human error, so estimating human reliability is important to define system reliability. Starting from literature studies, in particular from the model of Rasmussen, a cognitive and taxonomy model have been proposed and thanks to the System Dynamics approach a Causal Loop Diagram has been developed. The proposed analysis is preliminary to the development of a simulation model that allows to assess the impact of human error in a real system. A Causal Loop Diagram is proposed, deriving from literature analysis on taxonomy, in order to model the human error and, therefore anticipate the dynamics of a generic socio-technical system in certain situations and subject to several interacting factors.

References

1. Reason, J.: Human Error. Cambridge University Press, New York (1990)
2. Madonna, M., Martella, G., Monica, L., Pichini Maini, E., Tomassini, L.: The human factor in risk assessment: methodological comparison between human reliability analysis techniques. Prev. Today 5(1/2), 67–83 (2009)
3. IEC 62508: Guidance on human aspects of dependability (2010)
4. Di Pasquale, V., Iannone, R., Miranda, S., Riemma, S.: An overview of human reliability analysis techniques in manufacturing operations. In: Schiraldi, M. (ed.) Operations Management, pp. 221–240. INTech-Open Access Publisher, Osaka (2013)
5. Di Pasquale, V., Miranda, S., Iannone, R., Riemma, S.: A simulator for human error probability analysis (SHERPA). Reliab. Eng. Syst. Saf. 139, 17–32 (2015)
6. Cacciabue, P.C.: Guide to Applying Human Factors Methods. Springer, London (2004)
7. Harwood, K., Sanderson, P.: Skill, rules and knowledge: a discussion of Rasmussen's classification. In: Human Factor Society. A Cradle for Human Factors. Proceedings of the Human Factors Society 30th Annual Meeting, Dayton (OH), USA, p. 1002, September 29–October 3 1986
8. Rasmussen, J.: Human errors: a taxonomy for describing human malfunction in industrial installation. J. Occup. Accid. 4, 311–333 (1982). Elsevier Scientific Publishing Company
9. Forester, J., et al.: The International HRA Empirical Study – final Repot – lessons Learned from Comparing HRA Methods Predictions TO HAMMLAB Simulator Data. HPR -373 OECD Halden Reactor Project, Norway (2013)
10. Swain, A.D., Guttmann, H.E.: Handbook of Human Reliability Analysis with Emphasis on Nuclear Power Plant Applications. NUREG/CR-1278, US Nuclear Regulatory Commission. Washington, DC (1983)
11. Cacciabue, C.: Modelling and simulation of human behavior for safety analysis and control of complex system. Saf. Sci. 28, 97–110 (1998)

12. Mohaghegh, Z., Kazemi, R., Mosleh, A.: Incorporating organizational factors into probabilistic risk assessment (PRA) of complex socio-technical systems: a hybrid technique formalization. Reliab. Eng. Syst. Saf. **94**(5), 1000–1018 (2009)
13. Gregoriades, A.: Human error assessment in complex socio-technical systems- system dynamic versus Bayesian belief network. In: System Dynamics Conference, Manchester (2008)
14. Forrester, J.W.: Industrial Dynamics, p. 464. MIT Press, Cambridge (1961)
15. Sterman, J.D.: Business Dynamic: System Thinking and Modeling for a Complex Word. Irwin McGraw-Hill, Boston (2000)
16. Marchand, A., Demers, A., Durand, P.: Does work really cause distress? The contribution of occupational structure and work organization to the experience of psychological distress. Soc. Sci. Med. **61**(1), 1–14 (2005)
17. Hart, P., Cooper, C.: Occupational Stress: toward a more integrated framework. In: Anderson, N., Ones, D.S., Sinangil, H.K., Viswesvaran, C. (eds.) Handbook of Industrial Work and Organizational Psychology, vol. 2. Sage, London (2001)
18. Harvey, S., Courcy, F., Petit, A., Hudon, J., Teed, M., Loiselle, O., Morin, A.: Organizational interventions and psychological health in the work: a synthesis of Approaches. Report, Institute de Research enSante et Securitie au Travail (IRSST), Montreal (2006)

A System Dynamics Model for Bed Management Strategy in Health Care Units

Giuseppe Converso[1](✉), Sara Di Giacomo[1], Teresa Murino[1], and Teresa Rea[2]

[1] DICMAPI, University of Naples Federico II, Naples, Italy
{giuseppe.converso,sara.digiacomo,murino}@unina.it
[2] Department of Public Health, University of Naples Federico II, Naples, Italy
teresa.rea@unina.it

Abstract. Hospital overcrowding is a universal problem. Currently, Lean thinking is focused on removing process waste and variation. However, the high level of complexity and uncertainty inherent to healthcare make it incredibly challenging to remove variability and achieve the stable process rates necessary for lean redesign efforts to be effective. In this work, in fact, we proposed the Agile logic, which was developed in manufacturing to optimize product delivery in volatile demand environments with highly variable customer requirements. Agile redesign focuses on increasing system responsiveness to customers through improved resource coordination and flexibility. Furthermore, we propose a new method of bed management through the use of DRGs. System dynamics simulation is used to explore the impact of following an agile redesign approach in healthcare on service access and on diagnostic system and the effect of the Bed Manager application to the hospital.

Keywords: Lean · Agile · Healthcare · System dynamics · Bed management

1 Introduction

Public hospitals have, in general, more demand for health services than available capacity. Therefore it is important to forecast and manage demand with good precision in order to adjust capacity or take alternative courses of action. Furthermore, we identify two critical points that plagues most of the hospital structures: the first is overcrowding in the Emergency Department (ED), the second is the lack of free beds.

One of the causes of the overcrowding is demographic aging, which is a shift in the distribution of a country's population towards older ages. Another factor is the inability (real or perceived) of find general practitioner, which could act as a filter to the recourse to hospital treatment. Furthermore, the emergency room guarantees availability 24/7 and it is often considered as a general consultancy area where people go for every indisposition or disease.

Other problems are difficulty getting timely consultation from non-ED physicians and difficulty getting diagnostic procedures scheduled and results returned. It often

© Springer International Publishing Switzerland 2015
H. Fujita and G. Guizzi (Eds.): SoMeT 2015, CCIS 532, pp. 610–622, 2015.
DOI: 10.1007/978-3-319-22689-7_47

happens that a lot of patients are kept waiting in ED for a long time because of unavailability or reactivity of ambulance which have to transfer patients from ED to other wards.

The shortage of beds in the hospital, instead, is principally due to the fact that hospitals have the difficulty, if not impossibility, of balancing an unknown demand of treating and the available resources in terms of beds for patients, nursing staff and other facilities. In addition, it is important to note that the patients are admitted to hospital both for election and emergency cases.

In particular, an elective patient's admission is planned by the hospital, following a decision by a consultant to admit. In contrast, an emergency admission comes suddenly following an accident or the onset of an acute illness. Such a situation means that it is deeply difficult to predict in advance the number of people who needs care.

2 Literature Review

Many healthcare organizations adopt the Toyota Production System as the practices and the performance improvement that often called the Lean Healthcare management system [1]. There are many studies proven that implementation lean in healthcare given positively result for healthcare performances. Study by Koning [2], found that lean could controlling healthcare cost increase, improving quality and providing better in healthcare. Furthermore a better utilization of resources, rationalizing the layout and use of space may contribute to reduce significantly lead times, and consequently waiting lists, also with higher patient arrival rates [3].

T. Papadopoulas [4] take advantage from the deployment of continuous improvement (Kaizen) in healthcare system. The purpose of his work was to explore the link between continuous improvement and dynamic actor associations through a case of lean thinking implementation in healthcare, in particular his study was conducted in Pathology Unit of NHSCO hospital in UK NHS. Such a study demonstrates: the improvements in turnaround times for all specimens inpatients, outpatients and doctors; lower costs; help in quicker clinical decisions and more efficient patient care.

With the growing complexity of healthcare, providers are increasingly dependent on sharing care delivery activities with other, specialized healthcare professionals to provide adequate patient care. As well the relationship between pharmaceutical companies and hospitals is one of the most important key factors in healthcare system [5]. In Lean Healthcare, "energy efficiency" means also to make better use of the energy resources available, and try to achieve the main objective represented by the care of as many patients as possible, with the use of the smallest amount of energy possible [6].

However, the variability and unpredictability inherent to healthcare demand and internal operations render this assignment of taking care of patients, difficult to manage. Individual patient cases are variable and work cannot always proceed according to schedule or plan. New developments in a patient's condition, unexpected diagnostic findings or surprising reactions to medication may call for sudden changes in planned process with ripple effects throughout the service supply chain. J.Vries and R.Huijsman [7] in their paper "Supply Chain Management in health services: an overview" seek to concentrate on the question whether any parallels can be found between the industrial sector and health care services with respect to the developments that have taken place in the area of Supply Chain Management. In particular they proposed the alternative improvement paradigm of "agile" as a means to improve healthcare service delivery. Rust [8] in his work, highlight the importance of designing care systems that respond effectively to variability in patient demand; how improving demand responsiveness can also lead to reduced costs, as resources are matched more effectively to demand; and provide healthcare practitioners and leaders with practical insights for applying simple, effective operational plans to improve performance in their own healthcare delivery systems.

3   The Proposed Model

The System Dynamics (SD) is a method to the study of the behaviour of systems (in particular of socio/economic systems) which emphasizes the role of the plan between policies, decision-making structures and time delays that influence the dynamic phenomena.

In the last twenty years the SD approach has become an appropriate choice for modelling healthcare systems, as it encourages both a systemic view of the interactions of patient flows and a strategic perspective on the management of healthcare delivery systems.

The software chosen for the construction and representation of the model is the Powersim Study of Powersim Software. This software allows plotting any complex system to be analysed by the SD method, translating transparently to the user-entered information in mathematical equations necessary to the formulation of the model itself.

For each variable of *stock* (the stocks show the state of the model at each instant), it was given as start value a matrix type and not a scalar one. The matrix has a fixed size *(n x m)*, where *n* is the number of patients, which make access to the hospital during the period of the simulation and *m* is the number of the features associated with each patient.

The use of the matrices within the model prevents the loss of information, associated with each patient, allowing to view, instant by instant, all the rows of the matrix that crosses the entire structure. In any stock variable of the model, this matrix, of fixed size, will present all void lines except those corresponding to the patient present, at that moment, within the variable considered.

In Figs. 1, 2 are shown the two most important part of the simulation model achieved for our analysis.

As soon as a doctor, a surgeon or an orthopaedist is free, under our model, priority for input is first given to the patient with the highest priority triage code and then to the patient who has been waiting for the longest time.

In Fig. 2. two flow variables are shown: the former is *Elective Patient* that daily feeds the hospitalization of a certain number of patients depending on the availability of beds. The latter, *Recovery Start Status* fits, in the initial time of the simulation, 800 patients so as to create an initial state as verisimilar as possible.

The data used for this work have been collected from "Cardarelli" Hospital database (that plays a strategic role in the hospital emergency network of the metropolitan area of Naples, Italy) in a time range of three years (2011–2013).

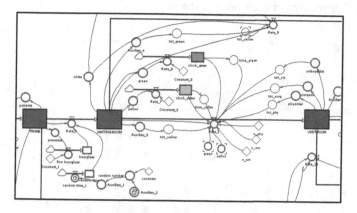

Fig. 1. The patient flow

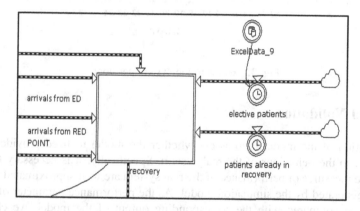

Fig. 2. Election input to the system

The collection of data related to a period even earlier would have been useless because the technological innovations, social and behavioural changes that have altered the characteristics of the healthcare system.

To model the daily patient flow of "Cardarelli" Hospital, we have analysed the distribution of access to the system per hour.

Making use of the data provided by the Hospital, on average, 250 patients come through the emergency department each day, distributed as in Fig. 3.

In this picture. we note that the inputs are highly variable throughout the day. The major peak of inputs is in the late morning, between 10 am and 12 am. Moreover, an arrival is a random event and thus the waiting time of a random arrival is distributed as an exponential random negative variable.

It is well-known that if the number of arrivals in an interval of time T is a random variable Poisson of parameter λ, then the time T between two consecutive arrivals is a exponential random negative variable having an average value of 1/λ. We have evaluated the rates λ from the real data. Such a rates represent the number of access to Emergency Department in each hour of the day.

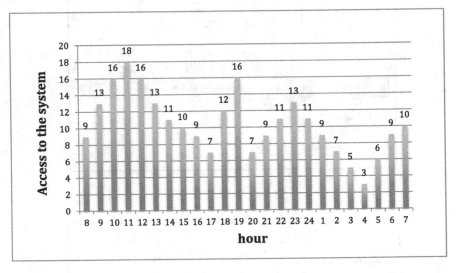

Fig. 3. Access to the system per hour

4 Model Validation

The validation of the model is to assess whether the model realized provides results comparable to the behaviour of the real system. Specifically, it is necessary to verify whether the measures of performance of the real system are well approximated from the measures generated by the simulation model. As the performance parameter of the real system to be compared with the corresponding output of the model, we chose the average number of gurneys present throughout the hospital during the day. The reason of this choice is due to the fact that the shortage of beds in the face of such a high number of accesses, both from the emergency room and election, means that the number of patients lying on a gurney is an important factor to understand the state of emergency of the hospital in terms of overcrowding.

For the validation of the model we make a hypothesis test for comparing the means of the two populations. The first test used is Student's t-test:

$$t = \frac{\bar{X}_2 - \bar{X}_1}{s\sqrt{1/n + 1/m}} \tag{1}$$

Where S^2 is the Pooled variance defined as:

$$S^2 = \frac{(n-1)S_1^2 + (m-1)S_2^2}{(n+m-2)} \tag{2}$$

and it is equivalent to the average of the two sample variances "weighted" with the respective degrees of freedom.

At this point, to perform the Student's t-test will proceed as follows.

We will define the null hypothesis H_0 and the hypothesis to be rejected H_1:

$$H_0 = [\bar{x}_1 = \bar{x}_2]; H_1 = [\bar{x}_1 \neq \bar{x}_2] \tag{3}$$

After the calculation of the degrees of freedom v, given by the difference between the number of observations and the number of compared groups, it defines the significance level of the test α and extrapolating from its tables the critical values $t_{0.025}$ and $-t_{0.025}$ that define the rejection region of H_0:

$$v = n + m - 2;$$
$$\alpha = 0.05;$$
$$t_{0.025} = 2,00039$$

The average number of gurneys was finally calculated at 3 pm and then has been made the average of 30 days (a single simulation run).

The main parameters of our samples are:

$$Real\, data : \bar{x}_1 = 230.8;\ S_1^2 = 111.9$$

$$Modelled\, data : \bar{x}_2 = 234.4;\ S_2^2 = 154.6$$

$$S^2 = 133.24;\ v = 58$$

$$t = 1.18$$

Since $|t| = 1.18$ in this case $t < t_{0.025}$, it implies that the Student's test is verified, with a confidence interval of $1 - \alpha = 0.95$.

In Fig. 4 has compared the performance of the real data and those obtained from the simulation.

Furthermore, it is possible to realize the hypotheses test of variance of the two populations, in fact, calling with S_1^2 and S_2^2 the estimations of variances of two independent Gaussian variables (σ_1^2 and σ_2^2), we get the Z Fisher variable:

$$Z = \frac{S_1^2 \sigma_2^2}{S_2^2 \sigma_1^2} \tag{4}$$

with $n-1$ and $m-1$ degrees of freedom, where n and m are the size of the two samples. Fixed assumptions $H_0 = \{\sigma_1^2 = \sigma_2^2\}$ and $H_1 = \{\sigma_2^2 < \sigma_1^2\}$, we assume that the function (4), in which we place $\sigma_1^2 = \sigma_2^2$ becomes:

$$Z = \frac{s_1^2}{s_2^2} = \frac{111.9}{154.6} = 0,72 < z_{0.95} = 1.86 \quad v_1 = v_2 = 29 \tag{5}$$

In accordance with the result of Fisher's test, the simulation model is proved to be validated.

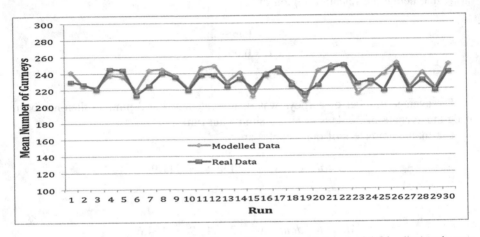

Fig. 4. Mean number of gurneys evaluated over 30 run of simulation model (blue line) and mean number of gurneys evaluated each month on real data (red line) (Color figure online)

5 Model Results

The aim of the simulation is to compare the results of the "to-be" simulation with the "as-is" one, in order to verify possible improvement of performance Fig. 5.

For this comparison, we used the same input data both for the "as-is" and "to-be" configuration. Currently the management of the hospital is based on a strictly Lean philosophy; therefore the sizing of the necessary resources was evaluated on a value of constant λ for 24 h Fig. 6.

The critical point that we can observe from the model simulation is the elapsed time in which the patients wait for the report consultation.

The logic Agile allows us to move resources within the hospital in certain time periods in which, given the influx of people, situations of overcrowding will be created.

If, as has been seen from the analysis of data related to the inputs to the Emergency Room, the peaks occur in late morning, so it is conceivable to introduce a medical resource that performs medical reports with some delay with respect to the phenomena of peak. This time lag is due to the time that the patient takes from the entrance to the emergency room to the instant in which he/she performed the examinations and he/she is awaiting the reporting by a physician. In the following figure it is represented the number of people in waiting.

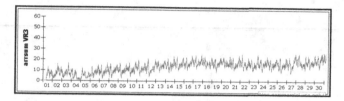

Fig. 5. "as-is" configuration of patients in waiting room 3.

This number achieves the value of 23 patients.

Below we show the results regarding the number of people in this visit room following the introduction of an additional medical resource.

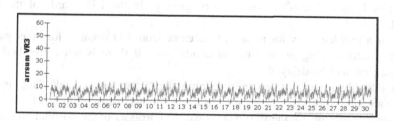

Fig. 6. "to-be" configuration of patients in visit room 3.

The maximum number of people who are waiting for the reporting is 13, while the average value is equal to 7, then the result obtained with this "to-be" is a substantial improvement in the performance of the system. This can be seen by a significant lowering of the number of people that in every moment are waiting for medical examinations or medical reports.

Another performance indicator is the mean number of people on gurneys every day, because how we have said earlier this an important factor to understand the state of emergency of the hospital in terms of overcrowding. In the "as-is" configuration we have in average 230 patients on gurneys per day as it is shown in the Fig. 7.

Having come to the conclusion that Agile logic improves the level of services in the Emergency Department (at least in the management of support system), we will examine what would happen to the number of patients on gurneys, with this hypothesis Fig. 8.

Fig. 7. Number of patients on gurneys with an "as-is" configuration of ED.

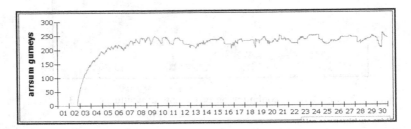

Fig. 8. "to-be" configuration of patients on gurneys.

The average number is unchanged, so this conclusion is not going to affect the problem of beds and thus the presence of gurneys in the ED, wards of the entire hospital.

This is a problem only for patients who came from ED because for other patients (elective patients) being in "non-urgent conditions", if there is not a free bed, their hospitalization will be delayed.

The difficulties encountered in managing the "emergency" and "programmed" involves a number of inefficiencies such as cancellations and/or slipping of admissions to election and patients (in the ED) that crowd the corridors of the hospital on gurneys.

The new professional figure of Bed Manager has a tack of place patients in beds on the wards that are most appropriate to their needs. However, bed availability within a hospital setting is constantly fluctuating and changing in response to the number of planned and emergency admissions, discharges and patient movement and transfer between specialities and ward areas. When patients need to be admitted to hospital in an emergency it is important they are admitted quickly and to an appropriate bed. For patients being admitted for routine surgery, it is important to minimise the number of occasions that admissions are cancelled as a result of there being no bed available.

The specific activities of the bed manager are:

- Programming activities of hospitalization;
- Management of waiting lists of specialist outpatient visits;
- Creation of a "pull" system for the use of beds for home care residents;
- Differentiation of beds of emergency and of election;
- Efficient and effective use of the Discharge Room aimed at making the bed available as soon as the patient can be discharged;
- Creating a system for predicting bed use during peak periods urgency;

Differently from what we founded in literature about application of Bed Manager in hospital system, in this work we want to give an instrument through which this figure could exhort the head department to discharge patients. This tool is a statistical estimate of the average time of hospitalization for each disease that is valuated in the Diagnosis Related Group (DRG) [9].

The grouping of hospitalizations in DRG is done by software called Grouper, which attributes the DRGs analysing a series of clinical and personal information on hospitalization. The information categories are: diagnosis codes and procedure, age and sex of the patient, duration of admission and discharge mode.

For each DRG there is defined a specific upper limit of duration of hospitalization, above which the patient's length of stay is considered anomalous. This upper limit is calculated by taking into consideration all hospitalizations for acute illness in the ordinary regime, according to the following formula:

$$T_{DRG} = \left[\sqrt[3]{q_3} + \left(\sqrt[3]{q_3} - \sqrt[3]{q_1} \right) \right]^3 \qquad (6)$$

Where T_{DRG} is the threshold value of the DRG in question (usually defined trim point), q_1 and q_3 are, respectively, the first and third quartile of the distribution of the durations of hospitalization [6].

The hospitalizations for abnormal length of stay are usually defined as admissions "above the threshold" or outlier.

Making use of the DRG value, the Bed Manager make a pressure on the departments heads of the hospital in order to discharge patients that have overcame the threshold value, thereby improving the turnover rate of hospitalized patients.

Without any doubt, the patient length of stay could pass the threshold value for worsening of the clinical condition, breakdowns in machinery (for example the CAT), late in availability of theatre rooms. In this case the hospitalization time will be not considered abnormal.

The proposed structure for the introduction of the Bed Manager within the model is described below: a vector containing the times of the DRG for each patient was introduced into the model. The variable level of "Bed turn around time" counts the length of stay of the patient within the department. As soon as the patient has a greater Bed Turn around Time (BTT) than his time defined by the DRG, the variable level "outlier" starts to count.

On the other hand, in the following structure the number of people who are on a gurney are compared with a value considered "physiological" in accordance with the number of gurneys within in the entire hospital. When the actual value exceeds the physiological, the level variable "level of pressure" increases so that we have an emergency situation with a high number of patients on gurneys.

The level variable "n_discharge" continuously raises only if "outlier" is greater than zero (there are people to discharge) and "level of pressure" is also positive. This is considered to be an emergency situation from the point of view of gurneys. As soon as this variable (n_discharge) is greater than zero, the system will discharge the patient who has passed the threshold value by more time Fig. 9.

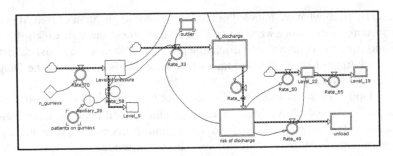

Fig. 9. Bed management

The variable level "Risk of Discharge" increases in a direct correlation to discharges made by the Bed Manager. There is a significant risk that a patient would be discharged in advance. After 24 h this level is cleared through the level variable "unload". Then analyse the results after applying the "Bed Manager":

From the graph it can be observed qualitatively that the number of gurneys, from an average value equal to 230 was reduced in some days of the simulation Fig. 10.

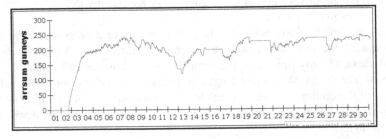

Fig. 10. "to-be 4" configuration of patients on gurneys after the implementation of BM.

Measuring the difference between the mean number of discharged per day between the two configurations "as-is" (blue line) and "to-be" (red line), we note that on average we get a decrease in the number of patients on gurneys by about 8 %. This value was calculated without taking into consideration several days of simulation, particularly the 1st and the 2nd day (since they represent a transition phase of filling of the hospital) and the 12th and 13th day (characterized by an excessive discharge from the simulation algorithm) Fig. 11.

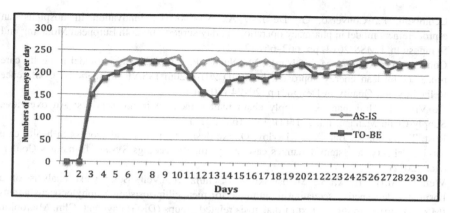

Fig. 11. Comparison between the "as-is" and "to-be" configuration

6 Conclusions

Main objective of this paper was the realization of a dynamic model of random access to hospital, we have, in fact, created a simulation model of schematization of matrix type representing the dynamics of complex systems such as the ED. Furthermore, this model can be used as a Decision Support System (DSS) because, running a series of experiments, we can evaluate what should be the delay in agile oversizing or as it must be brought the time cycle or how long it is necessary the oversizing of the solution agile. From the cycle time we could derive what are the number of resources needed with the known formulas.

At the end for the second problem that we have analysed that is the management of beds by the Bed Manager, what could make its work more efficient is to try to give this figure a tool that would allow him to accelerate the turnover of patients admitted. Indeed, we have talked about the DRG and hospitalization times average assessed for different pathology. The patient admitted that exceeded these time limits, unless of possible contingencies, had to be discharged. By operating in this way we have achieved a decrease in the number of patients on gurneys by about 8 %.

References

1. Poksinska, B.: The current state of Lean implementation in the health care: literature review. Qual. Manage. Health Care **19**(4), 319–329 (2010)
2. de Koning, H., Verver, J.P.S., van den Heuvel, J., Bisgaard, S., Does, R.J.M.M.: Lean six sigma in healthcare. J. Healthc. Qual. **28**(2), 4–11 (2006)
3. Gallo, M., Di Nardo M., Murino T., Santillo, L.C.: A simulation based approach for improving healthcare systems. In: Advances in Computer Science, pp. 387–392. WSEAS Press (2012)
4. Papadopoulos, T., Radnor, Z., Merali, Y.: The role of actor associations in understanding the implementation of lean thinking in healthcare. Int. J. Oper. Prod. Manage. **31**(2), 167–191 (2011)

5. Centobelli, P., Converso, G., De Iasi, A., Murino, T.: Innovation in hospitals: an e-procurement model in pharmacy operations in day surgery. In: 26th European Modeling and Symposium, EMSS 2014, pp. 662–667 (2014)
6. Converso, G., Ascione, M., Di Nardo, M., Natale, P.: An optimization model in health care processes by lean energy approach. In: RQD 2014, 20th ISSAT International Conference Reliability and Quality in Design, pp. 20–24 (2014)
7. De Vries, J., Huijsman, R.: Supply chain management in health services: An overview. Supply Chain Manage. Int. J. **16**(3), 159–165 (2011)
8. Rust, T., Saeed, K., Bar-On, I., Pavlov, O.: Re-designing policy and process in health care service delivery: a system dynamics case study. In: Proceedings System Dynamics Conference (2012)
9. Wernitz, M.H., Keck, S., Swidsinski, S., Schulz, S., Veit, S.K.: Cost analysis of a hospital-wide selective screening programme for methicillin-resistant Staphylococcus aureus (MRSA) carriers in the context of diagnosis related groups (DRG) payment. Clin. Microbiol. Infect. **11**(6), 466–471 (2005)

A Simulation Approach for Agile Production Logic Implementation in a Hospital Emergency Unit

Giuseppe Converso[✉], Giovanni Improta, Manuela Mignano, and Liberatina C. Santillo

DICMAPI - University of Naples Federico II, Naples, Italy
{giuseppe.converso, giovanni.improta, mignano, santillo}@unina.it

Abstract. The hospitals offer sweeping views of management ideas, as focus internally complex organizational structures, which can be improved in order to reduce waste and increase the effectiveness of the services provided. An analysis of the hospital system there are two characteristics: the demand variability and the variability of lead time. As a policy of innovative management of the health system is referred to Lean even though the characteristics identified do not allow you to get the continuous flow that is the strategic goal of Lean obtainable only with demand leveling and production lead time certain and repeatable. A management system that seems to contemplate these characteristics is the Agile Manufacturing applied to service sector, even though it has never been declined in health. Thus arises the need to simulate both policies so as to determine which best represents the health facilities.

Keywords: Healthcare · Lean production · Lean healthcare · Agile manufacturing · Agile healthcare · System dynamics · Simulation

1 Introduction

The problem of overcrowded facilities emergency/urgency is becoming one of the most important issue in healthcare management. Overcrowding means long waits for patients, it's the cause of increase of time spent at the hospital with the risk of infection, improper use of human resources.

For this reason, the research team of DICMAPI decided to develop a simulation model focused on the production dynamic of Emergency and Acceptance Departments. The goal of this work consists in understanding how the management acts to eliminate, or at least reduce, the critical issues that affect these health units.

2 State of Art

The most advanced studies about the production systems consider two methodologies: Lean Production (with healthcare applications) and Agile Manufacturing.

© Springer International Publishing Switzerland 2015
H. Fujita and G. Guizzi (Eds.): SoMeT 2015, CCIS 532, pp. 623–634, 2015.
DOI: 10.1007/978-3-319-22689-7_48

2.1 Lean Healthcare

The Institute for Healthcare Improvement affirms that Lean principles are applicable in the context of healthcare and that should be created the same gains, in terms of efficiency and quality, seen in other areas. However, in practice, the principles and lean tools translation in health care systems is very challenging. One of the main difficulties consists in establishing the "value".

The value concept underlying the clinical dimension is attributable to the achievement of the best result in terms of health for the patient.

The operational dimension regards the provision manner of benefits and services, whose evaluation is made in terms of cost/benefit ratio. The value in this context implies the satisfaction of needs at the lowest cost.

The experiential perspective is characterized from the ability of health facilities to maintain over time the relationship with patients, improving at the same time the level of satisfaction, trust and loyalty. This latter dimension draws extremely subjective and emotional aspects, related to the patient's outcome perception of received service, and the relationship quality, created with the providers of care.

The concept of multidimensional value is inclusive of the other two dimensions: economic and social.

The economic dimension is relative to the phenomenon of clinical risk; the concept of value is due, on the one hand to the potential cost reduction (in terms of damages) incurred by companies as a decrease result of clinical risk, on the other hand the increase in revenues, earned by virtue of the 'sale' performance (the patient prefers to head to the facilities which were generally more reliable). Value creation is directly linked, therefore, to the ability to achieve customer satisfaction which, in turn, is the perception that the customer feels about what and how his hopes and expectations have been realized [1].

The social value dimension refers to the ability to maintain and improve the overall health status of the population. In this case, the relational aspect of quality concerns both the relationships between professionals within the structures and users, both the creation of networks aimed at the dissemination and sharing of knowledge and exchange of experiences and best practices, within the health system.

The "global" value should help to simplify the process of identifying the main goal of a lean organization, or innovation, through the reduction of waste, conservation of resources and the overall system improvement [2].

Other studies, finally, demonstrated through empirical analysis, the actual improvement of business performance in terms of reduced costs, waiting times and response, increase in quality, patient satisfaction, staff and suppliers [3].

The goal of any Lean initiative is to focus on the needs of customers at the highest level, identifying and ultimately eliminating waste. Medical units recognize the patient as a critical factor to consider during the design process and in providing assistance.

Hagg et al., state that the Lean is an effective tool for the identification and elimination of waste from the process. The advantage and the aim of applying the Lean approach to the health sector is to a better approach to reduce waste, in addition to reducing the waiting time, and for the construction of quality, speed and flexibility in the organization [4].

According to Shrestha and Rexhepi, the implementation of the Lean is not possible without the support of top management. Therefore, leadership is recognized as critical to the implementation of quality systems in Lean approach. The organization cannot be successful in Lean if it hasn't the necessary culture, skilled workers, the buy-in from top management and strong leadership. Abdullah et al., pointed out that the involvement of employees is one of the most important factors for improving the quality. This is because the workers behavior plays an important role on customer perception of service quality [5].

Implemented in the context of health care, then, the Lean approach is commonly used to reduce the delays of the patients in the emergency room, doctors and eliminate medication errors, and prevent to inadequate procedures. This approach in the health sector focuses on improving process efficiency through the elimination of waste, or muda, defined as any activity that consumes resources but that generate no redeeming value to the patient [6].

Summarizing, the five critical issues with which all hospitals are called to face, are: resources allocation between Emergency Department (ED) and the other hospital units in the activities of patients receiving, treating, hospitalizing and discharging with the maximum suitability; surgical waiting lists management; overall costs reduction; length of hospital stays consideration; hospital acquired infections increase [7].

2.2   Agile Healthcare

In terms of production system, healthcare is particular field of service delivery composed by a wide number of different activities, whose demand is highly variable and unpredictable [8].

Precisely for this reason, the methodology Agile Manufacturing has recently been proposed as a means to improve the delivery of health care services. Despite of this vision, specific management policies and practices, have not yet been developed for services field including health assistance [9]. Moreover, the comparative effectiveness of Agile practices is unknown, while theoretical concepts Agile Manufacturing seem perfectly suited to improve healthcare organizations performances.

In order to maintain a competitive advantage and minimize costs, the common practice in the health sector is to define the staffing levels equal to the average demand of the service, as opposed to the concept of satisfaction of peak demand [10].

Although these management strategies help reduce personnel costs related to work, this trend leads to the undesirable consequence of deficient care units during periods of peak demand. This involves the use of excessive overtime as management solution to obtain the necessary flexibility. Excessive overtime involve higher rates of fatigue and error, contributing to increase risks to patient safety and to the deterioration of care quality. These considerations further strengthen the issue related to the changing of healthcare production system model.

The supply chain in the healthcare setting is characterized by some unique features that make it difficult to direct application of the knowledge gathered in the industrial sectors, to the health sector [11]. The unpredictable and stochastic demand, leads to the need for customized services. The impossibility of stocking finished products in a buffer, the wide number of care processes, and the good results of Lean method application to hospital units different to Emergency Department have so far prevented the implementation of the Agile Manufacturing methodology in ED unit [12].

In the paper "Adapting Agile Strategies to Healthcare Service Delivery" Rust, Saeed, Baron and Pavlov, the Agility is defined as a paradigm that improves the Healthcare environment, being the Agility a feature suitable for supply chain with volatile and unpredictable demand. In the same work they also define the Healthcare as one of the most complex systems to manage. The solution they proposed, consists in a clinical network of doctors and paramedics, abolishing the idea of medical staff composed by as individual operators, which deals with the provision of healthcare [13].

Kane et al. (2007) found that the mismatch between resources and demand peak is the main source of fatigue; it reduces quality of care in most health services. With management systems currently in place, this variable leads to errors in care delivery and increases risks to patient safety. In particular, the stresses posed by variability on the health system lead to an increase in medication errors, nosocomial infections, sicker patients, and are a major cause of adverse outcomes for the patient.

Ensure proper synchronization of resources to meet the peaks and troughs in demand, it is clearly crucial to provide high quality in health care.

The health managers, in fact, face a significant gap in knowledge about the optimal design and management of complex systems of care that ensure effective treatment of the patient.

As those issues are extensively described and well analyzed with great clarity in the literature, we put in evidence the lean and agile principles set out in the mentioned papers, in order to demonstrate the need to deepen the issues of implementation of services delivery Agile system to healthcare field and, furthermore, to indicate the utility of its use.

3 Proposed Model

The System Dynamics (SD) is a simulation methodology based on mathematical models development. The perspective of analysis is geared toward identifying, studying and understanding of systems, characterized by complex feedback relationships between different variables. The goal of the SD consists in combining into a single approach, the formal reconstruction of the causal structure of a system, reproducing the observation of the dynamic behavior of the same structure, generated through simulation. Among the tools used in System Dynamics, one of the most important to show and summarize the systems balance, is named causal loop diagram; for these reasons the SD logic well represents the interaction between dynamic elements (Fig. 1).

The causal loop diagram (CLD) is a representation that consists of a set of variables, interconnected by arrows, which indicate the influence between the random variables themselves. The CLD can provide a first graphical interpretation of the problem and provide a simple and schematic representation of the assumptions made in relation to the underlying causes of the performance problem, clearly illustrating the feedback mechanisms [14].

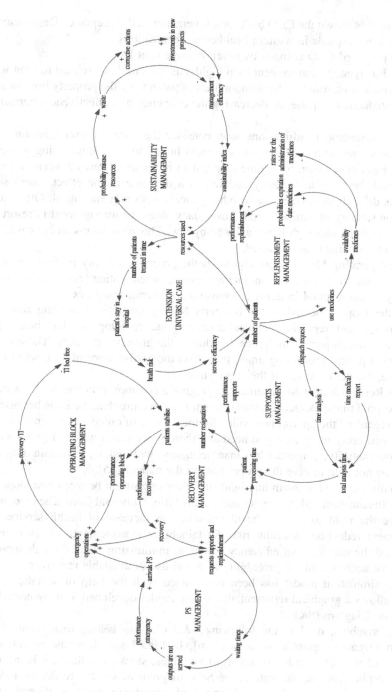

Fig. 1. Causal loop diagram

Below it is shown the CLD built for a Emergency and Acceptance Department, that characterizes hospitals in western healthcare organizations.

The proposed CLD is made by seven management loops.

The Emergency Management loop highlights the problems related to long waiting times, which often result in the abandonment of patients by the property itself or at least the dissatisfaction of patients, decreasing the efficiency and effectiveness performance of ER.

The Management Admissions loop consider the issue of execution timing and examinations reporting with its consequences linked to time lengthening of hospitalization. Beds occupation for a time longer than necessary, causes a waste in financial terms, and therefore inefficiency, as well as a decrease in the effectiveness since it becomes difficult to devote care to other patients with a greater need. Often, a compensation strategy of available beds inadequacy, does the management to resort to the use of stretchers, although is not allowed by law. This also entails an increased health risk to which patients are exposed.

The Operating Management highlights the process criticality in disposing surgery activities and hospitalization in intensive care, when patient accesses saturate the capacity of the hospital in terms of human and material resources.

In the loop dedicated to the Supports Management the execution time of the examination and reporting (clinical-chemical and radiological) has been split to understand which part of the process is due to the greatest criticality. These tasks are reflected in patient processing times, that affect the performance of such activities and, therefore, the performance of the entire structure.

The Replenishment Management highlights a common problem for a lot of operating hospital units; medication management is often a problematic issue because of the choice regarding the appropriate policy for the lot size of orders. The scenarios are two viable: you order more than you need and then undergoes a waste of goods for inactivity and maturity; you order less than necessary, with risking to remain drug devoid and to be not able to give the proper care to the patient [15].

Finally the CLD diagram highlights the clear opposition between two loops which are the Sustainability Management and Extensibility Universal Cure. The latter tends to preserve the right to citizens health, pushing an increase of health service with a consequent reduction in health risk. Sustainability management, however, tends to safeguard the management efficiency aiming at minimizing waste through appropriate corrective actions, and the probability of a bad use of available resources.

The simulation model has been constructed with the help of specific software, which allows a graphical representation of the model developed, usually named Stock and Flow Diagram (S&F).

The symbols, used in the following S&F diagram belong to a standard set of System Dynamics graphic semantics [16]. In Fig. 2 we show the model, even if because of its wide number of involved variables, stocks and flows, it is not easy to read. Despite this graphic feature, the S&F diagram makes the reader to understand from a qualitative point of view, which is high complexity grade of ED real operative model.

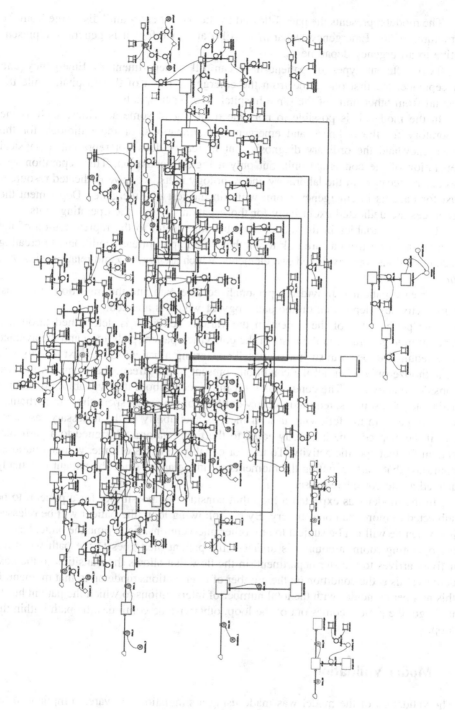

Fig. 2. Simulation model by S&F diagram

The model represents the path followed by the patient entry until discharge from the structures of the Emergency Department (ED) and therefore it is generally representative to all urgency departments.

Two different types of patient flow can fill a department to Emergency and Acceptance: the first one came from the emergency room of the hospital, while the second from other units of the same hospital or other hospitals.

In the model, it is possible to note the doubling of some activities, such as the laboratory for the ordinary and emergency examinations, or the radiology for the emergency and the ordinary diagnosis, but in reality does not represent a physical separation of the concerned unit, but only a logical separation. This separation was necessary because, in the laboratory and radiology units, we have dedicated resources just for patients in emergency room; while in the rest of Emergency Department the resources are dedicated exclusively for those patients within the operating units.

The flow variables in the model have become useful to the representation of the patient transition from a care task to another under appropriate conditions. In creating such conditions were exploited two elements, which are *for loop* and relationships *if...*, *then*.

For each patient is provided a personalized care path and the transition or at least some activities, depending on the pathology of which is affected.

The permanence of the patient in the various activities is determined through a random time generated in the basis of the concerned patient pathology and the average time required to perform such activities. Transferring a patient to the next activity will be authorize only when all the conditions present in the stream that connects the two considered activities. The conditions built into account both the availability of human and material resources, required to carry out both of the actual spent time. In particular, you can perform the following task, if there is availability of the necessary resources and if the elapsed time is exactly equal to the time randomly assigned to a particular patient for that specific activity. To test for equality in terms of time, you can build an hourglass that starts counting the moments of time elapsed since the patient is actually arrived at the considered asset.

In the model was expected a loop that consider the possibility for a patient, to be subjected to more than one surgery. By the following loop, the patient will be released just when he will not be subject to any other interventions. Each time the patient enters the operating room, a counter is updated; the patient then goes to the path when the activity arrives to transfer department, in the flow that allows the transition to the next activity; this is the condition on the number of interventions made up to that moment. If this number coincides with the total number of interventions to which the patient has to undergo, the patient comes out of the loop, otherwise he continues the path within the loop.

4 Model Validation

The validation of the model was made using a simulation software, compliant to the System Dynamics paradigm. We loaded an array of data, performed by the time series of access, of A.0.R.N. "A. Cardarelli" hospital, sited in Naples.

The first problem linked to the validation concerns to identify the minimum time frame such that they present a cyclical function of load. This horizon we choose, is equal to one day and must be divided into intervals statistically significant. They were considered 24 intervals of amplitude equal to 1 h. For each of these it can be stated that the distribution of access follows a Poisson distribution, each offering a different characteristic coefficient k. So, for each time horizon statistically significant it was possible to calculate a k which represents the rate at which you record accesses. At this point, the matrix was generated simulation data, refer to a time period of 30 days, taking into account the k found in the time series of real data. The data matrix used has a size of 7720 rows by 21 columns, i.e. 7720 patients were considered, this being the average number of accesses at the ED registered in 30 days, and of each patient.

Validation of the model was done by the aid of the two statistical tests: Student T test and Fisher F test.

From a historic series of collected data over a three years time horizon by making an appropriate stratification of them, and eliminating any outliers, the trends of the average load beds factor were regarded 30 time, each with a width of 30 days, being the month horizon simulation chosen. As simulated data, however, were considered trends of the average coefficient for 30 run simulation.

After a proper calculation related to exposed procedure, both hypothesis tests, T of Student and F of Fisher were satisfied.

5 Model Results

An analysis of the historic series of accesses at the Cardarelli Hospital Emergency Department, the accesses load wave appears to have not a level shape and resources have a configuration partially stationary or rather stationary within the work shift, but not stationary over of all day. In particular, the wave of the accesses load is distributed as a Poisson within each statistically significant interval, where the latter will have a width equal to 1 h. Therefore the hour is the minimum interval that it's possible to chose, so that al least a phenomenon (within that time frame) can be recorded.

The improvement is proposed is the re-engineering of the system, through the allocation of resources, allowing you to switch from a "partially stationary configuration of resources" to an "agile resources configuration". This changing needs to balance the accelerations that occur, and the demand peaks of accesses at the hospital.

The most critical problems have been recorded in management of supports units, because of the long time reporting, and management of operations, presenting the ED a wide number of patients in conditions of emergency surgery [17].

To balance the Δk_{max} we supposed to plan the availability of one more resource that will be scheduled in the time slot that corresponds to the demand peak over the lead time necessary to the patient in order to arrive at bottleneck activities, or activity where there is congestion of service requests [18]. For the re-engineering, we considered appropriate, moving a resource from the process of medical examination since it was possible to observe that, when there is a demand peak, you rather have a few requests for medical examination; under these phenomenologic hypothesis, it's possible the resource shift from the most "low charge" unit to the most "high charge" one.

This resource will be a doctor with versatile features or with flexible behaviors, so that he is skilled to perform multiple tasks with satisfying results [19].

Regarding the activities of surgery, we have simulated the disposition of an operating room and a operating team more, in the slot time, which corresponds to the demand peak over the lead time, necessary to ensure that the patient arrives in such activity, starting from the moment he accesses the hospital. Both the surgical team that the hall will be added to the emergency management and will be removed from the management of long term planned interventions [20].

The proposed improvement was evaluated through the simulation model, and in particular by monitoring the values of the beds load factor, which is configured as a primary indicator of reference, and by three other indicators during the execution of 30 runs with new resource configuration.

The four considered indicators are: the load factor of beds; the average residence time in the hospital; the maximum waiting time to which the patient may be exposed before being subjected to the intervention; the average time of (laboratory or radiology) exams reporting [21].

The reconfiguration of resources was performed considering separately the two critical processes (exam reporting and surgery interventions) by the simulations of related TO BE scenarios.

With the first scenario TO BE (referred to chemical laboratory and radiology improvement), has been possible to reduce the time required for the process of reporting, but no improvement is recorded on other indicators for the entire system.

Applying a agile configuration to the ED resources dedicated to the surgical unit, however, there were no improvements for what concerns the average time of reporting, but significant variations were noted for all other indicators, thus obtaining a partial solution to the problem of overcrowding in urgency structures of Emergency Department; in this scenario improved performance are obtainable on both single process and entire system.

Therefore it is clear that the agile logic fits structures urgent better than lean service system, resulting in improved performance of the units, as it is possible to read by the trend indicators of TO BE scenarios, represented in the Table 1, even because of the load wave is not level-shaped and the resource configuration is not stationary, both key assumptions for the applicability of the methodology lean.

Table 1. Results of the model TO BE (1) and TO BE (2)

INDICATOR	AS IS	TO BE (1)	TO BE (2)
Load factor of beds	117.867	117.8	106.7
Average residence time (days)	6	6	5
Max waiting for the surgery (minutes)	450	449.8	354
Average time of reporting (minutes)	37	28	37

6 Conclusions

We developed a simulation model that is able to solve, in terms of resources, the problem of Emergency Department managing processes and, therefore, to provide the business decision maker of an instrument able to compare different performance to vary the configuration of inputs adopted.

The mean result, therefore, consists in the conclusion that the performance of Emergency Departments does not depend on the diagnostic units subsystems, although they represent a criticality, but depends on the size of the resources allocated to the operating theater.

In accordance with the scientific literature, instead, the diagnostic units subsystems just determine the performance of Emergency Room.

In order to configure Agile production systems, it is possible to provide a phase shift of the load wave, that goes to support the request for production elasticity to the system.

Adopting agile configuration of resources, better performance can be achieve in terms of reducing the time needed to perform critical tasks, reducing the congestion of these processes, both in terms of the offered services effectiveness by reducing the number of used stretchers, resulting decreased in the load factor of beds.

Therefore, from the technological point of view, the encoding agile production factors can be the subject of a development in neural network that provides, in real time and according to the situation of simultaneous accesses, plus equipment of resources they have, in phase delay, in the wards for which it was read, in advance, the bottleneck.

References

1. Berwick, D.M.: Improvement, trust, and the healthcare workforce. Qual. Saf. Health Care **12**, 448–452 (2003)
2. Rust, T., Saeed, K., Bar-On, I., Pavlov, O.: Re-designing policy and process in health care service delivery: a system dynamics case study. In: Proceedings System Dynamics Conference (2012)
3. Brailsford, S.C.: System dynamics: what's in it for healthcare simulation modelers. In: Simulation Conference WSC 2008, pp. 1478–1483 (2008)
4. Hagg, H., Suskovich, D., Workman, J., Scachitti, S., Hudson, B.: Adaption of Lean Methodologies for Healthcare Applications, vol. 24, pp. 1–8. RCHE Publications (2007)
5. Rexhepi, L., Shrestha, P.: Lean Service Implementation in Hospital: A Case study conducted in University Clinical Centre of Kosovo, Rheumatology Department. Umea School of Business, Umea University, Sweden (2011)
6. Toussaint, J.S., Barry, L.L.: The promise of Lean in health care. Mayo Clin. Proc. **88**(1), 74–82 (2013)
7. Chiarini, A.: Risk management and cost reduction of cancer drugs using Lean six sigma tools. Leadersh. Health Serv. **25**(4), 318–330 (2012)
8. Fillingham, D.: Can Lean save lives? Leadersh. Health Serv. **20**(4), 231–241 (2007)

9. Frenk, J.: The global health system: strengthening national health systems as the next step for global progress. PLoS Med. **7**(1), e1000089 (2010). doi:10.1371/journal.pmed.1000089
10. Swafford, P.M., Ghosh, S., Murthy, N.: Achieving supply chain agility through it integration and flexibility. Int. J. Prod. Econ. **116**(2), 288–297 (2008)
11. Van Hock, R.I., Harrison, A., Christopher, M.: Measuring agile capabilities in the supply chain. Int. J. Oper. Prod. Manag. **21**(1/2), 126–148 (2001)
12. Yusuf, Y.Y., Sarhadi, M., Gunasekaran, A.: Agile manufacturing: the drivers, concepts and attributes. Int. J. Prod. **62**(1–2), 33–43 (1999)
13. Rust, T., Saeed, K., Bar-On, I., Pavlov, O.: Adapting agile strategies to healthcare service delivery. In: Proceedings System Dynamics Conference (2013)
14. Homer, J.B., Hirsch, G.B.: System dynamics modelling for public health: background and opportunities. Am. J. Public Health **96**, 452–458 (2006)
15. Centobelli, P., Converso, G., De Iasi, A., Murino, T.: Innovation in hospitals: an e-procurement model in pharmacy operations in day surgery. In: 26th European Modeling and Simulation Symposium, EMSS (2014)
16. Eden, C.: Cognitive mapping and problem structuring for system dynamics model building. Syst. Dyn. Rev. **10**(2–3), 257–276 (1994)
17. Milton, C.R., Donaldson, C.: Setting priorities and allocating resources in health regions: lessons from a project evaluating program budgeting and marginal analysis (PBMA). Health Policy **64**(3), 335–348 (2003)
18. Joosten, T., Bongers, I., Janssen, R.: Application of Lean thinking to healthcare: issues and observation. Int. J. Qual. HealthCare **21**, 341–347 (2009)
19. Mills, J., Platts, K., Bourne, M., Richards, H.: Strategy and Performance: Competing through Competences, pp. 149–162. Cambridge University Press, Cambridge (2002)
20. Moyano-Fuentes, J.: Learning on Lean: a review a thinking and research. Int. J. Oper. Prod. Manag. **32**(5), 551–582 (2012)
21. Womack, J., Jones, D., Roos, D.: The Machine That Changed the World: The Story of Lean Production, pp. 1–330. Simon and Schuster, New York (2008)

Author Index

Printed in the United States
By Bookmasters